What Is the Argument?

What Is the Argument?

Critical Thinking in the Real World

Steven P. Lee

Hobart and William Smith Colleges

Boston   Burr Ridge, IL   Dubuque, IA   Madison, WI   New York
San Francisco   St. Louis   Bangkok   Bogotá   Caracas   Kuala Lumpur
Lisbon   London   Madrid   Mexico City   Milan   Montreal   New Delhi
Santiago   Seoul   Singapore   Sydney   Taipei   Toronto

McGraw-Hill Higher Education

A Division of The **McGraw-Hill** *Companies*

1 2 3 4 5 6 7 8 9 0 DOC/DOC 0 9 8 7 6 5 4 3 2 1

Library of Congress Cataloging-in-Publication Data
Lee, Steven.
    What is the argument? : critical thinking in the real world / Steven Lee.
       p. cm.
    ISBN 1-55934-979-4
      1. Critical thinking. 2. Reasoning. I. Title.
    B809.2.L44 2002
    160—dc 21   2001030372

Sponsoring editors, Ken King and Jon-David Hague; production editor, Holly Paulsen; manuscript editor, Tom Briggs; design manager and cover designer, Susan Breitbard; art editor, Emma Ghiselli; text designer, Glenda King; illustrators, Rennie Evans and Emma Ghiselli; production supervisor, Pam Augspurger. The text was set in 10/12.5 Janson Roman by TBH Typecast, and printed on acid-free 45# New Era Matte by R. R. Donnelley & Sons Company.

Cover image: Peter Szumowski, Abstract Composition, 1996. © Peter Szumowski/Private Collection/Bridgeman Art Library.

Credits

Letters to the Editor reprinted with permission from the authors. **Figs. 1.3, 4.4 (right)** Courtesy of the Advertising Council. **Fig. 11.1** Courtesy of Public Campaign.

www.mhhe.com

To Amanda, Charlotte, and Lilah,
who never let a bad argument pass.

Preface

What Is the Argument? is a critical thinking textbook with a number of distinctive features designed to solve a variety of teaching problems characteristic of critical thinking courses. The book helps students to better understand the kinds of arguments they encounter in their everyday lives, both inside and outside the classroom, and develops an effective set of methods by which students can identify, understand, and evaluate those arguments. More than most texts, *What Is the Argument?* presents an interesting, integrated, skill-building approach that satisfies students and teachers alike.

ARGUMENT IDENTIFICATION   The main problem students have with critical thinking is understanding how statements in a text relate to one another so as to constitute an argument. While students may easily understand the relationship of words that give meaning to a sentence, they often do not understand the relationship of sentences that give meaning to an argumentative text. *What Is the Argument?* is designed to teach students how statements work together to create reasoning.

The book focuses on what arguments have in common, as well as what distinguishes different kinds of arguments. The common features of arguments are presented through a method (structuring) that helps students identify the parts of an argument in a prose text and understand the relationship of those parts (the support relationship) that make the text argumentative. Structuring is a method that can work for any argument. Based on this integrated approach to understanding arguments, different kinds of arguments are distinguished by such devices as the contrast between linked and convergent premises and the appropriate inclusion of implicit premises. In addition to deductive arguments, the book considers in detail inductive arguments, causal arguments, analogical arguments, and all-things-considered arguments. In the case of deductive arguments, both categorical logic and statement logic are presented.

ARGUMENT EVALUATION   Evaluating arguments shares importance with identifying and understanding them. *What Is the Argument?* focuses on the general ways that arguments go wrong, both in form and content, and four of these ways are identified as basic fallacies. Other fallacies in the standard canon are introduced as specific versions of one or another of the basic four. In evaluating an argument, students are asked not to simply name the fallacy, but also to justify a fallacy charge, to present an argument that the conditions of the fallacy are satisfied. This avoids the stale "fallacies" approach and provides students with a unified view of the strengths and weaknesses of arguments.

EXERCISES   Perhaps the most important aspect of a critical thinking text is the exercises, and here, too, *What Is the Argument?* is distinctive. It teaches students how to identify, understand, and evaluate the arguments they find in their everyday lives, in the "real world." To this end, while many simple constructed exercises are included to ease the students into an understanding of the skills, the main source of exercises is letters to the editor from major newspapers. These have been carefully chosen not only to serve as appropriate vehicles for students to sharpen their developing skills, but also as texts that will engage their interest. The letters cover a wide array of topics, including politics, education, cultural issues (traditional and popular), the arts, the sciences, law (criminal, tort, and constitutional), racial and ethnic issues, sports, military matters, economics, animals, the environment, sex and gender issues, reproduction, smoking, health care, drinking and drugs, and computers and the Internet. Most of them refer to recent events with which college students will be familiar, and many are written with humor. On topics with an ideological divide, efforts are made to include arguments from both sides. The subject matter of the exercises greatly facilitates class discussion.

This is a long book, and there may not be time to cover all of it in the typical critical thinking course. In recognition of this, while the material is well integrated, the book is designed so that some of the parts can be omitted from a course without detriment to those that are included. In particular, Chapters 2 through 8 present the heart of the structuring and evaluation technique, and it is important for a course using this book to include them. The remaining chapters can be included or excluded as time and energy permit.

OTHER FEATURES   Three other features of *What Is the Argument?* deserve mention: its attention to values arguments, its consideration of extended arguments, and its treatment of critical writing. Values arguments are a major portion of the arguments students encounter in their everyday lives, and no textbook that fails to adequately treat them can hope to prepare students to deal with arguments outside the classroom. *What Is the Argument?* gives considerable attention to values arguments and includes an extended discussion of the role of values in argument. This discussion is designed in part to shake students out of their unreflective values relativism and to provide a response to the frequent refrain in class discussion, "That's only your opinion." At the same time, values arguments are not handled separately from other kinds of arguments. Rather, they are presented as sharing the main feature of all arguments, namely, that the conclusion should be believed only to the extent that the supporting argument is strong.

The discussion of extended arguments and critical writing is contained partly in Chapter 12, "Extended Arguments," which is included on the Instructor's CD-ROM rather than in this text. To use this chapter in class, instructors can print the relevant portions from the CD-ROM or order a print version of the chapter from

Primis Custom Publishing through their McGraw-Hill sales representative or McGraw-Hill customer service. Following is a discussion of how extended arguments and critical writing are treated, both in Chapter 12 and the rest of the text.

Extended arguments, as they appear in both midlength and essay-length texts, are given careful consideration, and Chapter 12 shows how to apply the structuring and evaluation skills developed for short arguments to their longer cousins. For example, students learn how to structure complex arguments and to omit from consideration sections of the text that are not parts of the argument. But the structurings of extended arguments can become quite complicated, and for this reason students are shown how to extract and evaluate the main part of an extended argument without including all of the details.

Critical writing is treated not simply as an add-on, but in a way that flows naturally from the method of structuring and evaluation. First, when evaluating an argument to justify a fallacy charge, students are required to write a short argument. Second, in the chapter on extended argument, students are instructed in how to choose a thesis to defend and in the creation of longer arguments by being introduced to the method of initial structuring, a technique using the structuring and evaluation skills learned earlier to create a logical outline to use in the writing of an argumentative essay.

Students will find the answers to selected exercises (one-third of the total) at the back of the book. The remainder of the answers are found in the Instructor's Manual, published along with Chapter 12 as a CD-ROM to accompany the copies of the text sent to instructors. The Instructor's Manual will also include additional exercises for each chapter, useful in class discussion or as problems in quizzes or tests. The CD-ROM format of the manual allows instructors to easily print out any of the material for classroom distribution. In addition, the manual includes teaching tips and other material to assist the pedagogical enterprise.

Finally, please send me any comments, suggestions, questions, or objections that arise from your encounter with this text. My e-mail address is lee@hws.edu.

ACKNOWLEDGMENTS   Many others are due recognition in a project of this magnitude. First, let me thank my critical thinking students over the years, who have cheerfully been experimental subjects for earlier drafts of the book chapters, and who stimulated my efforts to provide an adequate response to the assertion "That's only your opinion." Students who were especially helpful include Jackie Augustine, Lyndsey Brown, Kyle Reynolds, John Rivera, Carol Rosenthal, Mike Simolo, Sky Stanfield, Amanda Vizedom, and Jeff Weisner. Much advice and encouragement was received from colleagues, including Andrew Altman, Scott Brophy, and Rosalind Simson, who provided comments on portions of the manuscript. In addition, assistance was ably provided by Bernadette Van Der Vliet, Susan Reece, Michelle Pickard, Pati Mattice, Melody Joyce, and Sue Yates. Erik van Slyke's generosity provided a workspace in which much of my work on the book was done. Thanks to them all, and to Hobart and William Smith Colleges, which provided me with both an excellent teaching environment in which to hone the methods presented in the book and generous support for the work of writing it.

Also due credit are the hundreds of authors who have generously given me permission to use their letters in the book. Often, they sent along notes expressing their interest in the project, offering encouragement, and asserting their belief in the importance of critical thinking. A number of them pointed out in their comments that weaknesses in their argument may have resulted from the habit of newspapers to edit and shorten submitted letters.

Thanks also to Ken King and the staff at McGraw-Hill. From the beginning Ken provided strong support and guidance for this project and this neophyte textbook writer, and somehow recognized, in the much cruder early incarnations, the promise that I hope this book has realized. Thanks go as well to Tom Briggs for his able and tolerant copy editing. In addition, many reviewers offered their advice and comments and made this textbook, as a result, better than it would have been. Among these are Jami L. Anderson, University of Michigan, Flint; Karen Bell, California State University, Fresno; Steven B. Cowan, University of Arkansas; Andrew Dzida, Saddleback College; Bruce Miller, Michigan State University; David V. Newman, Western Michigan University; Mark Schersten, Siena Heights University; Al Spangler, California State University, Long Beach; Helmut Wautischer, Sonoma State University; and Irene Woodward, Holy Names College.

Finally, special thanks go to my family, Cherry Rahn, Amanda, Lilah, and Charlotte, who chided, tolerated, encouraged, and supported my efforts, somehow in just the right proportions to give me the space and motivation to move this undertaking along to completion.

Contents

CHAPTER 3   Explanations and Value Arguments   59

CHAPTER 4   What Is *the* Argument?
Conclusions and Premises   94

CHAPTER 1

What Is Critical Thinking?

"Most people would sooner die than think—in fact, they do so."
—BERTRAND RUSSELL[1]

"In the last analysis, we are governed either through talk or through force."
—FELIX FRANKFURTER

In this introductory chapter, we discuss the nature of critical thinking. We also consider the importance and the role of critical thinking in our everyday lives.

1.1 What Is Critical Thinking?

Critical thinking is something you already know how to do. You learned to think critically while you were learning to talk. Think of how young children discover the question "why?" They begin to pester their parents by asking it repeatedly. And every time the parent gives an answer, the child asks the question anew. As the parent responds, the child is learning the basics of critical thinking. (However, parents are often driven to distraction by the constant questioning and terminate the conversation with a sharp "because I say so!" Thus ends the critical thinking session.)

What is the parent teaching the child by responding to the "why?" questions? Every time the child asks "why?" the parent gives a reason, so the child is learning about giving reasons. Consider this discussion:

Example 1.1

PARENT: You should go to bed now.
CHILD: Why?
PARENT: Because you need your sleep.
CHILD: Why?
PARENT: Because you have to go to school tomorrow.
CHILD: Why?

PARENT: Because you need to learn.
CHILD: Why?
PARENT: Because it is important to develop your mind.
CHILD: Why? . . .

With each response, the parent gives the child a reason that supports the parent's previous statement. Part of what the child is doing with each "why?" is asking for a reason. By giving the child reasons, the parent is teaching the child how to reason.

Critical thinking is reasoning. Critical thinking involves considering reasons in support of a claim about the world. When you give reasons for a claim, you seek to show that it is true. Reasons are themselves claims. In thinking critically, you seek to understand or explore the basis of the truth of a claim by considering other claims that may show the original claim to be true.

> ### Critical Thinking
>
> Critical thinking is reasoning. It involves seeking to establish whether claims are true by considering reasons that may show those claims to be true or show how they are true. Reasons are themselves claims. Therefore, critical thinking involves considering various claims and determining how some of them may show others to be true.

There are different ways to reason, but the main way is through **argument.** An argument is a unit or instance of reasoning. It is a reason or group of reasons that supports the truth of some claim. The claim that is supported by the reasons is the **conclusion** of the argument. In the exchange in Example 1.1, the parent presents a series of arguments. For example, the parent begins by making the claim that the child should go to bed and, at the child's request, provides a reason to support this claim. When the parent gives that reason, she or he gives an argument. The claim that the child should go to bed is the conclusion. Here is the argument:

Example 1.2

You need your sleep.
Therefore, you should go to bed now.

This bit of reasoning is an example of critical thinking.

> ### Argument (tentative definition)
>
> An argument is an instance of critical thinking or reasoning. It is an effort to show that some claim is true by giving reasons that support the claim. The claim that is supported by the reasons is the conclusion of the argument.

1.1.1 Skills in Critical Thinking

There are three main skills involved in critical thinking: (1) identifying the reasoning or arguments of others, (2) evaluating the reasoning or arguments of others, and (3) creating reasoning or arguments of your own. Let us consider the nature of these skills.

Main Skills Involved in Critical Thinking

1. Identifying the reasoning or arguments of others

2. Evaluating the reasoning or arguments of others

3. Creating reasoning or arguments of your own

First, you need to be able to identify the reasoning or arguments of others. You need to understand whether they are offering reasons and, if they are, what those reasons are and what the conclusions are. This is the activity the inquisitive child in Example 1.1 is beginning to appreciate. In asking "why?" she is asking her parent to give reasons to support the claim that she should go to bed.

Second, you need to be able to evaluate the reasoning or arguments of others. You need to determine when their arguments are strong and when they are weak. The child's mastery of this skill would be shown if she were to say to her parent, in response to the argument in Example 1.2, that she does not feel sleepy. She would then be implying, correctly or not, that the parent's reasoning is weak because it is based on a false claim—namely, that the child is tired.

Third, you need to be able to create reasoning or arguments of your own. You need to develop the skill of giving reasons that support the claims you make. When the child responds to the parent by claiming that she is not tired, she is creating an argument that is critical of the parent's argument.

These three skills build on and depend on each other. You cannot practice the second skill (evaluation) without mastery of the first (identification) because you cannot evaluate reasoning without first identifying what it is. Nor can you practice the second skill without mastery of the third (creation). To evaluate reasoning, you need to create reasoning of your own—namely, reasoning that supports the claim you make about the argument when you evaluate it. Moreover, to practice the third skill, you need to master the first two because your own arguments are often responses to the arguments of others. When you master these skills, your thinking about the world becomes more than mere thinking; it becomes *critical* thinking.

The purpose of this book is to improve your performance of these basic critical thinking skills. You do not need to *acquire* these skills since you already are a master of them to some extent. Nevertheless, you can learn to perform them better. Consider this analogy: The skills involved in reasoning are similar in some respects to those involved in any sport. For example, you begin to master the skills of baseball, such as catching, throwing, running, and hitting, as you develop physically, just as you begin to master critical thinking skills as you develop mentally and linguistically.

A baseball coach seeks to improve your mastery of the physical skills of the sport. As part of this effort, the coach might videotape you while you are hitting and then show you the replay so that you can see what you might do to hit better. You might learn that you can improve your hitting by changing your stance or the way you hold the bat. Before joining the team, you might not have thought much about how you batted. The videotape and the coach's instruction make you aware of this and so help you to improve. In a similar way, you may not have thought much about how you practice the reasoning skills you have developed. The purpose of studying critical thinking, like the purpose of the videotape and the coach's instruction, is to make you aware of how you perform reasoning skills and to show you how to improve them. Through a better understanding of your critical thinking performance, you will become a better critical thinker.

1.1.2 Critical Thinking and Language

You learned to think critically as part of learning language. Language has many uses, with reasoning one of the main ones. We can refer to reasoning as the **argumentative use of language.** Before considering the argumentative use, it will be helpful to examine some other uses of language, such as expressive, descriptive, directive, and interrogative. These are some of the things we do with language: (1) express ourselves, (2) describe the world, (3) direct others, (4) ask questions, and (5) argue.

Key Uses of Language

1. Expressive use

2. Descriptive use

3. Directive use

4. Interrogative use

5. Argumentative use

Considering the first, we often use language to express our feelings. For example, if you step barefoot on a sharp rock, you may yell "damn!" (or worse), using language to express the shock and pain. Expressive language, in its simplest form, can consist of a single word, as in this example.

Perhaps the most common use of language is the descriptive. We use language descriptively to describe the world and to make claims. The descriptive use, unlike the expressive, requires sentences. Suppose that John is taller than George.

To describe this fact, you must use separate words ("John" and "George") to refer to the two people in question and a phrase ("is taller than") to refer to the relationship between them, and you must put those words together in a sentence.

The next two uses of language also require sentences. In the directive use, we ask, instruct, order, plead with, or suggest to someone that she do something. The interrogative use involves asking questions. Though the descriptive, directive, and interrogative uses of language all require sentences, they usually take different grammatical forms—indicative, imperative, or interrogative.

Use of Language	Grammatical Form of Sentence
1. Descriptive	Indicative
2. Directive	Imperative
3. Interrogative	Interrogative

All claims are descriptive and involve indicative sentences. It follows that one important difference among the three grammatical forms is that only an indicative sentence is true or false. In contrast, a directive or interrogative use of language does not make any claim about the world, so an imperative or interrogative sentence is not true or false. If you ask, "Is it raining out?" or say, "Sit down," you have not made a claim or said something that is true or false.

It is not always easy to tell which use of language is at work, for two reasons. First, one type of language will sometimes borrow a grammatical form from another. For example, an interrogative sentence can be used descriptively.[2] Imagine a teacher saying to a student, "This is a directive use of language, isn't it?" The teacher would rightly be understood to be telling the student that the use is directive, not asking him whether it is. In other words, the teacher is using language descriptively, but doing so in the guise of an interrogative language form. The second reason is that language is often used in more than one way simultaneously. For example, a descriptive use of language can also be expressive, as in "that is a lovely sunset." The language of poetry is often both expressive and descriptive. When the expressive use occurs by itself, however, it involves a single word or a phrase, not a whole sentence.

Thus, grammatical form is not always an accurate guide to which use of language an author or speaker intends. Given this, how can you know which use of language an author or speaker intends? The key is to pay attention to the situation in which a sentence is used. In other words, you need to attend to the *context* in which a sentence occurs to understand which use of language it is. More generally, your understanding of context plays a crucial role in your comprehension of what other people are saying. For example, the interrogative sentence "This is a directive use of language, isn't it?" will sometimes be a genuine question and sometimes a descriptive statement, depending on the context in which it is uttered. (Tone of

Use	Linguistic Unit	Level of Complexity
Expressive	Word	None
Descriptive/directive/ interrogative	Group of words (sentence)	Grammar (relations of words)
Argumentative	Group of sentences (argument)	Logic (relations of sentences)

FIGURE 1.1   **Characteristics of Some Uses of Language**

voice is important here, as it often is.) We will have more to say about the important notion of context in Chapter 3.

The meaning of a sentence depends on the relations among its words. You must put the words together according to the rules of grammar to express meaning. Thus, language involving sentences (descriptive, directive, and interrogative) has a complexity that is not present in simple expressive language—the complexity of sentence structure or grammar. The expressive use, were it the only use, would not really be language at all. This is why many people argue that language is uniquely human. Other animals, while they make expressive noises, do not seem to have language, because the sounds they make are not grammatically structured.[3] The sentence, not the word, is the principal unit of language. Sentences sometimes contain a single word, as in the directive sentence "Go!" Nevertheless, this single word represents a multiple-word sentence because the "you" is understood.

1.1.3 The Argumentative Use of Language

How do the descriptive, directive, and interrogative uses of language differ from the argumentative use, the use involved in reasoning and argument? The first three consist of words connected in sentences according to the rules of grammar. The argumentative use is also based on rules. But the rules in this case show how sentences, not words, are connected. An argumentative use of language consists of at least two claims—one a reason and the other a conclusion, the claim that the reason is meant to support. The claims are usually presented in separate sentences. The sentences form an argument because they stand in a certain relationship to each other, just as a group of words constitute a sentence because they stand in a certain relationship to each other. There are rules for combining sentences or claims in an argument, just as there are rules for combining words in a sentence. The rules for combining sentences or claims in reasoning are rules of logic.[4] Logic is to arguments what grammar is to sentences. Figure 1.1 compares these different uses of language.

The unit of descriptive, directive, or interrogative language is the sentence; the unit of argumentative language is generally a group of sentences. Most arguments consist of a small number of sentences. But arguments can be much longer, extending over an essay or a book, over the life's work of a single writer, or over the works of a number of writers spanning hundreds of years.[5] At the other extreme, an instance of reasoning may consist of a single sentence, though that sentence will include more than one claim, as in this example:

Example 1.3

You should go to bed now, because you need your sleep.

Here, one claim ("you need your sleep") is offered in support of another ("you should go to bed now"). The two claims are contained in a single sentence, with each clause in the compound sentence containing a separate claim.[6]

EXERCISE SET 1.1

SECTION A: For each of the following sentences, taken from *Les Miserables* by Victor Hugo,[7] indicate which use of language is represented (expressive, descriptive, directive, interrogative, or argumentative), and briefly explain why. If a sentence seems as if it might have more than one use, choose the use that seems more important for it. (For any cases of the argumentative use, all the claims occur in a single sentence.) Because these sentences are, of necessity, taken out of context, it may not be possible to determine the best answer in all cases. (The answers for the exercises marked with an icon are given at the end of the book.)

EXAMPLE
"Inspector Javert, set this woman free."

ANSWER
Directive use. The sentence gives an order to Javert, telling him what to do.

PROBLEMS
1. "The darkness was serene." *Des*
2. "Oh my God!" *Ex*
3. "Pour away, old rain." *Ex*
4. "Alas! Alas!" *Ex*
5. "Give me my coin." *Dir*
6. "He was a charming young man, capable of being intimidating." *Des*
7. "I don't go to bed, because I'm busy making cartridges all night."
8. "He had a square face, a thin and firm mouth, very fierce bushy grayish whiskers, and a stare that would turn your pockets inside out."
9. "You irritate me." *Ex*
10. "Kill me instead." *Dir*
11. "Oh, I'm happy!"
12. "We're all going to die." *Ex*
13. "Break a pane of glass."

14. "It's a job we can do at night, so let's have a drink first."
15. "We must dwell on a psychological fact, particular to barricades."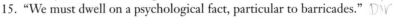
16. "The greatness of democracy is that it denies nothing and renounces nothing of humanity."
17. "Get back, or I'll blow up the barricade!"

SECTION B: Write a brief account of some episode in your life, using at least two examples of each of the three types of sentences we have discussed (descriptive, directive, interrogative) and at least one example of argumentative language. Underline the two sentences of each type and the argumentative use.

SECTION C: As far as we understand the behavior of nonhuman animals, none of them uses language, because the expressive noises they make do not count as language. Or so I have claimed. Do you agree with this conclusion? Write a brief argument for or against this claim, giving reasons for the position you take.

1.2 The Importance of Critical Thinking

People often enjoy critical thinking for its own sake. For example, many people like working on puzzles, proving mathematical theorems, or figuring out who committed the murder in a mystery novel. All these activities require critical thinking. When you work on one of these problems, you consider specific reasons for picking one solution over another. For example, in the case of the murder mystery, you ask yourself what reasons there are for thinking that Pat, and not Chris, is the murderer. In other words, you create arguments. And if the novelist is good, he or she will provide many false clues as to the murderer's identity, making it difficult to arrive at the correct solution. An activity that is valuable for its own sake has **intrinsic value.** If you enjoy the sorts of activities just mentioned, then critical thinking has intrinsic value for you. If an activity has intrinsic value for you, then the better you are at it, the more you enjoy it. Therefore, the better you become at critical thinking, the more likely you are to enjoy it for its own sake.

Intrinsic and Instrumental Value

Something (an event, an activity, an object) has intrinsic value if it is valuable for its own sake—for example, if it brings enjoyment or pleasure apart from its consequences. In contrast, something has instrumental value if it provides positive benefits. In addition, something can be valuable both for its own sake and for its consequences, in which case it has both intrinsic and instrumental value.

Of course, people practice critical thinking not only for its intrinsic value but also for its benefits. If an activity is valuable for the sake of positive consequences

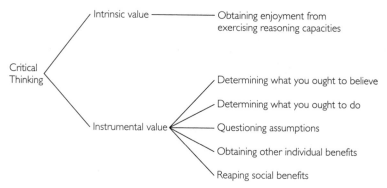

FIGURE 1.2   Value of Critical Thinking

that result from it, the activity has **instrumental value** (also referred to as extrinsic value). For example, some people do not enjoy exercise for its own sake but exercise anyway for the health benefits it provides. For them, exercise has instrumental value but not intrinsic value. Exercise is merely an *instrument* to achieve a purpose —namely, good health. Intrinsic value and instrumental value are not mutually exclusive; many activities are valuable in both ways. For example, some people enjoy exercising for its own sake, so for them, exercise has both intrinsic and instrumental value.

Critical thinking has instrumental value in different ways, as Figure 1.2 shows. First, critical thinking can help you discover what is true about the world. In general, it is beneficial for you to believe what is true, and to that extent, you ought to believe what is true.[8] Thus, critical thinking is of instrumental value because it helps you determine what you ought to believe. Second, critical thinking is useful in helping you decide what you ought to do in many of the situations you will face in life. When you deliberate about what to do, you call upon your critical thinking skills. These two purposes for critical thinking are often combined. Because actions are based on beliefs, determining what to believe helps you decide what to do.

Third, critical thinking can cause you to question assumptions, which is crucial in helping you determine what you ought to believe and do. Fourth, critical thinking has other significant benefits for you as an individual, beyond its intrinsic value. Finally, critical thinking provides important community benefits. Although these instrumental benefits of critical thinking overlap in various ways, it is of value for us to consider each of them by itself in more detail.

1.2.1 Determining What You Ought to Believe

Consider first the role of critical thinking in helping you to determine what is true, and hence what you ought to believe. You figure out what is true about the world in two ways. First, you can assess the truth of a statement *directly*, usually through the direct use of your senses. For example, you can determine through direct observation that the sun is shining or that the stove is hot. Second, you can assess the truth of a statement *indirectly*, in which case your belief in its truth is based on your belief in the truth of other statements.

To illustrate, consider two simple examples. First, you cannot base your belief that it is about to rain on direct observation of the rain, which has yet to start. Instead, you must base it upon other beliefs, such as that the midday sky is darkening and that there is lightning on the horizon. Second, you cannot base your belief that the tree that blew over in the storm is 150 years old on direct observation, since you were not around when it started to grow. Instead, you base your belief on your knowledge that trees accumulate one ring per year and your observation that the tree has 150 rings.

Now consider an additional, less simple case:

Example 1.4

1. The motion of a galaxy away from us causes the wavelengths of its light to appear shifted toward the red end of the spectrum.
2. The wavelengths of the light from the Andromeda galaxy are shifted toward the red end of the spectrum.

Therefore, Andromeda is moving away from us.

Again, in discovering new truths indirectly, you must explicitly think through the argument. In the two previous examples, you may not have been aware of the role of argument, but it was lurking in the background. Even when the arguments are not evident, they can be brought to the fore when someone asks for a **justification** of what you believe. A justification is the argument you give when what you believe is doubted by others. If someone doubted your claim that the tree was 150 years old, you could explain about the rings, even though you may not have been consciously aware of that argument when you made the claim.

> ### Justification
>
> A justification is an argument you present that has as its conclusion a belief or claim of yours (including a belief or claim about what someone should do) when there is some doubt about the truth of the claim. Usually, a justification is called for when someone disagrees with what you say or do and challenges its correctness.

Thus, argument plays a crucial role in what you come to believe indirectly. Critical thinking is a vital skill in extending your beliefs from what you already know to what you do not yet know. For example, science is based on argument. The formulation and testing of scientific theories is an exercise in argumentation and critical thinking. The better you are at critical thinking, the better you will be at understanding and doing science.

1.2.2 Determining What You Ought to Do

Correct beliefs are necessary in order to act effectively. But in deciding how to act, you need not only to have correct beliefs but also to be able to work through arguments based on those beliefs. Consider these examples:

Example 1.5

A.   Today is the first day of daylight savings time.
     Therefore, I should set the clocks ahead one hour.

B.   1. AIDS is a serious health menace to our community.
     2. We will probably not find a vaccine against AIDS in the near future.
     3. Our public health budget is limited.
     4. An educational campaign for safe sex would be relatively inexpensive.
     5. Such an educational campaign is probably the most effective thing we
        could do.
     Therefore, we should mount an educational campaign for safe sex.

In Example A, believing that today is the first day of daylight savings time is necessary in order to decide that the proper action is to set the clocks ahead. More precisely, that belief shows what the proper action is because it serves as a reason that supports the statement that the clocks should be set ahead one hour. When there are various actions you can take, selecting one amounts to deciding which of them has the best argument in its favor.

Of course, in deciding to set the clocks ahead, you are unlikely to have this consciously in mind, because the reasoning is so simple and straightforward. But the fact that you might need to justify setting the clocks ahead shows that there is an argument behind the action. Imagine someone saying, "Why are you fiddling with the clock?" This is a call for you to justify your action. In Example B, however, the reasoning is more complicated. Imagine that you are the head of the public health agency seeking to determine what your agency should do about the AIDS epidemic. You would probably run through in your mind (and present to others in the agency) something like the argument given here.

Example B reveals something else important about the relation between beliefs and actions. Not all of the reasons in this argument are beliefs of which you would be certain. As the word "probably" indicates, you would not be sure that a vaccine will *not* be discovered soon, nor that a safe-sex educational campaign will be effective. Many beliefs about the world have this character. People hold them with less than full certainty; they are beliefs that something is *likely* so. Still, as Example B shows, beliefs about what is likely so play a role in helping you decide what to do and to justify what you do.

1.2.3 Questioning Assumptions

When you are deciding what to believe or do, you often consider several alternatives. For example, as a jury member, should you believe the prosecution or the defense? For your vacation, should you travel to the beach, the mountains, or the city? When you are considering more than one alternative, each may have an argument supporting it. In such cases, you need to compare the different arguments and determine which is the stronger or strongest. This requires evaluation of the arguments.

One aspect of evaluating an argument is considering whether the reasons are true. If the reasons are doubtful or false, the argument is weak. The reasons that you might consider if you are deciding what to believe or do, or the reasons you offer in justification for what you believe or do, are referred to as **assumptions.** These reasons are what you *assume* to be true when you hold that belief or perform that action. Some assumptions are hidden. Frequently, people believe or do things without having consciously reasoned their way to such beliefs or actions but would be able to give reasons for these beliefs or actions if asked to justify them. These are **hidden assumptions.**

Many assumptions are **questionable assumptions.** Often, the assumptions that underlie your beliefs or actions are doubtful or questionable. In that case, you should question them, for if an assumption is questionable, so too is the belief or action it supports. One important critical thinking skill is rooting out and challenging questionable assumptions.

> ### Assumptions, Hidden Assumptions, and Questionable Assumptions
>
> An assumption is a reason that supports the truth of a belief or the correctness of an action. Assumptions are often hidden, meaning that they have not been consciously considered by the person whose beliefs or actions are based on them, but would be brought forth if the person were asked to give a justification for the belief or action. An assumption is questionable when there is reason to doubt it or regard it as false.

Consider this important historical example:

Example 1.6

The heavier something is, the faster it will fall.
Therefore, when two objects of different weight are dropped together, the heavier one will hit the ground before the lighter one.

In the seventeenth century, many people viewed the conclusion of this argument as true. But Galileo questioned the assumption that the heavier something is the faster it will fall. And in dropping two balls of different weights from the Leaning Tower of Pisa, he showed the assumption to be false. A questionable assumption, however, is not necessarily false. Upon investigation, it may turn out to be true. It is questionable because its truth cannot be taken for granted.

The justifications people give for their actions, like those they give for their beliefs, are sometimes based on questionable assumptions. It is often easier to see this at some historical distance, so consider the policy of denying women the vote. When those supporting this policy were challenged to justify it, one response might have been phrased this way:

Example 1.7

Women are inherently less interested in public affairs than are men.
Therefore, women should not have the right to vote.

It is clear now, though it was not clear to everyone a century ago, that this policy was based on a questionable assumption—as unjust social policies usually are. Social activists who fight such injustices seek to convince people of the falsity of the assumptions in the arguments offered to justify the unjust policies. Unjust policies, of course, do not result solely from faulty reasoning, but pointing out faulty reasoning historically has often led to change.

Note, by the way, that this argument against women's suffrage is different from the argument Galileo rejected. The suffrage argument has a conclusion that is a *value* claim, whereas the other argument's conclusion is a *factual* claim. Both factual and value claims can be conclusions of arguments. We consider this topic in detail in Chapter 3.

1.2.4 Obtaining Other Individual and Social Benefits

Critical thinking is also instrumentally valuable for other individual and social benefits it provides. Part of the individual benefit of critical thinking can be cast in economic terms. Critical thinking skills are among the most useful career skills you can possess. But critical thinking skills also are of immense value to your personal growth and to your ability to lead a fully human life.

The ancient Greek philosopher Aristotle argued that reasoning is an activity unique to human beings and that one cannot achieve happiness without the exercise of reason.[9] The development of reasoning skills is necessary for you to realize your humanness. You can realize yourself as a human being only when your life is your own. But your life is not your own if it is governed by outside forces. Your beliefs are determined initially by your upbringing, so they are initially not your own. Rather, they are the result of outside forces acting on you. You can make your beliefs your own only by determining whether they are justified. In holding your beliefs up to critical scrutiny, you make them your own, whether or not you choose to abandon them. Critical thinking is, of course, necessary for this.

In addition, critical thinking has important social benefits. In a large, complex society such as ours, people are constantly seeking to persuade others to do things that they might not otherwise do, such as buy a certain product or vote for a certain candidate. Such persuasion usually involves the use of argument. There are, after all, only two ways to get someone to do what he is otherwise not inclined to do: persuasion and force (or the threat of force).

The arguments involved in efforts at persuasion can be explicit or implicit. We need critical thinking skills to become aware of the arguments and to evaluate them. Only by being able to distinguish strong arguments from weak ones can you decide whether to allow yourself to be persuaded. To illustrate, consider the concept of logical self-defense.[10] The idea is that, just as you may need to learn certain physical skills, such as karate, in order to be able to defend yourself against an assault, you need to learn certain mental skills to defend yourself against poorly argued efforts to persuade you. These critical thinking skills are forms of logical self-defense.

Fortunately, most of us are not often called upon to defend ourselves physically, but we do constantly have to defend ourselves against efforts to persuade. (Think of how many TV commercials you have seen in your life.) If you do not possess critical thinking skills, you may be verbally manipulated by someone seeking to persuade you. Of course, you can also use critical thinking skills to persuade others to believe or do what they might have good reason not to believe or do. Critical thinking skills, like karate skills, can be misused. Those who are good at critical thinking can also be very good at making "the worse argument [seem] the stronger."[11] As the ancient Greek philosopher Plato observed, someone who has a highly developed skill can use it to do harm as well as good.[12]

The social value of critical thinking skills, as well as opportunities for their misuse, arise especially in the political arena. Democracy is based on the idea that citizens will exercise their critical judgment in voting and other forms of political participation. A democracy should involve vigorous public debate, and this can occur only when citizens have well-developed critical thinking skills. When such critical thinking skills are lacking, unscrupulous individuals can use their own persuasive skills to persuade people to support bad policies or vote for bad candidates. When citizens possess critical thinking skills, political discussion becomes more than mere disagreement; it becomes genuine debate.

1.2.5 Two Examples of Faulty Critical Thinking

To show more concretely the social value of critical thinking skills, consider two historical cases in which more effective application of these skills might have prevented serious policy mistakes—the Vietnam War and the Watergate scandal. In both cases, justifications for policies were based on weak arguments. These mistakes occurred not simply because of bad reasoning but also because of complex historical forces. Nonetheless, fuller critical scrutiny and more careful consideration of the justifications for the policies might have led to an avoidance of the mistakes.

The United States adopted a policy in the 1960s of sending troops (over a half million at one point) to support the government of South Vietnam in its struggle with local communist guerrillas and military forces from communist North Vietnam and to prevent a communist takeover of South Vietnam. It was believed at the time that a communist takeover not only would be harmful to the South Vietnamese but would lead other communist insurgents in the region to overthrow their governments (the "domino effect") and lead communists elsewhere to challenge the United States and the West, perhaps leading to a larger war. Moreover, given its sophisticated military capabilities in comparison with those of its communist foes, the United States expected to succeed. Thus, this argument would have been used to justify the policy:

Example 1.8

1. Victory for the communist forces in South Vietnam would embolden other communists in the region to overthrow their governments and communists elsewhere to challenge the West, perhaps leading to a larger war.
2. It would not be difficult for the United States to win a military struggle with the communist forces.

Therefore, the United States should commit its military forces to help defeat the communists in South Vietnam.

But each of these reasons was based on a questionable assumption. In fact, in hindsight, both assumptions clearly were false. The communists fought U.S. and South Vietnamese forces to a virtual draw, and the U.S. troops were withdrawn under domestic political pressure. By 1975, communist forces had seized control of South Vietnam and reunited the Vietnamese nation. Despite the massive troop mobilization and the superiority of U.S. military technology, the communists were not defeated. As it turned out, however, the fall of South Vietnam was not disastrous for the West in terms of its fight against communism. There was little or no "domino effect" of other nations falling to communism, as had been feared by proponents of the war.

If U.S. policy makers had worked through the justifications for the policy more carefully, they might have recognized that the assumptions were questionable, and, in fact, likely false, and so avoided the war.[13] Of course, there is no guarantee that, if the policy makers had more vigorously questioned these assumptions, they would have concluded that they were doubtful. Moreover, the decisions involved in the Vietnam policy were much more complicated than can be represented by any one argument. But the above argument was clearly one of the central justifications for U.S. involvement. Had policy makers recognized what a weak argument it was, they might have chosen not to commit U.S. forces to the region.

"Watergate" refers to the multifaceted political scandal that occurred during the administration of President Richard Nixon in 1972–74.[14] Watergate was an office and residential complex in Washington, DC, where in 1972 the Democratic National Committee had its offices. In the summer of 1972, seven burglars were arrested breaking into these offices. The burglars were, in fact, operatives from a group organized out of the White House as part of the effort to reelect Nixon. The president subsequently attempted to cover up the connection between his organization and the burglars. But tape recordings of conversations between Nixon and his aides in which they planned the cover-up proved to be his undoing. This clear violation of the law and subversion of the political process by the individual who, as chief executive, had primary responsibility for law enforcement, led to the efforts to impeach Nixon and so to his resignation. Watergate is the only political scandal in U.S. history that led to a presidential resignation.

We can imagine Nixon and his aides, deliberating about whether to engage in a cover-up, considering this argument:

Example 1.9

1. If our connection with the Watergate burglars becomes public, we will be damaged politically.
2. If we engage in a cover-up of this connection, we can keep it from becoming public knowledge.

Therefore, we should engage in a cover-up.

To the extent that such an argument was part of the decision-making process leading to the cover-up, the decision resulted from a failure of critical thinking. Certainly, Nixon and his aides should have recognized the second reason as a questionable assumption. Given all of the people who were aware of the connection between the White House and the Watergate burglars, Nixon and his aides should have realized how difficult it would be to keep the connection from becoming public. Moreover, they should have recognized that, were the connection and the cover-up efforts to become public, the political damage would be far greater than if the connection became public without the administration having tried to cover it up.

The point of these examples, as suggested earlier, is not to represent accurately the complex historical genesis of these mistaken policies. Nor is it to suggest that they necessarily resulted from bad reasoning. Rather, the point is that more effective critical thinking *might* have helped policy makers avert these disasters. To practice critical thinking is to question basic assumptions. This is critical thinking's greatest instrumental value.

Before leaving these examples, we should consider another aspect of critical thinking they reveal. We have already discussed evaluating arguments in terms of their questionable assumptions. There is, however, another way to evaluate an argument. Even if the justifications contain no questionable assumptions, an argument may be weak because the reasons do not provide *enough* support for the conclusion. Perhaps considerations that are not included in the argument should be.

For example, in the Watergate case, one of Nixon's aides should have said to him, "Mr. President, as chief executive you have sworn to uphold the law, and you have a fundamental legal obligation to do so, so we should not engage in a cover-up, even if it could save us from political damage."[15] This would have been a reason *not* to cover up the burglary. If this consideration had been incorporated into the decision-making process, Nixon might have decided not to engage in the cover-up. This consideration should have outweighed the two reasons given, even if they were not questionable. The fact that this consideration was not taken into account shows that the original argument was weak.

Likewise, in the case of the Vietnam War, an aide to President Lyndon Johnson, should have said, "Mr. President, to fight in Vietnam with all our military might would probably result in so much death and destruction that a victory would not be worth the cost, so it would be morally wrong to do so, even if we could win." As with the Watergate example, the existence of such a consideration, which undermines the original conclusion, shows the original argument to be a weak one. Had the policy makers considered this in the deliberations, they might have decided not to pursue the military intervention.

In these two cases, the considerations not raised in the original arguments were matters of legal and moral obligation. Nixon had a legal reason not to cover up the burglary, whatever the expected benefits from doing so. Johnson had a moral reason not to intervene in Vietnam, whatever benefits would follow from doing so. Often, the legal or moral reasons we have for (or against) a certain action outweigh the other reasons we have against (or for) it. Understanding the moral and legal dimensions of our actions is part of critical thinking.

≡ EXERCISE SET 1.2

SECTION A: Give three examples of beliefs that you hold that others might regard as doubtful. What reasons can you give to justify these beliefs?

SECTION B: Devise justifications with questionable assumptions for three beliefs that some people hold, and discuss how the assumptions are questionable. You might want to use beliefs you once held but have since abandoned.

SECTION C: The idea of logical self-defense is that you need well-developed critical thinking skills in order to protect yourself from efforts to persuade you with weak arguments. Many of these weak arguments come at you through advertising. Pick out and discuss three examples of advertisements from the print or electronic media that are based on weak arguments—whether explicit or implicit. In each case, discuss what the arguments are and why you believe they are weak.

SECTION D: Recall the claim that developing reasoning skills and living a life of reason are necessary for you to realize your humanness. Many people would object to this claim on religious grounds, viewing faith as more important than reason. They would argue that some of the most important beliefs in life must be accepted on faith. In a short essay, discuss this objection. Do you think that it is a good objection? Why or why not? Do you think that reason and faith are opposed in the way that the objection assumes, or is their alleged opposition a questionable assumption?

SECTION E: Discuss an example of weak reasoning leading to a mistaken action, as in the cases of Vietnam and Watergate. The example can be one from your own experience or one you know about; it can be real or fictional. Present an argument that might have led to the mistaken action and show how the argument is weak.

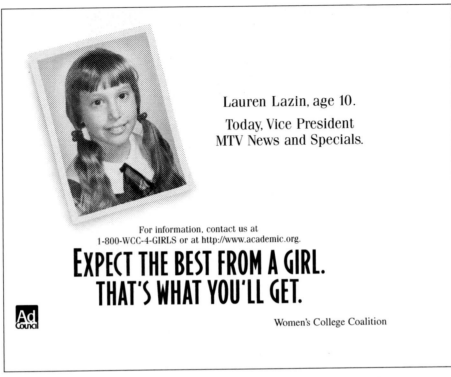

Lauren Lazin, age 10.

Today, Vice President
MTV News and Specials.

For information, contact us at
1-800-WCC-4-GIRLS or at http://www.academic.org.

EXPECT THE BEST FROM A GIRL.
THAT'S WHAT YOU'LL GET.

Ad
Council

Women's College Coalition

FIGURE 1.3   Public Service Advertisement. What argument does this ad make?

1.3 Critical Thinking in the Real World

Where do we find arguments? Everywhere! We are constantly encountering arguments in our everyday lives, though we may not always recognize them as such. The arguments we encounter are often not as obvious as those discussed previously. Figure 1.3 shows an example. The message of this public service advertisement is clear: We should have high expectations for girls, and we should not expect any less from a person because she is female. This message is contained in the sentence "Expect the best from a girl." But the ad is doing more than simply making this claim. If all it did were to make this claim, it would not present an argument, because it would not be giving a reason for the claim. The ad gives us a reason to support the claim that we should have high expectations for girls. The reason is represented by the second sentence, "That's what you'll get." If we want to make this argument completely clear, we need to reword it somewhat. Here is how this could be done:

Example 1.10

If you have high expectations of girls, then they will fulfill those expectations as much as boys do.
Therefore, you should have high expectations for girls.

FIGURE 1.4   Traffic Sign. What argument does this sign make?

Figure 1.4 gives another example of an argument in everyday life. We readily understand this traffic sign. Indeed, it is only useful as a traffic sign because it is so easy to comprehend. We can recognize that the sign is telling us not to speed, although it does not explicitly say this. In fact, the sign literally says exactly the opposite: "Exceed 25 M.P.H." Given that the sign says the opposite of what it means, how do we understand so easily what it does mean? We understand the sign precisely because we perceive it as an argument. The conclusion of the argument, in contrast to what the sign explicitly says, is that we should not exceed 25 M.P.H. Here is one way to formulate the argument:

Example 1.11

If you exceed 25 M.P.H., our judge will impose on you a legal penalty.
Therefore, you should not exceed 25 M.P.H.

The wording of the argument in the example is quite different from the wording of the sign. We saw this in the previous case as well, and it is true of many arguments we encounter in everyday life. The explicit wording of the argument has to be altered or reformulated to make it clear.

The argument in the traffic sign has another feature commonly found in arguments. To make the argument clear, we must not only change the wording but also include parts not included in its original presentation. In this case, we have to add the conclusion. In the original argument, the conclusion was left out because it was obvious. It is meant to be *understood*, as the "you" is understood in the sentence "go!" However, when we seek to make the argument clear, we must supply this missing part.

In these two cases, it is easier to understand the intended meaning than to identify the argument that is the basis of that meaning. This illustrates a point made previously about our reasoning skills: While we all understand the argumentative use of language, that understanding is largely "unconscious." Our critical thinking skills are often a matter more of intuition than of conscious understanding. In studying critical thinking, the goal is to make our intuitive understanding conscious understanding, thereby increasing it.

The real world presents us with many arguments that, unlike these two, are not so easy to understand. By the "real world," I mean simply our everyday lives beyond the classroom. Of course, the classroom is as much a part of the real world as anything else. But it is useful to use the term "real world" in this narrower sense because the arguments you encounter outside of the classroom are often more difficult than those presented inside. This textbook will prepare you to deal with the arguments you will encounter in the real world by including many such arguments. This is why, in the chapters to follow, many of the examples and exercises will be taken from newspaper letters to the editor, which provide many of the sorts of arguments you are likely to encounter in your everyday lives.

Consider three examples of arguments in letters to the editor:

Example 1.12

A. Background: For many years, the political relationship between the commonwealth of Puerto Rico and the United States has been a matter of controversy. Some have argued that Puerto Rico should be granted independence, and others that it should become the fifty-first state. This writer discussed the statehood option. (*Miami Herald*, 4/97)

> Puerto Rico should not become a U.S. state for several reasons. First, there is no way that English could become its official language—most Puerto Ricans speak Spanish. Second, Puerto Rican culture is too different from American culture. As a Cuban American, I know the differences between Latin and American cultures. Third, as a taxpayer, I do not want to subsidize the programs needed to raise Puerto Rico's standard of living.—R.R.

B. Background: This letter is addressing the issue of free speech as it applies to materials that encourage the reader to commit acts of violence. (*Los Angeles Times*, 5/97)

> Why is it against the law to print materials intended to assassinate a person's character, while it's not against the law to print material intended to assassinate the person? —A.S.

C. Background: During his administration, President Clinton adopted a policy of encouraging trade with China, despite China's weak record on human rights. Clinton argued for this liberal trade policy by claiming that a growing and prosperous economy in China would lead to improvements in respect for human rights. Also during this time, Switzerland came under criticism for the trade it carried on with Nazi Germany during World War II. This letter addresses these two facts. (*Boston Globe*, 6/97)

> The Clinton-Gore administration says of China that economic liberalization will over time increase the odds of political liberalization. Surely, such a theory would go far to explain the often-criticized trade between Hitler's Germany and Switzerland. It was only premature interference of Allied armies that prevented a fair test of that theory. Too bad.—P.C.

These three arguments represent a range of difficulty. They can be reformulated as follows:

Example 1.13

A. 1. English could not become the official language of Puerto Rico.
    2. Puerto Rican culture is very different from American culture.
    3. If Puerto Rico became a state, U.S. taxpayers would bear the burden of raising its standard of living.
    Therefore, Puerto Rico should not become a state.

B. 1. If it is against the law to print materials intended to assassinate a person's character, it should be against the law to print materials intended to assassinate a person.
    2. It is against the law to print materials intended to assassinate a person's character.
    Therefore, it should be against the law to print materials intended to assassinate a person.

C. 1. Clinton using a liberal trade policy to increase respect for human rights in China is like Switzerland using a liberal trade policy to increase respect for human rights in Nazi Germany.
    2. This Swiss policy was a failure.
    Therefore, Clinton's liberal trade policy with China will fail as well.

Argument A is quite straightforward. The author makes very clear what the conclusion is and what the reasons are. Argument B is more difficult to decipher. What point is the author trying to make? Apparently, she is claiming that it ought to be against the law to print materials intended to assassinate a person—presumably, materials advocating the use of violence against someone. This would be the conclusion of her argument, although it is not explicitly stated. What about the sentence that is given? It has the form of a question but is meant as a statement. The sentence is best understood as stating that, *if* it is against the law to print materials intended to assassinate a person's character, *then* it should be against the law to print materials intended to assassinate a person. This is one reason for the conclusion. The other reason, also not explicitly stated, is that it is a violation of slander or libel laws to print materials intended to assassinate a person's character. Thus, we have the conclusion and two reasons.

Argument C is more difficult still. Perhaps its main difficulty is that it employs irony. The author is making his point by saying the opposite of what he means (as with the traffic sign cited earlier). Specifically, what he says in literal terms is that the Swiss policy was a good one. He does this with the phrase "too bad." But he wants us to understand that he agrees with most of the rest of the world in condemning the Swiss policy. The second thing to note about the argument is that the author is making a comparison between Clinton's policy toward China and the Swiss policy toward Nazi Germany. Thus, given his intended condemnation of the Swiss policy, he also condemns the Clinton policy. Understanding this argument is a matter of formulating the argument he is making by interpreting his words so that the underlying logic of his argument, in contrast to the literal meaning of the words, becomes clear.

EXERCISE SET 1.3

"Real-world" arguments are often about the social, political, economic, or cultural issues. Some examples are gun control, prayer in public schools, euthanasia, cloning, race relations, immigration policy, humanitarian intervention, and genetic research. Pick one such issue that is of interest to you (you need not limit yourself to the ones listed here). Write a one-page argument defending some position on this issue. Be sure that you present an argument, with a conclusion and reasons supporting it. Do not simply discuss facts or attitudes about the issue.

Summary

Critical thinking is reasoning. Critical thinking involves the mental skills needed to understand how some claims (reasons) can support other claims. Three activities are important for critical thinking: (1) identifying the reasoning of others, (2) evaluating that reasoning, and (3) creating reasoning of your own. We use language in different ways. Language has, for example, an expressive use, a descriptive use, a directive use, and, most importantly for us, an argumentative use. Critical thinking is the understanding and mastery of this argumentative language.

Critical thinking has intrinsic value in that reasoning is an enjoyable activity in itself. Critical thinking also has instrumental value in that it provides positive benefits. Critical thinking can help you determine what you ought to believe and do. It can help you unearth and criticize questionable assumptions in your thinking. Moreover, because you have the ability to reason, practicing critical thinking is part of fulfilling your potential as a human being. In addition, critical thinking has considerable social benefits, especially the political benefit of allowing you to participate more effectively in democratic society.

Key Terms

critical thinking

argument

conclusion

argumentative use
   of language

intrinsic value

instrumental value

justification

assumption

hidden assumption

questionable assumption

Notes

1. Bertrand Russell, *The ABC of Relativity* (New York: Harper & Brothers, 1925), p. 166.
2. When a sentence that is grammatically a question is used descriptively, it is known as a rhetorical question. Rhetorical questions will be discussed in Chapter 4.
3. Whales, dolphins, and some specially trained apes may be exceptions to this rule.
4. Another use of language that involves multiple statements is the narrative. Here, the claims or sentences are related in a special way, but in a different way from that in which claims and sentences are related in argumentative language.
5. One example is the ontological argument for the existence of God, developed by the medieval philosopher Anselm and discussed extensively ever since. Roughly, the argument goes like this: There is a difference between concepts and reality. Normally, having a concept of something, such as visiting extraterrestrials, does not guarantee that such a thing actually exists. But this is not true in the case of one concept—our concept of a being perfect in every respect. Because it is more perfect to exist than not to exist, the fact that we have the concept guarantees God's existence.
6. Sometimes in the presentation of an argument, the conclusion is not explicitly stated but is left for the audience to draw for itself. This is an implicit conclusion, and it will be discussed in Chapter 4. An argument with an implicit conclusion might be given in a single sentence representing only one claim, which would be the reason.
7. Victor Hugo, *Les Miserables* (New York: New American Library, 1987), translated by Lee Fahnestock and Norman Macfee, based on the classic translation by C. E. Wilbour.
8. Sometimes it may be to our benefit to believe what is false. For example, believing that you are likely to do very well on a test may give you the confidence to do better than if you had correctly believed that you were not likely to do well. This is the power of "positive thinking." Despite such examples, the issue of whether it is always more beneficial to believe what is true is a matter of great controversy.
9. Aristotle, *Nicomachean Ethics* (many editions), book I.
10. This term is adopted from Ralph H. Johnson and J. Anthony Blair, *Logical Self-Defense* (New York: McGraw-Hill, 1994).
11. This quotation is taken from Plato's dialogue *Apology*, translated by G. M. A. Grube, in *Five Dialogues* (Indianapolis, IN: Hackett, 1981), pp. 18b–c. In this work, Plato presents the defense offered by his teacher Socrates at the trial that led to Socrates' execution. Socrates was defending himself against the charge that he had misused his formidable

critical thinking skills in this way, by making the weaker argument appear to be the stronger.

12. See, for example, *Republic*, pp. 333e–334a.

13. The questionable assumptions on which the decision to send U.S. troops to Vietnam were based are discussed by Robert McNamara in his book *In Retrospect* (New York: Random House, 1995). See, especially, pp. 319–324. McNamara, as secretary of defense, was one of the principal policy makers involved in that decision.

14. For an account of Watergate, see Fred Emery, *Watergate* (New York: Touchstone Books, 1995).

15. Nixon, in fact, publicly defended his actions as the scandal developed by claiming that he had said to his aides, when the idea of a cover-up came up in their discussion, "We could do that, but it would be wrong."

CHAPTER 2

What Is *an* Argument?

JACK: You always want to argue about things.
ALGERNON: That is exactly what things were originally made for.

—OSCAR WILDE[1]

Critical thinking is reasoning. We can think about any number of things, but we think *critically* about them when we use reasoning to understand them. We think critically because we want to determine what is best for us to believe or do and because it can be enjoyable for its own sake. The currency of critical thinking is mainly arguments. We reason in terms of arguments—arguments presented by others that we seek to understand and evaluate and arguments we create (which are, in turn, often evaluated by others). In this chapter, we develop our understanding of what an argument is. We consider how to distinguish arguments from nonarguments. We also discuss the social nature of the activity of reasoning. In this chapter, we learn how to determine *whether* an argument is present; in Chapter 4, we begin to determine *what* the argument is.

2.1 The Support Relationship

What is an argument? In Chapter 1, we discussed a tentative definition—namely, that an argument represents an effort to show that some claim is true by giving reasons that support the truth of that claim. Now we need to lay the basis for a more precise definition.

2.1.1 Statements

First, an argument is composed of two or more statements. A **statement**, also called a claim, is an assertion about the world. A statement is expressed in a sentence, but a statement is not the same as a sentence. A statement is *what* is expressed or asserted, while a sentence is *how* a statement is expressed or asserted. A statement is either true or false.

> ### Statements
>
> A statement is an assertion or claim about the world. A statement is either true or false, though we may not know or be able to discover which. Statements are expressed by sentences. A statement is what is expressed by a sentence, while a sentence is the way a statement is expressed. Statements are properly expressed in indicative sentences.

Not every sentence expresses a statement because, as we saw in the previous chapter, not every sentence is either true or false. For example, interrogative and imperative sentences are not true or false. Statements are properly expressed with indicative sentences. Consider these examples:

Example 2.1

A. Set your alarm.
B. I already did.
C. What time is it?
D. It is 5:30.

Sentences A and C are neither true nor false. If someone asked you whether they are true, you would be unable to respond. Such sentences do not normally express statements. In contrast, sentences B and D are either true or false. They are indicative sentences that express statements and that use descriptive language. Statements are properly expressed in indicative sentences, though sometimes, for stylistic reasons, they may be expressed with other kinds of sentences.[2]

An argument is a group of statements, one of which is supported by the others. In presenting an argument, you seek to establish the truth of a statement (the conclusion) by presenting reasons that support that statement. The statements that you present as supporting the conclusion are the **premises** (reasons). Some arguments have only one premise, but most have more than one.

> ### Premises
>
> In an argument, the reasons, or the statements presented in support of the conclusion, are called premises. Every argument has at least one premise and usually more than one.

2.1.2 Statements Supporting Statements

The idea that in an argument one of the statements is supported by the others is very important, for it is what distinguishes any random group of statements from an argument. What makes a group of statements an argument is the existence of a **support relationship** among the statements. A group of statements is an argument when a support relationship exists between some of the statements (the premises) and another of the statements (the conclusion). The support relationship holds between two statements when one of them is meant to provide evidence for the other.

We must be more precise about what a support relationship is, since it is the key to understanding what an argument is. Often, the truth of one statement (A) will provide evidence for the truth of another statement (B). In other words, if A is true, this may make it certain or likely that B is true. At the least, the truth of A makes it more likely that B is true (that is, more likely than if A were not true).

If statements A and B have this relationship, then the truth of B at least partly depends on or is a function of the truth of A. Even when we know nothing about the truth of B, when we know that A is true we can conclude that B is true or likely true—or at least that there is a greater likelihood that B is true. This is the support relationship. Put another way, the support relationship exists between two statements when one is *relevant* to the other or, more precisely, when the truth of one is relevant to the truth of the other. If no support relationship exists between two statements, they are irrelevant to each other.

Support Relationships

A support relationship exists between two statements when the truth of one provides evidence for or is relevant to the truth of the other. In other words, if the support relationship exists between two statements, the truth of one makes it certain or likely, or at least more likely, that the other is true as well.

The support relationship has different levels of strength. Consider these statements:

Example 2.2

A. Columbus's voyage in 1492 was the first visit to America by Europeans.
B. There were no Europeans in America before 1492.
C. Europeans did not know about America before 1492.
D. There were people living in America before 1492.
E. The Vikings visited America in the tenth century.
F. Americans had met Europeans before 1492.

Consider first the relationship between statements A and B. These two statements have a strong support relationship: A cannot be true without B's being true. A guarantees B. A provides not simply evidence for B but *conclusive* evidence. That is not to say that A is true. Columbus may not have been the first European to visit America. But the support relationship exists whether or not A is true. *If* A is true, *then* B must be true. That is, if Columbus's voyage in 1492 was the first visit to America by Europeans (and it may not have been), then it must be that there were no Europeans in America before 1492.

This is the strongest form of support relationship, called **implication.** With implication, the truth of one statement *guarantees* the truth of the other. Implication does not guarantee that either statement is true, but it does guarantee that if the one is true, then the other is true as well. To determine if two statements are related by implication, ask yourself this question: If the first it true, can the second be false? If the answer is no, the relationship between the statements is implication. For example, does "the flag has been moved from full staff to half-staff" imply "it is now closer to the ground"? Ask yourself, can it to be true that the flag has been so moved and false that it is now closer to the ground. The answer is no, so these statements are related by implication.

> **Implication**
>
> Implication is the strongest kind of support relationship. Implication exists between two statements (one implies the other) when the truth of one guarantees the truth of the other.

Implication generally works in one direction only. While implication goes from statement A to statement B, it does not go from B to A. Thus, the truth of A guarantees the truth of B, but the truth of B does not guarantee the truth of A.[3] Even if there were no Europeans in America before 1492, some other European besides Columbus might have led an expedition to America in 1492.

Consider now a weaker kind of support relationship. Does "the flag has been moved from full staff to half-staff" imply "someone has died"? It does not, for though the flag's being at half-staff is evidence that someone has died, it is not conclusive evidence. For example, the flag, while being lowered, may simply have gotten stuck at half-staff. So, in this case, the support relationship is weaker than implication.

Consider the relationship between statements A (Columbus's voyage in 1492 was the first visit to America by Europeans) and C (Europeans did not know about America before 1492). There is a support relationship between A and C, because the truth of A provides evidence for the truth of C. But it is a weaker connection than implication because the evidence is not conclusive. A provides some support for C, but A does not guarantee C. The truth of A makes it more likely that C is true, but it may be that A is true and C is false. That is, Europeans may have had other ways of knowing of the existence of America without having visited it. For example, debris from America may have floated over to Europe on the Gulf Stream and been identified as likely coming from a previously unknown continent. Or Americans may have visited Europe. While such historical events may be unlikely, they are possible, which means that it is not impossible that A is true and C is false.

Forms of the support relationship weaker than implication can vary in strength. Consider these statements:

Example 2.3

G. The dinosaurs died off suddenly 65 million years ago.

H. A layer of iridium, an element common in interplanetary bodies, has been found at various spots on the earth in sedimentary rocks dating back to 65 million years.

J. A large asteroid struck the earth 65 million years ago.

Statements G and H both have the support relationship to statement J by providing some evidence for J. But neither G nor H has the implication relationship to J, for either may be true and yet J be false. When we contrast G and H, however, we find that H provides much stronger support for J than G does. There are a number of other possible causes than the impact of a large asteroid for the sudden death of the dinosaurs. In contrast, it is harder to conceive of an alternative cause for the presence of the iridium.

Returning to the Columbus example, consider the relationship between statements A (Columbus's voyage in 1492 was the first visit to America by Europeans) and D (there were people living in America before 1492). There is no support relationship between A and D. Although it is a historical fact that people had lived in America for thousands of years before 1492, A provides no reason to believe that this is true. The truth of one statement has no relevance to the truth of the other.

Consider now a different kind of case, the relationship between statements A (Columbus's voyage in 1492 was the first visit to America by Europeans) and E (the Vikings visited America in the tenth century). The truth of A is relevant to the truth of E, but the truth of A does not support the truth of E. On the contrary, the truth of A implies that E is false. We can call this a **negative support relationship,** such that the truth of one statement supports the falsity of the other.

Like the positive support relationship, the negative support relationship has degrees of strength, from implication (as in the case of A and E) to weaker forms. When two statements, like A and E, have the strongest form of negative support relationship between them, then the truth of one implies the falsity of the other, so that there is an **inconsistency** between them. A and F (Americans had met Europeans before 1492) are an example of the weaker form of the negative support relationship. That Columbus was the first European to visit the Americas does not

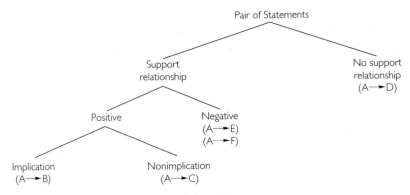

FIGURE 2.1   Types of Support Relationships

guarantee that Americans had not met Europeans previously, but it does provide some evidence for this.

> ### Negative Support Relationships and Inconsistency
>
> The support relationship between two statements is negative when the truth of one is evidence for the falsity of the other. The strongest form of the negative support relationship is inconsistency, such that the truth of one statement guarantees the falsity of the other. In weaker forms of the negative support relationship, the truth of one statement provides less than conclusive evidence that the other is false.

To summarize, the idea of the support relationship is key to understanding what an argument is. Two statements are connected by a support relationship when one of them provides some evidence, strong or weak, for the other. The strongest form of the support relationship is implication, such that one statement cannot be true without the other's being true. Some pairs of statements have no support relationship, and some have a negative support relationship. Figure 2.1 depicts these different possibilities, using statements A–F for illustration.

2.1.3 Two Kinds of Premises

The idea of the support relationship helps us to understand what an argument is. But arguments usually have more than one premise. So far, we have been talking about the support relationship between pairs of statements—specifically, between a premise and a conclusion. When an argument has more than one premise, however, the support relationship can exist between premise(s) and conclusion in two different ways. This is because there are two different kinds of premises.

Consider these arguments (henceforth, as in these examples, premises will be indicated by the letter "P," with multiple premises receiving the designations "P1," "P2," and so forth, and conclusions will be indicated by the letter "C"):

Example 2.4

A.   P1: Wetherbee was raised with loving care by his mother.
      P2: Wetherbee's mother is requesting desperately needed financial assistance from him.
      P3: Wetherbee can easily afford to provide his mother with the financial assistance she requests.
      P4: Wetherbee's mother has nowhere to turn for help other than Wetherbee.
      C: Therefore, Wetherbee should help his mother with the financial assistance she requests.

B.   P1: All humans are animals.
      P2: All animals are mortal.
      C: Therefore, all humans are mortal.

In the first argument, each premise by itself has a support relationship to the conclusion. Each premise provides at least some evidence for the conclusion, independently of the other premises. When this is the case, we may say that the premises together converge on the conclusion. Thus, premises of this kind are called **convergent premises.**

In argument B, each of the premises depends on the other to show how it supports the conclusion. Each supports the conclusion in conjunction with the other. The claim that all humans are animals shows how the claim that all animals are mortal supports the conclusion that all humans are mortal. Likewise, the claim that all animals are mortal shows how the claim that all humans are animals supports the conclusion. The two premises together support the conclusion. Each premise is dependent on the other for the support it provides to the conclusion. The support relationship holds between the premises together and the conclusion. The premises are linked together in their support for the conclusion. Hence, the premises in arguments of this kind are referred to as **linked premises.** While linked premises usually come in pairs, they can also come in larger groups. (As argument B shows, linked premises are connected by a bracket.)

This is different from the case of convergent premises, in which each premise provides support for the conclusion apart from the other premises. When there are several convergent premises, as in argument A, the premises taken together do provide stronger support for the conclusion than any one premise by itself. Still, each provides some support for the conclusion without needing any of the others to show how it does so. For example, the claim in P1 that Wetherbee was raised with loving care by his mother supports the conclusion that he should give her the help she needs, without reference to any other of the premises. None of the other premises shows how P1 supports the conclusion.

Most arguments have either convergent or linked premises, but some arguments have some premises that are linked and others that are convergent. These are known as **mixed arguments.**

Convergent and Linked Premises and Mixed Arguments

Arguments have two different kinds of premises: convergent and linked. An argument has convergent premises, if each of the premises supports the conclusion by itself without reference to the other premises. An argument has linked premises if the premises support the conclusion in groups. Each linked premise shows how a premise with which it is linked supports the conclusion. Most arguments have either convergent premises or linked premises, but some, called mixed arguments, have both kinds of premises.

The distinction between linked and convergent premises is connected with the distinction between implication and weaker forms of the support relationship. In an argument with linked premises, the support relationship between the premises taken together and the conclusion is usually (though not always) implication. In most arguments with linked premises, it is impossible for the premises to be true and the conclusion to be false, as argument B shows.

But things are different for arguments with convergent premises. The support relationship between the premises taken together and the conclusion may be quite strong, as in the case of argument A, but not implication. Thus, Wetherbee's mother might be deranged and want to use the money for something that could be harmful, such as purchasing firearms, in which case Wetherbee should not provide the funds, despite all the premises being true. This difference between arguments with linked premises and those with convergent premises will be very important when we consider the evaluation of arguments beginning in Chapter 6.

2.1.4 Author's Intention

Arguments are human creations, human artifacts. We formulate arguments and present them to others. Any argument we find (in conversations, newspapers, classrooms, talk shows, campaign speeches, and so forth) is presented *by* someone *to* others. In discussing this fact, certain terms will come in handy. A **text** is a piece of prose language, written or spoken, that may or may not contain an argument. A text that contains an argument is an **argumentative text.** An **author** is a person who creates a text. An **audience** is the group of people toward whom an author directs his or her text.

An author who presents an argument to an audience *intends* that the text express an argument. In understanding what an argument is, the author's intention

---

Text, Argumentative Text, Author, and Audience

A text is a piece of prose language, written or spoken, that may or may not contain an argument. A text that contains an argument is an argumentative text. An author is a person who creates a text, and an audience is the group of people toward whom an author directs his or her text.

---

is important. An author who presents an argument intends that a support relationship exist between some of the statements in the text. Thus, when you determine that a text contains an argument, you are judging the author's intention. Finding an argument is a matter of reading the intentions of the author, just as creating an argument requires having the intention to do so. All human communication works this way. For example, when you interpret someone's hand motion as a wave, you are judging that the motion was made with a certain intention.

Our definition of argument thus needs to be modified. In Chapter 1, we said that an argument is a group of statements that have a support relationship. But a group of statements having a support relationship and the author's intention for it to have the support relationship are not the same thing. The statements expressed in a text might have a support relationship without the author intending this, or, more likely, an author may intend that the statements have a support relationship without their actually doing so. We often do what we do not intend to do and fail to do what we intend to do.

This sometimes happens with arguments. While it is unlikely that there would be a support relationship among statements if the author did not intend to present an argument, it more often happens the other way around. That is, an author will intend to present an argument when the support relationship is absent. Consider this example:

Example 2.5

Background: Early in his first term in office, President Clinton proposed allowing homosexuals to serve in the military. In the 1960s, Clinton had opposed the war in Vietnam and avoided military service.

> We should reject Clinton's proposal to allow homosexuals to serve in the military. After all, Clinton was a draft dodger.

Clearly, this author intends to present an argument, which could be represented in this way:

Example 2.6

P1: Clinton refused to serve his country in Vietnam.
C: Therefore, we should reject his proposal to allow homosexuals to serve in the military.

The problem is that there is no support relationship here. The statement that Clinton refused to serve in Vietnam provides no evidence in favor of the statement that his proposal to allow homosexuals to serve in the military ought to be rejected. Whether an idea or proposal is good does not, in general, depend on the character of the person who advocates it. This text could not be said to contain an argument if "argument" were defined solely in terms of the existence of a support relationship. But if "argument" were defined in terms of the author's intentions, this text would count as an argument.

So, we must choose. Should we define "argument" merely in terms of the existence of a support relationship, or should we define it in terms of the author's intention? Should we define it in terms of actual or merely intended support relationships? Given that arguments are human constructions, we should choose the definition in terms of intended support relationships.

Arguments, Revised Definition

An argument is a group of statements in a text that the author intends to be connected by a support relationship. More precisely, a text contains an argument, if and only if, the author intends that some of the statements in the text (the premise[s]) support another of the statements (the conclusion). Usually, the statements in an argument will in fact have a support relationship, but not always.

In practice, the existence of the support relationship represents solid, though not infallible, evidence that the author intended to present an argument. So, the best way to determine whether a text contains an argument is to determine whether the statements have a support relationship. Even if there is no support relationship, however, this does not mean that there is no argument. As in Example 2.5, an author may intend to offer an argument but provide no support relationship.

How do we determine an author's intention? We cannot look inside her or his head, and the author may even be long dead. Therefore, we have to determine intentions from the text itself. The existence of a support relationship is one of the most important ways to determine that an author intends to present an argument. But it is not the only way. As our revised definition of argument suggests, we may need to consider more about the text than simply the potential existence of a support relationship.

Nevertheless, texts often provide inadequate clues about the author's intentions. There are two reasons for this. First, people often have not learned how to write or speak clearly or do not take the time or trouble to express themselves clearly. Second, people are often not clear in their own minds about precisely what they mean; their intentions are not clear to themselves.[4]

You may be unclear about the intentions of the author of a text in two ways. First, you may be unclear *whether* the author intends to present an argument. Does the author intend for there to be a support relationship among the statements expressed in the text? Second, even if you know that the author is presenting an argument, it may be unclear *what* the argument is. What is the conclusion? What are the premises? This is not simply a matter of identifying which sentences express the conclusion and the premises; you also must determine what those sentences mean and how the author intends them to be related. (This chapter is on the "whether"; Chapter 4 is on the "what.")

The difficulties in critical thinking are difficulties both of interpretation (the whether and the what) and evaluation. Problems arise in determining not only if an argument is strong or weak but also whether there is an argument and what the argument is. There is often room for controversy and legitimate disagreement about the "whether" and the "what."

This is not to say that any one interpretation is as good as another. Many interpretations are clearly wrong. But there may be more than one interpretation that could plausibly be correct. We may need to consider several plausible interpretations to determine which is the most plausible. The problem is one of *fairness* to the text and to the author. We seek to be as fair as possible to a text, to give it the best of its plausible interpretations.

When we struggle over which of several plausible interpretations is the best, we consider reasons in support of one or another of the interpretations. So, we are, in effect, constructing arguments about the correctness or fairness of these various interpretations. In this sense, even in interpreting the arguments of others, we are, at least implicitly, constructing arguments of our own.

EXERCISE SET 2.1

SECTION A: Consider the following pairs of sentences and answer these questions about each of them:

(1) Does a support relationship exist between the two statements?
(2) If there is a support relationship, is it positive or negative?
(3) If there is a positive support relationship, is it a case of implication or a weaker form of support relationship?

In all cases, assume that Pat and Chris are alive.

EXAMPLE
a. Pat is the oldest human being alive.
b. Chris is younger than Pat.

ANSWER
(1) A support relationship exists between a and b.
(2) The support relationship is positive.
(3) The relationship is implication, since if a is true, then b must be true.

PROBLEMS

1. a. Pat has the highest grade point average in the class.
   b. Pat is the most intelligent student in the class.
2. a. Pat has the highest grade point average in the class.
   b. Pat is the best-looking student in the class.
❖ 3. a. Pat is the only student with straight A's.
   b. Chris has straight A's too.
4. a. Chris is the principal's best friend.
   b. Chris knows the principal.
5. a. Chris is the star of the high school soccer team.
   b. Chris plans to play soccer in college.
❖ 6. a. Chris is the star of the soccer team.
   b. Chris knows how to kick a ball.
7. a. Chris is the star of the soccer team.
   b. Chris is a good student.
8. a. Chris is a good student.
   b. Pat is a good student.
❖ 9. a. Pat dresses in secondhand clothes.
   b. Pat is poor.
10. a. Pat is a constant liar.
    b. Pat cannot be trusted.
11. a. The Mount Saint Helens volcano has erupted in the recent past.
    b. The Mount Saint Helens volcano is likely to erupt again in the near future.
❖ 12. a. Pat has just flipped ten heads in a row with a coin.
    b. It is very likely that Pat will get tails on the next flip.
13. a. Chris is an unmarried adult male.
    b. Chris is a bachelor.
14. a. If euthanasia were legalized, it would be subject to abuse.
    b. Euthanasia should not be legalized.
❖ 15. a. Abortion is the killing of a human being.
    b. Abortion is not morally permitted.
16. a. There is too much sex and violence on TV.
    b. The government should control what is on TV.
17. a. Teachers are only human.
    b. You should not expect perfection from your teacher.
❖ 18. a. Genes are natural parts of all living things.
    b. Genes should not be patented.
19. a. Technology led to the atom bomb.
    b. Technology poses a risk to all life on this planet.
20. a. Celebrities advertise products they know nothing about.
    b. We should buy the products celebrities tell us to buy.

SECTION B: For each of the following arguments, answer these questions, giving reasons for your answers:

(1) Are the premises of the argument linked or convergent?

(2) If the premises are convergent, is the support relationship between the premises, taken together, and the conclusion strong or weak?

EXAMPLE

      P1: Kelly was not in class today.
      P2: Kelly visited the doctor yesterday.
      C: Therefore, Kelly is ill.

ANSWER

(1) The premises are convergent, since each supports the conclusion by itself.

(2) The support the premises together provide for the conclusion is not very strong. There are many other circumstances under which the premises would be true and the conclusion false. For example, Kelly might have been going to the doctor to be vaccinated for a trip overseas begun today.

PROBLEMS

1. P1: Sally and John were talking in the halls.
   P2: Sally and John walked home together.
   C: Therefore, John is Sally's new boyfriend.

2. P1: Stacy is Billy's mother.
   P2: Alice is Stacy's mother.
   C: Therefore, Alice is Billy's grandmother.

3. P1: Harry Potter was raised by muggles.
   P2: Harry Potter is a wizard.
   C: Therefore, Harry Potter was not raised by his own kind.

4. P1: The wealthy have more than they need.
   P2: The poor are starving.
   C: Therefore, the wealthy should provide more aid to the poor.

5. P1: A person can vote at age 18.
   P2: A person can serve in the military at age 18.
   C: Therefore, a person should be allowed to drink alcohol at age 18.

6. P1: All men are mortal.
   P2: Socrates is a man.
   C: Therefore, Socrates is mortal.

7. P1: Many have told tales of alien abduction.
   P2: There must be other civilizations more advanced than ours.
   C: Therefore, the earth has been visited by aliens.

8. P1: Drugs are available at rock concerts.
   P2: Authority is not respected at rock concerts.
   C: Therefore, people should not attend rock concerts.

2.2 Argumentative Texts

Not all texts are argumentative texts. In a nonargumentative text, the statements may be presented as true, but there is no attempt to *persuade* the audience that any one of them is true. In contrast, one of the purposes of an argumentative text is to persuade the audience of the truth of one of the statements, namely, the conclusion. The author of an argumentative text does this by providing statements that have a support relationship to the conclusion. The author of a nonargumentative text does not intend the statements to be related in this way.

Consider these examples, only one of which is argumentative:

Example 2.7

A. We should have our picnic today. The picnic basket is in the closet.
B. We should have our picnic today. Rain is forecast for tomorrow.

In which case is it likely that the author intended one of the statements to support the other? Clearly, text B is argumentative. In both cases, there are two statements, but the important difference is in how the statements are related. In text A, both statements are about the same subject, but they are not otherwise related in any relevant way. The statements in B, however, have a support relationship. The author clearly intended for the second statement (the premise) to provide support for the first (the conclusion). The fact that rain is forecast for tomorrow is a reason to have the picnic today. B is an argumentative text not because of the individual statements it contains, but because of the relationship intended between them.

Consider another pair of examples:

Example 2.8

A. It was 11:00 p.m. when Washington set out on his Christmas Eve crossing of the Delaware River. He took with him over a hundred men in a dozen large boats.
B. It was 11:00 p.m. when Washington set out on his Christmas Eve crossing of the Delaware River. He mentioned this departure time in his diary.

Which of these texts is argumentative and which is nonargumentative? Again, B is the argumentative text. A is nonargumentative because its two sentences, though they are about the same subject, do not have a support relationship. In contrast, in B, the second sentence provides evidence for the truth of the first, so the two sentences have a support relationship.

The argument in an argumentative text may be represented by writing out first the premises and then the conclusion, each on its own line. Sometimes, the wording needs to be changed to make the argument clearer.

Example 2.9

P1: Washington mentioned in his diary that he set out on his Christmas Eve crossing of the Delaware River at 11:00 p.m.
C: Therefore, he set out on that crossing at 11:00 p.m.

2.2.1 An Example of an Argumentative Text

Many argumentative texts have sentences that are not part of the argument. A text is argumentative if it contains an argument, even if some of the text is not part of that argument. As long as at least two statements are intended to have a support relationship, the text is argumentative. Consider a portion of Lincoln's Gettysburg Address. For our purposes, the sentences are numbered.

Example 2.10

① Fourscore and seven years ago our fathers brought forth on this continent a new nation, conceived in liberty and dedicated to the proposition that all men are created equal. ② Now we are engaged in a great civil war, testing whether that nation or any nation so conceived and so dedicated can long endure. ③ We are met on a great battlefield of that war. ④ We have come to dedicate a portion of that field as a final resting-place for those who here gave their lives that that nation might live. ⑤ It is altogether fitting and proper that we should do this. ⑥ But in a larger sense, we cannot dedicate, we cannot consecrate, we cannot hallow this ground. ⑦ The brave men, living and dead who struggled here have consecrated it far above our poor power to add or detract. ⑧ The world will little note nor long remember what we say here, but it can never forget what they did here. . . .

Do you recognize a support relationship between any of these statements?

Sentences 1–4 are a series of statements about the situation in which the author (Lincoln) and the audience finds themselves. None of these sentences stands in the support relationship to any of the others in this group. But sentence 4 seems intended to support sentence 5. It is fitting and proper to dedicate the field *because* the soldiers gave their lives there. Then, sentence 7 supports sentence 6. Lincoln clearly intends sentence 7 to provide evidence for the truth of sentence 6. The claim that those who fought in the battle have already consecrated the ground much more than the living ever could supports the claim that Lincoln and his audience cannot (in a larger sense, at least) themselves consecrate the ground.

Being able to distinguish argumentative texts from nonargumentative ones is a matter of learning to perceive whether the statements expressed by the sentences of the text are intended to stand in a support relationship. It means sharpening the ability you already have as a master of the argumentative use of language. At the most basic level, recognizing the presence of a support relationship involves a kind of intuition, an "aha, got it" experience. There is no set of rules that will invariably identify an argumentative text. But there are some rules that can help.

2.2.2 Reasoning Indicators

Once you have a grasp of a text from reading it carefully, you will often recognize immediately whether any of the statements have, or are intended to have, a support relationship. But what can you do if careful study of a text does not make this clear?

Authors often explicitly indicate their intention that a text is argumentative by including certain words and phrases, referred to as **reasoning indicators.** Familiarity with reasoning indicators will help you to determine not only whether a text is argumentative but also what the argument is. In other words, it will help you to determine which of the statements in the support relationship is meant to support which—that is, which is the premise and which the conclusion.

Reasoning Indicators

Reasoning indicators are common words or phrases that authors use to signal that a text is argumentative. Reasoning indicators may appear either in front of a conclusion (conclusion indicator) or in front of a premise (premise indicator).

Reasoning indicators appear in front of a premise or conclusion. The expressions themselves may appear at the beginning of a sentence or in the middle. In either case, what follows the expression is the premise or the conclusion. In many instances, the other part of the argument (that is, the premise in the case of a conclusion indicator and the conclusion in the case of a premise indicator) appears just in front of the indicator, whether as part of the same sentence or in the previous sentence. Conclusions often appear just in front of premise indicators, and premises just in front of conclusion indicators. For example, often the conclusion of an argument will appear just before "because" and the premise just after (x because y).

Common Reasoning Indicators

Conclusion (x) Indicators	Premise (y) Indicators
therefore x	because y
consequently x	for y
so x	since y
thus x	as y
hence x	for the reason that y
implies that x	inasmuch as y
the conclusion is that x	follows from y
accordingly x	is supported by y
indicates that x	is indicated by y
it follows that x	is shown by y
demonstrates that x	the reason is that y
(et cetera)	(et cetera)

Consider this example:

Example 2.11

Background: This letter is about fees at art museums. (*New York Times*, 4/99)

> The high entrance fees imposed by some New York City art museums will not only deprive museums of future patrons, but will also deprive all of us of future artists, *since* children who might become great artists need to spend a great deal of time studying art in museums.—S.A.

The reasoning indicator, "since," is italicized. Because it is a premise indicator, the clause that follows ("children who might become great artists need to spend a great deal of time studying art in museums") is a premise. In this case, the clause that precedes the indicator is the conclusion.[5]

However, the presence of an expression from the reasoning indicator list is not an infallible indication of an argument. Sometimes, the presence of a reasoning indicator does not indicate an argument. One reason is that these expressions are often used to indicate forms of reasoning other than arguments, such as explanations (discussed in Chapter 3). Another reason is that these expressions can be used in other ways. Some of them, such as "for" and "since," are ambiguous, having grammatical roles in addition to their role as reasoning indicators.

Consider these statements:

Example 2.12

A. He did the job *for* ten dollars an hour.
B. The earth is at least 4 billion years old, *for* some of its rocks have been shown to be this old.
C. She has been gone *since* the Fourth of July.
D. *Since* today is her birthday, we can expect cake and ice cream.

The italicized terms in statements B and D are reasoning indicators, but in statements A and C, they play a different grammatical role. A reasoning indicator is usually followed by a sentence or a clause. In contrast, when these expressions are playing a different grammatical role, they are often followed by a phrase that is not a sentence or a clause, as in A and C.

2.2.3 Reasoning Indicator Test

The absence of reasoning indicators does not guarantee that a text is nonargumentative. Argumentative texts frequently do not contain reasoning indicators. Look again at this example:

Example 2.13

It was 11:00 p.m. when Washington set out on his famous Christmas Eve crossing of the Delaware River. He mentioned this departure time in his diary.

This is an argumentative text without a reasoning indicator. There is, however, a way in which you can use reasoning indicators to help you to determine whether a text is argumentative even when no reasoning indicator is present. This is called the **reasoning indicator test.** To perform this test, you insert a word or phrase from the reasoning indicator list into the text. If the reasoning indicator seems to fit—that is, if the text with the added indicator makes sense—then the text is probably argumentative.

Any of the indicators can be used in performing the test, but the easiest one to use is the conclusion indicator "therefore." The issue is whether "therefore" can be inserted into the text in a way that makes sense. Because a conclusion immediately follows "therefore" and a premise often immediately precedes it, you may have to rearrange the sentences of the text to apply the test.

Reasoning Indicator Test

For a text that you think may be argumentative but that lacks reasoning indicators, choose (1) the sentence (or the part of the sentence) that expresses what you think may be a conclusion and (2) a sentence (or the part of the sentence) that expresses what you think may be a premise. Reposition, if necessary, the first sentence immediately after the second and insert "therefore" in front of the first one. If the revised text makes sense, the text likely is argumentative.[6] If you are unsure which sentence would be the conclusion and which would be a premise, you can try different combinations, applying the test to each one.

There is one other wrinkle: If you have to rearrange the sentences, you may also have to change the wording to maintain sense, especially if pronouns are involved.[7] Pronouns normally occur after their referent, the term to which they refer. Thus, in repositioning sentences, you may have to replace pronouns with their referents.

2.2.4 Applying the Reasoning Indicator Test

To illustrate, let's apply the test to the texts in Example 2.8, neither of which has a reasoning indicator. If we assume that the texts are argumentative, we can plausibly regard the first sentence of each as expressing the conclusion and the second sentence as expressing a premise. Because in each case the would-be premise sentence follows the would-be conclusion sentence, we have to reposition the second sentence in front of the first and insert "therefore." In doing so, we also have to change the wording of the sentences to make clear what is being referred to, as shown here:

Example 2.14

A. ORIGINAL TEXT: It was 11:00 p.m. when Washington set out on his Christmas Eve crossing of the Delaware River. He took with him over a hundred men in a dozen large boats.

REVISED TEXT: Washington crossed the Delaware with over a hundred men in a dozen large boats. [*Therefore,*] it was 11:00 p.m. when Washington set out on this crossing.

    B. ORIGINAL TEXT: It was 11:00 p.m. when Washington set out on his Christmas Eve crossing of the Delaware River. He mentioned this departure time in his diary.

    REVISED TEXT: Washington mentioned in his diary that he crossed the Delaware at 11:00 p.m. [*Therefore,*] it was 11:00 p.m. when Washington set out on this crossing.

With "therefore" added, revised text B makes sense, but revised text A does not. This means that there is a support relationship in B, but not in A. Thus, the test gives the proper results: B is an argumentative text and A is not.

If a text is nonargumentative, it may not, of course, be possible to identify a sentence that might be a premise or a conclusion, because the text in fact has no such sentences. But, in general, you can safely assume, without having to apply the test, that, if the text contains no sentences that are reasonable candidates for a conclusion or a premise, it is nonargumentative. Thus, you might have identified text A immediately as nonargumentative, without applying the test.

2.2.5 A Shorthand Method

Let us apply the reasoning indicator test to some real-world examples and in the process explore a shorthand method for applying the test. The sentences in these texts are numbered to make it easier to refer to them.

Example 2.15

A. Background: This letter is about the marketplace behavior of Microsoft that led to the government taking antitrust action against it. (*Los Angeles Times,* 5/98)

    ① Time was, when I thought of Microsoft, I'd think of innovation, continually improving a product until they got it right. ② Now I think of arrogance, greed and the need to be bigger without necessarily being better.—W.S.

B. Background: This letter is in response to a number of cases of school shootings by students. (*New York Times,* 5/98)

    ① Many reasons have been given to explain the epidemic of school shootings by youngsters, and many ideas have been advanced to prevent such incidents in the future. ② There is one characteristic common to the events. ③ The shootings have been carried out by boys, not girls. ④ The question should be asked: What is it in the upbringing of boys that is different from the upbringing of girls?—H.P.

C. Background: This letter is about candidates' debates. (*New York Times,* 10/88)

    ① The "debates" are a fraud committed by and for the news media to the detriment of the electorate. ② The questioned candidates are "tested" for their ability to think quickly on their feet and speak dramatically before an audience without the use of notes or reflectors. ③ These skills—useful for acting and electioneering—are no measure of planning ability or leadership.—O.L.W.

D. Background: This letter is about youth fashion. (*Chicago Tribune*, 4/97)

① Having just picked up my daughter at high school, I couldn't help but imagine the laughs today's high schoolers are going to have 20 years from now when they look back at pictures of themselves wearing pants large enough to envelop a well-fed pod of whales. ② I just hope these kids have the good sense to take plenty of pictures now. ③ (Hope they remember to use a wide-angle lens.)—C.T.

With the shorthand method, you don't actually write out the revised text, as we did earlier. Instead, first number the sentences of the text. Then, if you think the text may be argumentative, place the number of the sentence or sentence part that may contain the conclusion after the number of the sentence or sentence part that may contain a premise. (If a sentence part is used, label it, for example, as "2b," indicating the second part of sentence 2.) Then circle the numbers and place the letters "TF" (standing for "therefore") between them, as shown here:

Example 2.16

③ TF ②

Finally, indicate with a "Y" (yes) or an "N" (no) whether the "therefore" makes sense between the two sentences. If you are unsure which sentence is the conclusion and which is a premise, you can use this notation to apply the test more than once.

Consider text A. This text is nonargumentative, and if you were unable to identify either a conclusion or a premise, you were justified in judging it nonargumentative without actually applying the test. But if you thought it might be argumentative, you could test both possibilities:

Example 2.17

A. ① TF ② N
A. ② TF ① N

Because neither result makes sense, you can conclude that the text is nonargumentative.

Now consider text B, which seems to be argumentative. First, you need to identify a likely candidate for the sentence expressing the conclusion—the main idea that the author is trying to get across. Sentence 4 seems to fit the bill. The author is trying to make the point that we need to examine the differences in upbringings between boys and girls. Moreover, sentence 3 is a likely candidate for a premise.

How about text C? It too seems to be an argumentative text, whose main point is that the debates are a fraud, which is expressed in sentence 1. Sentence 3 seems a likely candidate for a premise. But, if sentence 3 expresses a premise, it would be a premise linked to another premise, namely, the premise expressed in

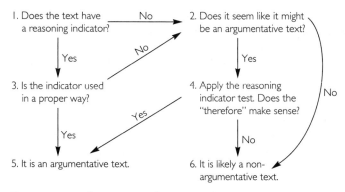

FIGURE 2.2   **The Process of Distinguishing Between Argumentative and Nonargumentative Texts**

sentence 2. If this text contains an argument, the statements expressed in sentences 2 and 3 each show how the other supports the conclusion. Thus, to apply the reasoning indicator test accurately, you should place both of these sentences in front of the sentence that expresses the conclusion. Here is how the test would be applied to texts B and C:

Example 2.18

B. ③ TF ④ Y

C. [② and ③] TF ① Y

In both cases, the Y indicates that the revised text (the text with the "therefore" added) makes sense. Texts B and C are indeed argumentative.[8]

Text D is more difficult. Sentence 1 can be divided into several parts. In the first part (call it 1a), the author talks about picking up her daughter from school. In the second part (1b), she claims that twenty years from now today's high schoolers will be laughing at pictures of themselves. In the third part (1c), she points out, with rhetorical exaggeration, how they are wearing extremely wide pants. This seems to be an argumentative text, and if it is, it seems that part 1b would be the conclusion and part 1c a premise.

Example 2.19

D. ①c TF ①b Y

This makes sense, so we may conclude that the text is argumentative.

Figure 2.2 contains a flowchart of the process of distinguishing between argumentative and nonargumentative texts.[9] The reasoning indicator test can help you determine whether a text is argumentative. But, in a sense, it cannot tell you more than you already know. You need to have some sense that a text is argumentative before applying the test because you must pick out possible conclusion and premise sentences. More difficult cases, like text C, make this clear. In addition, once you have inserted the "therefore," you must decide if the text makes sense. To do this, however, you must already have some awareness of the presence or absence of a support relationship. Without such an awareness, you would have no basis on which to judge whether the indicator made sense in the text. Thus, all the test does is to clarify your "intuition" about whether a text contains an argument.

EXERCISE SET 2.2

SECTION A: These exercises will give you practice in using the reasoning indicator test. All of the texts have two sentences.

    (1) Apply the test to each of the texts twice, once with the sentences in the order in which they are given and once with that order reversed. Apply the test whether or not you think that text is argumentative. Write out the revised texts; do not use the shorthand method.

    (2) As a result of your application of the test, state whether the text is argumentative and give a reason. If the text is argumentative, one of the two applications will make sense and the other will not. If neither application makes sense, the text is not argumentative.

EXAMPLE
The best musicians are the ones who truly feel the music. This is an ability that cannot be taught.

ANSWER
    (1) The best musicians are the ones who truly feel the music. [*Therefore,*] this is an ability that cannot be taught.
         The ability to truly feel the music cannot be taught. [*Therefore,*] the best musicians are the ones who truly feel the music.
    (2) Neither of the revised texts makes sense, so the text is not argumentative.

PROBLEMS
    1. On Sunday, the sun was shining and the birds were singing. In the evening there was a glorious sunset.
    2. The child was a genius. She could read Greek at 5 and do calculus at 8, and she also played a wicked game of chess.
    3. There is no greatness without the capacity to suffer. An easy life breeds complacency.
    4. I love the drama of the soaps. The conniving, backstabbing characters are the ones I like the most.
    5. In the musical *My Fair Lady*, the drama flows from the class conflicts in British society. Sparks fly between the two leading characters, Henry Higgins, an aristocrat, and Elisa Doolittle, a poor woman of the streets.
    6. Some are morning people and some are night people. Morning people do their best work when the sun rises, just as the night people are finished theirs.
    7. States have become addicted to the tax revenue gambling brings in. The poor suffer from gambling.
    8. Growing older is a matter of exchanging exuberance for wisdom. Imagine what it would be like if we could combine the two!

❖   9. TV today is filled with sex, violence, and trivial pandering. It is a vast wasteland.

10. New York City is the financial capital of the world. It is also the art capital of the world.

11. Some argumentative texts contain reasoning indicators. Those texts are the easiest to spot as argumentative.

❖   12. Microsoft should be condemned for putting solitaire into Windows. Millions of hours have been wasted playing that stupid game.

13. There is no element of chance in chess. Winning at chess is not a matter of luck.

14. The bigger they are, the harder they fall, and he is big. He'll fall hard.

❖   15. Fairy tales always begin with the same phrase, "once upon a time." Children can always tell at the beginning that a story is a fairy tale.

SECTION B: For the following texts, do this:

(1) Determine whether the texts are argumentative. Give reasons for your answer, applying the reasoning indicator test where appropriate and using the shorthand method.

(2) If the text is argumentative, write down the conclusion, using either the words in the text or your own paraphrase in cases in which this makes the conclusion clearer.

You should number the sentences in the textbook and use those numbers when applying the test on your answer sheets. Remember that in applying the test you sometimes need to break up a sentence into parts and put the "therefore" between them. Also, some of the nonindicative sentences will make a statement. Remember, in addition, that often an argumentative text will contain sentences that are not part of the argument.

EXAMPLE

Background: This letter discusses the role of computers in education. (*New York Times*, 5/97)

① One danger I see is the ability to quit a difficult lesson, simply by turning off the machine or switching to a different program with the click of a mouse. ② In a real classroom, or in a work environment, or in a family, there is training for staying with a task until it is complete. ③ Responsibility, a major part of real life, can often be avoided in cyber-life.—D.K.

ANSWER

(1) This text seems to be an argument, but it has no reasoning indicators. Sentence 3 is a likely candidate for the conclusion, and sentence 1, a likely candidate for a premise. Applying the test: ① TF ③. This makes sense, so the text is argumentative.

(2) The conclusion is: The use of computers does not provide training in responsibility.

PROBLEMS

1. Background: This letter is in response to an article on the Canada Goose. (*New York Times*, 5/95)

"Canada" comes from the Huron-Iroquoian word "Kanata," meaning (as you noted) village. The Canada Goose derived its name from the country by 1676. Canada has lent its musical name to more than 30 plants and animals.—C.L.C.

2. Background: This letter discusses one difference between judges and legislators. (*Los Angeles Times*, 4/98)

   Judges must decide cases, even those that by necessity have political overtones. Unlike legislators, judges have no control over the matters assigned to them and once assigned must decide them one way or the other. Judges cannot refer matters to committee or wait for political winds to subside.—R.J.S.

❖ 3. Background: This passage is from Charles Darwin's *On the Origin of Species*.[10] The varieties he is talking about are species or subspecies.

   Whatever part is found to be most constant, is used in classing varieties: *C/* Thus the horns are very useful for this purpose with cattle because they are less variable than the shape or colour of the body, etc.

4. Background: This letter is part of the debate over campaign finance reform. (*Los Angeles Times*, 2/98)

   It is not possible to have a president with high moral values in view of the vast amount of money that he must raise to get the office.—J.G.

5. Background: This is a letter to the *Miami Herald*. (5/97)

   Many years ago my husband, John D. Locke, was a prominent advertising manager. We lived a very interesting life and retired in Pompano Beach. One of his highlights and everyday pleasure is reading the *Herald*. He is now 80 years old.—A.B.L.[11]

❖ 6. Background: This letter is about children and violent films. (*New York Times*, 7/97)

   Your article on the increase of violence in family films failed to mention the "forbidden fruit syndrome." Often when parents forbid their children to see action-adventure films, it only spurs kids to see it on the sly. When something is forbidden, we desire it even more.—R.F.B.

7. Background: This letter is in response to an article about space exploration. (*New York Times*, 7/96)

   Your news article about Io, the moon of Jupiter, says Io is "pronounced either EYE-oh or EE-oh." Is that EYE-thr EYE-oh or EE-oh, or EE-ther EYE-oh or EE-oh?—J.G.

8. Background: This passage is taken from *The Federalist* 51, by James Madison.[12] He is speaking of the power given up by the people in the formation of the government.

   In the compound republic of America, the power surrendered by the people, is first divided between two distinct governments, and then the portion allotted to each, subdivided among distinct and separate departments. Hence a double security arises to the rights of the people.

9. Background: This letter is about the 1997 transfer of the British colony of Hong Kong to China. (*New York Times*, 7/97)

   The transfer of Hong Kong to Chinese rule and, with it, the effective end of the greatest empire in human history, leaves several ironies in its wake. One is the fact that the first country to break from Britain's colonial grasp—the United States—now rules the largest colony in the world by population: Puerto Rico.—J.C.

10. Background: This letter is about high-ranking military officers who are disciplined for adulterous relationships. (*New York Times*, 6/97)

    The real victims in the military adultery scandals are the wives of these generals. Many have spent their lives advancing their husbands' careers. Not only must they bear public humiliation, but they also may face a lowered standard of living caused by their husbands' forced retirements at reduced rank.—D.W.

11. Background: This letter offers advice about burglars. (*Los Angeles Times*, 7/97)

    Do not go in your house if you have any reason to suspect that a burglar might still be inside. Searching the house for a cornered burglar is extremely dangerous and is a job best left for the police.—S.Y.

12. Background: This letter is in response to an article on the removal of relics from a military park. (*Washington Post*, 6/98)

    You report that the attorney of a man convicted of digging up relics at a military park said, "Our ancestors are not going to be real upset if we remove a few mini-balls." He was no doubt referring to minie balls, named after French captain Claude Minie, who invented an elongated bullet with an expanding base that spun as it left the rifle for greater range and accuracy. Variations of this bullet were used throughout the Civil War. —S.T.S.

13. Background: This letter concerns postal rates. (*New York Times*, 7/97)

    Local mail sent to the same ZIP code should get a discount because the Postal Service has reduced handling and shipping costs for such mail. That would encourage more people to communicate by mail, which would mean more revenue for the Postal Service.—P.F.

14. Background: This is in response to an article on children's illiteracy. (*Atlanta Constitution*, 4/97)

    Why are the news media not asking the obvious questions: Why can't these children read? After all, they have been in school for several years. What have their teachers been doing? If professionally certified teachers cannot teach children to read, why do we think unprofessional volunteers can do it? —R.F.B.

❖ 15. Background: This letter is part of the debate over government funding of the arts through the National Endowment for the Arts (NEA). (*New York Times*, 7/97)

In your editorial, you say that the Republican right saw the vote to kill the NEA "as an important expression of opposition to any government arts program they could not control." On the contrary, the Republicans will control the NEA the next time they're in the White House just as the Democrats do now. We must abolish the NEA because the arts are too important to be controlled by politicians.—D.S.

16. Background: This letter is about squirrels and bird feeders. (*Washington Post*, 6/97)

Many bird lovers try to design feeders so squirrels can't get to them and eat all the food. There is a simple solution to this problem. All that is necessary is to sprinkle a little cayenne pepper on the birdseed. This does not bother the birds, and it is good for them. But a squirrel will take one sniff and run away without touching the food.—H.P.M.

17. Background: This letter is in response to an article discussing the efforts of physicists to confirm the existence of the "top quark," a subatomic particle predicted by atomic theory. (*New York Times*, 5/94)

You describe experimental verification of the top quark as "central to understanding the nature of time, matter and the universe." But in the same sentence you state that the discovery, in all likelihood, "will never make a difference to everyday life." How dispiriting.—D.B.

❖ 18. Background: This letter is part of the debate about former President Clinton's trial for impeachment in the Senate and whether the fact that he was not convicted meant he was acquitted of the charges against him. (*New York Times*, 2/99)

Failure to reach 67 votes to convict the President is not tantamount to acquittal. Since 67 votes are needed to convict, it would seem that 67 votes would be needed to reach a true verdict of acquittal. A split vote would be the same as a hung jury and thus be a mistrial. History would not perceive the President as acquitted but as having received a verdict equal to censure.
—A.J.B.

19. Background: This passage is taken from *The Federalist*, #34, by Alexander Hamilton.[13]

To judge from the history of mankind, we shall be compelled to conclude, that the fiery and destructive passions of war, reign in the human breast, with much more powerful sway, than the mild and beneficent sentiments of peace; and, that to model our political systems upon speculations of lasting tranquility, is to calculate on the weaker springs of the human character.

❖ 20. Background: This letter is in response to an article about efforts to develop a global wireless communications system based on satellites. (*Chicago Tribune*, 6/97)

The article said that, when completed, 66 satellites will comprise the global wireless network called Iridium. Your readers may be interested to know that iridium is the element that has 77 electrons circulating around the nucleus. The original design of the wireless system called for 77 satellites. Cute. Subsequent revision of the system, however, reduced that number to 66 satellites, and 66 is the atomic number of dysprosium.—P.L.

21. Background: This letter was written in 1998, before basketball legend Michael Jordan re-retired from the Chicago Bulls. (*Chicago Tribune*, 4/98)

Last night I dreamed that Michael Jordan left the Chicago Bulls forever. Flags were flying at half-mast. Many buildings were draped in black. Little children huddled together in schools and were being counseled by trained personnel. Men and women were sobbing openly all over town. Everyone wore a black arm band. Mayor Richard Daley proclaimed a day of mourning; President Clinton declared Chicago a disaster area. Thank God I woke up and realized it was only a dream!—D.S.

22. Background: This letter is in response to an article discussing sending humans to Mars. (*New York Times*, 7/97)

Important issues should be resolved before sending a manned mission to Mars. When men spend time on Mars, especially if they try to grow food and extract resources, they will likely taint the remains of whatever biota might have existed before the mission. We should thoroughly investigate Mars before taking a large risk of introducing Earth life.—M.F.

23. Background: This letter seeks to correct a mistake in a newspaper article discussing the discovery of insulin. (*New York Times*, 6/97)

It has long been established that insulin was actually discovered by Frederick Banting, a young surgeon, and his assistant Charles Best, a medical student. Dr. Macleod, the Scottish-born chairman of the physiology department at the University of Toronto, merely gave Banting laboratory space in the summer of 1921 and then shared credit with Banting when the validity of the discovery became apparent.—M.R.O.

24. Background: This letter is in response to an article discussing the photographs Charles Darwin took of facial expressions. (*New York Times*, 5/98)

The study of facial expressions is vital to the artist. How does an artist show a particular expression in painting and sculpture so that it will be successfully understood by the viewer? This question was of special interest in the seventeenth century, when the depiction of strong facial expressions was an essential feature of Baroque art. Emotions like fear, anger and surprise were described in detail so that artists could illustrate them with precision.—F.F.H.

25. Background: This letter is about a policy adopted by public transit officials in New York City. (*New York Times*, 7/97)

The Metropolitan Transportation Authority's new plan to provide free transfers between the subway and bus systems with a strict two-hour time limit is no favor to New Yorkers. In a city with so many neurotic and obsessive-compulsive residents, adding this deadline will only increase the level of craziness. Not wishing to increase the level of stress in my own life, I'll continue to use tokens and give up my right to the free transfer.—L.M.R.

2.3 Persuasion and the Social Nature of Arguments

There is another common meaning for the term "argument," a meaning different from though related to the one we have been discussing. According to this definition, an argument is simply an exchange of words, often heated, between people. Oscar Wilde may have had this sense of the term in mind in the quote given at the beginning of the chapter.

One way to highlight the difference between the two definitions is to observe that they are used with different verbs. When an argument is a heated exchange, we say that people *have* an argument—for example, between romantic partners or between an employee and her boss. When an argument is a form of critical thinking, we say that people *make* or *present* an argument—for example, a student presenting his case to a teacher. In addition, the two definitions tend to be used with different adjectives. An argument in the critical thinking sense can be strong or weak, clever or misleading, or fallacious, adjectives unlikely to be applied to an argument in the heated-exchange sense. Arguments in the heated-exchange sense are more likely to be referred to as vicious, air clearing, or tension increasing.

However, the two meanings have in common an attempt to *persuade*. In a heated exchange, each person is trying to persuade the other on the point about which there is disagreement. But an argument in the critical thinking sense is an attempt to persuade as well. In a critical thinking argument, people are generally attempting to persuade others of the truth of their conclusion. Because both senses of "argument" involve efforts to persuade, they may be occurring at the same time. When people are *having* an argument, they are often *presenting* arguments as well. Consider this case:

Example 2.20

CHRIS: You're much better at doing the dishes than I am. So, you should do the dishes.

PAT: It's unfair that I do the dishes all of the time. So, you should do the dishes.

Here, both Chris and Pat are presenting an argument. But when people make critical thinking arguments in the context of having a heated exchange, whether one side succeeds in persuading the other is likely determined by factors other than the merits of the individual arguments. Pat may have a better argument than Chris, but this is no guarantee that Pat will persuade Chris to do the dishes. In a heated exchange, emotions often prevent the participants from giving full consideration to each other's arguments.

In addition, participants in heated exchanges frequently seek to impose their positions on others by coercion or psychological manipulation. Thus, both Chris and Pat may seek in various subtle ways to threaten or intimidate each other into doing the dishes. The emotional intensity of heated exchanges makes the use of coercive tactics especially effective and especially likely. Participants in a heated exchange often seek to win concessions more through manipulation and coercion than through strong, well-thought-out arguments.

2.3.1 Two Questions About Arguments

Even when you present arguments in the critical thinking sense outside the context of a heated exchange, the strength of your argument does not guarantee success at persuasion. Here, you need to ask two questions: (1) *Should* others be persuaded by this argument? and (2) *Are* others likely to be persuaded by this argument? People *should* be persuaded by an argument only if the argument is a strong one. But whether people are likely to be persuaded is not always a matter of the argument's strength.

It is important to see the difference between these questions. The second is an empirical question, a question asking for a prediction about how others will react in response to the argument. It is a question of rhetorical effectiveness: How effective is the argument at the level of rhetorical power? Many factors may lead people to be persuaded or not persuaded by an argument other than how strong the argument is. People are often persuaded by weak arguments and not persuaded by strong arguments.

The first question, in contrast, is a normative question, a question not of how people *will* react, but how they *ought to* react. This is a question of rational effectiveness: How effective is the argument at the level of reason? Is the argument rationally persuasive? Rational people will be persuaded only by strong arguments —but, of course, people are not always rational.

To illustrate the difference between the two questions, consider the lyrics of an old advertising jingle:

Example 2.21

The bigger the burgers, the better the burgers. The burgers are bigger at Burger King.

This ad presents an argument. The conclusion, that Burger King burgers are better, is implied rather than explicitly stated. The two premises are that bigger burgers are better burgers and that Burger King Burgers are bigger. This brings us to question 1: Is this a strong argument? Should consumers be persuaded by it?

But the advertising agency that created this jingle was asking question 2: Will the ad persuade consumers? Will it lead them to choose to eat at Burger King? The agency was basing its advertising campaign on predictions about the effectiveness of the ad on consumer behavior. Unfortunately, presenting a strong argument is not always the most effective way to persuade.

If we consider the message at the level of reason, we will not be interested in how we are likely to respond to the advertisement. It would be rather odd for us to choose to patronize Burger King by asking ourselves whether we are likely to be persuaded by the advertising jingle. We cannot choose based on predictions of our own behavior. If we respond to this ad rationally, we will base our behavior on our perception of how strong the argument is.

2.3.2 *Two Purposes of Arguments*

One purpose of argument in the critical thinking sense is to persuade others through the use of reason. In other words, we use arguments to rationally persuade others. But we also use argument in order to discover the truth.

Two Purposes of Arguments

1. To rationally persuade others

2. To seek the truth

Arguments are used for the second purpose in science. Scientists' efforts to discover the truth about the world involve the creation and evaluation of arguments. Indeed, we might say that our understanding of the world simply represents the conclusions of the strongest arguments about the nature of the world currently available. Of course, efforts to discover the truth are closely related to efforts to rationally persuade, because we want to share the truth with others. But they are not the same. For one thing, we might seek the truth in isolation, without seeking to persuade others of what we have discovered.

But arguments are also social in a way other than their being meant to persuade others. Reasoning, like other forms of language use, is a social activity. We learn to reason in interaction with others, and much of our reasoning occurs in collaboration with others. Thus, a person's ability to use argument to seek the truth in isolation from others is dependent on his or her having had this social interaction. Collaborative reasoning is more fundamental than individual reasoning. We initially learn to reason collaboratively, since language learning is not a solitary effort. Later, we learn to internalize the dialogue that constitutes reasoning in its social, public form and to reason by ourselves.

Because reasoning is a social activity, it is subject to the pitfalls that characterize other forms of social activity, pitfalls that can deflect reasoning from the pursuit of truth. For example, all forms of social activity are subject to the human tendency to seek an advantage over others. People may try to persuade others of claims that it is in their own interest for others to believe, with little concern for whether those claims are true. The advertising industry is an example of this. In addition, people sometimes present arguments to others in an attempt to show their own superiority, as a kind of one-upsmanship. In presenting arguments, people often seek to win at all costs, regardless of the truth. But these uses of reason are corruptions of reasoning.

That reason can be misused in these ways helps to explain why people are often reluctant to be persuaded by a strong argument. They may suspect that a person presenting an argument to them is simply trying to beat them or trick them rather than to rationally persuade them. If they refuse to be persuaded, they cannot be beaten or tricked. In addition, refusing to be persuaded is often a way of protecting one's ego. People often invest their egos in the positions they hold; they identify themselves with their beliefs. So, to admit that they are wrong would be a blow to their self-esteem. Consequently, they refuse to consider any argument that challenges their beliefs. Instead of identifying themselves with the particular beliefs they hold, people should identify themselves with their capacity to reason. This will enable them to engage more enthusiastically in critical thinking. They can take delight in arguments that challenge their beliefs, seeing this as an opportunity to practice their reasoning skills.

People's tendency to use arguments as a form of one-upsmanship has led to some criticism of critical thinking and its underlying idea of reason. According to this criticism, reasoning is not really a matter of people working together to pursue the truth, but an often not-so-well-disguised form of social combat. This notion of reasoning, the criticism continues, is modeled on the idea that social relations are confrontational, a kind of warfare by other means, rather than genuinely collaborative. Indeed, competition should not have the upper hand over collaboration in the use of reason, but the two are not incompatible. There is competition involved in all genuine reasoning, but competition should be and often is treated as subordinate to the collaborative aspect of truth seeking.

2.3.3 An Ethics of Critical Thinking

This criticism shows that there is an important need for an ethics of critical thinking. An ethics is a set of rules for people to abide by in their interactions with others. Any social activity will include some notion of how participants should treat each other in order to further the purpose of the activity. The ethics of an activity is generally related to its purpose. So, an ethics of reasoning might consist of a set of rules to promote the use of reason in discovering the truth. The rules would be designed to foster the pursuit of truth. The idea is that there are rules that, if followed, will make people who use argument more effective at discovering the truth. Possible rules might include being open-minded, valuing the strength of arguments, respecting others' arguments, and being aware of your own assumptions.

An Ethics of Critical Thinking

1. Always be open to the possibility that what you believe is false.

2. Regard the strength of an argument as a more important consideration than whether you agree with the conclusion.

3. Respectfully hear out those arguing against you and take their arguments seriously.

4. Seek to be aware of and to test the acceptability of the assumptions that underlie your beliefs and the beliefs of others.

Alternatively, an ethics of critical thinking could be cast in terms of rules of character rather than rules of behavior. This ethics of critical thinking would recognize a set of character traits that critical thinkers ought to have, such as disinterestedness, open-mindedness, and fairness.

EXERCISE SET 2.3

SECTION A: Find some examples from the print or electronic media of advertisements or commercials that seem to contain arguments.

(1) Indicate what the argument is. That is, what is the conclusion? What are the premises?

(2) Answer these questions about it: Is it likely to persuade others? Why or why not? Should others be persuaded by it? Why or why not?

SECTION B: Consider the task of setting forth an ethics of critical thinking based on the idea that the rules of such an ethics should promote the effectiveness of argument in discovering the truth. Do you agree with the rules presented here? Would you add others or take some away?

Summary

An argument is a set of statements that have a support relationship among themselves. Specifically, one or more of the statements, called premises, have a support relationship to another of them, the conclusion. The support relationship holds between a pair of statements when one provides evidence for the other. The support relationship can be strong or weak. The strongest form of the support relationship is implication, which exists when the truth of one statement guarantees the truth of the other.

A text is a group of sentences written or spoken by a person (or group). Texts can be argumentative or nonargumentative. When determining whether a text contains an argument, it is important to take into account the intention of the author. Many times, authors will signal their intention to present an argument by including in the text certain words or phrases, referred to as reasoning indicators. But many argumentative texts do not have reasoning indicators. When a text does not contain any reasoning indicators, one way to determine whether it is argumentative is to insert a reasoning indicator at an appropriate place in the text and see if the resulting text makes sense. This is the reasoning indicator test.

The two main purposes of making arguments are to rationally persuade others and to seek the truth. There is an important difference between the question of whether someone should be persuaded by an argument and whether someone is likely to be persuaded by an argument. Critical thinking is concerned only with whether someone should be persuaded. Reasoning or critical thinking is primarily a social, collaborative activity. We collectively search for the truth and seek mutual persuasion. When we become able to reason by ourselves as individuals, we have internalized the exchange among people that characterizes reasoning as a social activity.

Key Terms

statement	inconsistency	argumentative text
premises	convergent premise	author
support relationship	linked premise	audience
implication	mixed argument	reasoning indicator
negative support relationship	text	reasoning indicator test

Notes

1. Oscar Wilde, *The Importance of Being Earnest*, Act 1.
2. The different uses of language, such as the descriptive use, are discussed in Chapter 1. The use of nonindicative sentences to express statements is discussed in Chapter 4.
3. Because the support relationship generally works in one direction only, when we speak of the support relationship between two statements, we mean a relationship that holds in one direction between the two statements, but not necessarily in the other. In other words, the implication relationship holds between ordered pairs of statements, the order in which the statements are listed being crucial. With some pairs of statements, however, the implication relationship works in both directions. This occurs in definitions and certain other logical statements, which will be discussed in Chapter 9.
4. These two reasons are closely related because taking care in writing and speaking is how we make our own intentions clear to ourselves.
5. A clause is a group of words containing a subject and a verb.
6. There is an exception to this. Sometimes, an author will say the same thing twice using different sentences. In this case, the author usually does not intend to present an argument, because a statement is normally not a reason for itself. But an argument indicator often makes sense when placed between two such sentences. So, when two sentences in a text make the same statement, the reasoning indicator test may not give the correct

result. Sometimes, an author does intend for a statement to be a reason for itself, but the resulting argument is then fallacious, an instance of "begging the question," to be discussed in Chapter 8.

7. Another factor to consider is whether the argument has linked premises. If it does, the test may not work unless the conclusion sentence is repositioned after all of the premises, and not simply one of them. The reason is that linked premises support a conclusion together, not individually. We will consider an example of this later.

8. Earlier, I said that for most arguments with linked premises, but not all, the premises taken together have an implication relationship to the conclusion. Text C is a case in which linked premises do not have an implication relationship to the conclusion.

9. This chart ignores the fact that the reasoning indicator test can pick out explanations as well as arguments. Explanations, which are another form of reasoning, are discussed in the next chapter.

10. Charles Darwin, *On the Origin of Species* (Cambridge, MA: Harvard University Press, 1964), p. 423.

11. This letter was written by Locke's wife. Locke is a descendant of the seventeenth-century British philosopher John Locke.

12. James Madison, *The Federalist* 51, in Jacob Cooke (ed.), *The Federalist* (Middletown, CT: Wesleyan University Press, 1961), p. 351.

13. Alexander Hamilton, *The Federalist* 34, in Cooke, p. 212.

CHAPTER 3

Explanations and Value Arguments

Some men see things as they are and ask why. Others dream things that never were and ask why not.

—GEORGE BERNARD SHAW

This chapter explores two important forms of reasoning. The first is explanation, a form of reasoning that differs from argument in some important respects. The second is arguments about values—that is, arguments with value statements as conclusions.

3.1 Explanations

People advance arguments primarily to rationally persuade others and to seek the truth. In both cases, you can assume that the conclusions of the arguments you create usually will not be believed in advance by others. Otherwise, in most cases, there would be little point in presenting the argument.[1]

In the case of **explanation,** however, this is not the case. Explanation is like argument in many respects and is often confused with it, but it is a distinct kind of reasoning. Consider this example, similar to one in Chapter 1:

Example 3.1

CHILD: Why is the sky blue?

PARENT: Because the atmosphere scatters some of the colors in sunlight more than others.

CHILD: Why?

PARENT: Because the molecules in the atmosphere scatter certain wavelengths of light more effectively than others.

CHILD: Why?

PARENT: Because the electrons in those molecules are normally at certain energy levels.

CHILD: Why? . . .

In the "why?" example in Chapter 1, the child and the parent disagree about whether the child should go to bed. The child is challenging the parent to give reasons for sending her to bed. This implies that the child does not believe the parent's claim that this is the appropriate time for bed.[2] Thus, the child is asking for an argument, asking to be given reasons to show that what her parent said is true. But, as in the example about the color of the sky, children often ask "why?" when they are seeking not an argument but an explanation.

What makes this an example of explanation rather than argument is that the child believes in advance that the sky is blue. Who could doubt it? What the child wants is for the parent to explain *why* it is blue. Here is one of the series of explanations offered by the parent:

Example 3.2

1. The atmosphere scatters some of the colors in sunlight more than others. Therefore, the sky is blue.

The child is not asking for reasons showing that the sky is blue (he already knows this), but rather for reasons showing why or how it is blue. In general, the purpose of an argument is to show *that* a claim is true, while the purpose of an explanation is to show *why* a claim is true or *how* it is true. Both explanation and argument involve giving reasons, which is why they are both forms of reasoning. But the purposes for the reasons differ.

In the case of explanation, the audience does not need the explanation to believe the conclusion. This may be so for two reasons. First, the audience may believe the conclusion prior to the encounter with the author of the explanation, as the child already believes that the sky is blue prior to engaging his parent in conversation. Second, the audience may believe the conclusion simply because the author says it is so, before the author gives the explanation. This happens when the audience recognizes the author as an authority in the subject that the reasoning is about. (The idea of authority in argument will be discussed in Chapter 8.) For example, a scientist might present a lay audience with some line of reasoning in which the conclusion is not common knowledge outside the scientific community. In most cases that reasoning will be an explanation because the scientist would assume that the audience will believe the conclusion based on her authority as a scientist. Or a doctor may explain to her patient why he needs to take a certain mineral supplement even though she knows that he probably has never even heard of that mineral and so has no beliefs about it at all. Again, the doctor assumes that the patient will believe that he should take the supplement simply because she says so. She feels free to explain why he needs to take it and does not need to argue to persuade him that he should take it.

We should note one special case of authority. Individuals are generally regarded as authorities in matters of their own thoughts and feelings and most of the facts about their own life. So, I can explain to you why I feel optimistic even when you did not believe in advance that I felt this way. Because I say that I do, you believe it. Here is an example of this:

Example 3.3

Background: This is a portion of a letter about the author's antiwar activity during the Vietnam War era. (*New York Times*, 8/94)

> What I saw in Vietnam and my study of the subject convinced me of the tragic mistake our country was engaged in.—S.B.

The author discusses his views about the war, but he does not try to persuade us that these are his views. Rather, he seeks to explain how he came to have these views. He explains rather than argues because he expects his audience to believe that these are his views simply because he says that they are.

Explanation

An explanation is a form of reasoning in which the conclusion is generally already believed by most or all members of the audience, whether in advance or because the author is accepted as an authority. In contrast, in an argument, the conclusion is generally not believed by most members of the audience before the argument is presented to them. The reasons in an explanation are meant to show how or why the conclusion is true, while the reasons in an argument are meant to show that the conclusion is true.

Once we begin to become aware of the world, we want to know why it is the way it is. As rational beings, we want to make sense of the world, to understand how things fit together. Explanations show us how things we already believe about the world connect up.

The conclusion of an explanation—the sentence the explanation is meant to explain ("the sky is blue")—is called an **explanandum.** A reason in an explanation ("the atmosphere absorbs some parts of sunlight and scatters others") is called an **explanans.** A premise is to a conclusion in an argument what an explanans is to an explanandum in an explanation. When an explanation has more than one reason, the explanans is the whole group of reasons taken together. So, an explanans can be

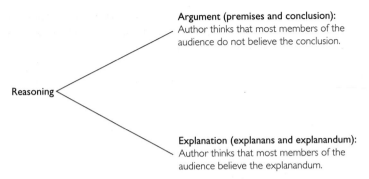

FIGURE 3.1   **Argument Versus Explanation**

a single statement or a group of statements. Figure 3.1 summarizes the two different types of reasoning.

> ## Explanans and Explanandum
>
> The conclusion of an explanation is known as the explanandum, while the
> group of reasons offered for the explanandum, whether one reason or
> several, is the explanans.

3.1.1 Qualified Explanations

Some explanations are **qualified explanations.** Consider these examples (in these
examples and in many others, the sentences of the text are numbered so that we can
refer to them more easily):

Example 3.4

A. Background: This is a letter about the problems with our society. (*Miami Herald*, 4/97)

> ① We have allowed reason to replace art, psychology to replace romance, and sci-
> ence to replace religion to an extent much greater than originally intended. ② We
> now realize that none of these is equal to the assigned tasks, nor collectively to the
> task of furthering human progress in general. ③ That is part of the reason why our
> civilization is in trouble.—S.M.S.

B. Background: This letter is about trends in public dress. (*New York Times*, 6/99)

> ① At our church, there is a noticeable increase in the number of people attending in
> shorts and T-shirts. ② At formal weddings there it is not unusual to see guests wear-
> ing jeans. ③ The trend toward too much informality may have begun in our class-

rooms when informal attire for teachers became acceptable. ④ It may be that such teachers seem to be "one of the guys," but in my day teachers wore suits and ties to reinforce their position as authority figure.—W.K.

The explanandum of text A, expressed in sentence 3, is that our civilization is in trouble. The explanans is expressed in sentences 1 and 2. But note how the author qualifies the explanation in sentence 3. She says that the explanans is *only part of* the reason for the explanandum, that the explanans only partly explains the explanandum. (In identifying the explanandum, the explanans, and the qualifying phrase in this example, and in many of the examples that follow, it is helpful to paraphrase the language of the text in order to make the meaning clearer. This topic of reformulation will be discussed in detail in Chapter 5.)

Now consider text B. The explanandum, reflecting the general point the author is making in sentences 1 and 2, is that there has been a trend toward increasing informality in dress. The explanans is expressed in sentence 3. But the author qualifies his explanation. As sentence 3 indicates, he is claiming only that the informality of teachers' attire *may* explain the trend toward increasing informality.

These are the two main ways in which an author can qualify an explanation. First, she might say, as in A, that the explanation is only partial, that the explanans only partly explains the explanandum. Second, he might say, as in B, that the explanation is only one possibility, that the explanans may or may not explain the explanandum. Authors use many phrases to qualify their explanations. For example, an author might say, "One of the explanatory factors of x is y," which would be a way of saying "y partly explains x." Or an author might say, "There is some reason to think that x explains y," which would be a way of saying "x may explain y." The phrases used in place of "may explain" or "partly explains" may indicate a stronger or weaker version of that kind of qualification.

Qualified Explanations *Megan C. Dunbar*

A qualified explanation is an explanation that is less than certain or less than complete. An author indicates that an explanation is possible by saying that the explanans *may* explain the explanandum (using "may" or some variant phrase). An author indicates that an explanation is only partial by saying that the explanans *partly* explains the explanandum (using "partly" or some variant phrase).

When you study a text that contains an explanation, you need to pay attention to the wording to determine whether the explanation is qualified in some way and, if so, whether the use of the stronger or weaker version of that qualification is appropriate. You can represent the qualification of an explanation by placing a phrase expressing the qualification between the explanans and the explanandum.

> **Qualifications of Explanations**
>
> 1. The explanans *may explain* the explanandum.
>   Stronger version: *likely explains*
>   Weaker version: *possibly explains*
>
> 2. The explanans *partly explains* the explanandum.
>   Stronger version: *largely explains*
>   Weaker version: *is a factor in the explanation of*

3.1.2 Explanatory Texts

Just as arguments are found in argumentative texts, so explanations are found in **explanatory texts.** In Chapter 2, we spoke of texts involving reasoning as argumentative texts. But some of these texts are explanatory rather than argumentative. How do you determine that a text is explanatory? You begin as you would in identifying an argumentative text: You look for reasoning indicators, which are explanation indicators as well as argument indicators. If there are no indicators, you can apply the reasoning indicator test. If the test is positive, you know the text is either argumentative or explanatory.

How do you decide if it is explanatory rather than argumentative? Unfortunately, there is not a stock set of phrases that authors use to signal whether the reasoning they are presenting is an explanation or an argument. Most of the reasoning indicators, such as "because," can be used in either an explanation or an argument. But the **explanation indicator test** sometimes can help you to distinguish between an explanation and an argument.

In explanatory texts, authors sometimes put the phrase "It is no wonder that" (or some variation) just in front of the sentence expressing the explanandum. The idea is that, given the explanans offered in the text, the audience should not be surprised that the explanandum is true. But, of course, people will be surprised that something is true only if they come to believe that it is true. Thus, this phrase indicates that the author thinks that the audience believes that the conclusion is true, which shows the reasoning to be an explanation. The test is for you to insert the phrase in front of the sentence that would express the conclusion in some text with reasoning. If the phrase makes sense there, the reasoning in the text is probably an explanation rather than an argument.

Consider this application of the test:

Example 3.5

Background: This is a passage from Charles Darwin's *On the Origin of Species.*[3]

> [*It is no wonder that*] our domestic animals were originally chosen by uncivilized man because they were useful and bred readily under confinement.

The presence of the reasoning indicator "because" clearly shows that this is a text with reasoning. Is it an argumentative text or an explanatory text? Because the "It is no wonder that" phrase makes sense inserted into this text, this is an indication that the reasoning is an explanation.

> **Explanation Indicator Test**
>
> This test involves inserting the phrase "It is no wonder that" in front of the sentence that would express the conclusion in some text with reasoning. If the phrase makes sense there, the reasoning in the text is probably an explanation rather than an argument.

Just as with arguments, the statements in explanatory texts will often not be expressed in indicative sentences. One common form of explanatory text begins with the conclusion expressed with an interrogative sentence, as in this example:

Example 3.6

Background: This passage is from *The Federalist* 15 by Alexander Hamilton.[4]

> Why has government been instituted at all? Because the passions of men will not conform to the dictates of reason and justice, without constraint.

This is an explanation because we all know that government exists, a truth that Hamilton expresses with an interrogative rather than an indicative sentence. When we formulate an explanation from an explanatory text, we often need to revise the wording of the text, as in this case.

3.1.3 Context

If the author of some reasoning thinks that the audience either already believes the conclusion or will believe it based on the author's authority, then in all likelihood he or she intends to present an explanation rather than an argument. So, understanding the author's intention is crucial in determining whether some piece of reasoning is an explanation. An author may intend that the reasoning persuade the audience that the conclusion is true, in which case it is an argument. Or the author may intend that the reasoning simply help the audience make sense of what most of its members already believe, in which case it is an explanation. The explanation indicator test works at least partially because it gives at least a rough indication of an author's intention in this regard.

In general, apart from the test, how do you determine the author's intention? In determining what kind of reasoning an author intends in a text—explanatory or argumentative—the **context** in which the text is offered is crucial. The context of a text (whether the text is a word, a phrase, a sentence, or something longer) is the

To understand what someone says, it is important to understand the context in which it is said. (© *1989 The New Yorker Collection Danny Shanahan from cartoonbank.com. All Rights Reserved.*)

surrounding circumstances that help to indicate what the intention of the author is or how the text should be interpreted. A host of factors can be part of the context, including other parts of the text or other texts, facts about the author or audience, the time the text was presented to the audience, and the history and culture of the social group of the author and audience.

Context is important in distinguishing whether the author intends a text to be explanatory or argumentative. In particular, context will give clues to the author's beliefs about what the audience believes. Does the author assume that the audience already believes the conclusion? Paying attention to context is important because often an argument and an explanation can be given in the same words. You have to consider who the intended audience is: What some audiences believe, other audiences do not. And the same audience will believe something at one time and not at another.

Consider this example:

Example 3.7

1. The economy in 2000 is/was strong.
2. Al Gore is/was perceived as more competent than George W. Bush.
3. Despite his scandals, Clinton is/was a very popular president.
Conclusion: Gore will be/was elected president in 2000.

Even though the wording is the same (with the exception of the verb tense), this reasoning could be an argument or an explanation, depending on when it is presented. If it had been presented in mid-2000, when I wrote it, it would have been an argument because no one knew at that time who would win the election. But if it is presented as you read it, long after the 2000 election, it counts as an explanation (if Gore had been elected, of course) because you will then know the conclusion to be true.

> ### Context
>
> The context of a text is simply the surrounding circumstances that help to indicate what the author's intention is or how the text should be interpreted. A host of factors can be part of the context, including other parts of the text or other texts, facts about the author or audience, the time the text was presented to the audience, and the history and culture of the social group of the author and audience members.

Sometimes, a text will be explanatory or argumentative depending on precisely what the conclusion is taken to be. For example, most conclusions are about something that the author believes. But some are about the fact that the author believes something; that is, they are a statement about her or his psychological state. Consider this example about whether schools should require students to wear school uniforms. Assume that the audience does not agree that students should be required to wear uniforms but knows that Jean thinks that students should.

Example 3.8

A. Argument

    P1: When students wear uniforms, they take their schoolwork more seriously.

    C: Therefore, students should be required to wear uniforms.

B. Explanation

    Explanans: *Jean thinks that* when students wear uniforms they take their schoolwork more seriously.

    Explanandum: *Jean thinks that* students should be required to wear uniforms.

The conclusion of the argument is that students should wear uniforms; the conclusion of the explanation is a psychological claim about what Jean thinks—that students should wear uniforms. These are two very different claims.

More generally, this example illustrates the need for caution in interpreting the way authors word their statements. Some conclusions related to something that the author believes (call it x) are worded as if they were about the fact that the author believes x. Authors will often express statement x by saying "I think x," "I know/believe x," "It seems to me that x," or something like this. In such sentences, the author is, if taken literally, talking about her psychological state. But in most cases, the author will be using this language not to talk about psychological states, but to express the statements indicating what she believes, knows, and so forth.

Consider this example:

Example 3.9

Background: This letter is in response to news reports of a partnership between Microsoft and Apple. Bill Gates is the CEO of Microsoft. Apple is located in Cupertino, CA, and Microsoft is in Redmond, WA. (*Los Angeles Times*, 8/97)

① The alliance between Microsoft and Apple comes as no surprise to me. ② Gates can't afford to let his technology engine go broke, or even get stale. ③ The new business arrangement only means he won't have to steal the concepts; there will now be an open pipeline between Cupertino and Redmond.—R.M.

The conclusion of this line of reasoning is in sentence 1. In that sentence, the author is literally speaking of his psychological state—specifically, his lack of surprise. But the statement that the author is most likely intending to make is not about his own psychological state. It is, rather, that the alliance occurred. This is an explanation because the author likely believes that his audience knows this. (The phrase "comes as no surprise" is a version of "it is no wonder that.")

3.1.4 Causal and Agency Explanations

Explanations can be of different kinds, but there are two main types: causal explanation and agency explanation. A **causal explanation** explains by stating a cause of some effect. The cause is the explanans, and the effect is the explanandum. The earlier example about the color of the sky is a causal explanation. The blueness of the sky is caused by the way that the atmosphere refracts light. Here is another example:

Example 3.10

Background: This letter is in response to news accounts of spring flooding in the upper Midwest. (*Chicago Tribune*, 4/97)

Your current coverage of the spring flooding in the upper Midwest has ignored a basic fact. The Red River that forms the boundary between North Dakota and Minnesota flows *north*. That phenomenon has accounted for flooding during many past springs. Snow, ice and rains along its south end cause waters to rush northward where the river bed may be narrowed and clogged by unmelted ice. Then the water is forced out of the riverbank.—J.M.K.

This is an explanation because the conclusion is about Midwest flooding, the fact of which would have been known to most of the readers. The author seeks to explain the flooding by giving its cause. The explanans is that, due to the northward flow of the river, the spring thaw comes to the upper parts before the lower, resulting in ice dams and consequent flooding.

Now consider this example:

Example 3.11

Background: This letter, written in response to a column, is part of the public debate over smoking. (*New York Times*, 2/99)

> Your columnist argues that smokers should be liable for their own tobacco-related illnesses since "people know smoking is risky but choose to do it anyway." In fact, nicotine, like most addictive substances, acts on reward centers in the brain that play a direct role in decision making. Once someone becomes addicted to nicotine, his brain is programmed to seek it.—H.T.B.

This letter gives two different explanations for the fact that people smoke. The first is that they choose to smoke, and the second is that an addiction to nicotine causes them to smoke. The second explanation is a straightforward causal explanation—the cause of the smoking is the nicotine addiction. But the first is an agency explanation. When a person chooses to do something, she has made a decision to do it. She has acted as an agent, exercising her powers of human action.

An **agency explanation** presents the factors that led to a person's choice of action or behavior. Such factors could be the character traits out of which an action grew, the motives that lay behind it, or the desires that prompted it. Such factors are the *reasons* for the person's action. So, for example, you might explain why your friend told a lie by giving the reasons he told a lie, which might include that he is cowardly (character trait), that he wanted to impress his friends (motive), and that he sought some benefit (desire). Thus, the fact that someone had a nicotine addiction would not be part of an agency explanation for smoking because having such an addiction leads people to smoke without being a factor they consider in choosing or deciding to smoke.

When an explanandum is some fact about the nonhuman world, the explanation is usually causal. When an explanandum is about human behavior, it is usually an agency explanation. But human behavior can also be explained causally, as when smoking is explained by addiction.

It is important, however, to distinguish between agency explanations and justifications. Recall from Chapter 1 that a justification is an argument that may have as its conclusion a statement that some action is the right thing to do, when there is some doubt about it. Thus, an agency explanation is not a justification because one is an explanation and the other an argument. But there is another difference between them. An agency explanation has as its conclusion that some individual or group *did* something. A justification about a human action has as its conclusion that someone or some group *should do* (or *should have done*) something, in situations in which the rightness of what they did or may do is a matter of controversy.

Even though justifications are different from agency explanations, it can be difficult to tell which one an author intends. Consider this example:

Example 3.12

Background: This letter is in response to a news account of victim impact statements, which are statements from crime victims considered by the court in the penalty phase of a criminal prosecution. (*New York Times*, 9/97)

> As the victim of a recent robbery, I took care in my communication to the court to make no mention of any loss that my family and I had suffered, but only to urge that the criminal, who had previously been imprisoned for rape and manslaughter, be seen as someone who posed a real threat. Our losses were not important; the safety of the community was.—D.S.W.

It is not clear whether the author intends to explain why he made no mention of his and his family's loss or to justify the fact that he did so. In other words, it is unclear whether this is an explanation or an argument. The conclusion would be different in each case. The conclusion of the explanation would be that he did not mention the loss. The conclusion of the justification would be that his not mentioning the loss was the right thing to do.

As this example illustrates, it is sometimes not easy to distinguish between explanations and arguments, as it is not always easy to tell an argumentative from a nonargumentative text. The main reason for this is the same in each case. Authors frequently do not make their intentions clear.

3.1.5 Explanations and Arguments Together

Explanations are often mixed with arguments. In other words, some texts are both argumentative and explanatory. Here are two examples:

Example 3.13

A. Background: This letter is in response to a complaint in the newspaper about high school mathematics education. (*Los Angeles Times, 2/98*)

> ① Your writer is right on in decrying the decline of Euclidean geometry in our high schools. ② Geometry is one of the few courses in high school that require you to think rather than just memorize facts. ③ I'm sure this is why some high school students don't like it, because thinking is hard—particularly if you're not used to it. ④ In my opinion, geometry should be required rather than phased out.—W.B.D.

B. Background: This letter discusses the prevention of heart disease. (*New York Times, 8/99*)

> ① The recent Centers for Disease Control and Prevention report on the decline in heart disease mortality in the last three decades offers inadequate reasons for this spectacular success. ② The improvements in smoking cessation, treatment of hypertension and lower blood cholesterol levels cited by the CDC are more recent than the onset of the decline in heart disease. ③ A better explanation is the introduction of synthetic folic acid and vitamin B6 into the American food supply beginning in the 1960s. ④ Increased amounts of these vitamins are consumed through voluntary fortification of breakfast cereals and supplements. ⑤ Major studies, including the Nurse's Health Study, have demonstrated that dietary deficiencies of these vitamins lead to increased blood homocysteine levels and increased mortality from heart disease.—K.S.M.

In text A, the main part of the text is an argument with the conclusion expressed in sentence 4 and a premise in sentence 2. But sentence 3 contains an explanation—of why students do not like geometry. The explanandum is in part 3a and the explanans is in part 3b. Although the argument and explanation in this text are about the same issue, high school geometry, they are separate pieces of reasoning.

The relationship between the argument and the explanation in text B is more interesting. The author presents two explanations for the decline in heart disease and argues that one is a better explanation than the other. One explanation, proposed by the CDC, is that heart disease has declined due to a decrease in smoking and better control of cholesterol and blood pressure. The other explanation is that the decline is due to a better vitamin intake. The conclusion of the argument, expressed in sentence 3, is that the second explanation is better than the first. Premises for the argument are expressed in sentences 2, 4, and 5.

An argument and an explanation are tied together in a text in other ways. For example, sometimes, an author does not offer two explanations and argue that one is better than the other, as in text B, but offers a single explanation and an argument supporting the claim that the explanation is correct. Other times, an author provides an argument for the explanans.

This completes our discussion of explanation. Explanation is clearly an important form of reasoning, but in the rest of this book, the focus will be primarily on argument.

EXERCISE SET 3.1

SECTION A: Some of the following texts are argumentative and some are explanatory. For each, do this:

    (1) Determine whether the text is argumentative or explanatory, giving your reasons.

    (2) Formulate the conclusion or explanandum (paraphrasing, if this makes it clearer), and give the premises if an argument or the explanans if an explanation.

Assume that the intended audience is composed of typical college undergraduates.

EXAMPLE

Many Americans have unhealthy lifestyles. This is because they are unable to control their desires.

ANSWER

    (1) The explanandum is in the first sentence. The text is explanatory because the audience believes this statement.

    (2) Explanans: Americans are unable to control their desires.
        Explanandum: Many Americans have unhealthy lifestyles.

PROBLEMS

    1. Clinton had so much trouble with scandals because a vast right-wing conspiracy was out to get him.

    2. Reagan was one of our greatest presidents because he stuck to his principles.

    3. The legal costs of death penalty appeals are tremendous. Thus, executing a person costs more than keeping him in jail for life.

4. Dogs are better pets than cats because dogs are much more affectionate than cats.

5. Walking under a ladder is considered bad luck. Maybe the reason for this is that doing so puts one at risk of being hit by a falling paint can.

❖ 6. An atomic bomb is no more deadly than an ice pick. It simply takes longer with an ice pick.

7. Alcohol gets you drunk because of the effect it has on the cognitive and motor centers of the brain.

8. Red wine can reduce the risk of heart disease due to its ability to reduce fatty deposits in the arteries.

❖ 9. Time seems to go faster when you're having a good time. The reason is simple: When you're having a good time, you are less likely to think about what time it is.

10. Atheists cannot be trusted to keep their word because they do not fear God's punishment.

SECTION B: The following are explanatory texts, some of which may contain arguments as well. For each, do this:

(1) Give the explanans and the explanandum, using your own words, if this makes them clearer (the explanans may include more than one reason). Some may contain more than one explanation.

(2) If it also contains an argument, identify what the argument is.

EXAMPLE
Background: This letter is about a psychiatrist who was held legally responsible for the crimes committed by one of his patients. (*New York Times,* 10/98)

① Why did the jury hold the psychiatrist accountable for the defendant's murderous acts? ② Because psychiatrists invented and perpetuate the myth of mental illness. ③ As long as people believe in mental illness as a cause for behavior, those who receive such a "diagnosis" will be exculpated—and someone else will be culpable. ④ Since psychiatrists removed the blame, it is only fitting that they should be saddled with it.—J.A.S.

ANSWER
(1) Explanans:
1. Psychiatrists promote the myth of mental illness.
2. If a defendant is mentally ill, he cannot be held accountable and someone else will.

Explanandum: The jury held the psychiatrist accountable for the defendant's, his patient's, criminal acts.

(2) In addition to the explanation, there is an argument in sentence 4. The argument is that blame should be assigned to the psychiatrist because psychiatrists promote the myth of mental illness that absolves the defendant from blame.

PROBLEMS
1. Background: This letter is part of the debate over the problem of voter apathy. Iowa and New Hampshire have traditionally been the first states to hold presidential primaries. (*New York Times,* 2/00)

The reason there's such voter apathy is that by the time the voters in Iowa and New Hampshire have had their say, the "race" is over. People throughout the country have no say in who will be the presidential candidates.—J.G.

2. Background: This is a passage from Charles Darwin.[5]

Thus we can easily raise plenty of corn and rape-seed, etc., in our fields, because the seeds are in great excess compared with the number of birds which feed on them.

3. Background: This letter is about TV weather forecasts. (*New York Times*, 2/89)

Why is it that television weather reporters, usually young and city bred, describe cloudy days and precipitation in negative terms, such as "nasty" or "unpleasant"? Central New York State needs rain or snow badly to fill the wells and store moisture for next summer. We are having a winter drought. Some of this comes from the weather reporters having little sense about the needs of farmers for rain and snow.—G.R.H.

4. Background: This letter is about the frequent unwanted calls people receive from telemarketers. (*San Francisco Chronicle*, 4/98)

Telemarketers often use computer systems that try to get you on the line even before a salesperson is ready. That's why you'll often hear a three-to-five-second delay before the salesperson starts the pitch. So as soon as you hear a delay, hang up. If it's an automated calling system, it won't call you back. And if it's a friend, he will. Works everytime.—C.A.

5. Background: This is another passage from Darwin.[6]

[It has been] shown that plants which have very wide ranges generally present varieties; and this might have been expected, as they become exposed to diverse physical conditions, and as they come into competition . . . with different sets of organic beings.

6. Background: This letter is about income disparities (the gap between the rich and the poor) and life expectancy in different nations. (*New York Times*, 1/00)

Recent research clearly indicates that countries with less income disparity have longer life expectancies and lower rates of mortality from specific diseases. This helps explain why people in countries less well off than the United States, where income disparity is greater, are in better health and live longer.—L.W.

7. Background: This letter is about belief in God. (correspondence submitted by author)

Primitive, barbaric people created the concept of an omnipotent God we don't know how many thousands of years ago as an ally in their vulnerable lives. Why is today's population, especially of the educated class, still suffering from impotence and in the need of an omnipotent God in this most scientific, industrialized and psychologically sophisticated epoch? Why is the explanatory concept of a God our primitive forefather's used still surviving today? The fear of death.—N.J.

8. Background: This letter was written during the prosperous late 1990s, when there was low unemployment and a low crime rate. (*Los Angeles Times*, 6/97)

   Am I the only one who sees a relationship between record low unemployment and record low crime rates in the U.S.? If people have jobs and hope, they turn less and less to crime.—A.N.T.

9. Background: Again, a passage from Darwin.[7]

   I strongly suspect that some well-known laws with respect to the plumage of male and female birds, in comparison with the plumage of the young, can be explained on the view of plumage having been chiefly modified by sexual selection, acting when the birds have come to the breeding age.

10. Background: This excerpt is from *The Federalist* 10, by James Madison.[8]

    From the protection of different and unequal faculties of acquiring property, the possession of different degrees and kinds of property immediately results: and from the influence of these on the sentiments and views of the respective proprietors, ensues a division of the society into different interests and parties. The latent causes of factions are thus shown in the nature of man.

11. Background: This letter is about the cost of software. (*New York Times*, 2/95)

    Software is expensive because the labor of experienced programmers does not come cheaply. Companies recruit and train software developers to work in teams. These teams work intensively over a period of months to write, test and debug a particular product. A lone programmer would have to spend years to achieve a comparable result.—E.H.

12. Background: This letter is in response to the wave of school shootings in the late 1990s. (*New York Times*, 4/99)

    It should be pointed out that liberal ideology has guided our educational system, judicial system and cultural compass for more than 30 years. Failing schools, a failing judicial system and the unrelenting assault on our religious foundations and values have resulted in a culture that can produce young people capable of evil that we could previously only imagine.—W.B.

13. Background: This letter appeared after the Columbine High School shooting when many people expressed concern about the way popular students treated the less popular. (*New York Times*, 4/99)

    How can we teach students to be good citizens without insisting that they practice civility toward other students? That is what good citizenship is: respecting the rights of everyone. We can certainly demand that students behave with courtesy toward other students. Many faculty members don't insist that popular students behave decently toward less popular students because they themselves are often as anxious to have the approval of the

popular students as the other students are. Teachers must demand civil
behavior from the student leaders as well as from the outcasts.—S.G.

14. Background: This letter is about former President Clinton and the Monica
Lewinsky scandal. (*New York Times*, 9/98)

Astute Republicans, right-wing independents and libertarians favor having
Congress throw the book at the President without bringing on removal
from his office. Their concern is that in the event that Mr. Clinton is
impeached or resigns, we would face an incumbent President Gore in 2000.
With the leg-up incumbency, Mr. Gore would be hard to defeat, but if Mr.
Clinton serves out his term, the Republican contender, running against
"damaged goods," would be a shoo-in.—W.V.

15. Background: This letter is about the 2000 Republican presidential primaries, in which John McCain ran against George Bush. (*New York Times*, 3/00)

In light of John McCain's primary losses to George Bush, I think I know
one big reason why negative campaigning is so effective in this country:
there is not enough substantive political debate. A more informed and
engaged electorate would be more difficult to sway with misleading, fly-by-
night blitzes of the sort that hurt Mr. McCain in New York.—M.S.

16. Background: This letter is about declining crime rates. (*New York Times*,
5/00)

Attributing crime reduction to "get tough" policing and mandatory sentencing policies, minor gun control legislation and baby boomers aging past
their crime-prone years ignores one very important determinant of crime in
the United States: improvements in economic opportunity. Crime rates are
very much a function of labor market opportunities, especially for minorities
and low-wage workers. The tight labor market that has prevailed since the
mid-1990s is an important reason for the steep fall in crime. Punitive factors
have contributed, but so has the increase in low-wage earnings and employment. Creating good-paying jobs is one of the best deterrents to crime that
money can buy.—E.H.

17. Background: This letter is in response to a report on India. (*New York
Times*, 8/97)

The story of post-colonial India is a dismaying one. And the key to a half-
century of misfortune in that benighted land can be found in one sentence
in your article: "Indians speak 17 languages and 22,000 distinct dialects."
How can any nation fragmented by a babble of languages and a patchwork
of antagonistic cultures hope to find the direction or generate the energy to
achieve anything at all?—W.M.G.

18. Background: This letter is about the decline in black enrollment at a California law school in the mid-1990s. (*New York Times*, 7/97)

This is not due to discrimination. Fourteen black students were actually
admitted but subsequently declined. Well-qualified black law school

applicants are at a premium and can command preferential treatment, for scholarships and other benefits outside of California now that the university has adopted race-neutral policies.—D.K.

19. Background: This letter is in response to a news article about Americans vacationing in Europe with their communications gear. (*New York Times*, 7/97)

    Anyone wondering why the French are opposed to economic globalization, and thus a common European currency, need only read your article on Americans who vacation with their cell phones and laptop computers. The French believe there is more to life than working 14 hours a day and continuing this obsession on vacation. They take time to enjoy family, friends, nature, food, music, art—the good life—in addition to making a living. Vive la France!—C.W.

20. Background: This letter is part of the debate over genetically modified food. (*New York Times*, 3/00)

    Your columnist argues that dietary supplements pose proven health hazards but have not raised much concern from the press or the public, while genetically modified food, allegedly safe, has set off an outcry. The divergent reaction is easily explained. A person takes a supplement only when he chooses to. Not so with genetically modified food. Whether or not such food is harmful, those who eat it—especially in poor countries—will have no choice, unless the choice is cast as eating potentially omnipresent genetically modified food versus starving.—E.P.S.

❖ 21. Background: This letter is about the expansion of NATO (the North Atlantic Treaty Organization) to include some nations in eastern Europe. (*New York Times*, 12/97)

    Following the West's success in the demise of the Soviet Union, Eurasia's natural resources are now being rediscovered by the rest of the industrialized world. With a potentially uncertain and unstable Middle East in the years to come and probable Russian fragmentation, there is a need for monitoring, containing and countering threats to foster businesses in these mineral-oil- and natural-gas-rich regions. The United Nations is turning out to be unwieldy with its global scope and focus, but a regional NATO is a viable substitute, hence NATO survives and expands.—S.V.N.

22. Background: This letter is about road rage. (*New York Times*, 7/97)

    While some aggressive behavior is surely gratuitous, much more is a natural human response to the passively aggressive behavior of far too many drivers. These are the folks who never pull over on two-lane roads no matter how many cars have stacked up behind them and who cruise in the passing lane of the Interstates at the same speed as the drivers in the right lane.—P.C.

23. Background: This letter is about feminism in the 1990s. (*New York Times*, 7/98)

    That feminism is stagnant now can be attributed to a lack of reliable, affordable child care and to the stubborn division of labor accorded to men and women at home. It can also be attributed to complacency among the boomer generation and to their children, who did not have to fight, as my generation did, for careers in professions dominated by men: law, medicine academia and science.—B.A.

24. Background: This letter is part of the public debate about violence in the schools. (*New York Times*, 5/98)

Proposed remedies for school violence have called for reducing the number of violent television shows, greater vigilance by teachers and stationing police in schools. The proposals are based on a false diagnosis. A correct analysis views the killings as accidents in areas where there are many guns. Angry people, including adults as well as children, may harm their fellows, and where guns are easily had, they use them. The shootings are part of a larger phenomenon, which includes post office shootings and domestic shootings, which are so frequent that we don't hear about most. The availability of guns leads to gun incidents.—D.S.

25. Background: This letter is in response to a letter that referred to those who disagree with popular views of morality as moral relativists. Moral relativism is the position that there are no absolute moral standards. It is related to a view, values subjectivism, discussed later in this chapter. (*New York Times*, 8/98)

The letter writer echoes the view that those of us who disagree with popular ideas about sexual morality and the rights of privacy are guilty of "moral relativism." He should be reminded that we dissenters may be just as "absolute" in our moral convictions as those who go along with prevailing conventions. We disagree because we think prevailing conventions are sometimes cruel or unjust. It is those who think that deep moral questions may be decided by majority vote who are the relativists.—D.R.L.

3.2 Facts, Values, and Opinions

When people discuss controversial issues, the term "opinion" often comes up. For example, if you are debating the issue of capital punishment with some friends, someone might say, in response to a remark of yours, "That's only your opinion" or "That's a matter of opinion." But what is an opinion?

People can mean different things by "opinion." For example, someone might use it dismissively as an "argument stopper"[9]—in other words, as a signal by the speaker that he wishes to end the debate. But more often, when someone labels a claim an **opinion,** she is saying that necessary support has not been provided for the claim. In this view, if someone labels your claim "just your opinion," that person thinks that you did not provide support for the claim when you should have. And when someone labels what you have said "your opinion," he is seeking not to terminate the argument, but rather to push the argument ahead by suggesting where it needs further development. Thus, a claim is an opinion not as a result of its content, but as a result of its not being supported.

> **Opinions**
>
> To label a claim an opinion is to say that the author should have provided support (or an argument) for the claim but did not do so. The author of the claim owes the audience an argument for it that has not been provided.

Consider the following statements:

Example 3.14

A. The North won the Civil War.
B. Politicians who are caught lying to the public should resign.

In response to statement B, it would not be surprising for someone to say, "That's your opinion." But this would be a very odd response to statement A. Because A is generally known to be true, someone who says that the North won the Civil War is not expected to provide support for the claim. In contrast, B is a controversial claim. The person who presents it cannot expect others automatically to agree, but rather owes the audience an argument in support of the claim.

3.2.1 Value Statements and Factual Statements

A statement is an opinion because it needs support and does not have it, not because it has any particular kind of content. In contrast, facts and values are represented in statements with different kinds of content. Factual statements have a different kind of content than value statements. A **factual statement** (or empirical statement) is a statement about the way the world is. A **value statement** is either (1) a statement about what action some person(s) should take (or should have taken), (2) a statement about how the world should be, whether it is in fact that way, or (3) a statement about how something should be evaluated, by itself or in comparison with something else.[10] Factual statements are descriptive, whereas value statements are prescriptive or normative.

As usual, it will help to look at some examples:

Example 3.15

A. Phoenix is warmer and drier than Chicago.
B. Picasso's famous 1937 painting *Guernica* hangs in Barcelona.
C. You should move to Phoenix.
D. It is wrong to deceive.
E. *Guernica* is the greatest work of art to come out of the 1930s.

The first two sentences express factual statements. They seek to say something about how the world is (or was or will be); they attempt to state facts.[11] In contrast, the last three sentences do not say how the world is, but rather, in one way or another, concern how people should act, how the world ought to be, or how something should be evaluated or compared with another. Sentence C is about an action you should take (moving to Phoenix). Even if you never move to Phoenix, this does not mean that you should not have done so. Sentence D states that no one should deceive others or that the world should be a place where no one deceives others. It does not make any claim about whether people actually engage in deception. Sentence E compares *Guernica* with other works of art from the 1930s.

Value statements are normative statements—statements that express norms or standards. Value statements are also called prescriptive statements because they *prescribe* how the world should be, how we should act, or how we should evaluate or compare things. Sentence D is normative because it states a norm against actions of deception. It prescribes acts of nondeception. Sentence E is normative because it reflects a standard by which we should evaluate works of art.

> ### Factual and Value Statements
>
> A factual statement is a statement about the way the world is. A value statement is either (1) about what action some person(s) should take (or should have taken), (2) about how the world should be, or (3) about how something should be evaluated, by itself or in comparison with something else. Factual statements are descriptive; value statements are prescriptive or normative.

How can you identify value statements? Value statements often contain certain words and phrases that serve as value statement indicators. Among these are "should/should not," "ought/ought not," "right/wrong," "good/bad," "better/worse," "best/worst," "moral/immoral," "duty," and "obligation." Clearly, these words and phrases indicate claims about how the world should be, how we should act, or how we should evaluate or compare things. Sometimes, however, people express value statements in sentences without using any of these terms (and some sentence with these terms do not express value statements). For example, the statements that are expressed in imperative sentences ("Let's go to the movies") are often value statements. Determining whether a sentence expresses a value statement is often not a simple matter.

There are different kinds of value statements, including moral statements, aesthetic statements, and prudential statements. **Moral statements** are among the most important and frequently occurring value statements. Morality concerns how we should live our lives, especially in our relationships with other people. Sentence D, expressing the moral statement that deception is wrong, is a rule about how we should relate to other people—with honesty. Morality concerns our duties and obligations toward others. Different kinds or standards may be represented in moral statements, such as justice, equality, and benevolence.

Most matters of public controversy involve moral issues, which means that arguments about these matters will include moral statements. You cannot seriously address issues such as capital punishment, abortion, or euthanasia without making moral statements. One reason that moral issues are controversial is that moral standards can come into conflict. For example, supporters and opponents of capital punishment will appeal to different moral values representing different standards to support their positions. A proponent of capital punishment might appeal to the moral value that a person must pay society back for his crimes, while an opponent might appeal to the moral value that human life is sacred. Standards of justice and equality are frequently at odds as they apply to particular situations.

Aesthetic statements either express or apply standards prominent in the arts, such as beauty, balance, symmetry, coherence, and simplicity. When you judge a Mozart opera as better than a Salieri opera, you are making an aesthetic statement that may involve an appeal to one or more of these standards. Sentence E expresses an aesthetic statement. Debates about art often involve conflicting aesthetic statements, just as moral debates involve conflicting moral statements.

Prudential statements concern what is best for a person or a group in terms of self-interest. Health and security are two important prudential values. The statement that you should take a good supply of vitamins each day, for example, is a prudential statement related to your good health. Sentence C, that you should move to Phoenix, is probably a prudential statement.[12] The weather is better there, so it would be in your best interest to move there. Prudential values can conflict as well. For example, living in the big city might be more exciting, but it is also more dangerous and stressful.

Moral, Aesthetic, and Prudential Statements

Moral statements are value statements indicating what actions a person or group should take or what characteristics they should exhibit in their actions; moral statements indicate their duties or obligations toward other people. Aesthetic statements are value statements that evaluate some human creation or natural object in terms of its beauty. Prudential statements are value statements that indicate what actions a person or group should take when those actions are concerned with taking the best interests of that person or group into account.

There are many other kinds of value statements, corresponding to different standards for evaluating or comparing things of different kinds. For example, the statement that x is a good ball team is neither moral, aesthetic, nor prudential.

Rather, there are standards for evaluating ball teams. Whenever we talk about a good such-and-such or say that x is a good such-and-such, we are making a different kind of value statement, one involving standards for judging such-and-suches. There are standards for evaluating and comparing cars, racehorses, golf clubs, wood, fountain pens, college teachers, and many other kinds of things.[13]

Conflicting value statements can arise not only within morality (justice versus equality), aesthetics (balance versus simplicity), prudence (security versus stimulation), and the other areas just discussed, but also between these different areas. Some of the most important value conflicts are those between moral statements and prudential statements. For example, should we do what is right toward others at the expense of our own self-interest? Many of the most troublesome conflicts in our own lives are conflicts between morality and prudence.

3.2.2 Value Arguments

A **value argument** is an argument with a value statement as its conclusion. We have seen many examples of value arguments already. Value arguments, in addition to having value statements as conclusions, often have value statements as premises. Consider this example:

Example 3.16

P1: Warm, dry weather is good for your health.
P2: Phoenix has a warm, dry climate.
C: Therefore, you should move to Phoenix.

This argument contains two different value statements, one in the first premise and one in the conclusion. In addition, as this example shows, value statements can appear in arguments in two different forms. The value statement in the conclusion is an **action recommendation.** It directly states that someone should do something—in this case, move to Phoenix. Contrast this with the value statement in P1. This prudential value statement is not itself an action recommendation, but it supports the action recommendation in the conclusion. It does not directly recommend an action, but there are a number of action recommendations for which it would provide support. So, value statements can be divided into those that directly recommend an action and those that can support an action recommendation.

The conclusions of most value arguments are action recommendations. For example, an argument with the conclusion that you should not lie to your friend has an action recommendation for a conclusion. One of its premises might be that deception is wrong. The statement that deception is wrong does not directly recommend an action, but as a premise in an argument, it could support many different action recommendations. Sometimes, though, a value argument will have as a conclusion not an action recommendation, but a value statement that supports an action recommendation. For example, the value statement that deception is wrong might itself be the conclusion, rather than a premise, of an argument.

> ## Value Arguments and Action Recommendations
>
> A value argument is an argument with a value statement as its conclusion. The value statement in the conclusion either is an action recommendation or supports an action recommendation. An action recommendation directly states that a person should do something.

Consider these examples:

Example 3.17

A.   P1: Deception is wrong.
      P2: Telling your friend that you like his new hat would be a deception.
      C: Therefore, you should not tell your friend that you like his new hat.

B.   P1: It is wrong to harm others and destroy social trust.
      P2: Deception harms others and destroys social trust.
      C: Therefore, deception is wrong.

Argument A has a conclusion that is an action recommendation. In contrast, argument B's conclusion is a value statement that can support an action recommendation. Notice that both arguments also have value statements as premises. In fact, most, if not all, value arguments have value statements as premises.[14] Sometimes, however, the value statement premises are not explicitly stated. In other words, value arguments sometimes have value statements as unstated or implicit premises. (Implicit premises will be discussed in Chapter 6.) In any case, when you have a value argument, you should look for a value statement among the premises.

Recall that one of the benefits of critical thinking is that it helps us determine what we ought to do. It does this through value arguments with action recommendations as conclusions. A statement about what we ought to do is, of course, an action recommendation. Consider an example of a value argument with an action recommendation as a conclusion:

Example 3.18

Background: This letter is about a proposal from former President George H. Bush to create a commission to strengthen ethics laws. (*New York Times*, 2/89)

> ① You listed names of Republicans and Democrats who will form the commission, but I regret to say none were women. ② Women are now recognized as valuable additions to government, business, higher education and management, and they have strong views about ethics in these areas. ③ I think President Bush should look for women members for the commission. ④ Let us give women a chance to contribute their expertise to a more ethical and fair America.—S.G.E.

This conclusion of this argument is expressed in sentence 3—that Bush should look for female members for the commission. It is an action recommendation directed at the president. One of the premises is also a value statement—namely, that women are already valuable members of such commissions. This premise is a value statement that can support an action recommendation, and this author uses it to support her conclusion.

When value arguments have as their conclusions value statements that are not action recommendations, they are often about the nature of morality itself. Consider this example:

Example 3.19

Background: This letter is critical of people who labeled as immoral the activities of former President Clinton that led to his impeachment. (*Boston Globe*, 9/98)

> In response to the president's recent personal problems, the term "moral" has been cropping up often in the various media and in the halls of politics. For example, Senator Trent Lott recently said that the office of the presidency has a "moral dimension [which] has been lost in scandal and in deception." The president's sexual transgressions are serious violations of trust and, in my opinion, do represent a moral lapse. However, I get outraged when I hear of someone like Lott pontificating about morality. Lott and his ilk in the Senate have blocked tobacco legislation, impeded health care reform, and brewed up a long list of other special-interest, antisocial actions. In Clinton's case, the victims of his errors will heal in time, and their lives will go on. The same cannot be said of those affected by Lott's misdeeds: Many people will be severely affected by his actions, physically and financially. Sorry for the melodrama, but health issues are often life-or-death issues. It makes me wonder, just what do we think morality is, anyway?—M.M.

As this letter shows, value arguments are not always about what someone should or should not do; they also can be about what counts as morality and what sorts of actions are more worthy of moral condemnation. What this author suggests is that the seriousness of a moral wrong depends on the amount of harm it causes.

3.2.3 Are Value Statements Subjective?

Despite the pervasiveness of value statements in our thinking and conversation, many people regard value statements with suspicion, for a number of reasons. Some people suggest that value claims are *relative to* the person making the claim or the culture within which the claim is made. In other words, value claims have no interpersonal, intercultural, or universal truth. Other people suggest that value claims, in contrast to factual claims, are *subjective*.

Consider the following letter:

Example 3.20

Background: This letter is part of a debate about who should judge which works of art are exhibited in public places. It is in response to a letter that found fault with allowing the public to do the judging. (*Boston Globe, 6/97*)

①The letter decried the practice of allowing art amateurs to make aesthetic decisions concerning public art projects. ②The writer seems to prefer that art snobs control the decision-making process. ③The reason we continue to believe that the judging of art is purely subjective is because it *is* purely subjective. ④How else does one explain why an artist and his work may be revered by one group, ridiculed by another, and yawned at by the third? ⑤Rather than belittling the judgment of those who must pay for and live with their works, prospective public artists would be better served by taking the time to learn about the needs and tastes of the neighborhood where a particular piece will be installed. ⑥Perhaps then they will be able to create something pleasing to both themselves and their prospective patrons.—O.D.

This is an interesting letter for several reasons. But we will focus on the author's statement, expressed in sentence 3, that artistic judgments (aesthetic statements) are subjective. It's not clear if the author endorses the broader claim that *all* value claims, and not simply aesthetic ones, are subjective. But the line of argument the author offers could be used to support the broader claim as well, and it is the broader claim that we will consider.

3.2.4 Values Subjectivism

The challenge that subjectivism poses to critical thinking is that, if all value claims are subjective, then there can be no legitimate value arguments. But what does it mean to say that a claim is subjective? What is the distinction between the subjective and the objective? The subjective is that which is characteristic of human thought or feeling, while the objective is that which is independent of human thought.

Consider what this difference is in terms of factual statements. You may think to yourself that the sky is blue. Your thinking that the sky is blue is subjective; it is something that occurs in your thought. But there is a sky, and there is the fact that the sky is blue, both of which are outside of your mind and independent of your thought. The fact that the sky is blue is what makes your thought true. It is only because the sky is blue that your thought that it is blue and the factual statement that it is blue are true. The fact makes the thought and statement objective. When this element of independence from thought is absent, then objectivity is absent, and a claim is subjective.

A statement is objective when there is some way to judge whether it is true or false. If Jones claims that the sky is blue and Wilson claims that it is green, the fact that the sky actually is blue makes Jones' claim true and Wilson's false. Without objectivity, we have no way to judge truth or falsity. If a claim is subjective, it lacks objectivity. As a result, we have no way to judge it true or false and no way to dispute someone who makes the claim.

Given this understanding of what makes a factual statement objective, some claim that *only* factual statements can be objective. In the case of a value statement, there is no fact corresponding to the statement (otherwise, the statement would be factual), and so no objectivity. Value claims thus are subjective. A value statement cannot be true or false because there is nothing objective to make it true or false. If it cannot be true or false, it cannot be a legitimate part of an argument, since all of the statements in an argument are true or false. A value statement is not even a real statement, since statements are always either true or false. This is the position known as **values subjectivism.**

Values Subjectivism

Values subjectivism is the view that all value statements are subjective. Claims are subjective when there is no fact—nothing objective, nothing independent of a person's thinking—that corresponds to them and makes them true or false. Because there is no fact corresponding to value claims, there is nothing objective about them. So, value claims are not true or false. Therefore, value statements are not genuine statements, and there are no genuine value arguments.

The problem with this line of argument is that it is guilty of the error or fallacy called begging the question, which means that it assumes what it is trying to prove. (This fallacy is discussed in detail in Chapter 8.) The argument assumes that only factual statements are objective and concludes that value statements (one kind of nonfactual statement) are not objective. For the argument to avoid this error, it would need to show that facts are the only basis of objectivity. But we have good reason to believe that value statements have a basis for objectivity as well.

Consider these sentences:

Example 3.21

A. Chocolate is the best flavor of ice cream.
B. It is wrong to torture babies for fun.
C. The temperature at the center of the sun is 10 million degrees centigrade.

Sentence A expresses a preference of the speaker—his subjective preference for chocolate ice cream. There is no objectivity to this claim. For some, vanilla is the best flavor; for others, it is Cherry Garcia. So, A is neither true nor false. It may be true that the speaker likes chocolate, but his declaration that chocolate is the best flavor is neither true nor false. Rather, he is simply expressing his attitude or preference. The sentence is grammatically indicative, but, despite this disguise, it is an expressive use of language rather than a descriptive use. What the speaker is really saying is something like "yea! chocolate ice cream." The indicative sentence may make it seem like he is expressing a statement, but he is not.

Sentence C, in contrast, expresses a factual statement. We know that it is either true or false, though we may not know which, because there is a fact out there that makes the statement objective and determines whether it is true or false.

But what about sentence B, the value claim? Is it, like sentence A, a subjective expression of preference? Or is it, like sentence C, an objective statement? The key to answering this question rests in the role of argument in relationship to each of these claims. In the case of A, argument has no role to play. Imagine two children arguing over which is the best flavor of ice cream. We would smile and think to ourselves that they do not yet get it. They understand argument as heated exchange, but not as an attempt to determine the truth. If we witnessed two adults having such an argument, we would conclude that they must be spoofing. To some-one who understands the argumentative use of language, arguing about the best flavor of ice cream makes no sense because claims about the best flavor of ice cream are subjective.

In the case of sentence C, argument has an important role to play. We cannot observe the center of the sun, so claims about what the center of the sun is like can only be assessed in terms of arguments. For example, there may be two competing theories about how the sun operates, and each may imply a different answer to the question of the central temperature of the sun. So, to determine whether C is true or false, we need to see the arguments that scientists would advance for the two theories. Whatever the best theory says about the sun's central temperature is the basis on which we would judge whether C is true or false.

Argument also plays an important role in sentences like B. We make value arguments all of the time. In contrast to sentences like A, sentences like B frequently appear as conclusions in arguments. Value arguments make sense. Value arguments are something we take seriously, something into which we put consider-able time and effort. This is especially evident when we think about how we should act. We use our critical thinking skills to help us to decide what to do. When we deliberate about what to do, we are considering value arguments; we are looking for the best action recommendation that applies to our situation. Thus, if value arguments were not legitimate, deliberation would make no more sense than the child's argument about the best ice cream flavor.

The appropriateness of argument in support of a given statement is what establishes the objectivity of that kind of statement. If some kind of statement can play a role as a premise or conclusion in an argument, then that kind of statement is objective. Claims like those about the best flavor of ice cream cannot play such a role, so such claims are subjective. But value statements, as well as factual state-ments, do play such a role, so both kinds of statements are objective. In fact, what sentence C shows is that factual statements are objective not necessarily because there are facts we can directly observe (though in many cases there are), but because it is appropriate to argue about what the facts are (facts that may not be open to direct observation). Ultimately, it is arguments that establish what the facts are.[15] More generally, arguments establish the truth or falsity of claims, and the fact that claims are argued about shows that the claims are true or false—and so, objective.

Imagine that someone whom you are speaking with says, in response to something you have said, "That is only your opinion." Earlier, we discussed how such phrases represent a complaint that what you have said needs support. But there is another interpretation: not that what you have said needs support, but that it *cannot* be supported, that it is subjective. This is what the phrase would likely mean, for example, if addressed to a child making a claim about the best flavor of ice cream. But we should use such phrases in this way only in response to subjective statements. We are entitled to demand support, or an argument, for a value statement, but not to dismiss it as subjective.

Finally, consider briefly the argument in Example 3.20 that aesthetic statements are subjective. The principal premise for the argument is in sentence 4: "How else does one explain why an artist and his work may be revered by one group, ridiculed by another, and yawned at by the third?" This argument, broadened to cover all value claims, could be formulated this way:

Example 3.22

PI: Value claims are sources of extensive disagreement.
C: Therefore, value claims are subjective.

Many who regard value claims as subjective find this argument very convincing. Debates about value claims may seem endless, but this argument is not a very strong one. The premise simply does not provide sufficient evidence to prove the conclusion. For one thing, there is agreement on some value claims, such as that it is wrong to torture babies for fun. In addition, some factual statements seem to be sources of deep and unending disagreement—for example, the claim that light is composed of waves rather than particles or that Lee Harvey Oswald was the lone assassin of John F. Kennedy.

EXERCISE SET 3.2

SECTION A: For each of the following, determine whether it is a factual statement or a value statement. Give a reason for your answer. For example, if it is a value statement, is it a value statement because it prescribes how we should act, states how the world should be, or presents an evaluation?

EXAMPLE
We ought to pull together and support our president.

ANSWER

This is a value statement because it prescribes how we should act.

PROBLEMS

1. You really should get that tooth looked at.
2. The best outcome of this fight would be a draw.
3. Max's Muffler has the lowest prices in town.
4. The oldest members of the community are the most susceptible to the infection.
5. The existence of hunger in a rich country like America is morally unconscionable.
6. Macs are better than PCs.
7. Parents have an obligation to send their children to college.
8. Most parents are willing to send their children to college.
9. If you live fast, you are liable to die young.
10. Stop and smell the roses.
11. The best colleges are not necessarily the most expensive.
12. The Internet has added to the stress of modern life.
13. The Internet is the best means of communication yet devised.
14. Thou shall not bear false witness against thy neighbor.
15. Frank Lloyd Wright designed some of the most beautiful buildings.
16. People should be allowed to vote at age 16.
17. Muhammad Ali was the greatest.
18. Daily exercise is healthful.
19. Wake up and smell the coffee.
20. When all else fails, read the manual.

SECTION B: The following argumentative texts express value arguments, so each has a conclusion that is a value statement. In each case, answer the following:

(1) What is the conclusion? Express it in a clear sentence.
(2) Do any of the sentences that are premises also express value statements? If so, express them in clear sentences. If not, can you identify any value statement that might be an implicit premise?
(3) If you were arguing the other side of the issue, what value statement(s) might you refer to?

EXAMPLE

Background: This letter is part of the public debate over whether it should be legal to burn the American flag as part of a protest. (*USA Today*, 5/99)

① This issue on flag burning burns me up. ② I am a U.S. Army veteran of 14 years. ③ It's painfully obvious flag burning is not a form of speech. ④ The flag represents the country that made us what we are today. ⑤ Plain and simple, the flag is a symbol. ⑥ When someone burns a symbol of something, the person should be prosecuted. ⑦ Prosecute those who dare desecrate our symbol of freedom, democracy, sacrifice and patriotism. ⑧ One who burns our flag is a disgrace to society. ⑨ Flag burning should be a criminal act and dealt with accordingly.—P.R.M.

ANSWER

(1) The conclusion is the value statement in sentence 9: "Flag burning should be made criminal and flag burners should be prosecuted."

(2) A premise value statement is in sentence 6: All those who burn a symbol should be prosecuted.

(3) The most likely value statement that would be appealed to by those arguing the other side of this position is that the right of protest and free speech should always be respected.

PROBLEMS

1. Background: This letter is on the sport of boxing. (*New York Times*, 1/00)

   The overriding problem in professional boxing is not that there is no central governing body but that it is a vicious "sport" that should be outlawed. A sport in which one of the participants is trying to hurt the other and render him or her—the sport now includes women—unconscious is immoral. While in other sports, like football, an injury to a participant is incidental, in boxing it is the essence of the contest. How many more deaths and serious injuries have to occur in the ring before this barbarism is ended?—J.F.H.

2. Background: This letter is in response to an editorial recommending that banking legislation before Congress include a basic banking requirement, such that banks would provide basic services to all customers at a reasonable fee. (*New York Times*, 10/98)

   You are right to insist that the Senate include a basic banking requirement in the financial services bill. This would insure that all Americans can afford a checking account. More than 12 million American families don't have bank accounts. Yet banks have reaped record profits each year for the last several years by creating new fees, raising existing fees, and making fees harder to avoid. Requiring banks to provide low-cost checking accounts is a fair obligation in light of the fact that taxpayers underwrite this country's banking system through deposit insurance.—R.H.

3. Background: This letter is about the decision of Maine to bring child abuse charges against a mother (V.E.) for the way she treated her son. (*New York Times*, 9/98)

   Child abuse under Maine law includes deprivation of health care "when that deprivation causes a threat of serious harm." Thus, the Maine Department of Human Services seemed justified in bringing an action against V.E. for refusing to provide HIV therapy drugs for her 4-year-old son. Yet this law and others like it in every state fail to account for the fact that many medical treatments themselves may be abusive to the child. The adverse reactions from cancer and HIV therapies may bring children close to death or cause them to be severely diminished. In such cases parents should be respected in their decision to withhold treatment. Allowing terminally ill children to live full lives unencumbered by debilitating treatment may be the most humane thing we can do for them.—N.K.

4. Background: This letter is about a New York City policy that seeks to control sex shops through zoning regulations. (*New York Times*, 3/95)

The change in zoning for sex shops in New York flies in the face of economic arguments presented by the United States government to the world. Our governments, both Republican and Democrat, have always endorsed the idea of a market economy. The policy on sex shops is contrary to this policy. If people patronize these shops and the shops are making money, they should be allowed to flourish. If people find them repugnant, they shouldn't buy from them. Lack of demand and related losses will cause the shops to close in order to stop losing money. This is a more efficient policy and furthers the idea of reducing government involvement.—J.P.K.

5. Background: This letter is about the quality of public schools. In the school systems in question, schools that have been found to be inadequate are allowed to continue to operate under "emergency circumstances." (*New York Times*, 4/00)

Why should our schools be allowed to operate at lower standards than hospitals? When a hospital has inadequate numbers of properly credentialed professionals, when its facilities are insufficient and substandard, and when its equipment is obsolete, the hospital must go on "divert," and send patients to other medical facilities. Schools should follow a similar procedure instead of continuing to operate under "emergency" circumstances. Our children deserve a certain standard of care. Why do we accept inadequacy in our schools? We don't in our health care system.—R.A.S.

❖ 6. Background: This letter is about the fact that U.S. and Russian nuclear weapons are maintained in a state of "high alert." (*New York Times*, 12/99)

Thousands of Russian and United States nuclear weapons remain on high alert, ready to be launched on a few minutes' warning. A slight miscalculation could bring unimaginable destruction. Because of the disarray in Russia, and because of the increased possibility of misreadings during the year 2000 rollover period, President Clinton should strike an agreement with Russia to remove all nuclear weapons from high-alert status.—W.P.[16]

7. Background: This is in response to a letter recommending that natural history museums should not give a "privileged status" to science, but should recognize the "sacred status" of its objects. (*New York Times*, 3/00)

It would be hard to think of a more disastrous prescription for museums. Science is an open-ended inquiry into nature, constrained only by the phenomena of nature itself. The great museums of natural history are among our premier institutions of scientific research and education. One shudders to think what would become of these institutions, and the important scientific work they carry out, if they were to be fettered by religious views. Should the fossils be taken off display, since they might offend those who hold a literal reading of Genesis to be sacred? There are churches and politicians enough to remind us of what is sacred. Let's allow museums of natural history to stick to science.—G.C.M.

8. Background: This letter is in response to news of the reduction in automobile thefts in New York City. (*New York Times*, 1/00)

   The cost to achieve this reduction is substantial, and is borne by all New Yorkers, not just motorists. Costly police protection, the sleep-disturbing noise of car alarms and the preemption of limited open space in the city are substantial societal burdens that are imposed by motorists who park their private property free of charge on public streets. In contrast, motorists who park their cars in secure off-street garages and lots, and pay taxes on these sites, do not impose this burden. Perhaps it is time for those who park on the street to pay for the extra city services they consume. After all, the majority of households in New York City do not even own cars.—G.H.

❖ 9. Background: This letter is in response to a proposal to extend the time for which copyrights provide legal protection against the unauthorized use of a work. (*New York Times*, 4/98)

   According to the Constitution, the purpose of patents and copyrights is to encourage invention and innovation by assuring that the innovator can gain financially by his or her efforts. Does anyone really believe that creativity will be enhanced if copyright protection extends for more than 50 years after the creator dies? A case can be made that the incentive effects of copyright call for protection for no more than 20 or 30 years at most. The right reform is to reduce, not expand, the copyright period.—D.N.

10. Background: This letter is in response to news that the beverage industry was considering the introduction of "self-cooling" beverage cans. (*Chicago Tribune*, 6/97)

    A recent news story on "self-cooling" beverage cans raises the serious fear of an attack on our environment. The can allegedly uses a hydrofluorocarbon, HFC134a, to cool itself when the consumer pushes its button. This gas will diffuse through the atmosphere, adding to the chemicals that cause "greenhouse" warming and the disruption of the ozone layer. Congress should not wait until the self-cooling can goes into production and the beverage industry's weight gets behind its sale to consumers. The threat to our atmosphere should be peremptorily stopped before it begins. It boggles the mind that someone could believe that an environmental catastrophe is worth one's short-term profit. Yet, the Faustian dilemma has been around for a long, long time. This time, however, it is we, our children and their children who will pay for someone's selfishness, unless Congress acts now to prevent the fouling of our air.—B.J.[17]

SECTION C: In Exercise Set 1.4, you were asked to write a short argument about a contemporary social, political, economic, or cultural issue of your choice. If you did that exercise, go back to the argumentative text you wrote, and list and discuss the value statements you made there. If you did not do that exercise, choose an issue now and discuss the value statements that would be made by authors on different sides of the issue.

Summary

Though similar to argument in many ways, explanation is a different form of reasoning. An argument seeks to show *that* the conclusion is true. An explanation seeks to show *how* the conclusion is true. In general, an author intends to present an argument when she believes that much of the audience does not believe or has doubts about the conclusion. In contrast, an author intends to present an explanation when he believes that most of the audience already believes the conclusion or will accept the conclusion as true on his authority. As in other aspects of reasoning, then, whether some reasoning is an argument or an explanation depends on the intentions of the author, which are revealed by the context. Causal explanations, which seek to reveal the causes of events, states of affairs, or human behavior, are distinct from agency explanations, which seek to reveal the reasons behind human actions.

We reason about both facts and values. In other words, our arguments are composed of both factual (descriptive) statements and value (normative or prescriptive) statements. A value argument is an argument with a value statement as its conclusion. An opinion, which may be represented by either kind of statement, is a claim that needs support the author has not provided for it. Value statements are true or false, just as factual statements are. Both factual statements and value statements can be matters of opinion, which means simply that the statement has not been supported by the argument it needs to show that it is true.

The view that value statements are not real statements and that value arguments are not legitimate forms of argument is called values subjectivism. The weakness of this position is that it fails to understand the role of argument in supporting both value statements and factual statements. Proponents of values subjectivism view value statements as mere expressions of preference. But there are no arguments defending expressions of preference (such as "chocolate is the best flavor of ice cream"). In contrast, arguments in defense of value statements, like action recommendations for ourselves and others, make eminent sense, and formulating and considering them is a constant human activity.

Key Terms

explanation	context	moral statement
explanandum	causal explanation	aesthetic statement
explanans	agency explanation	prudential statement
qualified explanation	opinion	value argument
explanatory text	factual statement	action recommendation
explanation indicator test	value statement	values subjectivism

Notes

1. This is, however, not always the case. You may enjoy presenting an argument to some-one who already believes the conclusion because you enjoy creating arguments as an intellectual exercise, the way people enjoy doing logical puzzles. Or you may present an argument to someone who already believes the conclusion as a way of testing the argu-ment, in preparation for presenting it to someone who does not believe the conclusion.

2. The Chapter 1 "why?" example is Example 1.1. There is another way to interpret the Chapter 1 "why?" example that would make it an explanation rather than an argument. The question is whether the child is challenging the truth of the parent's claim that now is the time for bed, as I am assuming, or accepts what the parent is saying but simply wants to understand why it is true. In the second interpretation, the parent would be responding with an explanation rather than an argument, even though what the parent said would be exactly the same in each case. It seems to me that the parent's response in the Chapter 1 example is more plausibly regarded as an argument than an explanation. This is because the typical child would be intending to challenge the truth of what the parent said, not accepting what the parent said as true without reasons being given, and the parent would understand the child to be doing this.

3. Charles Darwin, *On the Origin of Species* (Cambridge, MA: Harvard University Press, 1964), p. 140.

4. Alexander Hamilton, *The Federalist* 15, in Jacob Cooke (ed.), *The Federalist* (Middle-town, CT: Wesleyan University Press, 1961), p. 96.

5. Darwin, p. 70.

6. Darwin, p. 53.

7. Darwin, p. 89.

8. James Madison, *The Federalist* 10, in Cooke (ed.), p. 58.

9. Richard Feldman, *Reason and Argument* (Englewood Cliffs, NJ: Prentice Hall, 1993), p. 188.

10. The first of these three criteria is really a special case of the second. If people should take action x, the world should be a place where people take action x.

11. The sentences only *attempt* to state facts but may not succeed in doing so. In fact, *Guernica* hangs in Madrid rather than Barcelona.

12. Sentence C might be intended as a moral statement instead. It would be a moral state-ment if it were supported by other moral statements, like the statement that you have an obligation to your family to move to Phoenix. Usually, however, this statement would be supported by other prudential statements and so would be intended itself as a pru-dential statement.

13. One interesting question is whether the standards for evaluating and comparing human beings are moral standards.

14. It is a matter of great philosophical controversy whether all value arguments have value statements as premises, but, in any case, at least most do.

15. In fact, some philosophers who study morality have suggested that there are such things as moral facts, though these are different from the more familiar sort of fact.

16. The author of this letter is Wendy Perron, executive director of Physicians for Social Responsibility, New York chapter.

17. The author of this letter is Bruce Joffe.

CHAPTER 4

What Is *the* Argument?
Conclusions and Premises

Sir, I have found you an argument;
but I am not obliged to find you an understanding.

—SAMUEL JOHNSON[1]

As Samuel Johnson suggests, there is a difference between being presented with an argument and understanding the argument. There is a difference between knowing *that* there is an argument and knowing *what* the argument is. In Chapter 2, we discussed how to tell that there is an argument. In this chapter, we discuss how to determine what the argument is.

Determining what the argument is involves identifying the statements in the argumentative text that represent the argument and writing them down in a way that reveals the support relationships among them. The argument has a certain structure, represented by the support relationships, and knowing what the argument is means knowing what its structure is. This process of determining what the argument is, is known as structuring the argument, and the result of this process is the **argument structure.**

4.1 Argument Structure

An argumentative text normally differs in several ways from an argument structure. Consider this example of an argumentative text and its argument structure. After reading the argument, see if you can figure it out before looking at the structure.

Example 4.1

Background: This letter was written in response to a proposal to increase postal rates. (*New York Times*, 12/94)

Instead of raising the price of a stamp yet again and penalizing those who pay bills and write letters, why not reduce or eliminate the bulk-rate discounts for catalogues,

94

> ### Argument Structure
>
> An argument structure is a way of representing an argument that makes clear what statements compose the argument and what the support relationships are among the statements. Structuring an argument involves putting down the statements of the argument in a way that reveals the argument structure.

solicitations and fliers that cram our mailboxes and add to environmental problems? This would keep the price of sending letters down and reduce the amount of junk mail.—D.K.

P1: Raising the price of a stamp would penalize those who pay bills and write letters.
P2: Catalogues, solicitations, and fliers cram our mailboxes and add to environmental problems.
P3: Eliminating the bulk-rate discounts for catalogues, solicitations, and fliers would reduce the amount of these that are mailed out.
C: Therefore, instead of raising the price of a stamp yet again, the government should reduce or eliminate the bulk-rate discounts for catalogues, solicitations, and fliers.

How does the structure differ from the text? First, the sentences in the structure are worded differently than the sentences in the text. Second, the order of the sentences in the structure is not the same as the order of the sentences in the text. Finally, the number of sentences in the structure is different from the number in the text. Most argument structures differ from their argumentative texts in all of these ways, and almost all of them differ in at least one of these ways.

Argument structures need to differ from their texts in these ways to make clear *what* the argument is—that is, to reveal what statements are being made and what support relationships among them exist. When you structure an argument, you usually change the wording, the order, and the number of the sentences in the text to reveal the premises and conclusion. In this chapter, you will learn a method for creating an argument structure.

4.1.1 Sentences and Statements

Consider the first difference between text and structure—that the wording of the sentences in an argument structure will often differ from the wording of the text sentences. Why do the argument structure and the text differ in this way?

> ## How Argument Structure Differs from Argumentative Text
>
> 1. The sentences in the structure often are worded differently than the sentences in the text.
>
> 2. The order of the sentences in the structure is often not the same as the order of the sentences in the text.
>
> 3. The number of sentences in the structure often is different from the number in the text.

Structuring an argument, like identifying an argumentative text, requires that you understand the intention of the author. Structuring an argument is a matter of *interpreting* the text. Sometimes, the correct interpretation is obvious; other times, it is not. Often, you must dig below the surface of the text to clarify the author's meaning. This is why the wording of the argument structure often differs from the wording of the text itself.

To understand this, it is important to distinguish between sentences and statements. So far, we have not explicitly distinguished them, but doing so is of great importance for critical thinking. A **sentence** is a series of words written or spoken on some occasion that conforms to rules of grammar and so has meaning. A **statement** is what a sentence means. A single statement can be expressed by many different sentences.

While in everyday speech the terms "sentence" and "statement" are often used interchangeably, you should already be familiar with the difference between them. To illustrate, imagine that someone says something to you that you do not understand. You might reply, "What did you say?" This usually means that you do not understand the speaker's words. That is, you do not know what sentence she spoke. But you also might reply, "What do you mean?" This usually means that, while you understand the words, you do not understand the meaning. You do not understand what statement she is using the sentence to make.

The first question is normally a request for the speaker to repeat his words. It indicates that you heard the sounds but did not understand the words. The speaker may have been muttering, there may have been background noise, or the words may have been garbled. The second question, however, is normally a request for the speaker to repeat himself *in different words*, that is, with a different sentence. In that case, you understood the individual words but do not understand what the sentence means. It is the speaker's statement that you do not understand.[2]

A statement can be expressed with many different sentences, and some will express the meaning more clearly than others. The sentences chosen for the structure should express the meaning of the text sentences as clearly as possible. Thus, you will often use a different sentence in the argument structure than in the text—specifically, when the sentence used in the structure expresses the meaning of the text sentence more clearly than the text sentence itself does.

Sentences and Statements

A sentence is a series of words written or spoken on some occasion that conforms to rules of grammar and so has meaning. A statement is what a sentence means. A single statement can be expressed by many different sentences.

Consider this example:

Example 4.2

Background: This letter concerns two global trouble spots in the mid-1990s and the response of the United Nations to them. In Zaire, refugees from ethnic slaughter in Rwanda were subjected to further systematic attack by members of the same group that had committed the slaughter in Rwanda. (*New York Times, 4/97*)

> The United Nations' failure to deploy an international force in Zaire to curb attacks on Rwandan refugees contrasts sharply with the military deployment in Albania ostensibly to insure the delivery of humanitarian aid. What works in Europe is again dismissed in Africa.—A.C.H.

The conclusion of the argument is expressed in the last sentence, but what precisely is the conclusion? What statement is that sentence meant to express? Consider these possibilities:

Example 4.3

A. Peacekeeping policies that work in Europe are not applied in Africa.
B. In terms of peacekeeping policies, the world treats Africa differently than it treats Europe.
C. In terms of peacekeeping policies, the world shows greater concern for Europe than for Africa.

Sentence A is one interpretation of the author's meaning. It makes the meaning clearer than the original text sentence because it refers to the fact that the author is talking about peacekeeping policies. But sentence B is an even better interpretation of the meaning than A. The author is not saying simply that different peacekeeping policies are applied in Africa and in Europe, but that Africa and Europe are treated differently in this regard. Of the three sentences, however, C is the best interpretation. The author is not saying simply that the two continents are treated differently in regard to peacekeeping policies, but that they are treated differently in a way that is favorable to Europe. This is indicated by the claim that what "works" in one case is "dismissed" in the other. Of course, this does not mean that C is the *best* possible sentence to use in the argument structure. Other sentences may express the author's meaning even more clearly.

The full argument structure may be formulated this way:

Diagram:

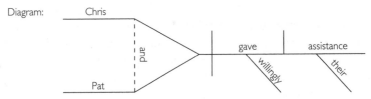

FIGURE 4.1   Diagramming the Sentence: "Chris and Pat willingly gave their assistance."

Example 4.4

P1: The United Nations' failure to deploy an international force in Zaire to curb attacks on Rwandan refugees contrasts sharply with the military deployment in Albania ostensibly to insure the delivery of humanitarian aid.

C: Therefore, in terms of peacekeeping policies, the world shows greater concern for Europe than for Africa.

Notice that the wording of the premise sentence is not changed. This is because the text sentence representing the premise, unlike the sentence representing the conclusion, expresses its meaning fairly clearly. Thus, there is not a strong reason to substitute a different sentence for it.

4.1.2 *Argument Structure and Sentence Structure*

Recall the second difference between argumentative text and argument structure: The order of the sentences in the structure often differs from the order in the text. To help explain this point, consider the contrast discussed in Chapter 1 between the descriptive and the argumentative uses of language. The unit of a descriptive (or directive or interrogative) use is a sentence, while the unit of an argumentative use is a group of sentences. In each case, the unit has internal complexity. In the descriptive use, the complexity is grammar, or the relations of words; in the argumentative use, it is logic, or the relations of statements. In each case, understanding the meaning requires understanding the complexity. That is, you must understand the relations among the parts, whether the parts are words or sentences.

In each case, it is helpful to have a method for representing this complexity. To represent the grammatical complexity of sentences, there is a standard method, one you may have encountered in high school English classes—namely, sentence diagramming. Figure 4.1 shows one example.

The point of sentence diagramming is to show the grammatical relationships that give the sentence meaning by putting the words into a certain spatial relationship. Each part of the sentence—subject, verb, object, adverb, modifier—has a different spatial location in relation to the others. By graphically organizing sentences this way, you can see what functions the different words serve and how they relate to the other words.

An argument structure does the same thing for an argumentative text. It labels the various sentences as particular parts of the argument (premises or conclusion), and it puts those sentences in a certain spatial relationship to show the support relationship. To illustrate, refer back to the argument in Example 4.1. This argument structure labels three statements as premises and places sentences expressing them *above* the sentence expressing the conclusion. This is simply a spatial representation of the support relationship that exists among them. Tree diagrams (to be discussed shortly) also show the support relationships in a spatial way. In fact, corresponding to the term "sentence diagram," we could adopt the term "argument diagram."

Understanding structure is crucial to understanding meaning, in sentences and in argumentative texts. Simply understanding the individual words of a sentence, without comprehending how they relate to one another, would not be to understand the sentence. Likewise, simply understanding the sentences of an argumentative text, without comprehending how they relate to one another, would not be to understand the argument. The main problem people have understanding argumentative texts is that, while they understand the sentences that compose the texts, they do not understand how the author intends the sentences to relate to each other.

4.1.3 Argument Structure as the "Bare Bones" of the Text

Now recall the third way in which argument structures differ from their argumentative texts. Not only are the sentences in the two often worded differently and put in a different order, but the number of sentences in each may differ. But this is not always true. The text and the argument structure for the letter in Example 4.2 each have two sentences. More commonly, however, the argument structure will have fewer sentences than the text.

The argument structure is the "bare bones" of the argumentative text. It contains the minimum number of sentences needed to represent the argument. Authors frequently put extra sentences into their argumentative texts, sentences that are not part of the argument, for a number of reasons—for stylistic flourish, as background information, as asides. In addition, authors often express a premise or the conclusion with more than one sentence. You clear all of this clutter away when you sketch the argument structure.

Sometimes, it works the other way, with fewer sentences in the text than in the argument structure. One reason for this is that the same sentence can express two or more statements. Another reason is that parts of the argument sometimes are not stated in the text; they are implicit rather than explicit.

Here is an example of a text, followed by its argument structure, in which different statements of the argument are expressed in a single sentence:

Example 4.5

Background: This letter was written in 1981, just after President Jimmy Carter had left office and a group of U.S. hostages held for over a year in Iran had been released. The letter refers to this release, as well as to the peace treaty brokered by Carter between Egypt and Israel. (*New York Times,* 1/81)

> For his efforts in achieving the Camp David Agreement and the release of the hostages, President Carter should be nominated for the Nobel Peace Prize.—D.L.

P1: Carter brought about the Camp David peace agreement between Israel and Egypt.

P2: Carter helped to secure the release of the U.S. hostages held in Iran.

C: Therefore, Carter should be nominated for the Nobel Peace Prize.

In this example, all three of the statements of the argument are expressed in a single sentence.

There is often room for disagreement about how the argument in a text should be structured. This is because structuring is a matter of interpretation. The need for interpretation, and the differences of opinion this can lead to, arises whenever you need to figure out the intentions of another person.

If a text is unclearly written, if it is complicated, or if it is taken out of context, you may have difficulty determining precisely what argument the author intended. In fact, the author may not have been clear about his or her own intentions. In such cases, several different argument structures composed of different sentences could plausibly be said to represent the argument. But this does not mean that any one interpretation is as good as another. Some interpretations are simply incorrect.

EXERCISE SET 4.1

SECTION A: Following is a list of well-known sayings. Express each one in a different sentence, a sentence that you think states the intended meaning more clearly, even if less poetically or memorably. Your sentence will almost certainly be longer than the sentence given because one of the virtues of these sayings is their economy of expression. If you are not familiar with the saying, ask someone or make your best guess.

EXAMPLE
Don't cry over spilt milk.

ANSWER
You should not spend time bemoaning mistakes that cannot be undone.

PROBLEMS
1. A stitch in time saves nine.
2. Too many cooks spoil the broth.
3. Fools rush in where angels fear to tread.
4. There's no fool like an old fool.
5. Time heals all wounds.
6. For want of a nail, the battle was lost.
7. Many hands make light work.
8. Don't be penny wise and pound foolish.
9. The bigger they are, the harder they fall.

10. You cannot see the forest for the trees.
11. Waste not; want not.
❖ 12. You cannot put Humpty-Dumpty back together again.
13. Life is what you make of it.
14. A penny saved is a penny earned.
❖ 15. Tomorrow never comes.
16. The grass is always greener on the other side of the fence.
17. Birds of a feather flock together.
❖ 18. Think outside the box.
19. The road to hell is paved with good intentions.
20. De gustibus non est disputandum.

SECTION B: Treat each of your answers in Section A as the conclusion of an argument, and supply one or more premises to support it.

EXAMPLE

P1: If a mistake cannot be undone, spending time bemoaning it is unproductive and will serve no purpose.

C: Therefore, you should not spend time bemoaning mistakes that cannot be undone.

4.2 Identifying the Conclusion

Structuring an argument is a matter of selecting the text sentences that express the statements of the argument and showing the support relationships among the sentences. An argument structure has two parts: (1) a tree diagram and (2) a PC structure ("PC" is short for "premise-conclusion"). We have already seen a number of PC structures, but we have not yet seen a tree diagram. The remainder of this chapter is concerned with tree diagrams; the next chapter focuses on PC structures.

The process of argument structuring can be described in four steps. The first three concern the tree diagram, while the fourth concerns the PC structure. Figure 4.2 summarizes the four steps.

4.2.1 What Supports What (WSW)?

To apply the four steps in argument structuring to a text, you must first, of course, determine that the text is argumentative. You do this by following the method discussed in Chapter 2.

First, there is the simple, mechanical step of numbering the sentences of the text. The purpose of this step is simply to create a common reference point for comparing the structuring work that you and others do on the same text. It is important that people working on a text number the sentences in the same way so that they can compare their work. Be sure that you number all of the sentences and that you number only whole sentences. Do not number parts of sentences, even if the sentence is long or contains a colon or semicolon.

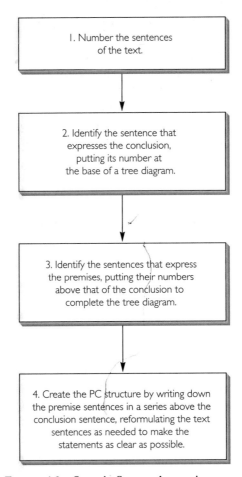

FIGURE 4.2   Steps in Structuring an Argument

Here is an example of how the sentences would be numbered in an argumentative discourse:

Example 4.6

Background: This letter is in response to a discussion of economic losses due to food wastage. (*New York Times*, 9/97)

① One of the major reasons not to use more food than we need is ecological. ② Agriculture and meat production are very hard on the environment. ③ So are processing, packaging and shipping. ④ The billions of pounds of food wasted annually represent vast amounts of other waste, including water, fertilizers, agricultural run-off and fossil fuels, to produce the energy used in production.—J.S.

Once you have numbered text sentences, you construct the tree diagram by identifying the sentence that expresses the conclusion (step 2) and the sentences that express the premises (step 3) and arranging their numbers in the form of a "tree." But before discussing steps 2 and 3, we need to consider an important topic: **What supports what (WSW)?**

WSW is the key question to ask in distinguishing between the conclusion and the premises in an argumentative text. The support relationship works in one direction only, from premises to conclusion.[3] It is the premises that support the conclusion, and not the conclusion that supports the premises. But when students begin a critical thinking course, they sometimes find it difficult to determine what supports what. They confuse premises and conclusions.

Consider these examples:

Example 4.7

A. Background: This letter is about the annoying use of cell phones in restaurants. (*New York Times*, 3/99)

> ① When someone answers a cellular phone in a restaurant or other public place, the intrusion is upon the ever-diminishing personal space of the other patrons of the establishment. ② The cellular phone universalizes the intrusiveness of every little phone call.—D.W.E.H.

B. Background: This announcement is made over the public address system toward the close of the day at the British Library in London. The "materials" referred to are texts retrieved by librarians from the closed stacks.

> ① Requests for materials to be delivered today will end in fifteen minutes time.
> ② Last orders for delivery today should be made in the next fifteen minutes.

In each of these argumentative texts, one sentence expresses the conclusion and the other a premise.

What Supports What (WSW)?

In argumentative texts, premises support conclusions, and not the other way around. Sometimes, however, it is difficult to determine in which direction the relationship goes—that is, which sentences express the premises and which the conclusion. When what supports what is not intuitively obvious, it can be helpful to apply the reasoning indicator test.

How do you tell what supports what? In many cases, it will be intuitively obvious. But if you have trouble telling the difference, you can fall back on the reasoning indicator test from Chapter 2. If there are two text sentences, one of which expresses a conclusion and the other a premise, but you are not sure which is which, place "therefore" between the first and the second. Then reverse the positions of the sentences and place "therefore" between the second and the first. Now ask yourself: Which of the two makes more sense?

Here is the reasoning indicator test applied to the two examples:

Example 4.8

A. 1. ① TF ②
   2. ② TF ①
B. 1. ① TF ②
   2. ② TF ①

In text A, version 2 clearly sounds more appropriate than version 1, so the first sentence is the conclusion and the second the premise. In contrast, in text B, version 1 sounds more appropriate than version 2, so the second sentence is the conclusion. Consider a different reasoning indicator applied to these examples. It is *because* cell phones universalize the intrusiveness of calls that talking on a cell phone in a restaurant intrudes on the other patrons (and not the other way around). It is *because* requests for materials will end in fifteen minutes that last requests must be made in that time (and not the other way around).

4.2.2 Identifying Conclusions

Interpreting an argument correctly is easier if you look for the conclusion first. This is the case even though, as the discussion of WSW indicates, you cannot really look for the parts of the argument separately. A statement is a conclusion only relative to a premise statement. It is not a conclusion unless another statement has a support relationship to it. Thus, in determining if a text is argumentative, whether you rely on your intuitions or apply the reasoning indicator test, you must already have at least a vague idea of what the conclusion and premises are.

Nonetheless, despite your initial sense of which sentences express which parts of the argument, determining this precisely is easier when you focus first on the conclusion rather than the premises. If the text contains a conclusion indicator, you can, of course, directly identify the sentence expressing the conclusion—namely, the one that follows this word or phrase. A premise indicator will also usually point you, at least indirectly, to the conclusion.

If there is no reasoning indicator, you can apply the reasoning indicator test, as discussed previously. But, in general, in identifying the conclusion, it is helpful to keep in mind what a conclusion is. A conclusion is the *point* that the author is making with an argumentative text. It is the statement that the author is trying to prove to be true. It is the claim that the author is trying to rationally persuade the audience of. Frequently, the sentence expressing the conclusion will appear either at the end or the beginning of the text, so it may help to check there. But as often as not, the conclusion is somewhere in the middle.

Recall that in structuring the argument you are *interpreting* the argumentative text. You are basing your judgment about what the argument is on your understanding of the author's intention. This means that *context* is crucial, just as in any situation in which you interpret the intentions of another. (Recall our discussion of context in Chapter 3.)

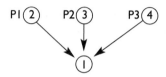

FIGURE 4.3   Tree Diagram for Example 4.6

Once you identify the sentence expressing the conclusion, you can begin to construct a tree diagram. A **tree diagram** is a spatial representation of the support relationships between premises and conclusion. The numbers representing the text sentences that express the premises and conclusion are connected to each other by arrows to show the support relationships. The number representing the conclusion sentence falls at the base of the "tree," and the numbers representing the premise sentences are above it and connected to it, filling out the branches of the tree. The premise circles are labeled "P1," "P2," "P3," and so forth.

Figure 4.3 shows a tree diagram for the argumentative text in Example 4.6 about the ecological effects of food wastage. The conclusion is expressed in the first sentence, so we place the number of that sentence in a circle at the base of the tree. We place the numbers for the other three sentences, each expressing a premise, above it and connect them to the conclusion with arrows. If you think of the bottom of the page as "down," then the direction of the support relationships follows the force of gravity. That is, the reasoning flows downward from premises to conclusion.

At this stage, since we are only on step 2, the tree is just beginning to grow. The branches come when we add the premises, in step 3. So, for now, we simply put a circle around the number of the sentence expressing the conclusion and await further growth.

Constructing a Tree Diagram

1. Place the number representing the conclusion at the base of the "tree" and the numbers representing the premises above.

2. Connect the numbers representing the text sentences that express the premises and the conclusion with arrows to show the support relationships; these are the "branches."

3. Label the premise circles "P1," "P2," and so on.

4.2.3 Some Special Cases

One special case, which we have seen before, involves an author who expresses the conclusion with an interrogative sentence. On the literal level, the author is asking a question, but she is really making a statement, which is why it can be the conclusion of the argument. The interrogative sentence is simply a rhetorical device for making the statement. To take a very simple case, you might remark, "Isn't this just glorious weather?" In most contexts, people would understand this to be a statement that the weather is glorious, despite the interrogative form of the sentence. For example, someone might respond to this sentence by saying, "That's false! It's raining cats and dogs." A genuine question cannot be either true or false, so the appropriateness of this response clearly shows that the sentence is understood to express a statement.

Such sentences are referred to as **rhetorical questions.** The interrogative form is simply rhetorical, not substantive. The substance is a statement. A rhetorical question is simply a stylistic way, often quite effective at the rhetorical level, of making a statement.

> ### Rhetorical Questions
>
> A rhetorical question is a statement expressed with an interrogative sentence. An author who uses a rhetorical question intends to be understood as making a statement, and not asking a question. Rhetorical questions often are used to express conclusions or premises.

How do you tell whether an interrogative sentence is a genuine question or merely a rhetorical question? As with other aspects of textual interpretation, you must rely on your sense of what the author intends to say, based on the context. In fact, this is usually not difficult because people tend to be quite adept at recognizing rhetorical questions. Here is an example:

Example 4.9

Background: This letter from 1999 is about a matter of great public controversy at that time: When would the new millennium begin? (*Houston Chronicle*, 12/99)

① Ask almost anyone how many years in a millennium and they will answer, "1,000, of course." ② And how many years in two millennia? "Why, 2,000 of course." ③ And how many years will we have completed in the second millennium at midnight on Dec. 31, 1999?: 1,999. ④ So, why is there so much talk about the "new millennium" when it is still more than a year away?—R.L.V.

Clearly, sentence 4 is meant to make the statement that the millennium does not begin until 2001 and is the conclusion of the argument.

Some other special cases are worth mentioning. In these cases, what goes in the circle at the base of the tree diagram is not a single number because the conclusion is not expressed in a single sentence. Rather, it is expressed either in part of a sentence or in more than one sentence.

Consider these examples:

Example 4.10

A. Background: This letter is about the court settlement reached between the government and the tobacco companies in the late 1990s. (*Los Angeles Times*, 6/97)

① The $368.5 billion tobacco industry settlement will be a monumental travesty of justice without stiff prison sentences for the tobacco company CEO's who lied to Congress about their knowledge of the deadly effects of their products.—G.H.

B. Background: This letter is the lament of a long-suffering baseball fan. (*Chicago Tribune*, 4/97)

① As a long-suffering diehard Cubs fan, I want to say thank you to the Chicago Cubs for their 0-12 start. ② In years past, the Cubs struggled at the beginning of the season and then played well enough to keep our hopes alive through the summer. ③ Then came August. ④ And each lost game tore another small piece from our hearts. ⑤ Like putting a sick animal out of its misery, the Cubs' miserable start has ended our hopes before the pain becomes too intense. ⑥ And for that I say, "Thank you!" ⑦ Just wait 'til next year.—C.D.D.

C. Background: This letter is about public education. (*New York Times*, 6/98)

① President Clinton said that "we shouldn't let a child graduate from middle school without knowing how to use the new technologies." ② Such a platitude obscures the real problems with education in a country in which an unconscionable percentage of middle-school students graduate without basic reading, writing and math skills. ③ Computer literacy is not an alternative to these skills but a further step in learning that is based on these fundamentals.—E.D.

Here is how the base of the tree diagram looks in each case:

Example 4.11

A: ⓵ⓐ
B: ⓵ or ⑥
C: ⓵ & 2a

In text A, the author expresses the whole argument in a single sentence, so the conclusion forms only part of the sentence. The first part of the sentence gives the conclusion, and the second part the premise. You can see this by breaking the sentence into two and applying the reasoning indicator text, as in this example:

Example 4.12

The tobacco company CEOs lied to Congress about their knowledge of the deadly effects of their products. [*Therefore*,] the tobacco industry settlement will be a monumental travesty of justice without stiff prison sentences for the CEOs.

Or, using the shorthand method: ⓵ⓑ TF ⓵ⓐ

As this example indicates, when you need to split a sentence up because it expresses more than one statement, you label the parts "1a," "1b," and so forth. In the case of text A, the sentence expresses only two statements, so all we need are "1a" and "1b." In any case, the base of the tree diagram for A has "1a" in the circle.

Text B has two different sentences—1 and 6—that say roughly the same thing. The sentences do not say exactly the same thing, but each makes the statement that is the conclusion of the argument—namely, that the Cubs should be thanked for their early season losses. Either of them may be taken as representing the conclusion, which is why B has "1 or 6" in the circle at the base of the tree diagram.

Text C differs from text B because the conclusion in C is a result of combining ideas from two different sentences, 1 and part of 2. It is not that these two sentences express the same statement, as in B, but rather that each contributes something to the statement that is the argument's conclusion. Sentence 1 reports Clinton's remark, and sentence 2 makes a claim about this remark. The conclusion is the claim about the remark, but to get this statement, we need to combine the remark in sentence 1 and the author's comment on it in sentence 2. The conclusion is that President Clinton's remark—that "we shouldn't let a child graduate from middle school without knowing how to use the new technologies"—obscures the real problems with education in the country. One of the premises of the argument is contained in the second part of sentence 2, so the portion that includes some of the conclusion is labeled "2a." As a result, what goes at the base of the tree diagram for C is "1 & 2a." The ampersand (&) indicates that the conclusion combines aspects from both of the sentences.[4]

You need to pay attention to cases in which the conclusion is not expressed in one whole text sentence because otherwise you may not correctly identify the premises. On the one hand, if the conclusion is expressed in only part of a sentence, as in text A, the other part may express a premise. If you indicate the conclusion in the tree diagram with "1" instead of "1a," you might not recognize that a premise is expressed in sentence 1b. On the other hand, if two sentences (or parts of sentences) are involved in expressing the conclusion, as in texts B and C, none of these sentences or parts expresses a premise. If you do not include both numbers at the base of the tree diagram, you might mistakenly regard the one you leave out as expressing a premise.

4.2.4 *Implicit Conclusions*

Sometimes, the conclusion of an argument is not explicitly stated in the text. Authors often leave it to the audience to draw or infer the conclusion of their argument and so do not express the conclusion in any of the text sentences. A good example is the following lyrics from an old advertising jingle, also cited in Chapter 2: "The bigger the burgers, the better the burgers. The burgers are bigger at Burger King." What is the conclusion or point of the argumentative text? Clearly, it is that Burger King burgers are better. But this is not stated in the text; it is merely implied. This shows how natural it is to have conclusions that are *not* stated.

In this case, the author (an advertising agency) is so certain that we will understand the unstated conclusion when we hear the ad that it feels no need to state it. When a conclusion is unstated in the text, it is an **implicit conclusion.**

Implicit Conclusions

An argument has an implicit conclusion when no sentence in the text actually states the conclusion. In this case, the author of the text believes that the audience will understand what the conclusion is even though it is not explicitly stated. The author intends the audience to infer the conclusion from the text.

Like rhetorical questions, implicit conclusions are often used for rhetorical effect. For example, the rhetorical strategy may be that, if the author presents the conclusion as so obvious that he does not even need to express it, the audience will be more likely to regard it as true. This idea is suggested in the following text:

Example 4.13

Background: This letter is about the so-called single-payer approach to health care insurance, which is a single health insurance system for everyone run or overseen by the government. (*Boston Globe*, 8/94)

① A recent editorial stated that we must "make sure that every American has the health protection that citizens of other wealthy nations take for granted." ② Most, if not all, of these wealthy nations employ the single-payer approach to obtain that health protection. ③ 'Nuff said.—R.D.

The conclusion is not stated, nor does it need to be. The premises in sentences 1 and 2 speak for themselves. After expressing the premises, this author signals that the conclusion is so obvious that he does not need to express it by including sentence 3: "'Nuff said." It is enough to state the premises. The audience can draw the conclusion for itself.

As with other aspects of interpreting texts, it is the context that reveals the author's intention to present an argument with an implicit conclusion. An interesting example of the role of context involves context provided by pictures that complement the words of a text. Figure 4.4 gives two examples. In each case, the pictures make obvious the implicit conclusion the author intends. In the example on the left, the implicit conclusion is roughly that people in poverty are of great value. In the example on the right, the implicit conclusion is roughly that we should provide an adequate education for all children. (We will discuss one of these photos further in Chapter 5.)

 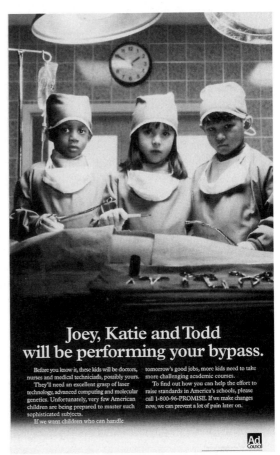

FIGURE 4.4   Implicit Conclusions. How do these pictures provide the context that, along with the words, reveals the authors' intent?

> ### Rule of Addition, Number 1[5]
>
> If an argument has an implicit conclusion, the text contains no sentence (or sentences) expressing the point the author is making. In that case, the conclusion must be added to the argument structure. In the tree diagram, the implicit conclusion is added by putting the letters "IC" in the circle at the base of the tree diagram.

When an argument has an implicit conclusion, the conclusion must be added to the argument structure. We can formulate this idea as a **rule of addition.** In the tree diagram, you indicate that the implicit conclusion is added by putting the letters "IC" in the circle at the base.[6]

Here is an example of a text with an implicit conclusion:

Example 4.14

Background: This letter is on the subject of requiring community service of high school students. (*New York Times*, 4/97)

> ① It is consistent with our model of education to require community service.
> ② There are multiple benefits to the requirement. ③ Our communities benefit from
> the intelligence and creative energies of young people. ④ Students learn that they
> have substantive contributions to make to adult society. ⑤ They learn about them-
> selves, discover career interests and abilities, and return to school more motivated
> and focused on academic studies. ⑥ In fact, requiring community service is an effec-
> tive way to instill values en route to graduation.—E.N.

This author makes a series of statements, all of which are reasons for requiring high school students to perform community service. But she never explicitly expresses what these statements are reasons for. It is obvious that the statements are reasons for requiring community service and that she intends to present them as such. Thus, this is an argumentative text with an implicit conclusion. The base of the tree diagram for this text would have an "IC" in the circle.

The fact that some arguments have implicit conclusions shows the impor-tance of considering the author's intention in determining whether a text is argu-mentative. With an implicit conclusion, no sentence in the text represents the conclusion.[7] A support relationship exists between statements expressed in the text and a statement that is not explicitly part of the text. Only by understanding the author's intention that the implicit conclusion be understood as part of the argu-ment can you recognize the existence of the support relationship that makes the text argumentative.

Consider a simple example to show how context is crucial to figuring out an author's intention. Imagine that at breakfast you say to your family, "The forecast is for beautiful weather today." Normally, of course, this would not be an argument. It contains only one statement, so there can be no support relationship. But sup-pose that the topic of the conversation preceding your remark was whether the family should go on a picnic that day. Given this context, your family members would naturally understand your remark as supporting the proposal to go on the picnic. In other words, they would interpret it as an argument with the implicit conclusion that the family should go on the picnic today. There is usually not much doubt, given the context, whether a text is meant to have an implicit conclusion. An author leaves out an explicit conclusion only when she or he is confident that the audience will recognize that the conclusion is implicit.

4.2.5 Value Conclusions

Value arguments, as discussed in Chapter 3, are arguments with value statements as conclusions. Many of the arguments you encounter are value arguments, so many of the conclusions you identify should be value statements. The majority of value arguments have action recommendations as conclusions. Action recommendations are value statements either that some individual(s) should take some action (such as quitting smoking) or that some group should adopt some **policy** (such as enacting strong gun control laws). Because policies are decisions by an organized body representing a group, such as a government, we may refer to them as collective actions.[8]

The most important examples of policy are found in law. For instance, the argument about the postage rate in Example 4.1 had an action recommendation as its conclusion: Instead of raising the price of a stamp yet again, the government should reduce or eliminate bulk-rate discounts for catalogues, solicitations, and fliers. This statement recommends that the government make a law that leaves the first-class postage rate the same and increases the bulk rate.

Authors often frame action recommendations in nonindicative sentences, especially imperative sentences. Consider this historical argument: "Slavery is an inhumane institution. Vote for Lincoln!" The conclusion is expressed in an imperative sentence, but, like all conclusions, it is a statement (specifically, a value statement). It could be rendered, "You [or everyone] should vote for Lincoln."

Policies

Some value conclusions that are action recommendations recommend not individual actions, but collective actions—that is, actions that groups take through an organizational or governmental structure of some kind. A collective action of this sort is a policy.

While conclusions of value arguments are usually action recommendations, they can be the other kind of value statement—namely, one that supports an action recommendation. (This kind of value statement was discussed in the previous chapter.) For example, the conclusion of a value argument might be this: "It is unjust to have a large wealth gap between the rich and the poor within a country." This is not an action recommendation, but a value statement that can support action recommendations, such as that the government raise taxes on the wealthy to support social services for the poor.

≡ EXERCISE SET 4.2

SECTION A: One of the most important critical thinking skills is determining which way the support relationship goes. What supports what? In the following argumentative texts, one sentence expresses the conclusion and the other a premise. Underline the sentence that expresses the conclusion.

EXAMPLE
Plato's *Republic* is a lively, readable text. It works well in the classroom.

ANSWER
Plato's *Republic* is a lively, readable text. It works well in the classroom.

PROBLEMS

1. The earth is made of material from dead stars. The universe is older than the earth.

2. The law should make divorces difficult to obtain. Marriage is our most important social institution.

3. Buying a baseball team is a good investment. After all, baseball is America's national pastime.

4. The public infrastructure is vital to the health of the economy. The public infrastructure must be well maintained.

5. One is the loneliest number. You had better go for two.

6. There is no joy in Mudville. Mighty Casey has struck out.

7. Liquid water is essential for life. Life cannot exist on the outer reaches of our solar system.

8. There is no effective way to control the distribution of music on the Internet. The Internet will revolutionize the recording industry.

9. I had better take voice lessons. I would like to teach the world to sing in perfect harmony.

10. Social Security is unfair. It amounts to the transfer of wealth from the young to the old.

11. Sally has a green thumb. Sally is the person to take your sick plants to.

12. Time seems to pass quickly when you're having fun. If you want to feel like you're having a long life, don't have any fun.

13. Who cares what we choose? There is little to win and little to lose.

14. Hamlet is a hero of the modern intellectual. Hamlet is intelligent, and his intelligence gets in the way of his taking action.

15. What doth it profit a man to win the world but lose his soul? Everyone needs to attend to matters spiritual.

16. Contrary to what one might expect, an extensive system of ballistic missile defenses would increase the risk of a nuclear war. We should not deploy an extensive system of ballistic missile defenses.

17. Dodos have been extinct for hundreds of years, killed off by humans. George must have been mistaken when he says he saw a live dodo.

SECTION B: Formulate the implicit conclusions in the following argumentative texts.

EXAMPLE

The bigger they are, the harder they fall. John is bigger than others.

ANSWER

John will fall harder than others.

PROBLEMS

1. The only instrument Betty plays is the piano. There are no pianos in the marching band.

2. All birds have feathers. The black-footed booby is a bird.

3. All Cretans are liars, and George is a Cretan.

4. Adults need at least 1000 calories a day, and Sally is 27.

5. The president must be at least 35, and Sally is 27.

6. It's after midnight, and good things happen after midnight.

7. Jim is a blonde. The old cliché is true that blondes have more fun.

8. Young people have an ironic detachment from politics. Jean is a young person.

❖ 9. Possums are the only marsupial native to North America. The animal in my backyard is a marsupial native to North America.

10. If the jails are getting fuller, then the crime rate must be going down. The statistics prove that the jails are getting fuller.

11. It is only fair that descendants of slaves should receive reparations for the uncompensated economic contribution their ancestors made to this country. Jessie is a descendant of slaves.

❖ 12. Only electric automobiles can save us from global warming. But electric cars are not feasible.

13. Birds of a feather flock together. Jamal and Aaron are alike. Duh?

14. You figure it out. The faster the film, the shorter the exposure, and this is very fast film.

❖ 15. All members of the Bennett family are prejudiced against Mr. Darcy. Elizabeth is a member of the Bennett family.

16. Humans should show humility in the face of what they cannot control. Humans cannot control the weather.

17. Given the great number of children in foster homes, it is vitally important to encourage adoption. One thing that the economists tell us is that increasing the dependent tax credit would encourage adoption.

❖ 18. The first atomic bombs were 1000 times more powerful than the largest nonnuclear bombs. The Blockbuster was the largest nonnuclear bomb.

19. The North Pole is the only location on Earth where anywhere you go is south. Wherever Matthew moves is south.

20. Collies have been especially bred for herding sheep. Slim is having trouble managing the sheep on his ranch.

❖ 21. The ivory-billed woodpecker is gone from all parts of the world with the possible exception of Cuba. Jane just saw an ivory-billed woodpecker.

SECTION C: For each of the following argumentative texts, do this:

(1) Identify the sentence (or the part of a sentence) that expresses the conclusion, and underline it. If the conclusion is expressed in more than one sentence, then underline each place it is expressed. If the conclusion is implicit, do nothing at this stage.

(2) Write down the conclusion statement using as clear a sentence as possible. The sentence you write down may be the same as or different from the one used in the text.

EXAMPLE

Background: This letter is on the ethics of human cloning. (*New York Times*, 12/97)

The product of cloning, or any other reproductive technology, should be regarded as fully human. Cloning a person to create an organ donor or a lost child is morally offensive because it negates the intrinsic value of the human being produced in favor of some other, previously born human.—M.C.

ANSWER

(1) The product of cloning, or any other reproductive technology, should be regarded as fully human. <u>Cloning a person to create an organ donor or a lost child is morally offensive</u> because it negates the intrinsic value of the human being produced in favor of some other, previously born human.

(2) Cloning a person to create an organ donor or a lost child is morally offensive. (no change of wording needed)

PROBLEMS

1. Background: This passage is from *The Federalist* 22, by Alexander Hamilton.[9]

   The treaties of the United States, under the present constitution, are liable to the infractions of thirteen different Legislatures. . . . The faith, the reputation, the peace of the whole union, are thus continually at the mercy of the prejudices, the passions, and the interest of every member of which it is composed.

2. Background: This letter is about the problem of motorists being killed at railroad crossings. (*Chicago Tribune*, 7/97)

   One way to keep drivers from driving around downed gates at railroad crossings is to close both sides of the crossing. Many crossings already have a pedestrian gate to keep people from crossing the tracks. The pedestrian gate could be extended to reach across the lane.—M.Z.

3. Background: This letter is about electricity use. (*New York Times*, 8/00)

   With an energy shortage in New York, why is there no law prohibiting retail establishments from running air conditioners full blast, with their doors wide open?—D.R.

4. Background: This text is from *On the Origin of Species* by Charles Darwin.[10] "Descent" refers to evolutionary ancestry. The issue is whether classification of a life form as a species relies on descent or, for example, appearance only.

   With species in a state of nature, every naturalist has in fact brought descent into his classification; for he includes in his lowest grade, or that of a species, the two sexes; and how enormously these sometimes differ in the most important characters, is known to every naturalist.

5. Background: This letter is about metal roofing. (*Boston Globe*, 5/00)

   I was disturbed to read in your editorial a brief mention of metal roofing as "aesthetically less pleasing" than other roofing options. Classifying metal roofing as unattractive is far from the truth. Metal roofing has made significant strides in the last few years. It now comes in slate, shingle, shake, and even tile designs and more and more is selected by top architects.—T.B.

6. Background: This letter is about the early 2000 decision of Illinois governor George Ryan to call a halt to executions in his state due to concerns that the system might allow an innocent person to be executed. (*New York Times*, 2/00)

Gov. Ryan has taken it upon himself to thwart the will of the people by calling a moratorium on executions. Since the beginning of the republic we have accepted the possibility that innocent people will be convicted of capital crimes and executed. We also accept that parole and bail will result in additional crimes, even the murder of innocent people.—W.B.

7. Background: This letter is about spending by universities. (*New York Times*, 6/97)

   Since 1945, the administrative share of university expenditures has increased 40 percent. Instruction and library shares are down, each about 15 percent. Research, after a peak in the 1960's, is up about 10 percent. The question is whether the bureaucracy that controls the budget can do the right thing, putting the money back into instruction and libraries. —A.H.

8. Background: This letter is about January in Chicago. (*Chicago Tribune*, 1/98)

   Ahhhh, January! Chicagoland is snow-covered, and the wind chills are sometimes minus 10 or lower. The holiday bills are already appearing to create as much dismay as some clothes that are now too tight due to holiday weight gains. The newness hasn't worn off many holiday gifts (read computers and related goodies), and logging on to one's favorite online service is as tough as finding a parking place at the health club. Truly, January is the month for reading!—S.W.

9. Background: This letter compares the response of the government in two different cases in which government security employees broke the rules by downloading classified data from their office computers. (*New York Times*, 2/00)

   The former director of central intelligence, John M. Deutch, is called "sloppy" by security officials and his security clearance is suspended. Wen Ho Lee, a Los Alamos weapons scientist, was indicted and is now held without bail. Has the concept of equal treatment before the law been discarded?—D.M.

10. Background: This letter is on the topic of same-sex marriages. (*New York Times*, 3/96)

    Same-sex marriages are not an assault on "the family," as is so often charged. They provide an option for gays, other than a life of loneliness of hiding, that is true to their real identities. Many gays and lesbians are forced into heterosexual unions that end in abandonment. Gay and lesbian unions can also be an instrument of reconciliation between children, their parents and their siblings.—J.K.D.

11. Background: This letter is about the role of the U.S. Senate in the impeachment of a president. (*New York Times*, 9/98)

    The Founders' original vision of the impeachment process involved a trial ultimately before a representative but as yet unelected body, the Senate. It was not until the 17th Amendment was ratified in 1913 that the Senate became an institution directly elected by the people. Thus, it is only in modern times that the electorate may play a nearly dispositive role in the outcome.—E.J.M.

12. Background: This letter responds to the newspaper's use of a famous phrase, "an eye for an eye," to mean retribution and retaliation. (*New York Times*, 7/97)

    Your reference to "the Old Testament credo of an eye for an eye and a tooth for a tooth" is out of place. The commandment originally was intended as a response to "might makes right," as expressed in Lamech's song of Genesis. Long before Jesus proposed nonretaliation, the Jewish people had substituted fines for such acts of retaliation.—L.E.F.

13. Background: This 1981 letter is about the proposal of former Governor Carey of New York State to allow alcohol sales 24 hours a day. (*New York Times*, 2/81)

    I want to go on record as being categorically opposed to Governor Carey's recommendation that 24-hour sales of beer, wine and liquor be allowed in the State of New York. Alcoholism is the greatest addictive problem in the United States, and the interrelationship between alcohol and mayhem on our highways is well known. The interplay of alcohol and other drugs is harmful to our residents—youths in particular. To permit the free flow of alcohol on a 24-hour basis would only exacerbate these problems. We all must oppose the Governor's destructive proposal.—H.E.A.

14. Background: This letter is in response to a discussion about leaving babies outside in the winter cold. (*New York Times*, 5/97)

    Your author describes the Scandinavian conviction that fresh, cold air is good for babies. There may be a scientific basis for this. Before vitamin D was discovered and used to fortify milk and other foods, babies born in the fall and unable to get adequate sunlight through the long, dark Northern European winter were at risk to develop and possibly die of rickets before spring. Keeping a baby outside, even in cold weather, maximized ultraviolet light exposure and vitamin D production.—S.J.G.

15. Background: This letter is in response to a letter claiming that it is unfair that sanitation workers are paid more than teachers. (*New York Times*, 8/83)

    The letter regarding the "unfairness" in granting higher salaries to sanitation workers than to teachers exposed the "degree syndrome" all too prevalent today. Participation in numerous pedagogical sessions does not entitle a person to a higher pay scale than others. Societal forces alone determine this.—E.S.K.

16. Background: This letter is part of the public debate over what to do about those in the United States who lack access to health insurance. (*New York Times*, 9/98)

Having no insurance does not mean that these patients do not get medical attention. Regrettably, many wait until they have a health crisis, then present themselves to emergency departments, with the tab being picked up by all of us in the form of charity care. That process is highly expensive and very inefficient. Prevention and wellness are less expensive. —J.J.B.

17. Background: This letter is about whether India, which has tested nuclear weapons, should be granted the status of a recognized nuclear weapons power under the Nuclear Nonproliferation Treaty, a 1967 treaty that seeks to stop the spread of nuclear weapons to nations that do not have them. (*New York Times*, 3/00)

India should not be given status under the nonproliferation treaty as a nuclear power for two reasons. First, doing so would break faith with countries that could have built nuclear weapons but have not done so and instead signed the nonproliferation treaty as nonnuclear states. Second, legitimizing India's nuclear status then makes it hard to reject any similar claims by countries that live with nuclear neighbors—nations like Japan, Taiwan and Vietnam, which border China, or Iran or Egypt, which may claim a nuclear need to balance Israel. International security is better preserved by diminishing the prominence of nuclear weapons rather than by legitimizing any enlargement of the nuclear club.—D.M.

18. Background: This letter is about the practice of fans at hockey games of throwing dead octopuses onto the ice. (*Washington Post*, 6/98)

The octopus is a living, feeling animal of fairly advanced intelligence. Tossing dead octopuses on the ice demonstrates a fundamental disregard for the sanctity of life and teaches children that life, especially animal life, is a disposable commodity. Is this the lesson we want our children to take with them to school? Furthermore, whether one eats them or not, octopuses are a source of food. Hockey fans who toss them away like garbage would do well to remember that there are hungry and starving people in the world, including here in the United States, and that food should not be wasted in such a nonchalant manner. This senseless, destructive ritual ought to end.—M.G.

19. Background: This letter is in response to a column about global warming. (*New York Times*, 7/00)

Your columnist could have mentioned another way to reduce global warming: policies that slow tropical deforestation. The destruction of rain forests causes approximately 20 percent of greenhouse gas emissions worldwide. By helping interested countries conserve their forests, Americans can also maintain an ecosystem that, in some cases, removes gases already in the atmosphere. These forests also buffer equatorial solar radiation. Rain forests also protect genetic diversity that may be helpful in countering some of global warming's possible ills, like outbreaks of pests and viruses from the tropics.—J.O.N.

4.3 Identifying the Premises

The next step in structuring an argument is to complete the tree diagram by tifying the text sentences (or parts of sentences) that express premises. Puttin numbers of these sentences or parts in the diagram as the branches of the shows the support relationships between premises and conclusion.

4.3.1 Completing the Tree Diagram

To identify the premises, ask, Which of the remaining sentences (or parts of sentences) in the text express statements meant to support the conclusion? Since you have already determined that the text is argumentative, you should have a good idea of where at least some of the premises are. Once you have identified the sentences expressing premises, you should put the numbers of those sentences in circles above the number representing the conclusion and connect each of the premise circles to the conclusion circle with an arrow pointing downward. (We saw an example of this in Figure 4.3.)

Consider this example:

Example 4.15

Background: This letter is in response to a news report that Amtrak, the national passenger train service, is close to bankruptcy. (*Boston Globe*, 6/97)

①I use Amtrak for traveling, as do many thousands of Americans—as well as Europeans who visit America, traveling to the cities by plane, then taking Amtrak across the country to view the beauty and grandeur of the United States, which is not possible from the air. ② Railroads are subsidized in Europe. ③ Why can't they be subsidized in America? ④ We subsidize tobacco farms and the military industry, so why not rail service, used by a large number of Americans, elderly and handicapped, and families with children who find it is cheaper and more comfortable to travel by train?—J.R.B.

Here, the author is offering reasons in support of Amtrak—more specifically, reasons in support of the statement that Amtrak should be subsidized by the government. The author expresses this conclusion in sentence 3 and also in part of sentence 4—specifically, part 4b. Sentences 1, 2, and 4 express premises, with sentence 4 expressing two of them. Figure 4.5 shows the tree diagram. Note that the premise circles are labeled "P1," "P2," and so on.

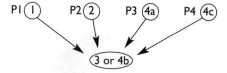

FIGURE 4.5   Tree Diagram for Example 4.15

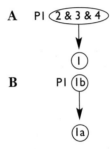

FIGURE 4.6   Tree Diagrams for Example 4.16

In identifying premises, the same sorts of special cases arise as in identifying conclusions.[11] Sometimes, a premise statement will be expressed in only part of a text sentence, in which case what goes in the circle will be a number and a letter—for example, "1b." Sometimes, two premise sentences will say the same thing, in which case what goes in the circle will be two numbers joined by an "or"—for example, "3 or 5." Sometimes, a premise statement will have contributions from different text sentences, in which case what goes in the circle will be, for example, "2 & 3a."

Consider these examples:

Example 4.16

A. Background: This letter is about the controversy following news that a 63-year-old woman gave birth. (*Chicago Tribune*, 5/97)

① The uproar about a 63-year-old woman giving birth is very sexist. ② Every day, wealthy older men, many of them CEOs or movie stars, marry women young enough to be their granddaughters. ③ Quite often they have children together. ④ Is this "sick and disgusting"?—J.L.

B. Background: This letter is in response to an assertion by a top official of the R. J. Reynolds tobacco company that the public would be the loser if his company was not allowed to market cigarettes. (*New York Times*, 6/97)

① The public is the loser if Reynolds is permitted to continue marketing a lethal and addictive product to children.—I.B.

Figure 4.6 shows the tree diagrams for these examples.

In text A, the conclusion, expressed in sentence 1, is that it is sexist to claim that a 63-year-old woman's giving birth is sick and disgusting. The premise is that the many prominent men who father children at an advanced age are not regarded as sick and disgusting. Each of the remaining sentences in the text contributes something to the premise, which means this premise is the result of combining ideas from three sentences. Thus, it is represented in the tree diagram by the three sentence numbers in a single circle, joined by the ampersand (&).

Text B is a different kind of case. The conclusion is that, if Reynolds continues to market its product to children, then the public will suffer. The supporting premise is that the product is lethal and addictive. The interesting thing about this premise is that it is not contained in a separate sentence, or even in its own clause in a compound sentence, but rather in a pair of adjectives in the middle of the sentence. As a result, the labeling in this case is not as straightforward as in other cases. Because the adjectives appear in the second half of the sentence, we can label the premise as "1b." We can also label the conclusion as "1a" in order to distinguish it from the premise, even though the conclusion takes up both parts of the sentence. Of importance here is not the numbering system, but the recognition that adjectives sometimes can express premises. They do in this case because the author clearly intends that they support the statement about the public being the loser.

You need to be especially cautious in identifying premises. Because arguments often contain more than one premise, it is important that you not run together into a single premise two premises that ought to be treated separately. A single premise is often expressed in more than one sentence, resulting in two or more numbers in a single premise circle, as in Figure 4.6A. But you must be careful not to include two numbers in a single circle that are better regarded as representing separate premises.

4.3.2 Convergent and Linked Premises

Recall the distinction made in Chapter 2 between convergent and linked premises. A convergent premise supports the conclusion by itself. The premises of the Amtrak argument in Example 4.15 are convergent—they are separate points that "converge" on the conclusion. In contrast, a linked premise depends on another premise to show how it supports the conclusion. Linked premises support the conclusion not individually but in groups, so the support relationship holds between *groups* of premises and the conclusion. Each linked premise shows how another premise with which it is connected supports the conclusion. In tree diagrams, linked premises are treated differently than convergent premises.

Consider these examples:

Example 4.17

A. Background: This letter is in response to former House of Representatives speaker Newt Gingrich's being unable to pay a fine he was assessed by the House Ethics Committee. (*Washington Post*, 5/97)

① I'm wary of having a person in charge of a $1.4-trillion budget—House Speaker Newt Gingrich—who, on a salary of $171,500 plus benefits and perks, has not managed his own money well enough to pay a $300,000 fine out of his pocket.—E.R.

B. Background: This letter is in response to an article discussing various views on the issue of clitorectomy, or female genital mutilation. (*New York Times*, 3/99)

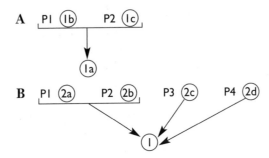

FIGURE 4.7   Tree Diagrams for Example 4.17

① Those who defend female genital mutilation as no more harmful than male circumcision are way off the mark. ② Unlike male circumcision, female genital mutilation subjects the girl or woman to risk of infection, which can lead to death, to a lifetime of difficulty and pain in urinating and menstruating, and to a reduction in or absence of sexual responsiveness.—A.J.W.

In text A, which contains only one sentence, the conclusion is expressed in the first part of the sentence (1a). This part of the sentence speaks literally to the author's psychological state, but it is meant to express a statement about Speaker Gingrich—namely, that it may not be safe to entrust a $1.4-trillion budget to him. The remainder of the sentence contains two linked premises. The first premise (1b) is that Gingrich receives a salary of $171,500 plus benefits and perks; the second premise (1c) is that he was unable to manage his own money well enough to pay a $300,000 fine without assistance. The fact that he receives the salary he does shows how his inability to pay the fine supports the conclusion. Likewise, the fact that he could not pay the fine shows how his substantial salary supports the conclusion.

Linked premises are represented in a tree diagram differently than are convergent premises. In the case of linked premises, the circles representing the premises in the linked group are bracketed, and the bracket is connected to the conclusion circle by a single arrow. Figure 4.7 shows how this argument and argument B, which also contains linked premises, can be represented in a tree diagram.

The same is the case for argument B, which also has two premises in a linked group. The conclusion, expressed in sentence 1, is that it is false that female genital mutilation is no more harmful than male circumcision. Sentence 2 contains four premises: that genital mutilation, unlike male circumcision, can lead to infection (2a), that the infection can lead to death (2b), that the mutilation can lead to a lifetime of difficulty and pain in urinating and menstruating (2c), that the mutilation can lead to a reduction in or an absence of sexual responsiveness. The first and second of these premises are linked rather than convergent, because each shows how the other supports the conclusion. The fact that the infection can lead to death shows how the fact that mutilation causes the infection supports the conclusion, and vice versa.[12] The third and fourth premises are convergent, each supporting the conclusion by itself. Therefore, this is a mixed argument (see Chapter 2).

How can you tell whether premises are linked or convergent? You need to ask yourself whether one of the premises shows how another of the premises supports the conclusion. In other words, does one of the premises show how another of the premises is relevant to the conclusion? If so, those premises are linked. In contrast, if none of the premises shows how any other premise supports or is relevant to the conclusion, then the premises are convergent.

One rough way to determine if a premise is convergent or linked is to apply the **so-what? test.** If you ask "so what?" about some claim, you are asking about its relevance to something else. To ask of a premise "so what?" is to ask to be shown how it is relevant to or how it supports the conclusion. So, if you ask the so-what? question about a premise and another premise in the text answers the question, those two premises are linked. In contrast, if you ask the so-what? question of a premise and no other premise in the text answers the question, then that premise is convergent rather than linked. This does not mean that a convergent premise is not relevant to the conclusion. Rather, it means only that the author has not supplied another premise that shows how it is relevant.

Consider Example 4.17. If you look at one of the premises—for example, that former Speaker Gingrich has a salary of $171,000 plus benefits and perks—and ask the so-what? question, you will find that the other premise is an answer to that question. This shows that the premises are linked.

The So-What? Test

When premises are linked, one of them shows how another supports, or is relevant to, the conclusion. In general, when we ask how something is relevant to something else is, we are asking, "so what?" To ask "so what?" of a premise is to ask how it is relevant to the conclusion. If another premise in the text answers this question, then the two premises are linked. Thus, to determine if the premises of an argument are linked, ask the so-what? question of each of them. If another premise answers that question, the premises are linked. If no premise answers that question, the premise is convergent.

Here is another example of a mixed argument, with both linked and convergent premises:

Example 4.18

Background: This letter is about the tendency for managed care organizations (health insurance providers) to delay reimbursing physicians for their services. (*New York Times,* 4/97)

① As a primary care physician, I must battle daily with managed care companies in order to receive payment on services rendered months ago. ② All providers of

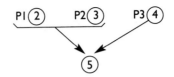

FIGURE 4.8   Tree Diagram for Example 4.18

health care are adversely affected by this practice. ③ This will continue to occur until there is legislation in place to penalize the managed care companies for late payment. ④ Who among your readers has been granted leniency for late payment of health insurance premiums? ⑤ Make the managed care companies pay a reasonable interest on claims greater than 45 days. ⑥ Wake up, Washington, and fix what can be fixed. —G.R.L.

The conclusion of this argument, expressed in sentence 5, is that legislation should be passed to make the managed care companies pay a reasonable interest on claims greater than 45 days. Sentences 2 and 3 each express a premise: that all providers of health case are adversely affected by managed care companies delaying payments and that this practice will continue until there is legislation in place to penalize the managed care companies for late payments. These premises are linked. (Try the "so-what?" test on them.) That is, the premise expressed in sentence 2 shows how the premise expressed in sentence 3 supports the conclusion, and vice versa.

But there is another premise, expressed in the rhetorical question, sentence 4, that leniency is not granted for late payments of health insurance premiums to the managed care organizations themselves. This statement is a convergent premise because it supports by itself the conclusion that managed care organizations should be required to pay a penalty for such behavior. Figure 4.8 shows the tree diagram. Note that linked premises should be put next to one another in the tree diagram and given adjacent designations (for example, P1 and P2, or P2 and P3) so that they can be bracketed.

4.3.3 Premises of Value Arguments

As mentioned in Chapter 3, value arguments usually have value premises supporting their conclusions.[13] For example, when the conclusion is an action recommendation, there will often be a value premise that supports the action recommendation. In addition, a value argument with an action recommendation as the conclusion will often have an effectiveness premise (or premises). An **effectiveness premise** shows how the action recommendation would achieve some desirable goal, how it would be a good means to some desirable end. Consider this argument:

Example 4.19

Background: This letter is in response to a letter complaining about the scalpers of tickets to Broadway shows. (*New York Times*, 11/98)

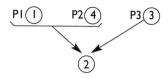

FIGURE 4.9   Tree Diagram for Example 4.19

① A letter writer complained that the profits reaped by Broadway ticket scalpers do not benefit the starved production budgets of Broadway shows. ② But if a Broadway show is in great demand, why shouldn't the producers auction off their best tickets to the highest bidder (who may include scalpers and brokers)? ③ In every other business, product is priced to meet market demand. ④ If Broadway show producers auctioned their tickets, they would reap the benefits previously reserved for scalpers. —J.O.M.

Figure 4.9 shows the tree diagram for this argument.

This argument has an action recommendation conclusion, expressed in the rhetorical question of sentence 2, that the producers of successful Broadway shows should auction off their best tickets to the highest bidder. What about sentence 1? On the surface, this sentence simply reports the view of someone else that Broadway show producers, and not ticket scalpers, should realize the profits the scalpers receive from the ticket sales. But the author of the argument seems to be not just stating the view, but endorsing it. Thus, this sentence expresses the value statement that the profits reaped by the scalpers of tickets to Broadway shows should benefit the shows' producers instead of the scalpers. Sentence 4 expresses the premise that if Broadway show producers auctioned their tickets, they would reap the benefits previously reserved for scalpers. This is an effectiveness premise because it states how the action recommendation would bring about the desirable goal of giving the profits of ticket sales to the producers and not the scalpers. Sentence 3 expresses the additional premise that ticket auctioning would allow the theater, like all other businesses, to price its product in accord with market demand.

Note that the value premise (P1) and the effectiveness premise (P2) are linked. This is the case because the effectiveness premise shows how the value premise supports the conclusion, and vice versa. The support each premise has for the conclusion is shown by the other. Often, value premises and effectiveness premises will be linked in this way.

Effectiveness Premises

Value arguments with action recommendation conclusions often have effectiveness premises—statements claiming that or showing how the recommended action will achieve some desirable goal. An effectiveness premise shows that the recommended action serves as a means to that end. Effectiveness premises are often linked with value premises.

Arguments with action recommendations as conclusions often have both a value premise and an effectiveness premise (or more than one of each). When an argument with an action recommendation conclusion does not have an explicit value premise or effectiveness premise, the premise may be *implicit*. (Implicit premises will be discussed in subsequent chapters.) In addition, a value conclusion will sometimes be implicit. As in all cases in which there may be an implicit conclusion, you need to judge whether the author intended to imply such a conclusion.

4.3.4 What to Leave Out

Argumentative texts will often have sentences or parts of sentences that are not part of the argument—neither conclusion nor premise. You simply leave their numbers out of the tree diagram. An argumentative text may have sentences that are not part of the argument for many reasons. Some sentences may be included in the text to help provide context for the audience. Others may report the author's own experiences or reaction to what he or she is talking about, without being part of the argument. Sometimes, authors simply have trouble sticking to the topic.

According to the **rule of omission,** when you are identifying premises, you should not assume that all of the sentences other than the one expressing the conclusion necessarily express a premise. If a sentence expresses neither the conclusion nor any statement intended to have a support relationship to the conclusion, you can omit it from the argument structure.

How do you tell what sentences should be omitted? For each of the remaining sentences in the text, you should ask yourself, Does it express a statement that the author intends as support for the conclusion? Does the author mean it to express a reason for the conclusion? If not, then the sentence is not a part of the argument and should not be included in the argument structure.

Rule of Omission

When you are identifying premises, you should not assume that all of the sentences other than the one expressing the conclusion express premises. If a sentence expresses neither the conclusion nor any statement intended to have a support relationship to the conclusion, you can omit it from the argument structure.

Consider this example:

Example 4.20

Background: This letter is in response to a news article. (*New York Times, 4/97*)

① I was appalled to read that rooftop water tanks may soon be wrapped in advertising. ② These charming round structures provide unique details in a chiefly angular

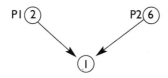

FIGURE 4.10   Tree Diagram for Example 4.10

urban landscape, adding a subtlety to the New York City skyline of which few people may be consciously aware. ③ My attention was first called to their aesthetic value as an architecture student at Pratt Institute. ④ My drawing teacher took our class to the rooftop of her Manhattan studio where we spent the day sketching water tanks. ⑤ I still have the drawings. ⑥ Is nothing in society safe from commercialism's greedy grasp?—E.K.P.

This argumentative text requires some careful interpretation. First, we look for the conclusion. Sentence 1, which expresses the conclusion, is literally about the author's feelings, but the statement it is making in the argument is not about these feelings. Rather, the author's talk of being appalled is simply a rhetorical way of making the value statement that the rooftop water tanks in New York City should not be wrapped in advertising. This is the conclusion. One premise is expressed in sentence 2. This value statement supports the conclusion by extolling the aesthetic beauty of the unadorned water tanks in the urban landscape. Another premise is expressed in sentence 6. This rhetorical question supports the conclusion by stating that putting advertising on the water tanks would be a case of greedy commercialism.

What of the remaining text, in sentences 3–5? They do not seem to provide support for the conclusion. They discuss how the author became aware of the aesthetic value of the unadorned water tanks, but these points do not support the conclusion. By the rule of omission, then, they should not be included in the tree diagram. Figure 4.10 shows the tree diagram.

This does not imply that these sentences should *not* be in the text. Certainly, the sentences are *related* to the topic, and it is not as if the author suddenly started talking about cabbages. It is completely appropriate for the author to tell the audience how she became aware of the value of the water tanks. This material makes the text more interesting, even if it is not part of the argument. The author set out to do two things in the text: (1) to present an argument and (2) to discuss her own personal involvement with the topic. There is nothing wrong with combining these two objectives in a single text. But when we seek to understand her argument, we should set aside the sentences that do not express that argument.

Deciding what parts of the text to omit from the tree diagram is part of the process of interpreting that text. In any case of interpretation, as mentioned previously, there is room for disagreement about what the argument is. This "room" will become even larger when we consider the issue of reformulation (step 4 in structuring arguments, discussed in Chapter 5). Though there is usually room for disagreement, this is not to say that any interpretation is as good as any other. Some interpretations are better than others, and some are simply wrong.

EXERCISE SET 4.3

SECTION A: Some of the following argumentative texts have convergent premises, and some have linked premises. Number the sentences in the text, and construct a tree diagram for each, indicating in the diagram whether the premises are convergent or linked.

EXAMPLE
Vitamins are important for the immune system. The restoration of connective tissue requires a good supply of vitamins. Everyone should get a proper dose of vitamins.

ANSWER
① Vitamins are important for the immune system. ② The restoration of connective tissue requires a good supply of vitamins. ③ Everyone should get a proper dose of vitamins.

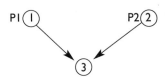

PROBLEMS
1. Pets make good companions. Having a companion is especially important for shut-ins. Shut-ins should have a pet.
2. Computers can be good educational tools. Computers provide great opportunities for entertainment. You should have a computer.
3. Critical thinking exercises the mind. The mind must be exercised to function effectively. Study critical thinking!
4. You should get a poodle. Poodles are good show dogs. You would enjoy participating in a dog show.
5. An ounce of prevention is worth a pound of cure. Plan z is an ounce of prevention. Plan z will avoid a pound of cure.
6. It is illegal to have a bear in our town. You should get rid of your bear. Bears do not even make good pets. Moreover, it takes a lot of money to keep a bear.
7. The owl of Minerva takes flight only at dusk. The owl of Minerva is not taking flight now because it is only noon.

8. The moon is not a proper place to picnic. No picnic is complete without ants, and there are no ants on the moon.

❖ 9. A day without orange juice is like a day without sunshine. Orange juice contains plenty of vitamin C. You should drink your orange juice.

10. Fools rush in where angels fear to tread. His mama raised no fools, so he will not rush in where angels fear to tread.

11. Parents should have as much choice as possible in the education of their children. So, we should adopt the proposal for school vouchers because this proposal would increase parents' choice in the education of their children.

❖ 12. We should not adopt the proposal for school vouchers. Vouchers would violate the constitutionally mandated separation between church and state, and they would hurt poor children the most.

13. Every child should have a pen pal because having a pen pal encourages a child to write and increases that child's knowledge of the wider world.

14. Supermarkets help to keep food prices low. Supermarkets offer consumers a great variety of choice. Cambridge should have a supermarket.

❖ 15. Whatever helps to keep food prices low is good for a community, and supermarkets help to keep food prices low. Cambridge should have a supermarket.

16. When ships sail into the horizon, their masts are the last part to disappear from view. By sailing far enough west, a ship can return to the place from which its voyage began. The world is round.

17. Cellular phones are a threat to human well-being because having time to oneself is essential for human well-being, and cellular phones make it harder to have time to oneself.

SECTION B: Each of the following argumentative texts has at least one sentence that is not part of the argument and should not be included in the argument structure. For each, number the sentences and construct a tree diagram.

EXAMPLE

I love ocean beaches. They are a great vacation site. They provide plenty of ways to relax. In addition, they provide plenty of ways to have fun. My favorite beaches are on Long Beach Island in New Jersey. But the accommodations there are getting more and more expensive and are definitely upscale.

ANSWER

① I love ocean beaches. ② They are a great vacation site. ③ They provide plenty of ways to relax. ④ In addition, they provide plenty of ways to have fun. ⑤ My favorite beaches are on Long Beach Island in New Jersey. ⑥ But the accommodations there are getting more and more expensive and are definitely upscale.

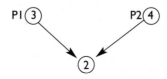

PROBLEMS

1. The United States has a capitalist economic system. Capitalism allows for maximum individual opportunity. In addition, it is the system that creates the greatest prosperity. Clearly, capitalism is the best economic system.

2. Rock 'n' roll came to wide public consciousness in the 1950s with Elvis Presley. It is based on African-American musical forms. There is no doubt that it is here to stay. It appeals to a wide diversity of audiences. Moreover, rock 'n' roll has a great capacity to renew itself each generation.

3. World War I began in 1914. At the time, however, it was not called "World War I" and would not be until the coming of World War II. Germany was to blame for the war. The first nation to do something that leads inexorably to war is to blame for a war. Germany was the first nation to mobilize its forces. It is the mobilization of forces that led inexorably to the war.

4. Chess is the most intellectually challenging of games. The number of moves is almost unlimited. There is no element of luck in the game, except for the decision about who goes first. Chess was invented in India many centuries ago. Chess championships have now become major sporting events.

5. The number of vegetarians is growing every day. People have been attracted to the vegetarian lifestyle. Vegetarianism helps to reduce the suffering of animals. Moreover, a vegetarian diet is healthier than a diet including meat. A vegetarian diet contains no harmful animal fats. It contains no cholesterol. It is easier to control one's weight on a vegetarian diet.

6. The circus act with the greatest draw is invariably the acrobats. Acrobats make their death-defying stunts seem easy. But they are really very hard. Acrobats must work long, hard hours to develop the strength, stamina, and flexibility their work requires. If a person must work long, hard hours to develop the physical skills needed for a vocation or avocation, she or he is an athlete. Circus acrobats are athletes.

7. I have suffered jet lag on a number of occasions. Jet lag makes me feel lousy for several days. It decreases my efficiency. It leads to insomnia and increases the risk of infection. Jet lag is the bane of the international traveler. Some say that it is worse flying west to east than east to west.

8. E-books—give me a break! Gutenberg must be turning over in his grave. E-books will never replace real books. The printed page is simply more appealing than the screen. Can E-books function when wet? Moreover, nothing can beat the smell of a freshly printed book.

9. The exchange rate advantage makes travel to Canada very affordable. Moreover, Canada is more civilized than the United States. Its cities are cleaner. It has a lower crime rate. It is more generous with its foreign aid. And it has a government-run universal health insurance system.

10. Did you ever see the movie *Jaws*? It is because of that movie that so many people have an intense fear of sharks. But that fear is greatly exaggerated. Many more people are killed or injured in other water accidents than are killed or injured by shark attacks. In fact, some species of shark are endangered.

11. One of the joys of the morning is a fresh cup of coffee. The aroma of coffee brewing is a wonderful and delicate alarm clock. Not only is coffee a pleas-

ure, but it has beneficial effects as well. It can improve concentration and provide mild stimulation. It can be an effective self-medication to control mood swings and moderate mild depression.

12. Sun exposure used to be thought of as healthy. The bronze glow of a good tan was thought to be an indication of good health. Now we know that the opposite is the case. Sun exposure can cause premature aging of the skin. Severe sunburns can increase the risk of skin cancer.

13. Harry Potter must spend his summers with muggles, much to his dismay. He would much rather be back at wizard school. Harry has a lightning-bolt scar on his forehead. He speaks the language of snakes. The powerful and evil Lord Voldemort failed in his efforts to kill Harry. Harry is indeed a very special wizard.

14. Some humans are simply evil. If you have ever known such a person, you will know what I mean. Moreover, if evil people achieve political power, their capacity for evil increases immeasurably, and they become super-evil. Hitler was evil. Hitler achieved political power. He was responsible for the deaths of over 50 million people, including tens of millions of civilians. Hitler was super-evil.

SECTION C: For the texts in Exercise Set 4.2, Section C, number the sentences and construct a tree diagram for each.

EXAMPLE
Background: This letter is on the ethics of human cloning. (*New York Times*, 12/97)

The product of cloning, or any other reproductive technology, should be regarded as fully human. Cloning a person to create an organ donor or a lost child is morally offensive because it negates the intrinsic value of the human being produced in favor of some other, previously born human.—M.C.

ANSWER
① The product of cloning, or any other reproductive technology, should be regarded as fully human. ② Cloning a person to create an organ donor or a lost child is morally offensive because it negates the intrinsic value of the human being produced in favor of some other, previously born human.

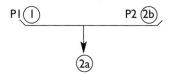

SECTION D: For each of the following argumentative texts, number the sentences and construct a tree diagram.

EXAMPLE
Background: This letter is about efforts to reduce gasoline prices. (*New York Times*, 2/00)

Would not the most practical, effective and immediate way to help reduce gasoline and diesel prices be to reduce consumption—hence demand—by enforcing speed limits on highways and roads? An added bonus: fewer traffic accidents, injuries and death.—D.J.S.[14]

ANSWER

① Would not the most practical, effective and immediate way to help reduce gasoline and diesel prices be to reduce consumption—hence demand—by enforcing speed limits on highways and roads? ② An added bonus: fewer traffic accidents, injuries and deaths.

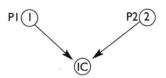

PROBLEMS

1. Background: This letter is in response to an editorial about the opposition of the U.S. government to an international treaty banning land mines. (*New York Times*, 9/97)

   I thought that a fundamental function of military troops was to put themselves at risk in order to defend unarmed civilians. When it comes to land mines, President Clinton and the Pentagon seem to have it the other way around: they want to put civilians at risk in order to keep soldiers safe.—E.B.

2. Background: This is a passage from Charles Darwin's *On the Origin of Species*.[15]

   Forms existing in larger numbers will always have a better chance, within any given period, of presenting further favourable variations for natural selection to seize on, than will the rarer forms which exist in lesser numbers. Hence, the more common forms, in the race for life, will tend to beat and supplant the less common forms.

3. Background: This letter is in response to a column claiming that the huge salaries received by the co-stars in *Seinfeld* was a symptom of yuppie greed. (*New York Times*, 5/97)

   Your columnist fails to explain why these actors, who labored for years before hitting it big, should voluntarily work for less than they can get in negotiations. It's not as if they extorted pennies from UNICEF. *Seinfeld* generates tremendous wealth, in part based on the talents of its cast members. Why shouldn't they share in it?—J.S.T.

4. Background: This letter is by a disappointed movie-goer in Dade County, Florida. (*Miami Herald*, 3/97)

   How is it possible that a wonderful and educational film such as William Shakespeare's *Hamlet* played in one Dade County theater for approximately two weeks and instead we get *Jungle 2 Jungle* and *Private Parts* released in most theaters? Is it commercialism that defines this area as a frontier town? —L.M.G.

5. Background: This letter is about the surpluses that developed in the federal budget in the late 1990s. (*Los Angeles Times*, 4/98)

   With an $8-billion federal budget surplus, the first surplus in 30 years, wouldn't it be refreshing to make a token $1-billion payoff on the national debt? Consider that, at 6%, a $1-billion reduction in debt would yield a $60-million reduction in interest. I propose that the first billion of every annual surplus should be applied toward the national debt, just so people and especially the Congress don't forget it is there.—R.P.

6. Background: This letter is in response to a proposal that the government promote economic development by funding research in computers and telecommunications. (*New York Times*, 3/99)

   History is not encouraging to those who would predict the future of innovation. Future breakthroughs in information technology may well come from research in optics, polymer chemistry or biology. Without a crystal ball, the best we can do is support the research and training of talented people in a wide range of fields.—R.G.T.

7. Background: This letter is in response to a column arguing that the "wealth gap," the growing disparity in wealth between the wealthiest and the poorest Americans, should not be a source of concern. (*New York Times*, 1/00)

   Your writers ask, "Why Decry the Wealth Gap?" First, inequality is correlated with political instability, one of the strongest findings of cross-national research. Second, inequality is correlated with violent crime. Third, economic inequality is correlated with reduced life expectancy, shown by a large and growing body of public health research. A fourth reason? Simple justice. There is no moral justification for chief executives' being paid hundreds of times more than ordinary employees. Social policies that reduce inequality, like progressive taxation and living wages, should be strengthened and expanded for the health and well-being of those not at the top of the pyramid.—R.H.

8. Background: This letter is about the decision of the North Atlantic Treaty Organization (NATO) in the late 1990s to admit some new members. NATO is a military alliance of the United States, Canada, and the countries of western Europe set up in the late 1940s to combat the Soviet Union. (*New York Times*, 3/99)

   Your news analysis on the accession of Poland, Hungary and the Czech Republic to NATO didn't mention that all NATO decisions must be made by unanimous vote. Every time a new country is admitted to the alliance, the chances of reaching unanimous decisions decrease and the probability of paralysis increases. In the wake of NATO's latest expansion, shouldn't its procedures be changed to eliminate the unanimity requirement and replace it with a two-thirds majority vote?—P.F.

❖   9. Background: This letter is part of the public debate over affirmative action in college admissions. By "social engineering," the author refers to all admissions decisions based on factors, including affirmative action, apart from merit. (*New York Times*, 3/00)

The best colleges have always practiced social engineering in addition to considering merit in the admissions process, and merit is itself a far-from-simple concept. Why is it that few complained when the social engineering was done to further the advantages of the already privileged?—K.D.

10. Background: This letter is a commentary on the vast amount of coverage and attention in the press given to National Secretaries' Day. (*San Francisco Chronicle*, 4/98)

You should know that following Secretaries' Day on April 22, is St. George's Day, the patron saint of England and an early Christian martyr, on April 23, which is also William Shakespeare's birthday, an event considered important in educated parts of the globe.—A.C.N.

11. Background: This letter is in response to a news story about a woman (A.M.) charged with killing her adopted child. (*Chicago Tribune*, 12/97)

I have never seen the headline "Biological parent kills child." How come, then, the sad story of A.M. has been reported under the banner "Adoptive mom charged in girl's death"? The headline suggests that the mother's adoptive status offers insight into the tragedy. The dark insinuation that adoptive parents are more likely to harm their children is statistically inaccurate and offensive.—M.T.S.

❖   12. Background: This letter criticizes the amount of coverage given by the *Chicago Tribune* to the 1997 death of Princess Diana of Great Britain. (*Chicago Tribune*, 9/97)

It would be interesting to know how the total number of column inches in the *Tribune*'s report on the death and funeral of John F. Kennedy compares with the total inches of the report on the death and funeral of Princess Diana.—D.A.

13. Background: This letter is part of the continuing debate over tax cuts. (*Chicago Tribune*, 4/97)

It has become popular for politicians to call for tax cuts. We would all like to see our taxes go down, but we must keep in mind one very important fact. The costs of government must be paid. If we do not pay now out of tax revenues, we (or our children) must pay later, plus interest. The time to talk of tax cuts is not when we have a $5.3-trillion national debt. We can simplify our tax system and make it more fair, but it will be irresponsible for politicians to be offering voters tax cuts as the next election draws near.—E.L.

14. Background: This letter is in response to a story of a boy (N.A.) who committed murder and was sentenced as a juvenile. (*New York Times*, 1/00)

The judge's sentencing of N.A., who was convicted of a killing committed when he was 11, to seven years at the maximum-security juvenile detention center, may have "stunned prosecutors and disappointed lawmakers." But it is cheering to those who are disgusted and outraged at the way our society can think of nothing to do with youthful offenders, themselves victims of abuse and neglect, except punish them severely.—B.S.

❖ 15. Background: This letter is in response to the death of the "Peanuts" cartoonist Charles Schulz. (*New York Times*, 2/00)

The plaudits to Charles M. Schulz stress how "Peanuts" was a sweet, simple comic strip that reflected its readers' lives. In my opinion, nothing could be further from the truth. In its golden age (mid-1950's to mid-60's), at least, "Peanuts" was a brilliant, quasi-surrealistic explosion of language and imagination. Many of its situations bore no resemblance at all to our lives, which made them all the more hilarious. And Charles Schulz, in his ingenious use of sophisticated language, became a major influence on a whole generation of comedy writers, myself included.—D.M.

16. Background: This letter is about inadequate toilet facilities for women at theaters. (*New York Times*, 6/97)

There is a simple interim procedure theater operators should take to improve the usage of ladies' rooms. The curtain should be held until the restroom lines have gone and no one remains inside. Many theaters maintain that they already do this. However, without prominent notices to this effect, many women abandon the lines (or attempt to use the men's room) at the first indication of the end of the intermission. The Paris Fine Arts movie theater seats 586, while its ladies' room seats three. When the four-hour *Hamlet* was shown, there was only one short intermission. Upon my protest the manager agreed to hold the curtain. Operating a theater entails a responsibility beyond providing entertainment.—A.P.S.

17. Background: This letter is about the issue of foreign intervention in countries where genocide is occurring. (*New York Times*, 2/00)

What about the possibility of a ground force under United Nations' command made up of volunteers from many countries, but with the use of such a force in particular cases requiring Security Council approval and logistical support by member nations? This would avoid loss of soldiers from the military force of any particular country (for example, the United States) yet preserve the right of the United States and other permanent Security Council members to approve or veto military action in specific cases.—H.S.

❖ 18. Background: This letter is in response to New York governor George Pataki's decision to seek the reinstitution of the state death penalty in the mid-1990s. (*New York Times*, 11/94)

As a longtime advocate of the death penalty for murderers, I concur with Governor Pataki's decision. However, the bill being prepared prescribes electrocution, a repulsive way of putting anyone to death, which should be replaced by injection. Lethal injection is procedurally not different from other injections. It is a painless and nonrepulsive way of doing justice and should be adopted.—E.V.D.H.

19. Background: This letter is about what the policy should be toward adultery in the military ranks. (*New York Times*, 7/97)

   Our sex-soaked culture must not pull the military into its slimy pit. Tough adultery laws promote military readiness. Two-thirds of military members are married, and Pentagon studies confirm that a strong family is key to military readiness. Another study found that respect for marriage decreases sexual harassment—allegedly a Pentagon objective. Adultery is not just about sex, but about breaking a vow. It is about honor—the military's bedrock. If the marriage vow means nothing to a soldier, can we trust his commitment to his country and his unit? Adultery is not a victimless crime. It creates resentment and damages families.—R.L.M.

20. Background: This letter is about conserving water. (*New York Times*, 8/99)

   The best solution to droughts is to give water users the proper economic incentive. This can be done by increasing water taxes by, say, $200 a year and by using the increased revenue to reduce property or other taxes by a similar amount. We would not pay a dime more in net tax revenue. But we would all use less water because wasting water would be expensive. As a result, reservoir levels would be significantly higher in times of rain failure. This has the additional advantage of preserving liberty: During droughts it would be less necessary to punish citizens for specific water uses.—T.O.

❖ 21. Background: This letter is about higher-education admission examinations. (*Los Angeles Times*, 1/00)

   I believe that the SAT, Graduate Record Exam and particularly the Medical College Admissions Test discriminate against slower readers. Knowing the material, not speed-reading, should be what the grade is based on. Many students are simply slow readers, but are tops academically. Slow reading does not only result from attention deficit disorders, dyslexia, etc. but also from English as a second language and simply from being a normal kid who is not a speed reader. All students should be given double time on all these standardized exams. That would result in a fair evaluation of knowledge and ability, not one based on discriminatory speed-reading.—S.B.O.

22. Background: This letter is about laws requiring seat belt use. (*Boston Globe*, 8/94)

   A seat belt law ensures that people riding in cars carry some legal responsibility for their own safety. A driver who contributes to an accident through carelessness has a legal defense against the worst charges that might result. A seat belt law not only protects us from collisions with the windshield, it also minimizes the impact of accidents on everyone else.—D.B.

23. Background: This letter is about affirmative action. (*New York Times*, 3/95)

Affirmative action is not a system for preferring unqualified individuals over qualified individuals. Nor is it a quota system. What affirmative action goals and timetables do is insure those qualified of all genders, ethnicities, races and abilities or disabilities that they will be fairly included in hiring and other decisions. Unfortunately, a history of discrimination against women, people of color and the disabled has for more than 250 years excluded qualified people from employment, housing, contracting and educational opportunities. Insuring all qualified people an equal opportunity by keeping the door open for white as well as nonwhite Americans is not un-American; it represents the best America can be.—J.A.F.

❖ 24. Background: This letter addresses the issue of whether mothers should work when their children are growing up. (*New York Times*, 6/98)

For 25 years now, I've listened to women snipe at each other about home versus work. The full-time mothers whine that no one appreciates all they do and everyone makes them feel unimportant. The working mothers whine that no one appreciates all they do and everyone makes them feel guilty. I have the same question for everyone: Are you doing what's best for your family? If the answer is no, change it. If the answer is yes, shut up about it. No self-respecting woman should care what some stranger thinks about the way she's chosen to care for her family.—N.R.

25. Background: This letter is about law school admissions. (*New York Times*, 6/97)

There is a problem with the importance that is given to the admission system. Acceptance to most law schools is almost a guarantee that the student will receive a law degree. Very little culling is done after admission. A better policy would be for schools to accept far more law students by lowering mandatory test scores and other criteria. That would remove most of the problems associated with who is and who isn't admitted. Then only those students who quickly exhibited the necessary aptitude and dedication to become lawyers would be retained.—A.S.N.

Summary

Identifying the argument in an argumentative text is a matter of identifying the parts of the argument—the conclusion and the premises—and presenting them in a way that shows the support relationship. The result is an argument structure.

An argument structure usually differs from the argumentative text in three ways. First, the structure may use different sentences than the text to express statements more clearly. Second, the order of the sentences will usually be different. Third, the structure will often contain a different number of sentences than the text.

Tree diagrams are a useful method of structuring arguments. The first step in constructing a tree diagram is to number the sentences of the argumentative text.

The second step is to identify the text sentence(s) that express the conclusion and put the sentence number(s) in a circle at the base of the tree diagram, to represent the trunk. In identifying the conclusion, the most important thing to recognize is what supports what. In general, the support relationship goes in one direction only, from premise to conclusion. The third step in the construction of a tree diagram is the identification of the premises—those statements that provide support for the conclusion. The numbers of the sentences that express premises are put in circles above the conclusion circle. Like conclusions, premises are not always expressed in the text in single whole sentences.

Sometimes, the author of an argumentative text will not include a sentence that expresses the conclusion of the argument. This is called an implicit conclusion. Implicit conclusions are usually easy to spot because authors generally leave out of the text a sentence expressing the conclusion only when they believe that the audience will have an easy time figuring it out. Value arguments have value conclusions, which are usually action recommendations. Action recommendations can be recommendations for individual action or for collective action, or policy.

Convergent and linked premises are treated differently in the tree diagram. One way to tell the two kinds of premises apart is to apply the so-what? test. When one premise provides an answer to the so-what? question asked about another premise, those premises are probably linked. If not, the premises are probably convergent.

Key Terms

argument structure	rhetorical question	policy
sentence	implicit conclusion	so-what? test
statement	rule of addition	effectiveness premise
what supports what (WSW)?	(number 1)	rule of omission
tree diagram		

Notes

1. In Bergen Evans (ed.), James Boswell, *The Life of Samuel Johnson* (New York: Random House, 1952), p. 506.
2. It is instructive that each question uses a different verb tense—the first, the past tense, and the second, the present tense. A sentence is tied to the occasion on which it was spoken, and that is now in the past. But a meaning is not tied to a particular time in the same way.
3. Sometimes, it works in both directions. This happens when the premise and conclusion say the same thing, when they make the same statement. This is normally taken to be a mistake (or fallacy) in an argument, a fallacy called "begging the question" (discussed in

Chapter 8). It is a fallacy because a statement cannot be used to support itself or to prove itself true.

4. There is another kind of case in which the base of the tree diagram has numbers for two text sentences joined by an ampersand. This is when there is a double conclusion. A double conclusion occurs when a text contains two conclusions supported by the same set of premises. Though it has two conclusions, it is a single argument because both conclusions are supported by the same set of premises. Here is an example: Sally is the valedictorian, so she has the highest grades and will get to give an address at commencement. This is one argument with two different conclusions drawn from the single premise. Double conclusions do not occur often, but it is important to recognize them when they occur.

5. Other rules of addition, which concern implicit premises, will be discussed in subsequent chapters.

6. This is analogous to the way in which the implicit "you" ("you understood") is included (in parentheses) in the subject position of the diagram of the sentence "Go!"

7. Implicit conclusions cause problems for the reasoning indicator test. If the conclusion is implicit, the sentence expressing the conclusion will not be available to put the "therefore" in front of. This is another reason for not taking the reasoning indicator test as an infallible guide.

8. Policies stipulate, at least indirectly, what actions individuals should take, so you might think that there is not a lot of difference between conclusions recommending actions and those recommending policies. But policies usually involve the coordination of many individual actions, which gives them an important dimension that individual actions do not have.

9. Alexander Hamilton, *The Federalist 22*, in Jacob Cook (ed.), *The Federalist* (Middletown, CT: Wesleyan University Press, 1961), p. 144.

10. Charles Darwin, *On the Origin of Species* (Cambridge, MA: Harvard University Press, 1964), p. 424.

11. This includes implicit premises, which will be discussed in subsequent chapters.

12. Sometimes linked premises come in groups of three or more. When this is the case, the basis of the link is usually that one premise in the group shows how each of the others support the conclusion, and they in turn show how the first one supports the conclusion. But none of these others show how the premises in their group support the conclusion. All the others are linked because of their relationship to the first one.

13. As mentioned in Chapter 3, it is a matter of some controversy whether all value arguments have value premises, but at least most do. Sometimes, the value premise will be an implicit premise.

14. The author of this letter is Dan J. Samuel.

15. Darwin, p. 177.

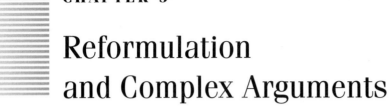

CHAPTER 5

Reformulation and Complex Arguments

The argument in an argumentative text is represented by an argument structure. An argument structure is a combination of a tree diagram and a premise-conclusion (PC) structure. Both tree diagrams and PC structures represent an argument by showing the support relationships among premises and conclusion. We discussed tree diagrams in the previous chapter; in this chapter, we consider PC structures.

Recall that our method of argument structuring involves four steps. The first three steps lead to the tree diagram, and the fourth step leads to the PC structure. Specifically, you create a **PC structure** by writing down a sentence that clearly expresses the conclusion and, above that, on separate lines, sentences that clearly express the premises. By listing the premises above the conclusion, you show that they have a support relationship to the conclusion. But you will have to reword many of the sentences to express the statements more clearly.

When premises are linked rather than convergent, you should note this in the PC structure by placing the linked premises one above the other and bracketing the premise numbers. Here is an example:

Example 5.1

P1: If the cat is away, the mice are at play.
P2: The cat is away.
C: Therefore, the mice are at play.

The key to creating a proper PC structure is the *reformulation* of the text sentences as necessary for the sake of clarity. We begin our consideration of reformulation by looking at some special kinds of sentences that frequently occur in arguments. We look first at general statements and then at conditional statements.

5.1 General Statements

Recognizing whether statements are general or singular and whether they are universal or nonuniversal is crucial to reformulation.

5.1.1 General and Singular Statements

A **general statement** makes a claim about the members of a group (or class) of things rather than about some particular thing. A **singular statement** makes a claim about a particular thing. Consider these examples:

> **Example 5.2**
>
> A. All birds have feathers.
> B. Most birds fly.
> C. Polly has feathers.
> D. The bird in my backyard cannot fly.

Statements A and B are general statements; they make claims not about a particular bird, but about birds in general—that is, the class or group of things that are birds. General statements claim that all or some members of a class have something in common. Statement A is a **universal generalization**—a general statement that makes a claim about *all* the members of a class. In contrast, statement B is a **nonuniversal generalization,** because it makes a claim that applies only to *some* members of the class.

> ### General and Singular Statements
>
> A general statement makes a claim about the members of a class of things (all or some of them) rather than about a particular thing. A universal generalization is a general statement that makes a claim about all the members of a class. A nonuniversal generalization is a general statement that makes a claim about only some members of the class. A singular statement makes a claim about a particular thing, identified by a proper name or definite description.

Statements C and D are singular statements because each makes a claim about a particular thing rather than a class of things. Statement C identifies the particular thing with a **proper name** (Polly)—a special word or phrase adopted by a group of people to refer to something with which they are familiar. Statement D, in contrast, identifies the particular thing with a **definite description**—a noun phrase that acts like a proper name in that it identifies one particular thing. All human beings have proper names, but many other things do as well, including pets, hurricanes, sports teams, and events (for example, Independence Day). Humans give proper names to all sorts of things in which they have an interest.

Proper Names and Definite Descriptions

A proper name is a special phrase adopted by a group of people to refer to something with which they are familiar. A definite description is a phrase that refers to a particular thing. The word(s) in a proper name are special words, usually not part of the general language, while the words in a definite description are all part of the general language.

Definite descriptions can be composed of descriptive terms (for example, "the oldest one") or demonstrative pronouns (for example, "that thing over there") or a combination (for example, "the tallest person on that team"). The important thing is that a definite description uniquely identifies a particular thing. Above all, a definite description must be phrased so that people understand the particular thing to which it refers. Clearly, context is crucial in understanding what particular thing a definite description is meant to refer to.

When identifying an argument in a text, you need to determine whether the relevant text sentences represent general or singular statements and, if general, whether they are universal or nonuniversal. The reason is that the strength of an argument, as well as its significance or importance, depends on the kind of statements of which it is composed. When you evaluate an argument, it is crucial, in fairness to the author, that you correctly interpret the kind of statements that make it up. Otherwise, you might either incorrectly criticize the argument or miss a potential criticism.

5.1.2 Scope and Quantifiers

The **scope** of a general statement is the portion of the class about which the claim is made. Universal generalizations have the widest scope. Nonuniversal generalizations have a narrower scope, but just how narrow the scope is can vary significantly. If a nonuniversal generalization is a claim about most of the members of a class, then it has a fairly wide scope. If it is a claim about a small portion of a class, it has a quite narrow scope.

The word or phrase that indicates the scope of a general statement is a **quantifier.** Quantifiers commonly used in general statements include "all," "every," "no," "almost all," "the vast majority," "most," "the majority," "many," "some," "a

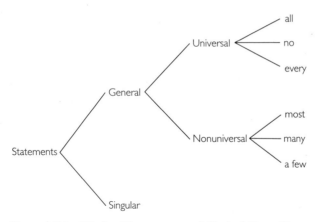

FIGURE 5.1   **Kinds of Statements and Typical Quantifiers**

few," and "at least one." The quantifier "no" is an interesting case. "No birds study critical thinking" is a universal generalization because it is equivalent to "all birds do not study critical thinking."[1] Quantifiers can take special forms as well. For example, there is the set of quantifiers used with respect to time, such as "always," "most of the time," "occasionally," and "sometimes." Most quantifiers, with the exception of those used in universal generalizations ("all," "every," "always," "no") are imprecise in their indication of scope. To say that most birds fly is not to say precisely what proportion of birds fly. "Most," like most quantifiers, is vague in its meaning. Figure 5.1 shows the different kinds of statements and some of the quantifiers they may involve.

Figuring out the scope of a general statement can be difficult because many sentences in argumentative texts are **incomplete sentences,** in that they express general statements but lack quantifiers. When a quantifier is lacking, the scope of a general statement is implicit. Consider these examples:

Example 5.3

A. College students are slobs.
B. All college students are slobs.
C. Most college students are slobs.
D. Many college students are slobs.
E. A small portion of college students are slobs.

Sentence A is an incomplete sentence. It expresses a general statement but lacks a quantifier and it does not explicitly indicate scope. As a result, A could express any of the statements in the remaining sentences. An incomplete sentence leaves it to the audience to determine the scope. Before reading on, see if you can determine which of the remaining sentences is the best interpretation of A. That is, which of them is most likely the one the author of sentence A meant to express?

This is a trick question, because the answer depends on the context in which the claim is made. We are given no context for sentence A, which makes it difficult to get a fix on the author's intent. But we can make some plausible assumptions about context and draw some conclusions about the scope from those assumptions. We may assume, for example, that the author probably does not intend statement B, simply because B is such an implausible claim. Who would believe that literally *all* college students are slobs? In addition, we can probably rule out statement E, but not because it is an implausible claim. Of the remaining statements, E may be closest to the truth. But it is unlikely that an author would use sentence A to express statement E. Even with B and E eliminated, however, statements C and D remain as strong possibilities. Until we see the actual context, we simply cannot decide which is a better interpretation of A.

Scope, Quantifiers, and Incomplete Sentences

The scope of a general statement is the portion of the class to which the claim applies. A quantifier is the word or phrase that indicates the scope of a general statement. An incomplete sentence is a sentence that expresses a general statement but lacks a quantifier, so that the scope is implicit.

Notice that in an incomplete sentence the *content* of the statement is important in interpreting its scope. For example, for the statement "Fish swim," the most likely interpretation would be "All fish swim," simply because this is such a plausible claim. But when a characteristic that not all humans share (like being a slob) is applied in an incomplete sentence to some large group (like college students), it is implausible that all members of the group have that characteristic and unlikely that the author intends to claim that they do. This is especially so when the characteristic has strongly positive or negative connotations.[2]

Incomplete sentences are quite common in argumentative texts and represent an important issue in interpretation. Here is an example:

Example 5.4

Background: This letter is in response to a column about the concern shown by Europeans over genetically modified foods. (*New York Times,* 6/99)

(1) Genetically modified crops in the United States have been documented as producing herbicide-resistant "superweeds" in related plants, causing the death of monarch butterflies feeding on milkweed contaminated with pollen from genetically engineered corn, and causing the contamination of organic corn, also by genetically altered pollen. (2) Moreover, scientists believe that genetically altered crops will result in the increased spraying of herbicides on "herbicide-ready" crops at a time when we are seeing headlines about the dangers of chemical-spray residues to children eating food from sprayed crops. (3) In light of these developments, one can only praise the Europeans' caution.—L.R.Q.

Sentence 1 expresses a premise of the argument in this text, but it is a general statement that lacks a quantifier. Thus, the scope is implicit. How should we interpret the sentence? In this case, the interpretation is fairly easy. The claim that *all* genetically modified (GM) crops have been documented as having the characteristics claimed in sentence 1 is highly implausible. The sentence claims only that some GM crops have been so documented. Sentence 2, also a premise, is likewise incomplete. Here, there are two questions of scope: What portion of scientists believe what the sentence claims? In the belief of the scientists, what portion of GM crops would have the effects indicated? The sentence leaves the answer to both of these questions implicit. But, here again, the author surely does not intend either generalization in this statement to be understood as universal. It would not be plausible to claim that *all* scientists believe that *all* GM crops would have those effects.

Here, then, is how these sentences may be interpreted:

Example 5.5

> *Some* genetically modified crops . . . Moreover, *many* scientists believe that *some* genetically altered crops will . . .

Clearly, the generalizations in the argumentative text are meant to be nonuniversal. The author does not include the quantifiers because the scope of the statements, at least roughly, is obvious. The author can leave the scope implicit with the expectation that the audience will not misunderstand.

5.1.3 Strength

General statements are strong or weak, depending on their scope. The wider the scope, the stronger the statement; the narrower the scope, the weaker the statement. Universal generalizations are the strongest general statements, and nonuniversal generalizations with quantifiers like "a few" or "hardly any" are the weakest. **Statement strength** refers to the strength or weakness of a general statement—and hence to its scope.

Imagine this conversation between two students:

Example 5.6

STUDENT A: In the class debate next week in environmental ethics, I plan to argue that some endangered species should be legally protected.
STUDENT B: Why defend such a weak position? Why not take a stronger stand? Why not say that *all* endangered species should be legally protected?

By saying that only *some* endangered species should be legally protected, student A is taking a weak position. If she instead planned to argue that *all* endangered species should be legally protected, as student B recommends, her position would be stronger.

Why are universal generalizations regarded as strong and nonuniversal generalizations as weak? Among nonuniversal generalizations, why is the statement, for example, that *most* birds build nests regarded as stronger than the statement of narrower scope that *many* birds build nests? The reason seems to be that, the wider the scope of a general statement, the easier it is to disprove. The claim that all birds build nests is easier to disprove than the claim that most birds build nests, because to disprove that all birds build nests, all you need to do is to find *one* species of bird that does not build nests.[3] Likewise, the claim that *most* birds build nests is easier to disprove than the claim that *many* birds do. You need to find more species of birds that do not build nests to show that it is false that *many* birds build nests than to show that it is false that *most* birds build nests. We can say that, the wider the scope, the stronger the statement, because if you make a claim that is easier to disprove, you have taken a stronger stand. The stronger a statement, the harder it is to prove; the weaker a statement, the easier it is to prove.

Statement Strength

All general statements have some degree of statement strength, depending on their scope. The wider the scope, the stronger the statement, so universal generalizations have the greatest statement strength. The narrower the scope, the weaker the statement, so nonuniversal generalizations have less statement strength than universal generalizations. Nonuniversal generalizations vary among themselves in statement strength depending on whether their scope is wider or narrower.

But there is another kind of strength: the strength of an assertion. An **assertion** is simply the making of a statement or claim by a particular person at a particular time. A statement can be asserted many times (in fact, an infinite number of times). When people assert statements, they do so with greater or lesser strength. Sentences in argumentative texts often contain words such as "certainly," "absolutely," "likely," "probably," "possibly," and "perhaps." Such words, usually adverbs, are normally *not* about what is being claimed, but about the author's degree of confidence in the truth of what he or she is claiming. These words characterize not the statement the author is expressing, but the author's assertion of that statement. These words are **modal phrases** because they indicate the mode or way in which a statement is asserted. An author may assert a statement as "certain," "possible," "likely," and so on.

The kind of strength represented by modal phrases may be referred to as **modal strength.** The higher the level of confidence with which someone asserts a statement, the higher its modal strength. Modal strength is greatest when sentences have modal phrases such as "certainly" or "absolutely," and it is least when sentences have modal phrases such as "possibly" or "perhaps."

Consider this text:

Example 5.7

Background: This letter is about hyperactivity in children. (*New York Times*, 12/99)

> ① In the search for causes and treatment of hyperactivity, has any consideration been given to the possibility that hyperactive children may be just plain worn out? ② Many children today are allowed to stay up until they fall asleep. ③ When my children were small, they became wired when they were sleep-deprived. ④ Perhaps the answer to hyperactivity is as simple as "It's time for bed."—S.C.

The conclusion of this argument, expressed in sentence 4, contains the modal phrase "perhaps," which indicates a low level of modal strength. Because this statement is the conclusion of the argument, the low level of modal strength indicates that the author views the support relationship between premises and conclusion as fairly weak.

Assertions, Modal Phrases, and Modal Strength

An assertion is the making of a statement by a particular person at a particular time. Assertions have degrees of strength independent of the strength of the statement that is asserted. The strength of an assertion, referred to as modal strength, is indicated by a modal phrase, which an author uses to indicate the degree of confidence she or he has in the assertion. The modal strength of an assertion is this degree of confidence.

When interpreting an argumentative text, you need to consider both statement strength and modal strength. Like statement strength, modal strength is sometimes implicit. Sentences can be incomplete regarding modal strength, just as they can be incomplete regarding statement strength.[4] Authors sometimes leave out modal phrases, just as they sometimes leave out quantifiers. But there is one important difference between the way authors represent the two kinds of strength. If there is no modal phrase indicating modal strength, the best interpretation is almost always that the sentence has the highest level of modal strength. In other words, an implicit modal phrase is almost always "certainly." Statement strength does not work this way. You cannot assume that a sentence with an implicit quantifier expresses a universal generalization; it is as likely to express a nonuniversal generalization. In other words, an implicit quantifier is as likely to be "some" or "many" as it is to be "all."

Statement strength and modal strength are independent of each other. A sentence may indicate strength in one area and weakness in the other. Consider these examples:

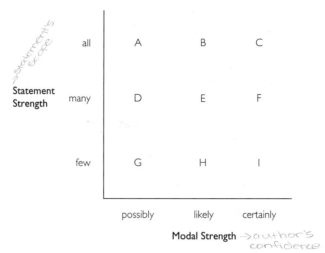

FIGURE 5.2   Strength Space Coordinate System

Example 5.8

A. Certainly, all college graduates will prosper.
B. Possibly, all college graduates will prosper.
C. Certainly, some college graduates will prosper.
D. Possibly, some college graduates will prosper.

In sentence A, the levels of both statement strength and modal strength are high, and in sentence D, they are both low. In sentences B and C, the level is high in one case and low in the other.

Because the two forms of strength are independent of each other, it is helpful to think of them as represented on a coordinate system (like the x- and y-axes in mathematics). We can refer to such a coordinate system as **strength space.** Every sentence expressing a general statement will have a position in strength space, which can be helpful in figuring out how to interpret and reformulate it.

Figure 5.2 shows a diagram of strength space, with statement strength on the vertical axis and modal strength on the horizontal axis. The terms "all" and "certainly" represent the highest level of strength in the two dimensions. The terms "few" and "possibly" represent the lowest level of strength. The terms "many" and "likely" represent rough midpoints between the highest and lowest levels. The letters plotted in the graph represent the positions in strength space that the following examples occupy.

Example 5.9

A. Possibly, all bankers are rich.
B. Likely, all bankers are rich.
C. Certainly, all bankers are rich.
D. Possibly, many bankers are rich.

E. Likely, many bankers are rich.
F. Certainly, many bankers are rich.
G. Possibly, few bankers are rich.
H. Likely, few bankers are rich.
I. Certainly, few bankers are rich.

> **Strength Space**
>
> Strength space is the diagrammatic representation of the statement strength and modal strength of a statement and its assertion by some author on some occasion. The y-axis indicates statement strength and the x-axis indicates modal strength.

For convenience, we can refer to the point in strength space where both levels of strength are highest as the top corner. Thus, in Example 5.9, sentence C is at the top corner. Correspondingly, the point at which both levels of strength are lowest is the bottom corner—sentence G in the example.

The trick of reformulation is to represent the argument in sentences that capture the place in strength space intended by the author. This is important because, if you misrepresent what the author intended in terms of either kind of strength, you may not be able to evaluate the argument fairly.

EXERCISE SET 5.1

SECTION A: Find the following kinds of sentences in other chapters of this book. For each, write down the sentence and its page number.

(1) Five sentences with quantifiers expressing general statements. Include a variety of quantifiers.
(2) Five sentences expressing singular statements, some with proper names and some with definite descriptions.
(3) Five incomplete sentences expressing general statements but lacking quantifiers. In each case, also write down an interpretation of the sentence, supplying the implicit quantifier.
(4) Five sentences with modal phrases indicating modal strength.

SECTION B: The following incomplete sentences express general statements. Express the statement in a sentence that supplies the missing quantifier. Because these sentences are out of context, you should base your judgment about the missing quantifier on which quantifier makes the statement most plausible. Give a brief reason for your choice of quantifier.

EXAMPLE
Sunsets are beautiful.

ANSWER

Many sunsets are beautiful. ("Many" because some sunsets are drab and because sometimes there is cloud cover at sundown.)

All, some,
most, none

PROBLEMS

1. Children are rewarding for parents. *most*
2. Human beings have lungs. *All*
3. European colonial officials at the height of imperialism were cruel toward the native populations of their colonies.
4. Men are potential rapists. *some*
5. Material objects are composed of fewer than 150 elements.
6. Human actions are selfish.
7. People on welfare are lazy.
8. Human beings came out of Africa.
9. Genetic engineering experiments are harmful.
10. Old dogs cannot learn new tricks.
11. Wood floats on water.
12. Houses of brick are stronger than houses of straw.
13. Women are paid less than men for the same work.
14. Chapters in this book contain exercises.

SECTION C: Refer to the diagram of strength space in Figure 5.2. Assess the statement strength and the modal strength of each of the following general statements by writing down the letter (A through I) that most closely represents its position in strength space and reformulating the sentence, expressing it in the terms used in the strength space diagram.

EXAMPLE

No one can doubt that every other writer is inferior to Shakespeare.

ANSWER

Position C: *Certainly, all* other writers are inferior to Shakespeare.

PROBLEMS

1. Perhaps not a single planet besides Earth has life.
2. Without a doubt, the majority of music CDs are overpriced.
3. In all likelihood, hardly any labor-saving devices have failed to save us time.
4. Unquestionably, American presidents have uniformly been men.
5. It seems likely that every mass die-off of species in the history of life has been caused by an asteroid hitting Earth.
6. The probability is good that most places on Earth will be warmer 50 years from now.
7. It is possible that some humans have been over 8 feet tall.
8. I can say with complete confidence that hardly any species of whale is absent from the endangered species list.
9. There is some possibility that a large number of Mozart's early works were written with his sister.
10. It is highly probable that the majority of future American presidents will be over 40 years old.
11. Can you doubt that every real man does not eat quiche?

12. One thing we can say for sure is that few presidential elections have been as close as the 2000 contest.

5.2 Conditional Statements

Part of making a proper tree diagram, as we saw in the previous chapter, is splitting up text sentences when they express more than one statement. But not all sentences that seem to express more than one statement actually do so.

5.2.1 Antecedents and Consequents

Consider these sentences:

Example 5.10

A. The cat is away.
B. The cat is away, and the mice are at play.
C. If the cat is away, then the mice are at play.

Sentence A expresses one statement. Sentence B expresses two statements. If B were a text sentence that was part of an argument, it would be broken into two in the argument structure. That is, it would be represented by "2a" and "2b" in separate circles in the tree diagram. Sentence C, like B, contains two statements. But unlike B and like A, it expresses a single statement, one that melds the two component statements into a single statement. The single statement is that *if* one statement (the cat is away) is true *then* another statement (the mice are at play) is true. In other words, C is a statement that expresses a relationship between two statements. It should be represented as a single statement in an argument structure. Because B does not express a relationship between the two statements (except that they are both true), it is best represented in the argument structure by the two statements it expresses.

Sentence C expresses a **conditional statement** (or a conditional for short), such that the truth of the first statement is a condition for the truth of the second. The conditional nature of the statement is represented by the "if . . . then . . ." language form. The first statement in a conditional, the one preceded by "if," is called the **antecedent.** The second, the one preceded by "then," is called the **consequent.**

Sentence C expresses one statement rather than two because the author does not claim that either of the sentence's two clauses is true. In contrast, in sentence B, the author claims that both of the statements are true. This is why B expresses two statements and C does not. The author of C does not say that either statement is true, but rather that *if* one is true *then* the other is as well. The statement expressed by C can be true even if both of the statements it contains are false.

> ### Conditional Statements, Antecedents, and Consequents
>
> Conditional statements (or conditionals) are compound statements that indicate a particular kind of relationship between two statements, an antecedent and a consequent. If one of the statements (the antecedent) is true, then the other (the consequent) is true. A conditional does not claim that either of the two statements of which it is composed is true.

Conditionals occur frequently and play an important role in arguments. Because a conditional says something different from either of its component statements, it is very important in identifying the PC structure to represent the conditional as a single statement, whether premise or conclusion. But conditionals are not always easy to spot. They can appear in argumentative texts in language forms other than "if . . . then . . ." Consider these examples:

Example 5.11

A. If the cat is away, then the mice are at play.
B. The mice are at play, if the cat is away.
C. When the cat is away, the mice are at play.
D. The cat's being away ensures that the mice are at play.
E. The cat is away only if the mice are at play.
F. The cat's being away implies that the mice are at play.

All of these sentences can be understood to express the same conditional. The standard way to express the conditional is sentence A. The other sentences are all variants of A. Notice that none of these statements asserts that either of its two component statements is true. These statements could be true even if it were false that the cat is away or that the mice are at play.

But not all sentences that contain the word "if" express conditional statements. Consider these examples:

Example 5.12

A. If you want to watch your favorite program, it is on now.
B. The senator has not decided if she will run for another term.
C. They do not know if they will draft a constitution.

These sentences are not conditional statements because they do not express a conditional relationship between two statements.

Given that a conditional statement can be expressed in a variety of different sentences and that not all sentences containing "if" express conditionals, how do you tell if a text sentence expresses a conditional statement? For a sentence to express a conditional, two conditions must hold. First, the author of the text is not claiming that either of the statements in the sentence is true. Second, the author intends to say that the truth of one of the statements is dependent on the truth of the other. If a text sentence meets these conditions, even if not in the "if . . . then . . ." form, then it should be treated as one statement in the tree diagram and represented in the PC structure using the standard "if . . . then . . ." form.

How to Recognize a Conditional Statement

A text sentence containing two statements is intended to be a conditional statement, and so should be treated as one statement in the argument structure, when these two conditions hold:

1. The author is not claiming (in that sentence) that either of the statements contained in the sentence is true.

2. The author means to say that the truth of one of the statements is dependent on the truth of the other.

5.2.2 Interpretative Problems

Two other kinds of interpretative problems regarding conditionals arise in argumentative texts. Sometimes there is a conditional statement where there does not appear to be one, and sometimes there is not a conditional statement where there does appear to be one.

Consider these examples:

Example 5.13

A. Background: This letter was written during the 1997 baseball season. (*Chicago Tribune*, 9/97)

① With still another three weeks to go in the baseball season, the Cubs, Phillies and Oakland A's each have already lost more than 80 games. ② Shouldn't this tell the major leagues that it's time to downsize by reducing the number of teams in each league? ③ This, in turn, would get rid of a slew of mediocre players while allowing the more talented ones to compete with their peers and improve the overall quality of the game.—M.H.

B. Background: This letter is a criticism of an organization known as the Family Research Council, which is committed to the preservation of American families and opposed to homosexual marriage. (*New York Times*, 10/98)

① The real enemies of the American family (as the Council defines it) are divorce and its causes, including adultery. ② If half of all the marriages in the United States end in divorce while gay men and lesbians constitute only 2 percent to 3 percent of the total population, why is the Family Research Council spending millions on television and newspaper campaigns to convert homosexuals to heterosexuality rather than pouring money into campaigns to fight divorce and adultery?—W.M.

Text A may at first seem to have no conditionals, but sentence 3 does express a conditional. The antecedent is represented by the pronoun "this," referring to the statement expressed by the rhetorical question in sentence 2. The conditional is this: If the major leagues downsized by reducing the number of teams, then a number of mediocre players would leave the league, allowing the more talented ones to compete with their peers and improve the overall quality of the game.[5] Often, argumentative texts like this one will include the antecedent and consequent in separate sentences and use a pronoun—most commonly, "this"—in one of the sentences to bring them together into a conditional. "So" is sometimes used for this purpose as well, as in the phrase "if so" at the beginning of a sentence.

Sentence 2 in text B seems to express a conditional, but it is actually better interpreted as expressing instead an argument. The sentence does not express a single statement, as it would if it were a conditional, but at least two statements standing in the support relationship. The author presents the statement that follows the "if" as true and as supporting the statement expressed later in the sentence. In a genuine conditional, as we have seen, the author does not mean to claim, in the sentence expressing the conditional, that either the antecedent or the consequent is true, although she or he may claim elsewhere in the text that one or the other is true (or false). But in this case, the author intends in sentence 2 to assert the truth of what follows the "if." In fact, the best interpretation is that sentence 2 expresses *three* statements, the first two being premises (half of all the marriages in the United States end in divorce *and* gay men and lesbians constitute only 2–3 percent of the total population) and the third the conclusion of the argument (a claim about how the Family Research Council should spend its money). In the tree diagram, "2a" and "2b" would be premises (along with "1") and "2c" the conclusion.

How can you tell whether a text sentence beginning with an "if" expresses a conditional or the premise and conclusion of an argument? Consider these sentences:

Example 5.14

A. If the cat is away, then the mice are at play.
B. Because the cat is away, the mice are at play.

An author might use sentences A and B interchangeably in a text, but they say different things. There is an important difference between the "because" and the "if." Sentence A is a conditional which does not claim that either of its component statements is true. In contrast, sentence B is an argument which claims that the statement following the "because" is true and supports the statement expressed later in the sentence. In general, if you find yourself wondering whether some text sentence that begins with "if" is a conditional, like A, or a whole argument, like B, ask yourself whether it makes more sense to substitute "because" for "if." If the "because" version makes more sense, then the sentence expresses not a conditional, but instead an argument. This test reveals that sentence 2 in text B is an argument rather than a conditional.

One reason it is important to represent a conditional in an argument structure as a single statement is that a conditional premise is always a linked premise (see Chapter 2), not a convergent premise. This makes conditionals especially important for understanding an argument's structure. For example, as we discuss in the next chapter, conditionals are helpful in identifying implicit premises.

5.2.3 Necessary and Sufficient Conditions

Once you have identified a conditional as part of an argument, you may need to reformulate it for the PC structure. As we have said, the standard way to express a conditional is in the "if . . . then . . ." form. If the text sentence(s) expressing the conditional does not have this form, reformulation is necessary. But this often raises the question of which clause is the antecedent and which is the consequent. To determine this, you need to understand the distinction between necessary and sufficient conditions and the ways in which these are related to conditionals. A **necessary condition** is one whose presence is needed or required for some fact to hold or for the statement representing that fact to be true. A **sufficient condition** is one whose presence guarantees that some fact holds or that the statement representing that fact is true.

Necessary and Sufficient Conditions

A necessary condition is one whose presence is needed or required for some fact to hold or for the statement representing that fact to be true. A sufficient condition is one whose presence guarantees that some fact holds or that the statement representing that fact is true.

Consider this example: Biologists believe that life can originate only in environments in which there is liquid water. Assuming that this is true, each of the following statements is true.

Example 5.15

A. The presence of liquid water is a necessary condition for the origination of life.
B. The origination of life is a sufficient condition for the presence of liquid water.
C. If life has originated, then liquid water is present.

Statement A says that without liquid water life could not have begun, and statement B says that life's having originated ensures that liquid water is present. But, when we consider A and B together, we see something else interesting. When the truth of one statement is a necessary condition for the truth of another, the truth of the second is a sufficient condition for the truth of the first. That is, water is a necessary condition for life, and life is a sufficient condition for water. Water can be present without life, but life cannot be present without water. Life guarantees water, but water does not guarantee life.

This brings us to statement C, the conditional, in which the order of the clauses is the same as in statement B. This indicates that in a conditional the truth of the antecedent is a sufficient condition for the truth of the consequent. The truth of the antecedent guarantees the truth of the consequent. Thus, life's presence guarantees water's presence, and the cat's being away guarantees that the mice are at play. But that relationship does not hold the other way around. As statement A indicates, when the statements of a conditional are reversed, the relationship shifts from one of sufficient condition to one of necessary condition. Thus, water's presence is necessary for life, and the mice's being at play is necessary for the cat's being away.

Notice something important about necessary and sufficient conditions: They do not necessarily mirror causal or temporal relationships. For example, in the case of statement B, life is a sufficient condition for water even though the water has to be present before the life begins. Or, in the case of statement C, if there is life, then there is water, even though the water comes first. Water is one of the causes of life, but the presence of life is still the antecedent and the presence of water is still the consequent. So you cannot rely on your sense of what causes what or what comes before what to determine which is the antecedent and which is the consequent in a conditional.

Distinguishing Antecedent from Consequent

If a sentence expresses a conditional, one of the clauses expresses the antecedent and the other the consequent. To tell which is which, you have to understand that the antecedent is a sufficient condition for the consequent and that the consequent is a necessary condition for the antecedent. Ask yourself two questions: Which statement's being true guarantees the truth of the other? That statement is the antecedent. Or, which statement is it whose truth is required for the truth of the other? That statement is the consequent.

Sometimes, the correct formulation of a conditional seems contrary to our sense of time and causation. Consider these sentences:

Example 5.16

A. When the signal is given, the race begins.
B. If the signal has been given, then the race has begun.
C. If the race has begun, then the signal has been given.
D. The race has begun only if the signal has been given.

Sentence A clearly expresses a conditional relationship between the two statements. But what is the formulation that expresses this relationship, B or C? To determine this, ask yourself which statement's being true guarantees the truth of the other. The race's having begun guarantees the signal's having been given; the race cannot start in the absence of the signal. This indicates that the race's having begun is the antecedent and that C is the proper formulation of A. To check, ask yourself which statement's being true is required for the truth of the other. The signal's being given is required for the race to begin; the race cannot begin without the signal's being given.

Think of the situation in terms of necessary and sufficient conditions. The race's having begun is a sufficient condition for the signal's having been given, and the signal's having been given is a necessary condition for the race's having begun. But the signal's having been given is *not* a sufficient condition for the race's having begun, *nor* is the race's having begun a necessary condition for the signal's having been given. For example, the signal might have been given without the race's having begun if there was a false start.

This example shows how the order of statements in a conditional may be contrary to our sense of time and causation. The signal comes first and causes the race to begin. Yet the race's beginning is the antecedent and the signal's being given is the consequent. This point may be easier to appreciate at an intuitive level if you consider sentence D. As we saw earlier, D expresses the same statement as C; it is simply an alternative rendering of C. But, to your ears, D may sound more in tune with the fact that the signal is the cause of the race's beginning, and not the other way around.

EXERCISE SET 5.2

SECTION A: For each of the following sentences, indicate whether it is a conditional. If it is, indicate which statement is the antecedent and which is the consequent by putting the conditional into standard "if . . . then . . ." form.

EXAMPLE
Light on the eastern horizon guarantees that the sun is about to rise.

ANSWER
If there is light on the eastern horizon, then the sun is about to rise.

PROBLEMS
1. When there is but a hint of light on the western horizon, the sun has just gone down.
2. People are atheists only if they do not attend religious services.
3. The Yankees are the best team, and they have the best pitching staff.
4. Our studying war ensures that our children can study peace.
5. When Joan is home and the phone rings, she answers it.
6. A dog cannot be trusted around children if it is a pit bull.
7. A black-footed booby is a bird only if it is an animal.
8. An event is contrary to the laws of nature if it is a miracle.

❖   9. Bill Gates is rich, but he is generous.

10. A being can love only if there is something it lacks.

SECTION B: For each of these argumentative texts, number the sentences and identify the sentence(s) that express(es) a conditional. Reformulate each conditional, if need be, into a clear sentence in standard "if . . . then . . ." form. (Many of these are excerpted from longer letters.)

EXAMPLE
Background: This is from a letter about campaign finance reform. (*Los Angeles Times*, 10/97)

① Being dependent on large contributions from wealthy interests, most of our representatives are afraid to defy the wishes of their benefactors. ② When we start electing representation that is less dependent on major contributions for reelection, the interests of the less affluent will be given greater consideration. —L.N.

ANSWER
Sentence 2: If we start electing representatives who are less dependent on major contributions for reelection, then the interests of the less affluent will be given greater consideration.

PROBLEMS

1. Background: This is from a letter about imprisonment. (*San Francisco Chronicle*, 12/97)

   Treating prison inmates humanely is in our own best self-interest. Over 96 percent of the people serving time will one day be released back onto the streets and into our communities. But if they are handled like animals while in custody they will come back at us crazier and more dangerous than when they went in.—R.K.

2. Background: This is from a letter about the "digital divide," the greater access to computers that the wealthy have in comparison with the poor. (*New York Times*, 3/00)

   ① While there is a wealth of information on the Web, most home computer use is limited to trivial pursuits like playing games, forwarding recycled jokes or downloading pornography. ② And everyday tasks like banking or filing tax returns can still be done in the traditional manner. ③ One can't help but wonder whether home computer use is a counterproductive activity that the "have-nots" are better off without. ④ If it is, then the existence of the digital divide might actually serve to bridge the general non-digital divide that plagues our society.—Z.B.

❖   3. Background: This is from a letter about what punishment should be given to Timothy McVeigh, convicted of the 1995 bombing of the Federal Building in Oklahoma City, in which a number of people were killed. (*San Francisco Chronicle*, 6/97)

   A hard man like Timothy McVeigh could take decades to repent. Instead we will cut short his time of reflection, send him to his death as pleased as if he were marching to war. The death penalty is no penalty at all to a fanatic. If we meant to deal justice, we should have forced him to live.—D.J.N.

4. Background: This is from a letter critical of a proposed change in the McCain-Feingold campaign finance reform bill, then before Congress. (*New York Times*, 7/99)

   This proposal undermines the purpose of campaign finance reform. The strength of the McCain-Feingold bill is that it treats all unregulated soft money as potentially corrupting, whether it goes to political parties or private groups. If soft money restrictions were applicable only to political parties, wealthy individuals and organizations would merely channel their donations to private groups, which through "issue ads" subtly endorse candidates.—K.A.

5. Background: This is from a letter about the death penalty. (*New York Times*, 9/88)

   I am opposed to capital punishment, but can find one strong case where it should be carried out: against terrorism and hostage taking. Jailing convicted terrorists only incites co-conspirators to take further hostages to bargain for a jailed terrorist's release. If death is the only penalty for terrorism or hostage taking, further escalation of that problem will stop.—S.W.

6. Background: This is from a letter about baseball. (*Chicago Tribune*, 4/97)

   Can't something be done to speed up baseball? Every other game I know of goes pretty much by the clock. I think the players and management should be reminded that they are being paid by the fans, and if they want to give the fans a "break"—speed the game up.—L.F.

7. Background: This is from a speech at a rally for striking teachers.

   We have had enough of unfair treatment. The school gives signing bonuses for student athletes. No signing bonuses for athletes without signing bonuses for teachers!

8. Background: This is based on the familiar cliché.

   The bigger they are, the harder they fall. There can be no doubt that Johnny's heading for a hard fall.

9. Background: This text by Alexander Hamilton is from *The Federalist*.[6]

   [From] the probability of incompatible alliances between the different States, or confederacies, and different foreign nations, and the effects of this situation upon the peace of the whole, this conclusion is to be drawn, that America, if not connected at all, or only by the feeble tie of a simple league offensive and defensive, would by the operation of such opposite and jarring alliances be gradually entangled in all the pernicious labyrinths of European politics and wars.

10. Background: This text is from Charles Darwin's *On the Origin of Species*.[7]

    A struggle for existence inevitably follows from the high rate at which all organic beings tend to increase. Every being, which during its natural lifetime produces several eggs or seeds, must suffer destruction during some period of its life . . . otherwise on the principle of geometrical increase, its numbers would quickly become so inordinately great that no country could support the product.

11. Background: This is from a letter about the introduction of a new telephone area code in the Boston area, which led to disputes about who should get to keep the old area code, 617. (*Boston Globe*, 8/97)

    Any experienced parent knows the right solution to the controversy over who gets the 617 area code: Nobody should get it. The 617 area code should be scrapped, and replaced with a totally new area code number at the same time the other new area codes are created. In this way no community could be perceived as receiving preferential treatment compared to the others, and there would be no basis for disagreement.—C.R.

12. Background: This is from a letter in response to an editorial critical of the plan to expand the North Atlantic Treaty Organization (NATO) into eastern Europe. NATO is a military alliance established in 1949 to defend against potential aggression by the former Soviet Union. (*New York Times*, 7/97)

    ①Your editorial says, "Expanding NATO now may well complicate, if not undermine, the transformation of Europe.②If so, why is there not more opposition to enlarging the alliance from the European members?③Some want to add two more new members, Slovenia and Romania, yet the Clinton Administration objects.④Maybe the Administration and you are being a bit parochial and looking at this issue from a narrowly American perspective. —K.W.R.

13. Background: This is from a letter about the school shootings that occurred in the late 1990s. (*New York Times*, 5/99)

    Unfortunately, most adults refuse to see the abuse that goes on daily in American high schools, or they try to brush it off as nothing more than adolescent pranks. The rage that we have seen and that is continuing to surface will continue as long as young adults are victimized, marginalized and made to feel worthless by their peers. When people feel worthless, everything around them seems worthless as well, often leading to disastrous consequences.—M.E.

14. Background: This is from a letter about the Vietnam War and the president's failure to avoid it despite his belief that it did not serve national interests. (*New York Times*, 4/00)

    ①It is indeed sad that President Lyndon B. Johnson did not follow his "simple impulse" and resist military expansion in Vietnam.②As you say, his failure to do so cost the nation dearly.③If there was no national interest to be served by military expansion in Vietnam, why did he order it anyway?④Johnson said his failure to act would be political suicide.—P.A.M.

15. Background: This is from a letter about the financial problems of our national parks. (*Washington Post*, 8/97)

American taxpayers of all income levels are being asked to subsidize the vacations of prosperous foreign tourists. The Park Service could easily solve a lot of its problems if it started charging foreigners a couple of dollars more than it charges American taxpayers. If the parks are really the property of the American people then this is only fair. It would raise revenue for park upkeep while keeping the parks affordable for all Americans and not requiring a shift of tax revenue.—M.P.

5.3 The Idea of Reformulation

Once you have a tree diagram, the most difficult part of structuring an argument is figuring out when and how to reformulate the text sentences. **Reformulation** involves rephrasing the sentences in an argumentative text to express the premises and conclusion of the argument as clearly as possible.

Reformulation is not necessary in all cases. Sometimes, the text sentences themselves express the statements clearly enough that you can transcribe them directly into the PC structure. Indeed, you should always use the language of the text when it is appropriate to do so. But, more often than not, you will want to reformulate the sentences. Sometimes, the phrasing of the new sentence will be quite close to that of the original, and other times it will be quite different. But the reformulation should always express the same statement as the text sentence it replaces.

Reformulation is paraphrasing, not for the sake of paraphrasing, but for the sake of clarity. This is exactly what you do in ordinary conversation. For example, if someone asked you to recount a conversation you had with a third person, in most cases you would not use the exact words of the conversation, even if you could remember them. Instead, you would paraphrase to communicate the *meaning* of what was said.

> **Reformulation**
>
> To express the statements of an argument clearly, it is often necessary to use different wording in the PC structure than that used in the argumentative text. Reformulation is the process of rephrasing sentences for the PC structure. The new sentences are paraphrases of the text sentences that express the statements of the argument more clearly.

5.3.1 Reasons for Reformulation

To create a PC structure, you need to understand *when* reformulation is necessary and *how* it should be done. To do this, you need to appreciate the reasons that reformulation is necessary. Understanding the reasons for reformulation will lead to an understanding of how text sentences should be reformulated. Reasons for reformulation include the following:

1. To change an interrogative or an imperative sentence to an indicative sentence
2. To capture the contribution of internal context to meaning (for example, pronoun reference)
3. To capture the contribution of external context to meaning
4. To express in separate sentences the multiple statements that may be contained in a single text sentence
5. To capture in one sentence a statement that is expressed in more than one text sentence
6. To omit the parts of text sentences that are not parts of the argument statements
7. To account for irony and other forms of meaning by indirection
8. To express general and conditional statements correctly — *if/then in PC structure*
9. To economize on language
10. To make the meaning as clear and straightforward as possible

These reasons are not exclusive, and in many cases, more than one of them will apply. But we will discuss them separately.

We have considered the first reason before. All sentences of a PC structure should be in the indicative, the grammatical form in which statements are normally expressed. An argument is composed exclusively of statements because the parts of the argument—premises and conclusion—must be true or false. Questions ("Is it raining?") and commands ("Open the door") are neither true nor false. So, when interrogative sentences (usually rhetorical questions) and imperative sentences (including action recommendations) express parts of arguments in texts, you need to reformulate them into the indicative in the PC structure.[8]

The second reason for reformulation is the need to reflect the contribution of **internal context** to meaning. Recall from Chapter 2 that context is the set of surrounding circumstances that help to indicate how we should interpret a text. The meaning of a sentence in a text is often dependent on other sentences in the text, which form the internal context. Internal context often requires reformulation because a sentence used in the PC structure appears outside the text, apart from the other sentences that may help to give it meaning. The part of the meaning of the text sentence dependent on other parts of the text must be incorporated into the wording of the sentence used in the PC structure to express the full meaning of the text sentence.

The simplest kind of case of reformulation due to internal context is when pronouns or pronoun phrases occur in text sentences. Sentences in the PC structure should contain no pronouns or pronoun phrases other than those whose referents are in other sentences of the structure. Suppose the following text sentence expresses the conclusion of an argument: "They should not have to undergo this kind of treatment." Obviously, we cannot know the meaning of this sentence without knowing to what the pronoun "they" and the pronoun phrase "this kind of treatment" refer. Normally, the rest of the text would make this clear. For example, suppose that the rest of the text indicates that "they" refers to federal prisoners and "this kind of treatment" to solitary confinement. So, for the PC structure, the sentence should be reformulated as follows: "Prisoners in U.S. federal prisons should not have to undergo solitary confinement."

The third reason for reformulation reflects the fact that meaning depends on external as well as internal context. **External context** is that part of the context that extends beyond the text itself, such as facts about the beliefs of the author and audience, the time at which the text is created, and information about the history and culture of the author and audience. An argumentative text, for example, might contain the sentence "The abortion decision should be overturned" without mentioning what the decision is. An understanding of the argument in that text might require the awareness that the decision referred to is the Supreme Court's 1973 landmark ruling in *Roe v. Wade*. If so, the reformulated sentence would read, "The Supreme Court's 1973 decision in *Roe v. Wade* should be overturned."

External context can contribute to the meaning of text sentences in many ways. In making meaning clearer, it is important to take account of some of these and to reformulate the sentences for the PC structure accordingly. At the same time, it is impractical, if not impossible, to take account of all aspects of external context. External context should play a role in reformulation only to the extent that it helps you avoid the most likely sorts of misunderstanding. The better your general background knowledge of the culture in all its dimensions—social, political, historical, ethical, aesthetic, ideological, scientific, philosophical—the better you will understand the contribution of external context to the meaning of texts written by members of the culture. Many of the examples and exercises of this book are preceded by a brief explanatory passage to fill in some of the external context.

Internal and External Context

Context that helps to determine the meaning of text sentences can be internal or external to the text. An example of internal context is the presence of a pronoun in a text sentence, the referent for which occurs elsewhere in the text. The audience can understand the meaning of the sentence only by considering that referent. An example of external context is the cultural understanding among the audience that the text phrase "the Sultan of Swat" refers to baseball immortal Babe Ruth. The meaning of the sentence in which that phrase occurs depends on an understanding of that cultural reference.

The fourth and fifth reasons for reformulation arise from the fact that premises and conclusions may be expressed either in only part of a text sentence or in more than one text sentence. (We discussed this in Chapter 4 in the case of tree diagrams, where the numbers in circles sometimes represent parts of text sentences, such as "2a," or multiple sentences, such as "3 or 4a" or "1 & 6." The need for reformulation in such cases is clear. If a premise or conclusion is expressed either in part of or in more than one text sentence, the sentence expressing that statement in the PC structure must be different from the text sentences from which it is derived.

When two or more sentences (or clauses) in a text make the same point or contribute to a single point, the sentence in the PC structure should be a reformulation that represents both (or all) of them. Sometimes, these sentences or clauses will be virtually identical in meaning, in which case a reformulation of one would be a reformulation of the other. Other times, each of them contributes something different to the argument statement, and the reformulation should reflect this.

The sixth reason for reformulation involves cases in which a text sentence expresses only one argument statement, but the sentence includes words or phrases that are not relevant to the argument. Reformulation is necessary to eliminate those features from the sentence included in the PC structure. For example, as discussed in Chapter 3, many text sentences begin with phrases such as "I think that," "I believe that," or "I propose that." In most cases, authors use such sentences not to make a point about their mental states (that they have certain thoughts, beliefs, and so on), but to make the point contained in the part of the sentence that follows the phrase. Consider this example:

Example 5.17

A. I think that welfare policy should be reformed.

B. The author thinks that welfare policy should be reformed.

C. Welfare policy should be reformed.

Sentence A says the same thing as sentence B, but in most cases, if A appeared in an argumentative text, then the premise or conclusion the author intended would be expressed by sentence C rather than B. C is the "that-clause" of A, the part of the sentence following the "that." Thus the phrase "I think" is in most cases simply a rhetorical device, perhaps interesting as autobiography, but not meant by the author to be part of the argument.

Consider an example in which creating the PC structure requires reformulation involving several of the reasons just considered.

Example 5.18

Background: This letter is in response to a column that referred to the late Diana, princess of Wales, the former wife of Charles, heir to the British throne, as an "airhead." (*Boston Globe*, 9/97)

① As an English teacher I spend considerable time trying to teach to students the importance of precision with words. ② That is why I was so disappointed with your columnist's particularly inept use of words when he labeled the Princess of Wales an "airhead." ③ Did she earn that label in his estimation because she asked simple questions instead of wallowing in ponderous statements? ④ Is it because she dared to ask why as she walked through mine fields in Angola and Bosnia? ⑤ Because she questioned the price paid by thousands of children in the loss of legs, arms, and eyes as dues for the waging of territorial wars? ⑥ Because she shunned political euphemisms and let her actions speak louder than her words? ⑦ Perhaps he labeled her that because he was sadly at a loss for words to explain the profound depths of her simply moving effect on many—especially the voiceless and those with few champions.—N.O.

Structure

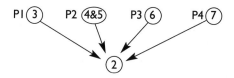

PI: Diana asked simple questions instead of wallowing in ponderous statements.

P2: She asked why thousands of children had to be injured by mines laid in territorial wars in Angola and Bosnia.

P3: She shunned political euphemisms and let her actions speak louder than words.

P4: She had a profound effect on many, especially the voiceless and those with few champions.

C: Therefore, it is wrong to call Diana an "airhead."

This PC structure illustrates reformulations that involve most of the reasons we have considered so far. First, the text sentences that express premises are all rhetorical questions, so we had to convert them into indicative sentences. Second, attention to internal context led us to substitute "Diana" for "she" in P1; the personal pronoun is used in the remaining premises because the referent is in P1. Third, external context is involved in interpreting sentences 4 and 5 as expressing a single premise. The external context in this case is the knowledge that the injuries to children discussed in sentence 5 occurred in the places referred to in sentence 4. The fifth reason comes into play because sentences 4 and 5 are interpreted as expressing a single premise (P2). Finally, the extensive changes in the phrasing of all the premise sentences require leaving out many features of the text sentences. Specifically, we omitted the terms "because" and everything that preceded them in the text sentences. This material is part of the rhetorical pattern, not the content.

The seventh reason for reformulation is the frequent use of **indirection** in language. That is, people often make some point indirectly rather than directly. One example of indirection we have already seen is the use of rhetorical questions. Through a rhetorical question, an author asserts something in a language form that, taken literally, asserts nothing. There are many other kinds of indirection and different reasons for speaking through indirection. Indirection may be due, for example, to politeness, a desire not to offend, modesty, humility, or a tendency toward understatement.

The role of indirection can be seen in the development of slang. Much slang involves taking a term already in the language and giving it the opposite meaning. For example, the terms "cool" and "wicked" have developed slang meanings that are directly opposite to their original meaning. Of course, once a slang term becomes well enough established in the language, its original meaning may be largely displaced by the slang meaning, so that using the term is no more a matter of indirection. The important point is to recognize that people often speak through indirection, and when they do, they expect to be understood. The sentences expressing premises and conclusion in PC structures, however, should express meaning directly rather than indirectly. So, indirection in a text requires reformulation.

The most interesting form of indirection, evident in indirection by slang, is **irony.** To speak ironically is to say something that is literally the opposite of what you mean to say and to expect your meaning to be understood nonetheless. It is to speak "tongue in cheek." Irony can be a strong and rhetorically interesting way to make a claim. Humans are deeply ironic creatures, frequently expressing themselves through irony.

Indirection and Irony

Authors often express themselves through indirection, by using a sentence whose literal meaning is different from what they intend to mean. The most interesting form of indirection is irony, where the literal meaning of what is said is the opposite of the intended meaning.

We are so attuned to indirection and irony in language use that authors are readily able to communicate their real meaning using these devices. Consider this example:

Example 5.19

Background: This letter is in response to a column that recommended reducing speed limits to cut down on auto accident fatalities. (*Washington Post,* 8/98)

> ① Your columnist is incorrect when he says that speed is the most significant factor in fatal automobile accidents. ② The most important factor is the very existence of automobiles. ③ It is absolutely undeniable that if cars did not exist there would be no fatal automobile accidents. ④ Anyone who is not for the abolition of automobiles is therefore pro-death. ⑤ The answer to highway carnage is abolition of the automobile. ⑥ We must do it for the children. ⑦ If we can just save one life it will be worth it.—S.K.

Sentence 5, taken literally, advocates the abolition of the automobile. But this is ironical. On the contrary, the author is clearly against restrictions on automobile use in the name of safety. Here, the ironical meaning is communicated by the absurdity of the proposal to abolish the automobile. The author relies on people recognizing this absurdity to understand that his meaning is ironical. More broadly, the author uses the irony to criticize the idea apparently suggested by the columnist that speed limits should be reduced or kept low to reduce the number of fatal accidents.[9]

The eighth reason for reformulation is to make sure that you identify general statements and conditionals and that you express them correctly in the PC structure. For example, as discussed previously, it is important to properly locate a general statement in strength space and to identify correctly the antecedent and the consequent of a conditional. One problem that arises here is that authors sometimes use, as a form of indirection, a sentence that, understood literally, expresses a singular statement in order to express instead a general statement. We will see an example of this shortly, and this kind of case will be discussed further in Chapter 8.

The ninth and tenth reasons for reformulation are more general than the others. As the ninth reason indicates, reformulation is often done simply to economize on language. Economy of language can be an aid to clarity. While sentences in the PC structure often need to be longer than the corresponding text sentences, they sometimes can be shorter. Text sentences often contain elaborate, flowery language that makes them less clear than they would be if they were shorter. In this case, you need to replace the longer version with the shorter one, which expresses the statement more clearly.

The nine reasons we have discussed so far all involve producing sentences for the PC structure that express argument statements more clearly than the text sentences. So, the tenth reason, which recommends reformulation for the sake of clarity, is, on the one hand, simply a summary of the previous reasons, and, on the other, a reminder that reasons for reformulation are not limited to those already discussed. Any reformulation of a text sentence that results in clearer expression of an argument statement should be adopted.

5.3.2 Value Statements and Implicit Conclusions

We should briefly consider two special cases of reformulation. The first is value statements. Many value statements, as we have seen, are expressed by text sentences in the imperative form and so need to be reformulated with a sentence in the indicative. What indicative sentence forms are best used to express value statements in PC structures? Consider these sentences:

Example 5.20

A. Congress should pass the free trade agreement.
B. We should be kind toward our neighbors.
C. Punishing the innocent is wrong.

Sentences A and B express the sort of value statement we earlier called action recommendations (see Chapter 3). Reformulations of action recommendations should indicate in the subject position the person or group for whom the action is recommended. If the action is recommended for everyone, as in B, the subject "we" or "everyone" is appropriate. The other sort of value statement, represented by sentence C, is the sort that supports action recommendations. These can be worded in many different ways. They usually are general statements attributing to a class of actions, events, people, or things a value characteristic such as good, bad, right, wrong, moral, immoral, preferable, or desirable.

A final aspect of reformulation is actually a matter of *formulation*—the formulation of an implicit conclusion. Of course, you cannot reformulate an implicit conclusion, given that it is absent from the text. Instead, you must identify the conclusion that the author intended the audience to draw and give a clear formulation of it. To illustrate, we will consider one of the public service advertisements reproduced in Figure 4.4.

The photograph shows a young, poor child in an unhealthy environment. The caption reads, "God made me and God doesn't make junk." If we took this literally, the implicit conclusion would be "I am not junk." But this is not an adequate formulation. First, the term "junk" is metaphorical. In formulating the conclusion, we should be more literal. By "junk," the author seems to mean something like being an inferior human. Second, the argument is clearly not meant to apply to this child only, but to all those in similar circumstances, that is, all those who are poor or who are poor and black. This is related to a third point. The premise "God made me" expresses a singular statement, but it is one of those cases in which, by indirection, a sentence appearing to express a singular statement is in fact meant to express a universal generalization.

Here are two plausible PC structures for this argument. The difference between them depends on whether the group to which the child belongs, for the sake of formulating the general statement that "God made me" is meant to express, is the group of those in poverty or the group of those who are black and in poverty. (Recall that "IC" indicates that the conclusion is implicit.)

Example 5.21

A.   P1: God made those living in poverty.
     P2: No one that God makes is an inferior human.
     IC: Therefore, those living in poverty are not inferior humans.

B.   P1: God made those who are black and living in poverty.
     P2: No one that God makes is an inferior human.
     IC: Therefore, those black and living in poverty are not inferior humans.

5.3.3 Fairness and the Straw Man

It is, of course, important that you represent the argument of a text as accurately as possible. When you misrepresent an argument, the misinterpretation is known as a **straw man**—a pretender, a creature of straw. Straw men are sometimes deliberate and sometimes not.

Some Rules for Creating PC Structures

1. Reformulate only when necessary. Keep the original text wording as much as possible.

2. Include only pronouns that already have referents in the sentences of the PC structure.

3. Express each premise and conclusion in the PC structure with a single sentence in the indicative mood.

4. Do not include reasoning indicators.[10] (We will have more to say about this in the discussion of complex arguments later in the chapter.)

5. Do not include in reformulations features that are not themselves parts of the argument statements (such as "I think").

6. Be attentive to meaning by indirection, such as irony.

7. Bracket linked premises.

A straw man leads to several problems. The misinterpretation may make it seem as if the argument is subject to criticism that it is in fact not subject to. This is a straw man that presents an interpretation that is *stronger* than the argument it claims to represent, which can make it seem to be an easier critical target than it is. But it is also important not to present a straw man that errs on the other side. This kind of straw man presents an interpretation that is weaker than the argument it claims to represent, which can make it seem less open to criticism than it is. The problem with a straw man that presents too weak an interpretation is that, the stronger an argument is, the more significant and interesting it is. So, to interpret an argument as weaker than it is presents it as less significant and interesting than it is.

Straw Men

A straw man is a misinterpretation of an argument.[11] A straw man may misinterpret an argument as stronger than it is, making it seem more open to criticism, or as weaker than it is, making it appear less significant or interesting than it is. A straw man may be deliberate, created to provide an easier critical target or to downplay the importance or significance of an argument.

To avoid straw men, you should check the PC structure against the text to make sure you have not misrepresented the argument. The PC structure should present an argument that reflects the author's intentions, as accurately as you can identify them. The frequent need for reformulation makes it easy to misinterpret an argument. Moreover, argumentative texts are often so unclearly written that there is room for reasonable disagreement about what the author intended the argument to be. In the end, structuring an argument is more a rough art than an exact science. For this reason, it may be better to speak of the goal as producing a *fair* interpretation than a *correct* interpretation.

> ### Rule of Fairness[12]
>
> In structuring an argument from an argumentative text, you should strive to give a fair interpretation of the argument and to avoid straw men. After structuring the argument, you should return to the text to compare it again with the tree diagram and the PC structure, including the reformulations you have given, to ensure that they are faithful to the argument the author intended.

To illustrate the problems involved in giving a fair interpretation, consider what is required in checking the accuracy of your reformulations of general statements. First, you need to make sure that the reformulations have the proper quantifiers and modal phrases—that is, that they are from the correct position in strength space. But this is difficult because quantifiers are often implicit. Even if the reformulations are from the correct position in strength space, they can still misrepresent the text sentences by misidentifying the class the sentences refer to or the property they attribute to the class.

This discussion of straw men and the rule of fairness calls our attention again to the fact that there is frequently room for disagreement about what is the best interpretation or structure. Often, there are **alternative reasonable interpretations** or structures for a text argument, ones that could reasonably be seen as correct. When people disagree over how to interpret an argument, each seeks to present an argument in favor of his or her interpretation. A reasonable interpretation is an interpretation with a strong argument behind it.

Reasonable people can disagree over which alternative reasonable interpretation is the best one. How is such a disagreement to be resolved? The best interpretation is the one that has the strongest argument in its favor. Many of the arguments we consider in this text have alternative reasonable interpretations.

In addition to alternative reasonable interpretations, there may be many unreasonable interpretations—interpretations or structures that are clearly mistaken. In fact, there are usually more ways to be wrong than right in interpreting an argument. An unreasonable interpretation is an interpretation that has no strong argument in its favor. A straw man is an unreasonable interpretation presented as the correct one.

The discussion of argument structuring in this chapter and the previous one has been presented in terms of a set of steps and rules. But, like any set of rules for a complicated activity, they can only serve as a rough guide. They cannot be mechanically applied to guarantee the correct result. Your ability to identify an

> ## Alternative Reasonable Interpretations
>
> Frequently, an argument in an argumentative text will have alternative reasonable interpretations or structures. This means that, even after you apply the rule of fairness, there will often be different interpretations or structurings that you can reasonably view as correct. In such cases, the best interpretation is one that has the strongest argument in its favor. An interpretation without a strong argument in its favor is an unreasonable interpretation or a straw man.

argument from a text will come not from knowing in the abstract these rules or any set of rules, but from getting lots of practice in applying them.

 ## EXERCISE SET 5.3

SECTION A: Return to Section B of Exercise Set 4.3. Complete the structuring of the arguments in these texts by formulating a PC structure for each.

EXAMPLE

① I love ocean beaches. ② They are a great vacation site. ③ They provide plenty of ways to relax. ④ In addition, they provide plenty of ways to have fun. ⑤ My favorite beaches are on Long Beach Island, NJ. ⑥ But the accommodations there are getting more and more expensive, and are definitely upscale.

ANSWER
P1: Ocean beaches provide plenty of ways to relax.
P2: Ocean beaches provide plenty of ways to have fun.
C: Therefore, ocean beaches are great vacation sites.

SECTION B: Return to Section C of Exercise Set 4.2. Complete the structuring of the arguments in these texts by providing a PC structure for each.

EXAMPLE

① The product of cloning, or any other reproductive technology, should be regarded as fully human. ② Cloning a person to create an organ donor or a lost child is morally offensive because it negates the intrinsic value of the human being produced in favor of some other, previously born human.

ANSWER
P1: The product of cloning should be regarded as fully human.
P2: Cloning a person to create an organ donor or to replace a lost child negates the intrinsic value of the human being produced in favor of some other, previously born human.
C: Therefore, cloning a person to create an organ donor or to replace a lost child is morally offensive.

SECTION C: Return to Section D of Exercise Set 4.3. Complete the structuring of the arguments in these texts by providing a PC structure for each.

EXAMPLE

① Would not the most practical, effective and immediate way to help reduce gasoline and diesel prices be to reduce consumption—hence demand—by enforcing speed limits on highways and roads? ② An added bonus: fewer traffic accidents, injuries and death.

ANSWER

P1: The most practical, effective, and immediate way to help reduce gasoline and diesel prices would be to reduce consumption—hence demand—by enforcing speed limits on highways and roads.

P2: Enforcing speed limits on highways and roads would lead to fewer traffic accidents, injuries, and death.

IC: Therefore, we should enforce speed limits on highways and roads.

SECTION D: Structure the arguments in the following texts, applying the four steps. Provide both a tree diagram and a PC structure for each.

EXAMPLE

Background: This letter is in response to an editorial recommending fishing as an activity for children. (*Miami Herald,* 5/97)

① How can anyone believe that any activity that aims to kill creatures is wholesome or ethical? ② You cannot teach children respect for life as you are teaching them how to kill. ③ Humans are not the only creatures who matter.—H.P.

ANSWER

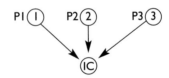

P1: An activity that aims to kill creatures is neither wholesome nor ethical.

P2: You cannot teach children respect for life when you are teaching them how to kill.

P3: Humans are not the only creatures who matter.

IC: Therefore, we should not allow children to fish.

PROBLEMS

1. Background: In the 2000 presidential race, the Republican candidate, George W. Bush, claimed that the Clinton administration should not be given credit for the economic boom of the 1990s because the administration did not do anything to bring it about. In a speech, President Clinton responded to this charge. (Quoted in *New York Times,* 8/15/00)

   To those who say the progress of these eight years was an accident, that we just coasted along, let's be clear. America's success was not a matter of chance; it was a matter of choice.

2. Background: This letter is part of the debate about how the SAT examinations should be considered in college admissions. (*New York Times,* 6/98)

In the absence of a national high school curriculum and uniform grading standards, a standardized test is necessary as a criterion for evaluating students from around the country and around the world.—E.S.

❖   x   3. Background: This is part of the debate over gun control legislation. The National Rifle Association, a group opposing such legislation, uses the slogan "Guns don't kill people, people kill people," meaning that the chief cause of gun deaths is not the guns themselves, but those who use them. (*Cleveland Plain Dealer*, 7/81)

The recently published reports concerning the worst rioting in the history of gun-free England do not include mention of a single death. The conclusion to be drawn should be obvious to everyone but the National Rifle Association: People don't kill people; guns kill people!—F.E.W.

4. Background: This is from Charles Darwin's *On the Origin of Species*.[13]

Grouse . . . are known to suffer largely from birds of prey; and hawks are guided by eyesight to their prey. . . . Hence I can see no reason to doubt that natural selection might be most effective in giving the proper colour to each kind of grouse.

5. Background: This letter is about dangerous bicyclists in cities. (*New York Times*, 7/97)

Licenses on bicycles would do more to help the anarchy on our sidewalks. Ever since curb cuts were installed for wheelchairs, bicycles have been zooming along sidewalks. A friend's shoulder was broken by a hit-and-run cyclist. Without a license to report, there was no recourse. Licenses might also insure a minimum exposure to traffic laws, of which far too many cyclists seem oblivious.—A.K.

❖   6. Background: This letter is about the difficulties in hiring women as firefighters in New York City. (*New York Times*, 2/00)

Women have far less upper-body strength and are less inclined to engage in physically risky activities than men. Although the department has not relaxed standards, it provides physical training for female applicants to improve their test performance. But why? Is a city with more female firefighters somehow better than one with fewer, assuming fair selection? —K.R.B.

7. Background: This letter is in response to a report that a school board in New Jersey had decided to abolish high school class rankings. (*New York Times*, 10/95)

The decision to abolish class rankings is one more symptom of the growing reluctance by schools to recognize excellence and reward achievement, coupled with a movement to sugar-coat failure. We are doing students a disservice by watering down the importance of excellence in learning and diluting the power of recognition of academic achievement as an incentive. —C.J.M.

8. Background: This letter is in response to an editorial expressing concern about the safety of American astronauts working in the Russian space station Mir. (*Chicago Tribune*, 9/97)

Your editorial assumes that working on Mir is more dangerous than riding the space shuttle. There is absolutely no evidence for that assumption. Mir has traveled hundreds of millions of miles farther than any other manned vehicle—without a single life lost. The space shuttle must take off and land, which is clearly more dangerous than simple orbiting. If Mir becomes uninhabitable, astronauts and cosmonauts can climb aboard an escape capsule and deorbit to Earth. The space shuttle has no escape facilities, and if it becomes uninhabitable, it is a virtual certainty that everybody abroad will die.—D.D.D.

9. Background: This letter is about the policies of a health insurance organization. Viagra is a drug that treats male impotence. (*New York Times*, 4/98)

Oxford Health Plan pays for six Viagra tablets a month for its patients. However, it has often refused to cover oral contraceptives for female patients, even when prescribed for the treatment of other medical problems like premature menopause, polycystic ovary disease or as a prophylaxis for women with a family history of ovarian cancer. I find this paradox difficult to justify, considering that impotence is not a life-threatening condition but that unwanted pregnancies, certain uterine cancers and ovarian cancer certainly are.—L.R.G.

10. Background: The Equal Rights Amendment (ERA) was a proposed constitutional amendment in the 1970s to secure equal rights for women. The amendment, ratified by Congress but not by the required number of states, did not become law. The letter is in response to statements by candidates for the 1984 Democratic nomination for president that, if elected, they would put pressure on the states to ratify the amendment. (*New York Times*, 7/83)

The necessity for state ratification in the amendment process is a critical element in a procedure designed to insure that constitutional change reflect the broadest possible consensus, and not merely the will of the Federal Government. It follows, therefore, that the intention of the proposed Democratic Presidential candidates if elected to use political and economic pressure and sanctions against the states to achieve ratification of the ERA is a blatant violation of the intention behind the amendment process.—T.E.D.

11. Background: This letter is in response to a column about politics and youths. (*New York Times*, 12/97)

Your columnist is right on the money in describing how America's youths are becoming more and more historically illiterate. He worries that if young people do not understand why democracy is worth preserving, they may not recognize when it is threatened. I would go further to say that it is exactly this group that constitutes the real threat to democracy by becoming the future generation of politically apathetic citizens who do not exercise the most basic component of democracy—that is, their right to vote!—M.H.

12. Background: This letter is in response to an article reporting a study showing that moderate drinking can lower the risk of heart disease. (*New York Times*, 12/97)

The headline has horrible implications for public health. People are likely to infer that habitual drinking is not only benign, but good for you! What an excuse to encourage incipient alcoholism. Your article reports that virtually the only people who benefit from regular drinking are people at special risk of heart disease (like sedentary, stressed-out, obese smokers). But there are infinitely healthier and even more pleasurable ways than drinking to relax and reduce every known risk factor for cardiovascular disease.—M.Y.

13. Background: This letter is in response to a column claiming that humans should be humble given how vast the universe is and how little we know about it. (*New York Times*, 4/99)

Why humility? We are becoming, as far as we can tell, the only creatures in the universe *aware* of the universe. As far as we can tell, here on our infinitesimal "speck of dust," we embody the only morality, the only esthetics, the only joy since time and space began. Humility? No; exaltation, excitement and pride.—B.W.

14. Background: This letter supports the position that Timothy McVeigh, convicted of the 1995 bombing of the Oklahoma City Federal Building in which 160 people died, should not receive the death penalty. (*Boston Globe*, 6/97)

When we condone the premeditated murder of a fellow human being we become, in a small but significant way, just like him. There is a better way to express our revulsion. We can reject doing to him what he has done to others and let him contemplate that fact for the rest of his life in jail.—T.S.

15. Background: This letter is in response to a letter asking why we should begrudge the students from wealthier school districts the educational advantages they enjoy. (*Los Angeles Times*, 4/98)

Uh, because this creates a mass of second-class citizens mired in poverty and despair? Because Americans believe in fair play and a level playing field? Because we disproved the doctrine of "separate but (un)equal" long ago? Some people still think only the rich deserve to get richer. So much for equal opportunity in America.—R.S.

16. Background: This letter is in response to a discussion of memoirists. (*Washington Post*, 3/99)

In a discussion of the American tradition of cashing in on fleeting fame, your columnist compares Ulysses S. Grant with others who made fortunes with well-timed memoirs. In this he does a disservice to one of this country's greatest soldiers and memoirists. The Civil War, in which Grant gained his enduring fame, was two decades in the past when he wrote his memoirs. At the time, Grant was destitute as a result of his own lack of financial acumen and the perfidy of a dishonest business partner. As he took up the task of writing *The Personal Memoirs of U.S. Grant,* he discovered that he had throat cancer. He completed them in a morphine daze scarcely more than a week before his death, thereby ensuring the economic well-being of his family. The posthumous income earned through this last act of courage represented Grant's only financial success.—M.C.P.

17. Background: This letter is in response to articles poking fun at student writing errors. (*New York Times,* 1/88)

Two articles by college English teachers point out the humor of student errors. Where are the articles about how it feels to be a young man or woman laughed at by one's instructors? Where are the articles about the numbers of students in our colleges who are hindered by undiagnosed disabilities in written language? Where are the articles about the deplorable conditions in which most urban high school English teachers work, conditions that guarantee student ineptitude? Where are the articles about the lamentable education of college English teachers, who are often assigned to teach writing courses without having had even a single semester of instruction in teaching methods?—J.M.P.

18. Background: This letter is about recycling policy in New York City. (*New York Times,* 1/93)

Why does New York City recycle certain items and not others? Why are newspapers, magazines and corrugated board recycled and gray cardboard, brown paper bags and general paper scrap not recycled? Why are plastics labeled 1 and 2 recycled, while other plastics, including those clearly labeled with higher numbers, rejected for recycling? I follow the regulations assiduously but I am offended by the seeming inconsistency and the failure of the city to provide an explanation. I do not see how recycling can gain intelligent or enthusiastic support from the citizen who is required to recycle certain materials and yet forbidden to recycle others of a seemingly identical nature.—S.J.

19. Background: This letter is about toll roads. (*Chicago Tribune,* 1/98)

①Some years ago (I don't want to say how many) I was a student at Valparaiso University and many times traveled, the Wisconsin-Indiana route through Chicago.②The Tri-State Tollway then was in its infancy.②currently have a son at Valparaiso.④My wife's sister lives in Wilmette, and my wife is a former Park Ridge resident.⑤It never ceases to amaze me how the good residents of Illinois (and the Chicago area) tolerate the waste in time that is created by the archaic process of toll-paying.⑥I remember some years ago a study was done indicating the manpower and fuel losses occasioned by the many delays at the toll plaza.⑦I would beg to suggest that the accident incidence at the toll plazas is probably higher than on any of the surrounding roadways.⑧Why can't these simply be eliminated?⑨Raise your fuel tax, raise your licensing taxes—something certainly more logical, simpler and safer.—S.P.S.

20. Background: This letter is about the pay of public school teachers. (*USA Today,* 1/99)

A teacher works nine months of the year in the classroom, often putting in as many as 10 or more hours a day. Teachers also spend many hours of their own time preparing for classes, grading papers, attending meetings and taking classes to keep up their credentials. Also take into account, when judging the salaries of teachers, the money they spend out of their pockets to buy supplies for their classrooms because school districts are so often underfunded. So, now what about teacher salaries? Are they high enough? Do they compare in any way to those of other highly trained professionals? I think not. And let's not forget that many teachers today are putting their lives on the line, thanks to a fragmented society.—G.M.

❖ 21. Background: This letter is in response to a column by Bill Gates, head of Microsoft, arguing in favor of the World Trade Organization (WTO), the international organization promoting free trade and globalization. (*New York Times*, 11/99)

As Mr. Gates noted, the WTO seeks to increase protection for intellectual property claims like copyrights and patents. These forms of protectionism are enormously costly to developing nations, raising prices of some goods by several hundred or even several thousand percent. And when patent protection involves vital drugs, it could cost lives. The WTO also seeks to make Internet commerce tax-free, an idea for which there is no economic or ethical justification. In short, the WTO agenda is clearly designed to help big corporations like Microsoft, to the detriment of much of the world's population.—D.B.

  22. Background: This letter is in response to a letter accusing Vietnam War protesters of acting out of self-interest. (*New York Times*, 8/94)

Accusing the Vietnam War protesters of self-interest ignores two important points: (1) at the height of the 1960's protests, students had the absolute protection of student deferments, and (2) a very large percentage of the protesters were women and not subject to the draft. Moreover, in my own case, I was expelled from my university because of my antiwar activities and immediately subject to the draft. No, protesting the war was by no means the safest course of action, nor was it the surest and most opportune path to successful and remunerative career. It was, however, for thousands of very young men and women, the only possible path to take, given the circumstances of the Vietnam War.—M.L.F.

  23. Background: This letter is about the much-criticized sexual behavior code adopted some years ago by Antioch College. The code stipulated that in sexual encounters between students verbal permission should be obtained by the party taking the initiative for every increase in level of intimacy. (*New York Times*, 1/94)

I am astonished that many people are horrified at prior verbal consent to sexual engagement. As a species that has chosen to eschew instinct for intellect, we use words as our major tool. Words define us as human. If we disassociate words from an activity of such survival importance as sex, it must mean that we think of sex as a lower-species act. Dialogue is not desired in dominance-submission cultures. Whereas in a society in which power struggle is a nonissue and mutuality is valued, exchanging words of honest substance not only sustains autonomy but also weaves shared sensuality. I speak to you guys who are afraid of prior verbal consent ("guys" is used here as a non-gender-specific word): believe me, if you have deprived yourselves of the conversational choreography of consensual exploration, you have before you much richness yet to discover in the pleasures of the dance—no matter what the final steps.—F.L.

5.4 Complex Arguments

One purpose of an argument is to rationally persuade the audience that the conclusion is true. To do this, the author provides premises that support the conclusion. However, if the audience does not regard the premises themselves as true, it may not be persuaded of the truth of the conclusion. Thus, whenever possible, authors should provide premises that their audience will regard as true. When the premises of an argument are themselves doubtful, an author needs to show that those premises are true. This means, of course, providing an argument for the doubtful premises. The argument for the premises then becomes part of the overall argument, which is referred to as a **complex argument.** In contrast, a **simple argument** has no parts that are arguments. All of the arguments we have considered so far have been simple arguments.

Complex and Simple Arguments

A complex argument has a part or parts that are arguments. In a complex argument, one (or more) of the premises itself has an argument supporting it. A complex argument has a single main conclusion and an argument supporting one or more of the premises that support that conclusion. A simple argument, in contrast, has no parts that are arguments.

Consider this example:

Example 5.22

Background: This letter is in response to criticisms of former President Clinton by Republicans for his allegedly inviting some Democratic Party campaign contributors to spend the night at the White House. (*Miami Herald,* 3/97)

① The White House is the president's home. ② He can invite anyone he wishes there. ③ The Republican Party should stop its witch hunting.—G.S.

Sentence 3 expresses the conclusion, and sentence 2 expresses a premise supporting the conclusion. What about sentence 1? This is clearly part of the argument, but its role is in support of sentence 2 rather than 3. We can imagine the author of this argument thinking in this way: Republicans should stop criticizing Clinton for inviting contributors to spend the night at the White House because the president should be able to invite anyone he wants to the White House. But my audience may not regard this premise as true, so I should provide support for it. The president should be able to invite anyone he wants to the White House because the White House is his home. This last sentence expresses an argument supporting the premise, with that premise in turn supporting the conclusion.

Here is the structure for this argument:

Example 5.23

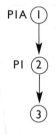

PIA: The White House is the president's home.

PI: The president can invite anyone he wishes to the White House.

C: Therefore, the Republicans should stop criticizing the president for inviting contributors to spend the night at the White House.

Previous simple arguments involved only the *width* of the tree diagram—that is, the number of premises supporting the conclusion. But with complex arguments, the tree grows *taller*. There are, in principle, no width limits on trees because an argument can have any number of premises. Likewise, there are, in principle, no limits on how high a tree can be. That is, the premises that support a conclusion can themselves be supported by arguments, and the premises of those arguments can, in turn, be supported by further arguments, and so forth. In reality, however, most complex arguments are only two or three levels high. In addition, in most complex arguments, only some of the premises supporting the conclusion have arguments of their own. But all of them may have such arguments. Note that in the PC structure of a complex argument each argument supporting a premise is indented and placed above the premise it supports.

Because discussions of complex arguments can become quite complex, it is helpful to adopt some standard terminology. The conclusion of a complex argument and the premises directly supporting it form the **main argument,** and those premises are the **main premises.** An argument supporting a premise is a **subargument,** and the premises of that argument are **subpremises.** A subargument is

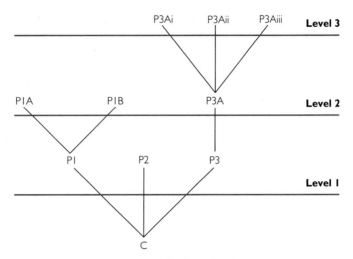

FIGURE 5.3   Tree Diagrams of a Complex Argument

labeled as "the subargument at P1" (or P2, or whichever premise the subargument supports).

Figure 5.3 shows a tree diagram of a complex argument. The conclusion and the premises directly supporting it—P1, P2, and P3—constitute the main argument, and P1, P2, and P3 are the main premises. All of the rest of the premises are subpremises. This complex argument has three subarguments—at P1, P3, and P3A. The horizontal lines indicate the levels at which the various premises and subpremises appear. (These lines need not be included in your tree diagrams; they are used here simply for illustration.) The diagram indicates the scheme for labeling subpremises. At the level above the main premises (level 2), all of the premises are labeled "PxA," "PxB," "PxC," and so on, where "x" indicates the number of the main premise it supports. At the next level up, level 3, the subpremises are labeled "Pxxi," "Pxxii," "Pxxiii," "Pxxiv," and so on, where "xx" indicates the subpremise at level 2 that those subpremises support. In this case, all the premises at level 3 are supporting subpremise P3A.

> ## The Parts of a Complex Argument
>
> The conclusion of a complex argument and the premises directly supporting it form the main argument; those premises are the main premises. An argument supporting a premise is a subargument, and the premises of that argument are subpremises.

5.4.1 What Supports What? Part 2

It is sometimes difficult to tell whether an argument is simple or complex. In addition, when structuring complex arguments, it is sometimes difficult to distinguish a subargument from the main argument and a subpremise from a main premise. In practice, this is a problem of distinguishing what level a premise or subpremise belongs on. This suggests a need to consider again the question, first raised in Chapter 4, What supports what?

To help answer this question, we can call again on the reasoning indicator test, introduced in Chapter 2 to distinguish between arguments and nonarguments. Here, we use the shorthand method for representing an application of the test, as discussed in Chapter 2, in which, for example, an argument is represented by ① TF ②. A version of the reasoning indicator test can be used to distinguish between simple and complex arguments, as well as to distinguish between a premise and a subpremise within a complex argument. This application of the test relies on the fact that, while the shorthand schema for a simple argument is ② TF ①, the shorthand schema for a complex argument is ③ TF ② TF ①.

Imagine that you have an argumentative text but are not sure whether the argument is simple or complex or that you believe the argument is complex but are not sure which sentence expresses a premise and which a subpremise. To apply the test, first identify the text sentence (call it A) that expresses the conclusion and a sentence (B) that expresses a main premise that you think may be supported by a subargument. Then pick out a sentence (C) that you think may be a subpremise supporting the premise expressed by B. Now, consider the schema: Ⓒ TF Ⓑ TF Ⓐ. If this makes sense, then the argument is complex, with C expressing a subpremise supporting the main premise B. Thus, the test tells you whether the argument is complex and which sentence expresses the premise and which the subpremise. If it does not make sense, either the argument is not complex after all, or you have not picked out the sentences from the text that show the argument's complexity. In the latter case, you can rule out the argument as complex only by picking out other sentences from the text and applying the test again.

To see how the test works, consider the complex argument presented earlier and a variation of it:

Example 5.24

A. ① The White House is the president's home. ② He can invite anyone he wishes there. ③ The Republican Party should stop its witch hunting.
B. ① Many White House guests were friends of as well as contributors to the president. ② He can invite anyone he wishes to the White House. ③ The Republican Party should stop its witch hunting.

Now consider this application of the reasoning indicator test:

Example 5.25

C. ① TF ② TF ③
D. ① TF ② TF ③

Application C makes sense. It accurately represents the structure of the complex argument in A, but application D does not make sense. Although sentence 2 in text

B has a support relationship with sentence 3, sentence 1 does not have a support relationship with sentence 2. Instead, sentence 1, like sentence 2, supports sentence 3. In B, there are two main premises and no subarguments, so B contains a simple rather than a complex argument.

Consider these other examples:

Example 5.26

A. Background: This letter is in response to a column on the problems of alcohol abuse. (*New York Times*, 6/00)

① Although alcohol is the drug that causes the most crime and violence in America each year, government officials responsible for the war on drugs don't include alcohol in prevention messages aimed at youth. ② Whither common sense?—H.W.[14]

B. Background: This is a portion of a letter written in response to a comment by a proponent of creationism that evolutionary theory is at odds with morality. Creationism is the view that the diversity of species is a direct result of God's handiwork rather than biological evolution. (*New York Times*, 12/99)

① But science only provides empirical explanations of how nature works. ② It provides no basis for a moral code and therefore poses no threat to Christianity.—J.F.S.

One of these is a simple argument and one is a complex argument. Here is an application of the reasoning indicator test to each:

Example 5.27

C. ⓛₐ TF ⓛᵦ TF ②
D. ① TF ②ₐ TF ②ᵦ

Application D makes sense. This means that text B expresses a complex argument, with sentence 1 expressing the single premise of the subargument supporting the main premise expressed by claim 2a. The claim that science provides only empirical explanations supports the claim that science provides no basis for a moral code, which in turn supports the argument's conclusion that science poses no threat to Christianity. In contrast, application C does not make sense. Claim 1a, that alcohol is the drug that causes the most crime and violence, does not support the claim 1b, that government officials do not include alcohol in their prevention messages. Instead, it is clear that, while claim 1b supports the conclusion, expressed by sentence 2, claim 1a does as well. Thus, text A is a simple argument with two main premises.

Now consider two examples that are more complicated:

Example 5.28

A. Background: This letter is part of the public debate over whether the use of automobile seat belts should be legally required. (*USA Today*, 4/86)

① The seat belt does more than prevent physical harm. ② It will prevent an accident and, therefore, possible injury. ③ It is designed not only to keep the motorist from

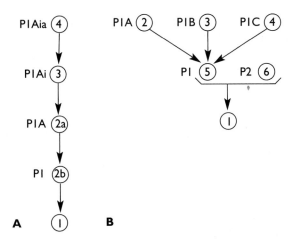

FIGURE 5.4   Tree Diagram for Example 5.26

being ejected, but also to keep him in control of his vehicle in an emergency.
④ Should your tires suddenly skid violently, or if you must make a sharp turn, your
seat belt will keep you firmly attached to your seat.—E.S.

B. Background: This letter is about the price of oil. (*New York Times,* 2/00)

① We are partially responsible for the rapid rise in oil prices. ② We drive heavy cars
and sport utility vehicles when more fuel-efficient cars are available. ③ We live in
houses that are much larger than we need. ④ We favor the automobile over public
transportation. ⑤ The American public wastes huge amounts of energy. ⑥ These
wasteful habits translate into higher demand for oil and are a major factor in the high
demand that produces the high oil price.—N.G.

Text A has four levels of premises and subpremises. Moreover, as Figure 5.4
shows, its tree diagram is all trunk and no branches. Each subargument, as well as
the main argument, has but a single premise. The conclusion, expressed in sentence 1, is supported by a single main premise (2b). The main premise is supported
by a subargument with a single subpremise (2a), which in turn is supported by a
subargument with a single subpremise (3), which in its turn is also supported by a
subargument with a single subpremise (4).

In the case of text B, as Figure 5.4 shows, we have two linked premises (5 and
6), one of which is supported by a subargument with three subpremises (2, 3, and 4).
Sentences 2–4 support the claim in sentence 5 that the American public wastes huge
amounts of oil, and that statement is a premise linked with the statement in sentence
6 that these wasteful habits result in the high demand that produces high oil prices.

5.4.2 Intermediate Implicit Premises

Earlier, we discussed implicit conclusions. There are also **implicit premises.** An
implicit premise, like an implicit conclusion, is a part of an argument that is not
explicitly stated. The author intends it as part of the argument but does not include

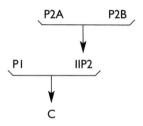

FIGURE 5.5   Tree Diagram for an Argument with an
Intermediate Implicit Premise

any sentence expressing it in the argumentative text. Thus, you need to determine the author's intent.

Implicit Premises

An implicit premise is a part of an argument that is not explicit. There is no sentence in the argumentative text that expresses an implicit premise. Figuring out when an argument has an implicit premise, like figuring out when there is an implicit conclusion, is a matter of understanding the author's intent.

We will discuss implicit premises in more detail in subsequent chapters, but it is important at this point to consider a special kind of implicit premise that arises in complex arguments. This is the **intermediate implicit premise,** so called because it comes between the conclusion of the argument and a subargument. An intermediate implicit premise is usually a linked premise in which case it needs to be included in the argument structure to show that the argument has linked premises. Figure 5.5 shows a typical tree diagram, in schematic form, for an argument with an intermediate implicit premise (labeled "IIP"). It may be helpful to think of an intermediate implicit premise as the implicit conclusion of a subargument.

Intermediate Implicit Premises

An intermediate implicit premise comes between the conclusion of an argument and a subargument, but it is not explicitly stated. It usually is a linked premise and needs to be included in the argument structure to show that the argument has linked premises.

Consider again the argument about high oil prices. As we said, this argument has a linked main premise, expressed by sentence 5, supported by a subargument.

The author might have left sentence 5 out, expecting the audience to recognize its role in the argument, even in its absence. If the author had done this, the statement expressed by sentence 5 would have been an intermediate implicit premise.

Consider this example:

Example 5.29

> ① All pornography should be banned. ② This allows us to infer that *National Geographic* should be banned, because anything that has pictures of naked people is pornographic, and *National Geographic* has pictures of naked people.

Here are the argument structures:

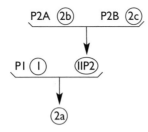

Example 5.30

P1: All pornography should be banned.
   P2A: Anything that contains pictures of naked people is pornographic.
   P2B: *National Geographic* contains pictures of naked people.
IIP2: *National Geographic* is pornographic.
C: Therefore, *National Geographic* should be banned.

The intermediate implicit premise, that *National Geographic* is pornographic, is linked with the explicit premise P1, that all pornography should be banned. Thus, the implicit premise needs to be included because, like all linked premises, it shows how the premise with which it is linked supports the conclusion.[15] The need to include intermediate implicit premises can be stated in a second rule of addition, the first being the one on implicit conclusions from Chapter 4.

Rule of Addition, Number 2

A complex argument sometimes contains an implicit premise supported by a subargument, an intermediate implicit premise. This occurs when the subargument supports the conclusion indirectly, through the implicit premise. Such an implicit premise is usually linked with an explicit premise and should be included in the structure to indicate that the argument has linked premises.

≡ EXERCISE SET 5.4

SECTION A: Determine whether the following arguments are simple or complex by applying the reasoning indicator test. Give a tree diagram for each.

EXAMPLE

① Whales have larger brains than do humans. ② The larger brain an animal has, the more intelligent that animal is. ③ Whales are more intelligent than humans.

ANSWER

Sentence 3 expresses the conclusion, so the following combinations may be considered to test whether the argument is complex.

A. ① TF ② TF ③
B. ② TF ① TF ③

Neither of these makes sense, so the argument is simple.

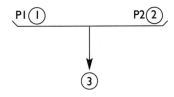

PROBLEMS

1. Radiation can cause cancer. Nuclear power plants can be harmful to humans. We should shut down all nuclear power plants.

2. A president has to understand the many complexities of a rapidly changing world. Understanding such complexities requires a high level of intellectual curiosity. We should not elect a president who lacks intellectual curiosity.

❖ 3. Sunspots can interfere with Earth's magnetic fields. Many types of communications depend on Earth's magnetic fields. Sunspots can cause poor communications.

4. Women should be treated as equals in the workplace. The only important difference between men and women is their roles in reproduction. Someone's reproductive life has little or no relevance for her ability to do a job well.

5. Summer is the best time of year. The pace is more relaxed. All of nature is in bloom. School is out.

❖ 6. The stock market influences the confidence that people have in the economy. When the stock market is high, people feel wealthier. An interest rate decrease will improve the stock market. The Federal Reserve Board should lower interest rates.

7. The Nobel science prizes should go to those who invent important technology, as well as to those who discover important scientific principles. Nobel himself was an important inventor. He invented dynamite.

8. Beauty pageants are simply meat markets. Portraying human beings as sex objects destroys their humanity. We should abolish beauty pageants.

❖ 9. Prior to the twentieth century, humans had no idea how the sun generated its energy. The sun is powered by nuclear energy, and nuclear energy was not discovered until the 1920s.

10. Summer is the best time of year. The pace is more relaxed. The heat makes everyone move more slowly.

11. Air bags can save lives. But for small people they can be deadly. It is a difficult choice for a small person whether to use air bags.

❖ 12. The foolish ask questions that the wise man cannot answer. It is easier to ask questions than to answer them. I am wise but cannot answer your question. 'Nuff said.

13. Every event has a cause. Human actions are events. So, there is no free will.

14. The central mission of a school is education. A school is only as good as its teachers. The first priority of any school is to attract good teachers. But teachers cannot be attracted without better pay. So, we should raise the salary of the teachers.

SECTION B: For those arguments you found to be simple in Section A, add one or more sentences to the text to make the argument complex.

EXAMPLE

Whales have larger brains than humans. Intelligence requires a very large number of neurons in the brain. The larger brain an animal has, the more intelligent it is. Whales are more intelligent than humans.

SECTION C: Construct an intermediate implicit premise for each of the following argumentative texts, indicating by a tree diagram which sentence(s) support that premise.

EXAMPLE

① Women are more interested in religion than men. ② It is important for the clergy to have a high degree of interest in the religion. ③ But your religion is opposed to women in the clergy. ④ Therefore, your religion should change its policy in this regard.

ANSWER

IIP: Women should be allowed in the clergy.

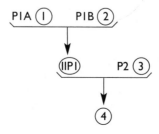

PROBLEMS

1. Wedding rings symbolize being bound to one's spouse. Those who are bound have a strong obligation. I see that you are wearing a wedding ring. You have a strong obligation.

2. ① Sexist language leaves some people out of the conversation, and whatever Ⓑ leaves some people out of the conversation is demeaning. ② We should all do what we can to avoid demeaning others. ③ You should work to remove sexism from your language.

3. Any problem created by humans can be solved by humans. Any problem that can be solved by humans is not something to worry too much about. The environmental problem was created by humans. It follows that we should not be too worried about the environmental problem.

4. There is no way to know that an event is contrary to the laws of nature. The Bible says that miracles occurred. So, you should not believe the Bible.

5. HIV can be contracted through sexual activity. HIV is deadly. Any activity that can be deadly should be discouraged. Schools should teach sexual abstinence.

SECTION D: Structure the complex arguments in the following texts. Some of them have implicit conclusions, and some may have intermediate implicit premises.

EXAMPLE

Background: This letter addresses our increasing tendency to focus media attention on the private lives of political and governmental leaders. (*San Francisco Chronicle*, 6/97)

① It is a matter of patriotism and concern for the welfare of our country that we appoint and elect people to serve our country who are the most qualified and capable. ② To eliminate such people on the basis of private matters that have nothing to do with their ability to serve is detrimental to our national interests. ③ Human nature is fallible. ④ In an active life there are few who do not have something they would prefer to keep private. ⑤ How will we ever get the most qualified people to run for office? ⑥ How many of the great leaders of our past could have passed such purity tests?—J.S.

ANSWER

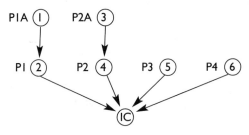

P1A: It is a matter of patriotism and concern for the welfare of our country that we appoint and elect people to serve our country who are the most qualified and capable.

P1: To eliminate such people on the basis of private matters that have nothing to do with their ability to serve is detrimental to our national interests.

P2A: Human nature is fallible.

P2: In an active life there are few who do not have something they would prefer to keep private.

P3: If we focus on private matters, we will not get the most qualified people to run for office.

P4: Many great leaders of our past would not have passed such purity tests.

IC: Therefore, we should stop focusing so extensively on the private lives of potential government officials.

PROBLEMS

1. Background: This letter is about the hypothesis that the Neanderthals, an early humanoid species, were unable to articulate the same sounds as early humans, and so had a different dialect. (*New York Times*, 5/98)

   The Neanderthal dialect may even have contributed to their extinction: *(1a)* recent genetic studies show that slight differences in dialect isolate humans, *(1b)* so the Neanderthals' dialect may have inhibited their mating with early modern humans.—P.L.   *3 explicit claims*

2. Background: This letter discusses the use of Internet filtering technology in public libraries. (*New York Times*, 6/97)

   This filtering technology creates more problems than it solves. Making it work requires some remote company—rather than the library itself—to keep up-to-date lists of objectionable sites. This is not how libraries work. Libraries allow access to what they themselves have approved as suitable.—S.W.

3. Background: This letter addresses the concern that tax increases on cigarettes will lead to a black market. (*New York Times*, 5/98)

   Concerns about contraband cigarettes and smuggling cigarettes as a result of proposed tax increases to help discourage teen-age smoking could be alleviated by imposition of the tax at the time of manufacture and before shipment to distributors. The distribution system would pass the tax on through the retailing network; thus, smugglers would be forced to pay the tax.—M.W.

4. Background: This letter is about the 1997 death of Princess Diana. (*New York Times*, 9/97)

   In the urgent attempt to place blame for the crash of the car carrying Diana, Princess of Wales, the authorities should not overlook the responsibility of French highway engineers for the magnitude of the impact. The columns down the center of the tunnel should have been spanned with steel rails. With a smooth tunnel wall and a continuous barrier, the car would have sideswiped its way through the tunnel until the driver (one would hope) had the sense to come to a stop.—W.H.

5. Background: This letter registers an environmental concern about preserving genetic diversity. "Charismatic fauna" refers to large animals, such as seals and tigers. (*New York Times*, 4/98)

   The public unfortunately is not very familiar with the consequences of the loss of the genetic wealth of plants—a wealth that includes genes resistant to pests, environmental stress and disease. With today's technology we have incredible possibilities to expand agricultural yields, and using plants for medicines contributes millions of dollars to the world economy. Plant diversities deserve the same recognition we grant to charismatic fauna; after all, no bamboo means no pandas.—B.B.

6. Background: This letter is about the price of gasoline. (*Los Angeles Times*, 9/97)

   To those complaining about gas prices, take a look at any of those birthday cards remembering one's birth year. I recently received one for 1945 when a stamp was 3 cents (now 32 cents); milk was 16 cents (now $1.20); bread was 9 cents (now $1); minimum wage was 40 cents (now $5.15); and a house was $10,131 (now $180,000). Gasoline cost 21 cents a gallon, including 6 cents tax, compared to today's price of $1.40, including 47 cents tax. Do the math and decide which are the bargains.—R.C.M.

7. Background: This letter is about an advertising campaign encouraging people not to drink milk. (*USA Today*, 3/00)

   People for the Ethical Treatment of Animals (PETA) correctly advocates elimination of milk from the diet. Even our close genetic cousins—the great apes—do not drink milk after weaning. Since milk drinking is unnatural, it surely is unnecessary for good health.—M.J.C.

8. Background: This is by James Madison, from *The Federalist Papers* 14.[16]

   It may be inconvenient for Georgia or the States forming our western or north eastern borders to send their representatives to the seat of government, but they would find it more so to struggle alone against an invading enemy. . . . If they should derive less benefit therefore from the union in some respects, than the less distant States, they will derive greater benefit from it in other respects, and thus the proper equilibrium will be maintained throughout.

9. Background: This letter is part of the public debate over South Carolina's flying the Confederate flag over its statehouse, in the face of the objections that it represented slavery. Defenders of the flag claimed that it should stay because it represented the state's southern heritage. (*New York Times*, 1/00)

   It should be pointed out that the Confederate flag was placed atop the South Carolina Statehouse only in 1962, as a rebuke to the civil rights movement. This fact is essential because many might assume that its flying in that location is a holdover from the Civil War, which it is not. Given the true motivation, there is hardly an argument for preserving "heritage" in continuing to fly the flag there.—J.H.

10. Background: This letter is in response to an article that asked whether bigotry was a form of mental illness or simply represented a different moral norm. The government of the former Soviet Union sometimes removed political dissidents from society by placing them in psychiatric hospitals. (*New York Times*, 1/00)

Your article illustrates the futility of trying to place moral problems into a medical category. It is clearly possible to be insane and moral, and it is equally possible to be sane and bad. Asserting that unpleasant people have mental illness poses the very real threat of medical treatment for those whose illness may be just an obnoxious opinion. Can we have forgotten the Soviet "psychiatric hospitals"?—A.P.

11. Background: This letter is in response to the 1999 Columbine High School shooting, committed by two students who were members of the so-called "trench coat mafia" school clique. (*New York Times*, 4/99)

School violence like the Colorado shooting is best answered not with punishment. Five out of six American secondary schools enroll 2,500 or more students, yet research consistently points to 600 to 800 as optimal. Because each school has but one football team, choir and Spanish club, the number of slots by which students may feel connected to the school is limited. In a school of 700, most students have an avenue for bonding and fitting in. In a school of 1,800, a large number of students will fail to find a slot, feel marginalized and be labeled "outcasts" and "misfits," the terms Columbine High School students applied to those in the "trench coat mafia."—A.P.G.

12. Background: This letter is about Benjamin Spock, the pediatrician, baby-book author, and peace activist, who died in 1998. (*San Francisco Chronicle*, 8/98)

One way to honor the life of Dr. Benjamin Spock is to award him a posthumous Nobel Peace Prize. The air that we breathe today is less contaminated because of his efforts, which eventually resulted in a Nuclear Test Ban Treaty between Russia and the United States. By lending his presence to peace demonstrations he made protests respectable and civil disobedience acceptable. Those of us who were privileged to be in his company will note with pride and gratitude that a gifted mind and intrepid heart has passed from the scene.—D.K.

13. Background: This letter is in response to an article discussing the concerns of some European nations about their declining birth rates. (*New York Times*, 7/98)

Europe is overpopulated. Virtually none of the great European forests survive. Roads, railroad corridors and urban sprawl have fragmented all wildlife populations that cannot fly. Ancient cities are crammed; beaches are jammed. Less is more holds true. A smaller population will allow a higher standard of living and make it possible to achieve an environmentally stable Europe (and planet).—G.D.

14. Background: This letter is critical of a newspaper headline. (*Atlanta Constitution*, 4/97)

The headline, "Women's gun death linked to depression, drugs," was not consistent with the content of the article. The most salient issue is that in 82 percent of the slayings of women by someone they know, guns are used. It is also revealing that two out of five women who commit suicide use guns. Clearly we have far too many guns in our homes, and when problems arise, women die by them. Perhaps that headline writer could use an update in Journalism 101 that would enable him to accurately portray a complicated issue without implying that the victims are to blame.—S.E.C.

15. Background: This letter joins the debate over the expansion of NATO, the military alliance established over 50 years ago to deter the former Soviet Union. The Holy Roman Empire was a federation of European states existing from about 800 to 1800 A.D. (*New York Times*, 7/97)

Rather than entering NATO Poland and Hungary should be admitted to the Holy Roman Empire. The Empire is more relevant to current European security problems than is NATO. For the foreseeable future, the threats to continental stability from ethnic discord and Islamic fundamentalism exceed any risk of Russian expansionism. The Holy Roman Empire, a multinational entity that combated Muslim autocracies, would be better suited to manage these problems than an alliance whose raison d'etre was to contain Russia.—B.R.

16. Background: This letter is about a proposal by then–Vice President Al Gore to place a satellite in stationary orbit that would beam back to Earth a view of our planet constantly available for the media and the Internet. (*New York Times*, 3/98)

Perhaps when we can all see at the flick of our remote controls just how tiny and precious this Earth is against the vast emptiness of space, and how our burgeoning humanity defaces it from day to day, we will modify our behavior to live within its limits before we destroy ourselves, other creatures and perhaps the planet itself. Mr. Gore's proposal seems a better use for my tax dollars than most others I can think of. I hope the world-watch system will be built.—S.R.B.

17. Background: This letter concerns a 1998 incident in which sections of concrete and steel fell into a seating area in Yankee Stadium, leading to calls for the venerable stadium to be replaced. (*New York Times*, 4/98)

Before anyone gets too carried away with the idea that a little falling concrete and steel prove that Yankee Stadium is too old and needs to be replaced, it should be noted that the materials fell from a section installed in a renovation that took place in the early 1970s. Maybe the real lesson here is that new construction methods are too unreliable to be trusted and that spending $1 billion of taxpayer money on a new stadium to help make a bunch of millionaires even richer is an expensive and dangerous gamble with the public's safety.—M.F.

18. Background: This letter is a criticism of the Vatican, the governing head of Roman Catholicism, on the issue of free inquiry. (*New York Times*, 10/98)

The Vatican is a source whose credentials on the subject of free inquiry are, to say the least, suspect. The Vatican is an institution that displays authoritarian tendencies, and which frequently busies itself with the suppression of the opinions that contradict its doctrine on subjects like birth control and gay rights. The Pope himself has been an enthusiastic censor—for example, placing discussion of the ordination of women beyond the pale by having his views on the matter declared infallible. The point is that the key ingredient in rational inquiry is skepticism, not faith. Honest and unfettered intellectual activity cannot be bound by doctrinal barriers, even when its results cause discomfort.—C.G.

19. Background: This letter is part of the debate over affirmative action. (*New York Times*, 6/97)

Nonwhite immigrants are themselves eligible for affirmative action, despite having no history of being discriminated against in the United States. American colleges and corporations are already using nonwhite immigrants to help meet affirmative-action goals, a trend that will only increase as the immigrant population grows. The nation's increasing diversity does nothing to help the descendants of slavery—the people for whom affirmative action was created—but instead robs them of the special status that offers the only conceivable defense for race-based preferences.—J.B.

20. Background: This letter is in response to an article on human consciousness. The Latin sentence "cogito ergo sum" is the famous argument of the French philosopher René Descartes. It translates as "I think, therefore I am." (*New York Times*, 4/96)

Those who argue that the conscious mind "doesn't exist except in the eye of the beholder" must be juggling words. The physical world may be an illusion—I may have been dreaming about it for 70-odd years. But Descartes was right: Consciousness exists. Cogito ergo sum.—H.A.F.

21. Background: This letter is about the tendency in Hollywood movies for older men to be paired up with younger women. (*New York Times*, 5/98)

Your article says that "to some degree, Hollywood mirrors reality" in coupling older men with younger women. A studio executive is quoted as saying that attraction is related to biology and that, unlike women, men can still procreate and "continue to be sexually attractive until their dotage." But does fertility make women attractive? In the 1960's the birth control pill caused an increase in sexual activity despite its role in decreasing female fertility. Moreover, if biology is linked to sexy roles for men, the popularity of the impotence drug Viagra casts doubt not only on the fertility of older men but also on their ability to perform sexually. Let's see film roles for what they are—a reflection of stereotypes, not biology. —M.S.M.

22. Background: This letter presents the economic theory of the nineteenth-century American political economist Henry George. (*New York Times*, 5/83)

Your editorial follows the significant logic espoused by Henry George over 100 years ago. A tax on production burdens producers who pass it on to the consumer, thereby reducing demand, hence the standard of living. A tax on rent of land confers no power on landowners to demand more in rent, therefore he must absorb the tax and is forced to put land to undelayed better use, thus increasing the supply of land, which in turn tends to reduce rent of land. Tax rent of land and you free it for use. Untax production and you increase supply at lower prices.—E.G.

23. Background: The following letter concerns a provision of the crime bill passed by Congress and signed by then-President Clinton in 1994. (*New York Times*, 9/94)

It is worth noting that one critical element of the law—the so-called assault weapons ban—contains a loophole that renders the law almost powerless by assuring there will be no successful Federal prosecutions for assault weapon possession. The law states that it is legal to possess or transfer an assault weapon that was lawfully owned on the date that the crime bill becomes effective. To convict someone of unlawful possession of an assault weapon, the Government will have to prove the entire chain of custody of the weapon at issue. Since there is no general national recordkeeping requirement for gun sales, this represents an almost impossible burden for the Government to meet.—C.J.A.

❖ 24. Background: This letter is about a proposal to reform the Medicare system by raising the age of eligibility. (*Washington Post*, 1/99)

The federal bipartisan commission's proposal to delay Americans receiving Medicare to age 67 is a regressive idea. Historically, legislation regarding health insurance intends to cover more people. This proposal intends to cover fewer people. Further, the number of uninsured (already more than 40 million) will go up. Let's hope the federal government will get on the right track and do what social legislation should do—help more, not fewer, people.—R.A.M.

25. Background: This letter is in response to a letter about the Y2K problem, the concern that the year 2000 would cause problems for computers. (*New York Times*, 4/97)

The writer states that while IBM may crash when going from Dec. 31, 1999, to Jan. 1, 2000, Macintosh systems will start the new century "without a blink." He is confusing applications software with operating software. The operating systems produced by IBM and Apple computers store the full date internally, so neither is likely to have significant problems when the turn of the century arrives. However, some applications software written by independent programmers, whether for IBM or Macintosh systems, stores only the last two digits of the year, and therefore cannot distinguish between the years 2000 and 1900. It is these applications programs that may crash (or produce incorrect results) when the century turns.—J.B.

Summary

In a PC structure, the premises and conclusion of an argument are written down one above the other and labeled "C," "P1," "P2," and so on. In many cases, this requires reformulating the sentences of the argumentative text to clarify the author's statements.

General statements say something about the members of a class or group of things, and singular statements say something about a particular thing. General statements can be divided into universal generalizations, which say something about all the members of a class, and nonuniversal generalizations, which say something about only some of the members of a class. In contrast, singular statements include a word or phrase that identifies the particular thing that the statement is about. That word or phrase can be a proper name or a definite description.

The scope of a general statement is the portion of the class about which it says something, and a quantifier is a word or phrase indicating the scope. All general statements have quantifiers, but in incomplete sentences, the quantifier is implicit, and we must rely on our understanding (from context) of the author's intentions to determine what it is. The strength of a general statement is determined by its scope, or statement strength. Statement strength applies to statements, while modal strength, as reflected in modal phrases, applies to particular assertions of a statement. In reformulating the sentences expressing the statements of an argument for a PC structure, it is important adequately to represent both the statement strength and the modal strength of the assertion in that argument. Strength space is a diagrammatic representation on two axes of these two dimensions of strength.

A conditional statement, or conditional, contains parts that are statements and asserts a truth about the relationship between those statements, not about the statements themselves. A conditional asserts that if the statement following the "if" (known as the antecedent) is true then the statement following the "then" (known as the consequent) is also true. A conditional can be true even when both the statements that compose it are false. For this reason, it is crucial to represent a conditional in the structure as a single statement rather than two statements. It is helpful to think about conditionals in terms of necessary conditions and sufficient conditions. A necessary condition is a condition without which some other possibility cannot be actual. A sufficient condition is a condition that by itself will guarantee that some other possibility is actual. The antecedent is always a sufficient condition for the consequent and the consequent is always a necessary condition for the antecedent.

Reformulation, or paraphrasing, is necessary when text sentences do not express their statements clearly. Whenever possible, it is better to use the same sentences in the PC structure as are used in the text. The need for reformulation, along with the need to determine the author's intention, makes it easy to misrepresent an argument. An argument or a statement that is misrepresented is referred to as a straw man.

A complex argument has parts that are arguments, known as subarguments. A simple argument does not have arguments as parts. The branches of a tree diagram of a complex argument extend upward as well as sideways, while those of a simple argument simply extend sideways. Authors present complex arguments because they do not think that the audience will regard the premises of the main argument as true. Identifying complex arguments creates special problems with regard to the question of what supports what?

Complex argument can create a special situation in which an implicit premise must be recognized. An implicit premise, like an implicit conclusion, is a part of an argument that is not expressed by any sentence in the argumentative text. In some complex arguments, a subargument will support a premise that is implicit. This is called an intermediate implicit premise because it is intermediate between the subargument and the main conclusion. An intermediate implicit premise is usually a linked premise.

Key Terms

PC structure

general statement

singular statement

universal
  generalization

nonuniversal
  generalization

proper name

definite description

scope

quantifier

incomplete sentence

statement strength

assertion

modal phrases

modal strength

strength space

conditional statement

antecedent

consequent

necessary condition

sufficient condition

reformulation

internal context

external context

indirection

irony

straw man

alternative reasonable
  interpretations

complex argument

simple argument

main argument

main premises

subargument

subpremises

implicit premise

intermediate implicit
  premise

Notes

1. Note that this sentence is not the same as "Not all birds study critical thinking," which means simply that some do not study critical thinking. These kinds of differences in meaning involving quantifiers will be further discussed in Chapter 7.

2. Part of the source of human prejudice may be the tendency for sloppy thinking regarding the implicit quantifier for incomplete sentences. Humans tend to think in terms of stereotypes. We often denigrate the members of some group of humans (women, men, blacks, whites, immigrants, and so on) by viewing all members of that group as having some negative characteristic (being slobs, being dishonest, being bad drivers, being stupid, being emotional, and so on) shared by only a portion of people. The use of incomplete sentences makes it easier for us to think in such ways. A person can think or say, "Members of group x are y," y being some negative characteristic, which may be true when the sentence is understood as having a narrow scope. Because the sentence is ambiguous as to whether the scope is wide or narrow, however, the prejudiced person will tend to understand the scope as wide, thereby engaging in stereotypical thinking.

3. The example that shows that a universal generalization is false is referred to as a counterexample. Such a use of counterexamples will be discussed in Chapter 8.

4. One difference between the two kinds of strength is that modal strength applies to both general and particular statements, whereas statement strength applies only to general statements.

5. This conditional may be separated into two conditionals: (1) If the major leagues downsized by reducing the number of teams in each league, then a slew of mediocre players would leave the major leagues, and (2) If a slew of mediocre players left the major leagues, then more talented players would compete with their peers and improve the overall quality of the game.

6. Alexander Hamilton, *The Federalist* 7, in Jacob Cooke (ed.), *The Federalist* (Middletown, CT: Wesleyan University Press, 1961), p. 43.

7. Charles Darwin, *On the Origin of Species* (Cambridge, MA: Harvard University Press, 1964), p. 63.

8. Things can work the other way, too. Although an indicative sentence normally expresses a statement, it may also express a question, command, or request. The indicative sentence "You're going out," for example, may express a question if spoken in a certain tone of voice and a command if delivered in another tone.

9. The overall argument is a special argument form, discussed in Chapter 8, known as *reductio ad absurdum*. With this argument form, an author seeks to reveal the falsity of some view by showing that it has absurd implications.

10. There are a few exceptions to this rule, such as, for example, an argument for an explanation, in which the conclusion may contain the reasoning indicator of the explanation.

11. A straw man can also refer to a misinterpretation of another's position, rather than another's argument.

12. Some authors of critical thinking books refer to this as the rule of charity rather than the rule of fairness. To the extent that the notion of charity suggests being more willing to err on the side of providing a weaker interpretation, I think that fairness is a better notion. Those who advocate charity are especially concerned about a straw man that presents an argument as stronger than it is, because a stronger argument is more open to criticism. But harm can also be done erring on the side of weakness, as the discussion of straw men suggests. To advocate charity in interpretation encourages the interpreter to be willing to view the argument as less significant or important than it is. A fair interpretation, unlike a charitable interpretation, does not favor erring on either side.

13. Darwin, pp. 84–85.

14. The author of this letter is Harvey Weiner

15. When an intermediate implicit premise is linked with another main premise, as in this kind of case, it is often possible to regard the structure in a different way. The premises

of the subargument could be treated as main premises linked with the explicit main premise, leaving out the intermediate implicit premise. In other words, this case could be treated not as a complex argument, but as a simple argument with claims 1, 2b, and 2c as linked main premises. Both ways of structuring the argument would be correct, though one may be preferred to the other in terms of clarity.

16. James Madison, *The Federalist* 14, in Cooke (ed.), p. 87.

CHAPTER 6

Evaluating Argument Form

He draweth out the thread of his verbosity finer than the staple of his argument.

—WILLIAM SHAKESPEARE[1]

Once you have identified the argument in an argumentative text, the next task is to evaluate the argument. After structuring comes evaluation. In this chapter, we begin to discuss the second and the third of the three activities of critical thinking outlined in the first chapter: (1) identifying an argument, (2) evaluating the argument, and (3) creating an argument. This chapter begins the focus on the second activity, but it introduces the third activity as well. When you evaluate an argument, you need to create an argument of your own to support your evaluation.

6.1 Argument Evaluation

When you evaluate something, you comment on its qualities. You assess it, grade it, or judge it; you make a value statement about it. You seek to determine whether it is a good or strong example of the kind of thing that it is. For instance, if you were to evaluate a car in terms of racing, you would assess the characteristics that make a good race car—speed, maneuverability, and so forth. But if you were a commuter trying to get good gas mileage, you would assess a car in terms of different characteristics. A good race car would be a poor commuter car.

6.1.1 Argument Strength

As there are different ways to evaluate a car, so there are different ways to evaluate an argument. For example, you could evaluate an argumentative text in terms of its originality, its historical importance or its literary merit—the way people speak very highly of the literary quality of the argumentative texts of Plato. But this is not the kind of evaluation we are interested in.

An additional type of evaluation focuses on the likelihood that an argument will persuade people of its conclusion, on the argument's rhetorical effectiveness. These two questions were introduced in Chapter 2: (1) Should you be persuaded by an argument? and (2) Is it likely that you will be persuaded by the argument? Question 2 concerns rhetorical effectiveness, but question 1 is the one critical thinking asks. When you evaluate an argument, you are seeking to determine whether someone *should* be persuaded by it. Someone should be persuaded by an argument if, and only if, that argument shows that its conclusion is true or likely true. This is the argument's rational effectiveness.

In critical thinking, the rational effectiveness of an argument is the extent to which the argument shows that its conclusion is true or likely true. So, as we will use the term, an **evaluation** of an argument is an assessment of it in terms of its rational effectiveness. Arguments are evaluated as strong or weak. A **strong argument** shows its conclusion to be true or likely true; it is rationally effective. A **weak argument** does not show that its conclusion is true or likely true; it is rationally ineffective.

> **Evaluating the Strength of an Argument**
>
> In critical thinking, an evaluation of an argument is an assessment of its rational effectiveness. An argument is rationally effective when someone *should* be persuaded by it. A strong argument shows that its conclusion is true or likely true; a weak argument fails to show this.

Note that when we describe a conclusion as "likely true," we are talking about the relationship between that statement and the argument for it. We are saying that the argument does not provide sufficient support or adequate evidence for us to regard with certainty the conclusion as true. The statement itself is either true or false, though we may not be sure which. A statement is true or false independent of the evidence for it and independent of our belief about it. Only when speaking about a statement in relation to the evidence for it can we say that the statement is "likely true."[2]

6.1.2 Being Critical

With our discussion of argument evaluation, we begin in earnest the *critical* part of critical thinking. We often think of the critical person as someone who finds fault. Some people are excessively critical, in the sense that they find fault with everything, especially other people. To be critical in this sense is a character flaw. But this is not the sense in which a good critical thinker is critical. A good critical thinker focuses on the argument, not on the arguer, and assesses the strengths and weaknesses (or faults) of arguments. A good critical thinker does not provide destructive criticism aimed at simply demolishing an argument or belittling the arguer. Instead, she or he seeks to provide constructive criticism and to understand an argument's strengths and weaknesses. The value of constructive criticism is that it helps us to see where our arguments need to be improved and so gets us closer to the truth.

From a critical thinking perspective, to criticize an argument is to accept an invitation to participate in public debate on issues. To criticize an argument is to take it seriously. If you do not adopt a critical attitude toward an argument, you are, in effect, dismissing the argument. Criticizing an argument is, thus, treating the arguer with respect. Though arguers often react negatively to criticism, they should recognize that those who offer constructive criticism are the ones who take them and their arguments seriously.

Students are often asked to write essays that critically examine some text. When the text is argumentative, which it usually is, their task, at least in part, is to evaluate the argument. But students often misunderstand what they are supposed to do in being critical of an argumentative text. They usually know enough to look for the author's conclusion but may be unsure of what to do next. After you have found the conclusion, there are three ways you might approach the assignment to be critical: (1) Simply claim that the author's conclusion is false, (2) give reasons the author's conclusion is or may be false, or (3) show the strengths and weaknesses in the author's argument for the conclusion.

Three Ways to Be Critical of an Argument

1. Simply claim that the author's conclusion is false.

2. Give reasons the author's conclusion is or may be false.

3. Show the strengths and weaknesses in the author's argument for the conclusion.

Consider this argumentative text:

Example 6.1

Background: The following letter is part of the public debate over the death penalty. (*Los Angeles Times, 4/98*)

> ① America must learn, as other civilized societies have, that killing the criminal is an inappropriate response to crime. ② The states set the example. ③ When they employ capital punishment as an instrument of revenge or as a de facto deterrent they tell us that killing is an acceptable social tool. ④ What does that say to the young man with a gun and a grievance?—C.D.

What does it mean to evaluate or criticize this argument?

The first thing you must do is to identify the conclusion. In this case, the conclusion, expressed in sentence 1, is that capital punishment is not an appropriate response to crime. But then what? Consider two responses, corresponding to items 1 and 2 in the box:

> Response 1: The author's claim that capital punishment should not be practiced is false.
>
> Response 2: The author's claim that capital punishment should not be practiced is false. We need capital punishment to deter potential murderers and to make sure that murderers do not murder again.

When students are asked to write a critical essay on an argumentative text, they often present a version of one of these responses. But neither response is a criticism of the *argument*. The first response is completely off track because it simply makes a claim, commenting on something said in the text but neither addressing the argument nor providing an argument of its own. The second response is partly on track—at least it presents an argument. All criticisms, in the critical thinking sense, are themselves arguments. To offer a criticism is to make a claim about an argument and to support that claim with reasons. The problem with the second response is that the argument it makes is about a claim made in the text (in particular, the conclusion), not about the argument in the text.

Now consider a third response:

> Response 3: The author argues that capital punishment is not an appropriate response to crime. The reasons offered for this conclusion are that (1) the state sets an example in its actions, (2) the message the state sends when it practices capital punishment is that killing is an acceptable social tool, and (3) this message will lead people to settle grievances by killing. But there are weaknesses in this argument. First, even if the premises are true, they don't show that the conclusion is true, because the deterrent role of capital punishment in discouraging murder may be a much stronger reason than capital punishment's alleged role in encouraging murder. Second, it is not clear that reason 2 is true because it is plausible to claim that the message sent by capital punishment is the precise opposite of what the author claims. The message may be that the law should be respected. If the public believes that a murderer deserves to die, the public will lose respect for the law if capital punishment is not practiced.

In criticizing an argument, you are not arguing that the conclusion is false, but rather that the author has not given sufficient reason to believe that it is true or likely true. Thus, to evaluate an argument is to present an argument of your own whose conclusion is a criticism of the argument under evaluation. This is what response 3 does. By the way, the argument you create in the evaluation is a value argument, because the critical claim(s) you argue for are value statements.

To criticize an argument, you need first to structure it, as in response 3. You need to structure it to identify the reasons the author is offering for the conclusion and to determine whether those reasons adequately support the conclusion.

> ### The Two Arguments Involved in Evaluation
>
> When you evaluate an argument, there are always two arguments involved, the argument you are evaluating and the argument that you create to support the critical claim(s) you make in the evaluation.

The following letter is an evaluation of an argument:

Example 6.2

Background: The following letter comments on a newspaper editorial concerning the effort to amend the Constitution so that it does not prohibit laws against the desecration of the flag. (*New York Times,* 7/98)

> You argue that the flag protection amendment that is currently before the Senate should be rejected because it represents an assault on the Bill of Rights. This is untrue. The text of the proposed amendment, "The Congress shall have power to prohibit the physical desecration of the flag of the United States," alters not a word of the First or any other amendment of the Bill of Rights. It simply gives back to the American people a power wrongly taken away by a razor-thin majority of the Supreme Court in its erroneous 1989 and 1990 decision holding that desecrating the flag was speech.—S.B.P.

The author does not deny that the flag protection amendment should be rejected (though this may be his opinion), nor does he give reasons it should not be rejected. Instead, he criticizes a particular argument that it should be rejected. According to him, that argument has as its premise that the amendment is an assault on the Bill of Rights, and he argues that that premise is false.

The difference between criticizing a conclusion and criticizing an argument provides an answer to a question students often raise: How can I criticize an argument when I agree with the conclusion? The problem with this question is its erroneous assumption that to criticize the argument is to try to show that the conclusion is false. Rather, to criticize an argument is to argue that the argument does not provide good reason to believe its conclusion. So, you can criticize an argument without taking a position on the truth of the conclusion. In other words, to show that an argument is weak is *not* to show that its conclusion is false.

Look at it this way: You may agree or disagree with the author's conclusion. If you disagree with the conclusion, you will, of course, want to find whatever faults there are in the argument, in order to show that the conclusion does not have sufficient support. But even if you agree with the conclusion, you will want to find whatever faults there are in the argument to ensure that the claim is not supported by a weak argument. It will clear the way for you to construct a stronger argument for that conclusion. This is how criticism is constructive. Criticism reveals the faults in an argument in order to show where it needs to be strengthened and how it can be strengthened. If you agree with the conclusion of an argument you are asked to criticize, think of your critical role as that of devil's advocate.

6.1.3 Two Kinds of Argument Strength

An argument is strong when it is rationally effective, when it should persuade its audience of the truth of its conclusion. There are two kinds of argument strength. The first kind of strength, a matter of **argument content,** concerns whether the premises are true or likely true. **Content strength** does not involve the support relationship between the premises and the conclusion, but rather each of the premises by itself. The audience should be persuaded that the conclusion is true or likely true only if it believes that the premises of the argument are true or likely true. The argument must provide adequate evidence. If the premises are neither true nor likely true, they provide no basis for accepting the conclusion.

The second kind of strength, a matter of **argument form,** involves how the statements of the argument are related to each other. The audience should be persuaded that the conclusion is true or likely true only if the premises provide sufficient support for the conclusion. The support the premises provide for the conclusion is independent of whether the premises are true. The question is, assuming the premises are true, is the support relationship between the premises and the conclusion strong enough for us to accept the conclusion?

In this sense, **formal strength** is about the support relationship. The form of something is the relationship among its parts. For example, the "form" of a sculpture is the relationship among its physical parts; the "content" of the sculpture is the material—for example, bronze or plaster—out of which it is made. An argument, although not a physical object, has parts—namely, its premises and conclusion. The relationship between the premises and the conclusion is the form of the argument. The form of a sculpture is important in evaluating it in aesthetic terms, and the form of an argument is important in evaluating it in critical thinking terms.

Two Kinds of Argument Strength

1. Content strength is a matter of argument content and concerns whether each of the premises, considered by itself, is true or likely true. If the premises are neither true nor likely true, they provide no basis for accepting the conclusion.

2. Formal strength is a matter of argument form and concerns the support relationship between the premises and conclusion. The question is whether the premises taken together, assuming they are true, provide sufficient support for the conclusion. If not, they provide little or no basis for accepting the conclusion.

For an argument to be strong overall, it must have both content strength and formal strength. For an argument to be strong overall, two questions must be answered in the affirmative: (1) Are the premises true or likely true? and (2) Do the premises provide sufficient support for the conclusion? If the answer to the first is yes, the argument has satisfied the content requirements and has content strength. If the answer to the second is yes, the argument has satisfied the formal requirements and has formal strength. When an argument is strong overall, its conclusion is true or likely true.

Argument Content and Content Strength; Argument Form and Formal Strength

An argument can be evaluated in two different dimensions: its content and its form. Argument content concerns the premises and whether they are true or likely true. Argument form concerns the support relationship between the premises and the conclusion and whether the premises provide sufficient support for the conclusion. An argument satisfies the content requirements (has content strength) when it has premises that are all true or likely true. An argument satisfies the formal requirements (has formal strength) when it has premises that provide sufficient support for the conclusion. An argument is strong overall when it has both forms of strength.

In this chapter and the next, we focus on the evaluation of formal strength; Chapter 8 takes up the evaluation of content strength.

EXERCISE SET 6.1

For each of these arguments, do *one* of the following, as appropriate:
  (1) Provide a content criticism (raise questions about the truth of a premise).
  (2) Provide a formal criticism (raise questions about whether the premise(s) provide sufficient support for the conclusion).
  (3) Provide both a content and a formal criticism.

(Hint: When you are considering formal criticisms, assume that the premises are true, and ask yourself whether the premises provide sufficient support for the conclusion.)

EXAMPLE

The United States has won every war it has ever fought. So, if the United States gets into a nuclear war, it will win that one, too.

ANSWER

We can give both a content criticism and a formal criticism of this argument. The content criticism is that the premise, expressed by the first sentence, is false.

The United States has not won every war it ever fought. It did not win the War of 1812 or the Korean War, and it lost the Vietnam War. The formal criticism is that the premise does not provide sufficient support for the conclusion. Nuclear weapons are so different from non-nuclear weapons that, even if the premise is true, it does not provide strong support for the conclusion. We cannot make reliable judgments about how a nuclear would go based on knowledge of how non-nuclear wars have gone.

PROBLEMS

1. All heroin addicts drank milk early in their lives. So, milk drinking leads to heroin addiction.
2. All heroin addicts drank wine regularly when they were young. So, early wine drinking leads to heroin addiction.
3. (Said in early 1992): A Republican has won every presidential race for the past 24 years. Certainly, a Republican will win in 1992.
4. A man falling from the top of the Empire State Building has fallen sixty stories without any harm coming to him. Therefore, he will fall the rest of the way without any harm coming to him. (Consider a formal criticism only.)
5. The United States has the best male soccer players in the world. The United States is certain to win the next World Cup.
6. All Berliners are Europeans. All Germans are Europeans. So, all Berliners are Germans.
7. My brother just got a nose ring. My boyfriend's sister just got a nose ring. So, most young people must have nose rings by now. (Consider a formal criticism only.)
8. In all societies throughout history, men have dominated women. It stands to reason that in our own society we cannot achieve true equality of the sexes.

6.2 Deductive Arguments and Validity

An argument that has the highest level of formal strength has **validity.** When the premises provide *complete* support for the conclusion, the argument is valid. In other words, an argument is valid when it is impossible for the premises to be true and the conclusion to be false. Validity is also known as deductive validity because, in a valid argument, the conclusion can be deduced from the premises. Recall our discussion in Chapter 2 of implication, the strongest form of support relationship. A valid argument is an argument in which the premises, taken together, have an implication relation to the conclusion.

To say that an argument is valid is *not* to say that the premises are true. The truth of the premises is a matter of content, not form. To say that an argument is valid is, rather, to say that *if* the premises are true *then* the conclusion is true. Consider these examples:

Example 6.3

A.   P1: If a being is human, it is a mammal.
      P2: If a being is a mammal, it is warm-blooded.
      C: Therefore, if a being is human, it is warm-blooded.

B.   P1: All men are 30 feet tall.
      P2: Socrates is a man.
      C: Therefore, Socrates is 30 feet tall.

Both of these arguments are valid even though argument B has an obviously false premise. Still, in the case of B, if the premises were true, then the conclusion would be true.

Arguments that are valid are **deductive arguments** because, as noted previously, we can deduce the conclusion from the premises. Arguments that look similar in their pattern of premises and conclusion to valid arguments but that are not valid are **invalid.** Consider this argument:

Example 6.4

        P1: All humans are creatures with backbones.
        P2: All reptiles are creatures with backbones.
        C: Therefore, all humans are reptiles.

Clearly, this argument is invalid. The premises are true, but they do not guarantee the truth of the conclusion, because the conclusion is in fact false.[3]

> ## Validity, Invalidity, and Deductive Arguments
>
> Validity (also known as deductive validity) is the highest level of formal strength. In a valid argument, the premises taken together have an implication relationship to the conclusion. If the premises are true, then the conclusion must be true. It is impossible for the premises to be true and the conclusion to be false; the truth of the premises guarantees the truth of the conclusion. A valid argument is called a deductive argument because the conclusion can be deduced from the premises. Arguments that look like valid arguments but are not valid are invalid.

6.2.1 Validity, Invalidity, and the Method of Counterexample

Validity is an all-or-nothing characteristic in the sense that a deductive argument is either valid or invalid. There is no in-between, no gray area. Deductive arguments are not more or less valid, or almost valid, or partially valid. One deductive argument cannot be more valid than another; a deductive argument is either strong, in which case it is valid, or weak, in which case it is invalid.

When you evaluate a deductive argument for formal strength, you consider whether its form is valid or invalid. An argument form is a pattern that can be repeated in different arguments with different content. Consider these arguments:

Example 6.5

A.   P1: If the universe began with the big bang, then it is between 10 and 20 billion years old.
     P2: The universe began with the big bang.
     C: Therefore, the universe is between 10 and 20 billion years old.

B.   P1: If Sally went rock climbing today, then she will be dead tired when she gets home.
     P2: Sally went rock climbing today.
     C: Therefore, Sally will be dead tired when she gets home.

Despite the fact that these two arguments are very different in content, they have the same form. Notice that in each case the first premise is a conditional statement, the second is the antecedent of that conditional, and the conclusion is the consequent. Recall that a conditional does not assert the truth of either of the statements that compose it. So, in these arguments, the first premise does not assert that either of its component statements is true. But the other premise asserts the truth of one component (the antecedent), and the conclusion asserts the truth of the other component (the consequent).

We can see this form more clearly if we abstract from the content of these arguments—that is, if we substitute variables for the statements that compose them. Let us use "x" for the antecedent and "y" for the consequent of a conditional. In making the substitution, we keep the terms "if" and "then" to show that the argument contains a conditional.

Example 6.6

     P1: If x, then y.
     P2: x.
     C: Therefore, y.

Any argument that has this form, whatever its content, is a valid argument. That is, it is impossible for the premises to be true and the conclusion to be false. This form occurs so frequently in deductive arguments that it has its own name—*modus ponens,* or "affirming the antecedent." The second premise asserts or affirms the antecedent of the conditional in the first premise.

But not all argument forms are valid. Consider this argument and its form:

Example 6.7

Argument

     P1: If the market goes up, then the endowment will prosper.

     P2: The endowment has prospered.

     C: Therefore, the market has gone up.

Form

     P1: If x, then y.

     P2: y.

     C: Therefore, x.

Any argument that has this form is invalid. To illustrate, consider another argument with the same form:

Example 6.8

P1: If my TV is working, then my TV is plugged in.

P2: My TV is plugged in.

C: Therefore, my TV is working.

The premises of this argument could be true and yet the conclusion still be false. That is, the TV might not work even though it is plugged in, perhaps because one of its components is burned out. Similarly, in the previous example, the endowment could be flourishing even if the market is down, perhaps because the college received a large donation.

This invalid form is known as "affirming the consequent." In this form, the second premise affirms the consequent, in contrast to *modus ponens*, in which the second premise affirms the antecedent. Because this form is invalid, any argument that has this form is faulty. A fault in an argument is called a fallacy. Thus, affirming the consequent is referred to as a formal fallacy.

Our discussion of affirming the consequent suggests one way of testing whether an argument is invalid. To show that an argument is invalid, you need to show that its form is invalid. For the argument about endowments, we devised a different argument with the same form, the one about my television, in which it is obvious that the premises could be true and the conclusion false. This proves that the form is invalid. Thus the argument about endowments is invalid because it has that invalid form.

This method of testing arguments for invalidity is known as the **method of counterexample.** The argument example you devise that has true premises and a false conclusion is an example that runs counter to the claim that the argument you are testing is valid. To say that an argument is valid is to say that *no* argument with that form can have true premises and a false conclusion. The counterexample shows that this claim is false. The method of counterexample, however, has one important limitation. You cannot use it to prove that an argument is *valid*. Even if you are unable to find a counterexample for some particular form, this does not show that there is not one out there yet to be found.

The Method of Counterexample

The method of counterexample is a way to test a deductive argument for formal strength, to determine whether the argument is invalid. To apply the test, you look for an argument with the same form that has obviously true premises and a false conclusion. If you find such an argument, then the argument form is invalid, as is the argument you are testing. If you cannot find such an argument, however, this does not show that the argument is valid.

In both the valid form *modus ponens* and the invalid form affirming the consequent, the second premise affirms one of the statements in the conditional. But many deductive arguments with a conditional as the first premise involve, not the affirmation, but the *denial* of the antecedent or the consequent. To deny a statement is to claim that it is false. (The denial of a statement x is often represented by "not x.")

Consider these arguments:

Example 6.9

A.　P1:　If the new president is to win our confidence, then he will pardon the old president.
　　　P2:　The new president will not pardon the old president.
　　　C:　Therefore, the new president will not win our confidence.

B.　P1:　If Samantha wins the lottery, then she will buy a new house.
　　　P2:　Samantha did not win the lottery.
　　　C:　Therefore, Samantha did not buy a new house.

In argument A, the consequent is denied; in argument B, the antecedent is denied. A has a valid form, known as *modus tollens,* or "denying the consequent." But B has an invalid form, known as "denying the antecedent." In order to see that B is invalid, we can apply the method of counterexample.

Here is an argument with the same form as argument B that has obviously true premises and a false conclusion:

Example 6.10

　　　P1:　If it is raining, then clouds are in the sky.
　　　P2:　It is not raining.
　　　C:　Therefore, there are no clouds in the sky.

Obviously, it is possible for the premises to be true and the conclusion to be false. There are many cloudy days when it does not rain. Thus, the argument form denying the antecedent is invalid.

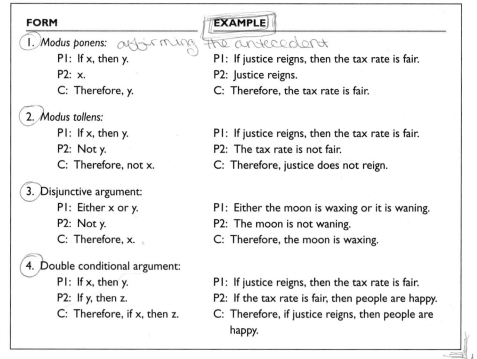

FORM   EXAMPLE

1. *Modus ponens:* affirming the antecedent
   - P1: If x, then y.   P1: If justice reigns, then the tax rate is fair.
   - P2: x.   P2: Justice reigns.
   - C: Therefore, y.   C: Therefore, the tax rate is fair.

2. *Modus tollens:*
   - P1: If x, then y.   P1: If justice reigns, then the tax rate is fair.
   - P2: Not y.   P2: The tax rate is not fair.
   - C: Therefore, not x.   C: Therefore, justice does not reign.

3. Disjunctive argument:
   - P1: Either x or y.   P1: Either the moon is waxing or it is waning.
   - P2: Not y.   P2: The moon is not waning.
   - C: Therefore, x.   C: Therefore, the moon is waxing.

4. Double conditional argument:
   - P1: If x, then y.   P1: If justice reigns, then the tax rate is fair.
   - P2: If y, then z.   P2: If the tax rate is fair, then people are happy.
   - C: Therefore, if x, then z.   C: Therefore, if justice reigns, then people are happy.

FIGURE 6.1   Some Valid Argument Forms Involving Compound Statements

6.2.2 Some Valid and Invalid Argument Forms

We have identified two valid forms so far, *modus ponens* and *modus tollens*. Figure 6.1 gives examples of these forms and of two other commonly occurring valid forms. All of these forms except for the disjunctive argument use conditionals. But a disjunctive statement (the first premise of that form), like the conditional, is a compound statement composed of two other statements, x and y. The term "disjunction" refers to a compound statement that connects simple statements with the term "or."

In addition to valid forms with compound statements, like conditionals or disjunctions, as premises, there are valid forms involving a universal generalization as a premise. Figure 6.2 gives examples of three of these. The variables in these forms refer not to statements, as the variables in the previous examples do, but to individuals or groups of individuals. As the examples illustrate, the lowercase variables m, n, and o refer to classes (groups) of individuals, such as stars, things that twinkle, and things that are far away. The uppercase variable A refers to particular individuals, in this case Betelgeuse or Venus.

As you may have noticed, there is a rough correspondence between some of the valid forms involving conditionals and the valid forms involving universal generalizations. For example, *modus ponens* (1) corresponds roughly to form 5, *modus tollens* (2) to form 6, and the double conditional (4) to form 7. (We will discuss these

FORM	EXAMPLE

5.   P1: All m are n.
      P2: A is an m.
      C: Therefore, A is an n.
	P1: All stars are twinkling things.
	P2: Betelgeuse is a star.
	C: Therefore, Betelgeuse is a twinkling thing.

6.   P1: All m are n.
      P2: A is not an n.
      C: Therefore, A is not an m.
	P1: All stars are twinkling things.
	P2: Venus is not a twinkling thing.
	C: Therefore, Venus is not a star.

7.   P1: All m and n.
      P2: All n and o.
      C: Therefore, all m and o.
	P1: All stars are twinkling things.
	P2: All twinkling things are far away.
	C: Therefore, all stars are far away.

FIGURE 6.2   Some Valid Argument Forms Involving Universal Generalizations

FORMS	COUNTEREXAMPLES

1. Affirming the consequent:
    P1: If x, then y.
    P2: y.
    C: Therefore, x.
	P1: If my TV is working, then it is plugged in.
	P2: My TV is plugged in.
	C: Therefore, my TV is working.

2. Denying the antecedent:
    P1: If x, then y.
    P2: Not x.
    C: Therefore, not y.
	P1: If it is raining, then clouds are in the sky.
	P2: It is not raining.
	C: Therefore, there are no clouds in the sky.

3.   P1: All m are n.
      P2: A is an n.
      C: Therefore, A is an m.
	P1: All court orders are things to be obeyed.
	P2: This is a thing to be obeyed.
	C: Therefore, this is a court order.

4.   P1: All m are n.
      P2: A is not an m.
      C: Therefore, A is not an n.
	P1: All court orders are things to be obeyed.
	P2: This is not a court order.
	C: Therefore, this is not a thing to be obeyed.

FIGURE 6.3   Some Invalid Argument Forms

two ways of representing arguments, one with conditionals and the other with generalizations, in detail in the next chapter.[4])

Figure 6.3 gives some examples of commonly occurring invalid forms. Two of these we have discussed already—affirming the consequent and denying the antecedent. Note that the examples are all counterexamples.

The arguments we encounter in our everyday lives are often deductive arguments that fit one of the forms discussed previously. But it can be difficult to perceive the form of the argument in the text. Often, you have to do considerable reformulation to create an argument structure that reveals the form. Deductive arguments in everyday contexts are seldom expressed in a way that makes their structure clear. When you find an argument that contains a conditional or a general 'statement, consider that it may be a deductive argument that fits one of these forms and see if you can structure it accordingly. These arguments often have an implicit conclusion. (They often have an implicit premise as well, as we discuss in the next section.) Consider this example:

Example 6.11

Background: This is a portion of a letter on the issue of whether the census should ask questions about race. (*New York Times,* 4/00)

> ① If the census stopped asking about race, we could not compare black and white unemployment, life expectancy or family wealth. ② Racial statistics remain essential to reveal how far we have progressed from our racialized past, and how far we still need to travel.—E.F.

Sentence 1 is a conditional, which suggests that this should be interpreted as a deductive argument. The premise expressed by sentence 1 is that, if the census did not ask racial questions, we would not be able compare blacks and whites in our society in terms of employment, life expectancy, or family wealth. The next important step in the interpretation is to recognize sentence 2 as a denial of the consequent. Because the consequent is a negative, its denial is a double negative, which, in general, is a positive. The statement expressed by sentence 2 is that we should be able to make such comparisons. Thus, the argument has the form of *modus tollens.* As a result, the conclusion, which is implicit, is that the census should ask racial questions—a denial of the antecedent. Here is the structure:

Example 6.12

P1: If the census did not ask racial questions, then we would not be able compare blacks and whites in our society in terms of employment, life expectancy, or family wealth.
P2: We should be able to make such comparisons.
C: Therefore, the census should ask racial questions.

Although the forms given above are among the most common deductive forms, there are others as well. In the next chapter, we will explore some other methods, besides the method of counterexample, to distinguish between valid and invalid deductive argument forms.

6.2.3 Sound Arguments

When a deductive argument is valid *and* has true premises, it is a **sound argument.** In contrast, when a deductive argument is either invalid or has premises not all of which are true, it is an **unsound argument.** Sound arguments have a special feature: their conclusions are always true. It is easy to show that this is so. If an argument is sound, it is valid, and if an argument is valid, then the following is true: If the premises are true, then the conclusion is true. But a sound argument also has true premises, which means that the antecedent of this conditional is affirmed. So, by *modus ponens*, the conclusion of a sound argument is true.

Sound and Unsound Arguments

Soundness and unsoundness are features of deductive arguments based on considerations of both formal and content strength. A deductive argument that is valid and has all true premises is sound. A deductive argument that either is invalid or has at least one false premise is unsound. A sound argument has a true conclusion.

EXERCISE SET 6.2

SECTION A: For each of the following deductive arguments, determine whether it is valid or invalid by structuring it (no tree diagram needed) and matching its form with one of the valid or invalid forms given in Figures 6.1, 6.2, and 6.3.

EXAMPLE
All smokers have heart disease.
Baker has heart disease.
Therefore, Baker is a smoker.

ANSWER
Invalid, pattern 3
> P1: All smokers are people with heart disease.
> P2: Baker is a person with heart disease.
>   C: Therefore, Baker is a smoker.

PROBLEMS
1. Abel did not go to law school because all lawyers go to law school and Abel is not a lawyer.
2. If Chris takes performance-enhancing drugs, Chris should be banned from sport. Chris should be banned from sport. It follows that Chris takes performance-enhancing drugs.
3. All those who participate in class discussion get good grades. Cain participates in class discussion. So, Cain gets good grades.
4. If Jonah's doctor gives Jonah a clean bill of health, Jonah is healthy. Because Jonah's doctor did not give Jonah a clean bill of health, Jonah is not healthy.
5. Jumbo is an elephant, and elephants have four knees. It follows that Jumbo has four knees.
6. All who surf the Internet are socially isolated. Diane is not socially isolated. Therefore, Diane does not surf the Internet.
7. Mona is rich because all rich people vote Republican, and so does Mona.

8. Humans are territorial animals, and all territorial animals fight members of their own species. It follows that humans fight members of their own species.

❖ 9. Either those who are now young will be denied Social Security when they retire or the government will go bankrupt. But the government cannot go bankrupt. The conclusion is obvious.

10. If Wilson is an adolescent, then she thinks she is immortal. If she thinks she is immortal, she will act imprudently. So, if Wilson is an adolescent, she will act imprudently.

11. All modern wars are unjust. World War II was not unjust. So, World War II was not a modern war.

❖ 12. Drunk drivers should be sent to prison. Why? Because all those who put others' lives in danger should be sent to prison, and drunk drivers do this.

13. Sarah cannot vote because the legal voting age is 18, and Sarah is only 3.

14. We know the stegosaurus is older than the saber-toothed tiger because if a fossil is buried deeper than another it is older than that other, and stegosaurus fossils are buried deeper than saber-toothed tiger fossils.

❖ 15. If a person is dead, that person cannot be harmed. This follows from two obvious facts. First, a person cannot be harmed if that person has no experience. Second, if a person is dead, that person has no experience.

16. Whenever I go to the restaurant, I have dessert. I did not have dessert. So, I did not go to the restaurant.

SECTION B: For the following arguments, try to determine whether they are invalid by applying the method of counterexample. Indicate the form of the argument, and give an example of that form in which it is obvious that the premises are true and the conclusion is false.

EXAMPLE

If a government is corrupt, the government is doing a poor job governing. If a nation is in poverty, the government is doing a poor job governing. So, if a government is corrupt, the nation is in poverty.

ANSWER

P1: If x, then y.
P2: If z, then y.
C: Therefore, if x, then z.

The argument form is invalid, as this counterexample shows.

P1: If it is raining, then clouds are in the sky.
P2: If it is snowing, then clouds are in the sky.
C: Therefore, if it is raining, then it is snowing.

Obviously, the premises of this argument are true, but the conclusion is false. While it may sometimes be snowing and raining at the same time, this is usually not the case.

PROBLEMS

1. All professional athletes are rich, and we know that all those with a good head for figures are rich. It follows that all professional athletes have a good head for figures.

2. If it is Halloween, the air is nippy. In addition, if it is Halloween, the hours of daylight are growing shorter. So, if the air is nippy, the hours of daylight are growing shorter.

❖ 3. If a course is popular, it will be heavily enrolled. If a course is heavily enrolled, the quality of the class discussion will be low. The quality of the discussion in this course is low. So, this must be a popular course.

4. All fast food is inexpensive, and all fast food tastes bad. Therefore, all inexpensive food tastes bad.

SECTION C: Consider the following deductive arguments, each of which fits one of the forms presented in Figures 6.1, 6.2, and 6.3. Structure the argument (no tree diagram needed) to show the form.

EXAMPLE

Background: This is a portion of a letter written in response to an editorial that criticized the "three-strikes" law, a law requiring that a person convicted three times of felonies be imprisoned for life, on the grounds that it can apply to minor criminals. (*Los Angeles Times*, 5/97)

As a taxpayer I believe in efficiency. As a person I believe in fairness. Most of us thought that the three-strikes law applied to violent crimes. The use of the three-strikes law to put away drug abusers with long jail sentences is stupid on both counts.—D.E.

ANSWER

The argument form is *modus ponens*. The argument is valid.

P1: If the three-strikes law is used to put away drug abusers with long jail sentences, that law is inefficient and unfair.
P2: The three-strikes law is used to put away drug abusers with long jail sentences.
C: Therefore, the law is inefficient and unfair.

PROBLEMS

1. Background: This is a portion of a letter about the 1999 war by the United States and its allies against Serbia over its antihuman policies in Kosovo. It is in response to a columnist who criticized the methods used in the war. (*New York Times*, 4/99) (Hint: Use a conditional.)

   I was amazed at your columnist's wondering why targets like bridges, communications installations and power stations are being hit. Yet if the Yugoslav military and police didn't use those resources, I doubt they would be high on the target list.—D.W.

2. Background: This is a portion of a letter about baseball. (*Chicago Tribune*, 4/97) (Hint: Use a conditional.)

   Can't something be done to speed up baseball? I think the players and management should be reminded that they are being paid by the fans, and if they want to give the fans a "break"—speed the game up.—L.F.

❖ 3. Background: This is a portion of a letter commenting on New York City's garbage policies. (*New York Times*, 2/99) (Hint: Use a conditional.)

New York City's plan to dump its garbage in other states' landfills would engender less ill will if our municipal government made a real commitment to reducing the amount of garbage we create. Legislation pending in the City Council would require agencies to practice waste prevention in the procurement of goods and services. Its passage would demonstrate that New York is making a good-faith effort to minimize the burden we ask communities with waste facilities—here and in other states—to shoulder.—N.C.

4. Background: This is a portion of a letter concerning the cause of death of a young boy memorialized in a New York City monument. (*New York Times*, 7/97) (Hint: Use a conditional.)

    The caption with a photograph of the Amiable Child monument says 5-year-old St. Claire Pollock drowned in 1797. It is more likely he died in the yellow fever epidemic. In a letter of Jan. 18, 1800, the father noted that an urn would be erected over the grave, but gave no indication of how the boy died. As many children died from yellow fever then, such a death would not have merited mention. An accidental tragedy would have.—A.A.

5. Background: This is a portion of a letter about the position on abortion of Rick Lazio, a 2000 candidate for the U.S. Senate from New York. (*New York Times*, 5/00) (Hint: Use a universal generalization.)

    A right is real only so much as it is available. Mr. Lazio's position is reminiscent of the pre-*Roe v. Wade* days when abortion, while illegal in most states, was always available to those who could pay for it.—G.E.S.

6. Background: This is a portion of a letter on the issue of campaign finance reform. It is about whether certain restrictions of contributions (on so-called soft money) should apply only to political parties or to private political advocacy groups as well. (*New York Times*, 7/99) (Hint: Use conditionals.)

    If soft money restrictions were applicable only to political parties, wealthy individuals and organizations would merely channel their donations to private groups, which through "issue ads" subtly endorse candidates. The result? Already weakened political parties would grow weaker while shadowy issue groups and their financial supporters increase their political influence over candidates.—K.A.

7. Background: This is a portion of a letter in response to an editorial critical of plans to expand NATO into Eastern Europe. NATO is a military alliance established in 1949 by the United States and the nations of western Europe to counter the former Soviet Union. (*New York Times*, 7/97) (Hint: Use a conditional.)

    Your editorial says, "Expanding NATO now may well complicate the transformation of Europe." If so, why is there not more opposition to enlarging the alliance from the European members? Some want to add two more new members, Slovenia and Romania.—K.W.R.

8. Background: This is a portion of a letter on capital punishment. (*New York Times*, 9/88) (Hint: Use a conditional.)

I am opposed to capital punishment, but can find one strong case where it should be carried out: against terrorism and hostage taking. If death is the only penalty for terrorism or hostage taking, further escalation of that problem will stop. This can be achieved if the United States gives a lead, with United Nations support, for all nations to pass legislation to make it understood that the death penalty in such cases will be universal.—S.W.

❖   9. Background: This is a portion of a letter on the violence afflicting American high schools. (*New York Times*, 5/99) (Hint: Use conditionals.)

The rage that we have seen will continue as long as young adults are victimized, marginalized and made to feel worthless by their peers. When people feel worthless, everything around them seems worthless as well, often leading to disastrous consequences.—M.E.

6.3 Implicit Premises

In Chapter 5, we introduced the idea of implicit premises, but the discussion there was limited to a special kind of implicit premise, an intermediate implicit premise. Now that we have introduced deductive arguments, we can broaden the discussion of implicit premises.

Implicit premises occur primarily in deductive arguments, because an implicit premise is always a linked premise. All deductive arguments with more than one premise have linked premises.[5] In addition, most arguments with linked premises are deductive arguments.

Many deductive arguments, as we have seen, contain a premise that is a conditional statement or a general statement. Often, an argument will have such a premise, but the text will not explicitly include the premise with which it is linked. So, if an argument has only a single explicit premise and that premise is a conditional statement or a general statement, the argument is probably a deductive argument with an implicit premise. Consider these examples:

Example 6.13

A. If human beings are the only animals that have a culture, then they are superior to other animals. It follows that human beings are superior to other animals.
B. If a planet has life, then it must have liquid water. Therefore, Mercury has no life.
C. All professors are argumentative. Thus, Norton is argumentative.

Each of these arguments has a single explicit premise that is either a conditional or a general statement, and each can be interpreted as a deductive argument with an implicit premise.

Here are the implicit premises:

Example 6.14

A. Human beings are the only animals that have a culture.
B. Mercury has no liquid water.

C. Norton is a professor.

In figuring out what the implicit premises are, notice that each of the arguments corresponds to one of the deductive argument forms discussed in the last section. That is, argument A corresponds to *modus ponens*, argument B to *modus tollens*, and argument C to form 5 in Figure 6.2. Those argument forms indicate what the implicit premise is.

Thus, the deductive argument forms show us how to find implicit premises. When an argumentative text contains a conditional statement or a general statement as the only (explicit) premise, then the argument is usually best interpreted as a deductive argument with an implicit premise. To determine what the implicit premise is, consider, in the light of what is explicit in the argument, which of the argument forms the argument fits. The form will indicate what the implicit premise should be. We can represent this as another rule of addition.

> ## Rule of Addition, Number 3
>
> When an argument contains a conditional statement or a general statement as its only (explicit) premise, it is usually best to understand it as a deductive argument with an implicit premise. The implicit premise is indicated by the form of the argument. Use the explicit parts of the argument (the one premise and usually the conclusion) to determine the form (from the earlier lists), and add the appropriate implicit premise.

Some of these deductive arguments with an implicit premise also have an implicit conclusion. An author will sometimes present, for example, a conditional statement in a way that makes clear from the context that either the antecedent or the consequent (or their denial) is meant as the (implicit) conclusion. The argument form will then indicate the implicit premise, although the correct form is often more difficult to identify in such cases.

According to this rule, we can interpret many everyday arguments as deductive arguments with implicit premises. But, as we saw in the last section, interpreting deductive arguments found in everyday contexts can be tricky. Following are some arguments that can be interpreted in this way. As we saw before, you often have to do extensive reformulation to show how arguments fit the deductive forms that reveal their implicit premises.

Example 6.15

A. Background: This letter is in response to an editorial critical of the proposal to expand into Central Europe the North Atlantic Treaty Organization (NATO), a military defense alliance formed in 1949 to oppose the former Soviet Union. (*New York Times*, 5/98)

① The lessons that you draw from history in your opposition to the expansion of the North Atlantic Treaty Organization are incomplete. ② The major wars that have been fought in Europe in the 20th century began in the region of Central and south-eastern Europe precisely when the interests of smaller countries were ignored in favor of their larger neighbors.—T.D.K.

B. Background: This letter is about the practice of working medical interns long hours without sleep as part of their residency training. (*New York Times*, 6/00)

① The problem with arbitrarily limiting hours that interns or residents must work relates to how they respond to stresses of their professions once their training is completed. ② If they are trained to make good decisions only when well rested, then that is the only time they will make them.—P.S.G.

Consider argument A. Given what we know of the context, as indicated in the background material, and in light of sentence 1, the author seems to be critical of an editorial that itself is critical of the expansion of NATO. Thus, we may assume that the argument has an implicit conclusion that is favorable about the expansion of NATO. Sentence 2, a universal generalization, talks about situations in which war has begun in Europe. To connect this claim with the implicit conclusion, we need a premise claiming that the expansion of NATO will avoid such situations. This is our implicit premise. Because sentence 2 expresses a universal generalization, we can use one of the forms involving such generalizations. The one that seems to fit is form 6 from Figure 6.2. This would be the resulting structure:

Example 6.16

P1: The major wars that have been fought in Europe in the twentieth century are conflicts that began when the interests of smaller countries in central and southeastern Europe were ignored in favor of their larger neighbors.

IP2: Expanding NATO is an action that would not ignore the interests of smaller countries in central and southeastern Europe in favor of their larger neighbors.

IC: Therefore, expanding NATO would avoid such conflicts beginning.

Now consider argument B. Here, it is clear from sentence 1 that the author's conclusion is in opposition to the idea of limiting the hours interns work in residency. The explicit premise, a conditional, expressed in both sentences 1 and 2, is that if interns are trained only when well rested, then they will not respond well to the stresses of their profession. The conclusion, because it opposes the policy of limiting hours, is a denial of the antecedent. This suggests that the pattern is *modus tollens* and that the implicit premise is the denial of the consequent. Here is the resulting structure:

Example 6.17

P1: If interns are trained to make good decisions only when well rested, then they will not respond well to the stresses of their profession.

IP2: Interns need to respond well to the stresses of their profession.

C: Therefore, interns should not be trained to make good decisions only when well rested.

The implicit premises discussed here apply to arguments in which the explicit premise is a conditional or a general statement. One question that arises is whether there are deductive arguments in which the conditional or the general statement is the implicit premise. This question is addressed in Chapter 10.

EXERCISE SET 6.3

SECTION A: Structure each of the following argumentative texts in terms of the argument forms (valid or invalid) listed in Figures 6.1, 6.2, and 6.3. Include the implicit premise. Many of them may be structured using either conditionals or universal generalizations.

EXAMPLE

All seniors think that they are wise. So, Sally is not a senior.

ANSWER

P1: All seniors are people who think that they are wise.
IP2: Sally does not think that she is wise.
C: Therefore, Sally is not a senior.

Valid; form 6.

PROBLEMS

1. All records of players who took bodybuilding drugs should be stricken from the record books. So, Mark McGwire should have his baseball records stricken from the books.
2. Surfing the Internet leads to social isolation. Clearly, Pat does not surf the Internet.
3. The lion is not the king of the jungle because the king of the jungle is always the largest animal.
4. In 2000, either Bush was going to be elected president or Gore was going to be elected president. It follows that Bush was elected president.
5. What you remember on your deathbed is what was most important in your life. So, Kane's sled was what was most important to him.
6. All intellectuals are absent-minded. Therefore, Henry is an intellectual.
7. Men are more intelligent than women because those with the bigger brains are more intelligent.
8. Ronald Reagan was a good president because all good presidents are actors.
9. If an actor comes from Indiana University, he is a great actor. So, Kevin is a great actor.
10. If a disease is devastating, it should be eradicated. It follows that the common cold should not be eradicated.
11. All who tire of London, tire of life. So, Jose does not tire of London.
12. The only way to get someone to do something he initially does not want to do is to persuade him or coerce him. So, Ed was persuaded into doing what he initially did not want to do.
13. The Federal Reserve Board will not raise interest rates because it raises rates whenever there is a serious threat of inflation.
14. If it is my birthday, I am getting presents. So, it must be my birthday.

SECTION B: Structure each of the following arguments (no tree diagram needed), adding the implicit premise. In some cases, an implicit conclusion will be needed as well. All of them can be structured in terms of either *modus ponens* or *modus tollens*. Indicate which form you are using. Assume in each case that it is clear from the context that the author intends to present an argument, even if only a single statement is presented. Most of these are passages from longer letters.

EXAMPLE

Background: This letter, which is critical of laws against "physician-assisted suicide," is part of the debate over euthanasia. (*Boston Globe*, 7/97)

Neither side in the controversy over physician-assisted suicide has confronted the basic question: Does a person's life belong to that person or to the state? In a democracy, does an individual person, if he is injuring no one, not have the right to be let alone?—E.B.

ANSWER

The form is *modus ponens*.

    P1: If a person is injuring no one, that person should be let alone by the law.
    IP2: A person practicing physician-assisted suicide is injuring no one.
    IC: Therefore, that person should be let alone by the law.

PROBLEMS

1. Background: This letter is in response to those who claim that the lack of new housing construction in New York City is due to rent regulation. (*New York Times*, 5/97)

   If they're not building new housing now, deregulation will do nothing to change that.—M.R.N.

2. Background: This letter is about the publicity sought by Marcia Clark, one of the lead prosecutors in the criminal trial of O.J. Simpson for the murder of his former wife, Nicole Brown Simpson, and her friend Ron Goldman. Simpson was found not guilty. (*Boston Globe*, 6/97)

   From where I come from, when your professional incompetence allows a murderer to walk the streets, you hide your face in shame. You don't start signing autographs.—T.J.C.

3. Background: This letter is about a proposed settlement between the government and the tobacco companies whereby the companies would agree to pay the government compensation for cigarette-related health care expenses. (*Los Angeles Times*, 6/97)

   When we the people (thanks to our elected official guardians and conservators) become putative stockholders in the tobacco industry, and get used to receiving dividends to the tune of $368 billion over the next 25 years and $15 billion per year thereafter, will future elected officials be so willing to control the marketing of this murderous drug? Not likely, since we too would be hooked then!—G.E.D.

4. Background: This letter is about Hooters, a chain of restaurants/sports bars that feature scantily clad women as servers. (*Boston Globe*, 10/97)

It's unfortunate that Boston will soon have a Hooters franchise. If we would not patronize a business that mocked minorities, why do we accept a restaurant that trivializes women for the amusement of men? —E.B.

5. Background: In this passage from *The Federalist* 7, Alexander Hamilton argues for the ratification of the Constitution.[6]

America, if not connected at all, or only by the feeble tie of a simple league offensive and defensive, would by the operation of such opposite and jarring alliances be gradually entangled in all the pernicious labyrinths of European politics and wars.

6. Background: This letter about the war over Kosovo is in response to those who argue that we had to fight the war because otherwise our credibility would suffer. (*New York Times*, 3/99)

Yes, if the United States keeps on using intemperate language in dealing with countries, it will find itself, sooner or later, the victim of a self-inflicted credibility loss when the bluff is called. The solution is to not conduct policy by the use of threats.—K.J.C.

7. Background: This letter is in response to a column on capital punishment. (*Los Angeles Times*, 1/98)

According to your columnist, punishment civilizes the appropriate desire for vengeance against lawbreakers and so supports civilization. Oh, really? If so, then shouldn't we encourage the slaughter, even genocide, in the Mideast and the Balkans, since that killing is predicated on vengeance for real (and imagined) wrongs?—K.R.

8. Background: This letter addresses the issue of the efficacy of prayer. The author asks how prayer can be effective. (*Miami Herald*, 5/97)

How can this be? If God is all-powerful and all-knowing, then God must be insulted by those suggesting, through prayer, that man knows more than God and what He should do.—T.C.R.

9. Background: This letter considers the economic implications of the fact that the stability of the economy requires that a certain portion of the population be unemployed. (*New York Times*, 3/85)

Policy makers and editiorialists have invented an entire new profession, that of joblessness, for the sake of maintaining economic stability. If this is necessary, then the unemployed should be suitably rewarded for doing the job that is assigned them.—F.C.T.

10. Background: This is a passage from Charles Darwin's *On the Origin of Species*.[7]

A struggle for existence inevitably follows from the high rate at which all organic beings tend to increase. Every being, which during its natural lifetime produces several eggs or seeds, must suffer destruction during some period of its life . . . otherwise on the principle of geometrical increase, its numbers would quickly become so inordinately great that no country could support the product.

6.4 Nondeductive Arguments and Formal Strength

Deductive arguments are distinguished from **nondeductive arguments.** Deductive arguments are valid arguments, in which the truth of the premises guarantees the truth of the conclusion. In addition, some arguments, such as those in Figure 6.3, that are similar in their formal pattern to valid arguments but in which the truth of the premises does not guarantee the truth of the conclusion, are also called deductive arguments—although invalid ones. All other arguments are nondeductive.

Nondeductive arguments are different in their formal strength from deductive arguments. Formal strength for nondeductive argument is not an all-or-nothing characteristic, as it is for deductive arguments, but a matter of degree. In terms of form, we can describe nondeductive arguments as "very strong," "rather strong," "not very strong," "weak," "very weak," and the like.

Nondeductive arguments cannot be valid. The formal strength of even the strongest nondeductive argument falls short of validity. If an argument is valid, the truth of the premises guarantees the truth of the conclusion. But no matter how strong a nondeductive argument is, the truth of the premises does not *guarantee* the truth of the conclusion. Instead, in a strong nondeductive argument, the truth of the premises shows only that the conclusion is *likely true*. The stronger the nondeductive argument (assuming that the premises are true), the more likely it is that the conclusion is true. Although nondeductive arguments are not valid, they are not referred to as invalid. The term "invalid" is reserved for those deductive arguments that are not valid, like those in Figure 6.3.

Nondeductive Arguments and Formal Strength

A strong nondeductive argument has a level of formal strength short of validity. In a valid argument, the truth of the premises guarantees the truth of the conclusion. In a strong nondeductive argument, the truth of the premises guarantees only the likelihood that the conclusion is true. In a nondeductive argument, it is always possible for the premises to be true and the conclusion false. The stronger a nondeductive argument (assuming the truth of the premises), the more likely the conclusion is to be true.

Consider again this nondeductive argument:

Example 6.18

P1: Jones had a strong motive to murder Smith.
P2: Jones had an opportunity to murder Smith.
P3: The murder weapon had Jones' fingerprints on it.
P4: Jones has no alibi for the time Smith was murdered.
P5: Jones was psychologically capable of killing Smith.
C: Therefore, Jones murdered Smith.

While this is a formally strong argument, the truth of the premises does not guarantee the truth of the conclusion. All the premises may be true without Jones being the murderer. The premises taken together do not imply the conclusion. Still, the argument is formally strong because, if the premises are true, the conclusion is likely true. Given the truth of the premises, while it is possible that Jones is innocent, it is not likely.

This argument shows how the formal strength of nondeductive arguments is a matter of degree. If you take away any one of the premises, the argument will be weaker but still fairly strong. The more premises you take away, the weaker it will get. You could also add premises to make it stronger, such as the premise that Jones knew where the murder weapon was stored. But no matter how many premises *like this* you add, the argument will never achieve the formal strength of validity.[8] It will never become a deductive argument.

The formal strength of a weak nondeductive argument, like that of a strong nondeductive argument, is a matter of degree. Nondeductive arguments are relatively weak or relatively strong. In contrast, deductive arguments are absolutely strong (valid) or absolutely weak (invalid). Figure 6.4 depicts these relationships.

When we first encountered the nondeductive argument about Jones and Smith in Chapter 2, it served to introduce the distinction between linked premises and convergent premises. This argument has convergent premises because each premise supports the conclusion on its own. In contrast, deductive arguments have linked premises because each premise shows how another premise supports the conclusion. This is an important difference between deductive and nondeductive arguments. The premises of a deductive argument are always linked. In contrast, the premises of a nondeductive argument are usually convergent. Sometimes, nondeductive arguments have linked premises, but deductive arguments never have convergent premises.[9]

When a nondeductive argument is formally strong and has premises all of which are true or likely true, it is a **cogent argument.** In contrast, when a nondeductive argument either is not formally strong or includes premises that are neither true nor likely true, it is a **noncogent argument.** Cogency for nondeductive arguments is like soundness for deductive arguments in that it concerns both form and

	Deductive Arguments	Nondeductive Arguments
Strong	Valid	Nondeductively strong
Relation Between Strong and Weak	All-or-nothing	A matter of degree
Weak	Invalid	Nondeductively weak

FIGURE 6.4   Deductive and Nondeductive Arguments and Formal Strength

content. When a nondeductive argument is cogent, its conclusion is true or likely true.

> ### Cogent and Noncogent Arguments
>
> Cogency and noncogency are features of nondeductive arguments based on considerations of both formal and content strength. A nondeductive argument that is formally strong and whose premises are all true or likely true is cogent. A nondeductive argument that either is not formally strong or includes premises that are neither true nor likely true is noncogent. A cogent argument has a conclusion that is true or likely true.

How can you tell the difference between deductive and nondeductive arguments? You need to ask yourself whether it is possible for the premises to be true and the conclusion to be false. If it is not possible, then the argument is deductive. If it is possible, but the argument has a form that is similar to one of the valid forms, then the argument is a deductive argument—but an invalid one. In all other cases, the argument is nondeductive. In practice, deductive arguments are arguments that fit one of the forms in Figures 6.1, 6.2, and 6.3 or other forms of a more elaborate but similar kind.

The most basic way to distinguish among arguments is the division between the deductive and the nondeductive, based, as we have seen, on the factor of formal strength. But there are several kinds of nondeductive arguments, shown in Figure 6.5, that we will examine later in the book. We consider deductive arguments fur-

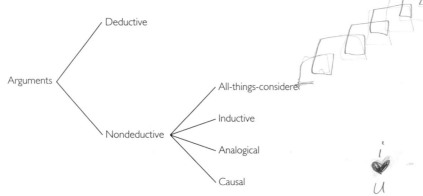

FIGURE 6.5   Types of Arguments

ther in Chapter 7, inductive and causal arguments in Chapter 10, and all-things-considered and analogical arguments in Chapter 11.

EXERCISE SET 6.4

SECTION A: The following nondeductive arguments are all rather weak. In each case, structure the argument (no tree diagram necessary) and indicate what premises you could add that would make the argument stronger. Make the argument as strong as you can. The added premises should not be linked premises and should be, as far as you can tell, true or likely true.

EXAMPLE

You should not burn the candle at both ends. Lack of sleep will cause you to get bags under your eyes.

ANSWER

P1: Lack of sleep will cause you to get bags under your eyes.
C: You should get a good night's sleep.

Premises to add to strengthen the argument:

P2: Lack of sleep will cause you to be more liable to get ill.
P3: Lack of sleep will cause you not to be at your mental and physical best.
P4: Lack of sleep will cause you to feel lousy the next day.

PROBLEMS

1. We should put criminals in prison because that keeps them from committing more crimes while behind bars.
2. The Beatles were the best rock group of the 1960s. Their movie *A Hard Day's Night* created the genre of the rock video.
3. Abraham Lincoln was our greatest president. His speech-making abilities were unparalleled.
4. The moon went through phases last month. So, it will go through phases next month.

5. Reading good literature is a valuable activity because it takes your mind off of your troubles.

❖ 6. It is obvious that the world is round. Note how when ships sailing away reach the horizon, their masts are the last part to disappear.

7. We should explore space so that we can find some place for the human race to go if Earth becomes uninhabitable.

8. Children can take care of you in your old age. Therefore, you should have them.

❖ 9. You should not drive drunk. This follows from the fact that driving drunk can lead to expensive body work on your automobile.

10. You should take a critical thinking course so that you can fulfill the humanities' requirement for your degree.

SECTION B: Consider the argument about Jones murdering Smith in Example 6.18. In a brief essay, describe how it might be possible for all the premises to be true and the conclusion to be false. To do this, you might imagine that you are writing a murder mystery and that the premises, although true, are all false clues planted to distract the readers' attention from the real murderer, whose identity you will reveal in the last chapter—which is your brief essay.

6.5 The Idea of a Fallacy

In both deductive and nondeductive arguments, a weak argument is a faulty argument. You can determine the strength or weakness of an argument in terms of whether it contains faults and how serious those faults are. A weak argument contains serious faults, and a strong argument does not. To evaluate an argument, you identify its particular faults, if any, and argue that it has those faults.[10] A fault in an argument is called a **fallacy.**

In this book, the term "fallacy" refers to any fault in an argument, any feature of an argument that shows it to be weak. A fallacy may be a weakness in form or a weakness in content. Some critical thinking textbooks use the term "fallacy" in a narrower way. For example, it sometimes refers only to faults that are designed to deceive an audience. Some fallacies are quite effective at masking the weakness of arguments, making the weaker argument appear the stronger. Other times, the term refers only to weaknesses in form, not weaknesses in content. But I will use "fallacy" to refer to any weakness, whether of form or content, whether designed to deceive or not.

6.5.1 Four Basic Fallacies

A fallacy is present when an argument fails to meet the requirements of argument strength. Formal requirements are met when the premises provide sufficient support for the conclusion, and content requirements are met when the premises are true or likely true. There are two formal requirements and two content require-

> ### Fallacies
>
> A fallacy is a fault in an argument that contributes to the argument's weakness. Some fallacies are weaknesses in form, and some are weaknesses in content. Some fallacies are effective at disguising weaknesses in arguments, and these fallacies may be deliberately used by authors to deceive. But most fallacies are simply weaknesses of which the author is unaware.

ments. Thus, an argument can fail to be strong in four ways, which means that there are four basic kinds of fallacy in arguments.

Consider formal strength. For an argument to be formally strong, the premises must provide sufficient support for the conclusion. But this requirement encompasses two more basic requirements: **relevance** and **sufficiency.** First, for an argument to be formally strong, the premises must each be relevant to the conclusion. An argument is formally strong only if the premises have a support relationship to the conclusion. When one statement has a support relationship to another, the first is relevant to the second. Second, not only must each premise be relevant to the conclusion, but the premises together must provide support sufficient to show that the conclusion is true or likely true.

Now consider content strength. An argument is strong in terms of content when each of its premises is true or likely true. As discussed previously, being true and being likely true are two different kinds of requirements. The first applies to the statement itself, and the second applies to how the statement is regarded by an audience. A statement is likely true when an audience has a high level of confidence in its truth. We may say that when a statement is likely true, the audience finds the statement *acceptable*—that is, it accepts the statement as true or has no serious questions to raise about its truth.

The source of these two different ways of assessing the content of an argument lies in the two main purposes of an argument, as discussed in earlier chapters: (1) to rationally persuade others and (2) to seek the truth. For an audience to be rationally persuaded of a conclusion, it must regard the premises as acceptable, or likely true. For an argument to further an audience's understanding of the truth, the premises must be true. As a result, there are two content requirements, one related to each of these purposes: **truth** and **acceptability.** For an argument to be strong in content, each premise must be both true and acceptable. Each premise must, in fact, be true and also be regarded by the audience as likely true.

There is a convenient mnemonic to help us to remember these four requirements: **TARS,** which stands for **T**ruth, **A**cceptability, **R**elevance, and **S**ufficiency. The first two are the requirements of content strength, and the last two are the requirements of formal strength. An argument is strong in both form and content if and only if it satisfies the TARS requirements. In terms of form, the premises must be both individually relevant to and collectively sufficient for the conclusion. In terms of content, each premise must be true and acceptable.

> ### The Four Requirements of Argument Strength
>
> For an argument to be strong, it must be strong in both form (relevance and sufficiency) and content (truth and acceptability). The premises of a strong argument must each be relevant to the conclusion and together sufficient to show the conclusion to be true or likely true. Each of the premises of a strong argument, considered by itself, and not in relation to the conclusion, must be both true and acceptable to the audience. The four requirements can be represented by the acronym TARS.

An argument has a fallacy when any of these requirements fails to be satisfied. Since there are four basic requirements, there are four basic fallacies. First, if an argument fails to satisfy the relevance requirement, at least one of its premises is not relevant to the conclusion. This is the fallacy of **irrelevant reason.** Second, if an argument fails to satisfy the sufficiency requirement, its conclusion is based on too little evidence or was drawn too hastily. This is the fallacy of **hasty conclusion.** Third, if an argument fails to satisfy the truth requirement, at least one of its premises is false. This is the fallacy of **false premise.** Finally, if an argument fails to satisfy the acceptability requirement, at least one of its premises is not acceptable to the audience. This is the fallacy of **problematic premise.**[11] Figure 6.6 shows a chart of the four requirements and their corresponding fallacies.

There are other fallacies, some of which will be discussed later, but almost all of them are specific versions of one of the four basic fallacies. Thus, if you understand these four fallacies, you will know what you need to do to evaluate an argument. Evaluating an argument in terms of these fallacies is a way to embody the sense you have about the weaknesses in arguments based on your understanding of the argumentative use of language. By approaching the evaluation of an argument in terms of these fallacies, you can both develop and sharpen your critical instincts.

In this chapter, we will consider the two basic formal fallacies: irrelevant reason and hasty conclusion. We will focus on the basic content fallacies—false premise and problematic premise—in Chapter 8.

6.5.2 A Real-Life Example of a Formal Fallacy

"If it doesn't fit, you must acquit," said Johnnie Cochran, defense lawyer for O.J. Simpson, in his summation to the jury in the famous 1995 trial of Simpson for the

Requirements of Formal or Content Strength	Fallacy of Failure to Satisfy That Requirement
Truth	False premise
Acceptability	Problematic premise
Relevance	Irrelevant reason
Sufficiency	Hasty conclusion

Content { Truth, Acceptability }

Form { Relevance, Sufficiency }

FIGURE 6.6   Basic Requirements of Formal or Content Strength and Their Corresponding Fallacies

murder of his former wife, Nicole Brown Simpson, and her friend Ron Goldman. Cochran argued that the prosecution's case did not fit together into an argument that showed Simpson to be guilty beyond a reasonable doubt.[12] What the defense at any criminal trial must do is to show that the prosecution's argument has some weaknesses—that is, show that there are fallacies in that argument.

Let us look at a rough version of the argument made by the prosecution at Simpson's trial and consider what formal fallacies the defense argued were present in that argument.

Example 6.19

P1: Blood found in Simpson's car, on his sock, and elsewhere is shown by DNA analysis to be the blood of the victims.

P2: A glove found on Simpson's property is the mate to a glove found at the crime scene.

P3: Simpson's whereabouts are unaccounted for during the time when he could have committed the murders.

P4: Simpson had a great deal of anger toward his former wife and a history of domestic violence against her.

C: Therefore, Simpson committed the murders.

How did the defense respond to this argument? Again, we consider only a rough summary.

The defense argued, concerning P1 and P2, that the physical evidence was planted by racist police investigators who were seeking to frame Simpson. The defense did not claim that P1 and P2 were false, but rather, because the evidence was planted, that they did not have a support relationship to the conclusion. If the evidence was planted by the police, then the presence of the evidence was not relevant to the question of whether Simpson was guilty. Thus, the defense claimed, the argument failed the requirement of relevance and thus committed the fallacy of irrelevant reason. P1 and P2 are both irrelevant reasons.

Another criticism offered by the defense was that the prosecution's argument should not be accepted because there were other people, such as drug traffickers, who might have committed the murders, a possibility the police chose not to investigate. In other words, the defense argued that the premises presented by the prosecution, even if true, were not sufficient to show that the conclusion was true. If there was a real possibility that the murders had been committed by someone else, and that possibility was not investigated by the police, all of the evidence the prosecution provided did not amount to a sufficient case. Thus, the defense accused the prosecution of committing the fallacy of hasty conclusion.

6.5.3 Justification

When a fallacy is present in an argument, the argument (or the arguer) commits or is guilty of the fallacy. When you claim that an argument commits a fallacy, you charge the argument with that fallacy, or you make a **fallacy charge.** Thus, you might say, "I charge this argument with the fallacy of hasty conclusion," or "I charge this argument with the fallacy of irrelevant reason at P2." (In the case of irrelevant reason, you need to indicate which premise you are charging.)

When you make a fallacy charge, you do not simply make a claim. As discussed previously, you also provide an argument to support that claim; you give an argument whose conclusion is the claim that the argument you are evaluating commits the fallacy. The argument you give is called the **justification** of the fallacy charge. A justification of a fallacy charge is an argumentative text, usually a paragraph or so in length, in which you give your reasons for the fallacy charge you make.

To illustrate, let's return to the O.J. Simpson case. The Simpson trial was a matter of great public interest and controversy. It was referred to at the time as "the trial of the century." One aspect of its notoriety is that Simpson was acquitted, though most people thought he should have been convicted.[13] So, while the jury thought that the defense had successfully shown fallacies in the prosecution's argument, the majority of the population apparently thought that the defense had not. Each group took a different view of the strength of the justifications that the defense had given for the fallacy charges it made against the prosecution's argument.

Let us consider the justification given by the defense for two of the fallacy charges it made. As discussed previously, the defense charged the prosecution's argument, given in Example 6.19, with the fallacy of irrelevant reason at P1 and P2 and with the fallacy of hasty conclusion. Here is a rough version of the justifications the defense offered for these charges, translated into our terminology:

Example 6.20

1. We charge the prosecution's argument with irrelevant reason at P1 and P2. The argument commits this fallacy because there are questions about the relevance of either premise to the conclusion. There is strong evidence that the blood referred to in P1 and the glove referred to in P2 were planted by the police. If the police planted them, then their presence would have no bearing on the truth of the conclusion; it would not increase the likelihood that Simpson committed the murders. The evidence that the blood and glove were planted by the police is the following: The police officers in question have been shown to have a racial bias against African Americans, and one of them had a strong personal dislike of Simpson as a result of an earlier confrontation. Moreover, the officers had an opportunity to plant the evidence. For example, one of them carried a vile of Simpson's blood to the site at which the evidence was recovered.

2. We charge the prosecution's argument with the fallacy of hasty conclusion. The argument commits this fallacy because the premises together do not provide sufficient support for the conclusion. There is a plausible alternative scenario for who committed the murders that the police did not investigate. Even if all the premises of the prosecution's argument were true, the fact that there is this uninvestigated alternative scenario—that the murders were committed by professional drug dealers—shows that the premises are not sufficient to support the conclusion. The plausibility of this scenario is due to the fact that a former resident of the house was involved with drugs.

Justification of a Fallacy Charge

A fallacy charge is a claim that an argument commits a particular fallacy, as well as an argument in support of that claim. To make a fallacy charge, you must both name the fallacy and argue that the argument commits that fallacy. The argument that you provide to support your claim that the argument you are evaluating commits the fallacy is called a justification.

It is helpful to begin your justifications by following this formula, as suggested in the preceding examples:

I charge this argument with [name the fallacy] at [indicate the premise if the fallacy is irrelevant reason]. The argument commits this fallacy because . . .

This formula is useful because it makes clear precisely what fallacy is being charged and reminds you (through the term "because") that you need to provide a justification (argument) to support the charge.

Arguments may commit more than one fallacy, as in the prosecution's case in the Simpson trial. We charged that argument with both formal fallacies; in fact, we charged it with one of the fallacies, irrelevant reason, twice. In a complex argument, you can make fallacy charges against both the subarguments and the main argument.

We need to make an important qualification to this discussion of formal fallacies: The requirements of formal strength apply differently to deductive arguments than to nondeductive arguments. In the case of deductive arguments, the fallacies of irrelevant reason and hasty conclusion become, in effect, a single fallacy. This is due to the difference between linked and convergent premises. Linked premises must be formally evaluated as a group, whereas convergent premises may, in the case of irrelevant reason, be formally evaluated individually. In the case of linked premises, which are present in all deductive arguments, this means that evaluating relevance becomes part of evaluating sufficiency. We will discuss this further in the next chapter, which is devoted to evaluating deductive arguments. In the remainder of this chapter, we focus on the fallacies of irrelevant reason and hasty conclusion as they apply to nondeductive arguments.

EXERCISE SET 6.5 (OPTIONAL)

Do some research on a famous trial in U.S. history, and write a short essay, like the discussion in sections 6.5.2 and 6.5.3, in which you formulate the argument offered by the prosecution and identify the fallacy charges and justifications offered by the defense. You should focus on formal fallacies, but you may consider content fallacies as well.

6.6 Irrelevant Reason and Hasty Conclusion

As discussed previously, irrelevant reason and hasty conclusion are the two basic formal fallacies. In providing a justification for a charge of irrelevant reason or hasty conclusion, you should argue in terms of the *conditions* for the fallacy being present. Associated with those conditions are justification strategies for arguing that those conditions are satisfied. Figure 6.7 lists the two formal fallacies, along with their conditions and recommended justification strategies.

6.6.1 Charging Irrelevant Reason

Consider the following argument:

Example 6.21

Background: This letter presents a proposal for reducing the size of government. (*Houston Chronicle*, 8/97)

① I have a unique idea on how to reduce the national debt without increasing taxes: Cut Congress in half. ② The constitutional law that provided for our present system

Formal Fallacy	Conditions	Justification Strategies
Irrelevant reason (lack of relevance)	A premise by itself has no support relationship with the conclusion. It is not relevant to the truth of the conclusion, or it supports the claim that the conclusion is false.	Show that the truth of the premise would have no bearing on the truth of the conclusion. Show that the premise and the conclusion concern different issues or that they do not stand in any functional relationship. Alternatively, show that the truth of the premise would actually support the claim that the conclusion is *false*.
Hasty conclusion (lack of sufficiency)	All the premises taken together (assuming they are true) do not provide sufficient support for the conclusion.	In the case of a nondeductive argument: Show what sort of premises are lacking in the argument—that is, what sort of premises should have been included in the argument but were not. In other words, discuss what other factors would need to be considered (in additional premises) before the conclusion would have sufficient support, whether or not you think the truth about those other factors would support the conclusion. The other factors may be of the same type as those discussed in the premises or of a different type. In the case of a deductive argument: Show that the argument is invalid.

FIGURE 6.7   Two Basic Formal Fallacies

was written during the days when the Pony Express was our best means of communication. ③ Today we have moved on to automobiles, airplanes, fax machines, computers, satellites, telephones and television, etc. ④ Cutting Congress in half would mean half as much paid for salaries, travel expenses, staffing, perks, office space, campaigns and half as much time arguing and fighting to pass a bill in Congress.—L.G.

The author's conclusion, expressed in sentence 1, is the action recommendation that Congress should be cut in half. The argument has three main premises, in sentences 1a, 2 and 3, and 4a. The first and third of these support the conclusion, but, it seems, the second does not. That is, the claim that communications are now much faster than when the Constitution was adopted does not seem to be relevant to the conclusion. Given this apparent lack of relevance we can charge this argument with irrelevant reason at P2. The author may have some basis for thinking that the speed of communication is relevant to the size of Congress, but he does not make this basis clear. As a result, a charge of irrelevant reason is in order.

The fallacy of irrelevant reason is often referred to by the Latin phrase "non sequitur," which translates as "it does not follow." When the conclusion of an argument does not follow from the premise in question, that premise is an irrelevant reason. Here is an example of a letter in which the author charges another's argument with irrelevant reason:

Example 6.22

Background: The following letter is in response to a letter by S.N. in support of allowing assisted suicide for those who are terminally ill. (*New York Times*, 1/97)

> ① The author's argument against the legal regulation of dying builds on a non sequitur. ② He contends that because the decision to live or die defies rational thinking and that the final stages of medical care are a "fear-filled" process, no legislature could think about assisted suicide as well as do those immediately at bedside. ③ The opposite conclusion is more sensible: Because the anxieties of such a decision are amplified by the suffering and the economic pressure of the moment, the patient, the physician and the family are often tempted to submit to the siren call of death as the easiest solution.—G.P.F.

The author makes a fallacy charge against S.N.'s argument and provides a justification. Sentence 1 names the charge—non sequitur or irrelevant reason. Sentence 2 explains S.N.'s argument, giving S.N.'s conclusion (that the government should not interfere in end-of-life decisions) and premises (that the decision to live or die in end-of-life contexts is not a rational one and that the dying process in such contexts is a time of fear). The first part of sentence 3 claims that the premises in S.N.'s argument not only fail to support the conclusion but actually support the opposite position. Finally, the second part of sentence 3 gives the justification for the charge: that the factors cited in the two premises lead to these bad end-of-life decisions. Because both premises are included in the charge, two charges of irrelevant reason are being made.

This justification is interesting because, in claiming that the premises of S.N.'s argument support the opposite conclusion, the author is arguing that the premises are not simply irrelevant but negatively relevant to the conclusion. One claim is negatively relevant, or has a negative support relationship, to another when the first supports the claim that the second is false. Although being irrelevant and being negatively relevant are not the same thing, both may be included under the charge of irrelevant reason because they both deny that the premise supports the conclusion.

Now let us consider how to present a charge of irrelevant reason, using the charge against the argument in Example 6.21 about Congress being cut in half.

Example 6.23

Structure

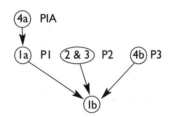

> P1A: If Congress were cut in half, then only half as much would be spent for salaries, travel expenses, staffing, perks, office space, and campaigns.
> P1: If Congress were cut in half, the national debt would be reduced without increasing taxes.
> P2: Communications today are much more rapid than when the Constitution was adopted.
> P3: If Congress were cut in half, then only half the time would be spent arguing and fighting to pass a bill.
> C: Therefore, we should cut Congress in half.

Fallacy Charge

> I charge this argument with irrelevant reason at P2. The argument commits this fallacy because the premise does not have a support relationship with the conclusion. The truth of the claim that communications are now much more rapid than when the Constitution was adopted has no bearing on the truth of the claim that Congress should be cut in half. The proper size of Congress has to do with issues such as how adequately the people are represented in lawmaking, not with how rapidly the representatives can communicate with their constituents. The speed of communications may support other proposals for change in Congress, but not a proposal to shrink it.

The first sentence of this justification simply states that the argument commits the fallacy. If the justification contained only this sentence, it would not be adequate because a justification must contain an argument. The second sentence does give an argument (note the "because"). However, if the justification contained only the first two sentences, it would still not be adequate because it would not give enough of an argument. The second sentence asserts that the conditions for irrelevant reason (see Figure 6.7) apply, but it does not go on to show that they do.[14] What is needed in the justification, which the subsequent sentences seek to provide, is a demonstration that the reason is irrelevant to the conclusion. These sentences seek to follow the justification strategy for irrelevant reason presented in Figure 6.7.

Here is another argument that could be charged with irrelevant reason:

Example 6.24

Background: This letter, written in response to a newspaper column, is part of the public debate about former President Clinton and his relationship with White House intern Monica Lewinsky. (*New York Times*, 9/98)

> ① I disagree with your columnist's assessment that President Clinton did not break any laws. ② If Mr. Clinton were not President but a corporate chief executive, his conduct would likely expose him to civil liability.—L.S.

First, we do the PC structure, and then the evaluation, including charge and justification. Three alternative justifications are included for the purpose of illustration and comparison.

Example 6.25

Structure

PI

PI: If Clinton were not president but a corporate chief executive, his conduct would likely expose him to civil liability.
C: Therefore, Clinton did break the law.

Fallacy Charge and Justification (three versions)
A. I charge this argument with irrelevant reason at PI.
B. I charge this argument with irrelevant reason at PI. The argument commits this fallacy because the premise does not support the conclusion.
C. I charge this argument with irrelevant reason at PI. The argument commits this fallacy because the premise does not support the conclusion. To break the law is to violate a criminal statute. Civil law is an area of law separate from criminal law. Breaking the law leads to a person's being prosecuted by the state. In the case of civil liability, one person sues another, and the state is not the prosecutor. Thus, the truth of the claim that Clinton would be subject to civil liability has no bearing on the truth of the claim that he broke the law.

Only version C is an adequate justification. Version A provides no argument, and version B provides an inadequate argument because it does not make clear how the conditions of the irrelevant reason fallacy apply to the argument in question.

In the case of the fallacy of irrelevant reason, it is especially important that you structure the argument correctly—in particular, that you correctly apply the rule of omission. According to this rule, the basis for excluding a statement from the text as part of the argument is that the statement is not relevant to the conclusion. Thus, on the one hand, if you include as a premise a statement that is not part of the argument, that premise will, of course, be irrelevant and so will lead to a mistaken charge of irrelevant reason. On the other hand, if a premise is irrelevant, it is easy to exclude it precisely because it is irrelevant. Again, the author's intent is crucial. All statements that the author intends to support the conclusion should be included as premises, even if they are irrelevant.

Consider these two simple examples:

Example 6.26

A. ① I have had experiences with poverty. ② The poor make it possible for the rich to acquire their wealth. ③ So, the rich should share their wealth with the poor.
B. ① You should not criticize my views, because my opinions are just as valuable as anyone else's. ② Besides, it is not polite.

In argument A, sentence 2 expresses the premise and sentence 3 the conclusion. Sentence 1, on the best interpretation, is not part of the argument. If you include sentence 1 as a premise in the structuring, you will open up the argument for a mistaken charge of irrelevant reason. In argument B, the reasoning indicator makes it clear that the author intends clause 1b to be a premise of the argument, so you should not exclude it from the structure even though it is irrelevant. If you exclude it, you will miss a fallacy that the argument does commit.

6.6.2 Charging Hasty Conclusion

In 1998, former President Clinton was charged with committing perjury and obstructing justice in his efforts to hide his sexual activity with White House intern Monica Lewinsky, charges that led to his impeachment by the House of Representatives and subsequent acquittal by the Senate. Here is an extremely simplified version (without the subarguments) of the argument put forth by those seeking to impeach the president:

Example 6.27

P1: The president committed perjury when questioned in court about his affair with Monica Lewinsky.

P2: The president obstructed justice by seeking to ensure that the truth about the affair would not come out in court.

C: Therefore, the president should be impeached.

The president's lawyers sought to defend him, in part, with the following argument: Even if the premises were true, the offenses would not justify impeachment because they did not fit the constitutional requirement of "high crimes and misdemeanors." In other words, the president's lawyers defended him by charging the critics' argument with hasty conclusion. Even if true, they argued, the charges would not provide sufficient support for the conclusion that the president should be impeached.

As this example shows, when a charge of hasty conclusion is made, the assumption is that the premises are true. A charge of hasty conclusion says that even if the premises are true, they do not provide sufficient support for the conclusion. The president's lawyers clearly believed that the charges of perjury and obstruction of justice were false. Yet, in making the hasty conclusion charge, they assumed, for the sake of that charge, that the claims made about the president's behavior were true. The need to assume the truth of the premises when making a hasty conclusion charge results from the distinction between form and content. Because the evaluation of form is different from the evaluation of content, when you criticize an argument's form the premises are assumed to be true.

To see how a hasty conclusion charge is made, consider this example:

Example 6.28

Background: The following letter is in response to a letter supporting an upper age limit for drivers. (*Finger Lakes Times*, 8/97)

① What about all the younger people who have many accidents. ② I think some of the older drivers are more cautious than young people.—C.H.M.

Structure

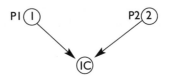

PI: Young drivers have many accidents.
P2: Some older drivers are more cautious than young drivers.
IC: Therefore, there should not be an age limit on driving.

Fallacy Charge

I charge this argument with hasty conclusion. It commits this fallacy because the premises do not provide sufficient support for the conclusion. Other factors need to be considered. First, the argument claims that young drivers have many accidents but does not consider evidence about how many accidents old drivers have. An argument for this conclusion would need to consider the per capita comparison of accident rates between old and young drivers. Second, the argument discusses one factor on the basis of which young and old drivers can be compared—namely, cautiousness. But there is another sort of factor not discussed that is relevant to a comparison of the driving abilities of the young and the old—namely, reaction time. The argument should have considered this factor.

As indicated in Figure 6.7, the justification strategy for a charge of hasty conclusion is to discuss the factors that should have been considered in the argument but were not. If some factors not discussed in the argument should have been discussed for the premises to have provided sufficient support for the conclusion, the argument is deficient. In justifying the charge, your job is to point out how it is deficient by discussing those other factors.

In the justification in Example 6.28, the other factors are the frequency of accidents involving elders and youths and the quick reaction times of youths. It does not matter whether you believe that the truth regarding the other factors would support the conclusion. You might think that evidence from these other areas would support the conclusion or that it would count against the conclusion, or you might not be sure what impact it would have on the argument. It does not matter. For example, you might not be sure whether a consideration of the per capita accident rate would favor old drivers or young drivers, and you might think that a consideration of reaction times obviously would favor the young driver. But in both cases, the argument is deficient because it does not discuss these factors. If an argument for the claim that there should not be an age limit on driving is to be formally strong, it must consider these factors.

Notice that the other factors discussed in the justification may be of the same type as or a different type from those discussed in the premises. The justification of the hasty conclusion charge against the argument about older drivers gives us an example of each. The first factor, a comparison of the per capita rate of accidents, is the same type of factor as those included in the argument. P1 discusses the number of accidents of younger drivers. The per capita rate of accidents is the same type of factor because it is also a matter of accident rates. The second factor mentioned in the justification, a comparison of reaction times, is another type of factor. It is about neither accident rates (P1) nor cautiousness (P2).

Consider these two simple arguments, both of which are ripe for a charge of hasty conclusion. What factors might you mention in a justification of a hasty conclusion charge against these arguments? Are the factors of the same type as or a different type from those considered in the arguments?

Example 6.29

A. Teachers should not receive a higher salary because they have a short working day and summers off.
B. The speed limit should be lowered to 50 MPH because if cars were traveling slower there would be fewer accidents.

In a charge of hasty conclusion, the justification should mention factors that are relevant to the conclusion but are not considered in the argument. In argument A, such factors might include the amount of time teachers spend working after the school day and at home (the same type of factor) and the importance of the job that teachers do (a different type of factor). In argument B, such factors might include the likelihood of compliance with the lowered speed limit (the same type of factor) and the extra amount of time that would be spent traveling with lower speed limits (a different type of factor).

The distinction between factors of the same type and of a different type is not precise, but it is important to keep in mind. In evaluating an argument, when you ask yourself whether more support is needed for the conclusion, it helps to remember that the missing support may be evidence of the same type as already included or evidence of a different type (or both).

Here is another example:

Example 6.30

This letter supports the medical use of marijuana. (*Boston Globe,* 8/97)

① Thank you for your sensible assessment of the medical use of marijuana. ② Doctors routinely prescribe drugs that are far more dangerous than marijuana. ③ In addition to being much safer than many of the possible alternatives, marijuana has another great advantage—it's relatively cheap.—S.W.

Structure

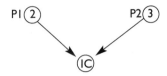

PI: Doctors routinely prescribe drugs that are far more dangerous than marijuana.

P2: Marijuana, in comparison with other drugs, is inexpensive.

IC: Therefore, marijuana should be available for doctors to prescribe.

Fallacy Charge and Justification

I charge this argument with hasty conclusion. The argument commits this fallacy because the premises do not provide enough support for the conclusion. There is an important issue that would have to be discussed before one could draw this conclusion—namely, the possible effect of medical marijuana on the rate of drug addiction. Allowing medical marijuana might lead to the general legalization of the drug, and this might lead more people to use hard drugs and become addicted to them.[15] If so, this harmful effect could outweigh the medical benefit. This is a question that the argument should address.

Here, the other issue cited is the social impact of legalizing medical marijuana. As before, if you are making this charge, it does not matter whether you believe that considering the social impact would support the conclusion. You might believe that the medical use of marijuana would have little or no effect on addiction rates, or you might believe that it would increase addiction rates. In either case, the absence of a discussion of this issue in the argument is the basis for a fallacy charge.

The idea of relevance is important in determining when a hasty conclusion charge is appropriate. To say that an author should have considered some other factors in an argument is to say that those other factors are relevant to the conclusion. The deficiency in the argument is that it did not discuss some relevant factors. A formally strong nondeductive argument is one that takes account of all relevant factors. An author's failure to consider some relevant factors opens up the argument to a charge of hasty conclusion.[16]

Remember that in charging hasty conclusion you are claiming not that the conclusion is false, but simply that the author has not done enough to support it. The main thing to do in justifying a hasty conclusion charge is to cite and argue for the other evidence or issues that the author should have considered. You may also discuss in the justification whether you think that the discussion of the other evidence or issues would support the conclusion, but you don't have to do this. The fallacy charge is based on the author's not considering the other factors, not on whether those other factors would support the conclusion.[17]

6.6.3 Counterconsiderations and Counterpremises

Something might seem a bit strange about this discussion of hasty conclusion: How can we claim that an author should have considered in an argument some factor that would clearly run counter to the conclusion? For example, how can we expect the author of an argument in favor of the medical use of marijuana to discuss the possibility that this would increase the number of drug addicts? After all, the author is arguing in favor of the medical use of marijuana, and raising this possibility would seem to undermine this effort.

This is a very important question, and it has a simple answer: When a factor that was not included in an argument appears to run counter to the conclusion, what the author should have done is claim or argue that that factor does not show that the conclusion is false. In other words, the weakness in the argument is that the author does not include a premise (perhaps with a subargument) designed to establish that the factor, which appears to show the conclusion to be false, does not do so.

To see how this works, consider this argument: "Abortion should be legally allowed because abortion helps to control population increase." Clearly, this is a weak argument, one that commits the fallacy of hasty conclusion. Here is a partial list of other factors that should have been considered:

1. The woman's ability to make choices about the direction of her life
2. The interests of the fetus
3. The disruption that an unintended pregnancy and child can cause in the life of the woman and her family
4. The reduction in the general respect for life that legalized abortion might cause
5. The deaths and disabilities that would arise from women's efforts to seek abortion if it were not legally available

This is not a complete list. You probably have other factors in mind that you would add. The point is that these are topics that should be discussed in an argument whose conclusion is that abortion should be legal.

> **Counterconsiderations**
>
> A counterconsideration is a factor that appears to be in opposition to the conclusion of an argument. It is a factor that would be cited by those who oppose or object to the conclusion.

If you consider this list, you can see that some of the factors seem to support the conclusion and others seem to oppose it. Specifically, factors 1, 3, and 5 seem to support the conclusion, while factors 2 and 4 seem to count against it. The factors that appear to be in opposition to a particular conclusion are called **counterconsiderations**—considerations that appear to run counter to the conclusion of an argument. A factor is, of course, a counterconsideration only relative to a particular conclusion. The claim that we should consider the interests of the fetus is a counterconsideration relative to the conclusion that abortion should be legal, but it is not a counterconsideration relative to the conclusion that abortion should be illegal.

An important part of presenting an argument is showing that any potential counterconsiderations do not, despite appearances, show that the conclusion is false. When you raise counterconsiderations as part of a charge of hasty conclusion, you are claiming that the argument has failed to do so.

Consider a situation in which you are seeking to get someone to do something that she or he does not want to do. Imagine, for example, that you want to persuade a younger sister to give up smoking. You probably will rehearse your argument in your mind before talking with her, including considering the kind of objections she is likely to raise. These objections are counterconsiderations to your conclusion that she should give up smoking. In presenting your argument to her, you are likely to include your response to these anticipated objections as part of your case. For example, she might respond that smoking is cool or that all her friends are doing it, so that part of your argument will be premises that seek to counter these objections. As a result, your argument might include the following points:

Example 6.31

A. Counterconsideration: The coolness of smoking
   Response: The fact that it seems cool to smoke cannot outweigh all of the harmful health effects of smoking.
B. Counterconsideration: The frequency of smoking among her friends
   Response: If all your friends jumped off a cliff, would you jump, too?

Failure to include responses to these counterconsiderations would be a weakness in your argument and should be cited as part of a hasty conclusion charge against that argument.

You should include as premises in your argument the responses to counterconsiderations, or **counterpremises**—premises that counter reasons against your conclusion. Regular premises provide evidence that directly supports a conclusion, and counterpremises indirectly support the conclusion by deflecting anticipated objections to the conclusion. Counterpremises are often supported by subarguments.

> ### Counterpremises
>
> A counterpremise is a premise of an argument that is a response to anticipated objections to the conclusion. It is a premise that claims that some objection to the conclusion does not in fact show that the conclusion is false. Such a claim itself often needs to be supported by an argument, so counterpremises often have subarguments.

Let us look again at the short argument about abortion and the list of other factors provided. As we said, factors 2 and 4 are counterconsiderations. What counterpremises could we have included in the argument in response to these counterconsiderations? Here are possibilities:

Example 6.32

A. Counterconsideration: The interests of the fetus
   Counterpremise (with subargument): The interests of the fetus need not be considered in the argument over abortion because a fetus is not a person and so has no interests.

B. Counterconsideration: The reduction in the general respect for life that legalized abortion might cause
   Counterpremise (with subargument): Legalized abortion would not reduce the general respect for life because societies that have legalized abortion do not show any increase in acts against human life.

The need to include counterconsiderations when you are making a charge of hasty conclusion shows the importance of distinguishing in your justification between factors of the same type as those included in the argument and factors of a different type. More often than not, a counterconsideration is a different type of factor. If you fail to include different types of factors in your justification, you will miss many counterconsiderations.

Of course, not all factors cited in justifications are counterconsiderations. For example, in the list of factors for the short abortion argument, factors 1, 3, and 5 are not counterconsiderations. They are factors that support the conclusion. Still, the argument is deficient for not including these factors. If the argument had included them, it would have been stronger. When you made a hasty conclusion charge, there may be factors that you think should have been considered in the argument, even though you are not sure whether they would support the conclusion. You may not know whether they are counterconsiderations. Still, you should include them among the factors cited in the justification.

Many arguments include counterpremises, including this example:

Example 6.33

Background: This letter was written in response to those who demanded that book series such as "Goosebumps," "The Babysitters Club," and "Sweet Valley High" be excluded from school libraries. (*Chicago Tribune*, 4/97)

① Although these books may not have provided my children with the insights of a Tolstoy or a Melville, they did teach them that reading is fun and entertaining, a lesson that has been the foundation of their now-broad reading interests. ② I say "thanks" to the authors because of the positive view my daughters have about reading. ③ Too bad those who would ban such books obviously are themselves so poorly read. ④ Otherwise they would know from history just how harmful their actions can be.—D.M.P.

Structure

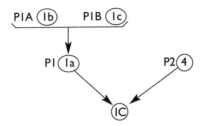

> P1A: Reading these books can teach children that reading is fun.
> P1B: Teaching children that reading is fun can lead to their having broader reading interests.

P1: The fact that these books do not provide the insights of great literature is not sufficient to show that they should be excluded from school libraries.

P2: Historically, banning books has had harmful effects.

IC: Therefore, book series such as "Goosebumps," "The Babysitters Club," and "Sweet Valley High" should not be excluded from school libraries.

Here, P1 is a counterpremise. In P1, the author attempts to address the main counterconsideration to her conclusion—that the books are without literary merit—by stating that even though this may be true it is not sufficient reason to ban them. The author includes a subargument to support this claim.

Many important and controversial subjects, like abortion, involve a large number and variety of factors that you need to carefully consider to ensure sufficient support for your conclusions. Many of the arguments for these subjects are incomplete, in the sense that they fail to address some of the relevant considerations. Hasty conclusion is a common charge because of incomplete arguments. We will discuss counterconsiderations and counterpremises in more detail in Chapter 11.

EXERCISE SET 6.6

SECTION A: Structure (no tree diagrams needed) and evaluate each of the following nondeductive arguments in terms of the fallacies of hasty conclusion and irrelevant reason, being sure to include justifications for the fallacy charges.

EXAMPLE

To my way of thinking, the United States should adopt the metric system. Just about every other country in the world uses it.

ANSWER

P1: Almost all of the other countries in the world use the metric system.

C: Therefore, the United States should adopt the metric system.

I charge this argument with the fallacy of hasty conclusion. The premise does provide some support for the conclusion, but not sufficient support. We need to consider other relevant factors. For example, how costly would it be to adopt the metric system? It may be that the costs outweigh whatever benefits it may provide. In addition, we need to consider whether the people want to change to the metric system. If the people are opposed to it, then it probably should not be adopted whatever the benefits it may provide.

PROBLEMS

1. The country is definitely the best place to live because the air is fresh and the spaces are wide open.
2. We should have nothing to do with the proposed policy of government-sponsored universal health insurance. After all, Castro approves of it.
3. If Earth warms up, growing seasons will be longer. It follows that we should encourage global warming. *hasty conclusion*
4. Now that we have VCRs and DVD players, we can watch whatever movies we want to at home. Going out to the movies is more expensive. It is time consuming. We should avoid going to the movie theater.
5. Phonograph records are the best way to listen to recorded music. This is the way that I listened to music when I was growing up.
6. Insects are a nuisance, as anyone who has had a picnic can attest. They can spread disease. In addition, they damage crops. We should try to destroy them all.
7. In nature, nothing is ever destroyed, only transformed. It is as plain as day that the soul cannot be destroyed.
8. God is aware of what you do and will reward or punish you according to your just deserts. So, you should be good for the sake of goodness itself.
9. Everybody deserves a day of rest. So, all businesses should by law be closed on Sundays.
10. You should definitely attend a large university. It offers so many more course offerings than a small college.

SECTION B: Structure and evaluate each of the following nondeductive arguments in terms of the fallacies of hasty conclusion and irrelevant reason, being sure to include justifications for the fallacy charges.

EXAMPLE

Background: This letter is about the national debt. (*Miami Herald*, 3/97)

① Not only must the budget be balanced, but the national debt must be eliminated. ② In this time of peace and relative prosperity, can there ever be a better time to do this? ③ The billions in interest that we pay on the national debt probably would cure all our financial ills if applied to entitlements, infrastructures, etc.—N.W.

ANSWER

Structure

P1: This time of relative prosperity is the best time to eliminate the national debt.
P2: The billions of dollars spent on interest on the national debt would likely solve all of our problems in areas such as entitlements, infrastructure, and so forth.

C: Therefore, we should not only balance the budget but eliminate the national debt.

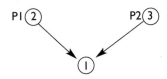

Fallacy Charge and Justification

I charge this argument with the fallacy of hasty conclusion. The premises taken together do not provide sufficient support for the conclusion because there is at least one other important issue that the author needs to consider—namely, the impact of diverting resources to pay off the debt. If the government sought to pay off the debt, it would do so by spending money that otherwise would go toward programs like entitlements and infrastructure repair. While it is true that after the debt were paid off there would be extra money for these programs, they might be severely damaged by their being starved for funds while the debt was being paid off. For example, if a family were to spend all of its money on paying off its mortgage as quickly as possible in order to save on interest payments, it might do serious damage to itself by the deprivation this policy would cause.

PROBLEMS

1. Background: This letter concerns the interaction between air and air conditioners. (*Miami Herald*, 3/98)

   Metals that rot away in coastal salt air are used in Florida air conditioners. In a few years, all that is left is a rusted, nonworking unit that can cost $500 or more to replace. Why doesn't a public agency regulate metals for salt-climate air conditioners?—J.M.C.

2. Background: This letter is in response to a jury's finding for the tobacco companies in a liability suit brought against the companies by individuals harmed by smoking. (*Miami Herald*, 5/97)

   Doesn't America know that the World Health Organization has predicted that by the year 2000 tobacco will be the No. 1 killer worldwide, responsible for more than eight million deaths? Don't jurors realize that they must find tobacco companies liable for the diseases that their products cause?—L.S.S.

3. Background: This letter is in response to another letter. (*New York Times*, 1/00)

   In response to the letter expressing preference for a culture in which people wait in line to complete a transaction with a real person rather than sit alone at home using a computer, I offer this quotation from the French philosopher Blaise Pascal: "I have discovered that all human evil comes from this, man's being unable to sit still in a room."—M.I.W.

4. Background: This letter is in response to a column concerning the sinking of the *Titanic*. (*Los Angeles Times*, 4/98)

The columnist states that the *Titanic*'s sinking is of "trivial historical consequence." In fact, it is of considerable significance. Some of the actions following the *Titanic*'s sinking were: An international ice patrol was established to warn seafarers of icebergs; sufficient lifeboats were required on all ships to accommodate every person aboard; ship design was changed to include double bottoms along the sides of the hull; emergency radio frequencies at sea were manned 24 hours a day.—R.V.

5. Background: This letter is in response to a column that derided abstinence-only sex education. (*Boston Globe*, 6/97)

Is abstinence such an unreachable goal that it should be treated with such disrespect and derision? Maybe it is possible to educate our children to respect their bodies and learn self-control. Maybe that respect will envelop the country, returning us to values on which this country was built. Let's give abstinence education a fair try and hope that it will reawaken our standards of decency, self-discipline, and conscience.—D.M.P.

6. Background: This letter is in response to an argument put forth by an abortion opponent. (*San Francisco Chronicle*, 12/97)

A pro-lifer recently claimed that abortion is evil because it "interrupts a natural process." By that ridiculously simplistic reasoning, we should let all disease rage unchecked, forget any medical research, and, heck, why do we even need doctors?—M.Z.

7. Background: This letter is about pedestrian right-of-way. (*Boston Globe*, 4/00)

I would like to know whose brilliant idea it was to give pedestrians the right of way over automobiles. A simple comparison of mass, inertia, and maneuverability clearly demonstrates that a locomotive should have the right of way over an automobile. Why then should a meeting of an automobile and a pedestrian be any different?—G.N.

8. Background: This letter was in response to the ranking of U.S. colleges by *U.S. News & World Report*, which lists one college as number 1. (*Chicago Tribune*, 5/98)

What could be more ridiculous? Obviously what's wonderful for one student is totally inappropriate for another, and vice versa. How can there possibly be a No. 1 college anywhere?—W.B.S.

9. Background: The following letter was written while former President Clinton was being investigated for his alleged relationship with Monica Lewinsky, a White House intern, but before he admitted that he had had an inappropriate relationship with her. (*New York Times*, 9/98)

Are we supposed to accept the idea that the president, who has a reputation as a womanizer, would have an affair with a 21-year-old intern at the White House? While he is being sued for sexual harassment? Bill Clinton did not become governor of Arkansas and president of the United States by being an idiot. For these allegations to be true he would have to be the dumbest man the world has ever seen.—D.C.M.

10. Background: This letter comments on an article on a proposal to launch a satellite that would send back pictures of Earth that would be constantly available to the media and through the Internet. (*New York Times*, 3/98)

Vice President Al Gore's proposal to send a satellite into space that would, as you put it, "beam back sunwashed images of the whole Earth [in order to] increase earthlings' appreciation of the planet" is poetic. However, it is misguided. The view from space will obscure and allow us to avoid seeing the poverty, racism, incivility, environmental injustices and loss of control that most in the universe experience with the growth of multinational capitalism, all of which are among the causes of the Earth's fragility. We do not have to sit in front of our television sets watching a Space Channel to see the environmental and social fragility of the planet. That can be seen wherever we live, work or play.—S.V.

11. Background: This letter is critical of a judge's ruling blocking a law requiring that parents be notified when their minor children receive government-funded contraceptives. (*New York Times*, 2/83)

The obvious truth about the startling (and quite saddening) number of teenage pregnancies is that there are very few, if any, moral sanctions against sexual promiscuity left. What rational people who hope for some kind of self-disciplined future citizenry want to see their children given license to do as they please? Children naturally do what is easiest and immediately pleasurable, not what is hardest and best; that is why teaching them is so difficult. For the Government to insist that parents of minor children be notified if those children received Government-funded contraceptives was a recognition that parental sanctions still do count and that the family is still respected for its ability to civilize its offspring. By blocking that ruling, a judge has once again made it possible for some children to avoid one of the few remaining moral sanctions: their parents' disapproval.—J.E.S.

12. Background: This letter is in response to a news story about a high school student who refused to recite the Pledge of Allegiance at school. (*Washington Post*, 6/98)

Excuse me? A high school sophomore chooses to sit out reciting the pledge because she "thinks the U.S. government is corrupt and that American society is too violent, so she shouldn't have to show respect for a country that has so many problems?" Yet she is invoking her First Amendment free-speech rights guaranteed her by that corrupt government and that violent society. What is wrong with this picture?—V.L.B.

13. Background: This letter is in response to a call by former President Clinton for the use of solar power to combat global warming. (*New York Times*, 7/97)

Solar power is the development that never developed. Billions of dollars have been spent on "renewable" energy ideas that have no place in our electric generation profile today. If they could work, we would have the reduction of emissions the Europeans call for. The reason for the failure: They have a political rather than a scientific base.—F.C.

14. Background: This letter is about the fairness of news coverage. (*Washington Post*, 5/98)

    On May 7 you gave front-page (top-left) coverage of a story stating that an unknown high-level U.S. official may have given sensitive data to Israel. The next day you printed strong denials of the story from top-level Israeli officials. That story appeared at the bottom of page 20. Considering the prominence given the first story, would it not have been equitable to give the second (and completely different opinion) story equal prominence? —H.K.O.

15. Background: The following letter is critical of government regulations banning smoking in restaurants. (*New York Times*, 10/95)

    Any number of polls have indicated that most U.S. adults would prefer to leave the smoking/nonsmoking issue up to the marketplace. If this country has an air-quality problem it lies in our addiction to fossil fuels. If it has a health problem, it lies in the way we eat and exercise (or, rather, don't exercise).—A.F.

16. Background: This letter is in response to a column calling for higher tuition fees at state colleges for students from higher-income families. (*Los Angeles Times*, 4/98)

    The commentary is highly discriminatory in its proposal to raise fees on the wealthiest families. First, it overlooks the return-on-investment that state taxpayers receive by educating the best and brightest. The relationship of the university to our economy seems self-evident. Driving the wealthy to private universities denies the good-looking middle-class female the opportunity to meet wealthy males and possibly marry them. Therefore the diversity of having wealthy students is needed.—B.K.

17. Background: This letter expresses concern about crime. (*Miami Herald*, 3/97)

    I am aghast at the release of so many criminals because our jails are too full. I propose that we pay some poor country such as Haiti or Guyana to house our surplus prisoners in acceptable conditions. Prisoners would be transported there for the length of their sentences and then returned. This would benefit the host country and provide jobs for its people, and it would deter potential criminals. It would also enable judges to pass sentences without considering if a sentence can be met with the current prison capacity. —B.G.P.

18. Background: This letter is about how the Census Bureau should treat the issue of race in conducting the census. (*New York Times*, 6/98)

    Federal officials are looking for ways to account for people with multicultural heritages on census and other forms. Instead, the Census Bureau could lead us into a new, enlightened era by eliminating the question about race.

After all, nearly all of us have mixed ancestry. Existing laws—and new ones —could protect us against crimes committed because of prejudice based on skin color, ethnicity, sex or sexual preference, without relying on "race" as a basis for anything.—M.H.

19. Background: This letter is by an oncologist (a cancer specialist) about a law enacted in Oregon to allow physicians to assist terminally ill patients in pain to commit suicide. (*New York Times*, 6/97)

   As an oncologist, I can tell you that the terminally ill patients with pain I see already have access to the lethal dose of medication for which the Oregon law provides. It is common practice to give patients at least a month's supply of pain medicines with each prescription. If that supply were taken at one time, it would be expected to be lethal. Prescriptions for monthly supplies of narcotics seem to be the rule. If so, I wonder what the Oregon law is doing that is new or different.—M.J.S.

20. Background: This letter concerns the efforts by the city of New York to control street vendors. (*New York Times*, 6/97)

   I read with great dismay that New York City is considering banning street vendors from midtown. Of the many odors that greet a commuter at Pennsylvania Station, the heavenly scents of roasted chestnuts and warm, yeasty pretzels are the most welcome. I also appreciate the fresh fruit carts that provide a quick alternative to superstores and groceries. Anyone who has walked the city streets can see that the carts do not significantly block pedestrian traffic. I hope the city reconsiders and preserves the carts, which reflect the pace and flavor of New York.—M.W.

❖ 21. Background: This letter is in response to an article advocating campaign finance reform. (*Boston Globe*, 5/98)

   There is a better way to fix the corrupt system; agitate for smaller government! With a smaller government, one that operates within the restrictions of our federal and state constitutions, there would be less money and power in the public domain and, therefore, less influence money trying to control that power.—D.L.B.

22. Background: In 1995, Harvard University rescinded its offer of admission to G.G., a young woman who had killed her mother 3 years earlier and hid this fact from the Harvard admissions committee. (*New York Times*, 4/95)

   As one of the premier universities of the world, Harvard has a special public responsibility to exercise moral leadership by example in its actions. The public interest, in this instance, is in the rehabilitation of people like G.G., so that they can become useful, productive citizens and realize their full potential. The individual or committee that made this egregiously incorrect decision should ask whether or not the public interest would be served if all other first-rate universities would follow Harvard's lead and reject G.G. Clearly the answer is no. I urge Harvard to rectify its error of policy and morality to the extent it is possible to do so.—R.D.

6.7 Some Specific Formal Fallacies

There are four basic fallacies, represented by the TARS acronym, but each of these general fallacies has more specific versions representing erroneous ways in which people frequently argue. But the kind of mistake represented by each specific fallacy is the same as that of the basic fallacy of which it is a version. It is not the name of the specific fallacy that is important, but the kind of mistake it represents. Being able to give a good justification for the charge you make is more important than getting the name right.

In this section, we look at one specific version of irrelevant reason, argument *ad hominem* (Latin for "to the person"), and one specific version of hasty conclusion, argument by anecdote. A case of **argument *ad hominem*** is a case of irrelevant reason because the premise does not support the conclusion. A case of **argument by anecdote** is a case of hasty conclusion because the premises do not provide sufficient support for the conclusion.

6.7.1 *Argument* ad Hominem

Sometimes, authors argue against a statement by turning the audience's attention away from the statement itself and toward a person or group that believes or advocates it, seeking to discredit the person or group in the hope that this will lead the audience to dismiss the statement. Argument *ad hominem* is a specific version of the fallacy of irrelevant reason because claims about a person or group that believes or advocates a statement are generally not relevant to its truth. Statements should be examined in their own right.

> **Argument *ad Hominem***
>
> Argument *ad hominem* is a fallacy that is committed when an argument concludes that some statement is false and supports this by "attacking the person"—that is, by making claims designed to discredit a person or group that believes or advocates that statement, rather than by addressing the statement itself.

Here is an example of argument *ad hominem*, including its structure and evaluation:

Example 6.34

Background: This letter is about the air attacks on Serbian forces by the United States and its allies to force the Serbians to stop their ethnic cleansing and forcible expulsion of Albanians in Kosovo. The author is critical of John Kenneth Galbraith, a well-known Harvard economist, who argued that the attacks should stop. (*New York Times*, 4/99)

① Galbraith says we should "suspend the bombing" and "isolate Serbia," counseling that patience is the best approach to Kosovo: "Time is the greatest of all curatives." ② Sitting within the comforts of Harvard, patience may seem like a good idea. ③ But would Mr. Galbraith be preaching the virtues of patience if he was living in a fetid refugee camp after having been forced out of his home?—A.R.

Structure

PI ②&③

IC

PI: Galbraith is making his recommendations from the comforts of Harvard rather than the discomforts of a refugee camp.

IC: Therefore, Galbraith's recommendation to stop the attacks on Serbia should be rejected.

Evaluation

I charge this argument with the fallacy of argument *ad hominem*. The argument commits this fallacy because the author seeks to discredit the person whose proposal the argument claims should be rejected, making the premise irrelevant to that conclusion. Galbraith's proposal may be correct whatever his circumstances. The fact that he is comfortable does not support the claim that his proposal is incorrect.

In this argument, the author supports the claim that we should reject the call to stop the war on Serbia by citing the fact that the person advocating this position lives in comfortable circumstances. But this "attack on the person" is not relevant to the conclusion.

6.7.2 Argument by Anecdote

Many times an argument will draw a general conclusion from singular premises. We will have more to say about such arguments in Chapter 10, but here we consider arguments of this sort that have only one singular premise. This premise is an anecdote, a story or narrative of a particular incident or episode, often one that the author is directly familiar with. There is nothing wrong with including anecdotes in argumentative texts. But when the conclusion is a general statement and the only reason offered is the anecdote itself, the argument is usually formally weak because one singular statement is seldom sufficient to support a general conclusion.[18]

Consider this argument and its evaluation:

Example 6.35

Background: This letter, in response to another letter, is about the author's encounter with baseball legend Joe DiMaggio. (*New York Times*, 10/00)

Argument by Anecdote

When an argument has a general statement as its conclusion and the only premise is an anecdote—that is, a claim about a single instance or episode—the argument may commit the fallacy of argument by anecdote. This is a specific version of the basic fallacy of hasty conclusion because the premises do not provide sufficient evidence to support the conclusion.

① The letter spoke of the supposed aloofness of Joe DiMaggio toward autograph-seekers. ② Now wait a minute! ③ It was in the late '50s and DiMaggio was leaving the old CBS building on East 52nd Street. ④ I was entering the building. ⑤ I asked him for his autograph. ⑥ It was one on one, and he said, "Sure." ⑦ Then I couldn't find a piece of paper, and I got flustered. ⑧ Joe said, "Take it easy." ⑨ I found a matchbook in my pocket and Joe signed it. ⑩ Enough about aloofness.—L.B.A.

Structure

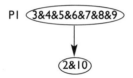

PI   ⟨3&4&5&6&7&8&9⟩

              ↓

          ⟨2&10⟩

    PI: In the late 1950s, I encountered DiMaggio alone and asked him for his autograph, which he willingly provided, being patient even while I had trouble finding a piece of paper.

    C: Therefore, DiMaggio is not aloof.

Evaluation

    I charge this argument with the fallacy of argument by anecdote at PI. The argument commits this fallacy because the anecdote that is the premise does not provide sufficient support for the generalization that is the conclusion. The premise does support the conclusion, but very weakly. The author needs to cite many more instances. One episode of nonaloofness does not show that a person is not aloof.

As the tree diagram indicates, it is generally better to include the entire anecdote in a single premise.

Anecdotes play different roles in argumentative texts, and their presence does not always indicate a fallacy. First, an anecdote indicates a fallacy only when it is the sole premise. Second, anecdotes are sometimes meant not as premises, but merely as illustrations to help the audience understand or appreciate what the author is saying. Anecdotes can play this role in argumentative or nonargumentative texts. Consider this example:

Example 6.36

Background: This letter is about tenure for faculty in higher education. (*Chicago Tribune*, 4/97)

① Tenure makes the long-term investment in people and projects needed for successful research and training of researchers. ② Research typically calls for long-term programs, often with a high chance of not succeeding (if something is easy, it usually has already been discovered). ③ For example, colleagues and I are seven years into a program to help understand the cause of great earthquakes in the Midwest, which may take 20 years to complete. ④ Without tenure, we wouldn't take on such a project.—S.S.

Here, we might interpret the anecdote, expressed in sentence 3, as a subpremise supporting the main premise expressed in sentence 2, in which case we could charge the subargument with committing the fallacy of argument by anecdote. But we would do better to view the anecdote as an illustration, meant simply to show the sort of thing sentence 2 is talking about, and not to be a premise in support of the statement expressed in that sentence.

Another kind of case in which the text contains an anecdote but a charge of argument by anecdote may be inappropriate is one in which a singular statement can be taken as a stand-in for a general claim. Consider this example:

Example 6.37

Background: This letter is from a subscriber to cable TV. (*Miami Herald*, 5/97)

① We should be able to order and pay for only the cable-TV channels that we want. ② I could easily eliminate 34 of our system's 63 channels.—J.O.

Here, the conclusion, expressed in sentence 1, is that cable subscribers should have to pay for only those channels they want. The premise is the anecdote that the author is not interested in many of the channels she gets. But this anecdote is clearly meant to be a stand-in for the general claim that subscribers in general are not interested in many of the channels they get. As a result, the premise should be reformulated in this way:

Example 6.38

P1: Cable subscribers do not want many of the channels that come in the packages offered by the cable companies.

C: Therefore, cable subscribers should have to pay for only those channels they want.

Even though we could charge the argument with hasty conclusion on other grounds, when interpreted this way, we cannot charge it with argument by anecdote.

How can you determine when to reformulate an anecdote as a general claim and when not to? You need to consider the context in which the anecdote is used and ask yourself whether the author is using the rhetorical form of an anecdote to express a general statement. The answer will usually be yes if there is no reason to think that what happened to the person in the anecdote would not happen to anyone who was in the circumstances in which the anecdote occurred.

> ### Anecdotes and General Statements
>
> Sometimes, an anecdote in an argumentative text should be interpreted in the argument structure as a stand-in for a general statement rather than as a singular statement. An anecdote should be interpreted in this way if it is obvious that the story would be true for all or most people who found themselves in the circumstances that the story describes.

Sometimes, of course, it is difficult to tell whether an author intended an anecdote as a stand-in for a general statement, but this is not always a serious problem. If you interpret an anecdote as a stand-in for a general statement, you would then not be able to make the charge of argument by anecdote, which you might have made had you interpreted the anecdote as an anecdote. But the argument with the general statement as a premise might be charged with a different fallacy— specifically, a content fallacy of false premise or problematic premise against the general statement. Either way, the argument is seen to have a weakness.[19]

EXERCISE SET 6.7

Structure and evaluate each of the following nondeductive arguments in terms of the specific formal fallacies of argument *ad hominem* and argument by anecdote. If an argument contains an anecdote that you think should be interpreted as a general claim, show this in the structure and argue that this is the case.

EXAMPLE
Background: This letter was written when former President Clinton was fighting to survive the Monica Lewinsky scandal and avoid being forced from office. (*New York Times*, 8/98)

① Those who say that a President's personal ethics and morals are relevant to his ability to perform the duties of the office should recall Jimmy Carter's Presidency. ② Mr. Carter's personal morals and ethics were admired and above reproach, but the public became highly displeased with his performance in office.—R.E.N.

ANSWER

Structure

P1: Though President Carter's personal morals and ethics were admired and above reproach, the public disliked his performance in office.

C: Therefore, a president's personal ethics and morals are not relevant to his ability to perform the duties of the office.

Evaluation

I charge this argument with the specific fallacy of argument by anecdote. The argument commits this fallacy because the anecdote about President Carter is the only premise, and that one instance is not sufficient to support the general claim of the conclusion. Just because Carter had strong morals and performed poorly does not mean that poor morals do not lead to poor performance. If he had had poor morals, his performance might have been even worse. We would need to consider many more instances before we could draw this conclusion.

PROBLEMS

1. Background: The following letter is critical of a vote by the House of Representatives to amend the Constitution to allow laws prohibiting the burning of the American flag. (*Chicago Tribune*, 6/97)

   The Beijing-"appointed" legislature for Hong Kong [recently] passed a law providing "fines and a prison sentence of up to three years for defacing or burning China's flag." Shall we compare our representatives to the Chinese communist government? I hope the Senate has more sense and ignores this simple-minded attack on a non-problem.—G.K.

2. Background: The following letter is in response to the singer Frank Sinatra's receiving a medal from Congress. (*Miami Herald*, 5/97)

   What great service to the country did Frank Sinatra do to earn the prestigious gold medal that Congress bestowed on him on his 81st birthday? He never served in the military, never was elected to office, and never served on any great national committee, except political ones. I'm 81. I served my country, but I've not received the same great honor given to Old Blue Eyes. —B.B.

3. Background: This letter defends a movie, *The Last Temptation of Christ*, that was strongly criticized by fundamentalist religious groups for its portrayal of Jesus. (*New York Times*, 8/98)

   What is it about this film that has created such fury and resentment in fundamentalists that they wish to obliterate it entirely and thereby force their views on the public. What curious behavior for individuals who claim to have such unshakable, rocklike faith! The matter bears further investigation, perhaps by psychologists and other specialists in behavior.—H.A.K.

4. Background: This letter is about a 1970s public service advertisement that used a Native American to deliver an antilittering message. (*Washington Post*, 1/98)

Often the advertising industry questions its effectiveness to truly influence behavior. The death of Oski "Iron Eyes" Cody brought to mind the personally powerful effect his "Keep America Beautiful" TV ad campaign had on me in the early 1970s. Until that time, I was a typical self-absorbed teenager, dumping McDonald's wrappers from my car windows and dropping candy wrappers wherever it was convenient for me to drop them. But then I saw that ad, and it stopped me dead in my tracks and brought tears to my eyes. I have never littered since, and to this day I still can remember watching that ad and its immediate effect on me. The use of Mr. Cody as a silent spokesperson was particularly powerful.—E.S.

5. Background: This letter is about the heavy burden children must bear. (*Chicago Tribune*, 12/97)

I got the surprise of my life when I picked up my grandson's schoolbag! I thought I would throw my back out! There were four textbooks, plus several notebooks and workbooks in the bag. This 5th grader has to lug about 20 pounds of books back and forth to school each day. I may be a meddling grandma, but my grandsons' backs are being strained far beyond reason. Why can't the books be bound with soft durable covers?—R.B.

6. Background: The following letter is part of the debate about "road rage" on American highways. (*Los Angeles Times*, 1/98)

The road rage story is part of a larger phenomenon that American society is facing. Winning. We see this on the football field, on the basketball court, in politics and in business. Winning is becoming the highest value in our society, to the detriment of a sense of justice, decency, and what some call "family values." I recall the words of Paul Joseph Goebbels, who said: "Important is not what is right but what wins."—H.B.L.

7. Background: This letter is about sports utility vehicles. (*New York Times*, 6/97)

Would someone tell me what people use these overgrown vehicles for? I know several people who own such vehicles, but most do not use them for anything more than driving to and from work or to other places where any car could venture. I'm not sure any of these folks I know have ever taken the car "off-road," where a high-riding, four-wheel-drive vehicle might be necessary, or camping, where the extra cargo space comes in handy, or have driven in the kinds of snowstorms that are common in North Dakota. Besides spending more on insurance, gasoline and the vehicle itself, what is the appeal?—S.T.

8. Background: This letter is critical of a column questioning the value of tenure in higher education. (*Chicago Tribune*, 4/97)

Without tenure as a drawing card and with such paltry recompense, who will compete at the level academia demands? In my quest for a humanities Ph.D., I've spent $120,000 in the last four years alone. I've trained rigorously for seven years, watched my friends go on to good-paying jobs and survived into my 30s on a four-digit salary. And, if I'm lucky enough to beat out thousands of equally qualified people for the one or two jobs open this year, I'll make less than a CTA bus driver. After six years, if I'm still in fashion, loved by my students and friendly with all my co-workers, maybe I'll get promoted a rung. Try selling that bill of goods without tenure.—S.J.H.

9. Background: This letter is about the proposed International Criminal Court, which could try individuals from any nation for war crimes. (*New York Times*, 7/98)

The issue has never been whether atrocities are committed in armed conflict. The issue is who should be responsible for supervising the situation. If the world community takes that responsibility, peace will suffer. For instance, would the new court try to arraign Yasir Arafat, the Palestinian leader, for complicity in undoubted Palestinian atrocities? Would it try to arraign Ariel Sharon, the Israeli cabinet minister, for complicity in what many believe to be atrocities against the Palestinian people? Would a trial of either or both help the search for peace on terms acceptable to the constituents of both?—A.P.R.

10. Background: This letter is in response to an editorial on the issue of tobacco advertising. (*New York Times*, 12/98)

Your editorial asserts that New York City's latest attempt to restrict outdoor tobacco advertising tramples "on principles of free expression." That is strictly the opinion of advertising's beneficiaries, not of those forced to see the ads. I can turn off or mute my television, close my newspaper or magazine. But I cannot avoid looking at a billboard or sign when walking or driving on a public thoroughfare. As I read the Constitution, free expression stops well short of intruding on the listener.—A.R.

11. Background: The following letter is in response to a column that discussed baseball fans as "dads and sons." (*New York Times*, 3/95)

The columnist's heartfelt remembrance of his father was charming; his description of baseball fans as "dads and sons"—and your emphasis of this category—was not. My 7½-year-old daughter, Andrea, has attended many baseball games with her father and me (another female fan!). She learned to understand large numbers by reading Barry Bonds's stats off a baseball card. Let's not make gender a requirement for mourning the state of baseball. The national pastime belongs to all.—E.R.G.

12. Background: This letter is a criticism of a claim by the bioethicist Peter Singer that infanticide is sometimes justified. (*New York Times*, 4/99)

Singer writes, "When the death of a disabled infant will lead to the birth of another infant with better prospects of a happy life, the total amount of happiness will be greater if the disabled infant is killed." As the mother of two, one with Down syndrome, I emphatically disagree with Mr. Singer's simplistic belief in happiness as a linear equation. Both of our children bring us joy and challenge. That one has Down syndrome has not made our family more or less happy. However, it has challenged us to think about what it means to be human, regardless of achievement.—E.F.C.

13. Background: This letter is in response to an article about the need to widen seats in public settings to accommodate overweight people. (*USA Today*, 4/00)

Obviously nobody has even remotely considered the alternative to spending millions and millions of dollars on new seating: Lose weight. I'm a 5-foot, 4-inch woman and weigh 113 pounds. I'm 32 years old and have two children. I'm a size 4. I don't diet. I eat burgers, ice cream and chocolate. But I eat with moderation. I eat whatever I want—in moderation. That is a key word. Instead of new diet fads and weight-loss pills, people only need to understand finally the signals of their own bodies. When your stomach is full, stop eating. Be moderate and be happy. Very simple.—U.F.

14. Background: The following letter is in response to an article about people getting rid of their TV sets. (*Denver Post*, 4/97)

At 32, I realized I had never been without television. My husband and I watched TV in separate rooms most evenings. We would speak only at the top of the hour, when commercials were broadcast all around. Curious about life without TV, I finally told my husband he could get me a birthday gift that wouldn't cost anything and wouldn't require any shopping: "Let's get rid of the TVs for one month and see what happens." He refused. We divorced, and I left both TVs with him. I had the most fun, exciting, fulfilling, productive, healthy and creative years I ever had—without television. I discovered a life I never had an inkling existed. What I would have missed had I kept watching! There's a great life waiting out there. Get rid of the TV set and see what happens.—A.L.

15. Background: This letter is about aggressive male behavior.[20]

I don't want to hear any more of this talk about how barbaric and brutal men are. I work in an emergency room. Allow me to tell you what I have seen lately. The other night, they brought in a man who had been beaten silly by his wife while he was sleeping. In another case, a man came in complaining of a headache that had lasted for several days. X-rays revealed a bullet in his head; later he found a note from his wife explaining that she had shot him while he was asleep and that he should go to the hospital. A young baby boy was brought in with bruises all over his body; his mother had beaten him. That's the kind of thing that makes me think this talk of men being the aggressive ones is overblown.

16. Background: This letter is about historians' ratings of presidents. (*Boston Globe*, 2/00)

President Clinton shouldn't lose any sleep over American historians rating him only the 21st-best president before he even leaves office. History shows that historians have no capacity to rank recent presidents. During the

Kennedy administration, they rated Eisenhower the fourth- or fifth-*worst* president. Now he's the ninth-best.—R.C.

Summary

One of the three major activities of critical thinking is evaluating arguments in terms of their strength as an instrument of rational persuasion. Criticizing an argument is different from, though often confused with, criticizing a conclusion. When you criticize an argument, you do not directly take a stand on whether the conclusion is true.

An argument should persuade its audience to believe the conclusion when the premises provide sufficient support for the conclusion (formal requirements) and the premises are true or likely true (content requirements). The form of an argument concerns the support relationship of the premises to the conclusion, while the content of an argument considers each premise by itself.

The highest degree of formal strength is validity. An argument is valid when it is impossible for the premises to be true and the conclusion to be false. A valid argument is a deductive argument. All arguments that have a valid form are themselves valid. Some arguments that have forms that look similar to valid forms but are not valid are invalid. The method of counterexample is a way of testing a deductive argument to determine if it is invalid.

Deductive arguments with more than one premise have linked premises, one of which will usually be either a compound statement, like a conditional, or a general statement, often a universal generalization. Two valid argument forms that have conditionals for premises are *modus ponens* and *modus tollens*. In *modus ponens*, the second premise affirms the antecedent of the conditional; in *modus tollens*, the second premise denies the consequent of the conditional. Deductive arguments often have implicit premises.

The formal strength of nondeductive arguments is always short of validity, for it is always possible for the premises to be true and the conclusion to be false. Whereas the formal strength of deductive arguments is all or nothing (valid or invalid), the formal strength of nondeductive arguments is a matter of degree. Deductive arguments are either strong or weak; nondeductive arguments are more or less strong or more or less weak.

A weak argument, whether deductive or nondeductive, has certain identifiable weaknesses, called fallacies. A strong argument must satisfy two basic formal requirements: (1) the relevance of the premises to the conclusion and (2) the sufficiency of the premises in their support for the conclusion. In addition, an argument must satisfy two basic content requirements: (1) the acceptability of the premises to the audience and (2) the truth of the premises. These four requirements can be represented by the acronym TARS, standing for truth, acceptability, relevance, and sufficiency.

Because an argument can be weak in each of these four ways, there are four basic fallacies. On the formal side, an argument that fails to satisfy the relevance requirement commits the fallacy of irrelevant reason, and an argument that fails to satisfy the sufficiency requirement commits the fallacy of hasty conclusion. On the content side, an argument whose premises fail to satisfy the truth requirement commits the fallacy of false premise, and an argument whose premises fail to satisfy the acceptability requirement commits the fallacy of problematic premise.

When you evaluate an argument, you structure it and charge it with whichever of these four fallacies is appropriate. To justify a charge of irrelevant reason, you argue that one of the premises does not have the support relationship or has a negative support relationship with the conclusion. To justify a charge of hasty conclusion, you argue that the premises, taken together, do not provide sufficient support for the conclusion. In arguments about important and controversial topics, hasty conclusion is a very common charge because such topics have a large number of factors relevant to them. Factors that would count against the conclusion are called counterconsiderations. Arguments often include counterpremises, which are premises meant to respond to the counterconsiderations for that conclusion.

Finally, the basic fallacies have a number of specific versions. One specific version of irrelevant reason is argument *ad hominem*, in which criticism of an argument is directed at the person making the argument rather than the argument itself. One specific version of hasty conclusion is argument by anecdote, in which the arguer seeks to draw a general conclusion from a single case, an individual anecdote.

Key Terms

evaluation

strong argument

weak argument

argument content

content strength

argument form

formal strength

validity

deductive argument

invalid

modus ponens

method of
  counterexample

sound argument

modus tollens

unsound argument

nondeductive
  argument

cogent argument

noncogent argument

fallacy

relevance

sufficiency

truth

acceptability

TARS

irrelevant reason

hasty conclusion

false premise

problematic premise

fallacy charge

justification

counterconsideration

counterpremise

argument *ad hominem*

argument by anecdote

Notes

1. *Love's Labor Lost*, act 5, scene 1.
2. One possible exception to this claim needs to be registered. If we are speaking of statements about future events (for example, "it is likely true that it will rain tomorrow"), it may be that the phrase "likely true" applies to the statement itself, rather than merely to our belief about it. This is a controversial issue in the study of probability.
3. Invalid arguments are not, strictly speaking, deductive arguments, because the conclusion cannot be deduced from the premises. But the term "deductive argument" is often used in a broader sense to refer to both invalid and valid arguments, and this is how I will use the term. However, not all arguments are deductive arguments, even in this broader sense of the term. Many arguments are nondeductive; we will consider these later in the chapter.
4. When deductive arguments are represented using compound statements, such as conditionals, this is known as statement logic. When general statements are used instead, this is known as categorical logic.
5. As our discussion of implication in Chapter 2 shows, a deductive argument can have a single premise. We will discuss such cases in Chapter 7.
6. Alexander Hamilton, *The Federalist* 7, in Jacob Cooke (ed.), *The Federalist* (Middletown, CT: Wesleyan University Press, 1961), p. 43.
7. Charles Darwin, *On the Origin of Species* (Cambridge, MA: Harvard University Press, 1964), p. 63.
8. The phrase "like this" in this sentence is important. There is a different kind of premise we could add that would make the argument valid. We will discuss this issue in Chapter 10.
9. As we discussed in Chapter 2, some arguments, called mixed arguments, have some premises that are linked and others that are convergent.
10. The *seriousness* of a fault depends, in part, on how easily it would be for the author to revise the argument in order to correct the fault.
11. Three of these fallacy names—hasty conclusion, irrelevant reason, and problematic premise—are borrowed from R. H. Johnson and J. A. Blair, *Logical Self-Defense* (Toronto: McGraw-Hill/Ryerson, 1977).
12. The phrase "if it doesn't fit, you must acquit" had a double meaning. In addition to being a comment on the prosecution's overall case, it also referred to one specific aspect of the defense's case. A glove that, according to the prosecution, was worn by Simpson when he committed the murders appeared not to fit Simpson when he tried it on in court.
13. Interestingly, public opinion largely split along racial lines. Most whites thought that he should have been convicted, and most blacks thought that the nonguilty verdict was correct. Unfortunately, this split may say something about the way that social factors get in the way of people fairly evaluating an argument.
14. If the justification were limited to the first two sentences, we could charge the argument with the specific content fallacy of begging the question. This fallacy is committed when the premise(s) simply repeats the conclusion. Begging the question will be discussed in Chapter 8.
15. This argument in the justification could itself be charged with a fallacy, the specific content fallacy known as slippery slope, discussed in Chapter 8.
16. This means that hasty conclusion is a kind of mirror image fallacy to irrelevant reason. An argument commits irrelevant reason when it includes premises that are not relevant. An argument commits hasty conclusion when it does not include premises that are relevant.

17. Please keep in mind that we are here discussing the hasty conclusion charge as it applies only to *nondeductive* arguments. The way in which you charge hasty conclusion in the case of a deductive argument will be considered in Chapter 7.

18. But a singular statement, sometimes in the form of an anecdote, is sufficient to *refute* a universal generalization. This is called refutation by counterexample, and it will be discussed in Chapter 8.

19. Content fallacies are discussed in Chapter 8. This is an example of a general point that arguments are often chargeable with one kind of fallacy if interpreted one way and another kind of fallacy if interpreted another. We will discuss this issue in Chapter 10.

20. This text is taken from Johnson and Blair, p. 91.

CHAPTER 7

Deductive Arguments

In this chapter, we continue our discussion of the evaluation of argument form by extending our focus to deductive arguments. Deductive arguments are distinguished by their form. Only deductive arguments are valid. An argument is valid only if it is impossible for the premises to be true and the conclusion false. But not all deductive arguments are valid. An invalid argument is one that only *seems* to have the form of a valid argument. To evaluate deductive arguments for formal strength is to distinguish between valid and invalid arguments.

We began our discussion of validity and invalidity in the previous chapter with a presentation of some common valid and invalid forms. In this chapter, we expand on the discussion of validity and invalidity.

Arguments that are not deductive are nondeductive. In formal terms, nondeductive arguments have two characteristics that distinguish them from deductive arguments. First, nondeductive arguments have more modest formal ambitions than deductive arguments. Nondeductive formal strength is always short of validity. The truth of the premises of a nondeductive argument, no matter how strong the argument is, can never guarantee the truth of the conclusion. Second, deductive formal strength is all-or-nothing, whereas nondeductive formal strength is a matter of degree. Nondeductive arguments are more or less strong or weak. Deductive arguments are strong (valid) or weak (invalid), with no in-between.

Our discussion of deductive arguments in this chapter focuses on the question of how to tell whether a deductive argument is valid or invalid. Because validity is a matter of form rather than content, it has nothing to do with the truth of the premises. Consider this argument:

Example 7.1

P1: If the moon is made of green cheese, then the moon is a dairy product.
P2: The moon is made of green cheese.
C: Therefore, the moon is a dairy product.

This is a silly argument because the second premise is absurd. Yet the argument is valid.

How do you tell whether a deductive argument is valid or invalid? In Chapter 6, we considered the method of counterexample. With this method, you determine the form of the argument you are evaluating and try to think of another argument with that form that has obviously true premises and a false conclusion. If you can do this, then the form, and the original argument, is invalid. But this "brute force" testing method has limitations. First, it is not always easy to exercise your imagination as required, especially when the argument is complicated. Second, and more important, while this method can show that an argument is invalid, it cannot show that an argument is valid. If you cannot imagine a counterexample, this does not guarantee that the argument is valid. Thus, we need better methods.

In this chapter, we explore two methods for determining validity: categorical logic and statement logic. These methods are how you consider a charge of hasty conclusion for deductive arguments. If an argument is found to be invalid, this shows that the premises do not provide sufficient support for the conclusion. Therefore, the argument has committed the fallacy of hasty conclusion. Applying the method to show that the argument is invalid is equivalent to the justification for the fallacy charge. This is how charging hasty conclusion differs in the case of deductive arguments. Instead of a written argument justifying the charge, you have the application of the method.

What about the other formal charge, irrelevant reason? In the case of deductive arguments, irrelevant reason does not apply as a charge separate from hasty conclusion, because deductive arguments have linked premises.[1] A linked premise, you will recall, shows how the premise with which it is linked supports the conclusion. So, a linked premise cannot be evaluated on its own for relevance to the conclusion. Because you must evaluate linked premises as a group, hasty conclusion and irrelevant reason become equivalent fallacies. To put it another way, irrelevant reason applies as a fallacy charge separately from hasty conclusion only when strength is a matter of degree, and not all-or-nothing, as it is with deductive arguments.[2]

Before beginning our discussion of categorical logic and statement logic, we need to say something more about logical form.

7.1 Formal Logic and Logical Form

Formal logic is the study of methods to test deductive arguments for validity. There are various methods of formal logic, two of which we will discuss here. The key idea in formal logic is logical form. We touched on this concept of logical form in the previous chapter when we considered some common valid and invalid forms. All deductive arguments have a **logical form,** and this is the feature that determines whether they are valid or invalid. The form of a deductive argument is independent of its content. Testing a deductive argument for validity is a two-step process: (1) determine its logical form, and (2) test that logical form for validity.

> ### Three Characteristics of Logical Form
>
> 1. A single logical form can be present in many arguments (that is, arguments with different contents).
>
> 2. Some logical forms are valid, and some are invalid. The validity or invalidity of a deductive argument is determined by its form alone, not its content.
>
> 3. Any argument with a valid form is valid, and any argument with an invalid form is invalid.

Here are two pairs of arguments. In each pair, the content varies because the arguments are about different subjects, but the form remains the same. Both of the arguments in each pair have the same logical form. The forms, both valid, are different from those discussed in Chapter 6.

Example 7.2

A1. P1: All mammals are warm-blooded creatures.
     P2: Some animals are mammals.
     C: Therefore, some animals are warm-blooded creatures.

A2. P1: All children are people who enjoy cartoons.
     P2: Some people who get up early on Saturday morning are children.
     C: Therefore, some people who get up early on Saturday morning are people who enjoy cartoons.

B1. P1: Either Shakespeare is the man of the millennium or Newton is the man of the millennium.
     P2: If Shakespeare is the man of the millennium, then the arts are the most important human activity.
     P3: If Newton is the man of the millennium, then the sciences are the most important human activity.
     C: Therefore, either the arts are the most important human activity or the sciences are the most important human activity.

B2. P1: Either we should keep the speed limit where it is or we should raise it.
     P2: If we keep the speed limit where it is, then many people will continue to break the speeding laws.
     P3: If we raise the speed limit, then the highways will become less safe.
     C: Therefore, either many people will continue to break the speeding laws or the highways will become less safe.

What is the logical form of these arguments? In a deductive argument, as we saw in Chapter 6, some words represent the content and some represent the form. Content is represented by groups of words (sentences, independent clauses, phrases, or single words), and each group of words, or synonymous expression, will occur more than once. To find the logical form of an argument, you replace with symbols the groups of words that represent content. The words that remain represent the logical form of the argument. The words that represent logical form are **logic words.**

Consider the arguments in Example 7.2. To show how you are replacing the content with symbols, you need to supply a table of symbols, which is simply a list that indicates which symbols replace which groups of words. Here is the table of symbols and the logical form for A1:

> **Example 7.3**
>
> Table of Symbols
>> M = mammals
>> W = warm-blooded creatures
>> A= animals
>
> Logical Form
>> P1: All M are W.
>> P2: Some A are M.
>> C: Therefore, some A are W.

The logical form is what results when you replace the groups of words with the symbols indicated in the table. (It does not matter what symbols you choose. But it is usually convenient, as in this case, to choose letters that are initials for the terms they represent.) After you substitute the symbols for the content, some words will remain; these represent the form. The logic words in this case are "all," "some," and "are."

The symbols for argument A2 are C = children, E = people who enjoy cartoons, and S = people who get up early on Saturday morning. Here is the logical form for A2:

> **Example 7.4**
>
> P1: All C are E.
> P2: Some S are C.
> C: Therefore, some S are E.

Note that A2 has the same arrangement of logic words and the same logical form as A1.

Now consider the B arguments from Example 7.2. The symbols for argument B1 are S = Shakespeare is the man of the millennium, N = Newton is the man of the millennium, A = the arts are the most important human activity, and C = the sciences are the most important human activity.[3] Here is the logical form for B1:

> **Example 7.5**
>
> P1: Either S or N.
> P2: If S, then A.
> P3: If N, then C.
> C: Therefore, either A or C.

Argument B2 has the same logical form, though it would probably be represented with different symbols. In the case of these two arguments, the logic words are different from those for the A arguments. The logic words for the B arguments are "either," "or," "if," and "then."

Logic Words

Logic words are words that represent logical form. They are the words that are left in deductive arguments after symbols have replaced the groups of words indicating content. For example, "if" and "then" are the logic words that represent a conditional; "all" and "are" represent a universal generalization. An important logic word is "not," which is used in both categorical and statement logic.

Although the procedure of replacing content with symbols sounds simple, it can be difficult in practice. The translation of the arguments from Example 7.2 was straightforward because these arguments were already expressed in a way that made their logical form apparent. However, outside a logic text, you normally will not find arguments written in this sort of partially formalized way. Consider how these arguments might have been presented in everyday contexts:

Example 7.6

A1. It is obvious that some animals are warm-blooded. After all, mammals are animals.
A2. Children sometimes get up early on Saturday morning, and all children enjoy cartoons.
B1. Shakespeare or Newton may be the man of the millennium. If so, the arts or the sciences are what is most important.
B2. People will go on breaking the speed limit if we leave it where it is, but if we raise it the highways will be less safe.

Content can be replaced with symbols in different ways. This is evident from the contrast between the way the A and B arguments are represented in Examples 7.3–7.5. The symbols chosen to represent the A arguments represent noun phrases, and the symbols chosen to represent the B argument represent sentences. Categorical logic represents content in terms of noun phrases (as with the A arguments), and statement logic represents content in terms of sentences (as with the B arguments). The method used to test any particular argument for validity will partly depend on the nature of that argument. Some arguments are better tested for validity using one method than another.

7.2 Categorical Logic

Categorical logic is the oldest method of formal logic. The Greek philosopher Aristotle developed categorical logic in the fourth century B.C.E., and until the nineteenth century, it was thought to be the only method of formal logic. Aristotle's achievement, producing a system of logic that dominated our view of the world for over two millennia, is perhaps unparalleled in the history of thought. **Categorical logic** is based on the idea that logical form is revealed when the statements of an argument are represented as **categorical statements.** We need to consider categorical statements before we can discuss the form of the arguments that comprise categorical statements.

7.2.1 Categorical Statements

When we think about the world, we often classify the things in it into categories or classes. For example, there are categories of babies, birthdays, and shades of blue. As in these examples, we often indicate categories in terms of common nouns. We also think about how the categories of things in the world relate to one another. In particular, a category may *include* some categories and *exclude* others. Categorical statements make claims about the inclusive and exclusive relationships of categories.

> ### Categorical Logic and Categorical Statements
>
> The world can be divided into classes or categories of things, events, properties, and so forth, and we seek to understand how these categories relate to one another in terms of inclusion or exclusion. Categorical statements indicate the relationships of inclusion and exclusion between categories or classes of things. Categorical logic is a way of understanding how categorical statements relate to each other as premises and conclusions of deductive arguments.

The idea behind categorical logic is that we can represent deductive arguments by statements about the relationships of inclusion and exclusion between categories and that when we formulate an argument in this way we can readily test its validity. A categorical argument is composed of categorical statements.

We need to introduce some terminology to our discussion of categorical statements. Let us consider two categories, S and P, that are related by inclusion or exclusion, and the possible relationships between them. Category S may include or exclude category P. In addition, if S includes or excludes P, it may do so completely or partially. This creates four possibilities, and four logical forms for categorical statements. When one category includes another, the statement representing this is an **affirmative statement;** when one category excludes another, the statement is a

Quantity \ Quality	Affirmative (inclusion)	Negative (exclusion)
Universal (complete)	Type A: "All S are P."	Type E: "No S are P."
Particular (partial)	Type I: "Some S are P."	Type O: "Some S are not P."

FIGURE 7.1 **The Four Forms of Categorical Statements**

negative statement. Whether a categorical statement is affirmative or negative refers to the **statement quality.** When inclusion or exclusion is complete, the statement representing this is a **universal statement;** when the inclusion or exclusion is partial, the statement is a **particular statement.** Whether a categorical statement is universal or particular refers to the **statement quantity.** As Figure 7.1 shows, the four possibilities can be represented in a grid or matrix.

These are the only four logical forms for categorical statements. The four types of categorical statement have traditionally been labeled "A," "E," "I," and "O."[4] The logic words in the four forms are as follows:

1. Universal affirmative (A): "all . . . are . . ."
2. Universal negative (E): "no . . . are . . ."
3. Particular affirmative (I): "some . . . are . . ."
4. Particular negative (O): "some . . . are not . . ."

The groups of words that fill in the blanks in these forms represent the categories the statements are about. All categorical statements refer to two categories, one in the subject position of the sentence (usually designated "S," as above) and the other in the predicate position (the term following a form of the verb "to be," usually designated as "P"). All categorical statements are general statements, some universal ("all" or "no") and some particular ("some"). Singular statements are not used in categorical logic, though, as we will see, there is a way of representing singular statements in categorical terms.

Note that as it is used in categorical statements "some" means "at least one." For example, it is appropriate to make the categorical statement "some people are president of the United States," even though only one person actually is. All of the following phrases that appear in categorical statements would be reformulated using the term "some": "many," "most," "a lot," "several," "a number," "a few," and "almost all." Thus, for example, to say that some children do not like spinach is to say only that there is at least one such child, even though we know that there are many. In this respect, particular categorical statements are not very precise in their meaning.

Like any statement, a categorical statement can be expressed in many ways. But categorical statements are most clearly expressed in sentences in which the verb is a form of the verb "to be," usually "is" or "are." In addition, each category should be expressed by a noun or a noun phrase. When representing categorical statements, you should formulate them in this way, even though this often requires extra words. Here are some examples:

Example 7.7

Universal affirmative (A): All liquor is an intoxicating substance.
Universal negative (E): No humans are creatures over 30 feet tall.
Particular affirmative (I): Some children are people who like peanut butter.
Particular negative (O): Some celebrities are not people who are egomaniacs.

Such sentences represent the standard form for categorical statements. Reformulation is frequently necessary to put the sentences representing categorical statements into standard form. You indicate the two categories, S and P, by nouns or noun phrases, and formulate the sentence with an "is" or an "are."

Here are examples of some sentences expressing categorical statements; the first sentence in each pair expresses the statement more casually, and the second one more formally.

Example 7.8

A: All birds have hearts.
   All birds are *animals with hearts*.
E: No airlines serve good food.
   No airlines are *companies that serve good food*.
I: Some politicians tell the truth.
   Some politicians are people *who tell the truth*.
O: Some Internet stocks are not overvalued.
   Some Internet stocks are not *investments that are overvalued*.

In the first A sentence, what is the second category? It is not hearts. Birds are not hearts. Rather, birds are *animals with hearts*, which is the second category. Usually, the expression in the subject position is already a noun or noun phrase, so it does not need to be reformulated. In the second sentence in all four types above, the noun phrase indicating the second category is italicized.

When you reformulate sentences representing categorical statements into standard form by substituting a noun or noun phrase for the predicate term, the

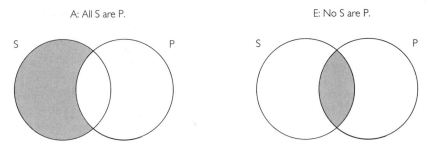

A: All S are P.   E: No S are P.

FIGURE 7.2   Venn Diagrams for Universal Statements

noun or noun phrase often represents a broader category than the one indicated by the noun in the subject position.[5] For example, in the second A-sentence, "animal" is a broader category than "birds"; in the second E-sentence, "company" is a broader category than "airline"; in the second I-sentence, "people" is a broader category than "politicians"; and in the second O-sentence, "investments" is a broader category than "stocks." If you can't think of a noun or noun phrase indicating a broader category, you can use the word "thing." For example, you could reformulate the statement "every event has a cause" as "all events are things with causes."

7.2.2 Representing Categorical Statements with Venn Diagrams

Categorical statements, as we have seen, are claims about inclusion and exclusion between two categories. Consider again how universal categorical statements represent the relationships of inclusion or exclusion between the categories. The universal affirmative—"all S are P"—indicates that the category of S is *included* within the category of P. The universal negative—"no S are P"—indicates that the category of S is *excluded* from the category of P.

To represent the idea of inclusion and exclusion for categories, we can use circles. For example, the category S can be represented by a circle, such that what is within the circle is part of S and what is outside the circle is not part of S (usually expressed by "non-S"). To represent a categorical statement and the relationship of inclusion or exclusion it asserts, we use two circles, one for each of the categories. The standard way to do this is to represent the statement with two intersecting, partly overlapping circles. This method of representation is referred to as **Venn diagrams**.[6] In the case of universal statements, we use shading to indicate the inclusion or exclusion relationship. Figure 7.2 shows how the two universal statements would be represented. Shading indicates an area within one or the other circle that is empty. In the case of the diagram of "all S are P," all of the S circle outside the area that overlaps the P circle is shaded. Since all S are P, there is nothing in that area. In the case of the diagram of "no S are P," the area of overlap of the circles is shaded because there is no S that is a P.

The particular categorical statements are also represented with two intersecting circles, but the inclusion and exclusion is indicated differently. Instead of shad-

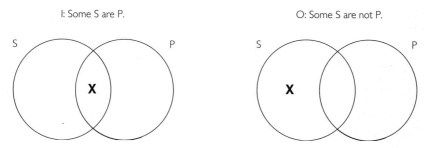

FIGURE 7.3   Venn Diagrams for Particular Statements

ing, an "x" is used. Recall that "some" means "at least one." The "x" represents that one, as shown in Figure 7.3. The affirmative particular statement ("some S are P") is represented with the "x" in the area of overlap because the statement says that at least one S is a P. The negative particular statement ("some S are not P") is represented with the "x" in the part of S that does not overlap with P.

We cannot put an "x" in any other of the areas of these diagrams because the statements do not give us enough information. The I-statement does not tell us that there is more than one S that is a P, nor that there are any S that are not P. If the I statement were "some politicians are charismatic," we would know that more than one is and that many are not, but the statement by itself does not tell us this. Similarly, the O-statement does not tell us that there is more than one S that is not a P, nor that there are any S that are P. If the O-statement were "some books are not boring," we would know that more than one is not and that some are, but the statement by itself does not tell us this. Categorical statements are concerned with the *fact* of inclusion in the case of the affirmative statement, and the *fact* of exclusion in the case of the negative statements. The *extent* of the inclusion or exclusion is another matter.

Venn Diagrams

Venn diagrams are a method of representing categorical arguments so as to determine their validity or invalidity. The method involves using partly overlapping circles to indicate what categorical statements say about inclusion and exclusion between categories.

7.2.3 *Reformulating Sentences into Categorical Form*

When a sentence express a categorical statement, you usually need to reformulate it to express the categorical form of the statement more clearly. Categorical statements seldom come in standard form. Previously, we saw the need to choose terms that are nouns or noun phrases. But more extensive reformulation often is required, because many categorical statements are expressed in sentences effectively disguising their form. Getting them into standard form requires recognizing that the sentences express categorical statements and then figuring out what categorical statements they express.

As we have seen in previous chapters, interpreting the meaning of a text can be difficult. Here, as elsewhere, there is no set of rules that will guarantee a correct interpretation, but there are some general guidelines. In any reformulation of a sentence expressing a categorical statement into standard form, you must (1) identify the two categories, determining which is S and which is P, (2) determine the quality of the statement (affirmative or negative), (3) determine the quantity of the statement (universal or particular), and (4) formulate the standard form sentence for that statement. It is not important that you follow these steps in this order, nor that you treat them as separate steps. But thinking of them as separate steps will help you recognize the tasks involved.

Steps for Reformulating Sentences Expressing Categorical Statements into Standard Form

1. Identify the two categories that the sentence is referring to, and determine which is S and which is P.

2. Determine the quality of the statement—affirmative (inclusion) or negative (exclusion).

3. Determine the quantity of the statement—universal (about the whole of the S category) or particular (about only part of the S category).

4. Formulate noun phrases for the two categories and express the statement in a standard form sentence.

Now let us examine some specific difficulties in carrying out these steps. Consider these sentences and their standard form reformulations:

Example 7.9

Nonstandard Form Sentence	Standard Form Reformulation
1. Every good boy deserves favor.	A: All good boys are people who deserve favor.
2. Humans do not hibernate.	E: No humans are creatures who hibernate.
3. Women are nurturing.	I: Some women are people who are nurturing.

4. Not all old people are cranky.   O: Some old people are not cranky people.

5. All bankers are not poor.   E: No bankers are poor.
or
O: Some bankers are not poor.

6. The beaver is a mammal.   A: All beavers are mammals.

7. A beaver lives in our pond.   I: Some beavers are creatures that live in our pond.

8. Only the good die young.   A: All people who die young are good people.

9. The only way to heaven is faith.   A: All ways to heaven are attitudes of faith.

10. Jockeys are all men.   A: All jockeys are men.

11. There are no motels on the moon.   E: No motels are buildings on the moon.

12. Water freezes.   A: All masses of water are things that can freeze.

13. Venn is a logician.   A: All people identical with Venn are logicians.

In sentences 1–7, we have to determine the quantity of the categorical statement they express. That is, we need to find the appropriate quantifier ("all/no" or "some") for the general statement. Sentence 1 uses "every" as its quantifier, which, like "each" and "any," is generally a synonym for "all." Sentences with any of these terms that express categorical statements are usually A-statements (universal affirmative).

Sentences 2 and 3 are incomplete sentences, expressing general statements with implicit quantifiers. For such sentences, we need to judge whether the author intends a universal statement (a statement of the A or E type) or a particular statement (a statement of the I or O type). Is the implicit quantifier "all" or "some"? Sentence 2 is almost certainly meant as a universal statement, since hibernating is a biological process that humans are not capable of. So, given that the quality of sentence 2 is negative, it expresses an E-statement. In contrast, sentence 3 is most likely meant as a particular statement, since, while many women are nurturing, not all are. So, it expresses an I-statement (particular affirmative).

Sentence 4 contains the frequently used phrase "not all." When you say "not all," you usually mean "some are not." To say that not all S are P is to say that some S are not P. Thus, sentence 4 expresses an O-statement (particular negative). Sentence 5 is ambiguous, because it is not clear how the "not" should be understood. In one interpretation, sentence 5 has the same form as sentence 4; that is, "not all bankers are poor," which is the O form: "some bankers are not poor." In the other interpretation, it is an E-statement (universal negative) saying something about all bankers—namely, that none of them is poor. In cases like this, you need to pay attention to context to determine which interpretation is best.

In sentences 6 and 7, as in sentences 2 and 3, the quantifiers are implicit. But whereas sentences 6 and 7 begin with articles ("the" and "a"), sentences 2 and 3 do not. However, the articles are, in these cases at least, of no help in determining the quantifier. In sentence 6, it is clear from the predicate term ("mammal") that the subject term refers not to some individual beaver, but to the species beaver, which is the class of all beavers. Thus, the quantifier is "all," and the statement is an A type. In contrast, it is clear that sentence 7 refers to one individual beaver, not to the species, so it expresses a particular statement of the I type rather than a universal statement. Recall that "some" means "at least one," so the I form is appropriate even though the sentence refers to only one member of the class. Note that it is not the article that indicates the quantifier in these cases. Either sentence could have begun with the other article, and the interpretation would have remained the same.

In sentences 8–10, we have to determine which category is the subject and which is the predicate. Sentence 8 refers to two classes—people who are good and people who die young—but which is the subject and which is the predicate? There is a rule for this kind of case. Generally, when "only" is used in this sort of sentence, a universal statement (A or E) is expressed and the predicate term is the one preceded by the "only." But things are usually different if the term is "the only," as in sentence 9. Sentences like this one also express universal statements, but the subject term, not the predicate term, is the one preceded by the phrase.

In sentence 10, the quantifier is included, but, in contrast to the standard case, it precedes the predicate term rather than the subject term. In such cases, it is usually obvious which is the subject term, despite the fact that the quantifier precedes the other term. One indication of this is that the sentence would clearly mean the same thing if the quantifier was placed in front of the subject term.

The final three sentences pose special interpretation problems. In the case of sentence 11, the grammatical subject of the sentence, "there," refers to no specific category. Both of the categories, motels and buildings on the moon, are referred to in grammatical predicate. So, proper interpretation of such a sentence involves figuring out which is the subject and which is the predicate in the standard form sentence.

The subject term in sentence 12, "water," is a mass noun. A mass noun, unlike most nouns, does not designate an individual unit. There is no individual water, as there are, for example, individual babies, birthdays, shades of blue. Mass nouns are used when there is no natural characteristic of a kind of thing that distinguishes some portion of it from other portions of it. When a mass noun is a subject term, you must invent a noun phrase that individuates, since this is what the standard forms of the categorical statements require. The reformulation for sentence 12 uses the term "masses" for this purpose. With another mass noun, it might be "instances" or "examples."

Sentence 13 expresses a singular statement. So, because categorical statements are general statements, it seems not to express a categorical statement at all. But we can understand singular statements as categorical statements by making up a class with only one member, the individual referred to in the sentence. Something is a member of that category only if it is identical with that individual. This is the source of the subject term in the reformulation. Because the predicate term applies to all members of the class referred to in the subject term, the statement is type A.

EXERCISE SET 7.2

SECTION A: Reformulate the following sentences so that they are in standard form for the type of categorical statements they express. Indicate clearly, using a noun phrase in the predicate position, what the two categories are. Also indicate the type of categorical statement the sentence expresses.

EXAMPLE
Some books have pictures.

ANSWER
Some books are objects with pictures.
Type I: Some S are P.

PROBLEMS
1. All computer chips are made of silicon.
2. Some Ph.D.'s are not very bright.
3. Some family gatherings have a tendency to go on and on.
4. Some fires have the potential for great destruction.
5. All energy comes from the stars.
6. All generalizations are false.
7. Some people cannot help meddling.
8. Some senior citizens are not feeble.
9. All categorical statements have one of four forms.
10. No meal should be eaten in haste.
11. Some wine has been aged a long time.
12. All critical thinking textbooks have exercise sets.
13. Some governments are not democratic.
14. No children should be out after dark.
15. No playwright can surpass Shakespeare.
16. No dispute is worth a life.
17. Some spirits are fairies.
18. Some dogs do not obey their masters.
19. All cats like to show their independence.
20. Some airlines have gone out of business.

SECTION B: Represent each of the statements in Section A with a Venn diagram.

EXAMPLE
Some books are objects with pictures.

ANSWER

S = books
P = objects with pictures

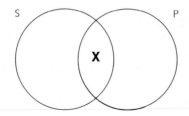

SECTION C: For each of the following problems, formulate two versions of the categorical statement based on the information given—a standard form sentence and a casual nonstandard form sentence.

EXAMPLE

Type A, S = bees, P = insects with stingers

ANSWER

All bees are insects with stingers.
All bees have stingers.

PROBLEMS

1. Type O,   S = chemical,   P = substance harmful to people
2. Type E,   S = ocean liner,   P = object made of paper
3. Type I,   S = story,   P = thing that is boring
4. Type A,   S = presidents,   P = person who is male
5. Type E,   S = grocery store,   P = place that sells circus animals
6. Type A,   S = bus,   P = vehicle with more than one wheel
7. Type I,   S = writers,   P = person with writer's block
8. Type O,   S = business,   P = establishment that is dishonest

SECTION D: For the following problems, follow the directions from Section A (no need to indicate statement type). If any of the sentences has an implicit quantifier, give what you think is the most likely interpretation of the author's intentions.

EXAMPLE

Rainbows occur only when it is raining.

ANSWER

All rainbows are events that occur when it is raining.

PROBLEMS

1. Old trees have many rings.
2. A person must be insane to commit murder.
3. Parents are older than their children.
4. Some college students would be better off not being in college.
5. Everything we know is subject to doubt.
6. Some fathers know best.
7. No politicians tell the truth.
8. No glass is a solid.
9. Any job is a job worth doing well.
10. Aristotle invented categorical logic.
11. There is nothing certain but death and taxes.
12. A chain is only as strong as its weakest link.
13. The British are eccentric.
14. Haste makes waste.
15. Home is where the heart is.
16. Only love can break a heart.
17. Some Broadway musicals are deadly dull.
18. A military draft is preferable to an all-volunteer fighting force.
19. Youth is wasted on the young.

20. An oak grows at the end of the drive.

❖ 21. Not all prizes are worth having.

22. Higher animals reproduce sexually.

23. An orchid is a flower.

❖ 24. Sewage is to be avoided.

25. Even cowgirls get the blues.

26. Whenever you feel sad, whistle a happy tune.

❖ 27. Every year, prices go up.

28. Some people would rather die than think.

29. There's a sucker born every minute.

SECTION E: Apply the instructions for Section D to the following problems, taken from letters to the editor.

EXAMPLE

A person seeking employment cannot take the chance that he or she is someone who can emerge from illness without intervention.—L.O. (*New York Times*, 5/97)

ANSWER

All people seeking employment are people who cannot take the chance that they are among those who can emerge from illness without intervention.

PROBLEMS

1. Every healthy adult should offer to donate a unit of blood.—V.H. (*New York Times*, 7/99)

2. Computer operating systems are inherently different from other intellectual property.—N.B.B. (*New York Times*, 5/98)

❖ 3. No society that began its history by defining a black person as less than a full person can expect the damage from this to be eliminated in one generation.—G.S.P. (*New York Times*, 7/99)

4. Physicians are forced by their employers to see more patients in less time. —M.R.G. (*New York Times*, 7/98)

5. The "reality" emergency shows are a completely unjustified invasion of the people's privacy.—D.J.A. (*Los Angeles Times*, 7/97)

❖ 6. Some of our military heroes were involved in long-term amorous relationships while in combat.—H.H.H. (*Boston Globe*, 5/97)

7. Traffic lights should never be set permanently to flash yellow in one direction and red in the other.—F.R.S. (*Miami Herald*, 1/98)

8. American judges must base their judgment on observable behavior and reasonably foreseeable consequences.—D.P.L. (*New York Times*, 1/97)

❖ 9. Some of the jury knew first-hand the fears of Mr. Goetz.—J.C.K. (*Washington Post*, 6/87)

10. The legislators who made this law have taken away one of the basic freedoms of life.—B.C. (*Atlanta Constitution*, 3/97)

11. Neo-Confederate partisans of decentralized authority overlook several salient elements in this history.—H.M. (*New York Times*, 3/98)

❖ 12. Most bureaucrats think that any writing style other than one that's turgid, impersonal, and convoluted will undermine their authority.—R.A.F. (*New York Times*, 6/98)

13. Colleges and universities should not be expected to change social patterns that are generally accepted in adult society.—J.F.Z. (*New York Times*, 1/88)

14. No, the real culprits are greedy large and small businesses in America. —R.M.C. (*Los Angeles Times*, 1/98)

❖ 15. Many religions do a great service to women by encouraging men to behave. —P.H. (*Boston Globe*, 3/99)

16. Whenever another man decides to go on a rampage and empties his rapid-firing gun into a group of uninvolved civilians, his maleness is not considered a motive.—P.S. (*New York Times*, 12/93)

17. In play, success and failure should be irrelevant concepts.—J.L. (*New York Times*, 6/99)

❖ 18. Let us rid ourselves of those silly fractions on our rulers and the unwieldy ounces and pounds on our scales.—D.S. (*New York Times*, 6/97)

19. All it takes are full lips, tousled hair, and a pack of Marlboros.—M.E.L. (*Boston Globe*, 7/97)

20. Let those who believe your columnist's assertion that "our country has been created by numerous wars, but we are not a warlike people" test their theory at the Pentagon.—R.E.P.[7] (*New York Times*, 7/98)

❖ 21. Life is a series of compromises.—L.S. (*New York Times*, 6/97)

22. In some foreign countries, schools teach less material but cover the topics in greater depth.—J.S. (*New York Times*, 2/00)

23. U.S. activities during the Nixon-Kissinger phase of the Vietnam War were behind the coup that destabilized Cambodia and paved the way for Pol Pot's rise.—L.R.U. (*New York Times*, 6/97)

❖ 24. Not all religions concern themselves with the worship of God.—A.D. (*New York Times*, 7/97)

7.3 Immediate Inference

The deductive arguments considered in Chapter 6 all had two premises. But sometimes deductive arguments have a single premise. We saw an example of this when we discussed implication in Chapter 2. A deductive argument with a single premise is referred to as an **immediate inference.** It is an implication of one statement by another. In an immediate inference, the truth of one statement guarantees the truth of another. The support relationship between the premise and the conclusion is called "immediate" because it is not mediated by the presence of another premise. Categorical logic gives us an easy way to examine and evaluate immediate inferences. Different kinds of immediate inference can be represented in categorical logic.

7.3.1 The Square of Opposition

Some kinds of immediate inference result from considering relationships among the four types of categorical statements. Categorical statements of the four types

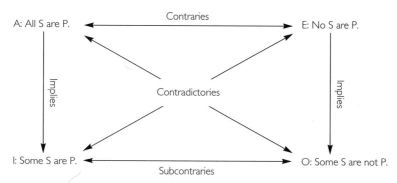

FIGURE 7.4   The Square of Opposition

with the same subject and predicate terms are said to be in opposition to one another. As Figure 7.4 shows, the relationships of opposition can be represented by the **square of opposition.** As the square indicates, the statements may be opposed as **contradictories** (A and O, or E and I), **contraries** (A and E), or **subcontraries** (I and O). Two statements are contradictories when the truth of one implies the falsity of the other (in other words, they cannot both be true or both be false). Two statements are contraries when they cannot both be true but may both be false. Two statements are subcontraries when they cannot both be false but may both be true. In addition, as the square indicates, there is an implication relationship from the universal affirmative (A form) statement to the particular affirmative (I form) statement, and from the universal negative (E form) statement to the particular negative (O form) statement.

To illustrate these relationships, consider these statements:

Example 7.10

A: All trees are evergreens.

E: No trees are evergreens.

I: Some trees are evergreens.

O: Some trees are not evergreens.

First, consider the contradictory statements. According to the square of opposition, A- and O-statements are contradictories. The statements that all trees are evergreens and that some trees are not evergreens are thus contradictories. If it is true that all trees are evergreens, it is false that some trees are not evergreens. But, if it is true that some trees are not evergreens, it is false that all trees are evergreens. In addition, E- and I-statements are contradictories. If it is true that no trees are evergreens, it is false that some trees are evergreens; and if it is true that some trees are evergreens, it is false that no trees are evergreens.

Now consider the contraries and subcontraries. According to the square of opposition, A- and E-statements are contraries, which means that both cannot be true though both may be false. The statements that all trees are evergreens and that no trees are evergreens are both false. According to the square, I and O are subcontraries, so they cannot both be false but may both be true. Indeed, the statements that some trees are evergreens and that some trees are not evergreens are both true. (In contrast, if the predicate term in these statements were "plants" instead of "evergreens," then one of the contraries and one of the subcontraries would be true and the other false.)

Finally, consider the implication relationship from A to I forms and from E to O forms. If all trees are evergreens, then some trees are evergreens; and if no trees are evergreens, then some trees are not evergreens.

The following list gives some of the immediate inferences traditionally thought to be based on the square of opposition:[8]

1. If the A-statement is true, then the E- and O-statements are false, and the I-statement is true.
2. If the A-statement is false, then the O-statement is true, and the truth or falsity of the E- and I-statements is undetermined.
3. If the E-statement is true, then the A- and I-statements are false, and the O-statement is true.
4. If the E-statement is false, then the I-statement is true, and the truth or falsity of the A- and O-statements is undetermined.
5. If the I-statement is true, then the E-statement is false, and the truth or falsity of the A- and O-statements is undetermined.
6. If the I-statement is false, then the E- and O-statements are true, and the A-statement is false.
7. If the O-statement is true, then the A-statement is false, and the truth or falsity of the E- and I-statements is undetermined.

8. If the O-statement is false, then the A- and I-statements are true, and the E-statement is false.

Consider examples of these:

Example 7.11

1. If it is true that (A) all trees are evergreens, then it is false that (E) no trees are evergreens, false that (O) some trees are not evergreens, and true that (I) some trees are evergreens.
2. If it is false that (A) all trees are evergreens, then it is true that (O) some trees are not evergreens.
3. If it is true that (E) no trees are evergreens, then it is false that (A) all trees are evergreens, false that (I) some trees are evergreens, and true that (O) some trees are not evergreens.
4. If it is false that (E) no trees are evergreens, then it is true that (I) some trees are evergreens.
5. If it is true that (I) some trees are evergreens, then it is false that (E) no trees are evergreens.
6. If it is false that (I) some trees are evergreens, then it is true that (E) no trees are evergreens, true that (O) some trees are not evergreens, and false that (A) all trees are evergreens.
7. If it is true that (O) some trees are not evergreens, then it is false that (A) all trees are evergreens.
8. If it is false that (O) some trees are not evergreens, then it is true that (A) all trees are evergreens, true that (I) some trees are evergreens, and false that (E) no trees are evergreens.

7.3.2 Conversion, Obversion, and Contraposition

We now consider three kinds of immediate inference among categorical statements that are not represented by the square of opposition. These three are based on *operations* performed on categorical statements, operations in which the subject and predicate terms are interchanged and/or negated. One of these operations is **conversion.** In conversion, you simply transpose the subject and predicate terms of a categorical statement.

Consider this example:

Example 7.12

Statement	Converse
A: All trees are evergreens.	All evergreens are trees.
E: No trees are evergreens.	No evergreens are trees.
I: Some trees are evergreens.	Some evergreens are trees.
O: Some trees are not evergreens.	Some evergreens are not trees.

Not all of these combinations are valid immediate inferences. There is such an inference for the E and I forms, but not for the A and O forms. For E and I forms, if a statement is true, its converse is also true; and if a statement is false, its converse is false. Thus, if it is true that no trees are evergreens, then it is true that no evergreens are trees. If it is false that no trees are evergreens, then it is false that no evergreens are trees. If it is true that some trees are evergreens, then it is true that some evergreens are trees. If it is false that some trees are evergreens, then it is false that some evergreens are trees. But there are no such inferences for the A and O forms. For example, the truth or falsity of the claim that all trees are evergreens tells us nothing about the truth or falsity of the claim that all evergreens are trees.

There is a valid immediate inference from the truth of an E- or I-statement to the truth of its converse because an E-statement and its converse and an I statement and its converse are logically equivalent. When statements have **logical equivalence,** they are either both true or both false. The truth of either one implies the truth of the other, and the falsity of either one implies the falsity of the other. Logical equivalence characterizes not only conversion but obversion and contraposition as well.[9] Unlike the kinds of immediate inferences we discussed in terms of the square of opposition, the immediate inferences represented by conversion, obversion, and contraposition are all from truth to truth or from falsity to falsity.

> ### Logical Equivalence
>
> Two statements have logical equivalence, or are logically equivalent, when the truth of either implies the truth of the other and the falsity of either implies the falsity of the other. In other words, logically equivalent statements are always both true or both false.

To understand **obversion,** we need to understand that the complement of a class is everything that is outside of that class. For example, the complement of the class of squirrels is everything in the universe that is not a squirrel. Thus, "nonsquirrels" is the complement of "squirrels." In the operation of obversion, you change the quality of the categorical statement from affirmative to negative or negative to affirmative, and you replace the predicate term with its complement.

Consider this example:

Example 7.13

Statement	Obverse
A: All trees are evergreens.	No trees are non-evergreens.
E: No trees are evergreens.	All trees are non-evergreens.
I: Some trees are evergreens.	Some trees are not non-evergreens.
O: Some trees are not evergreens.	Some trees are non-evergreens.

TABLE 7.1   Valid immediate inferences under the three operations.

	Conversion	Obversion	Contraposition
A	invalid	valid	valid
E	valid	valid	invalid
I	valid	valid	invalid
O	invalid	valid	valid

Unlike conversion, obversion yields a valid immediate inference in all four forms. In the A, E, I, and O forms, the truth of a statement implies the truth of its obverse. A categorical statement, in any of the four forms, and its obverse are always logically equivalent.

The third operation is **contraposition.** In this operation, you replace the subject with the predicate complement and the predicate with the subject complement. Consider this example:

Example 7.14

Statement	Contrapositive
A: All trees are evergreens.	All non-evergreens are nontrees.
E: No trees are evergreens.	No non-evergreens are nontrees.
I: Some trees are evergreens.	Some non-evergreens are nontrees.
O: Some trees are not evergreens.	Some non-evergreens are not nontrees.

Contraposition does not allow for valid immediate inference for all statement types. Immediate inference is valid in the A and O forms, but not in the E and I forms. Thus, if all trees are evergreens, then everything that is not an evergreen is not a tree. Likewise, if some trees are not evergreens, then some things that are not evergreens are trees. (This last point illustrates the rule of double negation. A double negative is a positive. That is, if something is not a nontree, then it is a tree.) But the E and I forms do not yield valid immediate inferences. For example, from the claim that no hawks are handsaws, you cannot infer that no nonhandsaws are nonhawks. In fact, a breadbasket is a nonhandsaw that is also a nonhawk. Table 7.1 summarizes the valid immediate inferences under the three operations.

Conversion, Obversion, and Contraposition

In conversion, the subject and predicate terms of a categorical statement are interchanged. In obversion, the quality of the statement is changed from affirmative to negative (or vice versa) and the predicate is replaced with its complement. In contraposition, the subject and predicate terms are interchanged and each is replaced by its complement.

EXERCISE SET 7.3

SECTION A: For the following, generate statements of each of the four categorical forms from the given subject and predicate terms. Then, assuming that the indicated statement is true, identify what, if anything, based on the square of opposition, can be said about the truth or falsity of the others. Be sure that you base your judgments not on your beliefs about the statements, but on the validity of the immediate inference.

EXAMPLE

S = endangered species, P = species worth saving; assume A true

ANSWER

A: All endangered species are species worth saving. True (as stipulated)
E: No endangered species are species worth saving. False
I: Some endangered species are species worth saving. True
O: Some endangered species are not species worth saving. False

PROBLEMS

1. S = consumers, P = satisfied people; assume E true
2. S = automobiles, P = gas guzzlers; assume I true
❖ 3. S = intelligent actions, P = things a computer can do better; assume O true
4. S = energy sources, P = renewable resource; assume I true
5. S = professional athletes, P = people who love their game; assume O true
❖ 6. S = octogenarians, P = mountain climbers; assume E true
7. S = former presidents, P = people with Secret Service protection; assume A true
8. S = cancers, P = fighting diseases; assume I true
❖ 9. S = breakfast foods, P = tasty meals; assume E true
10. S = maps, P = diagrams that use four colors; assume A true
11. S = politicians, P = people who say what they think; assume E true
❖ 12. S = oysters, P = creatures bearing pearls; assume O true
13. S = mushrooms, P = poisonous plants; assume I true

SECTION B: For each of the following categorical statements, generate the converse, the obverse, and the contrapositive, and state which of them can be immediately inferred from the given statement.

EXAMPLE

No oceanliners are sailboats.

ANSWER

Converse: No sailboats are oceanliners. Inference valid.
Obverse: All oceanliners are nonsailboats. Inference valid.
Contrapositive: No nonsailboats are non-oceanliners. Inference invalid.

PROBLEMS

1. Some people are firefighters.
2. Some animals are not pets.
❖ 3. No appliances are heirlooms.

   4. Some roommates are not friends.
   5. All books are treasures.
❖ 6. Some immigrants are Democrats.
   7. All waves are disturbances.
   8. No continents are islands.
❖ 9. Some wrestlers are women.
   10. All sneakers are shoes.
   11. Some recordings are CDs.
❖ 12. Some gamblers are not winners.
   13. It's always something.[10]

SECTION C: Assume the claim that all lizards are reptiles is true. Indicate how each of the following statements may be inferred from this claim and indicate whether the statement is true, false, or undetermined. (Hint: Some of these are based on square of opposition to the converse, obverse, or contrapositive of the original claim.)
   1. Some lizards are reptiles.
   2. No lizards are reptiles.
❖ 3. Some lizards are not reptiles.
   4. All reptiles are lizards.
   5. No lizards are nonreptiles.
❖ 6. All nonreptiles are nonlizards.
   7. All lizards are nonreptiles.
   8. Some lizards are nonreptiles.
❖ 9. No nonreptiles are nonlizards.
   10. Some nonreptiles are nonlizards.

7.4 Testing for Validity in Categorical Logic

Now that we have considered categorical *statements*, we need to consider categorical *arguments*. A categorical argument is an argument whose premises and conclusion are categorical statements. Just as categorical statements have specific forms (A, E, I, or O), categorical arguments have specific forms, known as **categorical syllogisms.**

7.4.1 The Categorical Syllogism

Here is an example of a categorical syllogism.

Example 7.15

P1: All horses are animals.
P2: All Clydesdales are horses.
C: Therefore, all Clydesdales are animals.

This example highlights several formal features of a categorical syllogism. First, it is composed of exactly three categorical statements—two premises and a conclusion. Second, although categories are referred to six times in the three statements (two times three), each is referred to twice, so that the number of different categories (also called terms) referred to is three. Third, one of the terms (the minor term, labeled "S") is in the subject position of the conclusion and in one of the premises. Another of the terms (the major term, labeled "P") is in the predicate position of the conclusion and in the other premise. The third term (the middle term, labeled "M") is in each premise.

In our example, there are three categorical statements and three terms (horses, animals, Clydesdales). Each of the terms is in two of the statements. The minor term is "Clydesdales," the major term is "animals," and the middle term is "horses." In presenting the syllogism, it is helpful to include a table of symbols indicating the three terms. The symbols you use can be S, P, and M, or ones chosen to help you remember the specific terms. Then you can present the argument itself in schematic form, using the letters you have chosen to represent the terms. The symbols for the argument in Example 7.15 are C = Clydesdales, A = animals, and H = horses. So, the form can be represented in this way:

Example 7.16

P1: All H are A.
P2: All C are H.
C: Therefore, all C are A.

This syllogism is composed exclusively of A-statements. But the statements of a syllogism can be any of the four types, and a syllogism can contain statements of different types.

> **Categorical Syllogisms**
>
> A categorical syllogism has exactly two premises and a conclusion, all of which are categorical statements. It has three different categories or terms: a minor term (S) in the subject position of the conclusion and in one of the premises, a major term (P) in the predicate position of the conclusion and in the other premise, and a middle term (M) in each premise.

Here is a syllogism composed of A- and I-statements: All humans (H) are warm-blooded creatures (W), and some warm-blooded creatures are creatures with four stomachs (F), so some humans are creatures with four stomachs.

Example 7.17

P1: All H are W.
P2: Some W are F.

C: Therefore, some H are F.

As you can see, this syllogism is invalid—the premises are true but the conclusion is false. We will study a method for determining the validity of syllogisms shortly, but we first need to consider the reformulation of arguments into standard syllogistic form.

7.4.2 Reformulating Arguments into Syllogistic Form

It's not always easy to recognize arguments as syllogisms. If an argumentative text containing a syllogistic argument does not present the argument in a way that makes its syllogistic form obvious, your task is to reveal that form in your structuring of the argument. If the argument cannot be reformulated in syllogistic form, it is not a syllogism. Not all arguments composed of categorical statements are syllogisms because not all such arguments can be put in the form of a syllogism. An argument composed of categorical statements can fail to be a syllogism in two ways: (1) It might have the wrong number of premises, or (2) it might have the wrong number of terms. But some arguments are syllogisms even though they seem to have the wrong number of terms or premises.

Consider these examples:

Example 7.18

A. Every dog will have its day. So, beagles will have their day.
B. Any friend of yours is a friend of mine. Everyone in Geneva is a friend of yours. No friend of mine should be turned away. So, no one in Geneva should be turned away.
C. All wealthy people should pay their fair share. A person's fair share is what that person can afford. So, the rich should pay what they can afford.

Each of these arguments appears not to be a syllogism because it contains the wrong number of either premises or terms. Text A seems to have only one premise, text B seems to have three premises, and text C seems to have four terms instead of the required three. But in each case, appearances are deceiving.

We know from the discussion in Chapter 6 that text A has an implicit premise—that beagles are dogs—so it really is a syllogism after all. In addition to implicit premises, some syllogisms have implicit conclusions. A syllogistic argument with an implicit premise or an implicit conclusion is an **enthymeme.** When you encounter an enthymeme, supplying the missing premise and/or conclusion should make clear its syllogistic form.

We also know from the discussion in Chapter 5 that text B is a complex argument, an argument with a subargument supporting one of its main premises. Two of the three explicit premises are premises of the subargument. The main premise that they support is an intermediate implicit premise—namely, that everyone in Geneva is a friend of mine. Thus, the main argument has two premises and is a

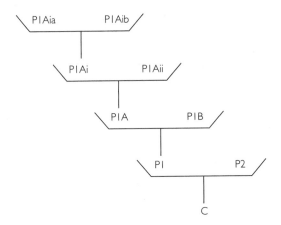

FIGURE 7.5   Tree Diagram of a Sorites

syllogism. The subargument is also a syllogism. Such arguments, common in categorical reasoning, are referred to as **sorites**.[11] They often have syllogistic subarguments extending in a "chain." In terms of the spatial representation of our tree diagrams, the chain extends upward through several levels. A sorites is a linked series of syllogisms in which one of the premises of each syllogism (except for the one at the highest level) is supported by a syllogistic subargument. Going down the chain, each syllogism is a subargument of one of the premises of the syllogism below it, with the chain terminating in the main argument. Going up the chain, beginning with the main argument, each syllogism is a subargument of one of the premises of the syllogism below it. Figure 7.5 shows a schematic tree diagram of a sorites.

Enthymemes and Sorites

An enthymeme is a categorical syllogism with an implicit premise or an implicit conclusion. A sorites is a complex argument in which the main argument and all of the subarguments are themselves categorical syllogisms. Often, there is a series of syllogistic subarguments, each one supporting a premise of another, creating a chain extending up several levels. Usually in a sorites, all of the arguments except for the one at the top of the chain contain an intermediate implicit premise.

Finally, in text C, there seem to be four terms instead of the required three. The apparent terms are wealthy people, those who should pay their fair share, what a person can afford, and the rich. But there are actually only three terms, one of them expressed by synonymous phrases, "wealthy people" and "the rich." But there is another possibility. Sometimes, when there seem to be too many terms and no two of them are synonymous, the argument is in fact a sorites. The addition of a syllogistic subargument to a syllogistic main argument adds one term to the three terms of the main argument.[12]

Consider how the arguments in texts A, B, and C should be structured so as to reveal them as categorical syllogisms:

Example 7.19

A. Table of Symbols

    B = beagles

    H = creatures who will have their day

    D = dogs

  Logical Form

    ⌈PI: All D are H.

    ⌊IP2: All B are D.

     C: Therefore, all B are H.

B. Table of Symbols[13]

    G = Genevans

    T = people who should be turned away

    M = friends of mine

    Y = friends of yours

  Logical Form

      ⌈PIA: All Y are M.

      ⌊PIB: All G are Y.

    ⌈IPI: All G are M.

    ⌊P2: No M are T.

     C: Therefore, no G are T.

C. Table of Symbols

    W = wealthy people

    A = people who should pay what they can afford

    F = people who should pay their fair share

  Logical Form

    ⌈PI: All W are F.

    ⌊P2: All F are A.

     C: Therefore, all W are A.

Detecting and Structuring Syllogistic Arguments

First, to determine whether an argument is syllogistic, you need to determine (1) whether its statements are categorical statements, (2) whether it has the proper number of premises, and (3) whether it has the proper number of terms. Second, to structure an argument, once you have determined that it is syllogistic, you need to (4) pick out the terms and (5) structure them in the syllogistic form.

Note that in detecting and structuring syllogistic arguments, you will probably not follow the process exactly as it is presented here. Instead, you will go back and forth as you work on an argumentative text that might contain a syllogism. You will try out different ideas for what might be terms or the premises and conclusion that would make the argument syllogistic before you work it out as a syllogism or decide that it is not a syllogism.

Consider some examples:

Example 7.20

A. All benefit from the arts. Those who benefit from the arts should provide support for them. So, all should support the arts.

B. Background: This is adapted from a letter about the value of knowing a second language. (*Los Angeles Times,* 6/97) (Hint: There is an implicit conclusion.)

Identifying words with things leads to all sorts of problems. As soon as one becomes aware that a "thing" can be called by a number of "names," that identification is reduced or eliminated.—W.B.B.

C. Background: This letter is about the issue of working women. (*Boston Globe,* 6/97)

Some women, of course, have to work to make ends meet. Many others work because we live in a kind of environment where women are not valued for their own power. The trouble began when women started to emulate men. Women are neither inferior to men nor superior to them. We are like a different species. Women set the standard of civility in society. When women are so eager to emulate men, it's no wonder that the moral fabric of our society is unraveling.—F.N.B.

Argument A is clearly syllogistic. Its sentences express categorical statements, and it has two premises and three terms. The symbols for A are P = people, S = creatures who should support the arts, and B = creatures who benefit from the arts. Here is its form:

Example 7.21

P1: All P are B.
P2: All B are S.
C: Therefore, all P are S.

Argument B is more difficult. One focus of the argument is the identification of words with things. The first sentence states that this leads to problems, and the second sentence discusses what can be done to avoid it. Thus, we have three potential candidates for terms, which are, roughly, the "identifying" and the "problems" in the first sentence and the "becoming aware" in the second sentence. The first of these occurs in both sentences, so, if the argument is a syllogism, the implicit conclusion would join the last two terms. The symbols for the argument are A = awareness that a "thing" can be called by a number of "names," P = cases that lead to problems, and I = identifying words with things. Here is its form:

Example 7.22

P1: All I are P.
P2: Some A are not I.
 C: Therefore, some A are not P.

The O form seems right for P2 because the text states that with the awareness the identification may be only "reduced." If the O form, more modest than the alternative E form, is the right one to use for P2, it is also appropriate to assume that the author intends the same kind of modesty in the implicit conclusion.[14]

Argument C is more difficult still. It contains some sentences that clearly express categorical statements, so it seems appropriate to explore the possibility that it is a syllogism. But the effort seems doomed. There are too many terms: women, those who have to work, environments where women are not valued, women emulating men, different species, and so on. Recall that there are two approaches to take when there seem to be too many terms. One is to try to find synonyms among the list of terms to reduce the number to three. This does not seem possible here. Another is to try to reconstruct the argument as a sorites, in which the extra terms are in the subarguments. That might be possible in this case, but it is difficult to see how it could be done. The appropriate conclusion is that this argument cannot be given a syllogistic interpretation. For the sake of structuring and evaluation, it should be treated as a different kind of argument.

7.4.3 Existential Import

According to the Aristotelian tradition of categorical logic, as indicated by the square of opposition, there is a valid immediate inference from A-statements to I-statements and from E-statements to O-statements. For example, the statement that all trees are plants implies that some trees are plants, and the statement that no trees are plants implies that some trees are not plants. We assumed this to be true when we discussed immediate inferences earlier. But modern logicians regard these two inferences as invalid. It is important to see why.

The problem these inferences raise is the one of **existential import**— whether categorical statements imply the existence of members of the category represented by the subject term. Consider these statements:

Example 7.23

A: All centaurs have hooves.
E: No centaurs have hooves.
I: Some centaurs have hooves.
O: Some centaurs do not have hooves.

There are, of course, no centaurs. How does this fact affect the truth or falsity of these statements? If this fact by itself makes any of these statements false, those statements have existential import. A statement has existential import when it implies that there exists at least one member of the class referred to by the subject term.

Do categorical statements have existential import? Aristotle seems to have assumed that they do. Modern logicians agree that *particular* statements (the I and O forms) have existential import. To say that some centaurs have hooves is to imply that centaurs (at least one) exist, so the fact that there are no centaurs makes the I and O forms in Example 7.23 false. Thus, any particular statement whose subject term refers to a class without any members (unicorns, round squares, Santa Claus's elves, assassins of George Washington) is false, no matter what term is in the predicate position.

But modern logicians do not accept the assumption that *universal* statements (the A and E forms) have existential import. On this view, the A and E forms in Example 7.23 are true, despite the absence of centaurs in the world, because they are based on the defining characteristics of centaurs, that they have the body of horses. Thus, we know that these statements are true even though no one has ever seen a centaur (because there are no centaurs to see).

We use the A and E forms in a way which shows that we do not, in general, regard them as having existential import. Consider these examples:

Example 7.24

A. All persons who roll a 300 game in this bowling alley receive a prize.
B. Quarks differ from each other in terms of properties known as "charm."

Sentence A can express a true statement even if no one has ever rolled a 300 game in that alley and even if no one ever does. It is the truth of the statement that encourages people to try to roll a 300 game. So, we do not regard this statement as having existential import. Sentence B is typical of statements found in science. Quarks are theorized subatomic particles for which there is not yet any solid observational evidence. So, from the perspective of contemporary science, it seems that universal statements are not regarded as having existential import.

There are two ways to interpret categorical statements. With an **existential interpretation,** we assume that they have existential import. The question is whether universal statements should be given an existential interpretation. Aristotle did, but today logicians, scientists, and people in general do not. Instead, we give the A and E forms a **hypothetical interpretation,** treating universal statements as conditionals. Thus, we can interpret the A-statement in Example 7.23 as "if there are centaurs, then they have hooves." This can be true even though there are no centaurs and the antecedent is false.[15]

The hypothetical interpretation of the A and E forms is also referred to as the Boolean interpretation, named after the English logician George Boole (1815–1864). Boole explicitly questioned what came to be called the Aristotelian or existential interpretation. So, returning to the square of opposition, under the hypothetical or Boolean interpretation of the A and E forms, we reject the inferences from the A form to the I form and from the E form to the O form that are accepted under the existential interpretations. This has important implications for our testing of syllogisms for validity, as we will see in the next section.

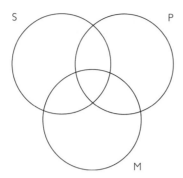

FIGURE 7.6   Venn Diagram for a Syllogism

**Existential Import: Existential
and Hypothetical Interpretations**

A statement has existential import when it implies that there exists at
least one member of the class referred to by the subject term, and it is
given an existential interpretation when it is understood to have existential import. Traditionally, all four forms of categorical statement were
given an existential interpretation. But the contemporary view, while it
continues to give particular statements an existential interpretation, gives
universal statements a nonexistential or hypothetical interpretation.

7.4.4 Testing Syllogisms with Venn Diagrams

We can use Venn diagrams to test syllogistic arguments for validity. There are other
ways as well to test syllogisms for validity, but we will focus on the Venn diagram test.

Recall that representation of categorical statements by Venn diagrams
involves two intersecting circles, with one circle representing each of the terms of
the statement. Because a syllogism has three terms, it can be represented with a
Venn diagram of three intersecting circles, as Figure 7.6 shows. Note that the figure has seven separate areas within it. The area in the upper left, for example, is an
area that is exclusively S, since it is not part of an overlap with P or M. Likewise,
the area in the upper right and the area at the bottom are exclusively P and M,
respectively. The other four areas are areas of overlap, three of them between two
of the circles and the one in the middle among all three. To see this more clearly,
Figure 7.7 labels the overlap or nonoverlap in each area. In this diagram "-" means
"not," so that, for example, "S(-P)(-M)" indicates the area that is exclusively S.

If you consider the circles two at a time, the three circles of a Venn diagram
represent three pairs of intersecting circles: (1) S and P, (2) S and M, and (3) P and
M. Each pair thus represents one of the three statements of a syllogism. You can

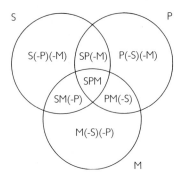

FIGURE 7.7   The Seven Areas in a Venn Diagram for a Syllogism

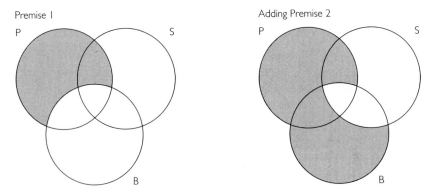

FIGURE 7.8   Venn Diagrams for Example 7.21

then follow a simple procedure to test a syllogism for validity. Here is a rough description of that procedure:

1. Label the three circles with the symbols of the terms of the argument (from the table of symbols).
2. Consider each premise and focus on the pair of circles representing that premise, diagramming the premise in that pair of circles with appropriate shadings or x's.
3. Focus on the pair of circles that represents the conclusion and determine if the pattern of shadings and/or x's already in the diagram represents what the conclusion claims. If so, the argument is valid. If not, it is invalid.

To see how this procedure applies, and how it can be more precisely formulated, recall how we structured the arguments in Examples 7.21 and 7.22. Figure 7.8 shows the Venn diagram for Example 7.21. After drawing the three circles, we diagram the first premise (all P are B). To do this, we focus exclusively on the two

Premise 1

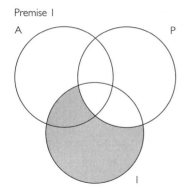

Adding Premise 2

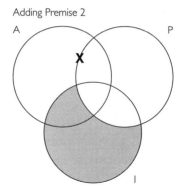

FIGURE 7.9   Venn Diagrams for Example 7.22

circles P and B. We shade the area of P outside of the overlap with B to indicate that it is empty. Next, we diagram the second premise (all B are S). So, focusing on just those two circles, we shade the part of B outside of S. Finally, we look at the resulting diagram, focusing on the two circles representing the conclusion, P and S, to see if the pattern of shadings already there represents the conclusion (all P are S). The diagram represents this claim because the only part of P that is unshaded is within S. According to the diagram, all P are S. So, the argument is valid.

Figure 7.9 shows the Venn diagram for Example 7.22. This argument contains both universal and particular premises. The first premise (all I are P) is universal, so we shade all the area of I outside of P. Because the second premise (some A are not I) is a particular statement, we need to put an "x" in the area of A outside of I. But here a problem arises. The area of A outside of I is divided by a line that is a portion of the P circle. Which side of this line should the "x" go on? The answer is that we do not know. The syllogism does not give us the information to answer the question. As a result, we put the "x" right on the line, indicating that it could be on either side. Is this argument valid? The conclusion (some A are not P) requires that there be an "x" in the area of A outside P. But the "x" is *on* the line, so the diagram does not represent what the conclusion says. If it did, the "x" would have to be clearly outside of P, which it is not. Thus, this argument is invalid.

Note, as this last example shows, that if an argument has a particular statement as its conclusion, an "x" must be in the appropriate area for the diagram to represent the conclusion and for the argument to be valid. This means that an argument with a particular conclusion can be valid only if it has at least one particular premise. Otherwise there would be no "x" in the diagram at all, only shading. This aspect of the Venn diagram technique shows its commitment to the hypothetical interpretation of universal statements. Because universal statements are not regarded as having existential import, while particular statements are, a syllogism with two universal premises cannot imply a conclusion that is a particular statement. The conclusion would have existential import and the premises would not.[16]

Here is another rule that should be observed: When a syllogism has mixed premises, one a universal statement (A or E) and one a particular statement (I or O), you should diagram the universal premise first. The reason is that this can affect the placement of the "x" in the diagram of the particular premise. Consider this example:

Example 7.25

Argument

    Some gamblers are not frugal, but all misers are frugal, so some gamblers are not misers.

Table of Symbols

    G = gamblers

    M = misers

    F = people who are frugal

Logical Form

    P1: Some G are not F.

    P2: All M are F.

    C: Therefore, some G are not M.

Venn Diagram

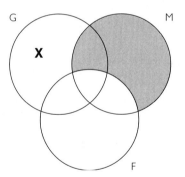

If the particular premise, P1, were diagrammed first, the "x" would go on the line of the M circle that divides the area of G that is outside F. But if the universal premise, P2, were diagrammed first, the resulting shading would indicate that, when P1 was diagrammed, it would be a mistake to put "x" on the line. Because of the shading, it is clear that the "x" should go completely outside the M area, not on the line. This turns out to be crucial, because only if the "x" is to the left of that line is it clear that the resulting diagram represents the conclusion and the argument is valid.

As a result of this discussion, we can more clearly formulate the procedure for applying the Venn diagram technique.

1. Structure the argument into syllogistic form, including a table of symbols.
2. Draw three interlocking circles, and using the letters from the table of symbols, label the top two circles with the letters of the minor term and the major term and the bottom circle with the letter of the middle term.
3. Represent each premise in the two circles that correspond to its two terms, using appropriate shadings or x's. Shade in empty space for universal premises, and put an "x" in the area indicated by the particular premises. If there is one universal and one particular premise, represent the universal premise first. If there are two areas in which the "x" could go, put it on the line between them.
4. Look to the two circles that represent the conclusion. If the pattern of shading and x's already in the diagram represents what the conclusion says, the argument is valid. If not, the argument is invalid. You do not actually diagram the conclusion, only the two premises.
5. Note that, as part of step 4, if the conclusion is a particular statement (an I or O form), then there must be an "x" in the appropriate area for the argument to be valid. In practice, this means that an argument with a particular statement as a conclusion cannot be valid unless at least one of the premises is also a particular statement. (This is a result of our adopting the hypothetical interpretation for statements of the A and E forms.)

EXERCISE SET 7.4

SECTION A: Structure the following arguments as syllogisms and then evaluate them using the Venn diagram technique. For the most part, these texts make clear the syllogistic form of their arguments. However, some have implicit premises or implicit conclusions. In the case of a sorites, each of the component arguments should be evaluated.

EXAMPLE
All rock stars take drugs, and some who take drugs die young. The implication is that some rock stars die young.

ANSWER
Table of Symbols
R = rock stars
D = people who take drugs
Y = people who die young

Logical Form
P1: All R are D.
P2: Some D are Y.
C: Therefore, some R are Y.

Venn Diagram

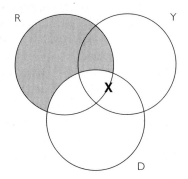

The argument is invalid.

PROBLEMS

1. All drugs have side effects, and anything with side effects should be treated with great care. Therefore, drugs should be treated with great care.

2. Some military heroes seek to solve problems through violence, but no one who seeks to solve problems through violence should be trusted with leadership. So, no military hero should be trusted with leadership.

❖ 3. All power corrupts. Politicians have power. 'Nuff said.

4. All teachers are professionals. We know that some professionals are very well paid. It follows that some teachers are very well paid.

5. Some chess players are eccentric because all chess players are brilliant, and some bright lights are eccentric.

❖ 6. Some software is not user-friendly. Everything on the market should be user-friendly. So, some software should not be on the market.

7. The government must approve all tobacco advertising. Everything that is approved by the government gets tied up in bureaucracy. So, tobacco advertising gets tied up in bureaucracy.

8. Whenever an activity is beneficial to students, they should be forced to do it. Some activities are of no benefit to students. So, some activities should not be forced on students.

❖ 9. No male legislator can know what it is like to be pregnant. All those who pass judgment on abortion should know what it is like to be pregnant. It follows that no male legislator should pass judgment on abortion.

10. All bread nourishes and no stone nourishes, so no bread is a stone.

11. All colleges have faculty accountability, because there is no college where a tenured professor cannot be fired, and wherever a tenured professor can be fired there is faculty accountability.

❖ 12. Some students don't take their work seriously. Some who do not take their work seriously should do something else instead. So, some students should do something else instead.

13. No first ladies are elected to their job, and only people elected to their jobs are accountable to the public. It is clear that some first ladies are not accountable to the public.

14. All public servants are in it for the money. Some of those in it for the money cannot be trusted. So, some government employees cannot be trusted.

❖ 15. All Greens are concerned about the environment. All those concerned about the environment drive fuel-efficient cars. No one who drives a fuel-efficient car is subject to road rage. As a result, no Greens are subject to road rage.

16. After 2050, there will be no majority race in America. Where there is no majority race, there is no room for racial prejudice, so in America in 2050 there will be no room for racial prejudice.

SECTION B: Structure the following arguments as syllogisms and evaluate them using the Venn diagram technique. Some have implicit conclusions or implicit premises, and, in many cases, the syllogistic form is not obvious, so that careful reformulation is needed.

EXAMPLE
Background: This passage is adapted from a letter on the issue of volunteerism being required by schools and corporations. (*Miami Herald*, 5/97)

When volunteerism is required, it becomes part of a big government. When this happens, our civil liberties decline.—L.M.C.

ANSWER
Table of Symbols
V = cases in which volunteerism is required
C = cases in which civil liberties decline
B = cases in which activities become part of big government

Logical Form
P1: All V are B.
P2: All B are C
IC: Therefore, all V are C.

Venn Diagram

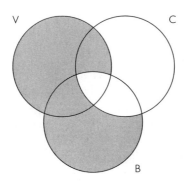

The argument is valid.

PROBLEMS
1. Background: This passage is an argument put forth by the seventeenth-century French philosopher René Descartes.

Animals have no souls and so cannot suffer.

2. Background: This is adapted from a letter about the nature and teaching of history. (*New York Times*, 2/94)

   All historical events were lived ideologically. So, any interesting discussion of them is ideological.—R.S.

❖ 3. Background: This is adapted from a letter about the need for stronger global authority to address the world's problems. (*New York Times*, 1/00)

   Some global problems cannot be solved at the national level. To solve these problems we need to create a limited global authority.—D.F.

4. Background: This is adapted from a letter expressing concerns about an amendment sponsored by Congressman Istook that would grant legal protections to certain religions. (*New York Times*, 7/97) (Hint: Treat Istook's amendment as a class with a single member.)

   Mr. Istook's amendment grants "the right to acknowledge God according to the dictates of conscience." Not all religions concern themselves with the worship of God, so that, under Mr. Istook's amendment, non-theistic religions would apparently fail to be deserving of the same protection afforded to theistic religions.—A.D.

5. Background: This is adapted from a letter on the role of women in the workplace. (*New York Times*, 8/98) (Hint: View the first sentence as the conclusion in need of significant reformulation, and include as an implicit premise "all mothers are those with a baby in their arms.")

   It is not only a mother's right to participate in the workplace but her responsibility. It is my view that all those who decide significant, future-determining issues should have a baby in their arms.—P.S.L.

❖ 6. Background: This passage is adapted from a letter critical of the attention afforded to "The King," rock-'n'-roll star Elvis Presley. (*Los Angeles Times*, 8/97) (Hint: Reformulate the first sentence as the conclusion, and include an implicit premise that takes Elvis as a class with a single member.)

   The continuing widespread adulation of non-role-model Elvis Presley on the 20th anniversary of his death is a sad comment on the so-called values of society today. We need no hero worship of a confirmed drug addict.—R.D.

7. Background: This is adapted from a letter that is part of the debate over capital punishment. (*New York Times*, 7/97) (Hint: Treat the first sentence as an O form, which [from the square of opposition] is the contradictory of the A form.)

   One implication [of the editorial] is that some murders—executions?—are less than brutal. But the sooner we accept that all killing is brutal, the sooner we may do away with the death penalty.—H.T.[17]

8. Background: This passage is adapted from a letter discussing spanking as a punishment for children. (*Houston Chronicle*, 8/97) (Hint: The third sen-

tence, the conclusion, needs significant reformulation, and one of the categories is "the wants of parents.")

The study indicates that spanking increases anti-social behavior. No parent wants this for their child. We need to show our children that we can resolve problems without violence.—J.D.

7.5 Statement Logic

The second method of formal logic we consider is **statement logic** (also called sentential logic, propositional logic, or truth-functional logic). It is called statement logic because the linguistic units that are replaced by symbols are whole sentences expressing statements, not phrases or parts of sentences, as with categorical logic. So, for example, the statement "all men are mortal" is represented in statement logic by a single symbol, whereas in categorical logic it is represented using two symbols, one for "humans" and one for "beings who are mortal." Logical form in statement logic is represented by logic words that connect sentences, such as "and" and "or."

The same deductive argument can often be represented using either method, but statement logic is a less restrictive method in some respects. There are deductive arguments that can be represented in statement logic that cannot be represented in categorical logic. Whereas a categorical argument must have only three terms and two premises, a statement logic argument can contain an unlimited number of statements and an unlimited number of premises.[18]

> **Statement Logic**
>
> Statement logic is a way of representing deductive arguments that takes statements as the basic units to which the symbols refer. In contrast, categorical logic takes the subjects and predicates of statements as the basic units.

7.5.1 Simple Statements and Compound Statements

The basic formal contrast in statement logic is between simple statements and compound statements. **Simple statements** are the basic units in statement logic; **compound statements** are constructed of simple statements. The means of construction are certain logic words, known as **logical connectives.** In categorical logic, logic words like "all" and "some" connect subject and predicate terms. In statement logic, logic words or logical connectives like "and" and "or" connect statements.

TABLE 7.2   Logical connectives and compound statement types.

Type	Symbol	Example
Negation	~B	Betty is *not* fishing.
Conjunction	B · H	Betty is fishing *and* Henry is sailing.
Disjunction	B ∨ H	Betty is fishing *or* Henry is sailing.
the Conditional	B ⊃ H	*If* Betty is fishing, *then* Henry is sailing.

Simple and Compound Statements and Logical Connectives

A simple statement does not have any components that are statements. A compound statement has at least one simple statement as a component. The components of a compound statement may be either simple statements or other compound statements, or a combination of these. Logical connectives are the logic words of statement logic, the means by which compound statements are constructed from simple statements.

There are four kinds of compound statements in statement logic, each with its own logical connective, and so four logical connectives as well. The four kinds of compound statements are **negation, conjunction, disjunction,** and (our old friend) the conditional. The corresponding logical connectives are "not," "and," "or," and "if . . . then." Each of these connectives has its own symbol representing it, as Table 7.2 shows. The table uses for illustration two simple sentences, "Betty is fishing" (represented by "B") and "Henry is sailing" (represented by "H").

The symbols for the logical connectives are usually given names. The "~" is referred to as the tilde, the "·" as the dot, the "∨" as the vee, and the "⊃" as the horseshoe. Negation is regarded as a compound statement even though, unlike the others, it is not composed of more than one simple sentence. A negation has a component that is a simple sentence, though the other three types, conjunction, disjunction, and the conditional have more than one simple sentence component.

7.5.2 Truth Values

The basic idea of statement logic is that arguments can be represented as combinations of simple sentences, using the four logical connectives, and that the truth value of a combination of simple sentences is a function of the truth value of its component simple sentences. To understand this idea, we need to say something about truth values.

To say that a statement, or a sentence that expresses it, is true or false is to say that it has a **truth value.** As the monetary value of a book might be forty dollars, the truth value of a statement might be "true" (or it might be "false"). For example, grass is green, so the sentence "grass is green" has a truth value of "true." Humans are never 30 feet tall, so the sentence "humans grow to be 30 feet tall" has a truth value of "false." The way the world is determines the truth value of statements. A statement has a truth value even if we do not know what the truth value is.

Both simple statements and compound statements have truth values. This raises the question of how the truth value of a compound statement is related to the truth values of the simple statements that compose it. The idea behind statement logic is that the truth values of compound statements are a function of the truth values of their component simple statements. This means that the truth values of the component simple statements completely determine the truth values of compound statements. All we need to know to determine the truth value of a compound statement is the truth values of its component simple statements. In other words, the basic idea of statement logic is **truth functionality.** Statement logic is truth functional because the truth values of the four kinds of compound statements of statement logic (negation, conjunction, disjunction, and the conditional) are a function of the truth values of the component simple statements.

Truth Value and Truth Functionality

The truth value of a statement (or a sentence that expresses it) is its status as true or false. Truth functionality is the characteristic of statement logic that the truth values of compound statements is a function of, or completely determined by, the truth values of the simple statements that compose them. In other words, the truth value of the compound statement in statement logic depends not on the content of the component simple statements, but on their truth or falsity.

Natural languages like English are only partially truth functional. The truth of many compound statements in everyday speech is not exclusively a function of the truth value of their component simple statements; it depends as well on their content. This is a limitation of statement logic. It cannot represent all of the meaning contained in everyday arguments.

Each of the four kinds of compound statements defines the truth value relationship between component simple statements and compound statement differently. The functional relationship between the truth values of the simple statements and the compound statement is different in each case. The easiest way to present these four kinds of truth-functional relationships is in terms of a **truth table.** A truth table for a compound statement displays all of the possible combinations of truth values of the component simple statements and then shows what the truth value of the compound statement is for each of those combinations. Figure

Negation

P	~P
T	F
F	T

Conjunction

P	Q	P · Q
T	T	T
T	F	F
F	T	F
F	F	F

Disjunction

P	Q	P ∨ Q
T	T	T
T	F	T
F	T	T
F	F	F

The Conditional

P	Q	P ⊃ Q
T	T	T
T	F	F
F	T	T
F	F	T

FIGURE 7.10   Truth Tables for the Four Basic Kinds of Compound Statements

7.10 shows the truth tables indicating the truth-functional relationships for each of the four kinds of compound statements; P and Q represent simple statements.

Truth Tables

A truth table is a graphical device for presenting the truth-functional relationships between the truth values of compound statements and their component simple statements. A truth table indicates a unique truth value of the whole for each possible combination of truth values of the components.

Let us first consider negation. When a statement is negated, it acquires the opposite truth value. Thus, as the figure shows, when P is true, ~P is false, and when P is false, ~P is true. With an important distinction from our discussion of categorical logic in mind, we can observe that a negation is a contradictory, not a mere contrary. For example, the negation of "Sally is tall" is not "Sally is short," which is the contrary, but "Sally is not tall" or "it is not the case that Sally is tall" (in slang, "Sally is tall—not"). The truth table for negation indicates the two possible truth values for P in the left-hand column and the corresponding values for the compound statement ~P in the right-hand column. One other point about negation is the rule in statement logic about double negation. As is often the case in everyday speech, a second negation turns a statement into an affirmation. Thus, symbolically, ~~P is equivalent to P. For example, to claim that it is not the case that he is not going is to claim that he is going.

To examine the next two kinds of compound statements, conjunction and disjunction, consider the following sentences:

Example 7.26

A. The moon orbits the Earth, and Shakespeare wrote *Othello*.
B. George Bush was elected president, and he moved into the White House.
C. Although the weather warmed up, the lake remained frozen.
D. Wallace and Gromit ate cheese.
E. Pat and Chris are in love.
F. Betty is going fishing or sailing.
G. Richard is staying in or he is going out.
H. Your money or your life! (said by a mugger to his victim)

The logical connectives are roughly based on the terms "not," "and," "or," and "if . . . then," but they do not exactly coincide with the way these terms are used in everyday speech. The main reason for this, as mentioned previously, is that these terms are not always used truth functionally. The logical connectives, being truth functional, ignore the non-truth-functional aspects of the terms.

Consider conjunction. A conjunction is composed of two simple statements. In the truth table, each simple statement is given a column in the left-hand side of the truth table. Because there are two simple statements, there are four possible combinations of truth values for them: (1) both are true, (2) the first is true and second false, (3) the second is false and the first true, and (4) both are false. So, as Figure 7.10 shows, the truth table has four rows. The right-hand column shows the truth value of the conjunction for the truth value combinations indicated in each of the four rows.

As the truth table indicates, this logical connective is largely consistent with the way we use "and" in everyday speech. Thus, a conjunction is true only when both of the component simple statements are true. If either component is false or both are false, the conjunction is false. Thus, in the right-hand column, the first row has a "T" and the three other rows have an "F." Consider sentence A. This compound statement would be true in everyday speech as it is in statement logic. But it is odd, in the sense that the "and" of everyday speech usually connects simple statements that have some relevance to each other, which these two do not. But this relevance cannot be part of the logical connective because if it were the connective would not be truth functional. For truth functionality to hold, a conjunction of any two true simple statements must itself be true.

This point also applies in the case of sentences B and C. In B, the order of the simple statements is an important part of the meaning. If the order of the statements were reversed, the compound statement would say something quite different, something that is false. But this part of the meaning is not part of the logical connective. Since each simple statement is true, the compound is true in whichever order the simple statements occur. In the case of C, the author is saying, in part, that both simple statements are true, so the entire statement is a conjunction (even though "and" is not used). But, again, this leaves out part of the meaning. The author is making a contrast between the two facts that the simple statements represent—that it is surprising that the second statement is true given that the first one is true. This element of contrast is not part of logical conjunction.

Sentence D illustrates an important point. The sentence is represented in statement logic as the compound "Wallace ate cheese and Gromit ate cheese." The rule is that when there is a double subject or predicate—that is, a sentence with two subject terms or two predicate terms connected by "and"—two simple statements are called for. The same is true when the double subjects or predicates are connected by "or," as in sentence F, which is rendered in statement logic as "Betty is going fishing or Betty is going sailing." But cases like sentence E are exceptions to this rule. This is another kind of case in which the sentence says more than a compound statement in statement logic would say. Specifically, E says that Chris and Pat are in love with each other, whereas the compound statement would say only that each is in love with somebody, not necessarily the other. If a double subject or predicate carries such extra meaning, you should leave it as a simple sentence rather than translate it into a compound.

Turning to disjunction, we find an important difference between the logical connective, as defined in the truth table, and the way "or" is used in everyday speech. As the truth table in Figure 7.10 indicates, the compound is true not only when one or the other of the simple statements is true but also when both are true. This is referred to as the *inclusive* sense of "or." In contrast, the "or" of everyday speech is *exclusive*, meaning that the truth of one of the simple statements excludes the truth of the other. In other words, in everyday speech, "or" means "A or B, but not both." This is indicated in sentence G, in which the implication is that Richard does one or the other, but not both (he cannot be in two places at once, after all).[19] The logical connective would be rendered in everyday speech as "A or B or both" or "A and/or B."

The contrast between the inclusive and exclusive uses of "or" is clear in sentence H as well. This is a threat intended to get the mugger's victim to turn over his money. But the victim will understand it as a threat only if he understands the "or" to be exclusive. The one prospect (his turning over his money) must be seen as excluding the other (his being killed). The victim has to believe that if he turns over his money, he will not lose his life.

The conditional is also partly at odds with the use of "if . . . then . . ." in everyday speech. This is clear if we consider the truth table for the conditional in the context of these examples:

Example 7.27

A. If the tooth is fixed, then the pain will stop.

B. If Tempe is in the United States, then it is in Nebraska.

C. If the summer Olympics are every 4 years, then water freezes at 0° C.

D. If the summer Olympics are every 3 years, then more medals are given out.

E. If the summer Olympics are every 3 years, then the Supreme Court has 10 members.

F. If the summer Olympics are every 3 years, then the Supreme Court has nine members.

Sentences A and B are standard uses of the conditional in everyday speech, the first being true and the second false. As the first two rows of the truth table in Figure 7.10 indicate, the truth value of the compound in statement logic is, for these two cases, the same as it is in everyday speech. But consider sentence C. Because both simple statements are true, C, like A, comes out true in statement logic. Otherwise, the conditional would not be truth functional. But in everyday speech, C would be regarded as strange or perhaps simply as false. The reason is that in C the simple statements have no relationship to each other.

In contrast, in everyday speech, the antecedent and consequent of a conditional are related in ways such as the following:

Example 7.28

A. If a person is a father, that person has a child.

B. If sugar comes into contact with water, it will dissolve.

C. If your king is in check, you cannot castle.

D. If you make a promise, you should keep it.

E. If you marry her, I will never speak to you again.

These are examples of just some of the ways in which the antecedent and consequent of a conditional are related in everyday speech. In sentence A, they are related in terms of a definition. In sentence B, they are related causally. In sentence C, they are related due to the existence of rules, the rules of chess. In sentence D, the relationship is in terms of moral rules. In sentence E, the relationship is in terms of the two simple statements being part of a threat. But, because there is no ready way to capture these kinds of relationships between the simple statements in a conditional in terms of truth functional connections, they are ignored in the statement logic conditional.

This shows an important difference between the conditional of statement logic and the conditional discussed in earlier chapters. The conditional discussed in those chapters is not truth functional. Rather, it depends on the content of the antecedent and consequent because there must be some relevance between them, as in the conditionals in Example 7.28. To mark this difference, the conditional of statement logic is referred to as the **material conditional.** Whenever we use the term "conditional" in our discussion of statement logic, we mean the material conditional.

> **The Material Conditional**
>
> The conditional of statement logic, represented by the "⊃" symbol (the horseshoe), is truth functional and is referred to as the material conditional to distinguish it from the other forms of the conditional. Other forms of the conditional are not truth functional because their truth depends on the meaning or content of the components—specifically, on their having some kind of relevance to each other, and not simply on their truth value.

The other three conditionals in Example 7.27 are examples from the last two rows of the truth table in Figure 7.10. The question is what the truth value of a conditional should be if the antecedent is false. The use of the conditional in everyday speech can offer little guidance, yet statement logic must provide a definite answer if it is to be truth functional. As the truth table indicates, in statement logic, whenever the antecedent is false, the conditional is true. This seems proper in cases like sentence D, which are referred to as counterfactuals. But, again, this is because of the relationship between the antecedent and consequent in D. In sentence E, there is no such relationship, and this statement would sound strange in everyday speech. But statement logic, ignoring any relationship between antecedent and consequent, treats D and E the same. Both are true. The last sentence, F, represents the third row in the truth table. It sounds as strange in everyday speech as E, because of the lack of relationship between the antecedent and consequent. Yet, in statement logic, it is regarded as true. It may help to alleviate any sense of unease to recognize that things would seem as strange if conditionals with false antecedents were regarded as false. Statement logic must give them some truth value, and this value is true.

Because the logical connectives in truth tables deviate in some respects from the way the corresponding terms are used in everyday speech, it is important to memorize them. They are the basis of the technique of testing arguments in statement logic for validity. Because the connectives depart in their meaning from everyday speech, statement logic cannot represent all of the meaning found in arguments in everyday speech. But statement logic is a powerful tool for exploring the idea of validity of deductive arguments. Statement logic represents a trade-off between this power and the ability to capture the full meaning of arguments in everyday speech.

7.5.3 Argument Form in Statement Logic

We need next to consider how to translate whole arguments into statement logic form. As compound statements are built out of simple statements, arguments in statement logic form are built out of statements, both simple and compound. Each premise of the argument will be a statement, simple or compound, and the conclusion will also be a simple or compound statement.

For an argument to be valid, at least some of the simple statements in it must appear more than once. Thus, in translating arguments into statement logic form, it is important to keep in mind the distinction between *statements* and *sentences*. Recall from Chapter 4 that a statement is what a sentence expresses or means and that a statement can be represented by different sentences. So, the same statement may appear at different places in the argument expressed in different sentences.

As we saw earlier, with Betty's and Henry's aquatic activities, when we represent arguments in statement logic, we assign a symbol to each simple sentence. Then we represent the compound statements using those symbols and the logical connectives. But, before we try this out with arguments, we need to discuss the use of parentheses. Parentheses are important in statement logic, as in mathematics, to keep the meaning clear. Consider these examples:

Example 7.29

A. If Joan does not run for class president, Amy and Ian will.
B. Either Joan and Keith will run, or Amy and Ian will.

Sentence A is a compound statement containing three simple statements. The symbols for A are J = Joan runs for class president, A = Amy runs for class president, and I = Ian runs for class president. Consider these two ways to represent the compound statement:

Example 7.30

1. $\sim J \supset I \cdot A$
2. $\sim J \supset (I \cdot A)$

The first rendering is ambiguous. It is unclear whether Amy's running depends on what Joan does. Of course, it is clear from the sentence that it does. Thus, we need to use parentheses, as in the second rendering, to make this clear.

Now, what about statement B in Example 7.29. Adding the symbol K = Keith runs for class president, we can represent the compound statement in two ways:

Example 7.31

1. $J \cdot K \vee A \cdot I$
2. $(J \cdot K) \vee (A \cdot I)$

Again, without parentheses, the result would be ambiguous. The use of parentheses in the second rendering removes the ambiguity and shows the meaning of B. The need to use parentheses arises from the fact that a compound statement can have as its components not only simple statements but other compound statements as well. Sentences A and B express compound statements that have other compound statements as components.

Now we move from this discussion of statements to a discussion of arguments. To structure an argument in statement logic, begin by identifying all of the simple statements in the argument, being sure to recognize when the same statement is repeated in different sentences. Assign a letter to each simple statement, and make a table indicating which letter represents which statement. Next, formulate the PC structure using these letters, either by themselves or as components of one of the four kinds of compound statements, to represent each premise and the conclusion.

Translating an Argument into Statement Logic Form

1. Identify all of the simple statements in the argument.

2. Assign a letter to each.

3. Create a table indicating which letter represents which statement.

4. Formulate the PC structure using these letters to represent each premise and the conclusion.

Consider some examples:

Example 7.32

A. If Johanna becomes an English professor, she will lead a fulfilling life but will not be wealthy. Johanna will become an English professor. It follows that Johanna will lead a fulfilling life but will not have a lot of money.

B. Background: This is adapted from a letter on the issue of abortion. (*New York Times,* 9/99)

Abortion opponents believe that rape should be an exception to any law making abortion illegal. If opponents of abortion really believed their argument for the sanctity of unborn life, why do they not assign this sanctity to the potential offspring of rape?—M.B.L.

Argument A contains three simple statements—(P) that Johanna becomes an English professor, (F) that she leads a fulfilling live, and (W) that she is wealthy (the same as her having lots of money). Here is the argument form:

Example 7.33

P1: P ⊃ (F · ~W)
P2: P
C: Therefore, F · ~W

Note the use of the parentheses.

In the case of argument B, there are two simple statements—(R) that abortion opponents believe that rape should be an exception to any law outlawing abortion and (S) that they believe in the sanctity of unborn life. Here is the argument form:

Example 7.34

PI: R
P2: S ⊃ ~R
IC: Therefore, ~S

The second premise is a reformulation of the rhetorical question in the text. The conclusion is implicit. The form of this argument is, of course, our old friend from Chapter 6, *modus tollens*, and the form of the first argument is our other old friend, *modus ponens*.

7.5.4 Testing for Validity Using Truth Tables

We have used truth tables already to define the truth functionality of the four kinds of compound statements. Now we will use them to test the validity of arguments in statement logic form.

The truth tables we used earlier to define the logical connectives had a column for each simple statement in the compound and a column for the compound itself. A truth table for an argument has a column for each simple statement and a column for each compound statement in the argument. The truth values for all of the compounds are based on the truth values of the simple statements. Among the simple and compound statements will be the premises and conclusion of the argument. Once you complete the table, it is easy to test the argument for validity. Recall that a valid argument is one in which it is not possible for the premises to be true and the conclusion to be false. So, if there are any rows in which the columns representing the premises all have the value T and the column representing the conclusion has the value F, the argument is invalid. If not, the argument is valid.

Here is a set of steps to apply the method:

1. Put the argument into statement logic form.
2. Create a truth table for the argument, with the number of columns equal to the number of simple and compound statements in the argument and the number of rows depending on the number of simple statements. If there are n simple statements, the truth table will have 2^n rows (the number needed to represent all the possible combinations of truth values of the simple statements).
3. Place each simple and compound statement that is part of the argument at the top of one of the columns, with the simple statements in the columns at the left of the table.

	R	S	~R	~S	S⊃~R
R1	T	T	F	F	F
R2	T	F	F	(T)	T
R3	F	T	T	F	T
R4	F	F	T	T	T
	P			C	P
	C1	C2	C3	C4	C5

FIGURE 7.11   Truth Table for Example 7.35B

4. Fill in the truth values for the simple statements so that all combinations of truth values are represented.
5. Fill in the truth values for the compound statements, as defined by the truth tables for the four types of logical connectives.
6. Indicate at the bottom of the appropriate columns (with a P or a C) all the premises and the conclusion of the argument.
7. Locate each row that has a T for all of the premises, and circle the truth value in the conclusion column for that row. If all the circled truth values are T, the argument is valid. If any are F, the argument is invalid.

Let us first try the method out on the two arguments from Example 7.32.

Example 7.35

A. ⌈P1: P ⊃ (F · ~W)
    ⌊P2: P
     C: Therefore, F · ~W

B. ⌈P1: R
    ⌊P2: S ⊃ ~R
     IC: Therefore, ~S

Because these forms are *modus ponens* and *modus tollens*, respectively, they had better be valid. Consider argument B first. It has two simple statements, S and R, and three compound statements, ~R, ~S, and S ⊃ ~R. (Remember that negations count as compound statements.) Thus, as Figure 7.11 shows, the table will have four rows (2²) and five columns (2 + 3). (For the sake of identification, the rows and columns have been labeled, R1, C1, and so on.)

The possible combinations of truth values for the simple statements, R and S, are all indicated in C1 and C2. The way to generate these combinations is as follows: If there are two simple statements (as in this case), you group the truth values for the one in the left-hand column (C1), with two Ts (in R1 and R2) and two Fs (in R3 and R4). Then you alternate the truth values in C2. (If there are three simple statements, as in argument A, you will have eight rows instead of four, grouping

	P	F	W	~W	F · ~W	P ⊃ (F · ~W)
R1	T	T	T	F	F	F
R2	T	T	F	T	(T)	T
R3	T	F	T	F	F	F
R4	T	F	F	T	F	F
R5	F	T	T	F	F	T
R6	F	T	F	T	T	T
R7	F	F	T	F	F	T
R8	F	F	F	T	F	T
	P				C	P
	C1	C2	C3	C4	C5	C6

FIGURE 7.12   Truth Table for Example 7.35A

four Ts and four Fs in the left-hand column. Four simple statements would require 16 rows, with the truth values in the first column grouped eight and eight.)

Once you have filled in the truth values of the simple statements, you enter the truth values of the compounds in C3, C4, and C5, one at a time, using the truth tables for the compounds presented earlier. In C3 and C4, the compounds are negations, so in each row you enter the truth value opposite to that listed in the corresponding simple statement. For example, the value for R in R1 is T, so the value for ~R in R1 is F. In C5, the compound is a conditional. So, you consult C2 (the antecedent) and C3 (the consequent) in the table. For example, at R1, the value of S is T and the value of ~R is F. The truth value of a conditional with a true antecedent and a false consequent is F, so you enter an F in C5 at R1, and so forth.

Once you complete the table, you put a P or a C at the bottom of the appropriate columns to indicate which represent the premises and which the conclusion. In this case, C1 and C5 represent the premises and C4 the conclusion. Then you look for rows in which both of the premises have the value T and circle the value of the conclusion in that row. In this case, the only row in which the premises are both true is R2, so the truth value of the conclusion is circled in this row. Finally, you inspect all of the circled truth values in the conclusion column. If none of them is false, the argument is valid. So, this argument is valid.

Now consider argument A. This argument has three simple statements and three compound statements. Thus, as Figure 7.12 shows, the truth table has eight rows (2^3) and six columns (3 + 3). You fill in the truth values of the three simple statements in C1, C2, and C3, according to the process just outlined. Then you fill in the values for the compounds in C4, C5, and C6. As before, you identify these values by consulting the values in each row for the components. In this example, some of the compound statements have compound statements as components. This means that you must fill in the compound statements in a certain order. In particular, because the compound in C5 has the compound in C4 as a component,

C4 must be filled in before C5, and C5 before C6. Once the table is completely filled in, you mark the columns representing the premises and the conclusion and circle the value in the conclusion column whenever all of the premises in that row are T. The only row in which this is the case is R2, and, because the value circled in this case is T, the argument is valid.

EXERCISE SET 7.5

SECTION A: Reformulate the following sentences, taken from letters to the editor, into proper statement logic form, using a table of symbols. Include parentheses where needed.

EXAMPLE
If the Pope recommended a vegetarian diet, human health would vastly improve, and millions of God's creatures would be spared the needless torture and killings that is required to support a meat-based diet.—R.C.R. (*USA Today*, 2/99)

ANSWER
Table of Symbols
V = The Pope recommended a vegetarian diet.
H = Human health would vastly improve.
C = Millions of God's creatures would be spared the needless torture and killings
     that is required to support a meat-based diet.
V ⊃ (H · C)

PROBLEMS
1. I hope that someone would loudly shout "fire" if there was a fire.—S.D.R. (*New York Times*, 5/95)
2. The wake of the Oklahoma City bombing is causing heated discussion of "hate speech" and its nexus to the right of free speech guaranteed by the First Amendment.—S.D.R. (*New York Times*, 5/95)
3. Neither the shooters' parents nor their teachers noticed warning signs in their behavior.—K.L. (*New York Times*, 5/99)
4. Only if the mental and the physical are ontologically distinct can there be any relationship of reciprocity between them.—A.K. (*New York Times*, 4/99)
5. While the author made an impressive argument for mental health counselors in schools, he did not mention an important factor leading to the recent schoolyard shootings.—K.L. (*New York Times*, 5/99)
6. If I'm having a heart attack, please don't send a volunteer—or a slew of former presidents, for that matter—with a box of Band-Aids.—D.B. (*Washington Post*, 5/97)
7. It is momentum, not merely speed, that determines the dangerousness of a moving vehicle.—M.L. (*New York Times*, 6/98)
8. Men account for 93 percent of all job-related deaths, although only 55 percent of the work force is male.—K.R.B.[20] (*New York Times*, 10/93)
9. This is appropriate for off-road vehicles, which is what the sports utilities were designed for.—M.L. (*New York Times*, 6/98)

10. The children would have been healthier in mind and body if they had focused their loose interest and energy on some sport of their own.—A.C. (*New York Times*, 5/99)

11. Cleaning up a vacant lot is not the same as having a decent well-equipped school, a comfortable house, or a job that pays more than minimum wage. —D.B. (*Washington Post*, 5/97)

12. If Congress had to appropriate money explicitly for such grants, the grants would be subject to closer scrutiny than the tax breaks, resulting in better government.—T.W. (*New York Times*, 10/97)

13. If we then take account of the differential representation of the sexes in the work force, we can see that a man is almost four times as likely to be murdered in the workplace as a woman and that a man is more than 11 times as likely as a woman to be killed on the job by all causes combined.—K.R.B.[21] (*New York Times*, 10/93)

14. In choosing to unionize, doctors will simply trade one rigid framework for another.—T.S.B. (*New York Times*, 6/99)

15. If children have to pay for their own college education, they will become much more responsible and take pride in their achievements.—B.D. (*USA Today*, 10/98)

16. When drivers see a yellow light, they speed up and will never let the stopped driver enter the intersection.—F.R.S. (*Miami Herald*, 1/98)

17. If the Soviet Union believes its nuclear submarines can be detected by the West, it might feel under great pressure to fire submarine-launched missiles if war appears imminent.—D.F. (*New York Times*, 8/87)

18. If proof of the efficiency of rail service is needed, one need only look at two of our greatest economic competitors, Germany and Japan, where fast, dependable trains are an integral part of the economy and are taken for granted.—T.S. (*New York Times*, 9/95)

19. With our Federal Government providing research and development and setting standards, each state could develop a network of high-speed railroads.—T.S. (*New York Times*, 9/95)

20. By setting the carding age as under 27, almost all persons under 18 will be carded.—P.D.F. (*Chicago Tribune*, 4/97)

21. The problem with the militia "movement" is not that it is anti-government but that it is anti-democratic government.—R.S.M. (*Los Angeles Times*, 6/97)

22. If children are not communicating with their parents concerning activities at college, while the parents are footing the bill, then parents should stop financial support.—B.D. (*USA Today*, 10/98)

23. Stopping payment on children's education, if they are not providing information to their parents and if they are not performing appropriately, is one way to get their attention and make them responsible for their actions. —B.D. (*USA Today*, 10/98)

24. If you are not certain about your definition of a human being, and if you are not certain what constitutes quality living, and what does not, is it not better to err on the side of saving a life, rather than destroying it?—A.B. & E.B. (*Washington Post*, 11/79)

SECTION B: Reformulate the following arguments into proper statement logic form, providing a table of symbols and the symbolic representation of the argument. Test the arguments for validity with truth tables. Some of them have an implicit conclusion or an implicit premise. Recall your work on the interpretation of conditionals in Chapter 4.

EXAMPLE
Either Ahab finds the white whale or he dies in the process. But, if he finds the white whale, he will die. So, Ahab will die.

ANSWER

Table of Symbols
F = Ahab finds the white whale.
D = Ahab dies.

Logical Form
P1: F ∨ D
P2: F ⊃ D
C: Therefore, D

Truth Table

F	D	F ⊃ D	F ∨ D
T	(T)	T	T
T	F	F	T
F	(T)	T	T
F	F	T	F
	C	P	P

The argument is valid.

PROBLEMS

1. You say you want to play on our team? If so, you have to have total commitment.
2. Old wine is good wine, and this is really good wine.
3. If you have both the ability and the drive, you can succeed in our firm. You have the drive, but your ability leaves something to be desired.
4. I know that he loves her. He casts her admiring glances and hangs on her every word. If he does these things, he surely loves her.
5. If you are discreet, you will be valorous. But you are not discreet.
6. In this business, you either sink or swim, and you do not know how to swim.
7. Cosmologists tell us that unless the universe has a sufficient amount of dark matter it will lack critical mass. If the universe lacks critical mass, it will expand forever. The universe does not have a sufficient amount of dark matter.
8. Either the universe will expand forever, or it will collapse into the "big crunch." But it will not collapse into the "big crunch." The conclusion is obvious.
9. If we permit human cloning, the human race is certainly doomed. But I know that we will not permit human cloning. So the human race is safe.

10. One hundred bottles of beer on the wall. One hundred bottles of beer. If there are 100 bottles of beer on the wall and one of those bottles should happen to fall, 99 bottles of beer on the wall. One just fell.

SECTION C: Reformulate the following arguments into proper statement logic form, including a table of symbols and a symbolic representation of the argument. Test the arguments for validity with truth tables. Some of them have an implicit conclusion or an implicit premise.

EXAMPLE
Background: This letter is about when the millennium should have been celebrated. (*Miami Herald*, 12/97)

If the current second millennium will end on Dec. 31 1999, then the first millennium had to end on Dec. 31 999 (1999–1000 = 999). Why would it be called a millennium if it lasted just 999 years?—M.N.

ANSWER

Table of Symbols
S = The current second millennium ends on Dec. 31 1999.
F = The first millennium ended on Dec. 31 999.

Logical Form
P1: S ⊃ F
P2: ~F
C: Therefore, ~S

Truth Table

S	F	~S	~F	S ⊃ F
T	T	F	F	T
T	F	F	T	F
F	T	T	F	T
F	F	Ⓣ	T	T
		C	P	P

The argument is valid.

PROBLEMS

1. Background: This passage is adapted from a letter written in response to a column. (*New York Times*, 1/00)

   Your columnist claims that those who fought under the Confederate flag were guilty of treason. If so, then Thomas Jefferson and George Washington were traitors.—H.M.G.

2. Background: This passage is adapted from another letter on capital punishment, written in response to a newspaper editorial. (*Miami Herald*, 4/97)

   While you defend executions, you favor carrying them out in a way that shields the executioners from what they are doing. If they are carrying out justice, they should not be shielded from what they are doing.—M.D.

3. Background: This letter is about a proposal to honor filmmaker Leni Riefenstahl for the propaganda films she made for the Nazis in the 1930s. Oswald was the assassin of former President John F. Kennedy. (*Los Angeles Times*, 9/97)

   If Leni Riefenstahl may be honored for her propaganda films, then I suppose Lee Harvey Oswald could be honored for sharpshooting. Despicable. —D.G.

4. Background: This passage is adapted from another letter on the trial of the man charged with bombing the Federal Building in Oklahoma City. The letter argues against the method of jury selection. Because it was a capital case, those opposed to the death penalty were excluded from the jury. (*Denver Post*, 4/97)

   When the only people being considered for the Timothy McVeigh jury are those willing to impose the death penalty, it means that a whole segment of those liberal and compassionate people in our society are automatically excluded.—M.R.

5. Background: This passage is adapted from a letter critical of a ruling by a Miami judge. (*Miami Herald*, 6/97)

   I reject the judge's decision that a convicted felon sleeping in a tent is cruel and unusual punishment. By this logic, the Boy Scouts and campground operators should be outlawed for inflicting such hardships on innocent children and law-abiding residents.—L.W.

6. Background: This passage is adapted from a letter critical of the anti-affirmative action stance of then Speaker of the House of Representatives, Newt Gingrich. (*New York Times*, 8/97)

   A news article quotes Speaker Gingrich as urging Senate reauthorization of preferences for veterans in awarding Federal contracts. If it is morally right to favor veterans, isn't it also right to give preferences to groups that have been denied full opportunity?—B.W.M.

7. Background: This passage is from a letter on illegal drugs and the fact that they are widely available in prisons. (*Los Angeles Times*, 9/97)

   With prisons full of smuggled drugs, is anyone asking about the whole principle of keeping drugs out of the U.S.? If prisons cannot keep them out, what is the justification for turning the good old U.S. into a prison?—R.S.

8. Background: This is a portion of a letter in opposition to the practice of a feminist professor of not allowing men to take her class. (*Boston Globe*, 3/99)

   Why shouldn't she allow any student to enroll in her class and ask questions? What is she afraid of? If she is speaking the truth, then she should be able to defend it.—P.H.

9. Background: This passage is adapted from a letter responding to a study of the attitudes of participants in an antipoverty program, Project New Hope. (*New York Times*, 5/99)

Two-thirds of Projects New Hope's participants report that they "were satisfied or very satisfied with their standard of living" in spite of having an annual package of earnings, wage subsidies, and welfare amounting to less than $12,000. Antipoverty programs like Project New Hope that rely on personal drive and ambition are indeed doomed if the life-style aspirations of the majority of the participants can be satisfied with this level of income. —R.S.

10. Background: This is a portion of a letter about comparing the length of human and canine lives. (*Washington Post*, 3/99)

   The notion that one canine year equals seven human years implies that, since dogs can breed at about 10 months, humans can do so at about 6 years old. Not so.—R.W.L.

11. Background: This passage is adapted from a letter written in response to reports that a proposed peace agreement between Israel and Syria would require $15 billion in U.S. support to the two nations. (*New York Times*, 1/00)

   The cost of the peace deal should not be borne by American taxpayers. Israel must take steps for its future and security with its own military and economic strength as its guarantee. Syria should negotiate for the sake of its future, not for a bribe by the United States. Otherwise, the treaty would be only a piece of paper.—S.D.L.

12. Background: This letter is in response to a columnist who argued that nuclear deterrence did not work during the Cold War. (*New York Times*, 1/88)

   According to your columnist, if there is no sane or sensible way of using nuclear weapons, they can't be used, and if they can't be used, they can't have prevented war for the last 40 years. But that there isn't any sane use of nuclear weapons doesn't mean they can't be used. Nor can it be said that they haven't prevented war.—R.L.H.

13. Background: This is a passage from *The Federalist* 22 by Alexander Hamilton in which he argues for the adoption of the U.S. Constitution.[22]

   If that plan should not be adopted . . . the probability would be, that we should run into the project of conferring supplementary powers upon Congress as they are now constituted; and either the machine, from the intrinsic feebleness of its structure, will moulder into pieces in spite of our ill-judged efforts to prop it; or by successive augmentations of its force and energy, as necessity might prompt, we should finally accumulate in a single body, all the most important prerogatives of the sovereign. . . . Thus we should create in reality that very tyranny, which the adversaries of the new constitution either are, or affect to be solicitous to avert.

14. Background: This passage is adapted from a letter on the garbage disposal practices of New York City. (*New York Times*, 5/98)

   To reach the goal of improving disposal practices, it is necessary to include in the price of the goods sold in New York the cost of their disposal and to develop a stable market for recycled goods. If the price of a product included its disposal cost, manufacturers would improve their competitive position by reducing the amount of packaging used and the cost of recycling. And if the disposal tax were eliminated when a product was packaged in recycled material, this would create a market for recycled products. Manufacturers have become used to the idea that their products will be disposed of at the expense of others, so changing the rules will not be easy.—B.L.

❖   15. Background: This letter is in response to a discussion of health insurance covering nonstandard forms of medical treatment. (*New York Times*, 9/97)

The fact that much of medicine is art rather than science doesn't mean that scientific proof of efficacy and safety is unnecessary. So it comes as a surprise to learn that many medical procedures are being done without sufficient testing and scant proof of appropriateness. Yet Federal, state and private health plans are willing to pay for many of these scientifically unproven techniques. This discourages research and proof of efficacy. If people want it and insurance will pay for it, why bother with scientific documentation? —S.Z.W.

Summary

In terms of formal strength, deductive arguments are either valid or invalid. Determining the validity of a deductive argument is a matter of judging the validity of its logical form, the structure of the argument after its content has been replaced with symbols. Formal logic is the study of methods of determining whether logical forms are valid or invalid.

Categorical logic studies arguments composed of categorical statements, which refer to two categories of things and make claims about one of these including or excluding the other and about whether the inclusion or exclusion is complete or partial. The quality of a categorical statement is about whether it claims inclusion (affirmative) or exclusion (negative). The quantity of a categorical statement is about whether the inclusion/exclusion is complete (universal) or partial (particular). Thus there are four kinds of categorical statements: the universal affirmative (A form—all S are P), the universal negative (E form—no S are P), the particular affirmative (I form—some S are P), and the particular negative (O form— some S are not P). The words that represent the statement's form ("all," "no," "some," "are," "not") are logic words.

Immediate inference is inference from one statement to another, a deductive argument with one premise. The relationships among the four forms of categorical statements can be represented by the square of opposition. In these relationships, the forms are contradictories (A and O forms, and E and I forms), contraries (A and E forms), and subcontraries (I and O forms). Additional forms of immediate inference result from operations done on categorical statements involving transposing and/or negating the subject and predicate terms of the statement. These operations are conversion, obversion, and contraposition.

The argument form in categorical logic is the syllogism, which is composed of exactly three categorical statements—two premises and a conclusion. Those three statements contain exactly three terms (that is, they refer to exactly three classes), each mentioned twice. A syllogism with an implicit premise or conclusion is an enthymeme. A complex syllogistic argument is a sorites. A statement has existential import when it implies the existence of members of the class referred to in the subject term. Modern logic does not regard universal statements as having existential import. This issue affects the validity of certain syllogisms—namely, those with a general statement as a premise and a particular statement as a conclusion.

Syllogisms can be tested for validity using Venn diagrams, a method of representing a syllogism with three partly overlapping circles. The premises are represented in the diagram by the use of shadings and x's. The syllogism is valid if the resulting pattern of shadings and x's represents what is claimed in the conclusion.

Statement logic, unlike categorical logic, takes its basic units to be statements. Simple statements are joined into compound statements of four kinds (using four kinds of logical connectives): negation, conjunction, disjunction, and the conditional. The logical connectives correspond roughly to the English terms "not," "and," "or," and "if . . . then." Every statement has a truth value, which is its status as true or false. Statement logic is truth functional, meaning that the truth value of compound statements is completely determined by the truth values of their component simple statements. Thus, the logical connectives differ in meaning somewhat from their English counterparts because the English terms are often used in ways that are not truth functional. The statement logic conditional is referred to as a material conditional to distinguish it from the conditionals used in everyday speech.

Because compound statements in statement logic are truth functional, the conditions for their truth can be defined by a truth table, a diagram that shows the truth value of a compound for all of the possible combinations of the truth values of its component simple sentences. Truth tables also provide a way to test the validity of arguments. For this purpose, a truth table displays the truth values of all of the component simple statements and the resulting truth values of the component compound statements. If there is any combination of these truth values under which the premises are true and the conclusion false, the argument is invalid.

Key Terms

logical form	negative statement	Venn diagrams
logic words	statement quality	immediate inference
categorical logic	universal statement	square of opposition
categorical statement	particular statement	contradictories
affirmative statement	statement quantity	contraries

subcontraries

conversion

logical equivalence

obversion

contraposition

categorical syllogism

enthymeme

sorites

existential import

existential
interpretation

hypothetical
interpretation

statement logic

simple statement

compound statement

logical connectives

negation

conjunction

disjunction

truth value

truth functionality

truth table

material conditional

Notes

1. Except for those deductive arguments with a single premise, which are discussed in the section on immediate inference.
2. The reason that hasty conclusion and irrelevant reason are the same charge in the case of deductive arguments is that formal strength for deductive arguments is all-or-nothing. In an invalid argument, the premises provide *no* support for the conclusion, which means that, as a group, they are irrelevant. So, to say that the premises provide insufficient support (justifying a charge of hasty conclusion) is to say that they provide no support (justifying a charge of irrelevant reason). Because the formal strength of nondeductive arguments is a matter of degree, there is a distinction between the two charges for these arguments, as we saw in Chapter 6.
3. "C," the second letter in "science," is chosen in this case because the "S" is already spoken for.
4. These letters are derived from the vowels in the Latin terms for affirmative and negative, *affirmo* and *nego.*
5. The predicate noun need not represent a broader category than the subject noun in cases in which the subject noun is qualified so as to restrict it. For example, consider "young people are people who are most idealistic." Here, the same noun can be used in the subject and predicate because its use in the subject is restricted by the adjective "young." Because of this restriction, the predicate category is still broader than the subject category.
6. Venn diagrams are named after English logician John Venn (1834–1923), who developed the method.
7. The author of this letter is Ruth E. Peterson.
8. Modern logicians question some of these inferences, as we discuss in the subsection on existential import.
9. The idea of logical equivalence is also used in statement logic. The kinds of immediate inference based on logical equivalence are valid, but they are chargeable with the fallacy of begging the question. In this fallacy, discussed in Chapter 8, a premise is the same statement as the conclusion. But this fallacy is a content fallacy, not a formal fallacy.
10. This was the line frequently uttered by Roseanne Roseannadanna, one of the characters created by the late comedienne Gilda Radnor on the original *Saturday Night Live.*
11. "Sorites" is a term derived from the ancient Greek word for "heap." This etymology is misleading, however, because a sorites has much more structure than a heap.

12. While both the main argument and the subargument have three terms, two of them are shared in the one statement that the two arguments have in common, the subargument's conclusion, which is also a premise of the main argument.

13. There are four terms in the two arguments of the sorites. The fourth term is the middle term of the subargument. The main argument and the subargument share two terms. The minor term of the subargument is the minor term for the main argument, and the major term of the subargument is the middle term of the main argument.

14. There is a more elaborate interpretation of this argument. If we assume that the author wants to say something about learning a second language, we could reconstruct the argument as a sorites with the above argument as the subargument. The other premise of the main argument would be that learning a second language leads to the awareness that a "thing" can be called by different "names," the conclusion being that some learning of a second language avoids the problems.

15. Why do we give the particular statements (I and O) an existential interpretation? There is little or no reason to use particular statements to talk about things that do not exist. When we want to talk about things that do not or may not exist, we usually want to say what properties *all* members of that class would have if they did exist. If we do not know whether any members of the class exist, it usually makes little sense to talk about properties that some members of the class would have and some would not. So there is little or no use for particular statements about such classes. It is interesting and important to know that centaurs have hooves, but it is not interesting, and perhaps makes no sense, to speculate about whether centaurs have freckles.

16. In the case of some categorical arguments, it may seem closer to the intentions of the author to understand the general statements as having existential import. For example, if an author spoke of "all teachers," we might assume that she intended to imply the existence of teachers. But, instead of regarding the general statements in such cases as having existential import, it would be better to treat the argument as if it had an implicit premise asserting that there are some teachers.

17. The author of the letter from which this is adapted is Howard Tomb.

18. Though, of course, a categorical argument can be composed of more than three statements, if it is a sorites.

19. There is a way in statement logic to represent the exclusive "or." It is by representing the phrase "but not both" and adding this to the inclusive sense of "or," like this: $(A \lor B) \cdot \sim(A \cdot B)$. The use of parentheses will be explained shortly.

20. The author of the letter from which this sentence is taken is Kingsley R. Browne.

21. See previous note.

22. Alexander Hamilton, *The Federalist* 22, in Jacob Cooke (ed.), *The Federalist* (Middletown, CT: Wesleyan University Press, 1961), p. 145.

CHAPTER 8

Evaluating Argument Content

Arguments can be evaluated in terms of both form and content. Formal evaluation assesses the adequacy of the support relationship between the premise(s) and conclusion. Content evaluation assesses the truth or acceptability of each premise. In the previous two chapters, we focused on formal evaluation—of nondeductive arguments in Chapter 6 and deductive arguments in Chapter 7. In this chapter, we turn our attention to content evaluation. Content evaluation, in contrast to formal evaluation, applies in the same way to both deductive and nondeductive arguments.

We consider in detail the two requirements of content strength—truth and acceptability—and the two fallacies that are present in an argument when these requirements are not satisfied—false premise and problematic premise. The discussion in this chapter will complete our consideration, begun in Chapter 6, of the four basic conditions for argument strength. As represented by the TARS acronym, these are, in addition to truth and acceptability, relevance and sufficiency.

8.1 Premises and Their Assessment

When you evaluate arguments in terms of content, you assess the premises in terms of their truth and acceptability. Consider this argument:

Example 8.1

Background: This letter is in response to the federal government's plan to purchase the presidential papers of Richard Nixon. In 1974, Nixon was forced to resign the presidency in disgrace as a result of the Watergate scandal. (*New York Times, 4/97*)

① Are we really about to spend $26 million of taxpayers' money to procure the papers of Richard M. Nixon? ② Are the papers of a disgraced President of more value than education, the arts, the environment and the many other worthwhile programs that Congress is cutting? ③ And what lesson are we sending posterity—that crime does pay?—M.K.

Structure

> P1: The papers of a disgraced president are of less value than what their $26 million cost could achieve in areas such as education, the arts, and the environment.
>
> P2: Purchasing the papers would send the message that crime pays.
>
> C: The government should not purchase the presidential papers of former President Nixon.

In terms of form, this argument seems quite strong. It is not valid because it is nondeductive, but P1 and P2 offer strong support for the conclusion. If the premises are true, the conclusion is likely true. So, if there are serious weaknesses in the argument, they are content weaknesses.

How, then, should we assess the two premises? Are the premises true or acceptable? First, the truth of P1 seems at least doubtful. The audience for the argument would not regard this as likely true without support, and there is an argument, independent of how the audience would view this claim, that it is doubtful. Specifically, an important function of our government is to keep a record of its activities. The activities leading to the Watergate scandal put our constitutional liberties at risk, and we need to have access to Nixon's papers so that we can learn how to avoid such episodes in the future. There is thus some reason to think that purchasing the papers would be of greater benefit to the public than what the $26 million could otherwise achieve in education, the arts, or the environment.

The argument just given is not sufficient to show that P1 is false, but it is sufficient to cast doubt on the truth of the premise. In other words, it shows that the premise needs support, which the author does not provide. Therefore, P1 is not acceptable. We have a justification for charging problematic premise against the Nixon papers argument at P1.

We take a different tack in our evaluation of P2, because P2 seems not merely doubtful but false. The purchase of the papers, rather than showing that crime pays, would help to establish that crime does not pay. Having access to these papers would enable the public to appreciate the nature of the crimes committed by the Nixon administration. Instead of concluding that there are reasons to doubt the premise, and thus that the author needs to provide support for it, this argument concludes that P2 is false. This argument is a justification for a charge of false premise against the Nixon papers argument at P2.

Before discussing the two content fallacies in greater detail, however, we need to consider some general issues regarding premises and their assessment.

8.1.1 Different Kinds of Statements

There are different kinds of statements that can appear as premises in an argument and that are assessed in different ways. We previously discussed some differences among statements, such as the difference between general and singular statements. Here, we look at some other relevant differences.

Consider these examples:

Example 8.2

A. It is raining or it is not raining.
B. A bachelor is unmarried.
C. Two plus two equals four.
D. Two plus two equals five.
E. A bachelor is married.
F. It is raining and it is not raining.

Each is an *a priori* **statement,** a statement whose truth value is known independently of experience. Experience is the awareness we have of the world through our senses. For instance, we know the truth value of the statement that the sun rises every morning only from experience. So, the statement that the sun rises every morning is not an *a priori* statement. In contrast, the truth values of statements (A–F) are not based on experience. We know the truth value of an *a priori* statement without any need to appeal to experience to determine or demonstrate it. To put it another way, no experience will ever lead us to question what we believe to be the truth value of an *a priori* statement. Statements A, B, and C are *a priori* statements that are true; they are known to be true *a priori*. Statements D, E, and F are false; they are known to be false *a priori*.

There are different kinds of *a priori* statements. One type is represented by statements A and F, which are true or false by virtue of their form alone. A is a **tautology,** an *a priori* statement that is *true* by virtue of its form alone. Using the letter P to represent a simple statement, the form of A is "P or not P." (Using the symbols from the previous chapter, we have "P ∨ ~P.") A tautology is true no matter what it is about, no matter what the content of P.

Statement F is a **contradiction,** which, like a tautology, has its truth value by virtue of its form alone. In the case of a contradiction, however, the truth value is false. We know F is false simply because of its form, whatever the content of its simple statements. The form of F is "P and not P." Symbolically, we have "P · ~P."[1]

Statements B and E are **analytic statements.** Each statement's truth value, unlike that of a tautology or a contradiction, depends on the meaning of the terms it contains, but only on the meaning of those terms. Whereas B is an analytic truth, E is an analytic falsehood. We know that B is true and that E is false based on the meanings of the terms they contain. That is, because "bachelor" is defined as "unmarried male," B must be true and E must be false, whatever our experience tells us about the world.

To put it another way, analytic statements are true or false *by definition.* That is, "being unmarried" is part of the definition of "bachelor." Analytic statements are often a source of humor—for example, in such questions as "Who is buried in Grant's Tomb?" The joke, of course, is that we know the answer to this question even if we know nothing from experience (including our study of history) about Grant. Analytic statements will be discussed further in the next chapter.

Tautologies, contradictions, and analytic statements tell us nothing about the world, which is why no experience can show them to be false. Tautologies and contradictions tell us nothing about the world because they are true or false no matter what they are about. Analytic statements tell us, not about the world, but rather about how we talk and think about the world. To know that a bachelor is unmarried is simply to know the meaning of the term "bachelor." To know that bachelors are unmarried does not tell us whether anyone is actually married or not, but simply that someone has to be unmarried to be a bachelor.

Though these *a priori* statements tell us nothing about the world, they are sometimes premises of arguments. Tautologies, for instance, often appear as premises in what are called arguments by dilemma (discussed later in the chapter), and analytic truths may be premises in arguments about how something should be classified. For example, if you were arguing that a whale is not a fish, you might include as a premise the analytic truth that fish are cold-blooded. Being cold-blooded is part of our definition of a fish.

Statements C and D are statements of mathematics, C being a mathematical truth and D a mathematical falsehood. Other examples of mathematical truths are the theorems of geometry. Some thinkers regard mathematical statements as analytic statements, or as tautologies or contradictions; others regard them as a separate kind of *a priori* statement. But, like all *a priori* statements, they are known to be true or false independently of experience. In the case of a mathematical truth, for example, no experience could show it to be false.[2] In geometry, we do not need to measure the angles to discover that the adjacent angles at the intersection of two lines equal 180 degrees. If we put two apples in a bag, then put two more in, and later discover five apples in the bag, we would never conclude that C is false. Rather, we would explain this unexpected event in some other way.

Now consider these examples:

Example 8.3

G. Alcohol consumption impairs motor coordination.
H. Smoking causes cancer.
I. Humans can survive for months without food and water.
J. Genes have little effect on personality.

In contrast to the previous examples, the truth values of these statements are known only through experience. They are not *a priori*, but *a posteriori* (so called because they are known posterior to, or following, experience). In the case of an *a posteriori* statement, we cannot know without experience whether it is true or false. Statements G and H are true, but they could have been false if the world were different. For example, they might have been false if human physiology were impervious to alcohol or to the carcinogenic effects of tobacco smoke. Since they could have been false if the world were different, we can know that they are true only through our experience of the world.

Likewise, while statements I and J are false, they could have been true if the world were different. For example, they might have been true if humans had a physiological mechanism for storing food and water for long periods, like animals that hibernate, or if genes did not have the major impact on our personalities we believe them to have. G has been known to be true and I to be false since early in human history, so they involve an appeal only to everyday experience. In contrast, the truth values of H and J have come to be known only fairly recently, through the specialized investigative experience of the scientific community. Still, we know all of them to be true or false only through experience.

A Priori and *a Posteriori* Statements, Analytic Statements, Tautologies, and Contradictions

In an *a priori* statement, the truth value can be known independently of experience. In contrast, in an *a posteriori* statement, the truth value can be known only through experience. Analytic statements are a kind of *a priori* statement in which the truth values depend on the meanings of the terms used to express the statement. Tautologies and contradictions are kinds of *a priori* statements in which the truth values depend only on the form of the statement.

Now consider a kind of statement with some similarities to the ones already considered but some differences as well:

Example 8.4

K. A fetus is a person.
L. A nuclear conflict is not a war.
M. Burning the flag is a form of speech.

These are **conceptual statements.** Conceptual statements resemble analytic statements in that they often seem to be a "matter of definition," but they differ from them in at least two respects. First, their truth value is not a straightforward matter, as it usually is with analytic statements, but often a matter of uncertainty or controversy. For instance, you cannot consult a dictionary to discover whether a fetus is a person the way you can to discover whether a bachelor is unmarried. Second, it is not completely clear whether the truth values of conceptual statements are *a priori* or *a posteriori*. Conceptual statements are not *a posteriori* statements in a direct sense. It is a mistake, for example, to think that we can determine, based on the factual information given us by medical specialists or biologists, whether a fetus is a person. But experience may be relevant to determining the truth value of a conceptual statement in at least an indirect way. Those who think that experience is involved have different views about how it is involved. In any case, we will discuss conceptual statements, as well as analytic statements, further in Chapter 9.

> ## Conceptual Statements
>
> A conceptual statement makes a claim about how we should understand and use some term that plays a role in how we think and talk about the world, in cases in which there is uncertainty or controversy about the meaning of the term. Conceptual statements are like analytic statements in their definitional character, but analytic statements generally occur when there is little or no uncertainty about the meaning of a term.

Consider this group of statements:

Example 8.5

N. Torturing babies is morally wrong.
O. Example 8.1 is a weak argument.
P. Mozart is the world's greatest composer.
Q. It was morally wrong for the United States to drop an atomic bomb on Japan.
R. A normal adult should not be allowed to make his or her own decisions about what career to pursue.

These sentences express value statements (see Chapter 3). Value statements, as we have seen, appear frequently as premises and conclusions and, like other statements, have a truth value. Here, statement N is clearly true and statement R is clearly false, but the truth values of the other statements are less certain, and perhaps controversial. How do we determine the truth value of a value statement? Just as we do for non–value statements: We see where the strongest argument lies. For example, the truth of statement O is argued for in the text following Example 8.1. The justifications sketched there for the fallacy charges of problematic premise and false premise constitute an argument that O is true. If this is a strong argument, then we can count O as true. These statements are about different kinds of values. For instance, statements N, Q, and R are about moral value, P is about aesthetic value, and O is about logical value.

Now consider some special cases:

Example 8.6

S. It ain't over 'til it's over.
T. Human beings evolved from more primitive life forms.
U. The release of carbon dioxide is causing global warming.
V. Property is theft.

Statement S, attributed to former New York Yankee player and manager Yogi Berra, seems to be a tautology, akin to "it is not raining until it is raining." Understood as such, it says nothing about the world. But Berra presumably did not intend to utter a tautology. Rather, he wanted to say something important about the world, and the fact that this has become a widely recognized saying shows that we understand it as more than a tautology. How could the statement be reformulated to make its meaning more explicit? What S means, apparently, is that no person or team in a contest should give up fighting until the very end—until the last out in the ninth inning or the last play in a football game. The game is not "over until it is over" in the sense that if there is time remaining winning is always possible.

Statement V is also ironic. The author is the nineteenth-century French political theorist Pierre Joseph Proudhon. It seems to be an analytic falsehood, since property ownership excludes the idea of theft in the same way that bachelorhood excludes the idea of being married. So what might Proudhon have meant by this claim? What he seems to be saying is that property should be publicly rather than privately owned, that private ownership is a form of theft from the population as a whole.

Finally, statements T and U are special cases for a very different reason. They seem like straightforward *a posteriori* statements, and, indeed, considered by themselves, they are. But today they are matters of political and ideological controversy. T has become a flashpoint in the debate between evolutionists and creationists, and U has become a flashpoint in the debate over how much we should restrict our economic activity for the sake of the environment. The proponents of the truth of T regard the critics of T as motivated by a belief in the literal truth of the Bible, and the proponents of the truth of U regard the critics of U as motivated by a blind opposition to any government regulation of the economy. In contrast, the critics regard the proponents of T as motivated by a quasi-religious position they label "secular humanism" and proponents of U as extreme environmentalists motivated by a blind opposition to economic growth.

Attacking the truth of a claim by impugning the motives of its proponents is not good critical thinking. It is, in fact, a case of the fallacy of argument *ad hominem*, discussed in Chapter 6. The motives of someone who puts forth a claim or an argument are irrelevant to the truth value of the claim or the strength of the argument. Statements that engender such political and ideological controversies usually do so for only a while. The claim that smoking causes cancer was once in this category, as was the claim that the Earth orbits the sun.

8.1.2 Different Kinds of Justifications

Imagine that you are an informal ethics advisor, someone to whom people turn for advice when facing troubling moral questions. They want you to help them to think through what they ought to do. Thus, they are asking for your help in formulating and criticizing arguments. Let us suppose, further, that one of your friends is Huckleberry Finn, the Mark Twain character. Huck comes to you in moral confusion about what to do about his friend Jim, an escaped slave. In the course of your discussion, Huck indicates that he is thinking of turning Jim in based on the following line of reasoning:

Example 8.7

P1: As property, all slaves belong to their owners.
P2: Jim is a slave who has escaped from his owner.
C: Therefore, Jim should be returned to his owner.

What Huck is asking you, in effect, is to help him to determine whether this is a strong argument. Focusing on the content of the argument, how would you assess these premises?

Consider P1. You could look at P1 in two ways. First, you could view it in terms of the accepted moral beliefs of your pre–Civil War American community, which Huck presumably shares. In this view, P1 would be true, for at the time the accepted sociocultural belief was that slaves were rightfully owned by their masters. Second, you could view P1 independently of whether it is accepted by society. You could attempt to look at it *in itself* to determine whether it is true or likely true, apart from what people generally believe. In this case, you might then question accepted moral beliefs. Thus, you might charge the argument with a false premise at P1, with the justification that human beings have an inherent right to freedom that precludes one person from owning another.

The first kind of assessment is a **conventional assessment,** one that focuses on the beliefs of the individual or group toward whom the argument is directed. It is "conventional" in the sense that it accepts the commonplace beliefs of the community or culture of the audience, on the assumption that these are the beliefs of the audience as well. Conventional assessment is based on what may be referred to as general belief—that is, the beliefs that are shared by most members of the general public from which the audience is drawn. A conventional assessment looks at a premise in the light of those beliefs, by asking whether the premise accurately represents them. A premise is inadequate when it is not in accord with those beliefs, when the audience does not regard it as true or likely true. Because the claim is at odds with what the audience would accept, the author should have provided support for it (with a subargument). So, the argument should be charged with problematic premise.

The second kind of assessment, a **critical assessment,** goes beyond conventional assessment because it attempts to consider the truth or likely truth of premises *in themselves*—that is, independently of, and sometimes at odds with, the accepted beliefs of the community. You should make a critical assessment of a premise when you have good reason to regard it as doubtful or false, even if the community would regard it as true.

> ### Conventional and Critical Assessment of Premises
>
> A conventional assessment is a judgment of the acceptability of a premise based on what is widely believed in the society or culture of the audience of the argument. A critical assessment is a judgment of the truth or likely truth of a premise in itself, apart from what is generally believed. A critical assessment involves an argument either that a premise is false or that it is not likely true, whatever the views of the community.[3] Conventional and critical assessment are different kinds of arguments that are used in the justification for content fallacy charges.

The distinction between conventional and critical assessment of premises applies not only to value arguments. Imagine that you are present in 1491 at an audience that Christopher Columbus has sought with Queen Isabella of Spain as part of his efforts to get funding for his proposed sea voyage west to India. Also present are two of the queen's advisors.[4] One of the advisors offers this argument to the queen:

Example 8.8

Your majesty:

    ⌜P1A: India lies to the east.
    ⌞P1B: Columbus plans to sail west.
⌜P1: If the world is flat, then Columbus will not reach India.
⌞P2: The world is flat.
  C: Therefore, you should not fund his voyage.

The queen turns to her second advisor, who tells her that this argument is strong, for, as everyone knows, the world is indeed flat.

The queen then offers Columbus a chance to respond. He says that the argument is weak in that it commits the fallacy of false premise at P2. He then offers a justification for this charge, offering arguments (by now quite familiar to us) supporting the claim that the world is round. The second advisor looks at the argument in terms of conventional assessment and finds no reason to criticize the premises. But Columbus offers a critical assessment, calling into question a belief that is widely accepted at that time, the belief represented in P2. The audience—in this case, the queen—presumably accepts this belief.

Today, accepted beliefs are being challenged in the same way that Columbus challenged the belief in a flat earth or abolitionists challenged the belief that humans should be owned by others. For example, it has long been an accepted belief in Western society that animals have little or no moral value. But that belief is being challenged by animal rights activists, who criticize arguments that support claims about how we treat animals. This does not mean that in the future such claims will be regarded as false, as we now regard the claim that humans can be owned. This depends, at least in part, on how strong the arguments are and how they play themselves out in the public debate.

The source of the contrast between conventional and critical assessment lies in the two main purposes of an argument, as discussed in previous chapters: (1) to rationally persuade others and (2) to seek the truth. The role of conventional assessment follows from the first purpose. To rationally persuade an audience of the truth of a conclusion, you have to present premises that the audience will find acceptable. Thus, you need to pay attention to what the audience believes, which normally will include the generally accepted beliefs of the broader society or culture. The complementary role of critical assessment follows from the second purpose of arguments. An argument with false premises cannot guarantee the truth of its conclusion and so cannot further our understanding of the truth. It follows that you should investigate premises for their truth independently of what the audience believes about them.

The set of beliefs widely accepted in a society or culture will, of course, contain many false beliefs. But this does not undermine the importance of conventional assessment. Because the role of conventional assessment is to determine whether an argument achieves its purpose of being rationally persuasive, it must be based on the beliefs of the audience, true or false. If you include as a premise in your argument a claim that you believe to be true but that your audience will believe to be false, you need to provide a subargument in support of its truth. If you do this, as we will see, your premise is not subject to a conventional assessment. You can use critical assessment to call attention to any false claims that the audience believes to be true. This is the division of labor between conventional and critical assessment.[5]

EXERCISE SET 8.1

SECTION A: It is important to understand how we acquire the beliefs that we share with others in our culture in order appreciate how reliable they are and to help us to determine when it is appropriate to critically assess them. The following statements are generally regarded as true. Explain how you acquired your belief in the truth of these statements, and, as a result, how reliable that belief is.

EXAMPLE
The Declaration of Independence was written in 1776.

ANSWER
This is something I know because I have read it in textbooks and been told it by my teachers throughout my primary and secondary education. These sources are reliable because the textbooks are written by recognized historical experts and the teachers have been certified as teachers by the college or university they went to.

PROBLEMS
1. The 2000 summer Olympics were held in Sydney, Australia.

2. My name is _____. (Fill in the blank.)

❖ 3. Nigeria is in Africa.

4. The legal drinking age is 21.

5. The sun will rise tomorrow morning.

❖ 6. My sex is _____. (Fill in the blank.)

7. I am younger than my mother.

8. The Internet is an abundant source of information about the world.

❖ 9. The press is much more willing to report on the private lives of politicians than it used to be.

SECTION B: For each of the following statements, indicate whether it is a tautology, a contradiction, an analytic truth, an analytic falsehood, an *a posteriori* truth, an *a posteriori* falsehood, or a value claim. Give reasons for your answer. Supply implicit quantifiers as needed.

EXAMPLE

The heart circulates the blood.

ANSWER

This claim is an *a posteriori* truth. It is not an *a priori* claim because it could have been false. In fact, for most of human history, people thought the heart had some other function. The role of the heart in the circulation of the blood was a great scientific discovery. Now, there is overwhelming medical evidence that the function of the heart is to circulate the blood. Much of the success of modern medicine is based on the truth of this statement.

PROBLEMS

1. The Internet has revolutionized the way we live.

2. All human beings are mortal.

❖ 3. The voting age should be raised to 25.

4. An avatar is a deity incarnate.

5. Pat is either coming to the picnic or not.

❖ 6. Second-hand smoke causes cancer.

7. Joe DiMaggio was a greater baseball player than Babe Ruth.

8. The government should not interfere in people's lives.

❖ 9. Rome had an empire in the ancient world.

10. The American Civil War began in 1860.

11. February follows January.

❖ 12. Illegal drugs are bad for you.

13. There are 70 seconds in a minute.

14. Not all those who wander are lost.

❖ 15. People with pierced noses listen to rock.

16. Hamlet is a fictional character.

17. Lynn is coming to the picnic and she is not.

❖ 18. A sanctimonious person is honestly devout.

19. This sentence is false.

Note: Sections C, D, and E refer to the list of statements presented earlier in the chapter (statements A–V).

SECTION C: Find an example of a statement that, like S and V, appears to be *a priori* but is used ironically to make some claim about the world. Briefly discuss the example.

SECTION D: Find an example of a statement that, like T and U, seems to be a straightforward *a posteriori* claim, but has become a political or ideological battleground. Discuss it briefly.

SECTION E: Provide a brief argument for the truth or falsity of statement P or Q.

SECTION F: Provide a justification for Columbus's charge of false or problematic premise against the argument of Queen Isabella's advisor (in Example 8.8).

8.2 The Fallacies of Problematic Premise and False Premise

The two content fallacies are false premise and problematic premise. Figure 8.1 lists the conditions and justification strategies for them. (This chart complements a similar one in Figure 6.7 for the two formal fallacies.) As the chart indicates, a charge of false premise is based on a justification showing that the premise is false in its own terms. A charge of problematic premise, in contrast, is based on a justification showing either that the premise is not acceptable in its own terms or that it not acceptable to the audience, or both. This suggests that critical assessment plays a role in justifications for charging either fallacy, whereas conventional assessment plays a role only in justifications for charging problematic premise.

8.2.1 Charging Problematic Premise

When you evaluate an argument for a charge of problematic premise, you assess its premises in terms of their acceptability, either in their own terms or in terms of the beliefs of the audience. To say that a premise is not acceptable is to say that there is significant doubt about its truth. In the case of a simple (noncomplex) argument,

Fallacy	Conditions	Justification Strategies
False premise (lack of truth)	A premise is false.	Show that the premise is false by refuting it through counterexample or false implication or by some other sort of argument.
Problematic premise (lack of acceptability)	A premise is (1) not supported by a subargument and (2) not likely true, in its own terms and/or in terms of the beliefs of the audience.	Point out that the premise is unsupported by a subargument and argue that there is reason to doubt the truth of the premise and/or that the premise is not accepted as true by the audience.

FIGURE 8.1   Fallacy Conditions and Justification Strategies

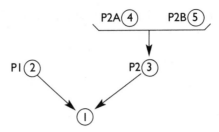

FIGURE 8.2   Tree Diagram with Three Top-Node Premises

any premise is open to investigation for a charge of problematic premise. But this is not the case for a complex argument. As Figure 8.1 indicates, a necessary condition for a premise's being charged with problematic premise is its *not* being supported by a subargument. The charge is that the premise is not supported and needs to be, because it is doubtful either in its own terms or in the view of the audience. So, in a complex argument, no premise supported by a subargument can be charged with problematic premise.[6]

A premise that is not supported by a subargument is a **top-node premise.** This term relates to the position of the circles representing premises in a tree diagram, with a top node a premise at the highest level of its branch on a tree diagram. Every premise of a simple argument is, of course, a top-node premise.

Consider the tree diagram shown in Figure 8.2. Premises P1, P2A, and P2B are top-node premises, and P2 is not. Top-node premises are assessed directly for acceptability, but any assessment of P2 for acceptability is indirect, through the evaluation of its subargument.

The top-node premises of an argument, taken together, are the **argument foundation,** the base on which it is built in terms of the beliefs of the audience.[7] An argument has to have a place from which to begin; otherwise, every premise would need to be preceded by a subargument to support it. Unless the foundation is rooted firmly in the beliefs of the audience, the argument cannot achieve its purpose of being rationally persuasive. An argument is a joining of a public debate, and a public debate has its foundation in what its participants accept or believe.

Top-Node Premises and Argument Foundation

Top-node premises are all the premises of an argument not supported by a subargument—that is, all the premises of a simple argument and all the unsupported premises of a complex argument. They are the premises that are represented by the circles at top branches of the tree diagram of the argument. Only a top-node premise can be charged with problematic premise. All of the top-node premises of an argument, taken together, form the argument foundation, the place from which the argument begins in terms of the audience's beliefs.

Authors of arguments are often well aware of the need to provide top-node premises acceptable to the audience. Consider the habit that many people have when presenting an argument, especially informally, of introducing a premise with the phrase "you know," as in "We should postpone the picnic because, *you know*, the forecast is for rain this afternoon." Inserting "you know" in this way indicates the author's recognition that the argument should be based on premises that the audience regards as true or likely true.

The audience of an argument, as we have seen, can be special or general. A **special audience** is a relatively small group of people who have certain levels of knowledge. Biologists, for example, are a special audience. Biologists who write for the professional journal *Cell Biology* do not need to provide subarguments for premises that other biologists will accept, even if members of the **general audience** (laypersons or nonbiologists) would not accept them (perhaps because they do not understand them). Authors in *Cell Biology* understand that the audience for their arguments will be other biologists, so their premises are not held to the same standards in terms of conventional assessment as they would be if their arguments were intended for a general audience. The conventional assessment of premises of an argument directed at a special audience is in terms of the beliefs shared by the members of that audience.

More important for our purposes is the general audience. Most of the arguments we encounter from day to day are meant by their authors for a general audience. A general audience is composed of people who are not experts in the subject matter of an argument. We assume a certain set of basic beliefs on the part of members of the general audience—what we referred to earlier as the general beliefs of a society or culture.

Special and General Audiences

A special audience is a group of people who have expertise or knowledge not shared by the general public. A general audience is a group of people who do not have expertise in the area that an argument is about. Whether an audience is general or special affects charges of problematic premise because what is acceptable to a special audience might not be acceptable to a general audience. Conventional assessment is appropriate only when an argument is directed at a general audience, like most of the arguments we encounter in everyday life.

One common occasion for charging problematic premise is when a premise may well be true but the truth of the premise would not be known to the general audience to which the argument is directed. In such a case, a conventional assessment is used in the justification.

Consider this example, with structure and evaluation:

Example 8.9

Background: This letter is in response to a proposal in Massachusetts to expand a law requiring deposits on bottles. (*Boston Globe*, 6/97)

> ① Common sense means recycling the most waste possible for the least amount of money. ② An expanded bottle deposit program would not even divert 2 percent of our state's solid waste stream and would cost over 10 times more to administer than curbside recycling programs. ③ That's a huge price to pay for a small amount of recycling.—M.M.W.

Structure

> P1: We should recycle the most amount of waste for the least money.
> P2: The expanded bottle deposit program would divert less than 2 percent of the state's solid waste stream and would cost ten times the amount of curbside recycling.
> P3: That is a large price to pay for little effect.
> IC: Therefore, we should not adopt the expanded program.

Evaluation

> I charge this argument with problematic premise at P2. The premise needs support but does not have it. The typical audience member would have no idea if these figures are accurate. This is something only a specialist would know about. Thus, the arguer should have given support for this premise—for example, by citing an authoritative source in a subargument supporting the premise.

Here, there is probably no basis for including a critical assessment as part of the justification for the problematic premise fallacy charge. As a member of a general audience, you normally would have no basis for arguing that the premise is false or not likely true. Of course, if you think that you could make an argument that the premise is false or not likely true, you should make the argument. But in most cases, as a member of the general audience, you would not be in a position to do so. In many cases, we have to rely on a conventional assessment to justify a problematic premise charge because we do not know enough to made a critical assessment or to determine whether a critical assessment is warranted.

If possible, however, in justifying a charge of problematic premise, you should include some critical assessment, either along with some conventional assessment or by itself. Here is an argument in which we can mix both types of assessment in justifying a problematic premise charge:

Example 8.10

Background: This letter addresses the problem of sexual harassment in the military. (*New York Times*, 9/97)

> The Army still seems unable to identify the cause of sexual harassment—a lack of respect for a fellow soldier, stemming from the different training standards for men

and women. Until the Army eliminates the different standards, the men will not respect the women and the Army will simply be a politically correct fighting force. —V.I.

Structure

P1: The cause of sexual harassment in the Army is the lack of respect soldiers have for each other due to the different training standards for men and women.

C: Men will not respect women in the Army until their training standards are the same.

Evaluation

I charge this argument with problematic premise at P1. This premise should have been supported by a subargument. First, the claim would not generally be regarded as true by the audience. Most members of the audience would be skeptical about the truth of this claim or have no view on the matter. Second, there are reasons to doubt its truth. Most men recognize that men and women on average differ in physical strength and that this difference has its source in biology. If so, it is unlikely that they would fail to respect women because the physical training standards were not as demanding for women. Men's lack of respect for women in the Army probably has a different source.

In this evaluation, critical assessment (second point) is mixed with conventional assessment (first point). The justification argues not only that the audience would not generally find the premise to be acceptable but also that there is reason to doubt that it is true. Both points indicate that the author should have provided a subargument in support of the premise.

Whenever you can provide some substantial reasons to think that a premise might be false, you have the basis of a critical assessment of that premise. In that case, you should charge problematic premise using the critical assessment as the justification or include a critical assessment in a problematic premise charge you were already making based on a conventional assessment.

We have spoken of cases in which a problematic premise charge can be justified based on a conventional assessment or on both a conventional and a critical assessment. There are also cases in which it can be justified solely on the basis of a critical assessment. This happens when the audience accepts a premise but you, in evaluating the argument, have significant reason to doubt its truth.

In terms of critical assessment, a problematic premise charge is appropriate when you can argue that there is substantial reason to doubt that the premise is true. If you believe that the premise is true or likely true, no critical assessment is needed. In that case, you should charge no content fallacy regarding the premise in question unless you can justify a problematic premise charge on the basis of a conventional assessment. But if you believe that a premise is not merely doubtful but is false or likely false, and if you can provide an argument to back this up, you should charge not problematic premise, but false premise.

	Charge of False Premise	Charge of Problematic Premise
Conventional Assessment (argument fails to be rationally persuasive)	—	If the audience would not accept the premise (would not regard it as true or likely true)
Critical Assessment (argument fails to move us closer to the truth)	If you have an argument that the premise is false or likely false	If you have an argument that there are reasons to doubt the premise

FIGURE 8.3   Content Fallacy Charges and Forms of Assessment

8.2.2 Charging False Premise

While a problematic premise charge can be justified by either a conventional assessment or a critical assessment (or both), a false premise charge is justified exclusively by a critical assessment. Figure 8.3 summarizes the conditions for content fallacy charges and forms of assessment.

Why does the justification for a false premise charge rely exclusively on a critical assessment and not on a conventional assessment as well? When you make a false premise charge, you are, in effect, saying that the premise in question should be dropped from the argument because you do not think that it could be successfully supported. But a conventional assessment is an invitation to provide such support. When you charge problematic premise, you are claiming that a premise needs support, but when you charge false premise, you are claiming that the premise is unsupportable.[8] Thus, a charge of false premise is not based on a conventional assessment.

To see the contrast between charges of problematic premise and of false premise, consider this pair of arguments:

Example 8.11

A. We do not have to conserve gasoline because, when the oil runs out, we will find some other energy source to use in its place.

B. We do not have to conserve gasoline because we will never run out of oil.

Both of these arguments have a content fallacy, but which content fallacy?[9] Consider the premises:

Example 8.12

A. When the oil runs out, we will find some other energy source to use.

B. We will never run out of oil.

Argument B warrants a false premise charge because premise B obviously is false. You would seek to provide a justification, based on a critical assessment, that supports the claim that it is false. Argument A probably warrants a problematic premise charge. Although premise A is not obviously false, both the audience and you, as the evaluator, would have serious doubts about its truth. The justification of the fallacy charge would be a combination of conventional and critical assessments. Here is a justification for the charge of false premise against argument B:

Example 8.13

I charge this argument with false premise at P1. The supply of oil is finite and nonrenewable. Oil was formed slowly millions of years ago by the decay of dead plant life. So, there is only so much that exists on Earth, even though we are not sure how much that is. Also, the supply, if it is being renewed at all, is being renewed at such a slow pace that, for human purposes, it is nonrenewable.

Here is an argumentative text that, in effect, offers a false premise charge against another argument:

Example 8.14

Background: This letter was in response to another letter that argued against strict controls on pornography. The first two sentences of this letter report one of the premises of that argument. (*Miami Herald*, 5/97)

> The author assures us that his own childhood encounters with smut left him none the worse, that it doesn't kill. It probably doesn't even injure. Can anyone with an ounce of common sense or decency believe that pornography, which is quickly rotting what's left of this nation's moral structure, is harmless? Pornography involving children doesn't harm them or others? Women are not degraded by this filth? Men who view it are encouraged to build intimacy within a marriage? Pornography's damage to adults, youth, and especially children is incalculable. The evidence is legion.—C.S.

The premise to which this author was responding is that pornography is probably not harmful. The argument of this letter is, in effect, a justification of a charge of false premise against that other argument based on a critical assessment of that premise. Through a series of rhetorical questions, the author makes the case that pornography is indeed harmful.

There are different ways to argue in a justification for a charge of false premise. One common and powerful way is to pose a counterexample to a universal statement, or a **refutation by counterexample.** In Chapter 7, we discussed the method of counterexample used to show that a deductive argument is invalid. Here, we use a strategy of counterexample to criticize argument content, not argument form. Refutation by counterexample applies only to universal premises. The idea is that any universal statement can be shown to be false by citing one case in which it does not apply. For instance, for the premise all x are y, you can show that it is false by pointing to one x that is not a y (the counterexample).

Likewise, for the premise no x are y, you can show that it is false by pointing to one x that is a y.[10]

A justification using refutation by counterexample often involves merely citing counterexamples, as in these examples:

Example 8.15

A. Universal statement: All great novelists have been men.
    Counterexample: Charlotte Brontë[11]
B. Universal statement: All plant life is healthy for humans to eat.
    Counterexample: hemlock

But sometimes you have to argue that the counterexamples cited are indeed counterexamples.

Consider an example of a text that criticizes the content of another argument using refutation by counterexample:

Example 8.16

Background: This letter was written during a congressional debate about whether the government should provide health care for all citizens. Newt Gingrich was then a Republican member of the House of Representatives. A police state is a society in which basic human rights are not respected. (*New York Times*, 8/94)

> Representative Gingrich has said that "you cannot get to universal coverage without a police state." Are Canadians living in a police state? Are Norway, Australia and Japan—which has had universal coverage since 1961—police states too? Are all the countries where people receive medical care without regard to income actually police states? If Republican leaders have to stoop to assertions like this, there can't be much rational support for their position.—F.B.

Gingrich was arguing that the government should not provide universal health care because doing so requires a police state. The author seeks to show that the premise is false by presenting a counterexample—in fact, several of them. The author cites several nations that provide universal health care without being police states. The letter is, in effect, a justification of a charge of false premise against Gingrich's argument.

Refutation by Counterexample

Refutation by counterexample is a method of showing that a universal statement is false by pointing out one or more cases in which it does not apply, sometimes along with an argument that those cases the universal statement does not apply. This is a simple and powerful way to provide a critical assessment to justify a false premise charge.

8.2.3 Refutation by False Implication and Reductio ad Absurdum

Refutation by counterexample is a special case of a more general strategy known as **refutation by false implication.** With this strategy, you seek to show that a statement is false by showing that some implication of that statement is false. This is a version of the valid argument form *modus tollens* (see Chapter 6). If the consequent of a conditional is false, the antecedent is false as well.

Refutation by False Implication

Refutation by false implication is a method of showing that a premise in an argument is false by showing that some implication of that statement is false. It makes use of *modus tollens*: if the consequent of a conditional (the implication) is false, the antecedent (the premise) is false as well.

Here is how refutation by counterexample fits the pattern of refutation by false implication:

Example 8.17

P1: If all great novelists are men, then Charlotte Brontë is not a great novelist.
P2: Charlotte Brontë is a great novelist.
C: Therefore, it is false that all great novelists are men.

Consider these examples of refutation by false implication:

Example 8.18

A. Background: This letter is in response to criticism of some U.S. political leaders for receiving campaign contributions from China. (*Atlanta Constitution,* 3/97)

① Why are we surprised and outraged that the Chinese have attempted to influence the American political process by contributing to political candidates? ② If this is wrong, the United States is guilty for supporting Shimon Peres over Benjamin Netanyahu in Israel, for attempting to influence elections in Bosnia and South Africa, for supporting Boris Yeltsin in Russia and for interfering in Haiti. ③ Our outrage is ill-founded.—E.J.F.

B. Background: This letter is in response to a letter that argued in favor of abortion rights. (*New York Times,* 2/00)

① The letter writer asserts: "Women need abortion options for physical, emotional and financial reasons. ② Abortion empowers women by providing an alternative to an unwanted pregnancy." ③ Although an abortion-rights supporter, I find this reasoning appalling. ④ By this logic, a woman should have the right to terminate the life of her month-old baby if doing so would improve her emotional or financial well-being, or "empower" her by providing an alternative to unwanted motherhood. ⑤ In the abortion debate, the question of when sentient human life begins, not the question of what's convenient, must remain primary.—D.K.

Argument A seeks to refute the claim that it is wrong for China to have tried to influence the American election. Sentence 2 provides the first premise: If it is wrong for China to try to influence the American election, it is wrong for the United States to have tried to influence elections in Israel, South Africa, Bosnia, and Russia. The second premise is implicit: It is not wrong for the United States to have tried to influence these elections. The conclusion is that it is not wrong for China to have tried to influence the American election.

Argument B is also an example of refutation by false implication, but it has a special character that makes it a case of ***reductio ad absurdum.*** The implication in this case is not only false but absurdly false. This argument refutes a claim by reducing it to absurdity by showing that it has implications that are absurd. Sentence 4 gives the implication: If women are allowed to kill their fetuses for the reasons stated, they should be allowed to kill their infant children for the same reasons. But this consequent is false because it is absurd. Therefore, it is false that women should be allowed to kill their fetuses for those same reasons.[12]

There is no sharp line between cases of *reductio ad absurdum* and other cases of refutation by false implication, because there is no sharp boundary between claims that are absurdly false and claims that are false without being absurd. Cases of refutation by false implication are sometimes presented in ironic terms. An author will suggest, tongue in cheek, that she or he accepts the truth of the consequent of the conditional P1 while intending the audience to understand that the consequent is clearly false. In addition, in many refutations by false implication, the claim to be refuted, along with the implication drawn from it, is an action recommendation. In such cases, the implication drawn is false because it clearly would be a bad action or a bad policy.

Reductio ad Absurdum

Reductio ad absurdum is a version of refutation by false implication. It has the same argument form as refutation by false implication, but it differs in that the implication drawn from the claim is not only false but absurdly so. The clearest form of absurdity is a contradiction, but an implication that falls short of being a contradiction can still be regarded as absurd.[13]

The examples we have looked at so far in this section have been cases in which authors offered justifications that would be part of a charge of false premise against another argument. In this example, we can make the charge ourselves:

Example 8.19

Background: The following letter is part of the debate over affirmative action in higher education. It concerns the steep decline in the number of African Americans admitted to the University of Texas Law School after it was forced to abandon its affirmative action admission policy. (*New York Times*, 5/97)

> ① Rather than dwelling on the decline in admissions of blacks to the University of Texas Law School, why not devote our energies to celebrating the achievements of the 10 highly motivated, highly qualified blacks who have been offered admission based solely on merit. ② These individuals will be the leaders of tomorrow. ③ Let's not forget that it is the quality, not the quantity, of the leaders that matters.—A.J.S.

Structure

P1: The ten highly motivated, highly qualified blacks who have been offered admission to the University of Texas Law School based solely on merit will be the leaders of tomorrow.

P2: It is the quality, not the quantity, of the leaders that matters.

C: Therefore, we should celebrate the achievements of those ten students and not be concerned with the decline in the number of admissions of blacks to the law school.

Evaluation

I charge this argument with false premise at P2. This premise is false because it is not only the quality but also the quantity of leaders that matters. A large nation like the United States needs to train a large number of people to take over leadership roles in the future. If it is only quality that matters, we should have a single law school for the whole country that trains only a few lawyers, the best of the best. Because the consequent of this conditional is clearly false, so is the antecedent. In addition, because this argument is about black admissions in particular, it is important to note that the leadership in our society should reflect our social diversity. Thus, even among a specific group, like blacks, the quantity as well as the quality of leadership is important.

This justification adopts, in part, the strategy of refutation by false implication.

By now it may be clear that there is no sharp line between cases in which you should charge problematic premise and cases in which you should charge false premise. What is most important is to recognize the difference between the two fallacies in terms of the kind of justification argument each requires. Often, the difference comes down to how well you, as evaluator, understand the issue being discussed in the argument. The key is to develop your critical thinking abilities and to use those abilities to offer the strongest justification possible for whichever content fallacy charge you find appropriate.

EXERCISE SET 8.2

SECTION A: Structure the following arguments and evaluate them in terms of problematic premise and false premise (no tree diagram needed). To justify a problematic premise charge, use a conventional assessment, a critical assessment, or both. To justify a false premise charge, use a critical assessment.

EXAMPLE

Technology has led to the average employee working more hours rather than fewer. It clearly follows that we should avoid introducing more new technology into the workplace.

ANSWER

P1: Technology has led to the average employee working more hours rather than fewer.

C: We should avoid introducing more new technology into the workplace.

> I charge this argument with problematic premise at P1. This premise is problematic, given that it is not supported, both because it is not acceptable to the general audience and because it is in itself doubtful. Most members of the audience would not believe that this claim is true. It is counterintuitive—that is, contrary to what people would tend to think—given that technology is thought of as labor-saving. The premise is in itself doubtful because there are many examples of technology being labor-saving, such as the word processor eliminating the need to retype documents. It is hard to believe that technology overall requires that we work longer hours. For all of these reasons, the author needs to provide support for this premise.

PROBLEMS

1. Every U.S. president elected at 20-year intervals since 1860 has died in office, so George W. Bush better be careful.
2. So many of the movies that come out of Hollywood are unoriginal. In addition, they are all full of mindless sex and violence. We should watch only foreign films.
3. People should think carefully about their automobile purchase. After all, an automobile is the most expensive thing that most of us will ever buy.
4. Parents should threaten violence against their children, for all children should learn respect for their parents, and no one can learn respect who is not threatened with violence.
5. Traveling by commercial airliner is the most dangerous way to travel. So, you should drive instead whenever you can.
6. The higher a college places in the *U.S. News & World Report* ranking of colleges, the better the educational experience it provides. So, of all the colleges a student is admitted to, she or he should attend the one highest on that list.
7. Members of Congress should be allowed to serve only a limited number of terms because no long-term member of Congress has ever been an effective legislator.
8. All a fire needs to keep burning is more fuel and more oxygen. So, if there is more fuel and oxygen available, there is no hope of extinguishing a fire.
9. The Sears Tower in Chicago is the tallest building in the world. So, the tallest building in the world is in the United States.
10. Mitochondrial DNA is passed down unaltered through the maternal line, so it has become possible to trace all of humanity back to a single female progenitor from early in the history of the species, a woman appropriately dubbed "Eve."

SECTION B: Following are arguments that seek to refute some claim using refutation by false implication, including refutation by counterexample and *reductio ad absurdum*. In each case, put the argument into the form for refutation by false implication and indicate whether it is a case of a general refutation by false implication, a refutation by counterexample, or a *reductio ad absurdum*.

EXAMPLE

Background: This letter is about whale hunting. (*New York Times*, 8/00)

Why do some people think that certain cruel practices—like whale hunting and eating—are justified simply because they're traditional? Given this convoluted line of thought, we should condone child labor, the oppression of women and slavery—all customary in some societies.—S.C.

ANSWER

P1: If people are allowed to hunt and eat whales simply because it is traditional, then people should be allowed to practice activities such as child labor, oppression of women, and slavery simply because they are traditional.

P2: It is false that people should be allowed to practice activities such as child labor, oppression of women, and slavery simply because they are traditional.

C: Therefore, it is false that people should be allowed to hunt and eat whales simply because they are traditional.

This is a case of *reductio ad absurdum* because the consequent of the conditional in P1 is not merely false but absurdly so.

PROBLEMS

1. Background: This letter addresses the claim of a columnist that the language of radical writings must be challenging or obscure. (*New York Times*, 5/99)

   Your columnist's claim that radicalism requires challenging, if not obscure, language cannot stand. There are too many counterexamples. Thomas Paine's *Common Sense*, Jefferson's introduction to the Declaration of Independence, Lincoln's Gettysburg Address, the Rev. Dr. Martin Luther King Jr.'s sermons and Betty Friedan's *Feminine Mystique* were all clearly written radical documents.—E.B.B.

2. Background: This letter is about white journalists writing about the lives of blacks. (*New York Times*, 6/00)

   I reject the argument that a white journalist should not write about a black drug addict because it is not "his story to tell." This assumes that only black people can or should write about black people, and implies that there exists a single, unanimous perspective that all black Americans hold. Many black Americans did not grow up in an inner-city community, so they would not be any better "witnesses" than a white journalist to such a story.—I.R.

3. Background: This is a continuation of the letter in the previous example.

   If the philosophy that whites cannot write about blacks is pushed to its fullest conclusion, only autobiographies will become acceptable representations of life. If we accept that race and ethnicity have trumped our ability to understand, empathize and write about the sufferings or joys of those with whom we share this country, we are finished as a society.

4. Background: This letter is in response to an argument against a proposal to raise the minimum wage. (*Los Angeles Times*, 4/98)

I was startled to read that "sound economic reasoning" mandates that we be opposed to raising the minimum wage to $6.75 an hour. If we think about it, free labor would be the cheapest way to go and very sound economically. Unfortunately, a Republican president did away with slavery a long time ago.—W.M.

5. Background: This is a criticism of the investigations of former President Clinton's relationship with a White House intern. (*Boston Globe*, 12/98)

All members of Congress and Supreme Court justices should be held to the same high moral and legal standards as the president has been this past year. This would entail their all being required to swear a sexual loyalty oath as well as their oaths to obey the laws and tell the whole truth and nothing but the truth. The sexual loyalty oath would consist of each senator, representative, and Supreme Court justice swearing that they had not ever engaged in extramarital sexual activity with other consenting adults.—C.C.A.

❖ 6. Background: This letter is about the issue of government regulation of the labor market to aid workers. (*Boston Globe*, 9/97)

Your columnist writes that "government intervention in the labor market to mandate wage rates and other employer practices does not work even at a national level." Oh really? Has he never heard of the laws on minimum wage, the 8-hour day, child labor, health and safety, pension management . . . ? Most have been in effect for most of this century. In what way, and for whom, do they "not work"?—C.C.B.

7. Background: This letter is about a female student's suing Duke University for not being allowed to participate in its varsity football program. (*New York Times*, 9/97)

I hope that the student wins her suit against Duke University for not being allowed to participate fully in its varsity football program. The suit's success would not only open the door for women to participate in other collegiate varsity sports like lacrosse, baseball and water polo, but it would also open the door for men to participate in softball and field hockey. Wouldn't it?—J.M.

8. Background: This letter is in criticism of another letter favoring euthanasia, the right of a terminally ill individual who is suffering to choose to end his or her life. (*Boston Globe*, 7/97)

The letter writer gives a strong argument in favor of the right to die. But his logic leads to a conclusion so unpalatable the letter writer himself avoids it. He says that the great unasked question in this debate is, "Does a person's life belong to that person or to the state? In a democracy, does an individual, if he is injuring no one, not have the right to be let alone?" It is a powerful argument. But why does he then back off? He says that of course this ownership does not apply to the unsound of mind. But why not? Does the state own the life of the mentally ill? And isn't the clinically depressed person the one who would benefit from help in ending his life peacefully and painlessly? By this logic of ownership an unhappy father would be morally in the right to kill himself, leaving his children destitute. It's his life, isn't it? But it is not his life, not absolutely. Our lives are owned in common by ourselves, our families, and our community.—G.P.

❖ 9. Background: This letter was in response to an argument that no government funding should go to support the arts. (*Chicago Tribune*, 7/97)

   In an editorial, the *Tribune* declares, "No citizen ought to be compelled to support expression to which he or she objects." Well! This is a stunning, even revolutionary concept. There is quite a bit of governmental "expression" that I object to: B-2 bombers that the Pentagon doesn't even ask for, ethanol and sugar subsidies, welfare programs that dispense unearned cash, tax credits that reward the middle class for the achievement of reproducing, etc. According to the *Tribune*, I am not compelled to fund these! This is wonderful news.—K.C.

10. Background: This letter is critical of a columnist's argument that nuclear deterrence is a good way to avoid war. (*New York Times*, 5/98)

   Your columnist says that "nuclear weapons are a superb deterrent" because "no state is likely to attack the homeland or vital interests of a nuclear-armed state for fear that such a move might trigger a horrific nuclear response." Then the United States could head off such conflicts with a pilot distribution program of nuclear weapons. If it seemed to work, we could expand the program so that each country in the world would in time be given nuclear weapons. We could eventually be able to announce that war has been eradicated. We have sufficient weapons to carry out the program, and the benefits to mankind could be inestimable—but don't count on it.—B.D.

11. Background: This letter in response to a report that administrators of Carnegie Hall, a famous New York City concert hall, were refusing to allow pianists to unhinge the lower lid of the grand piano to improve the sound. (*New York Times*, 12/97)

   It sounds as if the underlid is not all that has become unhinged at Carnegie Hall, whose administrators are skeptical about allowing the sounds of pianos to be augmented by a lower lid. Are these guardians of purity also going to inspect all clarinets to be sure that holes have not been undercut to improve intonation, all flutes to be sure that someone is not trying a new footjoint to allow the lower register to project, all violins to be sure there isn't a radical new bridge being tested? What about baffle boards for horn players or resonator boxes for cellists? The administrators should return to what they do so well—filling the hall with wonderful musicians. Let those musicians choose their own instruments.—G.A.

❖ 12. Background: This letter is critical of the policy of the administration of former President Ronald Reagan, which eliminated requirements that automobile manufacturers include certain safety devices in all their cars. (*New York Times*, 5/81)

Although advocates of free enterprise may applaud the recent demise of numerous restrictions on automobile manufacturers, it would seem that the Reagan Administration has missed a golden opportunity to confer even more significant benefits. This could be achieved by eliminating requirements for brakes, a substantial expense, especially when multiplied by the number of cars in which they are installed.—R.M.M.

13. Background: This letter is in response to the claims of some thinkers that the truths of mathematics are dependent on human minds and do not exist independently of human minds. (*New York Times*, 2/98)

It does not follow that mathematical truths are mind-dependent. The proponents of this claim must contend with two questionable consequences of their views: (1) Although the Earth and the Sun were around long before humans and other animals were, the fact that two plus two equals four was not. (2) If brains had developed differently, then two plus two might not have equaled four.—T.A.

SECTION C: Apply the instructions from Section A to these arguments. Include a tree diagram with your structuring.

EXAMPLE
Background: The following letter is part of the debate over the "war on drugs." (*New York Times*, 4/97)

① Prohibition is the reason that children have easy access to drugs. ② It is time to end this 20th-century folly.—A.L.

ANSWER

PI ①

②

P1: The prohibition of drugs makes drugs easily available to children.
C: The policy of criminalizing drugs should be abandoned.

I charge this argument with problematic premise at P1. P1 is a problematic premise because it needs support that is not provided. Most members of the audience would regard this claim as doubtful or false, as is shown by the widespread support for the war on drugs. Moreover, there is reason to doubt the claim's truth. The claim is not plausible. What is plausible is that heavily penalizing those who possess and sell drugs would deter their use and sale and so diminish their availability. This does not show that the premise is false, but it does show the need for support.

PROBLEMS
1. Background: This letter is about whether the right to an abortion should be considered part of women's rights. (*Chicago Tribune*, 1/98)

Isn't it time to make a distinction between women's rights and abortion? Let's keep it clear that the movement for women's rights does not inherently include tolerance for—or support of—abortion.—L.L.

2. Background: This letter is in response to problems of school violence. (*Miami Herald*, 12/97)

So the high school shootings in Kentucky were motivated in part by the movie *The Basketball Diaries*. There's just too much free expression in this country. We need to license reporters, moviemakers, editors, and columnists to be sure that no more children are hurt because of what they read and see. There has been enough talk of gun control. It's time to pass laws restricting the First Amendment. If only one child's life is saved, it's worth it.—G.A.M.

❖ 3. Background: This letter is in response to a letter discussing sociology textbooks. (*Los Angeles Times*, 9/97)

Students find almost all social science textbooks to be forgettable. Such books are characterized by shallowness and simplicity. They make no attempt to intellectually engage students. They have no "life" beyond the classroom. The damage that textbooks do is to turn off students to education. Textbooks function to "numb" the minds of students.—B.M.D.

4. Background: This letter is about how to increase the work benefits for low-skill workers. (*New York Times*, 6/98)

Wages and benefits for low-skilled workers could be improved by decreasing their numbers—through changes in our immigration policy. Over the past three decades the increased number of low-skilled immigrants to the United States has helped depress wages and job benefits for all low-skilled workers. —B.R.C.

5. Background: This letter is in response to the debate over requiring public school students to wear uniforms. (*New York Times*, 10/88)

There is an even more important matter concerning dress and its impact on students. I refer to the manner in which the teacher dresses, particularly male instructors. Male instructors who come to their classes in jeans, in sport shirts with no ties or jackets do little to justify the role-model image they should provide. A dress code for teachers could do much to earn them the respect they require if their instruction is to be effective.—D.L.L.

❖ 6. Background: This letter is part of the debate over the war on drugs. (*Los Angeles Times*, 1/98)

If we stopped the insane war on drugs—which has accomplished nothing, except to severely erode the constitutional rights on which this country was founded—and instead devoted all those billions to drug and alcohol rehabilitation, we would all be better off.—L.C.

7. Background: This letter is in response to an article about the families of the victims of the bombing of the Oklahoma City Federal Building and their feelings about the punishment of the convicted bomber, Timothy McVeigh. (*New York Times*, 6/97)

You say the families have learned "that justice in a far-away courtroom is not satisfactory. That healing might come only at Mr. McVeigh's grave." Why would this bring healing? It's a common fantasy of the victim's loved ones that killing a killer will somehow heal the loss. True healing comes from a different phenomenon you report: the pulling together of Oklahoma City residents in mutual love and support.—D.L.

8. Background: This letter discusses a proposed agreement between state governments and the tobacco industry that would, among other things, reduce the tar and/or nicotine content of cigarettes. (*New York Times*, 6/97)

   The proposed tobacco agreement misses the most important public health requirement: to guarantee a decrease in cigarette consumption. Experience has shown that reductions in tar and/or nicotine content do not necessarily reduce cigarette health problems. Only with a required annual reduction in cigarette production could we be sure that the cigarette-related health problems would disappear.—H.A.

9. Background: This letter addresses the issue of whether the United States should continue to have a private system of health care insurance or should instead adopt a government-sponsored "single-payer" system. (*New York Times*, 9/98)

   For-profit health insurance is inherently costly. The Congressional Budget Office found years ago that reducing the number of insurance payers to 1 (the Government) from 1,500 would save more than $100 billion a year in administrative costs. Moreover, only 70 percent to 75 percent of health maintenance organizations' premium dollars go to benefits. The rest goes to administration, advertising, huge executive salaries, and profit. By contrast, both Medicare and the Canadian single-payer system spend 97 percent of their income on benefits.—J.S.B.

10. Background: This letter is in response to an article on the availability of drug information on the Internet. (*New York Times*, 6/97)

    It is unfortunate that, under the current drug prohibition, potent psychoactive drugs are available to any teenager with money. But given the reality of the black market, far better that they learn to reduce the danger of the experiences they seek. How many more young people must come to grief before we realize that ignorance hurts them far more than the drugs they experiment with?—A.F.

11. Background: This letter is part of the debate over whether smokers should be allowed to sue tobacco companies for the health effects of smoking. (*New York Times*, 5/94)

    It is a sinister political portent, rather than a rational legal remedy, for courts to let smokers sue tobacco manufacturers for the unwanted consequences of a habit they chose, cultivated and enjoyed. Our political economic system has withstood much, but it is unlikely to withstand the consequences of substituting caveat vendor [let the seller beware] for the principle of caveat emptor [let the buyer beware].—T.S.

12. Background: This letter is part of the debate over gay rights. (*New York Times*, 3/96)

    This redrawing of the male-female design doesn't make life more fruitful, only more barren. It is a mind game, cloaked in the false raiment of the discrimination issue, that dares to exempt humankind from the sexual bipolarity that runs up the evolutionary ladder of earthy beings.—C.W.S.

13. Background: This letter is part of the debate over whether wealthy nations should forgive the debt of poor nations. (*USA Today*, 4/00)

    The idea of forgiving the poor nations' debt would have one sure effect—that no more loans would be made available to the world's poorest countries. No country, or person, can borrow money and not expect to repay the loan. Otherwise, no future loans will be available despite even the most worthy of causes.—J.C.

14. Background: This letter is in response to the policy of government regulation of what barbers charge. (*Miami Herald*, 5/97)

    Barbers should have the right to charge as much as the free market allows. — Problematic
    It's a surprise to hear, in the midst of so much clamoring for democratic government, that our local government will dictate how much a barber is allowed to charge for his or her services. Such measures are acceptable only — False premise
    in totalitarian regimes.—C.G.L.

15. Background: This letter is in response to the policy that excludes from juries individuals opposed to capital punishment in trials of defendants who may receive the death penalty. (*New York Times*, 6/97)

    Imagine being tried for a serious crime knowing that those charged with determining your guilt have all expressed a willingness to kill you if you are guilty! This makes a mockery of the Sixth Amendment guarantee of an impartial jury.—P.D.W.

16. Background: This letter is about the issue of capital punishment. (*Chicago Tribune*, 7/97)

    It was with disgust that I read about family members of the victims of a convicted murderer being allowed to witness his execution. Murder, whether done by a cold-blooded killer or by the state, should not be a spectator sport. The killer demonstrated a callous disregard for human life when he killed two people during a robbery. The victims' family's participation in his execution demonstrated a blood-thirsty revenge that is beneath the dignity of a civilized people.—R.G.

17. Background: This letter is critical of India for testing nuclear weapons. (*Boston Globe*, 5/98)

    By exploding nuclear devices, India thinks the world might finally accept it into the club of great powers. India will never get the respect of the world until it addresses the serious human condition under which its people suffer. India won't be elected to the club of great powers until it stops spending outrageous resources on mischievous nuclear devices, and improves the human condition of its people.—E.Q.

SECTION D: Go back to the letters in Section B. For each, you provided an argument with a premise that stated the implication that was the basis of the refutation by false implication contained in the letter. Now, look for letters in which you would charge that premise with either problematic premise or false premise, and make such a charge.

8.3 Appeals to Authority

If an argument is to avoid a charge of problematic premise, its top-node premises should be statements that the audience will find acceptable. If there is a premise in your argument that the audience will not find acceptable, you can avoid a problematic premise charge by supporting that premise with a subargument. But this is not always easy to do. Fortunately, you can also provide support for such a premise by indicating that the premise is endorsed by an **authority,** someone (or some organization) with special knowledge of the truth of a claim.

8.3.1 Expert Authority and Personal Authority

One kind of authority is **expert authority,** a person (or organization) that has expertise in the subject matter of the premise. For example, individual physicians and the American Medical Association are authorities in medicine. Expert authorities have special knowledge in their fields of expertise that is not derived primarily from their own personal experiences. Instead, the knowledge has been developed by a number of people over time and transmitted to the experts through some kind of training process. The training process may be formal, like medical school, or informal, like the interaction of a group of hobbyists. What's most important is that the expert knowledge has been developed and tested over time and through the experience of many persons. An expert authority that is an organization consists of a group of individuals, many of whom are themselves experts in that field, who are devoted, at least in part, to the acquisition, development, and communication of the special knowledge.

When an author of an argument supports a premise by appealing to an authority, it is an **appeal to authority.** Consider this argument:

Example 8.20

Background: This is a portion of a letter on the issue of sweatshops, which are manufacturing facilities, often in Third World countries, in which workers labor long hours for low wages. (*New York Times*, 6/97)

① Labor costs represent a small percentage of the retail price for clothing and athletic shoes. ② Nike reports that shoes retailing for $68 and made in Asian plants require only about 3.2 hours of labor (costing less than a $1).—J.D.J.

Structure

PI: According to Nike, shoes retailing for $68 and made in Asian plants require only about 3.2 hours of labor (costing less than a $1).

C: Labor costs represent a small percentage of the retail price for clothing and athletic shoes.

The phrase "according to Nike" signals an appeal to authority that is part of the premise of this argument. By making this appeal to authority, the author of this argument seeks to avoid a charge of problematic premise. The idea is that Nike is an organization with expert knowledge about the cost of manufacturing athletic shoes, so that what this organization says about this subject should be taken as likely true. It should make the premise acceptable to the audience.

Appeal to authority plays an important role in arguments. Only a small portion of what people know is general knowledge. Appeal to authority is the way that we can make use in the premises of our arguments of that vast body of human knowledge that is not general knowledge. The alternative to an appeal to authority is to provide subarguments, but this is not always easy or even possible to do. To provide the proper subarguments, we would need to understand and to re-create the special knowledge that authorities have. In addition, in many cases, providing subarguments in cases in which an appeal to authority is available would be like reinventing the wheel—that is, going through the same scientific process of investigating the world that the experts have already gone through. In making arguments, we need a way to appeal to the special knowledge that others have but that our audience does not. This is what appeal to authority accomplishes.

Citing expert authority in more formal writing means including formal citation, such as footnotes, to indicate to readers the source of some of the ideas and claims made. Such citations represent more formalized appeals to authority. In less formal writing, such as the examples and exercises in this book, the appeals to authority are found in the text of the arguments themselves.

Sometimes, an author will cite him- or herself as an authority. This may be because the author is, in fact, an expert authority—for example, "As a doctor, I can tell you that the best treatment for a cold is such-and-such." Alternatively, however, the author may be appealing to **personal authority**—for example, "As a mother who has raised four children, I can tell you that the best treatment for a cold is such-and-such." Personal authority is authority based on one's own experience, not on a body of knowledge developed by or with the help of others. When personal authority is cited in an argument, it is usually the authority of the author, but it may be the personal authority of someone else.

Consider this example:

Example 8.21

Background: This letter is about famine in the Third World. (*New York Times*, 1/93)

① The causes of famine in China, India, and Bangladesh are exacerbated by too many people competing for too few resources. ② As a soil scientist, population and public health professional who has lived and worked in Asia and north Africa for most of the last 30 years, I assure you that famine will continue to control population growth so long as populations in Africa double every 18 to 23 years and in Asia every 23 to 32 years.—R.W.G.

Here, the author makes an appeal to authority that cites himself as the authority. The basis of that appeal is partly expert authority and partly personal authority. He cites his personal experience (working in the areas of the world discussed) and his area of expert knowledge (his training as a soil scientist and a population and public health professional).

> ### Authority, Expert Authority, Personal Authority, and Appeal to Authority
>
> An authority is a person (or organization) that can vouch for the truth of a claim when that claim is not part of general knowledge. An expert authority is an authority recognized as having expert knowledge in some subject matter—knowledge developed over time and transmitted to those who will become experts by some kind of training process. A personal authority has knowledge based on personal experience. An appeal to authority occurs when the author of an argument cites an authority in support of the truth of a premise. Appealing to authority, like providing a subargument, is a way of avoiding a charge of problematic premise.[14]

When an argument is structured, an appeal to authority can generally be represented in this way: "According to x, who is y, z." The "x" refers to the person or organization that is the authority, the "y" includes information about the authority of x, and the "z" refers to the claim that the premise is making. Here is how the premises of the arguments considered earlier would look when structured in this way:

Example 8.22

A. According to Nike, which is a large manufacturer of athletic shoes, shoes retailing for $68 and made in Asian plants require only about 3.2 hours of labor (costing less than $1).

B. According to me, a soil scientist and population and public health professional who has lived and worked in Asia and North Africa for most of the last 30 years, famine will continue to control population growth so long as populations in Africa double every 18 to 23 years and in Asia every 23 to 32 years.

This format can be awkward, especially in the first-person case (B), and premises that involve an appeal to authority need not always have this precise form in the argument structure. But these sentences should normally refer to the three elements x, y, and z, unless y is itself part of general knowledge. In argument A, for example, the y element is part of general knowledge: Most people in our society know that Nike is a manufacturer of athletic shoes. So, in formulating the premise, this bit of information can be left out, as it is in the argument structure presented in Example 8.20.

8.3.2 Acceptable and Faulty Appeals to Authority

But not all appeals to authority work. When an appeal to authority is not acceptable, the argument commits the fallacy of **faulty appeal to authority.** An argument commits this fallacy when its appeal to authority does not meet the following three conditions:

1. In the case of expert authority, the claim the authority makes must involve a field in which there are experts, and the person or group cited as an authority must have genuine expertise within that field. In the case of personal authority, the person cited as an authority must have personal and reliable access to knowledge about the claim. It is up to the author to make these facts about the authority clear to the audience (if it is not part of general knowledge).
2. Among authorities, there must not be significant disagreement about the claim. In the case of expert authority, the experts in the area must generally agree about the claim. In the case of personal authority, those with personal knowledge of the claim must generally agree about it.
3. The authority must not have a substantial personal interest in getting others to believe that the claim is true.

Faulty Appeal to Authority

An argument commits the fallacy of faulty appeal to authority—expert or personal—when the appeal is not acceptable. For an appeal to be acceptable, the person or group must have genuine expertise in the area in question (for expert authority) or must have had reliable personal access to the knowledge in question (for personal authority). In addition, there must not be significant disagreement among experts on the matter in question, and the expert must not have a significant personal stake in getting others to believe the claim.

We can refer to these as the acceptability conditions for an appeal to authority. A faulty appeal to authority is an appeal to authority that fails to meet all of these conditions.

Consider condition 1. For an appeal to expert authority to be acceptable, the claim for which the authority is cited must be from an actual area of authority, the person or group cited must be a genuine authority, and their authority must be in that area. The latter point is often violated when the views of someone who is well known in one field are cited in support of a claim in a different field. Such cases are often attempts to trade on the visibility and popularity such people have in the eyes of the public to support claims in areas in which their opinion should carry no more weight than anyone else's. This often happens when celebrities such as movie actors or pop musicians appear in advertisements. For an appeal to personal authority to be acceptable, the authority must have had the experience that would give her that authority and that experience must have been reliable.

Conditions 2 and 3 come into play less frequently, but they are equally important. Condition 2 is required because, within areas of expertise, certain issues may be intensely debated by the experts. Clearly, appeal to authority cannot be relied on when such disagreement exists. For example, anthropologists disagree about whether modern Europeans are descended from Neanderthal, a species of humanoids that lived in Europe 50,000 years ago, or whether they are part of a completely separate species. So, it would not be an acceptable appeal to authority to cite an anthropologist on this question. Analogously, if the people who have personal experience with some event disagree about its nature, none of them could be cited in an acceptable appeal to authority about that event.

Condition 3 is meant to cover situations in which some authority has a personal stake in whether others believe the claim. For example, people may be excluded from testifying when their spouses are on trial, at least partly on the grounds that a person's personal interest in getting a jury to believe certain things about his or her spouse would make that person's personal testimony unreliable. Likewise, an expert who is employed by a company has a personal interest in consumers buying the company's products, so his or her claims about those products are not reliable.

Finally, it is up to the author of an argument involving an appeal to authority to make clear to the audience that the authority cited is indeed an authority in the area in question. As mentioned earlier, only when the audience would be aware of the fact that the authority cited actually has authority in the required area (as with the Nike example) can this be omitted from the argumentative text.

To see these conditions at work, consider these examples:

Example 8.23

A. Background: This letter is in response to a columnist who argued that formal clothing is a sign of respect. (*New York Times*, 6/99)

> I certainly don't want my children to think they must buy fancy clothes for an occasion. I want them to know that respect requires proper behavior, not "proper" dress. Why are comfortable sandals less respectful than shoes with stilt heels on which we totter precariously? Henry David Thoreau had it right when he said: "Beware of all enterprises that require new clothes."—R.G.K.

B. Background: This is a portion of a letter critical of proposals to decriminalize drugs. (*New York Times,* 4/98)

> As a neuroscientist, I study the effects of addictive drugs on the brain. The greatest risk factor for drug abuse and addiction is the availability of drugs. If marijuana and other drugs are legalized, more people will become addicted or suffer other drug-related problems.—D.P.F.

C. Background: This letter concerns an Air Force pilot who was dismissed from the military for committing adultery. (*San Francisco Chronicle,* 5/97)

> I'm an Air Force veteran. I flew bombers in World War II. I got shot down on my 35th mission. I think the Air Force's treatment of Lieutenant Kelly Flinn, the pilot charged with adultery, is outrageous. From what I've read and seen, she's a fine officer. What on earth does her sex life have to do with her ability to fly an airplane? Besides, he that is without sin . . .—W.C.

D. Background: This is a portion of a response to an article quoting someone who claimed that pornography is worthwhile. (*New York Times,* 11/88)

> Consider the research conducted by Profs. Neil Malamuth of U.C.L.A. and Edward Donnerstein at the University of Wisconsin. Their long line of well-designed experimental research has produced cogent evidence of the link between violent pornography and anti-social effects, such as males' greater acceptance of interpersonal violence against women.—S.D.

E. Background: This is a further portion of the previous letter.

> The risk of rape is shockingly high in this country. For example, Diana Russell, using a probability sample of San Francisco households, estimated a 26 percent lifetime risk for women in that city.

Argument A concludes that formal clothing is not a sign of respect, or at least is less of a sign of respect than proper behavior. One of the premises cites Henry David Thoreau as an authority on the issue of the importance of formal dress. This appeal to authority fails because in this area there are no experts. There are experts on formal dress, but not on whether formal dress is a sign of respect.

The appeal to authority in argument B involves a genuine area of expertise and a person who is clearly an authority in that area. But the appeal fails because the field the claim is from is not the field in which the authority has his expertise. The claim expressed in the second sentence is that the availability of drugs is the greatest risk factor in people becoming addicted. But the area of expertise of the authority is the effect of drugs on the brain.

Whereas A and B concern expert authority, argument C concerns personal authority. The appeal to authority fails in this case because the area in which the author has personal authority, military airplane piloting, is different from the area of the claim for which he cites his authority. The claim is that the Air Force was wrong in its treatment of the pilot charged with adultery. The claim concerns, not her qualities or abilities as a pilot, but her private behavior. Thus, the claim is outside the area of personal authority of the author.

Argument D includes what seems to be an acceptable appeal to authority. The claim z is that a link exists between violent pornography and antisocial behavior. The claim comes from a field of social science that is a genuine area of expertise, and the authorities cited appear to be experts in that field. But if this to be an acceptable appeal to authority, it must meet condition 2 as well. This may be the kind of claim about which there is some disagreement among experts in the field, with some experts finding links between violent pornography and antisocial effects and others not finding such links. However, because this claim was supported by a "long line of well-designed experimental research," it seems fair to say that condition 2 is satisfied as well.

Finally, argument E contains an appeal to authority that fails. According to condition 1, the authority cited must be an expert in the field from which the claim comes. But we have no idea whether this is true. The author does not tell us who Diana Russell is, nor what her credentials are as an expert. Russell may indeed be an appropriate authority, but if this is not general knowledge, it is up to the author to make this clear to the audience. Unless she is someone the general audience will recognize as an authority, this appeal to authority is not acceptable as it stands. Thus, the fallacy of faulty appeal to authority is chargeable in all of these arguments expect D.

Faulty appeal to authority is a specific version of the basic fallacy of problematic premise. It is a special way in which a premise can fail to be acceptable. An argument can be charged with problematic premise when one of its premises is in itself doubtful or is not believed by the audience to be likely true. If the author includes an appeal to authority as part of a premise to make the claim in the premise acceptable but the appeal does not satisfy all of the three conditions discussed previously, the appeal fails and the premise remains unacceptable.

To make a charge of faulty appeal to authority, you show in the justification how the appeal to authority included in a premise fails to satisfy one or more of the conditions and so fails to make the claim in the premise acceptable. By the nature of what is involved in an appeal to authority, there is considerable room for disagreement both on whether it is appropriate in particular cases to charge this fallacy and, when it is charged, on the arguments that may be used in the justification. There is also much disagreement as to what counts as a field of expertise, when a person is an expert in such a field, what issues are subject to significant disagreement within such a field, and when there is a significant conflict of interest. Thus, in evaluating an argument that involves an appeal to authority, simply make your best judgment as to whether or not the appeal is acceptable and offer the strongest justification you can for it being unacceptable when you judge it to be so.

≡ EXERCISE SET 8.3

SECTION A: The following arguments contain appeals to authority. In each case, indicate who the authority is and what claim the authority is cited as supporting (the x, the y, and the z). You need not structure the arguments. If you conclude that the appeal to authority is acceptable, argue for this conclusion, showing that the appeal satisfies the conditions. If you conclude that the appeal is not acceptable, provide a fallacy charge of faulty appeal to authority. In your justification for the fallacy charge, be sure to argue which acceptability condition the appeal fails to meet.

EXAMPLE

The noted nuclear physicist Professor Smith, who worked on the original atom bomb, says that nuclear deterrence is a dangerous policy. So, we should get rid of our nuclear weapons.

ANSWER

The authority (x) is Professor Smith, who (y) is a noted nuclear physicist and someone who worked on the original atom bomb. The claim (z) is that nuclear deterrence is a dangerous policy.

I charge this argument with faulty appeal to authority. The argument commits this fallacy because, though Smith is an authority, the claim is from an area different from that of Smith's authority. Smith is presumably an expert authority in the physics of nuclear explosives, but the issue whether nuclear deterrence is a dangerous policy is from the field of military policy or international relations.

PROBLEMS

1. According to Wilson, lifelong ice cream connoisseur, strawberry is the best flavor. This is the flavor you should eat.

2. Dr. Quackenbush, Bear Corporation's medical consultant, claims that Bear aspirin is the most effective pain reliever. You should use Bear aspirin.

❖ 3. We should abolish capital punishment. According to Mr. Simon, celebrated lawyer, legal expert, and death row resident, the death penalty is not an effective punishment.

4. Bennett, a world-class sailor, says that a figure-eight knot is the right knot to use in this situation. So, you should use a figure-eight knot.

5. Simpson, who has been observing the habits of his boss for a decade, says that she always gets a cup of coffee first thing in the morning. So, if we lie in wait in the coffee room at the beginning of the day, we should be able to catch her to voice our concerns about the new office policy.

❖ 6. Dr. Spaulding, professor of chemistry, says that argon is a noble gas. Thus, since noble gases are inert, argon can be added to the list of chemicals that are inert.

7. While there is much debate among cosmologists about whether the universe began 12 billion years ago or closer to 15 billion years ago, Dr. Stars, Nobel

Prize–winning cosmologist, claims that 12 billion is the proper age. Thus, we need not search the universe for any objects older than 12 billion years.

8. Joe DiMaggio, the baseball great, endorsed Mr. Coffee coffeemakers. This is clearly the brand of coffeemaker to get.

9. Although other eyewitnesses disagree, Gilbert claims that the bank robber had blonde hair. So Ryan, who has dark hair, could not have been the bank robber.

SECTION B: The following arguments include appeals to authority. Follow the directions from Section A.

EXAMPLE

Background: This letter, about astrology coverage in the newspaper, was written in response to the 1997 mass suicide of members of the Heaven's Gate religious cult in California. (*Miami Herald,* 4/97)

Is it any wonder that Heaven's Gate followers believed that their suicides would get them to a spacecraft and another life? Didn't the prestigious *Herald* devote two pages on March 27 to astrology and the foods that the zodiac mandates? What nonsense. Like the late Carl Sagan, I am horrified at the space accorded astrology in the media compared with the amount devoted to science.—R.J.K.

ANSWER

The authority is Carl Sagan, and the claim is that the media should give less attention to astrology and more to science.

This is an acceptable appeal to authority. Carl Sagan is known to the general public as a noted and respected astronomer. His area of expertise is the stars. If he claims that astrology, which is a view about the stars, has no basis in fact, and therefore that it should not receive much attention in the media, he speaks from his own area of expertise.

PROBLEMS

1. Background: This letter is about the controversy over offensive remarks made by baseball player John Rocker in an interview. (*New York Times,* 1/00)

   As a psychiatrist who has practiced professionally for more than 20 years, I am alarmed by the decision by Bud Selig, the baseball commissioner, to order John Rocker, a pitcher from the Atlanta Braves, to undergo psychiatric counseling before deciding whether to discipline him for racist and homophobic remarks he made to *Sports Illustrated* last month. Many of my colleagues in the field share this concern. In a society in which seeking professional help for one's emotional problems is still viewed with suspicion and stigma, this punitive and coercive misuse of psychiatry does little to contribute to creating an environment in which everyone (including Rocker and other sports figures) can get the help they need to develop more healthy emotional lives.—H.P.

2. Background: This letter is about reactions to the mapping of the human genome, the DNA structure in each cell that is the basis of life. (*New York Times,* 6/00)

President Clinton's comments regarding the deciphering of the human genome—"Today we are learning the language in which God created life"—could not be further from the truth. As a molecular biologist directly involved in sequencing and analyzing DNA, I find this statement to be misleading and in some ways dangerous, as it could give more ammunition to creationists to further their destructive social and political agenda. What the sequencing and subsequent analysis of DNA tell us is that we are much closer to every living organism than we previously thought. They provide further conclusive evidence (at a molecular level) that complements our existing fossil (anatomical), physiological and biochemical evidence in support of evolution.—M.H.

❖ 3. Background: This letter is in response to proposals that federal judges, instead of being appointed, be directly elected by the public. (*USA Today*, 3/99)

The suggestions that appointed federal judges be elected tear at the foundation of our constitutional system. An independent judiciary preserves the delicate balance between the will of the majority and individual liberty. Judges are bound by the Bill of Rights to protect the individual's fundamental right no matter how unpopular it is to the majority. As a former U.S. Supreme Court Justice Robert Jackson wrote, "The very purpose of a Bill of Rights was to withdraw certain subjects from the vicissitudes of political controversy, to place them beyond the reach of majorities and officials and to establish them as legal principles to be applied by the courts."—C.G.G.

4. Background: This letter is about whether Americans should be required to recite the Pledge of Allegiance. (*New York Times*, 11/88)

Those who would require pledges of allegiance by law reveal their ignorance of republican government. Dictators, kings and lords require allegiance. Thomas Paine, an architect of American independence, said when a government requires the support of loyalty oaths it is a sign it is not worth supporting. "Make government what it should be and it will support itself," he said. The word allegiance (look it up) comes from the word liege, as in liege lord. It harks back to the feudal system, vassal owing allegiance to lord. But we as free citizens are not vassals of the republic. Nor are we subjects of the republic. We *are* the republic.—L.W.J.

5. Background: This letter is about employment in the United States. (*New York Times*, 10/97)

We must take advantage of our prosperity to help those with low skills move into jobs with good pay and benefits. The Education Department's National Adult Literacy Study found, in 1992, that almost 40 million adults had extremely low literacy and math skills. The way to increase productivity, and contain inflation, is to give workers a chance to improve skills, enter vocational training or community college, and then succeed at high-skilled jobs. —J.P.C.

❖   6. Background: This letter addresses the issue of student evaluations of college and university courses. (*New York Times*, 8/98)

Since the 1960s students have assessed and graded their professors. Recent studies have indicated that poor and mediocre students routinely use these evaluations to exact revenge on professors they label "difficult." For untenured faculty, especially adjuncts, the stakes can be high, as contract renewals are often based on favorable evaluations. For tenured faculty, the stakes are equally high, as evaluations are often used to calculate a pay raises. As a result, those of us who choose to enforce standards often find it difficult to do.—A.M.L.

7. Background: This letter is about the U.S. policy of sending troops as peace-keepers to Bosnia. (*New York Times*, 10/97)

More than 150 years ago the military strategist Carl von Clausewitz wrote that "when the motives and tensions of war are slight we can imagine that the very faintest prospect of defeat might be enough to cause one side to yield." What this means in the case of our Bosnia commitment is that as soon as things go wrong there will be a public demand for withdrawal. There will be an incident, American soldiers will be killed, and then the commitment will end. Let us not wait until that happens. Bring the troops home now.—B.A.H.

8. Background: This letter addresses the issue of the proficiency of immigrants to the United States in English. (*USA Today*, 3/97)

As a Roman Catholic priest working with Hispanics in Atlanta and northern Georgia, I am among those who have the privilege of serving the area's bur-geoning immigrant population. Those of us who work with Hispanics wholeheartedly agree it is essential that our immigrant brothers and sisters who so deeply enrich our common American heritage learn English. How-ever, it is not always easy for them to take English-language courses or to study the language systematically. It is difficult for many adult Hispanics to attain even limited fluency in English because of their limited formal educa-tion; their long hours of demanding labor; proximity to their native lands, making periodic visits possible; cherished hopes of one day returning home; the growing presence of Spanish-language TV, radio and press; heavily pop-ulated Hispanic neighborhoods; a large transient population; and often the great distance to English classes.—J.A.F.

❖   9. Background: This letter is about the issue of reliance on standardized test scores for college admissions. (*New York Times*, 6/97)

You may be surprised to learn that the president of the world's largest edu-cational testing organization agrees that we must not use college admission test scores as the sole yardstick of individual merit. Individuals differ in their performance on various measures of qualification; no single measure can stand alone. The diversity of talent that colleges should be looking for

is too great to let a few narrow measures carry the weight of such decisions.
—N.S.C.

10. Background: This letter is in response to legislative proposals to try more juvenile offenders as adults. (*Los Angeles Times*, 5/97)

    Based on my more than 20 years' experience as a chaplain in both juvenile and adult correctional facilities, and based on the experiences of our L.A. Archdioceses staff chaplains and hundred of volunteers who help us in the ministry, I know that no child, especially at the age of 13 or 14, becomes involved in violent crime all by himself or herself. Many and often appalling failures of adults in these children's lives, as well as failures of social and governmental policies, contribute to the problem of juvenile violent crime. I am deeply disappointed and saddened that members of Congress voted to spend $1.5 billion to make permanent determinations that these children, like trash, have no redeemable value, and not one cent to correct the adult failures.—S.J.

11. Background: This letter is part of the debate over "alternative" medicine. (*Washington Post*, 10/97)

    The proponents of conventional, supposedly "scientific" medicine have short memories. Just a few years ago, they were sneering at the "quacks" who claimed that diet was an important influence on the susceptibility to heart disease and cancer. The "quacks" were right, as they often have been in the past, and are once again today, but that doesn't stop the self-anointed mainstream medics from their holy war against dissent. A 1978 Office of Technology Assessment study reported that only about 25 percent of the practices of conventional medicine were based on scientific evidence. That hasn't changed much, and things may well have worsened. The reason that the public—and Congress—supports alternative medicine is that conventional medicine, despite its arrogance, is far too ineffective, far too harmful and far too costly. Nonconventional medicine is a rational alternative to much greater evil—conventional medicine.—B.R.

8.4 Some Specific Content Fallacies

Faulty appeal to authority is a specific version of the basic fallacy of problematic premise. In this section, we consider some fallacies that are specific versions of both problematic premise and false premise. These specific fallacies are versions of the two basic content fallacies because they all involve, in one way or another, claims that a premise is false or unacceptable. We give them special attention because they are kinds of arguments that tend to recur. We will look at only some of the fallacies that could be included as specific versions of the two basic content fallacies. First, we will examine two traditional specific fallacies: slippery slope and false dilemma. Then, we will consider two special cases: begging the question and appeal to force.

8.4.1 Slippery Slope and False Dilemma

Sometimes, arguers seek to refute a claim that some action should be taken or some policy adopted by claiming that the action or policy might lead, often through a series of events, to a very bad outcome. This is referred to as a **slippery slope argument,** so called because taking the action or adopting the policy in question would be like standing at the top of a slope whose slipperiness would send us all the way to the bottom, a place where we do not want to be. If the slope really is slippery enough to ensure our trip to the bottom, then the argument is not fallacious. But, more often than not, either it is not obvious that the slope is slippery (in which case the fallacy is a specific version of problematic premise) or it is obvious that the slope is not slippery (in which case the fallacy is a specific version of false premise). In either case, the argument can be charged with the **slippery slope fallacy.**

Slippery slope arguments are usually value arguments with an action recommendation for a conclusion. One example of this fallacy is the so-called domino theory, one of the main arguments used to support U.S. involvement in the Vietnam War. According to the theory, if we had allowed Vietnam to fall to Communist forces, the Communists would then have taken over the neighboring nations, the neighbors of those nations, and so forth, like a series of dominos. Ultimately, the United States would have faced a world largely dominated by the Communists— the bottom of the metaphorical slope. This was a slippery slope fallacy because the premise that nations would fall like dominos to the Communists either was not acceptable or could be shown to be false.

To charge slippery slope, you provide a justification that shows that the premise that embodies the "slippery slope" claim is either unacceptable (in a critical or conventional assessment) or false. There are different kinds of slippery slope arguments. Consider these two examples:

Example 8.24

A. Background: The letter is about experimentation on animals. (*Boston Globe,* 12/97)

> The French philosopher René Descartes argued that animals had no souls and they could not suffer. Descartes' philosophy led directly to medical experimentation on animals, a process of questionable medical value, which has caused enormous pain being inflicted on these helpless creatures. In turn, animal experimentation led directly to the "medical" experiments conducted on Jews and Gypsies by the Nazis. Like animals, Jews and Gypsies were considered soulless and thus the appropriate subject of medical experimentation. In this country, similar barbarisms were perpetrated on African-Americans in the South. This experimentation proceeds from Descartes' false premise.—A.E.R.

B. Background: This letter is about the efforts of the Federal Trade Commission (FTC) to ban cigarette advertising featuring the cartoon character Joe Camel. (*Boston Globe*, 6/97)

> If Joe Camel does not have a right to exist, who's next? Certainly Spuds MacKenzie and the Bud frogs will be out. Maybe the Clydesdales will go, too, because someone might think that encourages drunken driving. The ultimate solution would be for all ads to get FTC approval. Under our Constitution, everyone has the freedom to do as they want (regardless of whether it's politically correct or popular) without interference from the government.—T.K.

One kind of slippery slope, represented by argument A (and by the domino theory) presents the slide down the slope as a series of events, with one causing the next. In contrast, argument B does not claim that the series of events representing the slide down the slope will necessarily occur. Instead, according to this kind of slippery slope argument, if the action is taken or the policy adopted, there will be no reason for other events not to occur. In other words, the same reasons that justify the action or policy in question will justify all those other events as well.

Slippery Slope Argument and Slippery Slope Fallacy

A slippery slope argument is usually a value argument with an action recommendation for a conclusion. The argument opposes an action by claiming that taking that action either will lead through a series of events to a very bad outcome or will serve as a precedent that could justify a series of bad actions. When that premise is unacceptable or false, the argument is guilty of the slippery slope fallacy.

Here is an argument that gives a justification for a charge of slippery slope fallacy against an argument similar to the Joe Camel argument:

Example 8.25

Background: This letter is in response to an editorial on Joe Camel. (*San Francisco Chronicle*, 6/97)

> In your editorial opposing the FTC's effort to protect children from exposure to Joe Camel you ask, "if the government bans Joe Camel, why should it not also forbid Budweiser from using the 'Bud-Wei-Ser' frogs and Spuds McKenzie to sell beer or other cuddly advertising mascots from selling greasy burgers, sugary cereals and other unhealthy comestibles officials disapprove?" If the FTC decides that manufacturers of age-restricted, addictive products should not advertise to children, the frogs will have to go. But, Ronald McDonald and the Lucky Charms Leprechaun don't need to worry about sliding down any "slippery slope" until we make it a crime to sell hamburgers and sweetened cereals to children.—L.L.

The author is arguing that it is false that banning Joe Camel would serve as a basis for the banning of characters selling burgers and cereal because, unlike cigarettes, burgers and cereal are not illegal to sell to children.

In general, when justifying a charge of slippery slope fallacy, you should distinguish between the cases—the one the argument opposes and the ones the argument claims will follow from it—showing that it is doubtful or false that the others will follow. In other words, you need to show either that there is a break in the chain of events the argument claims will follow from adopting the action it opposes or, as in Example 8.25, that one action will not serve as a precedent for other actions.

Another kind of argument that can be fallacious is an **argument by dilemma.** A dilemma is a pair of alternatives that, under specified conditions, is exhaustive. A pair of alternatives is exhaustive when there is no possibility outside of those two alternatives. Consider these examples:

Example 8.26

A. Either it is raining or it is not raining.
B. Given that he has a blockage in his windpipe, either the blockage will have to be cleared or he will die.
C. Either intelligence is completely determined by heredity or it is completely determined by environment.

Arguments A and B are genuine dilemmas because they satisfy the requirement that the alternatives be exhaustive. A is exhaustive because it is a tautology, which is exhaustive under any conditions. But some dilemmas, like B, are exhaustive only under certain conditions. That is, it is only because his windpipe is blocked that the two alternatives mentioned are exhaustive. But argument C is not a genuine dilemma because the alternatives are not exhaustive. There is a third possibility, namely, that intelligence is determined partly by heredity and partly by environment.

An argument by dilemma begins with a dilemma as a premise, from which different possibilities emerge. Consider these cases:

Example 8.27

A. You must register or you will not be allowed to vote. You want to vote. So, you must register.
B. We must either pass the tax bill or not do so. If we pass the tax bill, the public will lose confidence in the government. If we do not pass it, the government will be forced into deficit spending. So, either the government will lose the confidence of the people or will be forced into deficit spending.

Argument A has a premise that rules out one of the alternatives presented in the dilemma and so concludes that the second alternative is true. Argument B draws an implication from each of the alternatives and concludes that one of those implications must be true. In B, the conclusion is a dilemma as well.

An argument by dilemma is guilty of the **fallacy of false dilemma** when the dilemma it contains is not exhaustive. So, you should charge an argument with the fallacy of false dilemma when you can show that it has a premise that contains a dilemma that is false. You should also charge false dilemma when you can show that that premise is not acceptable.

Argument by Dilemma and the Fallacy of False Dilemma

A dilemma is a statement of alternatives that is exhaustive. A dilemma is genuine when the alternatives are exhaustive and false when the alternatives are not exhaustive. An argument by dilemma contains a dilemma as a premise. An argument by dilemma is chargeable with the fallacy of false dilemma when the dilemma is either false or not acceptable.

Consider these examples:

Example 8.28

A. Background: This letter is in response to an editorial about the efforts to impeach former President Clinton. (*New York Times,* 10/98)

> You write that "where plain citizens are prosecuted for lying, there cannot be a special standard for Presidents who lie under oath." That is most certainly true. But then has there ever been a single case in the history of American law in which a plain citizen has been prosecuted for the perjury regarding inadmissible evidence in a dismissed civil case? If so, who, when and where was that plain citizen? If not, then why is this extraordinary exception to our standard of prosecution OK with you when applied to the President's case?—B.C.S.

B. Background: This letter is about a tax repeal proposal. (*New York Times,* 5/99)

> Is it really in the self-interest of commuters to repeal the New York City commuter tax? Without the $360 million a year the tax represents, the city would have to choose between reducing services and raising taxes on city businesses or residents. Either action would weaken the city's ability to compete with other cities, putting commuter jobs and incomes at risk.—C.J.

The dilemma in Argument A is that there either has or has not been a case in the history of American law in which an ordinary citizen has been prosecuted for perjury regarding inadmissible evidence in a dismissed civil case. This is a genuine dilemma because it is a tautology. Thus, A is not guilty of the fallacy of false dilemma. Things are different with Argument B. The dilemma here is that, if the city loses the $360 million a year it receives from the commuter tax, it will have to either reduce services or raise taxes on city businesses or residents. We could charge this argument with the fallacy of false dilemma because the dilemma may not be exhaustive. For example, the city might reduce salaries or increase efficiency so that it would have to neither cut services nor raise taxes.

8.4.2 Two Special Cases: Begging the Question and Appeal to Force

This is an appropriate place to discuss two special cases: the fallacies of begging the question and appeal to force. These are specific versions of problematic premise, but in these cases, a premise is problematic in a special way.

The **fallacy of begging the question** occurs when an author assumes in a premise what she is trying to prove in the conclusion. This can happen because the conclusion is actually included as a premise or because the truth of the conclusion is assumed by one of the premises. The name of this fallacy comes from one of the meanings of "beg," which is to evade or sidestep. In committing this fallacy, a person evades the question by assuming the truth of what she is claiming to prove. This fallacy is also known as circular reasoning.

Consider again a typical parent–child dialogue:

Example 8.29

PARENT: You should go to bed now.
CHILD: Why?
PARENT: Because you need your sleep.
CHILD: Why?
PARENT: Because you need your sleep!
CHILD: No, really, why?

In his last comment, the child is questioning the parent's reasoning. The child asked for a reason in support of the claim that he needed his sleep, in response to which the parent simply repeated that he needed his sleep. The child recognizes that the parent has begged the question by simply repeating what she was asked to give a reason for.

Consider these examples:

Example 8.30

A. That's all there is 'cause there ain't no more.
B. The Bible is true because it is the word of God, and we know that the Bible is the word of God because the Bible itself says so.

In argument A, the premise simply repeats the conclusion, though using different words. But the two parts of the sentence make the same statement, so the question has been begged. When begging the question is this blatant, it is easy to spot, which is why this sentence in most contexts would be understood as a joke. The fallacy in argument B is more subtle because this is a complex argument. The conclusion is that the Bible is true, the main premise is that the Bible is the word of God, and the subpremise is that the Bible says that it is the word of God. But the subargument assumes that the conclusion is true, because the claim that the Bible is the word of God follows from the claim that the Bible says that it is the word of God only if what the Bible says is true, which is the conclusion.

> ### The Fallacy of Begging the Question
>
> The fallacy of begging the question, also known as circular reasoning, occurs when an argument has a premise that either is identical with or assumes the truth of the conclusion.

Why is begging the question a fallacy? To include in an argument a premise that either is the same as or assumes the truth of the conclusion undermines the two main purposes of an argument: (1) to rationally persuade others and (2) to seek the truth. If the conclusion is included in or assumed by the premises, an argument cannot rationally persuade an audience because the premises are no more acceptable than the conclusion. To rationally persuade an audience is to move it from what its members already accept (the premises) to what they do not yet accept (the conclusion). This is impossible if the conclusion is included in or assumed by the premises themselves. Similarly, an argument that includes or assumes what it is purporting to prove cannot move us toward the truth. It leaves us stuck where we are. For this reason, a premise that is identical with or that assumes the truth of the conclusion is a problematic premise.

Begging the question is an important fallacy, but it is not often found. One reason is that, in its unsubtle forms at least, it is easy to spot and so an unlikely mistake for an arguer to make. Another reason is related to the way in which we have learned to structure arguments in this book. When a statement is repeated in different words in different sentences in a text, all instances of it are taken to represent the same part of the argument. We show this by putting two or more numbers in the same circle of a tree diagram.

Here is a short example:

Example 8.31

Background: This letter is about Mother's Day. (*Chicago Tribune*, 5/97)

> Instead of Mother's Day, let's honor all females who love and care for others. We should say "Happy Nurturer's Day" to all of them!—B.P.

The two sentences make roughly the same point in different words. As such, we should treat the text as nonargumentative, rather than as an argumentative text that commits the fallacy of begging the question. In effect, we give the benefit of the doubt to the author by not treating the occasions when she repeats the conclusion in different sentences as cases in which the conclusion is also included among the premises. We should regard such repetitiveness as evidence of begging the question only when the arguer clearly intends for the two sentences making the same statement to be separate parts of the argument—one a premise and the other the conclusion. This is normally the case only when the author has included a reasoning indicator in such a way as to indicate this.

The other special case of a special content fallacy is the **fallacy of appeal to force.** Consider these examples:

Example 8.32

A. POLICE OFFICER TO PROTESTER: If you do not leave, I will arrest you. So, you had better move on.

B. MUGGER TO VICTIM: Your money or your life.

These look like arguments. In A, the second sentence seems to express the conclusion and the first a premise; in B, the implicit conclusion seems to be that the victim should surrender the money. These seem not to be chargeable with any basic fallacy. The premises are relevant and sufficient, and presumably they are both true and believed to be true by the person being addressed (unless the officer or mugger is or is thought to be bluffing). But there is something wrong with them.

One of the most important features of argument is that, as a form of persuasion, it is distinct from coercion. The problem with appeals to force is that they collapse this distinction. Threats are acts of coercion, and the premises in these two arguments are *threats*. If the officer says to the protester that she will arrest him unless he leaves, she gives him a reason to believe that he should leave, but the reason is identical to an act of coercion. Acts of coercion presented as arguments are fallacious because the premise is in fact a threat.

> ### The Fallacy of Appeal to Force
>
> The fallacy of appeal to force occurs when the premise of an argument is a threat, the author is the person making the threat, and the audience includes the parties threatened. A threat should not be regarded as an argument because, if it were, the important distinction between persuasion and coercion would be lost.

For this fallacy to occur, the person making the threat must be the author of the argument and the person(s) being threatened must be in the audience. The fallacy of appeal to force occurs only when the premise is itself a threat. But language is a threat only if issued by the person making the threat to the person being threatened. Imagine, for example, one protester saying to another, If we don't move, we will be arrested, so we had better move. The protester, unlike the officer, is presenting a genuine argument because she is simply reporting the threat, not making it.

Actual examples of the fallacy of appeal to force, unlike the two cases in Example 8.32, are often quite subtle. Here is one:

Example 8.33

Background: This letter speaks in favor of restricting public areas in which smoking is allowed. (*Houston Chronicle*, 8/97)

① Some smokers claim they are losing the "right" to smoke and we are supposed to sympathize with them. ② These victims can no longer smoke in most workplaces and soon may lose the "right" to smoke in restaurants and nightclubs. ③ Shouldn't smokers be happy "we the people" haven't decided all smoking-related disease should be exempt from Medicare and other publicly supported medical treatment? ④ After all, it is their choice to smoke and risk getting sick. ⑤ Let's applaud the movement to reduce the smokers' so-called rights.—A.R.

The author intends as part of the audience of this argument those smokers who are complaining about losing their rights. Sentence 3 seems to be a threat, however subtle and indirect, directed at those smokers: Remember, if you continue to complain, the people could decide to play rougher, for example, by denying you government-supported medical benefits for smoking-related illnesses. Charging this argument with the fallacy of appeal to force would require making an argument like this in the justification that that premise constitutes a threat.

EXERCISE SET 8.4

SECTION A: The following arguments contain examples of the four specific fallacies discussed in this section: slippery slope, false dilemma, begging the question, and appeal to force. In each case, structure the argument (no tree diagram needed) and make the appropriate fallacy charge. Not all of the arguments may be fallacious in these ways. If they are not, argue that this is the case.

EXAMPLE

Either we execute murderers or they will eventually be out on the streets again. Having someone who has committed murder walking the streets again is clearly intolerable. We must retain capital punishment.

ANSWER

P1: Either we execute murderers or they will eventually be out on the streets again.

P2: Having someone who has committed murder walking the streets again is clearly intolerable.

C: We must retain capital punishment.

I charge this argument with the fallacy of false dilemma. The dilemma, stated in P1, is false because the options are not exhaustive. Murderers could be given a sentence of life without parole.

PROBLEMS

1. People have free will because their choices are not determined.

2. Sleep with me. I am your boss.

❖ 3. You have to take the final examination because it is a course requirement.

4. Repent or burn in hell! Clearly, you don't want to endure eternal fire.

5. For lack of a nail, a horseshoe will be lost. For lack of a horseshoe, a horse will be lost. For lack of a horse, the battle will be lost. For lack of victory in this battle, the war will be lost. We cannot tolerate even one cavalry soldier missing a horseshoe nail.

❖ 6. You had better sleep with your boss. He has said that if you do not you will be fired.

7. Stealing is clearly immoral. Therefore, theft is wrong.

8. Euthanasia is the right policy. This is clear from the fact that terminally ill people should be allowed to choose to kill themselves.

❖ 9. Either there will be 6 feet or more of snow this winter or there will not be. If there is, the skiers will be happy. If there is not, snow shovelers will be happy. So, either skiers or snow shovelers will be happy.

10. A person either believes in God or has no scruples against acting immorally. It follows that atheists cannot be trusted.

11. If you contract HIV, it will latch on to your immune cells and inject its genetic material into them. The HIV material will then take over the cell and use it as a factory to produce many copies of itself. These copies will, in turn, attack other immune cells and repeat the process. Eventually, your immune system will become so weakened that you will easily contract dangerous infections. The result will be your eventual death or the need to take many very expensive drugs for the rest of your life. The message is clear: Avoid becoming infected with HIV.

❖ 12. Either aliens frequently visit Earth or the many people who claim to have been abducted by aliens are lying. But so many people could not all be lying. So, aliens must frequently visit Earth.

13. I think that you should vote for my proposal. I will make sure that those who do not support me live to regret it.

14. I think that you should vote for my proposal. I will make sure that my supporters are handsomely rewarded.

❖ 15. America—love it or leave it. It is clear that you protesters do not love America. So, get out.

16. If you know the truth, there is no need to look for it. If you do not know the truth, you would not know it when you find it. But, either you know the truth or you do not, so there is no point in looking for it.

SECTION B: The following arguments contain examples of the slippery slope fallacy and the fallacy of false dilemma. Structure and evaluate the arguments, charging those fallacies where appropriate. Not all of the arguments are fallacious in these ways. If the slope is not slippery or the dilemma not false, argue that this is the case.

EXAMPLE

Background: This is in response to a letter that reacted to a fatal shooting incident by recommending that gun controls be stiffened. (*New York Times*, 3/00)

① The letter writer's comment that the United States should end unlimited access to firearms is nonsense. ② What happened in Michigan is a tragedy, but suspending constitutional rights won't solve the problem. ③ Once you twist the Constitution, you are headed down a slippery slope from banning public ownership of knives to banning free speech.—K.C.

ANSWER

Structure

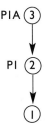

P1A: Once you twist the Constitution, you are headed down a slippery slope from banning public ownership of knives to banning free speech.

P1: Suspending constitutional rights won't solve the problem of gun violence.

C: The United States should not end unlimited access to firearms.

Evaluation

I charge this argument with the fallacy of slippery slope at P1A. The author claims in P1A that the interference with the Constitution that would result from stronger gun control laws would lead to other very problematic forms of interference, such as a ban on the ownership of knives and on free speech. The author refers to this as a slippery slope, but it is not. Even assuming that tighter controls on gun ownership would be an interference with constitutional rights (a controversial claim), it would not lead to these other forms of interference because the reason that guns would be more tightly controlled does not apply to the other cases. The ownership of knives or freedom of speech in no way results in the massive amounts of harm that the readily availability of guns does.

PROBLEMS

1. Background: This letter is about how the United States should respond to the devastation caused by a hurricane in Central America. (*New York Times*, 11/98)

   It should be obvious that the conditions in Central America in the wake of Hurricane Mitch will cause much sickness. The sickness will spawn epidemics, and then the epidemics will spread to the United States. In our own defense, we must do everything in our power to help these hurricane victims.—T.G.

2. Background: This letter concerns those who advocate a larger role for the government in regulating what citizens are allowed to consume. (*Miami Herald*, 3/97)

I can see it coming—weigh-in at supermarkets for anyone who appears to be overweight, followed by a ban on buying food products containing more than 2 percent saturated fat. Oh, what a healthy nation we will be. Hurrah for our public-health vigilantes.—B.H.

❖   3. Background: This letter is about whether printed condemnations of homosexuality are an incitement to violence against gays and lesbians. (*New York Times*, 10/98)

Moral disapproval of an act or life style is not bigotry; it is freedom of conscience. Publishing one's views on such matters is not inciting others to violence, but free speech.—S.G.

4. Background: This letter is in response to critics of a proposal that the government in certain cases keep a registry of DNA samples of citizens. (*Houston Chronicle*, 8/97)

Do these government-haters think that their fingerprints are their private matter? Do they object to registering for the vote? Did they register their automobile? Just what exactly is private about DNA? These people need to realize that this country is no longer a Wild West frontier.—J.S.M.

5. Background: Like the previous letter, this is about a proposal for the government to keep a registry of DNA samples of citizens. (*Houston Chronicle*, 8/97)

So your columnist thinks every American should be required to give a sample of his DNA to a national database. Why stop there? Why not require hair samples, fingerprints, monthly urine samples and photographs, too? Why not require a global positioning system that would implant transmitters in every citizen to track their whereabouts at all times? Where will this invasion of privacy stop? People who think Americans must give up their rights for their own protection give me the creeps. Catch criminals, not the honest citizens.—C.E.B.

❖   6. Background: This letter is in response to efforts by New York City to sue the tobacco companies to recover funds spent to treat patients for medical conditions brought about by smoking. (*New York Times*, 10/96)

New York City has decided to sue tobacco companies to recover money spent caring for cancer patients. Will the city now go on to sue General Motors and the Ford Motor company to recover all the money spent on fuel for gas-guzzling city vehicles. Or Anheuser-Busch for money spent caring for liver patients in city hospitals?—A.J.S.

7. Background: This letter concerns the federal government's suit against the Microsoft Corporation in the late 1990s. (*New York Times*, 12/97)

The principal issue in this suit—whether Microsoft's operating system and its browser constitute one product or two—is not one the Government has the information to resolve because it is a determination that depends on the preferences of millions of consumers. Without such information the Government is likely to make its decision on the basis of political considerations.

The real question in *United States v. Microsoft* is whether we should trust entrepreneurs or bureaucrats to structure and package technological advances. The historical success of markets and the failures of government intervention make the answer clear.—J.O.M.

8. Background: This letter is critical of Gen X fashions. (*San Francisco Chronicle*, 5/97)

   Let the word go forth across the land—to every Gen Xer, to every thirty-something who has yet to grow up, and to every Boomer who is wallowing in second adolescence—that the only proper times to wear a baseball cap on one's head backwards are when riding in a fast-moving open vehicle or when squatting behind home plate. Period. At any other time, the wearer simply looks like an idiot. It is symbolic of dorkiness, geekiness, nerdity and dweebitude. It's not sexy or masculine or stud-like, it's merely silly.—D.D.

9. Background: This letter is about an effort to get the Washington Redskins football team to change its name because it is an affront to Native Americans. (*USA Today*, 5/99)

   The story about the crusade to force the Washington Redskins National Football League franchise to change its name describes a perfect example of political correctness run amok. History indicates that the name was intended as an honor and not as a slur. Moreover, regardless of past usage of the word, to most Americans today, the word "redskin" connotes a member of the Washington football team. The radical agenda behind this crusade is evident: It seeks not only to change the Redskins name, but all team names that refer to Native Americans as well. Where does this nonsense end? As an Irish-American, should I sue the University of Notre Dame for using "Fighting Irish" as its nickname and Boston's National Basketball Association franchise for its use of "Celtics"? Certainly French Canadians could attack hockey's Vancouver "Canucks" team for its nickname, and Canadians in general might object to the "Canadiens" nickname of Montreal's National Hockey League franchise. And perhaps Catholics should object to the use of "Padres" by the San Diego baseball team, "Angels" by Anaheim's club and "Saints" by the New Orleans NFL franchise. How about very large people suing the New York and San Francisco "Giants" for disparaging them? Silly? Of course. The entire issue is.—J.D.

10. Background: This letter is part of the debate over whether the United States should pay reparations to African Americans for the enslavement of their ancestors. (*Washington Post*, 6/97)

    In law we have something called the statute of limitations. In common sense we have something similar. It is neither possible nor desirable to attempt to rectify every wrong, no matter how far in the past. What shall we do about our ill-gotten gains from the Native Americans? What should the Christians do about all the things they did to the Jews over the past 2000 years? How do we persuade the Japanese to pay the Koreans for their invasion and vandalism of 300 years ago? And so on ad infinitum. White America is indeed sorry for some of the actions of our parents and ancestors. We have even tried to do something about it (affirmative action, for example). Enough is enough.—R.E.M.

Summary

In evaluating the content of an argument, you assess the premises themselves for acceptability or truth. The two basic content fallacies are problematic premise and false premise.

The assessment of a premise depends on which kind of statement it is. Some statements, including tautologies and contradictions, analytic statements, and mathematical truths, are *a priori* statements, meaning that their truth values are known independently of experience. In contrast, knowledge of the truth or falsehood of *a posteriori* statements, which are more frequently found in arguments, depends on experience. Conceptual statements concern how terms should be used when there is not general agreement.

Justifications for content fallacy charges can use critical assessment or conventional assessment. Critical assessment considers whether a premise is false or doubtful independently of how it is viewed by the audience. Conventional assessment, in contrast, considers whether a premise is doubtful in the eyes of the audience. For a general audience, conventional assessment focuses on the general understanding of the world held by the members of that society or culture. The need for these two forms of assessment arises from the two main purposes of argument: to rationally persuade the audience and to seek the truth.

In evaluating an argument for problematic premise, you assess only the top-node premises, which are the argument's foundation. In charging problematic premise, you need to consider whether the audience is general or special. A special audience has knowledge or expertise not possessed by the general population. Conventional assessment is appropriate for a general audience only.

In your justification for a problematic premise charge, you argue that a premise needs support but does not have it. The justification should contain either a critical assessment, a conventional assessment, or a mixture of both. In a critical assessment, you argue that the premise is not acceptable apart from what the audience believes and so should have been supported. In a conventional assessment, you argue that the audience would not regard the premise as true or likely true without support.

A justification for a false premise charge is based exclusively on a critical assessment. In the justification, you argue that the premise is false or likely false. The most frequent type of justification is refutation by false implication. One version of this is refutation by counterexample, in which you point to an instance that contradicts a premise that is a universal statement. Another is *reductio ad absurdum*, in which the implication drawn from the premise is not only false but absurdly so.

Arguments frequently involve appeals to authority in support of their premises. Expert authorities have a special knowledge or expertise based on training in a discipline; personal authorities draw on their own experience of the world for special knowledge of the truth of certain kinds of claims. The standard appeal to authority is, According to x, who is y, z. In this formula, "x" represents the authority, "y" the nature or basis of that person's authority, and "z" the claim that the authority is being cited in support of.

An appeal to authority is acceptable only if the claim is in an area of recognized expertise or personal authority, the alleged authority is in fact an authority in that area, authorities in that area are in general agreement on the truth of the claim, and the authority is not in a significant conflict of interest in offering support for the claim. When these conditions are not all satisfied, the argument is guilty of the fallacy of faulty appeal to authority. To charge this fallacy, you argue in the justification that the conditions are not satisfied.

Like the two basic formal fallacies, the two basic content fallacies have some specific versions. The fallacy of faulty appeal to authority is a specific version of problematic premise. Two other fallacies, the slippery slope fallacy and the fallacy of false dilemma are specific versions of either problematic premise or false premise. A slippery slope argument is one that seeks to show that taking a certain action will lead (through a series of events) or could lead (through serving as justifying precedent) to an unfortunate outcome. When the claim that this is the case is false or not acceptable, the argument commits the fallacy of slippery slope. A dilemma is a statement of two alternatives that are exhaustive. An argument by dilemma reasons from a dilemma as a premise. A dilemma is false when the two alternatives are not exhaustive, and an argument commits the fallacy of false dilemma when the dilemma it is based on is a false dilemma.

The fallacy of begging the question and fallacy of appeal to force may also be regarded as specific versions of problematic premise, but in a special way. An argument begs the question when a premise either restates or assumes the truth of the conclusion. An argument involves an appeal to force when the conclusion is an action recommendation addressed to the audience and one of the premises is a threat issued by the author of the argument to the audience.

Key Terms

a priori statement

tautology

contradiction

analytic statement

a posteriori statement

conceptual statement

conventional
  assessment

critical assessment

top-node premise

argument foundation

special audience

general audience

refutation by
  counterexample

refutation by false
  implication

reductio ad absurdum

authority

expert authority

appeal to authority

personal authority

faulty appeal to
authority

slippery slope
argument

slippery slope fallacy

argument by
dilemma

fallacy of false
dilemma

fallacy of begging
the question

fallacy of appeal to
force

Notes

1. We discussed contradiction in the last chapter as well. When the contradictories in the square of opposition are conjoined with an "and," the resulting statement is false by virtue of its form alone: All S are P *and* some S are not P.

2. Some think that mathematical statements are not *a priori* at all, but rather are based on experience in some very abstract way. The American philosopher W. V. O. Quine (1908–2000) discusses this in his essay "Two Dogmas of Empiricism," in Quine, *From a Logical Point of View* (Cambridge, MA: Harvard University Press, 1953).

3. The claim that a premise is "not likely true" means that it is not the case that the premise is likely true. "Not likely true" is different from "likely not true."

4. I make no claims that this speculative encounter is consistent with the historical facts regarding Columbus's efforts to receive funding from the Spanish Crown.

5. Given the division of labor between conventional and critical assessment, there is no need to put a normative condition on what counts as the beliefs of the audience. Audience members' beliefs are their actual beliefs, true or false, because one purpose of argument is to persuade them. There is a normative condition on the audience, as implied in the idea that one purpose of an argument is to be *rationally* persuasive, but this condition is in terms of argument form rather than content.

6. Instead, the subargument for that premise should itself be evaluated. The strength of the subargument will indicate whether the premise is likely true and whether it should be so regarded by the audience.

7. We should be careful not to mix the metaphors of tree diagram and foundation because, for the premises to be the foundation, the tree would have to be turned upside down.

8. This leads to another difference between the two content fallacy charges. A premise's being unsupported by a subargument is a necessary condition for charging problematic premise, but not for charging false premise. So, while problematic premise is charged only with regard to top-node premises, it is sometimes appropriate to charge false premise against premises that are supported by a subargument. The idea is that if a premise is false there is no need to consider the adequacy of an argument meant to support it, because the point of such an argument is to show that the premise is true or likely true. In practice, however, you should consider the strength of a subargument before jumping to the conclusion that the premise that it supports is false.

9. Both of these arguments should be charged with the formal fallacy of hasty conclusion as well. The arguments do not consider the pollution effects of burning gasoline, nor do they consider the greenhouse effect.

10. Recall from our discussion in Chapter 7 of the square of opposition that A and O forms and E and I forms are contradictories. If one is true, the other is false.

11. There are, of course, others as well, such as Jane Austen and George Sand. You need only one for a counterexample, but you can cite as many counterexamples as you wish.

12. This argument is a good reminder that to charge an argument with a fallacy is not to imply that the conclusion is false. The author, while making this criticism, acknowledges that she remains a supporter of abortion rights. This argument supporting that conclusion may be weak, and another argument supporting the same conclusion may be strong.

13. The strongest, and truest, form of *reductio ad absurdum* is a case in which the consequent of the implication is a contradiction. One example of this is the so-called argument from evil for the nonexistence of God. The claim to be refuted is that there is a being who is both all-powerful and all-good. An implication of this, given the existence of evil in the world, is that such a being would both desire and not desire to eliminate this evil, but this is a contradiction, so such a being cannot exist.

14. It is interesting to contrast appeals to authority with arguments *ad hominem*, as discussed in Chapter 6. Roughly, an argument *ad hominem* says that such-and-such is false because so-and-so believes it. An appeal to authority says that such-and-such is true because so-and-so believes it. But arguments *ad hominem* are fallacious, whereas appeals to authority are perfectly acceptable, at least in many cases (we discuss cases in which they are not shortly). The difference is that in the one case we are asked to believe that x is *true* because someone believes it is true, whereas in the other case we are asked to believe that x is *false* because someone believes it is true. If we call the first case "positive authority" and the second "negative authority," it seems that there can be no negative authority. A lack of expertise does not imply that what one believes is false.

CHAPTER 9

Language and Meaning

"It depends on what you mean by . . ." This phrase is frequently heard when people are debating issues and trading arguments. Individual terms or groups of words can mean different things. As we have seen, it is often not clear exactly what an author means by a group of words. To know *what* a person is saying and to determine whether it is true, you need to know the meaning of the words. The "it" in "it depends on" refers to the truth value of a sentence.[1] Consider the simple statement "he met her beside the Amazon." Is the statement "he met her by the bank" true as well? It all depends on what we mean by "bank." If we mean the land beside a river, the statement is true. If we mean the place where they keep the money, the statement is false. Of course, not all cases of uncertainty about meaning are this easy to sort out.

An understanding of the meaning of the words plays a central role in our efforts to identify and evaluate arguments. The truth value of a statement depends not only on the way the world is but also on the meanings of the words that express the statement. "The sky is blue" is true because of the composition of the atmosphere. If the atmosphere were different—for example, if it contained significant amounts of chlorine—this statement might be false. But, equally, "the sky is blue" is true because the words mean what they do. If "blue" meant the same as "red" or "short," then the sentence would be false or meaningless.

When you are fluent in a language, its use is second nature. You see the world transparently through that language, so to speak. As a result, you usually do not think consciously about the meanings of the terms in what you say or hear. This ease of use, though necessary for fluency in a language, can lead to mistakes in identifying and evaluating arguments. Sometimes, you need to think consciously about the meaning of the terms in arguments, rather than take the meanings for granted.

By this time, you should have a great deal of experience with meaning in argument. For example, reformulation requires finding a different sentence that expresses the meaning of the text sentence more clearly. The text sentence and its reformulation must have the same meaning. In this chapter, we continue our work on meaning. This chapter is mainly an extension of our discussion of the evaluation of argument content in the previous chapter. For example, we examine how to assess premises that are conceptual statements and how to charge some specific content fallacies that depend on the meaning of terms. In addition, we consider further analytic statements as they occur in definitions.

9.1 Concepts and Their Role in Arguments

A **concept** is what a word or phrase means. The connection between words and concepts is like the connection between sentences and statements (see Chapter 4). The meaning of a sentence is the statement that the sentence expresses; the meaning of a word or phrase is the concept that the word or phrase expresses.

> ### Concepts
>
> A concept is the meaning of a term—a word or phrase. Terms express concepts the same way that sentences express statements.

9.1.1 Some Conceptual Issues

We begin by looking at some of the difficulties that arise when the concepts involved in an argument are unclear. Sometimes, an apparently trivial difference in the wording of a sentence can change its meaning. Consider this example:

Example 9.1

Background: This letter is about a speech given by former President Ronald Reagan. The Strategic Defense Initiative (SDI) was an expensive military research effort, championed by Reagan, to develop a defense against a ballistic missile attack from the former Soviet Union. Critics argued that, given social needs, the SDI was too expensive. (*New York Times,* 2/85)

> In your transcript of the State of the Union Message, you confirm that he said: "Proverbs tell us, without a vision the people perish." That is not what Proverbs tell us. Proverbs 29:18 says: "Where there is no vision, the people perish." Not "a" vision. Just "vision." "A" vision can become tunnel vision, as in not seeing the domestic needs clearly in focusing on a Strategic Defense Initiative in space. "Vision" works just the other way around.—J.A.

The author argues that there is an important difference in meaning between "vision" and "a vision," one that is crucial for understanding Reagan's argument.

According to the author, Reagan argued for the SDI as "a vision" and cited Proverbs on the importance of "a vision." But, the author claims, the passage from Proverbs, properly understood, refers to "vision" rather than "a vision." "A vision" can be any particular goal, like the SDI; "vision" is the balancing of all considerations. It requires, for example, not sacrificing social needs for the sake of military needs. Whether you agree that the SDI showed a failure of vision, you can appreciate that although these two phrases use the same word they express very different concepts. Arguments involving them can be understood only by recognizing this difference. An argument that confuses the two commits the fallacy of equivocation (discussed later in the chapter).

In the SDI example, the difference between two concepts is represented by a small difference in wording (you cannot get much smaller than "a"). But often different concepts can be expressed in the same words. Consider the scandal involving former President Clinton and his relationship with White House intern Monica Lewinsky. In early 1998, in a legal deposition filed by his lawyer, Clinton agreed with the statement that there "is no sex of any kind in any manner, shape, or form" between him and Lewinsky. In August 1998, Clinton appeared before a federal grand jury investigating, among other matters, his relationship with the young woman. He was asked whether that statement had been false. Clinton, who had by this time publicly acknowledged a relationship, replied, "It depends on what the meaning of the word 'is' is. If 'is' means is and never has been, that is one thing. If it means there is none, that was a completely true statement."[2]

According to Clinton, the word "is" expresses two different concepts, and the truth of the statement in the deposition depends on which of those concepts is involved in that statement. The distinction he seemed to be making is that "is" can mean either (1) having existed in the past or (2) existing in the present. When his lawyer denied the sexual relationship, that relationship had in fact been over for some time. Thus, the lawyer's claim is true if "is" is understood in the second sense but false if understood in the first sense. Clinton apparently was arguing that he was not guilty of perjury because he understood the "is" in the first sense.[3]

Many legal arguments depend on concepts referred to in the Constitution, in statutes, or in judicial opinions. This is why a great part of legal debate is about the meanings of terms. The resolution of such disputes is not merely an academic exercise but is often of great practical importance, especially to the defendants, whose guilt or liability is at stake. The law is in large measure a tradition and a method for arguing about the concepts expressed by terms in legal writings.

Here are some examples. In San Francisco, in 1994, a woman was served with a summons for violating a local antinoise ordinance that outlawed "willful sound that disturbs the peace." She was snoring.[4] In Bowling Green, Kentucky, in 1992, an individual was charged with drunk driving. He was a double amputee who was heading home from a bar in his motorized wheelchair.[5] In New York City, in 1999, a person who caused serious injury to another in a fight was charged with first-degree assault, a charge that can be brought only when a dangerous instrument is used in the attack. The injury was caused by biting.[6] Is snoring a "willful sound"? Is a wheelchair a "vehicle"? Can teeth be a "dangerous instrument"?

These are questions about concepts, and they are often difficult to answer. When cases like these come before the courts, the prosecution and the defense must present arguments about the meaning of these terms that support arguments for the guilt or innocence of the defendants. Judges must evaluate the strengths of these arguments. The fate of the defendants depends on the outcome.

Often, in such debates about the meanings of terms, people will cite a dictionary in support of their view. But in cases like these, a dictionary will not resolve the disputes, and so other kinds of arguments are needed. In the next section, we consider why a dictionary does not settle such disputes and what kinds of arguments are needed to do so.

9.1.2 Three Kinds of Questions About Meaning

The meaning of a word or phrase in a sentence can be unclear in at least three ways. Imagine that you have just attended a trial with three friends. As you come out of the courtroom, your friends comment on the trial:

Example 9.2

A. "The judge acted in a supercilious manner."
B. "The judge should not have given the defendant's behavior sanction."
C. "The judge is evil."

They then ask you if you agree. In each case, you might respond, "It depends on what you mean by 'supercilious' (or 'sanction,' or 'evil')." In other words, you are uncertain about the meaning of a term. But, though you might respond in this way to the three statements, the basis of your uncertainty about the meaning is probably different in each case.

Consider how your friends might respond to your responses:

Example 9.3

D. "If a person shows haughty disdain, then she is supercilious."
E. "If a person gives encouragement, then he gives sanction."
F. "If a person subverts the law to further her own political ambitions, then she is evil."

With statement A, when you say to your first friend, "It depends on what you mean by 'supercilious,'" the most likely reason is that "supercilious" is a word that you do not know. You do not know the meaning of the sentence because it contains a word with which you are not familiar. Your friend, in response D, simply gives you the dictionary definition of the term.

In contrast, with statement B, you may be familiar with the term "sanction" but know that it has two different meanings and not be sure which of them your friend had in mind. "Sanction" can mean either "encouragement" or "punishment." In other words, the term "sanction" has **ambiguity.** A term is ambiguous when it has two or more meanings, when there are two or more concepts to which it may refer.[7]

Often, the context in which a term occurs will clear up potential ambiguity. But in our example, we are assuming that this is not the case. Your friend may have meant either that the judge should not have encouraged the defendant's behavior or that the judge should not have punished the defendant for this behavior. Thus, in response E, your friend indicates which of the two meanings she had in mind and clears up the ambiguity. But, like your first friend, your second friend is simply reporting a dictionary definition.

When you say to your third friend, "It depends on what you mean by 'evil,'" you likely mean something quite different. It is not that you do not know the term "evil," which is a very common term in the language. Nor are you likely puzzled by any ambiguity in the use of the term. Instead, you are probably asking your friend to clarify what he means by the term "evil." You need clarification because the term, as used in this context, is characterized by **vagueness.**

Ambiguity and Vagueness

A term has ambiguity when it has two or more clear or definite meanings. Sometimes, the context will clear up the ambiguity. In contrast, a term has vagueness when, as used in a particular context, it has no clear or definite meaning. The vagueness of a term is a matter of degree and a function of the context in which it is being used.

Cases like A and B, in which uncertainty about meaning is due (as we are assuming) to ignorance ("supercilious") or ambiguity ("sanction"), share an important feature. The terms in question—"supercilious" and "sanction"—are fairly definite and clear in the concepts they express. This is why uncertainty is cleared up by an appeal to a dictionary definition. Your first friend gives you a dictionary definition, and your second friend tells you which of two dictionary definitions she has in mind. This is also why responses D and E, which address the uncertainty about the meanings of the terms, are analytic statements (discussed in Chapter 8).

In case C, the uncertainty about meaning is due not to ignorance or ambiguity, but to vagueness. Your friend can clear up the uncertainty only by going beyond what the dictionary says about "evil." The dictionary gives you a *general* idea of what "evil" means, but the general idea is not enough, in this particular context, to make your friend's meaning clear.

In order to appreciate how vagueness is a function of the context in which a term is used, consider these examples:

Example 9.4

A. The Yankees won the 2000 World Series.

B. The United States won the Cold War.

In statement A, the term "won" has a clear and definite meaning; there is no vagueness about it. But in statement B, the same term has a significant degree of vagueness. So long as we know the relevant facts, we can say without any doubt whether A is true or false. But even if we know all of the relevant facts, we cannot say whether B is true or false without a clearer understanding of what "won" means in that sentence.

A statement that clarifies the meaning of a vague term, like that expressed in response F in Example 9.3, is a conceptual statement. Recall from Chapter 8 that a conceptual statement makes a claim about how we should understand some term when there is uncertainty or controversy about its meaning. When terms are vague, the concepts they seek to express are unclear. Conceptual statements, in contrast with analytic statements, are not reports of dictionary definitions.

> ## Conceptual Statements (Revised Definition)
>
> A conceptual statement clarifies a term when the term is used in a context in which its meaning is vague or controversial. A conceptual statement seeks to make clear what concept the term is meant to express. In contrast, when a term has a clear meaning (when any uncertainty about the meaning is a matter of ignorance of the term or a matter of the term's ambiguity), an analytic statement is used to indicate the meaning.

There is no sharp line between terms that are clear and terms that are vague.[8] As we said, a term can be vague in some contexts and not in others. All terms have some degree of vagueness to them, and the vagueness becomes evident in some contexts but not in others. One way to understand this is to think of terms as having a core of settled or clear meaning and a boundary or periphery of unsettled or unclear meaning. At the core, there is little doubt about the term's meaning, as in the use of "won" in "the Yankees won the 2000 World Series." At the periphery, this term is vague, as in "the United States won the Cold War."[9]

Because vagueness is a matter of degree, and because there is no sharp line between cases in which that vagueness causes problems with understanding an argument and cases in which it does not, there is no sharp line between conceptual statements and analytic statements. The point of distinguishing between them is that conceptual statements play a role in arguments that analytic statements do not.

9.1.3 Conceptual Statements and Conceptual Arguments

Consider again response F in Example 9.3. That response makes the original sentence (C in Example 9.2) clear. Now you understand what statement it expresses, and you can consider whether you agree with it. But when the meaning of a statement is clarified by a conceptual statement, the conceptual statement becomes an assumption on which the original statement is based. And that assumption, like any assumption, is open to question. Thus, when a statement assumes a conceptual statement, there are two dimensions on which the original statement can be assessed: (1) the facts or values the statement asserts and (2) the conceptual statement assumed by that statement.

In the case of your reaction to statement F in Example 9.3, you can, first, agree or disagree about the facts, affirming or disputing your friend's claim that the prosecutor was subverting the law to further her own political ambitions. In this case, you are assessing the factual dimension of your friend's statement.[10] Second, you can take issue with the conceptual statement, with the way in which your friend specified the term "evil." For example, you might respond that you disagree because, although the prosecutor did subvert the law to further her own political goals, such wrongdoing is not serious enough to label her "evil." The term "evil," you might argue, is reserved for deeds of greater immorality, like those of the Nazis. In this case, you are assessing the conceptual dimension of the statement.

When your third friend offers a conceptual statement to clarify the original statement, he has, in effect, given a *reason* for his original statement, thereby offering an argument. The conceptual statement is a premise supporting the original statement. The argument looks like this:

Example 9.5

P1: If a person subverts the law to further her own political ambitions, then that person is evil.
P2: The judge subverted the law to further her own political ambitions.
C: Therefore, the judge is evil.

To assess the conclusion in terms of its factual dimension would be, in effect, to consider whether to charge a content fallacy at P2. To assess the conclusion in terms of its conceptual dimension would be, in effect, to consider whether to charge a content fallacy at P1. Conceptual statements, like other kinds of statements, are subject to debate. Some conceptual statements are acceptable and others are not. The situation is different with analytic statements. They can be true or false, but mainly by virtue of whether they get the dictionary definition right.[11]

The truth value of most sentences (those that do not express *a priori* statements) depends, as we have said, on both the meaning of the terms in the sentence and the way the world is. For most sentences, however, the meaning of the terms is not controversial. The terms, as used in those sentences, do not have a significant degree of vagueness, so the meanings of the terms (say, to someone who does not speak the language well) would be given in analytic statements. And the statements expressed in the sentences would be assessed in the factual dimension only. But when the terms in a sentence have a significant degree of vagueness, their meanings need to be given in conceptual statements, and the statements expressed by the sentences are open to both conceptual and factual assessment.

Consider these statements:

Example 9.6

A. New York City is at 40.43 degrees north latitude.
B. The United States is the greatest nation in the world.
C. Pluto is the planet farthest from the sun.

In statement A, none of the terms, as used in that sentence, has a significant degree of vagueness. The statement expressed by A does not assume any conceptual statements, so we can assess it in the factual dimension alone.

To assess the truth value of statement B, however, we need a conceptual statement clarifying the term "greatest." Any such statement would be controversial. Some might say that greatness is a matter of a nation's wealth, others that it is a matter of its military power, others that it is a matter of the moral force of its conduct, and so forth. Suppose someone offers in support of the truth of this statement the conceptual statement that greatness is a matter of a nation's military power. Another person might charge this statement with problematic premise or false premise, arguing that real greatness is a matter of the moral force of a nation's conduct.

With regard to statement C, recent discoveries suggest that it must be clarified by a conceptual statement. Given what we now know, the use of "planet" in this sentence is vague and requires a conceptual statement to make it more precise. Astronomers have discovered a large group of objects, each much smaller than the planets, orbiting the sun beyond the orbit of Neptune. These "trans-Neptunian objects" inhabit what is called the "Kuiper Belt." Pluto is in the same region of space and is similar to these objects in its composition and orbit, although, unlike them, it has an atmosphere. At the same time, Pluto is smaller than all the other planets (smaller even than Earth's moon) and unlike them in composition or orbit. Thus, it is unclear whether we should regard Pluto as a planet.[12]

Consider these conceptual statements:

Example 9.7

A. If an object is a planet, then it is orbiting the sun and is identical with or similar to (in composition, orbit, and size) either the inner terrestrial objects (Mercury, Venus, Earth, Mars) or the outer gas giants (Jupiter, Saturn, Uranus, Neptune).
B. If an object is a planet, then it is orbiting the sun and is of a significant size (so as to exclude the asteroids, comets, and so on).

Statement B is a conceptual statement assumed by statement C in Example 9.6, and statement A would show C to be false, because it would exclude Pluto from the planets. Each of these statements would have arguments offered in its favor.

Whether we view Pluto as a planet may seem a trivial matter, but many conceptual statements have clear and important practical implications. Consider this pair of statements concerning the concept of death:

Example 9.8

A. If the heart has ceased to function, then the person is dead.
B. If the higher brain has ceased to function, then the person is dead.

These conceptual statements have an important practical implication with regard to organ donation. Someone whose higher brain has ceased to function but whose heart is still beating makes a better organ donor. If the organs cannot be removed until the heart has stopped, they are much more likely to have deteriorated and so to be unsuitable for donation. But we should not, of course, remove the organs from someone who is still alive. So, often the lives of potential organ recipients depend on whether we accept statement A or B as the correct understanding of death.[13]

Here is another case of great practical import. In the disputed presidential election of 2000, the contest came down to whether George Bush or Al Gore would win the electoral votes of Florida. The popular vote in that state was very close, with Bush holding a slim lead. Gore supporters claimed that all the votes had not been counted and sought court rulings to allow the counting to continue. Bush supporters countered that the votes had already been counted and that there was no need for a recount.

The conflicting conceptual statements at the root of this dispute were these:

Example 9.9

BUSH SUPPORTER: If a ballot has been run through a vote-counting machine, then the vote has been counted.
GORE SUPPORTER: If a vote has been counted, then every effort has been made to determine the intentions of the voter.

When the ballots were run through the voting machines in Florida, many of them were rejected by the machines as not indicating a vote. Gore supporters wanted the rejected ballots to be examined by hand to determine if they indicated a vote that the machine had missed. Bush supporters did not want this. Much of the debate that occurred at that time involved arguments supporting one or the other of these conceptual statements.

A conceptual statement, like any statement, can be supported by an argument. Consider two arguments that might be offered for the two conceptual statements in Example 9.8 about the meaning of death:

Example 9.10

A. Death in humans occurs when the heart ceases to function because the heart is the organ that, in pumping blood, keeps the rest of the body alive. When the heart has ceased to function, no other part of the body can function. Hence, when the heart has ceased to function, the person is truly dead.

B. Death in humans occurs when the higher brain ceases to function, because a human being is not simply a body. A human being is a personality, and the functioning of the higher brain is crucial for the preservation of a personality. When the higher brain has ceased to function, the personality is gone and cannot return. Therefore, when the higher brain has ceased to function, the person is dead, even though other parts of the body may continue to function.

An argument, like A or B, given in support of a conceptual statement is a **conceptual argument,** also known as a conceptual analysis. A conceptual argument, like other arguments, can be evaluated for strength. The conceptual statement that should be accepted is the one supported by the strongest argument. The truth value of conceptual statements is not a matter of personal preference. Rather, their acceptability, like that of any statement, is a function of the strength of the arguments given in support of them.

A conceptual argument can occur by itself, but it is usually a subargument in a complex argument, in which case the conceptual statement that is its conclusion is a premise in a larger argument. When a conceptual statement is a premise in an argument, it is a **conceptual premise.** An argument for any conclusion that contains a term with a significant degree of vagueness should contain a conceptual premise. The conclusion cannot be understood without such a premise.

Consider these examples:

Example 9.11

A. Background: This letter is in response to an article about a sexual harassment suit. (*New York Times,* 8/94)

> In your news article on the sexual harassment suit, a lawyer not involved in the case offers that "if your idiosyncrasy is liking women, everybody says, 'That's the way he is.'" But wouldn't a man who truly likes women conduct himself in the opposite fashion?—T.J.H.

B. Background: This letter is in response to stories of two bears who were killed in Yosemite National Park for being a menace to humans. (*New York Times,* 12/97)

> If the National Park Service continues to modify the environment to suit tourists, it is preserving access for them at the expense of the park and its natural inhabitants, the bears. If tourists really appreciated Yosemite and its creatures, they would demand that their access be limited rather than have it plastic-wrapped for them.—S.J.L.

These texts involve conceptual statements—about the phrase "liking women" in text A and "appreciating nature" in text B. Both texts have a feature typical of conceptual statements: A refers to "truly" liking women and B refers to "really" appreciating nature. Conceptual statements often use terms like "truly" and "really" preceding the term expressing the concept that the statement is about. The point

> **Conceptual Premises and Conceptual Arguments**
>
> A conceptual statement may be a premise or a conclusion in an argument. An argument with a conceptual statement as its conclusion is a conceptual argument. A conceptual argument may stand alone or, more commonly, be a subargument in a complex argument, in which case its conclusion is also a conceptual premise of that larger argument. A conceptual argument is subject to evaluation like other arguments, and the acceptability of the conceptual statement it supports is dependent on the argument's strength.

is to claim that some other understanding of the concept is not a real or true understanding.

Here are the conceptual statements:

Example 9.12

C. If a person likes women, then he treats them with respect, rather than annoy or harass them.

D. If we appreciate nature, then we protect it from harm from tourists, rather than make it accessible to tourists.

In text A, the conceptual statement C stands on its own, and not as part of an argument. But in text B, the conceptual statement D is a premise in an argument whose conclusion is that the national parks should not be made more accessible to tourists. Neither text, however, contains a conceptual argument. Neither provides an argument for its conceptual statement.

9.1.4 Conceptual Premises

If the conclusion of an argument (or one of its premises) contains a term that has, in that context, a significant degree of vagueness, the argument should include a conceptual premise. The job of the conceptual premise, as we have said, is to clarify that term so that the argument can be understood. A conceptual premise is often linked with a nonconceptual premise. Sometimes, an argument contains a vague term that should be clarified by a conceptual premise, but no such premise is included. In that case, the argument may be treated as having an *implicit* conceptual premise. We may represent this as another rule of addition. The content of this implicit premise is usually evident from the text's internal and external context.

Consider this example:

Example 9.13

Background: This passage by Charles Darwin was in response to the claim that humans, in breeding pigeons, have *made* a fantail (a kind of pigeon with a large tail).[14]

> But to use such an expression as trying to make a fantail, is, I have no doubt, in most cases, utterly incorrect. The man who first selected a pigeon with a slightly larger tail, never dreamed what the descendants of that pigeon would become through long-continued, partly unconscious and partly methodical selection.

The conclusion, expressed in the first sentence, is that it is incorrect that humans made a fantail pigeon. The second sentence gives a premise. But this premise is not a conceptual statement; rather, it is a factual statement about how the fantail came to be. The "made" is vague in this context and shows that a conceptual premise is required. The implicit conceptual premise could be formulated this way: If something is made, then the maker envisions the end product. The explicit premise claims that those who began to breed pigeons selectively for a large tail did not envision the end product.

Rule of Addition, Number 4

When an argument includes a vague term that needs to be clarified by a conceptual premise, but none is explicitly included, the appropriate conceptual statement should be added as an implicit premise. The content of this implicit premise is usually evident from the text's internal and external context.

Several steps are involved in evaluating arguments with conceptual statements:

1. Determine what the conceptual premise is. (It may be explicit or implicit.)
2. If there is no conceptual subargument supporting that premise, charge a content fallacy regarding the premise.
3. If there is a conceptual subargument offered, determine what it is and evaluate it.

As step 2 indicates, one feature of conceptual premises is that, if they are unsupported, it is always appropriate to make a content fallacy charge, either problematic premise or false premise. This is, of course, not true of other kinds of premises, many of which are acceptable as they stand. Conceptual premises, if unsupported, are not acceptable—and thus require support—due to the controversial nature of conceptual statements.

Consider these examples:

Example 9.14

A. Background: This letter is about capital punishment. (*New York Times*, 7/97)

> Your editorial criticizing the Supreme Court for upholding a death sentence refers to "a brutal rape and murder." One implication is that some murders—executions?—are less than brutal. But the sooner we accept that all killing is brutal, the sooner we may do away with the death penalty.—H.T.

B. Background: This letter is about the 1998 chess match in which world champion Garry Kasparov lost to an IBM computer. (*Los Angeles Times,* 5/98)

> What is the "machine" that beat the chess champ? A team of IBM programmers, humans all, beat Garry Kasparov. The machine did only what they told it to do.—J.S.

There are different ways to formulate the conceptual premises in these arguments. Here is one way:

Example 9.15

C. If an action is a killing, then it is brutal.
D. If an entity is a machine, then it cannot be a contestant in a game of chess.

In the case of text A, the conclusion is that we should abolish the death penalty. Applying step 1, we have determined that the conceptual premise is C. No conceptual argument is offered for this statement, so we apply step 2 instead of step 3. Here is the fallacy charge:

Example 9.16

I charge this argument with problematic premise at conceptual premise P1. This conceptual statement, like all conceptual statements, is controversial and needs support that is not provided. There are important differences between legal executions and other killings that could lead one to the view that the legal executions are not brutal in the way that other killings are. For example, legal executions are performed with a different motive than other killings, namely, to pay back the victim for taking another life. Also, legal executions are usually done in a way that seeks to minimize the physical suffering for the victim as much as possible. The conceptual statement cannot stand unless such concerns are addressed in a subargument.

In the case of text B, the conclusion is expressed in the second sentence: A team of human IBM programmers beat Garry Kasparov. Applying step 1, we have determined the implicit conceptual premise to be D. There is a conceptual argument for this premise, so we skip step 2 and move to step 3. The subpremise supporting the conceptual statement is expressed in the third sentence. Reformulated, this could be: If something is a machine, it does only what it is told to do.

How should we evaluate the subargument in text B? Note first that the subargument seems itself to include a conceptual premise (in this case, an implicit one), namely, that if an entity is a contestant, then it is capable of making its own decisions. It is not unusual to have a conceptual premise as a premise of a conceptual argument, whether explicit or implicit. This conceptual subpremise, like all unsupported conceptual premises, would be the basis of a content fallacy charge against the subargument. In addition, the explicit premise (if something is a machine, it does only what it is told to do) may be the basis for such a charge. The debate joined by the arguments in the justifications for these fallacy charges would be about the differences between humans and machines. This is, in part, the debate over free will. Do humans have free will? Is it impossible for a machine constructed by humans to have free will? This is a complicated and fascinating debate indeed.

Here are two arguments, each with a conceptual premise devoted to clarifying the term "free society":

Example 9.17

A. Background: This letter is part of the 1970s debate about whether military forces should be raised by conscription (the draft) or by exclusive reliance on volunteers. (*Washington Post*, 3/80)

> In a free society there cannot be such a thing as compulsory military service. A truly free society uses the device of majority rule only to decide those issues that do not infringe on fundamental freedoms. Military service is not such an issue. A free society is militarily defended by volunteers.—D.J.C.

B. Background: This is in response to the first letter. (*Washington Post*, 3/80)

> The author's view is symptomatic of a wrong-headed notion that, if widely held, can lead to the eventual loss of our freedom. In a free society there can be and must be such a thing as compulsory military service—and a good many other obligations, as well—to preserve the freedom we now have. How free would we be today if we, and the rest of the free nations, had relied on volunteers to preserve our freedom in World Wars I and II? About as free as the French under Nazi rule, I would guess. The handwriting on the wall is clear. We will have a draft, or we will lose our freedom. —B.S.W.

In this exchange, the first author concludes that military service should be voluntary, and the second, taking issue with the first, concludes that military service should be compulsory. Each supports his conclusion with a conceptual premise about the idea of a free society. (Notice the first author's use of "truly.")

The conceptual premises may be reformulated as follows:

Example 9.18

C. If a society is a free society, then matters of fundamental freedom are not decided by majority rule.
D. If a society is a free society, then it is able to preserve its freedom against foreign aggression.

Each argument also makes some factual assertions that could be challenged, but the important issue here is the conceptual one. Neither author offers a conceptual argument in support of his conceptual premise. For this reason, both arguments should be charged with a content fallacy. If the authors were to continue the debate, they would have to present and evaluate conceptual arguments for these premises.

9.1.5 Formulating Conceptual Statements

Conceptual statements may be formulated in terms of necessary and sufficient conditions, which, as we saw in Chapter 5, are represented by conditional statements. Given the conditional "A ⊃ B," A is a sufficient condition for B, and B is a necessary condition for A.

Consider some of the conceptual statements presented earlier:

Example 9.19

A. If a person subverts the law to further her own political ambitions, then she is evil.
B. If a ballot has been run through a vote-counting machine, then the vote has been counted.
C. If we appreciate nature, then we protect it from harm from tourists, rather than make it accessible to tourists.
D. If something is made, then the maker envisions the end product.

As you may have noticed earlier, although all of these conceptual statements have been formulated with conditionals, the term to be clarified is sometimes in the antecedent and sometimes in the consequent. In statements A and B, the terms to be clarified are in the consequent and the clarifying features are in the antecedent. The features are thus given as sufficient conditions for use of the terms "evil" and "counted vote." In contrast, in statements C and D, the terms to be clarified are in the antecedent and the clarifying features are in the consequent. These features are given as necessary conditions for the use of the terms "appreciating nature" and "made."

When you identify the conceptual premise (whether explicit or implicit) in an argument, you need to determine what form of the conditional to use—that is, whether to put the term to be clarified in the antecedent or in the consequent. This is, again, a matter of understanding the author's intentions: In this context, does the author mean to clarify the vague term through necessary conditions or through sufficient conditions?

Consider statements A and B. In A, the author means to say that someone's subverting the law for political purposes is sufficient to label that person evil, but not that it is necessary. After all, there are many other ways to be evil besides this. In B, the author is saying that a ballot's having been run through a vote-counting machine is sufficient for the vote to have been counted, but not that it is necessary. This is because votes still count in districts that do not use vote-counting machines.

Now consider statements C and D. In C, the author is saying that protecting nature from harm from tourists is a necessary condition for appreciating it, but not that it is sufficient. There are many other things we have to do to appreciate nature —for example, avoid destroying it through global warming. Likewise, in D, the author is saying that the maker's envisioning the end product is a necessary condition for making, but not that it is sufficient. There are many other conditions that need to hold for something to be made—for example, the maker's ensuring that what she envisions becomes a reality.

In addition, however, there are some conceptual statements formulated not with a conditional, but with a **biconditional.** A biconditional is a compound statement like the ones discussed in Chapter 7. It is formulated with the phrase "if and only if" between the two statements, and it is indicated symbolically with a double arrow ("$\leftrightarrow$"). In a biconditional, the standard conditional relationship works both ways, meaning that the truth of each of the statements is both a necessary and a sufficient condition for that of the other. Here is an example: A person passes the course if and only if she or he receives at least a D– as a final grade. That is, receiving at least a D– as a final grade is both a necessary and a sufficient condition for passing the course.

Biconditionals

A biconditional is a compound statement in which the standard conditional relationship works both ways: The truth of each component statement is both a necessary and a sufficient condition for the truth of the other. It is usually indicated with the phrase "if and only if" between the component statements, and, symbolically, with a double arrow, as in "A $\leftrightarrow$ B." The truth values of the component statements are always the same.

Consider these other conditionals from our earlier discussion:

Example 9.20

A. If a person is dead, then his heart has ceased to function.
B. If the higher brain has ceased to function, then a person is dead.
C. If a vote has been counted, then every effort has been made to determine the intentions of the voter.
D. If a person likes women, then he treats them with respect, not annoys or harasses them.

Although these conceptual statements were formulated in conditional form, they would likely be more accurately represented by biconditionals. In statement A, the author probably means to say that the stopping of the heart is not only necessary for death but sufficient as well. In other words, all cases of death are cases of the heart having stopped, and all cases of the heart having stopped are cases of death. Likewise, the author of statement B likely means to say the same thing about the cessation of higher brain function. And the conditions presented by the authors of statements C and D probably are meant to be both sufficient and necessary for the terms whose meaning is being clarified. In addition, the conceptual statements in Example 9.7 clarifying the term "planet" likely are meant as biconditionals.

A conceptual statement expressed with a conditional is a **partial conceptual statement,** and one expressed with a biconditional is a **full conceptual statement.** A conceptual statement is partial when it indicates only necessary conditions or only sufficient conditions, but not both, for the use of a term. It is full when it indicates both necessary and sufficient conditions.

Partial and Full Conceptual Statements

A partial conceptual statement is expressed with a standard conditional, with the term being clarified contained in either the antecedent or the consequent. A partial conceptual statement gives either the necessary or the sufficient conditions (but not both) for the proper use of the term. A full conceptual statement is expressed with a biconditional, and it gives the necessary *and* sufficient conditions for the proper use of the term. A partial conceptual statement gives the partial meaning of the term, and a full conceptual statement gives the complete meaning of the term.

Most conceptual premises (whether explicit or implicit) are partial rather than complete because a partial conceptual statement is usually all that is needed to clarify the meaning of the vague term in the context of that argument. Given the context, an author may need to clarify the term through necessary conditions or through sufficient conditions. But occasionally, an author will include a conceptual premise that indicates both necessary and sufficient conditions for the use of the term, in which case the conceptual statement should be formulated as a biconditional. More often, conceptual premises contained in conceptual arguments are formulated in biconditionals.

9.1.6 Merely Verbal Disputes

Sometimes, when people are debating some topic, the disagreement among them is said to be a **merely verbal dispute.** Consider the following disputes:

Example 9.21

A. Imagine two people disagreeing about how many life forms there are in the world. One says that there are many trillions, while the other says that there are only a few tens of millions.

B. Imagine two people disagreeing (in 1999) about how many presidencies there
   have been in U.S. history. One says 42, and the other says 43.

What is going on in dispute A? Probably, one party understands the term "life
form" to mean individual living beings and the other understands it to mean
individual species.[15] What about dispute B? The basis of this dispute is likely the
question of whether to count Grover Cleveland twice. Cleveland's two terms
(1885–1889 and 1893–1897) were separated by the presidency of Benjamin Harri-
son. The question is whether to understand the term "presidency" to mean a continuous period of time in the office, in which case Cleveland gets counted twice (for
a total of 43) or to mean particular individuals' occupancy of the office, in which
case Cleveland, like everyone else, gets counted only once (for a total of 42).

These are referred to as merely verbal disputes because the disputants probably do not disagree on the facts. They may think that they are disagreeing on the
facts, but actually they have adopted a different definition of a key term. Once this
point is clarified, their disagreement will disappear. The use of the label "merely
verbal dispute" suggests that the debate is not important and that the disputants are
not *really* disagreeing after all.

But notice something about these two cases. The terms at issue are not vague
but ambiguous. As "sanction" could mean either encouragement or punishment, so
"life form" can mean either individual or species and "presidency" can mean either
a continuous time in office or a particular person's holding of the office. If you had
gotten in a dispute with your second friend about whether the judge gave the
defendant sanction, it would likely have been a merely verbal dispute. In merely
verbal disputes, the terms that are the source of the disagreement typically are
ambiguous rather than vague.

> ### Merely Verbal Disputes
>
> In a merely verbal dispute, the disputants adopt different definitions of a
> key but ambiguous term. The dispute is "merely verbal" because in most
> such cases there is no disagreement about the facts of the case, but only
> disagreement about which of the definitions of the ambiguous term is
> being used.

Because of their nature, merely verbal disputes are often trivial and should
not be confused with conceptual disputes, which often are far from trivial. The
debates continue even after the parties understand that the nature of their disagreement is, in some sense, about the definition of terms. Think about the debate
involving the term "free society" (see Examples 9.17 and 9.18). This debate is not
just a matter of how we might define the term. How we define "free society" will

determine the kind of society we choose to live in. This is a conceptual (and value) debate over what form of government is best, and how this debate is resolved will help to determine what kind of government we have. Certainly, this is not a trivial matter.

Implicit in the idea of a merely verbal dispute is that the only important disagreements are disagreements about facts. But conceptual disputes are important as well, and they are not simply disagreements about facts. They are disagreements about how we should apply our categories of thought to the world.

EXERCISE SET 9.1

SECTION A: The following exercises are based on examples used in this section.

1. In Example 9.1, the author argues that there is an important distinction between the term "vision" and the term "a vision." Discuss whether you agree with the author, and argue for your position.
2. Example 9.4B is the statement "the United States won the Cold War." Provide a conceptual statement clarifying the term "won" as used in this sentence, and argue whether the original statement, as thus clarified, is true or false.
3. The pair of conceptual statements in Example 9.9 seek to clarify the term "counted" as this applied to the controversy over the Florida vote in the 2000 presidential election. Provide an argument for the one you think gives the better clarification of this term.
4. Example 9.12C is a conceptual statement clarifying the term "to like women." First, state what is likely the conceptual statement assumed by the people this author is criticizing (in Example 9.11A). Second, provide a conceptual argument for the conceptual statement in Example 9.12C.
5. Discuss the issue of how we should understand the term "free society" in the light of the debate presented in Examples 9.17 and 9.18.

SECTION B: The following texts raise questions that require a conceptual statement to resolve them. The term requiring clarification is italicized. Draft an appropriate conceptual statement to resolve the issue, and indicate what the resulting resolution should be. Formulate the conceptual statement using either a conditional in terms of necessary or sufficient conditions or a biconditional.

EXAMPLE
Federal law makes it a crime to take a stolen *vehicle* across state lines. Jones steals an airplane in Chicago and flies it to Fargo, North Dakota. Should Jones be charged with that crime?

SOLUTION
Conceptual statement: If an object is a vehicle, it travels over land.
Resolution: Jones should not be charged with this crime.

PROBLEMS
1. In this neighborhood, each of the homes is limited by law to a single *family*. We have received two applications from people seeking to move in, one

from a gay couple and another from a man, his nephew, and his third cousin. Should their applications be approved?

2. You are on the selection committee for a major area *art* show. The rules stipulate that only true works of art are to be included. Among the submissions are a urinal to be hung from the wall, a realistic painting of a soup can, and a piece of driftwood exactly as it was found on the beach. Some members of the committee want to exclude these works on the grounds that they are not art. What is your view on the matter?

3. You are a member of the city council. The welfare agency of the city wants to take two children out of their home because they had been subject to *child abuse*. The law requires that children subject to child abuse be removed from their homes. It turns out that the children in this case had been locked in their rooms and not fed for long periods because they had been disobedient. The parents ask the city council to intervene and order the agency not to remove the children, claiming that their actions were not abusive. How would you vote?

4. An art museum recently hung a contemporary painting of the Last Supper in which the artist had replaced the Jesus figure with a nude image of herself. Some members of the museum's board of directors want the painting taken down on the grounds that it is a case of *pornography*. The rules of the museum exclude pornographic art from being shown. Do the rules of the museum require that the painting be taken down?

SECTION C: Give a conceptual argument (in prose form) for each of the conceptual statements you put forth in Section B.

EXAMPLE

Conceptual statement: If an object is a vehicle, then it travels over land.

SOLUTION

Conceptual argument: Humans have built various conveyances to move things from one place to another. A vehicle is a kind of conveyance. A boat is another kind of conveyance. Vehicles and boats are distinguished by the medium in which they travel. A boat travels on water and a vehicle travels on land. Because an airplane travels in a different medium, the air, it should be regarded as a separate kind of conveyance. So, a necessary condition for use of the term "vehicle" is that the object in question travels on land.

SECTION D: The following texts contain arguments that include or assume conceptual statements. In each case, state the conclusion of the argument and then follow the three steps for evaluating arguments with conceptual premises:

(1) State the explicit or implicit conceptual premise, using the conditional or biconditional form that seems closest to the author's intention.

(2) If there is no conceptual argument offered in support of that premise, charge that premise with a content fallacy.

(3) If there is a conceptual argument offered in support of the premise, state what that argument is and evaluate it.

You need not formally structure either the main argument or the conceptual argument (if any), unless you find it helpful to do so.

EXAMPLE

Background: This letter was written when George W. Bush was governor of Texas and his brother Jeb was governor of Florida. In both states at that time, affirmative action programs were under attack. (*New York Times*, 6/00)

I find it paradoxical that the governor of a state in which affirmative action is under such heavy attack is himself a beneficiary of one of the most insidious forms of the practice: the "legacy" system, through which the children of the elite are admitted into competitive schools and colleges, fraternities and private clubs. Your article says that "Yale, like Andover, gave a helping hand to alumni sons in the admission process . . . and it seems unlikely that Mr. Bush would have been admitted into Yale otherwise." For the white and the rich, it was called a "helping hand"; for minorities, it is called affirmative action and is in danger, especially in states led by the brothers Bush.—M.K.

ANSWER

The (implicit) conclusion of this argument is that affirmative action should not be under attack, especially in states led by the Bushes.

(1) The conceptual premise is that if college admission is based on the legacy system, then it is a form of affirmative action.

(3) There is a conceptual argument, the premise of which is that the legacy system is like affirmative action in that it allows the admission of people who would otherwise not be admitted based on their qualifications. The conceptual argument may be charged with hasty conclusion. The justification for this charge is that the argument does not consider one important difference between affirmative action and the legacy system, namely, that the legacy system allows the school to have much better success at raising money from wealthy former students, thereby helping to secure the success of the school.

PROBLEMS

1. Background: This letter is about traffic policy in New York City. (*New York Times*, 1/00)

   Bravo to Mayor Rudolph W. Giuliani for his new policy of confiscating the vehicles of reckless drivers. As for the response that such measures are "unfair and excessive," I would ask only that a recklessly driven automobile be treated plainly for what it is—a weapon.—S.M.O.

2. Background: This letter is in response to a judge's ruling that classified "secular humanism" as a religion. (*Washington Post*, 3/87)

   The judge's decision calling secular humanism a religion is a semantic joke. Secular humanism draws on 2500 years of Western thought regarding man's ability for self-realization through his capacity for reason. Religion requires faith in a supreme being to understand man's relation to the universe.—T.B.

3. Background: This letter is about the economy. (*New York Times*, 2/00)

   In your article about the 5 percent rise in productivity in the last six months of 1999, you point out that the economy can grow without igniting inflation because "workers, in effect, are producing much more without having to be paid more." Is that cause for self-congratulation? I call it exploitation.—E.B.

4. Background: This letter is about capital punishment. (*Chicago Tribune*, 4/97)

   Punishment usually assumes a lesson is learned so as not to repeat the offense. How does a dead convict learn anything? This raises the old question: Why do we kill people who kill people to tell them that killing people is wrong?—F.I.

5. Background: This is in response to a letter on Northern Ireland, a region of Great Britain that is split between Protestants and Catholics. (*Boston Globe*, 7/97)

   The author argues that Britain should return the northeastern corner of Ireland to the Irish and claims that it's all about democratic values and principles. But in every single election held in Northern Ireland since the 1920s, a clear majority has voted for parties favoring continued union with Great Britain. In other words, Britain governs Northern Ireland because that is what most people who live there want. What could be more democratic than that?—H.L.

❖ 6. Background: This letter is in response to a column about so-called corporate welfare, the tax breaks governments extend to corporations. (*New York Times*, 5/99)

   Your columnist makes the logical mistake of conflating a tax reduction with welfare. A welfare recipient by definition produces little or no wealth, pays little in taxes, if anything, and thus is "entitled" to the fruit of others' labor. He is a net recipient of government wealth transfers. A large company, on the other hand, generates wealth and as a rule pays copious taxes. For New York City or any other taxing body to reduce taxes as a bribe for companies to stay in that taxing body's domain is not welfare since those companies are still net payers of taxes.—T.S.

7. Background: This letter is in response to the pope's stand against the death penalty. (*USA Today*, 2/99)

   Pope John Paul II made clear that he wants Americans to expand the definition of "pro-life" to include a stance against the death penalty. Why limit that definition to one single species on Earth? The Pope should expand his compassion and pro-life advocacy to include all of God's creatures. If he recommended a vegetarian diet, for example, human health would vastly improve, and millions of God's creatures would be spared the needless torture and killings that is required to support a meat-based diet.—R.C.R.

8. Background: This letter is about the closing off of the street in front of the White House due to fears of a terrorist attack by a car or truck bomb. (*Washington Post*, 6/97)

   Once again, *The Post* has repeated that canard about Pennsylvania Avenue in front of the White House being "sealed off" to traffic, which *The Post* deems "an affront to open democracy." The street is not closed to traffic—only to motor vehicles. Other forms of traffic, including bicyclists, rollerbladers, pedestrians, tourists and the usual assortment of people wishing to present grievances, are all welcome.—J.A.S.

9. Background: This letter is in response to an article reporting that a main street in Beijing was closed to bicycles for the benefit of "traffic." (*New York Times*, 11/98)

Why do you consider the city's six million bikes not to be in this category, and why is the dominance of "gas vehicles" inevitable? Motor vehicle crashes are a leading cause of death worldwide. The polluting emissions of cars are a major source of greenhouse gases and other toxins that we'd be far better off without. A car takes up 12 times the space of one bicycle, and the energy used in building it could instead build a hundred bicycles. Bikes are the most efficient form of transportation ever invented. I am saddened that so many people consider their disappearance to be progress.—H.B.

10. Background: This letter is about the allegations that former President Clinton stole the 1996 election because he received illegal campaign contributions. (*New York Times*, 9/98)

Even if it is true that the Clinton campaign did use illegal contributions, how does that constitute the stealing of the election? As far as I know, there have been no allegations of election fraud, the only thing that would constitute the stealing of the election. American citizens elected Mr. Clinton. We may have been misinformed about his character, and illegal contributions may have been used to sell his candidacy, but the election was not stolen.—D.S.W.

11. Background: This letter is about media coverage of cybersex, the exploration of the sex-oriented aspects of the Internet. (*New York Times*, 5/00)

Your coverage of cybersex is a perfect illustration of how the term "addiction" has become politicized. There are millions of equally compulsive Internet users who spend their time shopping, day trading, chatting or playing games rather than looking at sexually oriented material, but we don't call them addicts because we don't disapprove of the underlying behavior. That interest in sex is singled out for especially derogatory attention says more about the sickness of society than about the "addicts."—M.D.

12. Background: This letter is in response to an article about California's growing population. (*San Francisco Chronicle*, 5/97)

The reporter must moonlight for housing developers. He tells us the 1.6 percent expansion of the state population in 1996 marks an "improvement" over more sluggish growth earlier. Surely we can "improve" even faster. At that snail's pace we'll have only about 37 million a decade from now. There are entire nations that double their population every 25 years. Let's not rest on our laurels.—J.P.

13. Background: This is in response to a letter arguing that a successful ballot initiative prohibiting gay marriages should be enforced. (*Boston Globe*, 3/00)

Democracy exists to protect the minority from the tyranny of the majority. The fact that gays who wish to marry must petition the government of a "free society" should offend everyone who believes in personal freedom. In the author's world, only heterosexuals seem to be entitled to life, liberty, and the pursuit of happiness.—C.A. & C.A.

14. Background: This letter is about standardized testing in high schools. (*New York Times*, 4/00)

   People opposing new requirements for students to pass standardized exams before graduation assert that the tests are discriminatory. Indeed they are. They discriminate against people who can't read, write or do arithmetic. When it comes to schooling, that's exactly the kind of discrimination we should practice rigorously.—J.G.

❖ 15. Background: This letter is about hormone replacement therapy for post-menopausal women. (*New York Times*, 6/97)

   We are told that hormone replacement therapy can reduce a woman's risk of death as long as she continues it. But then we learn that after ten or more years of hormone use women face a 43 percent increase in their risk of death from breast cancer. How has it become acceptable for medicine to advocate the use of a drug that increases a woman's chance of developing any disease, let alone cancer? How is it that we are expected to accept this preposterous either/or: Cancer? Or heart disease? What happened to "First, do no harm"?—J.A.

16. Background: This letter is in response to an article suggesting that environmental education is propagandistic. (*Christian Science Monitor*, 5/97)

   I found the article interesting but hardly balanced. It didn't give comparisons to the teaching of other, more traditional subjects. Doesn't history have a slant toward wars (specifically U.S. interests) in an effort to avoid them? Aren't children taught not to cheat in math and not to swear in English? Why should natural science values be any different? Why is it "propaganda" when we teach children not to pollute, not to consume more than their share? These are community values just like honesty and integrity.—G.M.

17. Background: This letter is about the boxer Mike Tyson, who has had trouble controlling himself both inside and outside of the ring. (*USA Today*, 10/98)

   Mike Tyson is no longer a boxer. He should not have been given back his boxing license. Boxing, no matter how one feels about it, is a sport. As in any sport, it requires a certain amount of mental discipline. If boxing were totally dependent upon size and strength, the fight would be decided at the weigh-in. A boxer needs to be in control, both mentally and physically, and Tyson is not. He cannot control himself in the ring, and he definitely cannot control himself outside of the ring.—N.K.

❖ 18. Background: This letter is about the tradition of recognizing "unknown soldiers," in the light of recent developments in genetic technology. (*New York Times*, 7/98)

The recent identification of the remains of the Vietnam Unknown and the unlikelihood, because of genetic testing, of there being a totally unidentifiable replacement presents us with an opportunity to redefine "unknown soldier." Unknown not only means unidentified, it can also describe that which is not capable of being known. It seems appropriate, then, to place in the Tomb of the Unknown a scroll or book inscribed with all 58,000 names of those who did not return from Vietnam. This would honor all of our Vietnam heroes as well as the "unknown" of what they might have been.—M.L.

19. Background: This letter is in response to an editorial on the Monica Lewinsky scandal that rocked the second term of former President Clinton. (*New York Times*, 10/98)

In your editorial, you support an "unfettered investigation of all allegations against Mr. Clinton." I submit that no citizen of the United States should be subject to an "unfettered investigation." Rules of law defining the relevant standard of conduct, granting protection against unreasonable invasions of privacy and creating privileges like attorney-client privilege, executive privilege and even the privilege against self-incrimination are not "fetters." They are what make us a society of free people.—A.I.

20. Background: This letter is part of the debate over a proposed constitutional amendment prohibiting the desecration of the American flag. (*New York Times*, 7/98)

The amendment to prohibit physical desecration of the flag, by using the term "desecration," elevates the flag to an emblem of a state religion. The word "desecration" means to strip away the sacred nature of a religious object. Since the Constitution prohibits the establishment of a state religion, the amendment is clearly unconstitutional.—J.A.B.

21. Background: This letter is in response to reports of crime rates in winter. (*New York Times*, 2/85)

I'd like to point out an unintended irony in your article about the record cold weather. A police spokesman is quoted as saying, "Usually crime does go down in this kind of weather," yet you mention 10,189 calls about inadequate heat and two people who froze to death in their apartment. Why is a teenager's demanding $5 on the subway considered a crime and a landlord's allowing people to freeze to death thought of as something else? A more accurate statement would have been: "Usually the type of crime changes in this kind of weather."—H.L.A.

22. Background: This letter is in response to a column arguing against euthanasia or physician-assisted suicide. (*New York Times*, 1/97)

Your columnist refers to self-preservation as a basic instinct. Surely he is right, not only in the physical sense but also in the psychological or emotional one. I believe that physician-assisted suicide is essential today because science has been so much more successful at keeping bodies alive than minds. I would rather be dead than psychologically unrecognizable to my descendants. Self-preservation thus means that their memories will be of my true self, warts and all, rather than of some helpless, unresponsive, money-devouring relic.—J.B.

9.2 Definitions

Recall, in our fictional example, the statements made by your three friends after you all attended a trial, and the uncertainty you had about what each of the statements meant (see Examples 9.2 and 9.3). While your uncertainty in the case of your third friend required a conceptual statement to clarify the meaning (for the term "evil"), your uncertainty in the case of your other two friends' statements required an analytic statement to clarify the meaning (for the terms "supercilious" and "sanction"). In these two cases, your friends responded with analytic rather than conceptual statements. They simply reported a dictionary definition. In this section, we focus on definitions and the analytic statements used to present them.

A **definition** is the meaning of a term as based on convention, a rule of behavior accepted by a group of people. The conventions of a language are the accepted rules of linguistic behavior among the people who speak that language. These rules cover both how words are used (the meaning of the words) and how words are combined with other words (grammar). A natural language is a large, complex set of such conventions.

A definition usually provides both necessary and sufficient conditions for the use of a word. Thus, definitions are often expressed with biconditionals. There are also, however, **partial definitions,** which indicate only part of the convention for the use of a word. Whereas a definition provides both necessary and sufficient conditions for the use of a word, a partial definition provides either necessary or sufficient conditions, but not both. Partial definitions, like partial conceptual statements, are expressed in conditionals.

Example 9.22

Definition: A person is a bachelor if and only if he is an adult, unmarried male.
Partial definition: If a person is a bachelor, then that person is unmarried. Being unmarried is a necessary condition for being a bachelor.

9.2.1 The Nature of Definitions

Definitions are primarily *reports* on how a word is actually used. Dictionaries contain these reports. The task of dictionary writers is to report how a language group uses the words of their language. If the writers do their job well, the meanings in the dictionary correctly report the conventions of the language group. Language does change over time, requiring new reportive definitions and new editions of the dictionary, but this change is a collective process. The language users gradually adopt new conventions for the use of words, and the meanings of words change.

Definitions are given for the **general terms** of a language, the words that apply, at least potentially, to more than one thing. Thus, "tall," "western," "run,"

Definitions and Partial Definitions

A definition is a convention or rule, accepted by a group of people who speak a language, about how they use the words of that language. Definitions are expressed in analytic statements. Definitions usually provide both necessary and sufficient conditions for the use of the word, so they may be expressed with biconditionals. A partial definition indicates only part of the convention or rule for the use of a term—either the necessary or the sufficient conditions for its use—so it may be expressed with conditionals.

"ape," "envelope," and "democracy" are all general terms and have definitions. Many different objects can be tall or be envelopes, and many different events can be cases of running. A definition specifies the conditions under which the general term may be used to refer to something. In contrast, definitions are not given for proper names, which are words meant to apply to only one thing.[16] "Fred," for example, is a proper name because, even though there are many people named "Fred," whenever we use the term we refer to some particular person. A proper name applies to something whatever its characteristics. In other words, something need have no particular characteristics to be given a particular proper name. In contrast, a general term applies to something only if the characteristics of that thing satisfy the conditions specified by the definition of that word.

General Terms

A general term is a word that applies, at least potentially, to more than one thing. In contrast, a proper name applies to only one thing. A general term applies to things based on the characteristics of those things. General terms have definitions that indicate the characteristics a thing must have for the general term to apply to it.

The kind of definitions found in dictionaries are reports of conventions about the use of words, and so are known as **reportive definitions.**[17] Most definitions are reportive definitions, but some are not. **Stipulative definitions** do not report on existing uses of a word, but instead offer revisions in our understanding of the meaning of words. Still, stipulative definitions, like reportive definitions, have to do with conventions. But whereas reportive definitions indicate existing conventions, stipulative definitions propose new conventions for the use of words. Thus, a reportive definition is *descriptive*, in that it describes how people actually use a term; a stipulative definition is *prescriptive*, in that it recommends how a term should be used.

Here is an example of a stipulative definition:

Example 9.23

Background: This is a passage by James Madison from *The Federalist*.[18]

> A pure Democracy, by which I mean, a Society, consisting of a small number of citizens, who assemble and administer the Government in person, can admit of no cure for the mischiefs of faction. A common passion or interest will, in almost every case, be felt by a majority of the whole . . . and there is nothing to check the inducements to sacrifice the weaker party or an obnoxious individual.

Madison here introduces the term "pure democracy" and gives it special meaning. He is recommending or prescribing that the term be used in this way.

Reportive and Stipulative Definitions

Most definitions are reportive definitions. Reportive definitions, which appear in dictionaries, are reports or descriptions of how words are actually used in the language. In contrast, stipulative definitions either recommend new meanings for existing words or introduce meanings for new words. Reportive definitions are descriptive and present existing conventions; stipulative definitions are prescriptive and recommend new conventions.

We can distinguish among stipulative definitions in several ways. First, some stipulative definitions are general and some are limited. A *general* stipulative definition proposes a convention for use beyond the text in which it is introduced. For example, a specialist in some field may propose a definition and recommend that it be adopted by the community of specialists. Or, a stipulative definition may be meant for adoption by the general community of speakers of that language. In contrast, a *limited* stipulative definition proposes a convention that is meant to apply only within the text in which it is introduced. For example, an author often will offer a stipulative definition in a text that is meant to apply to that text only.

Second, stipulative definitions may be offered either of existing words or of new words. A proposed definition of an existing word may be meant either as a replacement definition or as an additional definition. The author of a replacement definition hopes that the new definition will displace the old one. The author of an additional definition does not seek to replace the existing definition, but rather hopes that the new definition will serve as an alternative to the existing one. Any proposed definition of a new word must, of course, be a stipulative definition because there is no existing convention for its meaning. Figure 9.1 summarizes these distinctions.

Consider these examples of stipulative definitions proposed by physicists:

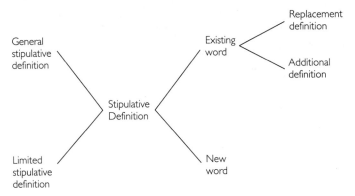

FIGURE 9.1   Stipulative Definitions

Example 9.24

A. The term "atom" is defined as a unit of matter with a certain kind of internal structure.
B. The term "quark" is defined as a certain subatomic particle.
C. The term "charm" is defined as a certain property of that particle.
D. The term "laser" is defined as a certain kind of light radiation.

All of these (we may assume) were meant as general stipulative definitions. In other words, the authors who introduced these definitions meant for them to be adopted beyond the context in which they were introduced. Indeed, at least two of them ("atom" and "laser") not only have been adopted by the physics community but have become part of the general language. Examples A and C are stipulative definitions of existing words, words already in the language. A is proposed as a replacement definition for the one that already existed, according to which atoms lacked internal structure. In contrast, C is proposed as an additional definition for an existing word. It was not intended to replace the established definition of "charm," which applies to people and other large objects, and not subatomic particles, but rather to supplement it, to exist alongside the established definition.

Examples B and D, in contrast, introduce new words. "Laser" was coined based on an acronym of a phrase that explains the nature of the kind of light in question (**l**ight **a**mplification by **s**timulated **e**mission of **r**adiation). When stipulative definitions are given of new words, the words are often based on acronyms.

Stipulative definitions are sometimes successful and other times not. They are proposed conventions, and they succeed only if they become existing conventions. That is, they succeed only if a group of language users comes to use the term the way the stipulative definition recommends. But this group need not be *all* of the speakers of that language. If a term is recommended for use only by a group of specialists (say, literary critics or sociologists), success results when that smaller group adopts the new meaning of the term. Moreover, if the stipulative definition is limited rather than general, success comes more easily. For example, in Chapter 6, I introduced the term "TARS" and gave it a limited stipulative definition. The success of this definition results simply from the fact that the readers of this text adopt this definition in their reading of the text.

One special kind of stipulative definition is **persuasive definitions,** which use terms that are designed to affect the beliefs of the audience by playing on their attitudes and feelings. Persuasive definitions seek to persuade the audience to adopt certain beliefs by appealing to members' emotions rather than their reason. Recall our discussion of the uses of language in Chapter 1. One of these is the expressive use of language, in which words express feelings rather than describe or argue. Many words have an expressive or emotive meaning in addition to their regular meaning (the concept to which they refer). The expressive meaning may be positive or negative. For example, "freedom," "motherhood," "truth," and "real" generally have a positive expressive meaning, and "hack," "dismal," and "obscure" generally have a negative expressive meaning.

> ### Persuasive Definitions
>
> Persuasive definitions are a kind of stipulative definition that include words that have positive or negative expressive meaning. The point of a persuasive definition is to turn the audience in favor of or against what is being defined by the use of such words. A persuasive definition is often deceptively presented as if it were a reportive definition. The author needs to argue for the claim being made, and not present it as simply "true by definition."

An author who gives a persuasive definition includes in that definition words that have either a positive or a negative expressive meaning in order to influence the beliefs of the audience about what is being defined. Thus, there is usually an element of deception in persuasive definitions. In most cases, the author of the persuasive definition tries to hide the fact that a stipulative definition is being offered by pretending that the stipulative definition is a reportive definition. In other cases, the author makes clear that it is not a reportive definition that is being offered. We might say that a persuasive definition is an *implicit* stipulative definition.

Here are some examples:

Example 9.25

A. Abortion is the murder of unborn children.
B. Abortion is exercising the right to choose.
C. Socialism is economic democracy.
D. Capitalism is market freedom.[19]

Because "murder" has a negative expressive meaning, an opponent of abortion may offer definition A in order to turn an audience against the practice. In contrast, because "right to choose" has a positive expressive meaning, a proponent of abortion might offer definition B to turn an audience in favor of the practice. Similarly, because "democracy" and "freedom" have positive expressive meaning, proponents of socialism may offer definition C, and proponents of capitalism definition D, to orient the audience in favor of these political/economic arrangements.

This is not to say that persuasive definitions are false. The point is that they need to be argued for, not accepted as true "by definition." Those who present persuasive definitions need to shift from the expressive to the argumentative use of language and to give reasons to believe that the claims they make under the guise of offering definitions are true. In this respect, a persuasive definition is akin to the fallacy of begging the question. It is, in effect, an effort to show that something is true simply by claiming that it is true. Persuasive definition is one situation in which an author will use terms with expressive meaning to seek to avoid giving an argument when an argument is needed. We discuss this more later in the chapter in the context of the fallacy of tendentiousness.

9.2.2 How to Define

We turn now from a discussion of different kinds of definition to a consideration of how precisely to construct a definition. The first thing to say is that a definition can be constructed in terms of intension or extension. The intension of a word is the set of properties that characterize all and only those things to which the word applies—in other words, the necessary and sufficient conditions for applying the word. Thus, an **intensional definition** lists the necessary and sufficient conditions for the application of a term. In contrast, the extension of a word is the set of all the things to which the term applies. Thus, an **extensional definition** is simply a listing of all the things to which the word applies. For example, the extensional definition of "president of the United States" would be a list of those who have been president. In contrast, an intensional definition of the term would be a list of the necessary and sufficient conditions for someone's being president.

> **Intensional and Extensional Definitions**
>
> Definitions may be constructed intensionally or extensionally. An intensional definition indicates the necessary and sufficient conditions for the application of a term. An extensional definition is a listing of all the individual things to which a term applies.

The definitions examined so far and those to be considered next are all intensional definitions. How is an intensional definition constructed? As discussed earlier, a definition is an analytic statement that provides necessary and sufficient conditions for the application of a general term. A definition may be divided into two parts: (1) that which is being defined, or **definiendum**, and (2) the list of necessary and sufficient conditions for the term's application, or **definiens**. (We are speaking here of complete rather than partial definitions.)

Consider these examples:

Example 9.26

A. An event is breakfast if and only if it is a meal eaten in the morning.
(Alternative formulation: Breakfast is a meal eaten in the morning.)

B. A facility is a library if and only if it is a building housing books.
(Alternative formulation: A library is a building housing books.)

In definition A, "breakfast" is the *definiendum* and "meal eaten in the morning" is the *definiens*. In definition B, "library" is the *definiendum* and "building housing books" is the *definiens*. In a definition, the *definiendum* is usually the first part of the sentence and the *definiens* the second part. But note the alternative formulations. A definition, as a listing of necessary and sufficient conditions, is fully formulated as a biconditional, using the phrase "if and only if." The alternative versions of A and B given are simply shorthand forms. They are shorter and easier to use because, while the "if and only if" connects sentences, the "is" connects subjects and predicates. We will use this shorthand form below, but keep in mind that, because definitions indicate necessary and sufficient conditions, the "is" is simply a stand-in for "if and only if."[20]

> ### *Definiendum* and *Definiens*
>
> In an intensional definition, the *definiendum* is what is being defined, and the *definiens* is a list of its properties or of necessary and sufficient conditions for the application of the term. In the formulation of a definition, the *definiendum* is connected to the *definiens* by "if and only if" or, in shorthand form, by a form of "is."

The question of how to construct an intensional definition is the question of how to formulate the *definiens*. There are different ways to do this, but the most often used method is **definition by genus and species.** According to this method, there are two aspects of a *definiens*. Imagine a definition of "chair." First, the *definiens* would indicate the general category to which chairs belong (say, furniture). This is the genus. Second, the definiens would indicate how chairs differ from other items in that category (meant to be sat on). This is the species. Thus, a chair is furniture meant to be sat on.

Consider the definitions in Example 9.26. In definition A (shorthand form), "meal" is the genus, the general category to which breakfast belongs, and "eaten in the morning" is the species, the feature that distinguishes breakfast from other meals. In definition B (shorthand form), "building" is the genus and "housing books" is the species. According to this definition, what is *general* about a library is that it is a building, and what is *specific* about a library is that it houses books. The fact that a library houses books distinguishes it from other buildings.

In these examples, the word or phrase in capitals is the genus, and the word or phrase in italics is the species.

Example 9.27

A. A child is a *young* HUMAN BEING.
B. A college is a *four-year* INSTITUTION OF HIGHER EDUCATION.
C. A coin is a UNIT OF MONEY *made of metal.*
D. A human being is a *rational* ANIMAL.
E. A human being is a *featherless* BIPED.

Definitions D and E are from the ancient Greek philosopher Aristotle. They show that different definitions by genus and species can sometimes be offered for a term. Humans are those animals that are rational. Also, humans are those bipeds (creatures who walk on two legs) that are without feathers (the other bipeds being birds). But D is a better definition than E, because D defines "human being" in terms of properties that are more important to being human. It says something more important about humans to characterize us as rational than as featherless. If we happened to grow feathers, we would still be human, but if we lost our rationality, we would not be.

9.2.3 Assessing Definitions

We can assess definitions in different ways. For example, we might assess them for clarity. Definitions should, of course, be as clear as possible. In addition, we can criticize definitions for circularity. A definition is circular when the *definiens* contains the same term (or a variant) as the *definiendum*. For example, a definition of a gambler as a person who spends considerable time gambling is circular. The same term occurs in the *definiendum* and the *definiens*, so this definition does not inform us as it should. A definition is not adequate if it is circular.[21]

But perhaps the most important form of assessment is for accuracy. Reportive definitions may be assessed in terms of how well they indicate the way in which words are actually used by speakers of the language. We often rely on dictionaries to give us accurate reports of how words are used. But the ultimate source for assessment of a reportive definition is the way in which the words are actually used. Reportive definition may be inaccurate in two ways. First, the definition can be *too broad*, meaning that it represents a word as applying to things that the word does not in fact apply to. Second, the definition can be *too narrow*, meaning that it represents a word as not applying to things that the word does in fact apply to.

In other words, a definition should represent a word as applying to *all and only* the things to which speakers of the language apply it. When a definition violates the "only" part of this formulation, it is too broad. When it violates the "all" part, it is too narrow. In an accurate definition, there is an identity between what is covered by the term being defined (the *definiendum*) and what is covered by the conditions set forth in the definition (the *definiens*). This reflects the fact that the two parts of the definition are connected by "if and only if." This identity holds only so long as the definition is neither too broad nor too narrow.

One way to determine whether a definition is too broad or too narrow is to apply the **method of counterexample,** as this applies to definitions.[22] In applying this method, you seek to find some real or hypothetical example that is included in the definition but should not be (showing the definition to be too broad) or that is not included in the definition but should be (showing the definition to be too narrow). Earlier, we offered the following reportive definition: A library is a building housing books. Let us test the accuracy of this definition by the method of counterexample.

Example 9.28

Definition: A library is a building for housing books.
Counterexamples showing the definition to be too broad: a textbook warehouse, a bookstore
Counterexamples showing the definition to be too narrow: a library that is a room in a mansion, a mobile library in a van visiting outlying communities

As you can see, a definition can be both too broad and too narrow at the same time. This might seem strange unless you recognize that the genus and the species can both be the source of error. In this case, the genus (building) leads to the definition being too narrow, and the species (housing books) leads to its being too broad.

Method of Counterexample (for definitions)

The method of counterexample is a way of assessing the accuracy of reportive definitions. A definition is not accurate if it has a counterexample, an example either to which the definition applies but should not (showing the definition to be too broad) or to which the definition does not apply but should (showing the definition to be too narrow). A definition can be both too broad and too narrow at the same time.

In applying the method of counterexample, it is important to avoid using counterexamples that represent *metaphorical* rather than *standard* uses of the term in question. A standard use of a term is its application to the sorts of things to which it is usually applied. A metaphorical use of a term has two characteristics: It is an application of a term (1) in an area different from that of its standard use and (2) to something that resembles in some respect the things to which the term is applied in its standard use.[23] For example, some people have recently begun referring to our genetic code as a library. But this is a metaphorical use and so should not be raised as a counterexample to a proposed definition.

There is no sharp line between metaphorical and standard uses of a term. Indeed, what was once a metaphorical use can become, in time, a standard use. This transition over time from metaphorical to standard use is an indication of the flexibility and adaptability of language. It is also an indication that the method of counterexample is not a precise and infallible method, because definitions do not remain fixed over time.

If your assessment reveals that a reportive definition is inaccurate, you can seek greater accuracy by revising it to avoid the counterexamples you have discovered. Here is one way, based on the counterexamples cited, to improve our definition of "library": "A library is an enclosure housing books for consultation or borrowing." In replacing "building" with "enclosure," we avoid the counterexamples that showed the definition to be too narrow. In replacing "housing books" with "housing books for consultation or borrowing," we avoid the counterexamples that showed the definition to be too broad. Of course, this definition *still* may be inaccurate, because there may be other counterexamples.

What about the assessment of stipulative definitions? With the exception of persuasive definitions, the reasons for introducing them usually involve practical considerations related to the argumentative purposes of the text in which they are introduced. For example, consider again the text from Madison in Example 9.23, in which Madison offers a stipulative definition: A pure democracy is "a Society, consisting of a small number of citizens, who assemble and administer the Government in person." What were his reasons for introducing this definition? He might justify introducing it in the following way:

Example 9.29

In order to argue for the federal system of government proposed by the Constitution, I need to show its virtues by comparing it with a faulty system and showing how a federal system avoids those faults. Some of the main features of the federal system are its representative character and the various checks and balances it includes on the exercise of political power. A nonrepresentational system in which political power is exercised directly by the citizens does not have these features. It would be helpful in my argument to have a label for such a system to make it easy to compare the system with the federal one. So, I will label this other system "pure democracy" and proceed in my argument to compare pure democracy with a federal system.

In general, to assess a stipulative definition is to consider the adequacy of the practical argument, such as this one, that is or could be offered for it. Will the definition achieve the practical purposes it is supposed to achieve? Does the author even need to introduce a special term? Or, more commonly, is the stipulative definition the author offers best suited for his or her purposes? Would a different definition serve these purposes better?

But this kind of practical argument is different from the typical conceptual argument given in support of a conceptual statement. Earlier in the chapter, we suggested that a conceptual statement seeks to clarify or sharpen the meaning of a term at the boundary—that is, as the term applies to cases at the periphery, rather than the core, of the use of the term. A conceptual argument typically compares the core use of the term with the peripheral case in question to show how the term should be applied at the boundary. In contrast, when you offer a stipulative definition, you are not bound by the standard meaning of the term. (Indeed, if the word is a new one, there is no standard meaning.) For example, when I introduced the term "TARS," the definition I offered had no relation to the reportive definition of the term. My argument for the definition would make no reference to the sticky petroleum product. Conceptual arguments have a substantive element to them that is not present in arguments for stipulative definitions.

EXERCISE SET 9.2

SECTION A: Without consulting a dictionary, provide short genus and species definitions of the following terms.

EXAMPLE
Flag

ANSWER
Genus: a rectangular piece of cloth
Species: symbolic of a nation

PROBLEMS

1. Table
2. Weapon
3. Overcoat
4. Star
5. Book bag
6. Computer
7. War
8. Leader
9. Hearing aid
10. House
11. Pebble

SECTION B: Evaluate the following definitions using the method of counterexample to show which are either too narrow or too broad (or both). For some of the definitions, there may be more than one kind of counterexample, so you should include all the kinds you can find. Where you find the definition to be inaccurate, propose a revised definition. Remember to avoid metaphorical uses of the term as counterexamples.

EXAMPLE
A "compact disc" is a circular piece of plastic for recording music.

ANSWER
Counterexample: a computer program stored on a compact disc. This shows the definition to be too narrow.
Counterexample: an old phonograph record. This shows the definition to be too broad.

Revision: A compact disc is a circular piece of plastic approximately 4.5 inches in diameter for recording information.

PROBLEMS

1. A "watch" is a timepiece worn on the wrist.
2. A "plant" is something that can be eaten in a salad.
3. A "class" is an educational activity that occurs in a room designed for that purpose.
4. A "song" is a musical vocalization accompanied by instruments.
5. A "guitar" is a hollow, stringed musical instrument.
6. A "crime" is any action that can cause a person to be required to appear in court.
7. A "language" is a set of rules for vocalizations that communicate meaning.
8. An "election winner" is the man who gets the most votes.

SECTION C: Apply the instructions in Section B to your answers in Section A. Alternatively, exchange answers with a classmate and apply the instructions in Section B to that person's answers.

EXAMPLE

A "flag" is a rectangular piece of cloth symbolic of a nation.

ANSWER

Counterexample: a flag of a state, such as Iowa. This shows the definition to be too narrow.

Revision: A flag is a rectangular piece of cloth symbolic of a political entity.

SECTION D: Consider the world of personal computing. Based on your experience with computers, try to think of some aspect of computing—for example, hardware, software, Internet activity—that could use a term of its own but (as far as you know) has not yet been given one. Propose a term for it, and give the term's stipulative definition. Give a brief argument for your definition.

9.3 Some Specific Fallacies of Language Use

In some cases, the incautious or incorrect use of language in an argument is a fallacy. Such fallacies of language use are specific versions of the four basic fallacies. In this section, we explore three of these—ambiguity, equivocation, and tendentiousness—all of which are specific versions of the basic content fallacies (problematic premise or false premise).

9.3.1 Ambiguity

There are two kinds of ambiguity: semantic ambiguity and syntactic ambiguity. The kind of ambiguity discussed earlier in the chapter is **semantic ambiguity,** ambiguity in the meaning of terms. "Bank" and "sanction" are terms with semantic ambiguity. Semantic ambiguity occurs when a term has two or more clear meanings.[24]

Syntactic ambiguity is ambiguity in the meaning of a sentence resulting from improper or confusing sentence construction or from bad grammar. Here is an example:

Example 9.30

Background: This letter is in response to an article on misplaced modifiers. (*Chicago Tribune*, 5/97)

> My favorite is: "Abraham Lincoln wrote the Gettysburg Address while traveling from Washington to Gettysburg on the back of an envelope."—M.F.

The sentence is syntactically ambiguous because the modifying phrase "on the back of an envelope" is in the wrong position. Literally, the sentence says that Lincoln traveled to Gettysburg on the back of an envelope, but clearly this is not what the author meant. The unambiguous expression of this meaning would require placing the phrase "on the back of an envelope" after the term "Address."

> ### Semantic and Syntactic Ambiguity
>
> Ambiguity occurs when a term or sentence has two or more clear meanings. Semantic ambiguity results when a term has more than one clear meaning. Syntactic ambiguity results from bad grammar or improper or confusing sentence construction.

A ripe, and often amusing, source of ambiguity, both semantic and syntactic, is newspaper headlines. It is easy to pick on headlines. They are such a ready source of ambiguity because there is such a demand for economy of expression placed on the headline writer, given the obvious space limitations. Consider these examples:

Example 9.31

A. Killer sentenced to die for second time in 10 years.
B. Never withhold herpes infection from loved one.
C. Deer kill 17,000.
D. Cold wave linked to temperatures.

Headline A is a case of syntactic ambiguity. As with the Lincoln example, it results from a misplaced modifying phrase—in this case, the phrase "for second time in 10 years," which should have been placed at the beginning of the sentence. The ambiguity is between the killer's being twice sentenced to die (the intended meaning) and the killer's being sentenced to die twice. Headline B is also an example of syntactic ambiguity, but it reveals a different kind of grammatical problem, namely, elision. Elision is the leaving out of material in an effort to compress a text. The full sentence would be "Never withhold *knowledge of your* herpes infection from loved one." In eliding this sentence into B by leaving out the italicized phrase, the author made the sentence ambiguous, allowing it to be understood as recommending that you allow your loved one to share the infection.

Headline C is primarily a case of semantic ambiguity. Here, "kill" can be read either as a noun referring to an event involving killing or as a verb referring to an act of killing. Thus, in one interpretation (yielding the intended meaning), "deer" is an adjective, implying that 17,000 deer were killed. In another, "deer" is a noun and the subject of the sentence, implying that the deer have killed 17,000 (presumably humans). As this example shows, there is not always a sharp distinction between semantic and syntactic ambiguity. The semantic ambiguity of "kill" leads to the syntactic ambiguity of "deer" being taken as either an adjective or a noun. In one interpretation of headline D, likely to lead to a response of "duh," this is an analytic statement telling us that "cold" has to do with temperature. This is probably not the intended meaning. The intended meaning, which presumably would be clear from the article, might be that the cold weather is due to temperature variants in the jet stream. This interpretation would make the sentence a case of elision. The full sentence would be "Cold wave linked to temperature *in the jet stream.*"

Not all cases of semantic or syntactic ambiguity in an argument result in a fallacy. The **fallacy of ambiguity** occurs when an argument contains an ambiguous term or sentence *and* the context does not make clear what meaning the author intended. The fallacy of ambiguity is a specific version of problematic premise because when a premise contains an ambiguity its meaning is uncertain, and a premise cannot be regarded as acceptable until its meaning is clear.[25] When you structure an argument that expresses a premise with an ambiguous sentence, you should clarify the meaning in the reformulation of the premise to the extent that the meaning is made clear by the context. If the context does not make the meaning clear, the reformulation should include the ambiguity and the argument be charged with the fallacy of ambiguity.

The Fallacy of Ambiguity

The fallacy of ambiguity occurs when a term or phrase (in the case of semantic ambiguity) or a sentence (in the case of syntactical ambiguity) in the expression of an argument is ambiguous, and the context does not resolve the ambiguity.

Many government documents, including the founding documents of the United States, are ambiguous, often deliberately so. Consider the Second Amendment of the Bill of Rights, which reads, "A well-regulated militia, being necessary to the security of a free State, the right of the people to keep and bear arms, shall not be infringed." Disputes about the meaning of this text reveal its ambiguity. Here is an example of this dispute:

Example 9.32

A. Background: This letter advocates gun control and criticizes the position of the National Rifle Association (NRA), a group that cites the Second Amendment in support of its strong opposition to gun control. (*New York Times, 6/98*)

> In the NRA ads, the full amendment will never be seen or heard. Why not? Because the first half of the amendment's "well-regulated militia, being necessary to the security of a free State" clearly limits the meaning of the second half, "the right of the people to keep and bear arms, shall not be infringed." If the NRA is going to hang its hat on the Second Amendment, it shouldn't shy away from quoting it in full.—W.H.D.

B. Background: This letter takes the other side of the debate. (*New York Times, 8/89*)

> If only the militia should be able to bear arms, the Second Amendment should have said so. It does not! When a militia is called up, the people must be able to bear arms and to know how to use them. If the "people" were not to bear arms the amendment would have said: "A well-regulated militia, being necessary to the security of a free state, the right of the militia to keep and bear arms, shall not be infringed."—D.H.W.

Though neither author sees ambiguity in the Second Amendment, the texts together make a strong case that it is there. According to argument A, the reference to a "well-regulated militia" in the opening clause of the sentence qualifies the right to bear arms referred to in the main clause, granting that right only to members of a militia. According to argument B, the fact that the main clause refers to "the people," rather than repeating the reference in the opening clause to the militia, shows that the right extends to all people, not merely militia members. The text contains a complicated mixture of semantic ambiguity, in the phrase "the people," and syntactic ambiguity, in the grammatical issue of whether the opening clause qualifies the main clause. When we come across arguments on gun control that appeal to the Second Amendment, we should be aware of this ambiguity.

Legal and constitutional documents are often ambiguous because they are the result of political compromise. Their authors seek to gain the support of competing political factions by including wording that opposing groups can interpret as in accord with their own points of view. It is frequently said, for example, that forging treaties is a practice in studied ambiguity, involving the use of ambiguous language that allows each side to read the treaty as favorable to its interests. Perhaps this can be said of bureaucratic documents in general.

9.3.2 Equivocation

Equivocation is closely related to semantic ambiguity and is, in fact, the way in which ambiguity most often causes problems in arguments. **Equivocation** occurs when an ambiguous term is used with two of its meanings in the same text. The **fallacy of equivocation** occurs when there is equivocation in an argumentative text and the argument's apparent strength depends on understanding the term in more than one way. An argument that commits this fallacy *trades on* the ambiguity of the term. Here is a simple and obvious example:

Example 9.33

P1: Only man is rational.
P2: No woman is a man.
C: Therefore, no woman is rational.

The apparent persuasiveness of this argument, such as it is, depends on the term "man" being understood in two different ways. "Man" is, of course, ambiguous, meaning either "humankind" or "male." The argument trades on this ambiguity because the plausibility of P1 depends on the term's having one of these meanings ("humankind") and the plausibility of P2 depends on the term's having the other meaning ("male"). The author takes advantage of this ambiguity to create an argument that appears sound, but only so long as one does not notice the shift in meaning of the ambiguous term.

The fallacy of equivocation is a specific version of either problematic premise or false premise. Unmasking this fallacy requires pointing out that the ambiguous term is being used in two different ways. This can be done in the justification by showing that, when the term is understood in one premise to have the meaning it has elsewhere in the argument, that premise is unacceptable or false. In Example 9.33, you could justify a fallacy of equivocation charge by arguing, with regard to P2, that, when the term "man" is understood in this premise in the way it is meant to be understood in the other premise, the premise is false.

Equivocation and the Fallacy of Equivocation

Equivocation is the use of an ambiguous term in two different ways—that is, according to two of its meanings—in the same text. The fallacy of equivocation occurs when there is equivocation in an argumentative text and the force of the reasoning depends on the term's being understood in the two different ways. This fallacy is a specific version of problematic premise or false premise because revealing the fallacy requires showing that one of the premises is unacceptable or false when the ambiguous term in it is understood in the way it is meant elsewhere in the argument.

Unfortunately, most cases of the fallacy of equivocation are not as easy to spot as in Example 9.33. The two occurrences of the ambiguous term may go unnoticed, the ambiguous term may appear in different forms, or one of its occurrences may be implicit. Moreover, not all cases of the fallacy are deliberate. Sometimes, they result from sloppy thinking, rather than any attempt to deceive the audience.

Calvin and Hobbes   by Bill Watterson

CALVIN AND HOBBES © 1995 Watterson. Reprinted with permission of Universal Press Syndicate. All rights reserved.

This *Calvin & Hobbes* cartoon is an example of the fallacy of equivocation. Calvin's strategy in taking the examination relies on the ambiguity of the phrase "your own words." Loopholes often depend on ambiguity. When he is later accused of not following the instructions, he might argue: "The question said to use my own words, and I used my own words, so I followed the instructions." Because of the ambiguity of "your own words," this argument commits the fallacy of equivocation. (Calvin's strategy also throws light on the role of conventions in language, discussed in the section on definitions. "Your own words" does not mean what Calvin takes it to mean because a person can communicate only with words whose meanings are conventional, and so shared with others. Rather, "your own words" means your own *combination* of words to express an idea expressed by someone else in different words, as when you reformulate a sentence in a text by choosing a different sentence to express the same statement.)

Consider this example in which the author, in effect, charges an argument with the fallacy of equivocation:

Example 9.34

Background: This letter is in response to a columnist who argued that nuclear deterrence did not work during the Cold War. (*New York Times*, 1/88)

> According to your columnist, if there is no sane or sensible way of using nuclear weapons, they can't be used, and if they can't be used, they can't have prevented war for the last 40 years. But that there isn't any sane use of nuclear weapons doesn't mean they can't be used. They obviously can still be used to punish an adversary who strikes first or to insure that such an adversary never attacks anyone else again.—R.L.H.

The author points out that the columnist's argument depends for its force on an equivocation on "used." The implicit conclusion of the columnist's argument is that nuclear weapons did not prevent war. The two conditional premises of that argument, cited in the first sentence of the text, each contain the term "used," but for the premises to be true, the term must mean something different in each case.

In one case it means sensible employment, and in the other it means employment, sensible or not. The author points out this difference in meaning.[26]

Here is an example of a fallacy charge of equivocation:

Example 9.35

Background: In the 1988 presidential campaign, candidate George H. Bush pledged to avoid new taxes, saying, "Read my lips; no new taxes." This letter was in response to that pledge. (*New York Times*, 12/88)

> As far as I can see, nothing will prevent Bush from proposing income tax increases to Congress, yet without violating his pledge of "no new taxes." Our income tax is an old tax dating back to 1913 and can hardly be called a new tax. George Bush did not promise no increase of existing taxes.—R.H.P.

Structure

> P1: Bush pledged no new taxes.
> P2: The income tax, dating back to 1913, is not a new tax.
> C: Therefore, Bush can propose increasing income taxes without breaking his pledge.

Evaluation

> I charge this argument with the fallacy of equivocation. The argument commits this fallacy because it contains an equivocation on the term "new tax." In P2, the term means "new kind of tax." But if "new tax" is interpreted in this way in P1, the premise is clearly false. Bush's pledge was clearly intended to mean "no increase in taxes."

9.3.3 Tendentiousness

Generally, a sentence is tendentious when it communicates a strong implicit point of view. Often, a sentence is tendentious because one of its terms has a strong expressive meaning, positive or negative. The point of view of such a sentence is implicit because it is hidden in the expressive meaning of a term. Sometimes, with the **tendentious use of language,** an author attempts to affect the beliefs of an audience by using such terms. We have already seen one kind of tendentiousness, namely, persuasive definition. But most cases of the tendentious use of language are not persuasive definitions.

Consider this example:

Example 9.36

Background: This letter is in response to an article reporting on an art auction. (*New York Times*, 5/99)

> Your article reports that when a Cezanne painting sold for $60.6 million at Sotheby's, "the salesroom burst into applause." Why this happens when unconscionable amounts of money are spent for works of art is mysterious.—J.W.

The author seeks to affect the beliefs of the audience about the purchase of paintings by referring to the amount paid in this case as "unconscionable." This is a term with a strong negative expressive meaning. Many terms in our language have strong expressive meanings, and so are tendentious, and we would have difficulty not using them even if we tried. But the problem with using a tendentious term is that it may mask the effect it can have on our beliefs. It may be true that too much money is spent on certain works of art, but we should consider whether this claim is true by considering the reasons for it. Labeling the money spent as "unconscionable" can tend to get us to accept the claim without considering the reasons.

Here is an example that makes this clear:

Example 9.37

Background: This is a portion of a letter about a newspaper's reporting on violence against abortion providers. (*New York Times*, 9/93)

> The use of the word "abortionist" in the headline of your report on the doctor who was shot and wounded outside his clinic was highly offensive to many physicians such as myself who provide abortion services. It is a highly charged word that is pejorative, derogatory and defamatory. It is most often used by anti-abortion fanatics in close company with words like "murderer," "baby-killer" and other slanderous phrases to describe physicians who perform abortions. The term "abortionist" has been used most often to describe illegal actors in a sleazy world of avaricious, incompetent criminals exploiting immoral women in a sordid and hazardous procedure. The world has changed, and I would hope your usage reflected that.—W.M.H.[27]

The author argues that referring to abortion providers as "abortionists" is a tendentious use of language, given the strong negative expressive meaning of the term. Given the term's expressive meaning, he claims, its use in this context is misleading. The term originally referred to the often unscrupulous persons who provided illegal, and often crude and dangerous, abortions prior to the legalization of the practice. This is the source of the term's negative expressive meaning. Clearly, the illegal abortions that had these characteristics should be condemned. But to use the term to refer to contemporary abortion services, which do not have these characteristics, is to imply that they too should be condemned. As in the previous case, we need to see the reasons for this claim.

Tendentious terms have different degrees of expressive meaning. Those with the highest degree of negative expressive meaning are described in a passage taken from the previous letter:

Example 9.38

> There are some words that are so laden with historically stigmatized meanings that they cannot be separated from the context, no matter how hard people may try to bring them into accepted use. Examples are "final solution," "ethnic purity" or "racial purity," or other terms associated with political totalitarianism or group discrimination.

This passage shows how the issue of tendentiousness is related to the contemporary controversy over hate speech. Some derogatory terms used to refer to groups of people have such strong negative expressive meaning that the question arises of whether, despite our concern for freedom of speech, we should prohibit their use in certain public contexts.

Often, a tendentious use of language does not stand alone, but is clearly part of an argument. Here is a simple example: "You cannot trust stupid Pat with elective office. So, do not vote for Pat." The first sentence is tendentious because it reflects the strong implicit point of view, represented by the term "stupid," that Pat is unworthy. By using the term, the author is presumably trying to convince the audience that Pat is unworthy. But here, the sentence involving the tendentious term is a premise of an argument, with the conclusion expressed in the second sentence. The author wants the audience to accept the alleged unworthiness of Pat as a reason not to vote for Pat, but there is no *evidence* that Pat is unworthy. The premise makes a claim that is not acceptable, a claim that needs support that it does not have. Thus, the argument is guilty of problematic premise. When an argument commits the fallacy of problematic premise due to the inclusion of terms of strong expressive meaning in its premises, this is an instance of the specific **fallacy of tendentiousness.**

Recall from our discussion of argument structuring in Chapter 4 that a single adjective in a text sentence can represent a claim that needs to be treated as a separate premise. This is often the case with arguments that commit the fallacy of tendentiousness. When an adjective or other term in an argumentative text has a strong expressive meaning that is relevant to the conclusion, the argument commits the fallacy of tendentiousness. The fallacy charge claims that that premise is not acceptable without a subargument, that is, without reasons to support what is implied by the tendentious term.

Here is another example, along with an evaluation:

Example 9.39

Background: This letter is about endangered species. (*Chicago Tribune,* 9/97)

> I'm very happy to hear that scientists *can't* get enough funds in order to *supposedly* save these "three-horned wartyback mussels" discussed in your article. To me, it shows that our society is finally starting to value human beings over and above animals and funneling money to help people rather than the overfunded, bleeding-heart liberal environmentalists movement.—T.G.

Structure

    P1: This lack of money shows that our society is finally starting to value human beings over animals.

    P2: The overfunded, bleeding-heart liberal environmentalists movement should not get more money.

      C: Therefore, it is good that scientists can't get enough funds in order to supposedly save these "three-horned wartyback mussels."

Evaluation

    I charge this argument with the fallacy of tendentiousness. P2 includes a tendentious use of language in referring to environmental groups as "overfunded,

bleeding-heart liberal." These terms have a strong negative expressive meaning, and their use is clearly meant to get the audience to accept the conclusion. But the premise needs support. The author needs to give reasons to
show that the criticism represented by these terms does apply to the groups
seeking to save endangered species. Part of the problem here is that the term
"bleeding-heart liberal" seems not to have any clear meaning, beyond its negative expressive meaning. The use of the term "supposedly" in the conclusion
is another instance of the tendentious use of language. It disparages the work
of the environmentalists without providing any evidence that their work is
less than sincere and effective.

This argument reveals two characteristics of many arguments that commit
the fallacy of tendentiousness. First, the tendentious terms involved are often very
unclear in their meaning, beyond the clear negativity of their expressive meaning.
The difficulty in clarifying the meaning of such terms is an additional problem with
many arguments that commit this fallacy. Without clarity of meaning, a strong subargument cannot be deployed. Second, the fallacy of tendentiousness is often
closely related to the fallacy of *ad hominem* (discussed in Chapter 6). Often, the tendentious term is applied to a person or group (such as environmentalists) that supports the position or view rejected in the conclusion. Some arguments that could
be charged with the fallacy of tendentiousness might also be charged with the fallacy of *ad hominem*, and vice versa.

> ### Tendentious Use of Language and the Fallacy of Tendentiousness
>
> The tendentious use of language is the use of a term or phrase that has
> strong expressive meaning, usually negative, in a way that is meant to
> affect the beliefs of an audience. The problem with a tendentious use of
> language is that it masks the fact that reasons need to be offered in sup-
> port of the implicit claim. When a tendentious use of language occurs in
> the premise of an argument and the expressive meaning has a bearing on
> the conclusion, the argument commits the fallacy of tendentiousness. This
> fallacy is a specific version of problematic premise because the premise
> needs support that is lacking.

There is one other use of language we should discuss: euphemisms, which are
a close cousin to tendentiousness. Tendentiousness involves an author labeling
something with a term that has a strong expressive meaning in order to influence
the audience's thinking about that thing. **Euphemisms,** in contrast, involve labeling something that an audience is already inclined to view negatively with a term
that has little or no expressive meaning to seek to counter the negative impression.
For example, because people tend to have a negative view of used cars, used car
salespeople have come to label them "pre-owned cars." Similarly, because people

tend to have a negative view of mobile homes, mobile home salespeople have come to label them "manufactured homes."

Euphemisms are often innocuous and no great source of critical concern. No one objects, for example, that a bowel movement is euphemistically labeled a "number 2." But sometimes it is important to call a spade a spade. In many cases, the use of euphemisms raises the same kind of problems as tendentiousness. They seek to affect our view of something without giving reasons. This occurs often in the military arena. For example, when civilians are killed in a military operation, this is often referred to as "collateral damage." During the Vietnam War, the destruction of rural villages and the transfer of their inhabitants to special camps was often referred to as "pacification." Such labels, by masking the nature of such policies and events, tend to blunt critical scrutiny of them. These events and policies may or may not have a strong argument in their favor, but we need to *see* the arguments, not simply have them relabeled.

Here is an example of an author being critical of a euphemism:

Example 9.40

Background: This letter is critical of the movement promoting greater volunteerism among citizens, such as put forth at a presidential summit under former President Clinton. (*Denver Post,* 5/97)

> Your columnist asks why conservatives are opposed to volunteerism as espoused by the presidential summit. There is a simple answer: Replace the term "volunteerism" with "involuntary servitude," and you may begin to understand the objection. That's what is really being proposed, after all.—E.F.

The author claims, in effect, that "volunteerism" is a euphemism for a policy that is in fact coerced service, or "involuntary servitude."

Euphemisms

Euphemisms involve the use of terms that lack expressive meaning (or are neutral in expressive meaning) to label things that people tend to have a negative view of, in an effort to ignore or mask what is negative about those things. Euphemisms are often innocuous, but they can be problematic in the same way that tendentiousness is. The label is a substitute for giving reasons to support the view that the thing in question should not be viewed negatively.

EXERCISE SET 9.3

SECTION A: For the following headlines, discuss any ambiguity you find.

EXAMPLE
Eye drops off shelf.

ANSWER

The double meaning in this headline results from ambiguity in the term "drops." One meaning, presumably the intended one, is of "drops" as a noun referring, in conjunction with the adjective "eye," to a liquid used to ease eye irritation. The second meaning, in which "drops" is a verb, is the event of falling, in which case "eye" becomes a noun, the thing that falls off the shelf.

PROBLEMS

1. Teachers strike idle kids.
2. Miners refuse to work after death.
❖ 3. Juvenile court to try shooting defendant.
4. Two sisters reunited after 18 years in checkout counter.
5. Red tape holds up new bridge.
❖ 6. Police begin campaign to run down jaywalkers.
7. Safety experts say school bus passengers should be belted.
8. Drunk gets nine months in violin case.
❖ 9. Farmer bill dies in House.
10. Stud tires out.
11. Panda mating fails; vet takes over.
❖ 12. British left waffles on Falkland Islands.
13. Squad helps dog bite victim.
14. Women are more interested in religion than men.

SECTION B: Charge the following arguments with the fallacy of equivocation.

EXAMPLE

No cat has two tails. But every cat has one more tail than no cat. So every cat has three tails.

ANSWER

P1: No cat has two tails.
P2: Every cat has one more tail than no cat.
C: Therefore, every cat has three tails.

I charge this argument with the fallacy of equivocation. The term "no cat" has a different meaning in each of the premises, and the reasoning depends on this shift in meaning. In P1, the term means "there is no cat," and in P2, it means "that which is not a cat." If the term meant in P1 what it means in P2, P1 would be "that which is not a cat has two tails," which is clearly false.

PROBLEMS

1. Hamburger is better than nothing, and nothing is better than steak. So, hamburger is better than steak.[28]
2. There's nothing wrong with stimulants such as amphetamines because, as psychologists tell us, everyone needs stimulation in life.
❖ 3. The end of things is their perfection, and the end of human beings is their death. So, the perfection of human beings is their death.
4. All people are equal, and if people are equal, there is no reason to treat them differently. So, no one should be treated differently than anyone else.
5. Everyday we witness the miracles of modern science. So, no one should reject the literal truth of the Bible because it contains reports of miracles.

❖   6. Mother to child: Now that you have discovered that I did not intend to become pregnant when I had you, you are concerned about your having been an accident. But this should not worry you. Everyone is an accident, since anyone's parents might never have met.

7. A convicted criminal is not innocent. Therefore, no convicted criminal who proclaims his innocence can be telling the truth.

8. GLENDOWER: I can call spirits from the vasty deep.
HOTSPUR: Why, so can I, or so can any man;
But will they come when you do call for them?[29]

SECTION C: The following texts criticize others for using incorrect terms to label things. Often, the criticisms amount to claims that the incorrect labeling is tendentious. Discuss the criticisms and any arguments provided for them. Also indicate whether the authors would regard the labeling they criticize as tendentious (including euphemistic). You need not consider fallacy charges because most of the authors do not report arguments of those they criticize.

EXAMPLE

Background: This letter is critical of a label used by a columnist. (*New York Times*, 3/00)

I believe that what your columnist and many other Americans refer to as the "moral meltdown" in this country is rather a moral diversification. In the last century this country has undergone profound changes, both in social structure and, more impressively, in the variety of its members' heritage. Yet some see this as nothing more than a moral failure. The morals of a time are and always have been subject to change.—T.M.

ANSWER

The author criticizes the columnist for referring to the United States as being in a state of "moral meltdown." Instead, the author claims, the state is one of moral diversification. There is an argument for this, which is that the moral views of a society are always subject to change over time, due, in the case of the United States, to major social changes and immigration of people from diverse cultures. The author clearly regards the term "moral meltdown" as tendentious, in that it indicates failure. The moral changes, in the eyes of the author, do not indicate failure.

PROBLEMS

1. Background: This letter is about the use of seat belts in automobiles. (*New York Times*, 6/97)

   Narrowly defining seat-belt usage as driver "self-protection," overlooks the restraint's safety role in keeping a driver in place: at the vehicle controls during multiple-event collisions and severe maneuvering in accident avoidance. In these cases, a vehicle with an unbelted driver flung from its controls has the potential of becoming an unguided missile. Viewed in this light, seat belt usage is not a matter of libertarian choice but a civic responsibility.—M.C.B.

2. Background: This letter is about a newspaper description of a suspect in a shooting that took place at a fast-food restaurant. (*New York Times*, 6/00)

Your reference to a suspect in the Wendy's massacre as the person "who is thought to have been the architect of the crime" is a most unfortunate analogy that many in my profession would take issue with.—P.S.

3. Background: This letter is in response to news of a knee injury suffered by former President Bill Clinton. (*Miami Herald*, 3/97)

   I object to your headline "Clinton faces grueling rehab." I am disabled, and I have some knowledge of rehabilitation. President Clinton is unfortunate to have suffered a physical injury, but, by his own admission, his life has been free from serious injury. He is dealing with a temporary inconvenience and will get better. The *Herald* prides itself on not being sensational, but it needs to look closer at its use of language when reporting a story.—D.N.

4. Background: This letter is about the vice-presidential candidate on the Democratic ticket in 2000. (*New York Times*, 8/00)

   As a nonagenarian who could recite a litany of personal anti-Semitic episodes, I am proud, as an American, and pleased, as a Jew, by Joseph I. Lieberman's vice-presidential candidacy. But I am critical of its foundation in "tolerance," a term I have always associated with the ethnocentric condescension of a "we" group toward a "they" group. Mr. Lieberman's candidacy is but a step in the direction of the country's maturation. Our democratic processes will really be mature when religious affiliations play little or no role in determining a candidate's qualifications.—D.L.C.

5. Background: This letter is about the law. (*New York Times*, 1/98)

   Your article about Pepperdine Law School quotes a student as saying that professors urge them not to "try and get off on your little technicalities." That is bad advice. A lawyer's obligation is to fight for the client zealously. More important, there is no such thing as a "technicality." In common parlance the word "technicality" refers to a law that the user of the term believes to be trivial or unimportant; it is most frequently used in the context of a criminal defendant whose rights have been violated.—D.R.D.

6. Background: This letter is about the Monica Lewinsky scandal that plagued the second term of former President Clinton. Kenneth Starr was the special prosecutor who investigated the scandal. (*New York Times*, 10/98)

   Your columnists describe the numerous allegations in the Starr report in only nine words: "having and concealing an affair in the White House." Another description of the Starr allegations might be: "repeated lying, and encouraging other witnesses to lie, in grand jury and discovery proceedings." Such conduct subverts the judicial process, which collapses if witnesses testify falsely.—P.E.

7. Background: This letter responds to an article on pesticides and produce. (*Boston Globe*, 6/97)

   You put the wrong headline on your story about the very low levels of pesticide residues found on fruits and vegetables ("Pesticides on produce leave residue of worry"). The title should have read "Don't Worry, Eat Healthy," since your investigation found only traces of pesticides. Instead, you seem to want to scare people away from the fruits and vegetables that have proven health benefits. For the good of public health we must encourage people to eat more fruits and vegetables not discourage them with scare stories about trivial risks.—G.M.G.

8. Background: This letter criticizes a columnist who objected to President Bush's proposed tax cut on the grounds that it favored the wealthy. (*New York Times*, 8/00)

Your columnist may be correct that George W. Bush's tax-cut plan provides greater tax savings to high-income Americans. But he does not mention the important fact that the tax increases of [former] Presidents Bush and Clinton disproportionately affected higher-income families, and they—on a dollar basis—have contributed most of the money that makes up today's surplus. To reduce taxes now primarily for lower-income Americans is tantamount to government-sponsored wealth distribution. If this is what your columnist and Al Gore want, they should simply say so.—D.S.

 9. Background: This letter is in response to a report on the work of a scientist who had done research on the relationship between mother and fetus. (*New York Times*, 8/93)

The scientist's work on the "conflict" between fetus and pregnant woman, which you describe, provides a useful example of the extent to which readers need to become conscious of the amount of interpretation that occurs in supposedly "scientific" studies. In the "tug-of-war" the scientist describes, he speaks of fetuses out to "protect" their "own interests," of woman and fetus involved in an elaborate series of "move" and "countermove." Why such images of war to describe chemical reactions in the body? In "Illness as Metaphor" Susan Sontag offered a startling critique of the destructiveness of using warlike metaphors to describe cancer. Is there something about the representations of women by patriarchal societies and perhaps the particular status of women in our culture today that feeds these fantasies of war in the womb?—K.M.

10. Background: This letter is about the economic sanctions imposed on Iraq as a result of the 1991 Persian Gulf War, sanctions designed to guarantee that Iraq eliminate its weapons of mass destruction. (*Chicago Tribune*, 3/98)

The U.S.-backed sanctions are responsible for the deaths of more than 70,000 Iraqi children, according to UN estimates. Almost the same number of adults—particularly seniors and other vulnerable people—also have perished since 1991 in this cruel war of starvation and disease against Iraq's people. It's high time to lift these horrible sanctions. Holding civilians hostage for political goals is often described as "terrorism." Isn't that precisely what we have here? State terrorism by our own government against an Arab people?—M.A.

SECTION D: Examine the following arguments for equivocation and tendentiousness. Structure and evaluate (no tree diagrams necessary) those that can be so changed.

EXAMPLE

Background: This letter is in response to a column critical of U.S. educational policy. (*Boston Globe*, 9/97)

The column captures the essence of what is wrong with education in America today. Our eggheads have changed education from a process of learning about a definite body of knowledge into a process of learning about an indefinite process of learning. We need to teach content, not process.—E.J.F.

ANSWER

P1: Egghead policy makers have changed education from a process of learning about a definite body of knowledge into a process of learning about an indefinite process of learning.

C: Therefore, we should return to teaching that focuses on content rather than process.

I charge this argument with the fallacy of tendentiousness. In P1, the author refers to those responsible for educational policy as "eggheads." This is a somewhat derogatory term applied to those who are intellectuals and out of touch with everyday reality. The author suggests that, because the policy makers are out of touch, so is the policy, leading to the conclusion that it should be rejected. It may be true that the policy makers are out of touch, and this may be a reason for rejecting the policy, but the argument needs to be made. The premise needs support that it does not receive.

PROBLEMS

1. Background: This letter is in response to a column recommending that Christmas trees be placed in a bag when discarded. (*New York Times*, 1/88)

    To save the homeowner two or three minutes of sweeping or vacuuming, you suggest wrapping or "bagging" a tree in plastic ("white vinyl," I'm sure was your choice of words to make it appealing). To suggest that the public should add millions of large vinyl bags to the ecosystem for the sake of a few fallen pine needles pangs the heart.—L.C.S.

2. Background: This letter is in response to the government's policy of asking that those who fill out certain forms indicate their race. (*Finger Lakes Times*, 9/97)

    Many Americans don't know that the U.S. government has five official racial classifications, which appear on census forms and hundreds of other government documents. Libertarians believe the government of a country dedicated to liberty and equality under the law has no business asking Americans about their race. By boycotting the census question on race, you can help bring the politicians' framework for American Apartheid crashing down to the ground.—J.R.

3. Background: This letter, from an alumnus, is critical of Dartmouth College's decision to force its fraternities and sororities to become coed. (*USA Today*, 2/99)

    The board's decision to embark on such a profound and rash course without input from alumni or the student body is indicative of irresponsible leaders who warrant removal from their positions. Dartmouth's action indicates college administrators are willing to pander to a small, vocal minority while sacrificing the needs and wishes of the majority.—T.K.S.

4. Background: This letter is about the government's antitrust action against Microsoft. (*New York Times*, 5/98)

   William H. Gates, the chairman of Microsoft, has frequently demonstrated his ignorance of the reasons for our antitrust laws. His statement that the Government "would put everything we've worked for and built for the last 23 years at risk" shows he believes that Microsoft's having achieved success, it no longer should be at risk. But the essence of business is that there is return for risk and that if there is no risk, there should be no return. Let Mr. Gates sell his stock and buy Government bonds if he wants to be free from risk. If he still desires the potential for further gains, he should be willing to accept the risk of loss.—A.C.D.

5. Background: This letter is about the role of international organizations in the transition of the former Soviet Union from communism to a market economy. (*New York Times*, 7/98)

   Russia's ostensible transition to a free market economy leads it to stop paying salaries and pensions and to destroy its social safety net. The international money police argue that the eventual benefits of this shift justify what amounts to the sacrifice of the older generation of less endowed Russian workers.—E.S.

❖ 6. Background: This letter is part of the debate over capital punishment. (*New York Times*, 2/95)

   The district attorney contends that there is no credible evidence that executions deter crime. Nonsense! The inescapable fact is that no convicted murderer executed by the state has ever killed again. It's too bad we can't say that about all the convicted murderers who are later set free. While it might make us feel better if we knew the death penalty deterred others, that's beside the point.—C.B.

7. Background: This letter is in response to proposals to ban some forms of gambling. (*Boston Globe*, 9/97)

   I grow increasingly frustrated by media and government notables who have decided that they know what is best for me. I am in a low-income bracket, and I gamble. The national busybodies have decided that I shouldn't do this, so the push is on to ban Keno, casinos, scratch tickets, and the like. Why am I not free to choose to waste my money? Why is it that the only choice people are allowed to have concerns abortion? There are loud, nasty little groups that want to ban gambling, smoking, fatty food, gas-burning cars, perfume, beauty contests, hunting, fishing, etc. These people must be taught a lesson. They must be taught to leave people alone.—K.I.B.

8. Background: This letter is part of the debate over gun control. (*Chicago Tribune*, 4/97)

In your editorial you say that the idea of permitting citizens to carry concealed weapons is nonsense. I disagree. Our streets are crawling with violent criminals created by disgracefully asinine social policies and unpunished and undeterred by an insane and ineffectual criminal law system. At the same time, government has no duty to—and indeed cannot—protect its citizens against crime. As our once-great nation has slid ever deeper into collectivist quicksand, the right to own and carry firearms has deteriorated to the point that now we must fight even to be allowed to beg our rulers for permission to protect our own lives.—D.V.W.

❖ 9. Background: This letter is in support of the National Endowment for the Arts, a federal agency providing funding for artists. (*San Francisco Chronicle*, 7/97)

The issue is purely one of free speech. The essence of any art form is freedom of expression. This is supposedly the country where that is an inalienable right granted us by our forefathers. What more appropriate use of government funding than to support artists so that they may be free to express themselves without the constraints of the commercial marketplace where the lowest common denominator becomes the standard and is often mislabeled art.—M.M.

Summary

Understanding the meaning of the language of an argument is crucial to understanding the argument and to evaluating its content. Concepts are the meaning of terms (words or phrases), as statements are the meanings of sentences. Uncertainty about the meaning of terms has different sources. First, it may be due to ignorance. Second, it may be due to ambiguity, when a term has different meanings and the context in which it is used does not make clear which meaning is intended. Third, it may be due to vagueness, when the term, in the context in which it is used, does not have a clear meaning and clarification of the meaning is called for. A conceptual statement goes beyond a dictionary definition to clarify the meaning of a term that is vague in the particular context in which it is used.

Conceptual statements are often expressed in conditionals, indicating either necessary or sufficient conditions for the use of a term. When a conditional is used, the conceptual statement is partial. Complete conceptual statements, expressing both necessary and sufficient conditions for the use of the term, are expressed in biconditionals. Biconditionals are compound statements in which the component statements are connected with the logical connective "if and only if."

Conceptual statements, like other statements, can be supported by arguments known as conceptual arguments. Conceptual statements also may be premises of arguments, though conceptual premises are frequently implicit. Conceptual statements are controversial, so they are not acceptable if not supported by an argument. So, whenever a conceptual premise lacks a supporting subargument, this is grounds for a charge of problematic premise or false premise. Disputes over conceptual statements are serious matters, unlike merely verbal disputes, in which the disputants use an ambiguous term in different ways.

Definitions are statements of the conventions regarding the use of terms. Usually, these are conventions that exist among the speakers of the language, in which case the definition reports them and is referred to as a reportive definition. Sometimes, the conventions are not existing conventions, but proposed conventions, or stipulative definitions. One important kind of stipulative definition is a persuasive definition, in which an author seeks to influence people's beliefs about something by offering a stipulative definition of it that contains terms with strong (positive or negative) expressive meaning.

The part of a definition that contains the term being defined is the *definiendum*, and the part that indicates the conditions for the term's use is the *definiens*. Definitions are extensional when they refer to all of the things to which the term applies, and they are intensional when they refer to the conditions for the use of the term. One important form of intensional definition gives the conditions in terms of genus and species. The genus is a general category to which the things referred to by the term belong, and the species is the characteristics that distinguish these things from other things in the general category. A reportive definition can be too broad, too narrow, or both. Accuracy can be assessed through the method of counterexample (for definitions).

Sometimes, the incautious or incorrect use of language in the presentation of an argument is a fallacy. The fallacy of ambiguity occurs when a term in an argument has semantic ambiguity or a sentence in an argument has syntactic ambiguity, and the context of the argumentative text does not make the meaning clear. The fallacy of equivocation occurs when an ambiguous term is used in two different ways in the same argument, and the apparent strength of the argument depends on the change in meaning. The fallacy of tendentiousness occurs when a premise of an argument contains terms with strong expressive meaning, and the author relies on that meaning to lead the audience to accept the conclusion. The author fails to give reasons to support the claim implicit in the expressive meaning of the term.

Key Terms

concept

ambiguity

vagueness

conceptual argument

conceptual premise

biconditional

partial conceptual statement

full conceptual statement

merely verbal dispute

definition

partial definition

general term

reportive definition

stipulative definition

persuasive definition

intensional definition

extensional
definition

definiendum

definiens

definition by genus
and species

method of
counterexample
(for definitions)

semantic ambiguity

syntactic ambiguity

fallacy of ambiguity

equivocation

fallacy of
equivocation

tendentious use of
language

fallacy of
tendentiousness

euphemisms

Notes

1. Recall that the truth value of a statement is its status as true or false. For example, the truth value of "ice is frozen water" is true. For a discussion of the notion of truth value, see Chapter 7.
2. Clinton's grand jury testimony as recorded at <washingtonpost.com/wp-srv/politics/special/clinton/stories/bctest092198_4.htm> in May 1999.
3. A different confusion about the meaning of the verb "to be" is at work in this children's joke: Sally says, "I'm hungry"; Fred responds, "No you're not; you're Sally!"
4. *New York Times*, February 25, 1994.
5. *New York Times*, June 28, 1992.
6. *New York Times*, May 14, 1999.
7. Earlier in the chapter, we used an example of another ambiguous term, "bank."
8. That terms are vague in some of their uses is not necessarily a defect in language. Rather, it seems to be that in describing the world we need the flexibility that vague terms provide. We need vague terms that we can in context seek to make more precise. This seems to be an essential part of the way that language relates to the world and the basis of our ability to use language to talk about the world.
9. For a discussion of this idea, see H. L. A. Hart, *The Concept of Law* (Oxford: Oxford University Press, 1961), Chapter 7.
10. For the purposes of this discussion, the factual dimension should be understood to include matters of value as well. As argued earlier, value statements can be objectively disputed. Values are part of "the way the world is" in a broad sense.
11. More generally, as we shall see, it is whether the analytic statement corresponds to an existing convention, the dictionary being one source of such conventions.
12. For a discussion of the status of Pluto, see Malcolm Browne, "A Minor Fracas over a Small, but Not Quite Minor, Planet," *New York Times*, February 9, 1999, and Kenneth Chang, "Pluto's Not a Planet? Only in New York," *New York Times*, January 22, 2001.
13. Another example in which the practical effects of the adoption of one conceptual statement rather than another are evident is the abortion issue. Is a fetus a person? Whether we should allow abortion may depend in part on which conceptual statement making more precise the vague term "person" we adopt.
14. Charles Darwin, *On the Origin of Species* (Cambridge, MA: Harvard University Press, 1964), p. 39.
15. In logic, this is the distinction between token and type.

16. Proper names are discussed briefly in Chapter 5. One interesting issue sometimes raised in theological discussions is whether "god" is a general term or a proper name.

17. Reportive definitions, because they are contained in dictionaries, are also referred to as lexical definitions ("lexicon" being another word for dictionary).

18. James Madison, *The Federalist* 10, in Jacob Cooke (ed.), *The Federalist* (Middletown, CT: Wesleyan University Press, 1961), p. 61.

19. The second and third of these definitions are adapted from Irving Copi and Carl Cohen, *Introduction to Logic*, 9th ed. (New York: Macmillan, 1994), p. 176.

20. As we saw earlier, "is" is an ambiguous term. Indeed, it is ambiguous in several different ways. The relevant ambiguity here is between what is called the "is" of identity and the "is" of predication. The "is" of identity, which is the one in definitions, indicates that the subject and the predicate of the sentence refer to the same thing. In contrast, the "is" of predication indicates only that the thing referred to by the subject has the property indicated by the predicate.

21. A circular definition is like an argument that begs the question; see Chapter 8.

22. Recall that in Chapter 6 we discussed a method of counterexample that applies to argument forms rather than definitions.

23. The metaphorical use of a term is based on an analogy between the sorts of things to which the term applies in its standard use and the things to which it is applied in its metaphorical use. The topic of analogy is discussed in Chapter 11.

24. Recall that ambiguity is different from vagueness. Whereas ambiguity is more than one clear meaning, vagueness is lack of any clear meaning.

25. Ambiguity can occur in a conclusion as well as in a premise. As a result, it is possible to charge a conclusion with the fallacy of ambiguity.

26. This argument raises the issue, much discussed during the Cold War, of the *credibility* of nuclear threats. If the weapons could be used only irrationally, could the threat to use them be effective at deterring an opponent?

27. The author of this letter is Warren M. Hern, M.D.

28. This exercise and the example exercise are borrowed from Robert Martin, *There Are Two Errors in the the Title of This Book* (Peterborough, Canada: Broadview Press, 1992), p. 57.

29. Shakespeare, *King Henry IV*, part 1, act 3, scene 1, lines 52–53.

CHAPTER 10

Induction and Causal Arguments

Those who cannot remember the past are condemned to repeat it.

—GEORGE SANTAYANA[1]

Arguments are either deductive or nondeductive. This distinction is drawn, as we have seen, in terms of argument form. Deductive arguments, when successful, are valid, but nondeductive arguments cannot be valid. Validity is the highest degree of formal argument strength. An argument is valid when it is impossible for the premises to be true and the conclusion to be false. Nondeductive arguments invariably fall short of this degree of formal strength.

In this chapter and the next, we take a closer look at nondeductive arguments. Specifically, we examine inductive and causal arguments in this chapter, and all-things-considered and analogical arguments in the next chapter.

10.1 Inductive Arguments

An **inductive argument,** in its most basic form, is an argument that generalizes from claims about individual cases known from experience. An induction goes from singular statements (premises) to a general statement (the conclusion). Consider this argument:

Example 10.1

Background: This letter is part of the debate about blame and responsibility for African American slavery. (*Boston Globe,* 12/97)

> Not only did Africans capture and sell slaves during the slave trade, but Jews betrayed Jews in Nazi Germany, Colonials became collaborators during the American Revolution, and brother betrayed brother in the Civil War. There will always be a Judas as long as there's a market.—V.G.

This is an inductive argument in that it *generalizes* on what we know from experience. Its conclusion thus is an **empirical generalization.**

10.1.1 Empirical Generalizations

The author of the preceding letter makes claims about four particular groups of people—that each has included traitors. Based on these claims, he draws a conclusion, expressed in the last sentence, that all groups contain traitors. Here is a reformulation of that generalization: All groups have members who are willing to betray other members of the group. The argument moves from a set of singular claims to a general claim—in this case, a universal generalization. Here is one way the argument might be structured:

Example 10.2

P1: Africans betrayed other Africans to slave traders.

P2: Jews betrayed other Jews to the Nazis.

P3: Colonials betrayed fellow Colonials to the British during the American Revolution.

P4: Family members betrayed their families during the Civil War.

C: Therefore, all groups have members who are willing to betray other members of the group.

The conclusion of this inductive argument is a universal generalization, but inductive arguments may also have conclusions that are nonuniversal generalizations. For example, if the author of this argument had concluded that *most* groups have traitors or that *many* groups have traitors, the argument would still have been inductive. One common way of expressing a conclusion that is a nonuniversal generalization is to use the phrase "tends to," as in "groups tend to have traitors."

Inductive Arguments and Empirical Generalizations

An inductive argument is a nondeductive argument. In its basic form, an inductive argument has premises that are singular statements and a conclusion that is a universal or nonuniversal generalization. The reasoning is from the particular instances discussed in the premises to the general case. An inductive argument is based on experience, as reflected in the claims of the premises, and has a conclusion that is a generalization about that experience. The conclusion is, thus, an empirical generalization.

In an inductive argument, the conclusion is usually expressed in a categorical statement. It is a generalization about *some category of thing*, a claim that all or many members of that category have some *characteristic* in common. In the case of the preceding argument, the category is human groups, and the characteristic is having members who are traitors. The **population** is all the members of the category that an inductive argument is about. In this case, the population is human groups. The premises refer to some particular members of that population, claiming that each of them has the characteristic. Those members of the category referred to in the premises are known collectively as the **sample.** So, in its basic form, an inductive argument generalizes from a sample to the population. The premises *enumerate* the members of the sample, claiming that each of them has the characteristic. Thus, the basic form of an inductive argument is an **induction by enumeration.**

> ### Populations, Samples, and Induction by Enumeration
>
> In an inductive argument, in its basic form, the premises make claims that some members of a category have some characteristic, and the conclusion makes a claim that that characteristic applies to all or most members of that category. The members of the category referred to in the premises are known collectively as the sample, and all the members of the group are known collectively as the population. The premises enumerate some members of the category, so this kind of argument is referred to as induction by enumeration.

In an inductive argument, in its basic form, the premises and the conclusion are all empirical statements, claims based on our observation and experience about the way the world is. The premises of the argument about group traitors are empirical statements about actions that some people have taken in the past. Like all empirical statements, they are based on observations. For example, if I look out of the window and then say that the sun is shining, this is an empirical statement based on my own observation. If I claim that the sun is shining because someone has told me it is, this is still an empirical statement, based on observation, even if the observation is not my own. While the premises of the argument about betrayal are obviously not based on observations by the author, they are based on the author's beliefs about history, and these beliefs are based on the observations of others. In addition, the premises, as is true in general of nondeductive arguments, are convergent.

The conclusion in the betrayal argument is also an empirical statement, a claim about the way the world is. But, because it is a generalization, the conclusion is not based *directly* on experience and observation in the way that the singular claims in the premises are. Rather, it is a generalization on that experience. We make such generalizations precisely by formulating inductive arguments—that is, by generalizing from our experience of a sample of a population to the population as a whole. The premises and conclusion are empirical claims, and the conclusion is a generalization supported by the singular claims of the premises. In an inductive argument, we go from the observed to the unobserved, because the conclusion makes a claim about all or most members of the category, including those that have not been observed, at least not yet.

10.1.2 The Role of Inductive Arguments

Generalizing from experience is the way in which we *learn* from experience. Consider this argument:

Example 10.3

Background: This letter is about the 1999 NATO military campaign against Serbia over its treatment of the ethnic Albanians in the province of Kosovo. It is in response to a report that the bombing by NATO forces had angered the Serbs and increased their commitment to the war. (*USA Today*, 3/99)

> The article suggests that philosopher George Santayana was correct in his observation that those who cannot remember the past are condemned to repeat it. During World War II, the Nazis bombed England, hoping to subdue her, yet the raids had just the opposite effect. Bombing Iraq does not appear to have seriously affected its regime. Can we really expect different results by bombing the Serbs?—L.W.Z.

This author gives an inductive argument, but as a subargument rather than the main argument. Its conclusion is implicit, an intermediate implicit premise (see Chapter 5). The main argument has as its conclusion that NATO's bombing of Serbia will not be effective. The conclusion is supported by the generalization that bombing is ineffective in winning a war, which in turn is supported by an inductive subargument. The inductive subargument has two premises, that the Nazi bombing of England was counterproductive and that the bombing of Iraq has been ineffective. These are the members of the sample, with the population being all policies of military bombing.

We can structure the argument in this way:

Example 10.4

PIA: The Nazi bombing of England was counterproductive.
PIB: The bombing of Iraq has not been effective in changing its government.
IIP1: Bombing is not an effective military policy.
C: NATO's bombing of Serbia will not be effective.

Appropriately, the author cites the famous aphorism of the American philosopher George Santayana that appears at the beginning of the chapter. This should be a motto for all those who recognize the importance of learning from experience. According to the author, we should have learned from experience that bombing is not an effective military policy. In other words, because bombing has been ineffective in the past, as indicated by P1A and P1B, NATO should have recognized the truth of the universal generalization IIP1 that bombing is not an effective military policy. (As it turned out, however, NATO bombing led Serbia to withdraw from Kosovo.)

Learning is largely learning not to repeat mistakes—for example, not to touch the hot stove again, not to rely again on a faithless companion, or not to eat the bitter fruit again. The long-term survival prospects of a species are greatly enhanced by the ability of its members to learn from their mistakes, which is why intelligence is in evolutionary terms a valuable survival trait. In humans, intelligence has developed to the point at which learning from experience is given linguistic representation in inductive arguments. That is, we can make explicit what other animals seem to do implicitly. Our ability to formulate generalizations, and the inductive arguments through which we do so, permit a much more powerful form of learning from experience. Not only can we learn more from experience, but we can pass on what we learn to each other and to future generations. We pride ourselves on our ability to learn from experience ("Fool me once, shame on you; fool me twice, shame on me").

We derive empirical generalizations through inductive arguments based on singular claims arising from experience. This is true even of the most common and commonsensical empirical generalizations—for example, that the sun rises every morning, that bread nourishes and a stone does not, that concrete is hard and pillows are soft, or that the pavement on which we walk will support our weight. Without taking such generalizations for granted, we could not live our day-to-day lives.

Some empirical generalizations are based on only a few instances. The inductive arguments for these have only a small number of premises, as in Examples 10.2 and 10.4. Others, like the commonsensical ones mentioned in the previous paragraph, are based on a very large number of instances. Each of us has eaten bread many times, and the number of instances in which other persons may have communicated to us their experience of eating bread is, of course, larger still. As a result, the inductive argument with the conclusion that bread nourishes could have a very large number of premises indeed. Often, especially when a large number of potential premises support an inductive generalization, the inductive argument is presented with a **condensed premise** that refers collectively to all members of the sample. Consider this example:

Example 10.5

P1: All the pine trees I know of have kept their needles in the winter.
C: Therefore, all pine trees keep their needles in the winter.

P1 is a condensed premise that refers to a very large number of pine trees. P1 takes the place of perhaps hundreds of premises, each of which would attribute the characteristic of keeping its needles in the winter to some particular pine tree.

> ### Condensed Premises
>
> A condensed premise in an inductive argument is a single premise that refers collectively to all members of the sample. A condensed premise stands in for a series of premises, each of which would refer to one member of the sample.

As the preceding examples show, inductive arguments are nondeductive. That is, even if the premises are true, it is possible for the conclusions to be false. For instance, for all we know, there may be some groups that do not contain traitors, some bombings that have been militarily effective,[2] and some pine trees that lose their needles in the winter. Inductive arguments cannot be valid. Therefore, when we evaluate them in formal terms, we rate them in terms of degrees of strength short of validity. Even if the form of an inductive argument is strong and its premises are all true, the truth of the conclusion is not guaranteed. We can never know *for certain* that a universal empirical generalization is true. A cliché of inductive logic is that there is no absolute guarantee that the sun will rise tomorrow or that all humans are mortal. Not only are we not acquainted with all the humans who have ever existed, but those who will exist in the future cannot be known now.[3] The fact that inductive arguments are nondeductive is closely related to our inability to predict the future with unerring reliability. After all, it is possible that the sun will *not* rise tomorrow.

In the process of generalization, we move from cases we know about (the sample, as referred to in the premises) to cases we do not know about (the rest of the members of the population, as referred to in the conclusion). If the form of an inductive argument is strong and its premises are true, it may give us very good reason to think that all of the members of the population share the characteristic. In fact, we have good reason to think that other humans will turn out to be mortal and that the sun will rise tomorrow.[4] The key point is simply that an inductive argument, no matter how many true premises it contains, cannot show that it is impossible for the conclusion to be false. This is because the enumeration that is the basis of an inductive argument is only *partial*. The premises enumerate some cases, but not all.

The force of inductive arguments is based on the **regularity of nature.** The idea here is that nature functions in a regular way, and through inductive logic, we can discover the regularities. These regularities are often referred to as the laws of nature. But even if nature is uniform in this way, operating invariably according to laws or regularities, this still does not allow us to assert that it is impossible for the conclusion of a strong inductive argument with true premises to be false. The reason is that we can never be sure that we have the regularities right.

One example of the difficulty in getting the regularities right involves Newton's and Einstein's theories of motion. Specifically, Newton claimed that the mass

> ## The Regularity of Nature
>
> Nature is regular. Events in nature repeat themselves according to patterns that we can discover. In other words, nature operates according to rules, referred to as the laws of nature, represented by empirical generalizations. Often, these empirical generalizations express general causal statements.

of an object does not vary with its speed. There was much inductive evidence for this argument, because prior to the twentieth century no variation in mass had ever been observed among objects moving at different speeds. Einstein argued that mass does vary with motion, but measurably only at speeds approaching that of light. Indeed, once scientists developed techniques for measuring the mass of objects (subatomic particles) moving that fast, empirical observation supported Einstein's rather than Newton's claim. Newton was wrong, not because nature turned out not to be regular, but because he got the regularities wrong.

10.1.3 Nonuniversal Generalizations

To this point, our examples of inductive arguments have had universal generalizations as conclusions. This is not always the case. Instead of concluding that "all A are B," we may conclude that "many A are B" or that "A are often B." Consider this argument:

Example 10.6

Background: This is part of a letter on capital punishment, regarding cases in which the radical political views of those executed played an important role in public perceptions. (*Washington Post,* 1/89)

> The death penalty is often misused for political purposes. Would John Brown have been hanged if abolition had not been an issue then? Would the Haymarket defendants or Joe Hill have been executed, if they had not been labor organizers when that was considered a crime? Sacco and Vanzetti if they had not been foreign-born anarchists and if their trial had not taken place during one of our periodic Red scares? Julius and Ethel Rosenberg, if they had been convicted of spying for, say, England instead of Russia? Or if their trial had not taken place at the height of the Cold War?
> —R.E.H.

The conclusion, expressed in the first sentence, is that capital punishment is often misused for political purposes, a nonuniversal generalization. The author presents several cases in which capital punishment has been misused in this way but does not conclude that capital punishment is always so misused. He apparently does not regard the evidence as sufficient to show that capital punishment is always misused for political purposes.

The claim that capital punishment is often misused for political purposes is *weaker* than the claim that it is always so misused. In this sense, a nonuniversal generalization is weaker than the corresponding universal generalization. It is located closer to the origin point in strength space (discussed in Chapter 5). When a statement is weaker, it is easier to prove. Authors generally offer a nonuniversal generalization as the conclusion when they do not regard the evidence as strong enough to establish the corresponding universal generalization.

This shows again that careful reformulation of the conclusion in the argument structuring is important. If you misrepresent the author's nonuniversal generalization as a universal generalization, you make the conclusion harder to prove and so open up the argument to a fallacy charge that might not be fair or appropriate. Here, as elsewhere, however, an author's intentions are not always clear. Quantifiers are sometimes implicit. As discussed in Chapter 5, if a sentence that expresses a general statement lacks a quantifier, you need to determine, as best you can from the context, what quantifier the author intended. This applies as well for general statements that are conclusions of inductive arguments.

Moreover, we saw in Chapter 5 that strength space is two-dimensional. Strength can vary not only in the scope of the quantifier (such as "all" and "many"), which distinguishes universal from nonuniversal generalizations, but also by the inclusion of modal phrases, such as "likely" and "possibly" that indicate how certain the author is of the truth of the conclusion. The conclusions of inductive arguments can vary in both of these ways, and it is important to represent the conclusion correctly in both respects.

One quantifier merits special mention. The quantifier "some," as we saw in Chapter 7, means "at least one." Thus, "some" would not be an appropriate quantifying phrase for the conclusion of an inductive argument. If the conclusion of an inductive argument used the quantifying term "some," the conclusion would be an immediate inference from any one of the premises (If any particular A is B, then some A are B). Such an argument would thus not be inductive; it would be deductive. For example, it would be an immediate inference, not an inductive argument, to conclude from the fact that Kofi Anan is secretary general of the United Nations that some people are secretary general of the United Nations.

10.1.4 Statistical Inductive Arguments

In the inductive arguments we have considered so far, the premises refer only to instances of the category that have the characteristic in question. In other words, all members of the sample have the characteristic. Whether or not the conclusion asserts that the characteristic is universal among the population, the characteristic is universal among the members of the sample. This is a basic inductive argument.

A different type of inductive argument, known as a **statistical inductive argument,** has two features that distinguish it from the basic case. First, the sample includes members that have the characteristic and members that do not, and the premise makes a claim about the proportion of the sample that has the characteristic. Second, the conclusion is a nonuniversal generalization that indicates that the same portion of the population has the characteristic.

Consider these three inductive arguments, each with a condensed premise:

Example 10.7

A. All the people I have known have tried alcohol.
   Therefore, all people have tried alcohol.
B. Most (but not all) of the people I have known have tried alcohol.
   Therefore, most people have tried alcohol.
C. Eighty percent of the people I have known have tried alcohol.
   Therefore, 80 percent of people try alcohol.

The first two are basic inductive arguments, and the third is a statistical inductive argument. Argument C has the two features of a statistical inductive argument. The premise indicates that a certain proportion of the sample short of 100 percent has the characteristic, and the conclusion indicates that the same proportion of the population has it. Statistical inductive arguments usually have a condensed premise.

> **Statistical Inductive Arguments**
>
> A statistical inductive argument is an inductive argument in which (1) the premises, usually a single condensed premise, indicate that a certain proportion (short of 100 percent) of the sample has the characteristic in question, and (2) the conclusion indicates that the same proportion of the population has that characteristic.

Statistical inductive arguments occur frequently. They are pervasive in our information age, used especially for drawing all sorts of conclusions about how people are likely to behave, how they will vote, what products they will buy, what TV programs they will watch, what Internet sites they will visit, and so on. Researchers poll a sample of the population and tally the proportions of the sample having certain attitudes or beliefs. The conclusion drawn is that the population as a whole will exhibit those attitudes or beliefs in the same proportions. The strength of statistical inductive arguments obviously depends a great deal on how the sample is chosen. We will consider later how inductive arguments, including statistical inductive arguments, are to be evaluated.

10.1.5 The Standard Model and Variations

Based on the discussion so far, we can now refine our earlier definition of an inductive argument with an expanded and revised list of standard features:

1. The premises and conclusion are empirical statements.

2. The premises are singular statements or condensed reports of a series of singular statements.
3. The conclusion is a generalization, universal or nonuniversal.
4. It is always possible for the premises to be true and the conclusion to be false, so the argument is nondeductive.
5. The premises are convergent rather than linked.

But some arguments usually regarded as inductive arguments do not fit this model completely. Three types are worth considering: (1) arguments with a singular conclusion, due to an intervening generalization, (2) induction to a collective property, and (3) inductive arguments with complete enumeration.

We have already seen an example of the first type of variation. Some inductive arguments, like Example 10.3, have a singular statement rather than a general statement as a conclusion. Here is another example: "All the humans ever known have been mortal, so Socrates is mortal." These are inductive arguments with some parts left out. In this case, the implicit intermediate premise is the generalization that all humans are mortal. Here is the structure:

Example 10.8

PIA: All the humans ever known have been mortal.
IIP1: All humans are mortal.
C: Therefore, Socrates is mortal.

The inductive argument proper is the subargument. Many inductive arguments leave out the generalization and draw a direct conclusion about an individual member of the population.

In the second type of variant, the characteristic referred to in the conclusion is not a characteristic attributed to the members of the sample in the premises. Instead, it is a characteristic that the population has as a result of the members of the sample having certain other characteristics. The characteristic mentioned in the conclusion is a **collective property.**

Consider this example:

Example 10.9

Background: This is in response to a reporter's complaint that there is a lack of diversity in the Washington radio market. (*Washington Post*, 6/98)

> Your reporter's lament over the alleged lack of program diversity in radio has no basis in fact. Local radio formats listed daily by the *Post* include four Spanish-language stations along with stations offering the following formats: Korean, smooth jazz, gospel, progressive rock, ethnic, black talk, contemporary Christian, Christian talk, alternative rock, urban hits, country, oldies, all news, all sports, easy listening, top 40, modern adult hits, soft rock and classic rock. That's not diversity?—D.W.

The conclusion of this argument is that the radio market in Washington has diversity. But diversity is a characteristic possessed by the population as a whole, not by any of its individual members. The population has this characteristic because its members have certain characteristics, but these characteristics of the individual members are different from the characteristic of the population. The individual radio stations each have the characteristic of being different from many of the others, which means that the whole has the characteristic of being diverse. In contrast, in a basic inductive argument, the characteristic referred to in the conclusion is possessed by many or all of the members of the population individually.

Collective Property

A collective property is a characteristic that is possessed only by a group considered collectively. Groups have collective properties because their members have certain other properties, but the properties of the members are not the same as the resulting collective property of the group.

The third variation on the standard inductive argument results when the premises completely enumerate the population—that is, when the sample is the same as the population. As we have seen, a standard inductive argument is a partial enumeration, in which the sample is smaller than the population. But, in some cases the population is small enough that all of its members can be discussed in the premises. Consider this argument: "Joe is a bad driver, Bill is a bad driver, and John is a bad driver, so all the men in that family are bad drivers." If there are only the three men in this family, this is a case of complete enumeration.

But such an argument is not really an inductive argument because it is deductive. Assuming that there are only three men in the family, the premises guarantee the truth of the conclusion.[5] It is impossible for the premises to be true and the conclusion false. The conclusion does not generalize on the premises, but simply repeats what they say in a condensed form.

EXERCISE SET 10.1

SECTION A: Indicate which of the following are empirical generalizations and which are singular empirical statements. For those that are empirical generalizations, reformulate, when necessary, to indicate whether they are universal or nonuniversal, paying special attention to any implicit quantifiers. For some of them, it will be helpful to think of how you might formulate them in categorical logic (as discussed in Chapter 7).

EXAMPLE
America has usually won its wars.

ANSWER
This is nonuniversal empirical generalization. Reformulation: Most wars America has been in, America has won.

PROBLEMS

1. New York is a world-class city.
2. Clouds are composed of water vapor.
❖ 3. The new medical technologies present us with difficult moral choices.
4. The Beatles are the biggest-selling rock group ever.
5. U.S. presidents have been men.
❖ 6. Many people have the name "Jennifer."
7. Abstract paintings are often misunderstood.
8. Class consciousness is talked about by Marxists.
❖ 9. According to geologists, the continents used to have a different configuration.
10. The great American novel has yet to be written.
11. The person who will discover the cure for cancer is alive today.
❖ 12. No one comes close to her in IQ.

SECTION B: Construct an inductive argument for any three of the exercises in Section A that you found to be generalizations. Take your reformulation of the sentence as the conclusion, and provide at least two or three premises. Do not worry at this point whether the argument is strong.

EXAMPLE
America has usually won its wars.

ANSWER
P1: America won the Revolutionary War.
P2: America won the Spanish-American War.
P3: America was on the winning side in World War II.
C: Most wars America has been in, America has won.

SECTION C: Structure the following inductive arguments. Indicate those arguments that are statistical, that have a condensed premise, that have a singular conclusion (with an implicit intermediate generalization), or that have a conclusion indicating a collective property.

EXAMPLE
Santa Claus left presents for me and all of my friends, so he must leave presents for my cousin Eddy, too.

ANSWER
Features: condensed premise, singular conclusion
     P1A: Santa Claus left presents for me and all of my friends.
IIP1: Santa Claus leaves presents for all children.
C: Therefore, Santa Claus will leave presents for my cousin Eddy.

PROBLEMS

1. New York has skyscrapers. San Francisco has skyscrapers. The skyscrapers in Chicago are a wonder to behold. Thus, all big cities have skyscrapers.
2. Monday, I took my umbrella to work, and it did not rain. Tuesday and Wednesday, the same thing happened. So, it always rains only when I do not take my umbrella.
❖ 3. All societies throughout history that I can think of have fought wars. So, humanity will never put an end to war.

4. Fifty-five percent of the people in our neighborhood are voting for the Democratic candidate for mayor. Therefore, that candidate will win with 55 percent of the citywide vote.

5. My daughter studies very hard in college, and the same is true of my son. The neighbors say the same thing about their children in college. College students today work very hard.

❖ 6. Although I am still a child, I have had a chance to see several operas. I saw *Cosi Fan Tutti* and did not like it. I saw *Aida* and did not like it. I saw *La Boheme* and did not like it. It is clear that I will never enjoy opera.

7. All the women in my family are bad drivers. So, all women must be bad drivers.

8. When the local country music station conducted a poll, 85 percent of the respondents said that country music was their favorite kind of music. Can anyone doubt that country music is the most popular form of music in the nation?

❖ 9. Carl does engine work. Betty works on transmissions. Grady handles suspensions and electrical systems. Lewis's specialty is cooling systems. Our shop has your whole car covered.

10. In all the towns I know of, most of the residents are white. So, in all towns, most of the residents are white.

11. Most of the winters I know have been colder than this winter. Thus, most winters are colder than this winter.

10.2 Evaluating Inductive Arguments

Inductive arguments, like other arguments, are strong only if they satisfy the TARS conditions (see Chapter 6). The premises must each be true and acceptable, and they must individually have relevance to the conclusion and collectively have sufficiency in their support of the conclusion. The basic fallacies of irrelevant reason and false premise apply to inductive arguments in the same way that they apply to other nondeductive arguments. But we should say something about how the fallacies of hasty conclusion and problematic premise apply to inductive arguments.

10.2.1 Inductive Arguments and Hasty Conclusion

In an inductive argument, the conclusion is a generalization based on the premises. The premises make the claim that all or most of the sample, or a specific proportion of it, have a certain characteristic. The conclusion is, in most cases, that the members of the population have that characteristic to the same extent.[6] The form of an inductive argument is the relationship between the sample and the population. A hasty conclusion charge against an inductive argument is a judgment that the sample is inadequate to support the claim made about the population in the conclusion.

Consider this argument and a structuring of it:

Example 10.10

Background: This letter is on the topic of global warming. (*Chicago Tribune, 4/97*)

> While skidding my way downtown recently, I thought it bizarre that large segments of the American public still believe in global warming when in Chicago the temperature was 22 degrees: Duluth, 12; Fargo, 9; Pittsburgh, 20; Albany, 19. Des Moines was balmy at 27. And this in April. Wind chills reached 70 below in the Midwest this winter, killing tens of thousands of cattle and forming ice covers four feet thick. There have been countless power outages, snowbound motorists and disrupted businesses and schools.—G.M.F.

Forming a condensed premise out of the several city temperature reports contained in this text, we can structure the argument as follows:

Example 10.11

P1: In April 1997, cities in the midwestern United States were unseasonably cold.

P2: The previous winter in the Midwest, wind-chill temperatures went as low as minus 70.

C: Therefore, the world is not warming up, as proponents of global warming believe.

To understand this inductive argument, we first need to identify the sample and the population. The sample is the temperatures of various locations in the Midwest during the winter and during a part of April of one particular year. But what is the population? The claim that the Earth is not warming up seems to be a claim about average temperatures for all locations on the planet into the indefinite future. The argument is a bit tricky because average temperature is a collective property. We can simplify things by formulating a condensed premise that also talks about averages:

Example 10.12

P1: The average temperatures for certain locations in the Midwest during certain periods of one portion of a year were lower than normal.

C: Therefore, it is false that the average temperatures for all locations on the Earth from now into the indefinite future will be higher than normal.

This argument is ripe for a charge of hasty conclusion, in that the premise does not give adequate support to the conclusion. The sample is simply not large enough or representative enough, given the claim about the population in the conclusion. In other words, the **sample size** and the **sample representativeness** are inadequate. If the author is going to draw a conclusion about the world as a whole, clearly he ought to have included more temperature reports (size). In addition, he should have considered a broader range of locations and times to draw a conclusion about the world as a whole over a long stretch of time (representativeness). These two ideas come together in terms of the process of **sample selection,** the method by which the sample is chosen.

> ### Sample Size, Representativeness, and Selection
>
> Sample selection, the method by which the members of the sample are chosen, has two important features. One is sample size, which concerns whether the sample is large enough, given the population and the characteristic that is claimed for it. The other is sample representativeness, which concerns whether the members of the sample, given the nature of the population and the characteristic in question, are chosen from an adequate variety of areas of the population membership.

10.2.2 Sample Selection

In terms of sample selection, how can you avoid a charge of hasty conclusion against an inductive argument? Anyone who presents an inductive argument has selected some sample on which to base the argument. In other words, this person has selected some members of the population for scrutiny in the premises in order to draw a conclusion about the population as a whole. Whether the premises provide sufficient support for the conclusion depends on what the sample is, which, in turn, depends on how the sample is selected. The sample should be large enough and representative enough, given the population and the characteristic the conclusion attributes to its members. If it is not, a charge of hasty conclusion is in order. Consider first representativeness.

A representative sample is, ideally, a **random sample.** A sample is random when each member of the population from which it is selected has an equal chance of being chosen. Suppose you have a bag of thoroughly mixed marbles, fifty red and fifty blue. If the marbles are of uniform size and weight, then the group of marbles you draw sight unseen from the bag will at least approximate a random sample. For a host of practical and theoretical reasons, however, it is seldom possible to achieve this level of randomness in selecting a sample.

One reason that this group of marbles is close to a random sample is that the population from which it is drawn is homogeneous. Thus, a marble selected from anywhere in the bag is as likely to be blue as it is red. But populations are very seldom homogeneous. Imagine that the red marbles are heavier than the blue ones. Then the population would not be homogeneous, because the red ones would be more likely to be at the bottom of the bag than would the blue ones. So, if you tend to reach all the way to the bottom of the bag to choose, you are more likely to pick red than blue, and your sample will not be random.

Of course, if the selector adopts a random method of selection, then the lack of homogeneity in the population will not be a bar to a random sample. But randomness in selection method is usually an unattainable ideal. Selectors will generally apply some principle of selection, some way of making the selection, whether consciously or unconsciously. A method of selection that is nonrandom is known as a **bias.**

If randomness is next to impossible, how are we to achieve representativeness? We can do nothing about the lack of homogeneity in the populations we study, but we can do something about our method of selection. Nearly every method of selection will have a bias. But only some bias is harmful, in the sense that it diminishes representativeness; other bias is benign, in the sense that it does not diminish representativeness. Thus, the search for representativeness in a sample is the search for a method of selection in which the bias is not harmful.

Consider this example of a question to be addressed by a statistical inductive argument:

Example 10.13

Question: What portion of Americans attend religious services regularly?
Population: All Americans
Characteristic: Attend religious services regularly

Note, first, that there is no practical way in a study like this to select a truly random sample. All methods of selection will have a bias. Even if the names of individuals to include in the sample are chosen by a computer using some software that guaranteed randomness, bias will still be present. For example, what list will the computer choose names from? Unless the list is complete, including everyone in the United States, this will be a source of bias. But there is no complete list—even the government census does not include *everybody*. In addition, once the computer generates its list of people, they do not become members of the sample until they have been surveyed about their religious practices. Bias then enters in because some members will be successfully surveyed and others not, and the distinction between these groups is not random.

If you were investigating this religious issue, how would you select your sample? Your options might include the following:

1. Survey among, or in a way that favors, your friends and relatives.
2. Survey among, or in a way that favors, people living Seattle.
3. Survey among, or in a way that favors, college graduates.
4. Survey among, or in a way that favors, elected officials.
5. Survey among, or in a way that favors, parents with young children.
6. Survey among, or in a way that favors, people with driver's licenses.

Each of these methods of selection would result in a form of bias. The question is whether the bias would undermine the representativeness of the sample. Clearly, the bias in method 1 would do so. Chances are, if you are religious, most of your family members and friends will be, and if you are not, most of them will not be either. So, religious people are likely to be either more or less common among this sample than they are in the general population. Method 2 is problematic as well, though less so. There are regional variations in how religious people are, with people in Seattle probably either more or less likely to be religious than the general population (though we may not know which). There are problems with method 3 as well, because college graduates may be less likely to be religious than members of the general population.

Method 4 is problematic for a different reason. Elected officials, not wanting to lose the votes of the religious among their constituents, may misrepresent their own religious activity in a survey. Method 5 is probably problematic as well, because parents with young children may be likely to be more religiously active than others for the sake of their children. But method 6 may yield a fairly representative sample. It does not seem likely that people with driver's licenses are either more or less likely to be religious than those without licenses.

We can say that selection methods 1–5 are *relevant* to the characteristic being investigated: attending religious services regularly. The question is whether the bias involved in the selection of a sample is relevant to the presence or absence of the characteristic being studied. Bias is harmful—that is, it undermines the representativeness of the sample—only if the principle of selection is relevant to the characteristic in question.

Sometimes, it is difficult to find a method of selection that is not relevant to the characteristic in question. In such cases, one strategy is to choose a **stratified sample,** one that selects the sample from different parts of the population to overcome the bias that would result from selecting the sample from only one part. To illustrate, look again at method 2. This method undermines the representativeness of the sample because it selects members of the sample on the basis of region, and we have reason to think that the level of religious commitment among people varies by region. But we can take this into account by dividing the population into regional groups and selecting a sample that includes members from each group in proportion to their overall numbers in the population. For example, if the South (suitably defined) has 26 percent of the overall population, then 26 percent of the stratified sample would be people from the South.

We could create stratified samples in regard to the other methods as well. In the case of method 3, for instance, we could divide the nation into educational attainment groups, such as those with advanced degrees, those with a college degree, those with a high school diploma, and those with less than a high school diploma. The stratified sample would be one that had members from each of these groups in proportion to the percentage of the entire population these groups represented. Of course, the issue of how the subgroups were chosen and how many were chosen would arise. If there were, for example, substantial differences in religious commitment in different areas of the South, we would have to choose a larger number of subgroups for the stratified sample to ensure representativeness.

Polling organizations use stratified samples to determine how elections may turn out, what television programs are most popular (and with which age or income groups), how many people would buy a new brand of soap powder, and so forth. Stratified sampling has been refined to a sophisticated science in which the size of the sample is usually very low in comparison with the size of the population. That is, a sample of but a few thousand can quite accurately determine the proportion of a population of tens of millions that has a certain characteristic.

This suggests that size is a less important factor than representativeness in selecting a sample that avoids a charge of hasty conclusion against an inductive

> ### Random Samples, Bias, and Stratified Samples
>
> A random sample of a population is one in which each member of the population has an equal chance of being selected for the sample. Bias is the tendency of a method of sample selection to make it more likely that some members of the population will be selected than others. Bias is harmful when it undermines the representativeness of a sample, and this occurs when the method of selection is relevant to the characteristic being investigated. One way to avoid harmful bias is to use a stratified sample. This involves (1) choosing a method of selection that leads to harmful bias (such as regionalism), (2) dividing the entire population into groups based on that method, and (3) including in the sample members from each group in proportion to their numbers in the overall population.

argument. The size does not need to be very large, so long as the representativeness of the sample is assured. At the same time, a larger size normally cannot make up for a lack of representativeness.

To illustrate this, consider again Newton's and Einstein's theories of motion. If we had set out prior to the twentieth century to test with an inductive argument whether the velocity of an object affects its mass, no matter how large the sample, the argument would have supported Newton's conclusion that there is no such effect. The reason is that all of the members of the sample would have been instances in which the velocities of the objects were far below that of light. Only in the twentieth century, with Einstein's theory, would we have become aware that the reason the inductive argument supported Newton is that the sample was not representative.[7] That is, there were no members of the sample in which the velocity was close to that of light, and to use a method of selection that excludes such members turned out to be a harmful bias. Of course, prior to the twentieth century, physicists had no reason to think that this bias in the method of sample selection was a harmful one. The reason is that they had no reason to suspect that the mass of an object depended on its velocity.

If sample size is too small, the premises are not sufficient to support the conclusion, no matter how representative the sample is. In fact, when an inductive argument has a sample that is too small, a hasty conclusion charge against it is similar to a specific version of hasty conclusion discussed in Chapter 6, namely, the fallacy of argument by anecdote. While that fallacy occurs when an argument has, in effect, a sample with only one member, an inductive argument may have too small a sample even when the sample has more than one member. In any case, the error is the same. In fact, one way to think of an inductive argument, at least the basic kind discussed earlier, is that it is an argument made up exclusively of anecdotes, individual claims based on experience. But there is nothing wrong with basing an argument with a general conclusion on anecdotes, so long as you include a sufficiently large and representative sample of them.

10.2.3 Inductive Arguments and Problematic Premise

Inductive arguments can be charged with problematic premise, just like any other argument. But two points are of special relevance in the case of inductive arguments. First, the premises of inductive arguments are often direct reports of observations. Because inductive arguments are based on empirical claims, they are ultimately dependent on such observations. There are a number of psychological reasons to be cautious about the reliability of human powers of observation. Human observation is often unreliable. For example, in psychology courses, instructors often stage an incident in which actors rush into the classroom, pretend to assault a confederate, and then rush out again. The students are then asked to "help the police" by providing a description of the "assailants." The variety of descriptions offered by the students demonstrates that human observation cannot always be trusted. When the sample includes observations of others, we must, like good historians, be cautious about the reliability of their testimony. This is why science relies on observations that can be repeated.

The second point is related to the first. To report an observation, to make an observational claim, is to categorize what was observed. An observation can become the basis of an inductive argument only by being categorized in some way. But an observed phenomenon can be categorized in different ways. For example, it is said that when the original inhabitants of Mexico first saw the invading Spaniards, they categorized the men on horseback as a single animal. Or the same cry might be categorized by some as a scream and by others as laughter. Or people who are paranoid might classify certain kinds of observations very differently than those who are not paranoid, and an experienced observer may classify things differently than an inexperienced observer.

☰ EXERCISE SET 10.2

SECTION A: Discuss the issues of representativeness in the selection of samples raised by the following problems.

PROBLEMS

1. Imagine that you are preparing a statistical inductive argument using as a sample people you know. This method of selection will, of course, introduce a bias into the sample, but the bias might or might not be harmful, depending on the characteristic you are looking for. List two characteristics for which the bias would be harmful and two characteristics for which it would not be harmful. Explain in each case why the bias would or would not be harmful. (For example, if you were a member of the basketball team, the bias would likely be harmful if the characteristic you were investigating were "being over 6 feet tall" because your teammates would tend to be taller than the average person.)

2. Imagine that you are doing a survey for an assignment in a college social psychology class to determine the proportion of the population that has a certain characteristic and that your sample is other students in the college.

As in problem 1, list two characteristics for which the bias of the method of sample selection would be harmful and two characteristics for which it would not be harmful, giving an explanation for your answer in each case.

3. This problem is the reverse of the first two. Imagine that you are preparing a statistical inductive argument to determine the proportion of people who watch wrestling regularly on TV. Indicate two methods of sample selection that would lead to harmful bias and two methods that would not lead to harmful bias, explaining your response in each case. If you cannot think of any method of selection not leading to harmful bias that does not involve a stratified sample, answer the question by explaining how you would stratify the sample.

4. Until recently, almost all medical research was done on males, and conclusions drawn by inductive argument from this research were applied in the treatment of women as well as men. Discuss some reasons this bias might be harmful.

5. Imagine that your student newspaper assigns you to do a survey for an article on student attitudes toward the current presidential administration in Washington. Discuss how you might devise a stratified sample that would avoid harmful bias in the sample selection of students to interview for the survey.

SECTION B: Evaluate each of the inductive argument structures you provided in Exercise Set 10.1, Section C. Consider formal fallacies only. Pay special attention to the issues of sample size and representativeness.

EXAMPLE

P1A: Santa Claus left presents for me and all of my friends.

IIP1: Santa Claus leaves presents for all children.

C: Therefore, Santa Claus will leave presents for my cousin Eddy.

ANSWER

I charge the inductive argument of the subargument for P1 with the fallacy of hasty conclusion. First, the sample size is not sufficiently large to support a universal generalization. There are millions of children in the world, and only a dozen or so are referred to in the premises. More seriously, there is a harmful bias in the sample selection. The sample is not sufficiently representative. The property in question, being left presents by Santa Claus, is part of a religious holiday, Christmas, that is celebrated by only a portion of the world's population. All the members of the sample are from families that celebrate this holiday.

SECTION C: The following either are inductive arguments or contain inductive arguments as subarguments. In each case, structure the argument and evaluate the inductive argument for formal strength (no tree diagram needed).

EXAMPLE

Background: This letter is in response to a column about defensive (or antiballistic) missiles, which are designed to destroy incoming missile warheads. (*New York Times*, 7/98)

Your columnist does not mention that a defensive missile with a nuclear warhead and using its neutron flux would have melted the fissile material in any incoming nuclear warhead whether that warhead were surrounded by a balloon or not. The blast and heat would also decompose any chemical warhead and burn up any biological agents being carried. Therefore, the only effective warhead for any real missile defense has to be nuclear.—H.M.A.

ANSWER

Structure

P1: A defensive missile with a nuclear warhead would melt the fissile material in any incoming warhead, whether or not it were surrounded by a balloon.

P2: Such a missile would decompose any chemical warhead and burn up any biological agents being carried.

C: Therefore, the only effective warhead for any real missile defense has to be nuclear.

EVALUATION

I charge this inductive argument with hasty conclusion. The premises do not provide sufficient support for the conclusion because the sample is not sufficiently representative. The conclusion claims that a nuclear defense missile would be effective, but there are many different factors in judging effectiveness beyond the ability of a missile to destroy incoming warheads. Other factors would be, for example, reliability, cost, and potential harm to one's own military forces. In the absence of premises discussing such factors, the conclusion is not adequately supported. In addition, the conclusion states not only that nuclear defensive missiles are effective but also that only such missiles are effective. But no evidence is provided to show that other kinds of defensive missiles are not effective.

PROBLEMS

1. Background: This letter is about young people as employees. (*USA Today*, 12/98)

   I cannot agree more with the complaint that employers cannot find suitable young employees. The youth of today is a pathetic entity. My two-year experience in the service station/car wash business has galvanized my opinions. I encountered bad attitudes, poor dress, theft, violence and social behavioral problems in a team setting. This certainly is a far cry from the day my 15-year-old father and four friends in 1934 rode the boxcars out West looking for work in the fields.—R.W.D.

2. Background: This letter is about the failures of the intelligence services. (*New York Times*, 12/00)

   It is interesting that the "intelligence community" has issued a report about how the world will look in 15 years. This intelligence community is the same one that missed predicting the collapse of the Soviet Union and the dismantling of the Berlin Wall, and overestimated Soviet military strength. On the basis of their published past performance, a prudent person would view intelligence officials' divinations about the world 15 years from now with a great deal of skepticism.—W.J.K.

❖   3. Background: This letter is in response to a gardening column. (*New York Times*, 12/00)

Your column fails to mention one effective deer deterrent for at least parts of the garden if not the entire landscape: Use plants the deer don't like to eat. In one corner of my yard I recently replaced some evergreen euonymus and yew—two top favorites of deer—with American holly (too prickly), Chinese juniper (too scratchy) and Japanese andromeda (like mountain laurel, distasteful and possibly poisonous). All thrive undisturbed. Short of starvation, deer will avoid a long list of thorny, fuzzy, aromatic and toxic plants. —S.M.S.

4. Background: This letter is about *Contact*, a movie about the search for extraterrestrial intelligence. (*Houston Chronicle*, 8/97)

I just saw the movie *Contact*. I thoroughly enjoyed it. One thing bothered me quite a bit about what was implied on the screen, though. They seem to be putting forth the thesis that if you are a scientist, you must not believe in God. I am currently an engineer and in the past have been a biochemist/microbiologist, and I believe in both God and science. I've known many other scientists, and although I didn't take a poll, only three or four espoused atheism and maybe a handful more were agnostics. By far, the largest number of scientists I've known practiced a religion. God put us here with brains to wonder at the universe and to marvel at the complexity of his creation.—B.R.

5. Background: This letter is about information on drugs available on the Internet. (*New York Times*, 6/97)

Thanks to the Internet, people can read and decide for themselves what to believe. Antidrug lobbyists widely publicize the work that purports to show the grave dangers of marijuana. On the Internet, however, one can read a critique of this work from two researchers and perhaps conclude that it may be an unreliable source of information. On the Internet, one can also read a copy of the LaGuardia Committee Report, published in 1944, that thoroughly debunked most of the common marijuana myths.—S.W.

❖   6. Background: This letter is about a proposed gun control measure. (*New York Times*, 2/00)

The creation of an intrusive new government bureaucracy could turn the right to keep and bear arms into an overly arduous undertaking for honest citizens. A perfect example is the once efficient handgun-licensing process in New York City, which has developed over the years into a nine-month ordeal costing prospective gun owners hundreds of dollars. Antigun groups may view an additional layer of bureaucracy as a laudable goal, but it would not prevent criminals from obtaining guns, nor would it serve the interests of a free society.—R.N.

7. Background: This letter is about equality between men and women. (*New York Times*, 6/97)

According to many women, men make the rules to suit themselves. It's funny how the rules haven't changed to suit us. As a working professional, I am obliged to wear a suit to work. It presents a formality to clients that speaks of a company that means business. But the women I work with do not have to wear suits and are considered no less professional. Meanwhile, when summer comes and I'm walking into work wearing a dress shirt, suit jacket and tie in 90-degree weather, my female co-workers are wearing short-sleeved blouses. I fail to see the equality in that.—M.A.

8. Background: This letter is about the "war on drugs." (*New York Times*, 3/99)

Harmful drug use tends to be self-limiting. In the 1960s we had a speed epidemic that caused great concern. As word got out on the street that "speed kills," the use of speed decreased. The same thing happened with crack. When people learned of its dangers, its popularity decreased. The drug warriors would like to take the credit for the decrease in crack use, of course, but I doubt if all the arrests and billions of dollars spent waging the drug war had much of anything to do with it. Our current drug policy seems geared to insuring that drugs ruin people's lives. What is the point of that? —S.W.

9. Background: This letter is about the risks of genetic engineering. (*New York Times*, 7/98)

Unpredicted effects can occur when a new gene is introduced to an organism through genetic engineering. An example is salmon genetically engineered with growth hormone that developed deformities and bone overgrowth. Although the males had been engineered to be sterile to keep them from passing on their deformities, the injected sterility gene did not take effect. Another example of an unanticipated effect is that of a genetically engineered bacterium that was created to produce ethanol from agricultural waste as a way of generating fuel. When it was added to soil, there was a significant decrease in the growth of both roots and shoots of wheat, and a decrease in beneficial soil fungi, which are necessary for fertile soil and healthy plants.—M.A.

10.3 Causal Arguments

Many arguments have as a conclusion a **causal statement,** a claim that something caused something else. An argument with a causal statement as a conclusion is a **causal argument.** Causal statements and causal arguments play a very important role in our thinking about the world.

10.3.1 Causal Statements

The basic form of a causal statement is "C causes (or caused) E," where C is the cause and E is the effect. C and E thus stand in a causal relationship. Different sorts of things can be referred to by the phrases represented by C and E. Consider these causal statements:

Example 10.14

A. The assassination of Archduke Ferdinand caused World War I.
B. The cigarette caused the forest fire.
C. Hitler caused World War II.
D. Wilson's exhaustion caused him to crack.
E. Lack of watering caused the plant to die.
F. The invention of the automobile caused the rise of the suburbs.
G. Joan's smoking caused her lung cancer.
H. Smoking causes (or tends to cause) lung cancer.
I. The *Titanic's* collision with an iceberg caused the *Titanic* to sink.
J. Ships' colliding with icebergs cause (or tend to cause) those ships to sink.

In sentence A, the C and E phrases refer to events: an assassination and a war. A war is, of course, a complex event, consisting of many smaller events. But an assassination is a complex event as well, even though it occurs over a much shorter period than a war. For example, an assassination may consist of the events of a gun being fired, a bullet being expelled from a gun, the bullet's flying through the air, the bullet's entering the body of the victim, the bullet causing certain physiological damage to the victim's body, and life ebbing from the victim. Notice that many of the events that are parts of the assassination are themselves related as causes and effects. For example, the bullet entering the body causes the physiological changes, which in turn cause the death.

So, in sentence A, the cause and effect are events. However, in sentences B and C, though the effects are events, the causes seem instead to be objects.[8] But, despite what B and C suggest, most thinkers who study causation believe that causes and effects are not objects. Instead, an object in a sentence expressing a causal statement is a stand-in for an event in which that object is involved. In B for example, "a cigarette" is shorthand for "the burning of a cigarette." As a result, B should read, "The burning of a cigarette caused the forest fire," because the cigarette is an object involved in the event of its burning. Similarly, in the case of C, "Hitler" is a stand-in for "certain actions of Hitler."

But not all causes and effects are events. Some seem to be *states* of objects, or states of affairs. In sentence D, for example, the cause is a state of Wilson—his exhaustion, the state of affairs of his being exhausted. Here is another example: the dullness of the knife causes the jaggedness of the wound. Here both cause and effect are states of affairs. So, in its basic form, a causal statement refers to events or states of affairs as causes and effects. The causal relationship is between events and/or states of affairs.

In sentence E the cause seems to be, not an event, but the absence of an event. The absence of a watering causes the plant's death. Apparently, the absence of an event, at least when such an event is a normal occurrence, often can be regarded as a cause. For example, the lack of a proper upbringing can cause bad character, and a lack of sunlight can cause a vitamin D deficiency.

> ### Causal Statements
>
> A causal statement indicates a causal relationship between events (or, in some cases, absences of events) or states of affairs. The basic form of a causal statement is "C causes E," where "C" refers to the cause and "E" to the effect. If a sentence expressing a causal statement uses phrases referring to objects, the objects are stand-ins for events or states of affairs in which those objects are involved.

In sentence F, the cause is at a considerable distance in time from the effect. Some causes are close in time (and space) to their effects; these are **proximate causes.** Other causes are distant in time (and/or space) from their effects; these are **remote causes.** There is no sharp dividing line between proximate and remote causes. When a cause is remote from its effect, a series of causes and effects come between the two. For example, suppose v causes w, which causes x, which causes y, which causes z. In this series, y is a proximate cause of z, and v if it is sufficiently far off in time or space, is a remote cause of z. Such a series or string of causes and effects is referred to as a **causal chain.**

> ### Proximate and Remote Causes and Causal Chains
>
> A proximate cause is close in time and space to its effect. A remote cause is distant in time and space from its effect. Remote causes are separated from their effects by a series of causes and effects, referred to as a causal chain.

Sentences G and H and sentences I and J represent an important contrast. G and I express singular causal statements, as do all the previous sentences in Example 10.14, and H and J express general causal statements. A **singular causal statement** indicates a causal relation between two particular events, such as the *Titanic's* colliding with an iceberg and the *Titanic's* sinking. A **general causal statement** indicates that there is or tends to be a causal relationship between events of one kind and events of another kind—for example, between smoking events and lung cancer events. General causal statements are often expressed with the phrase "tends to cause" because not all events of the one kind cause events of the other kind.[9] For example, some people who smoke do not get lung cancer, and some ships that collide with icebergs do not sink. (The reason for this will be discussed shortly.) Our focus in the rest of the discussion is on singular causal statements (and arguments with singular causal statements as conclusions) rather than general causal statements.

> ### Singular and General Causal Statements
>
> Singular causal statements indicate a causal relationship between particular events, like the assassination of Archduke Ferdinand and World War I. General causal statements indicate that events of one kind cause or tend to cause events of another kind, as in the claim that humans coming into contact with certain viruses tend to catch colds.

Thus far in our discussion of causal statements, we have considered cases in which the sentences expressing the statements use the verb "cause." But many other verbs indicate a causal relationship. For example, sentence B in Example 10.14 could have been worded "The cigarette started the forest fire" or "The cigarette led to the fire." The verbs that can be used in place of "causes" in sentences expressing causal statements are **causal verbs.**

> ### Causal Verbs
>
> Causal verbs can indicate a causal relationship in sentences expressing causal statements. Common causal verbs (using the past tense) include "produced," "brought about," "led to," "started," "was responsible for," "created," "resulted in," "was the event behind," "determined," "affected," "triggered," "initiated," and "made happen."

10.3.2 Causes and Conditions

A causal statement indicates two important features about the events in question (the cause and effect) and their relationship. First, causes can be distinguished from conditions. A causal statement often singles out the cause from a number of other events or states that might also have been designated as the cause of that effect. These other events and states, along with the cause, are the **conditions** of the effect.

Second, causation is distinguished from correlation. There is a **correlation** between a cause and its effect, meaning that the two events occur together. But causation is more than mere correlation. All cases of causation are cases of correlation, but not all cases of correlation are cases of causation. A cause, in addition to being correlated with its effect, brings about or produces that effect. We will look at the contrast between causes and conditions in this section and at the contrast between causes and correlations in the next.

Consider these examples:

Example 10.15

A. Background: This letter is in response to an article on assertive patients. (*New York Times, 8/97*)

> Patients no longer reverently listen to their physicians without question or comment. Instead they are researching their illnesses and challenging their doctors' directives. You attribute this change in patient behavior to a growing distrust of managed care incentives that favor withholding care. That may be a catalyst, but the seeds of patient activism were sown long ago. The pioneers of this change are the students of the 1960s who talked back to their professors then and started talking back to their physicians a decade ago.—L.S.W.

B. Background: This letter is in response to a column that discussed the role of feminist activism in the women's movement. (*Los Angles Times, 1/00*)

> Your column on the women's movement omits the crucial technological and scientific developments that made it possible: Myriad labor-saving devices nearly eliminated the value of upper-body strength that previously advantaged men in many livelihoods. Medical science saved many children's and mother's lives and gave women so much control over reproduction that the great majority of women in developed nations were freed from relentless childbearing in their fertile years. Without these changes in material conditions, women's activism could not have taken the course described in the column.—D.E.B.

Both texts discuss social trends. Text A speaks of the trend of patients being more assertive in their relationship with their physicians, and text B speaks of the movement for women's rights. Each of these trends may be regarded itself as an event, though an event of a very complicated kind with many events as parts (like World War I). The question then arises what is the cause of these events.

Both texts are responding to articles or columns that discussed the cause of these trends. Text A refers to the claim that the cause of patient assertiveness is the growing distrust of managed care (for example, HMOs) in health care delivery. Text B refers to the claim that the cause of the women's movement is feminist activism. But both letters say that there is more to the story. Text A points to the role of student activism of the 1960s, and B points to the role of technological advances in health care and in the introduction of labor-saving devices. Notice that both authors seem not to want to deny the causal claims in the texts they are responding to, but rather to add to the account, to fill in more of the story.

What these authors point to are other conditions behind patient assertiveness and the women's movement, in addition to the conditions represented by the causal claims in the texts they are responding to. As these examples show, any event has a number of other events (or states) that are necessary for it to occur. These events and states are the conditions of that event. Different conditions might, given the circumstances, be identified as the cause of the event.

For example, for a fire to start, three factors are required: fuel, oxygen, and heat. In the absence of any one of these, the fire will not start. If a fire starts, these three factors are the conditions of that event. But which of them is the cause of the fire? Each of them might be the cause. The one that we identify as the cause depends on the context in which the fire occurs.

Consider these situations:

Example 10.16

A. Someone throws a burning cigarette out of a car window while driving through a hot dry forest, and a fire ensues.
B. Someone bumps into a glowing lightbulb, which then separates slightly from its base, allowing air into the bulb and resulting in the incineration of the filament in a flash of flame.
C. Someone sets his damp clothes over a lamp to dry them, and they later burst into flame.

In each case, the three factors of fuel, heat, and oxygen are necessary conditions for the fire that results. But we would probably pick out a different one as the cause in each case. For example, in scenario A, the introduction of heat from the burning cigarette was the cause of the fire. In scenario B, the introduction of oxygen from the break in the bulb was the cause of the fire. In scenario C, the introduction of fuel, in the form of the clothing, was the cause of the fire. Why would a different factor be singled out as the cause in each case? Doesn't fire always have the same cause?

Two features characterize the factor identified as the cause in each case. First, the causal factor was introduced into a situation that already contained the other two factors. The cause was the trigger that brought about the effect. In scenario A, the fuel and oxygen were already present, and the fire began after the introduction of the heat from the cigarette. In scenario B, heat and fuel were already present in the lightbulb, and the filament burned when the break at the base of the bulb allowed oxygen to enter. In scenario C, oxygen and heat were already present, and the fire started when fuel, in the form of the clothing, was introduced into the situation. Second, the causal factor was introduced by human action. A person threw the cigarette out of the window, bumped the lightbulb, and hung clothing over the lamp.

As these examples show, we tend to designate one of the conditions of an effect as the cause and tend to make this choice based on the two features just discussed. First, if all other conditions for an event (like a fire) are already present and the final condition is then introduced into the situation, triggering the event, we usually view that condition as the cause. Second, if one of the conditions is introduced by a human action, we usually view that condition as the cause. These two features often go together because it is often a human action that introduces the final, necessary condition, as in our three examples. But not always.

Consider these cases:

Example 10.17

A. The rising of the sun caused the garden flowers to open.
B. The shoddy workmanship caused the bridge to collapse.

In text A, the sun simply supplies the last of a set of conditions necessary for the flower to open and so is the cause. Here, we label it the cause because it is the *final* condition introduced, even though a human action such as a gardener's care was also a condition. In text B, the shoddy workmanship is a human action and so is the cause, even though it was not the last of the conditions introduced (which might have been, say, the spring flood's swelling the river below the bridge).

When events happen, we often seek to explain them, and a full explanation of an event lists a set of conditions, each of which is necessary (and together that are sufficient) for the event's having occurred. But we sometimes seek something short of a full explanation. For example, we may be especially interested in the condition that *makes the difference*. In most cases, this is the final condition to come on the scene, the condition introduced against a background in which the other conditions are already present. We single this condition out for special attention by labeling it as the cause. Thus, while the forest may have been tinder dry and there may have been oxygen in the air, the condition that made the difference was the burning cigarette.

But there is another reason that we label the burning cigarette as the cause. It came on the scene as the result of a human action. If the event we seek to explain has negative consequences, we want to know whether to blame anyone. And if it has positive consequences, we want to know whether we should praise anyone. This is why the condition introduced by human action, if any, often is labeled as the cause, whether or not it is the final condition on the scene. In the case of the collapsed bridge, for example, we can label the condition involving human action (the shoddy workmanship) as the cause even though it may have occurred years earlier and another event (the swelling river) is the last necessary condition.

Conditions and Causes

A cause is often a necessary condition for its effect. A cause in this sense is one member of a set of conditions, each of which is necessary for the effect. Given the circumstances, different members of that set of conditions might be labeled as the cause. One consideration is whether a condition is the "last on the scene," an event that occurs when all the other conditions are already present and thereby triggers the effect. Another consideration is whether a condition is the result of human action.

The *set* of necessary conditions for an event—all the conditions taken together—is generally a sufficient condition for that event. A cause, as indicated previously, is often regarded as one member of that set. But sometimes, instead, a cause is taken to be the whole of the set. In that case, the cause would be, instead of a necessary condition, a sufficient condition for its effect.

Consider these relationships:[10]

Example 10.18

A. E ⊃ C

B. C ⊃ E

The relationship between cause and effect indicated by relationship A is that of cause as a necessary condition for the effect. As we have seen, in a conditional, the consequent is a necessary condition for the antecedent.[11] This relationship allows us to infer the cause from the effect (by *modus ponens*). If the effect is present, we know that its necessary conditions are present as well, and the cause is one of these. But it does not allow us to infer the effect from the cause (this would involve the fallacy of affirming the consequent). Thus, we cannot infer that the burning cigarette will start a fire, because fuel and oxygen may be absent. This partly explains our earlier observation that general causal statements often claim only that a kind of event *tends to cause* another kind of event. If a cause is a necessary condition, its occurrence does not guarantee the effect. Thus, the case of lung cancer may have been caused (in the sense of a necessary condition) by heavy smoking, but not all cases of heavy smoking cause lung cancer (since other necessary conditions may be lacking in some cases).[12]

But sometimes, we want to be able to infer the effect from the cause. Here, the cause must be a sufficient condition for the effect, as in relationship B. In B, we can use *modus ponens* to infer effect from cause. In this case, we identify the cause as the full set of necessary conditions, and not only one member of that set.

Whether we regard a cause as a necessary or as a sufficient condition depends, in part, on our practical interests. Knowledge of causes allows us to have a measure of control over nature, but the kind of control we are interested in can vary. Often, we want to be able to stop bad things from happening—for example, to cure a disease. In that case, we want to know about necessary conditions because, to cure a disease, all that we need to do is to eliminate one of its necessary conditions. (Here we use relationship A and *modus tollens*.) So, when we think about the causes of diseases and other bad things, we tend to think of causes as necessary conditions. In contrast, if we want to bring something good about that would not happen otherwise, like having a child receive a good education, we need to ensure that all of the necessary conditions are present. In this case, we tend to think of a cause as a sufficient condition.

10.3.3 Causes and Correlations

Now we address the second feature mentioned previously, the distinction between causation and correlation. Consider this letter:

Example 10.19

Background: This letter is about bicycle helmets. (*New York Times, 6/99*)

> Has it occurred to anyone that the declining use of bicycles correlates with the increasing insistence on the use of bicycle helmets? Although intended to save lives, the bike helmet could be the cause of increasingly fat, immobile children and adults. The pressure to wear a helmet reduces the spontaneous pleasure of a casual ride and often is the rationale for not bothering to hop on the bike.—J.R.G.

The author speaks of two events: the increasing pressure on people to wear bicycle helmets and the declining number of bike rides that people take. She says two things about these events. In the first sentence, she says that these events are correlated, that they are occurring together. And in the second sentence, she says that these events are causally related, that the pressure to wear helmets may be causing the decline in bike riding.

To say that two events are correlated is different from saying that they are causally related. All causally related events are correlated, but not all correlated events are causally related. Consider these examples:

Example 10.20

A. Each spring, my snowdrops come up and then my crocuses come up. These are correlated events. But the snowdrops' coming up does not cause the crocuses to come up.

B. In the 1962 movie *Dr. Strangelove*, the mad general Jack D. Ripper, having just launched a nuclear attack against the Soviet Union, points out that there was a correlation between the rise of the communist effort to subvert the United States and the campaign to put fluoride in the drinking water (both occurred about the same time). But his claim that the communists caused the fluoride campaign is not plausible.

C. Jones noticed that there is a correlation between a person's being well educated and that person buying many books, so he devised a scheme to become educated by buying books. His assumption that buying books causes people to be educated is false.

In all three cases, the claim about correlation is true but the corresponding causal statement is false. How do we determine which sets of correlated events are causally related? If event x is correlated with event y, how do we determine whether x causes y? In other words, how do we distinguish between causation and *mere* correlation? This is the main task of a causal argument.

With correlation, it is important to recognize that when two events, x and y, are correlated there are only four possible ways they can be related. It may be that x causes y. The three other possibilities are illustrated by the arguments in Example 10.20. First, it may be that x and y are not directly causally related but have a common cause. To say that they have a common cause means that some event w causes both of them and neither one of them is in a causal chain from w to the other one.[13] In the case of argument A, the snowdrops' coming up does not cause the crocuses to come up, but the onset of spring causes both events. Instead of being directly causally related, they are indirectly causally related by their having a common cause.

Second, it may be that events x and y are coincidental, that they are not causally connected, directly or indirectly. This is what is most plausibly the case in argument B. The Soviet effort to undermine the U.S. government occurred at about the same time that the move to fluoridate drinking water gained momentum, but the one event is unlikely to have anything to do causally with the other. The belief that they were connected is the result of a highly implausible conspiracy theory. Third, events x and y may be causally related, but with y's causing x rather than x's causing y. In argument C, Jones's belief that buying books would cause him to become educated is false, because it is being educated that tends to cause people to buy books. To become educated, you have to read the books, not simply buy them.

Correlation

Two events are correlated when they occur together, in roughly the same time period. When x and y are correlated events, sometimes, x causes y. But there are three other possibilities: (1) x and y share a common cause, (2) x and y are coincidental, or (3) x and y are directly causally related, but y causes x.

Clearly, then, causation cannot be established by correlation alone. One of the most common fallacies in causal arguments is the conclusion that event x causes event y based on premises showing only that x and y are correlated. Consider these examples:

Example 10.21

A. Background: This letter is about teaching abstinence in sex education classes. (*New York Times,* 12/00)

> ① Kudos to the abstinence-only educators featured in your article. ② They are doing the right thing. ③ After all, what has secular comprehensive sex education given us over the years? ④ Nothing but rampant promiscuity and millions of abortions. ⑤ But then, keeping teenagers sexually active by instructing them on "safe sex" is big business in this country. ⑥ Try abstinence. ⑦ It works every time!—M.C.A.

B. Background: This letter is about prayer in schools. (*New York Times,* 6/98)

> I'm getting tired of assertions like the one you quoted—"As prayer has gone out of schools, guns, knives, drugs and gangs have come in"—with the unsupported implication that there is some causal connection between these events. This is the *post hoc ergo propter hoc* fallacy. The association of two events does not prove that one caused

the other. We could just as well say, "After we threw God out of the schools, we put a man on the moon." Students may or may not need more faith, but Congress could certainly use more reason.—D.E.M.

Argument A is an example of the fallacy of confusing correlation with causation. The author refers in sentences 3 and 4 to two recent events: an increase in sex-education programs in schools and an increase in promiscuity and abortion. The author then moves immediately, in sentence 5, to the claim that the first event is the cause of the second (or, more precisely, is the cause of an increase in teenage sexual activity, which the author presumes to be the cause of an increase in promiscuity and abortion). Thus, the author has inferred causation from correlation without considering the other three possibilities. The causal relationship claimed in the argument may be correct, but in providing evidence only of correlation, the author has not given the claim adequate support. Thus, this fallacy is a specific version of hasty conclusion.

Text B is a criticism of an argument that commits the same fallacy. In this case, the author quotes someone who concludes that a lack of prayer in the schools has caused a rise in school violence merely because these two events are correlated. The author gives this fallacy its proper name: ***post hoc ergo propter hoc,*** Latin for "after that, therefore because of that." It is often referred to as the *post hoc* fallacy, for short. Simply because one event follows another (showing correlation), we cannot conclude that the one caused the other.

> ### *Post Hoc Ergo Propter Hoc* Fallacy
>
> The *post hoc ergo propter hoc* fallacy occurs in a causal argument when the only support given for the conclusion that event x causes event y is that x and y are correlated. The fallacy lies in the fact that there are three other possibilities for the relationship between correlated events x and y. This fallacy is a specific version of the fallacy of hasty conclusion.

10.3.4 Presenting and Evaluating Causal Arguments

Showing that event x causes event y requires showing that x and y are correlated events (or states of affairs) *and* that the other three alternatives for how x and y are related are not the case. This leads us to a definition of cause: Given that x and y are correlated events or states of affairs, x causes y if and only if it is not true that (1) x and y have a common cause, (2) x and y are coincidental, or (3) y causes x. Based on these factors, we can provide two basic forms of causal argument:

1. Argument to show that x causes y:
   - P1: x and y are correlated.
   - P2: Likely, x and y do not have a common cause, x and y are not coincidental, *and* y does not cause x.

C: Therefore, x causes y.
2. Argument to show that, though x and y are correlated, x does not cause y:

P1: x and y are correlated.
P2: Likely, x and y have a common cause, x and y are coincidental,
    or y causes x.

C: Therefore, though they are correlated, x does not cause y.

Note that these arguments have singular causal statements as their conclusions. This means that x and y are particular events. Also, in these arguments, a cause is being understood as a necessary condition of its effect. We may refer to P2 in the first argument as the **elimination premise** because it seeks to eliminate the other three possibilities. P2 in the second argument is the negation of the elimination premise. In the case of correlated events x and y, to show that x causes y, you must (using argument 1) show that the elimination premise is true. To show that x does not cause y, you must (using argument 2) show that the elimination premise is false. The elimination premise contains the modal phrase "likely" because the available evidence can never completely rule out the other three possibilities. Thus, causal arguments are nondeductive despite having linked premises.

> ### Elimination Premises
>
> In the case of a causal argument with the conclusion that event x causes event y, the elimination premise seeks to exclude the other three possibilities, namely, that x and y are coincidental, that x and y have a common cause, and that x causes y.

A third basic form of causal argument is worth mentioning. Sometimes, an argument for a singular causal statement does not use the elimination premise, but instead cites a general causal statement. In this case, the singular causal statement is an instance of, or is covered by, that general causal statement. For example, the singular causal statement that a particular bad economic report caused the stock market to decline could be argued for by citing the general causal statement that bad economic reports tend to cause stock market declines. Thus, when the conclusion is a singular causal statement, the premise would be a general causal statement.[14] Here is the form:

3. Another argument to show that x causes y:
    P1: Events of kind x cause (or tend to cause) events of kind y.
    C: Therefore, x causes y.

Before discussing causal arguments in more detail, we should say something about **causal explanations.** Often, instances of reasoning involving causal statements are explanations rather than arguments. Recall from our discussion of explanations in Chapter 3 the main difference between arguments and explanations. In general, an argument is reasoning in which the author believes that most of the audience does not already believe the conclusion, whereas an explanation is reasoning in which the author believes that most of the audience does already believe the conclusion.

In most causal explanations, the conclusion (the explanandum) is a statement that an event occurred rather than a causal statement; the causal statement is one of the premises. Suppose some event occurs that needs explanation: How did it happen? A statement that the event occurred would be the explanandum, and a causal statement, along with a statement that the cause occurred, would be the explanans. For example, how is some explosion to be explained? Here is the explanans: Gas can cause an explosion, and there was a gas leak.

Sometimes, causal explanations, like causal arguments, have a causal statement as a conclusion. This kind of causal explanation is similar to the third form of causal argument, presented above. The reasoning explains how a singular causal statement is included in or covered by a general causal statement. For example, we may all believe that George's rubbing a balloon in his hair is what caused the balloon to stick to the wall, and someone may explain this causal relation for us by citing the general causal statement that rubbing objects against certain surfaces tends to cause them to build up a positive charge.

Causal Explanations

A causal explanation is reasoning that seeks either (1) to explain an event by citing a causal statement or (2) to explain a singular causal statement by citing a general causal statement.[15] As in all explanations, the author believes that the audience already believes the truth of the explanandum (event y occurred). Thus, the explanans (event x occurred, and event x caused event y) explains the explanandum.

Now let us return to the discussion of causal arguments that involve the elimination premise. Assuming that events x and y are correlated, the focus is on showing the truth or falsity of the elimination premise. This is the most interesting and difficult part of most causal arguments. While we can directly observe that events are correlated, we cannot directly observe that any of the four possibilities is true or false. Thus, we cannot directly observe the truth or falsity of the elimination premise. Instead, we must argue for its truth or falsity. The key to a causal argument, whether type 1 or type 2, is, thus, the subargument for P2. How can this premise be supported? What kinds of subarguments can be offered for it?

The first question is whether events x and y are coincidental. The other three possibilities all involve some kind of causal connection between x and y: Either x causes y, y causes x, or x and y have a common cause. If x and y are not coincidental, then we need to figure which of these three kinds of causal connections holds between x and y. But the first step is to investigate the possibility of coincidence.

So, how can we argue whether events x and y are coincidental? Superstitions are coincidental events falsely thought to be causally linked. Consider these examples:

Example 10.22

A. When I hit my last home run, my second shirt button was unbuttoned, so the second must have caused the first.
B. When I broke my leg last month, it was Friday the 13th. My bad luck was caused by its being that unlucky day.

How do we show that the events in these cases are coincidental? The answer is that we look for repetition of the correlation among events of the same kind. In argument A, if event x (my second shirt button being unbuttoned) and event y (my getting a home run) are *not* coincidental, there is good reason to expect that another instance of an event of kind y would be correlative with another instance of an event of kind x. In other words, I would expect a correlation between other cases of my button being unbuttoned and other cases of my hitting a home run. The basis of this expectation is the regularity of nature (discussed in the section on inductive arguments). Causation acts according to laws. When there is a causal relation between particular events x and y, this is an instance of a general causal relationship between events of kind x and events of kind y.

It is not always easy to see the link between a causal law and an instance in which that law applies, for several reasons. First, as mentioned previously, if we think of a cause as a necessary condition, even when event x causes event y, correlation between other instances of these kinds of events will fail when another of the necessary conditions for event y is lacking.[16] For example, not all events of burning cigarettes thrown out of car windows are correlated with fires. Second, our awareness and discovery of causal laws is dependent on how we describe events. Events can be described in different ways, and recognizing that the relationship between events x and y is an instance of a causal law may depend on how we describe those events.

Despite these difficulties, however, the best way to determine whether correlated events are coincidental is to see if there is a correlation between other instances of those kinds of events. Are other cases of the unbuttoned button correlated with home runs? Are other Friday the 13ths correlated with unfortunate happenings? If we are trying to decide whether events x and y are coincidental, we need to look for other instances of these kinds of events to see whether they are correlated. In order to do do, we can simply look around for other instances, or we can create those other instances by intervening in nature. Such interventions are experiments.

Consider this example:

Example 10.23

Background: The outcome of the 2000 presidential contest came down to who (Bush or Gore) would win the electoral votes of Florida. Because less than a thousand votes separated the two candidates there, recounts were undertaken in some precincts. In those precincts, voters punched out tiny pieces of punch cards (called chads) to register a vote. Critics complained that the recounts were unfair because chads may have been knocked from the punch cards by the handling they received during the recount. This letter is in response to these complaints. (*New York Times*, 11/00)

> Not one of the many complainers about the confetti that is supposed to be raining out of Florida's ballots seems to have done the crucial experiment. They haven't tested what it takes to knock chads out of cards. I did it years ago. I shuffled punch cards, I riffled them, I hit their edges individually and in groups against a table top, I waved them vigorously through the air. I bent them and twisted them and dropped them on the floor. I wiped them off with my palm. The only stuff that fell out of them was from holes that had already been punched. Before grumblers report that finding bits of paper on the tabletops is evidence of wickedness, perhaps they ought to collect some facts about the stability of the cards themselves.—J.V.T.

The complainers that the author refers to claim that the handling of the punch cards in the recount process caused chads to fall out of the cards. This would, of course, mean that the recounts were not an accurate representation of the original vote. Their causal claim is based on a correlation between two events or states: (1) the handling of the punch cards in the recount process and (2) the presence of the chads around the recounting area. The author reports on an experiment in which he tried to dislodge chads from punch cards by handling them in the same way they were handled in the recount process. In other words, the author created other instances of event x to see if they would be correlated with other instances of event y. They were not. The results were that no chads were dislodged.

In this author's experiment, the lack of a correlation between events of kind x and kind y in this experiment suggests that correlation between events x and y during the recount process was a coincidence. In contrast, if the author had found other instances of the correlation, this would have been good evidence that x and y were not coincidental but were causally related.

To help us to develop these ideas further, consider this example:

Example 10.24

Ashley develops a severe stomach illness one evening (call this event S). Among the events correlative with her falling ill are her eating the main course at the college dining hall (D), her eating raw shellfish at a college party (P), and her having recent contact with someone just coming down with the flu (F). It turns out that five other students got a similar illness that evening. These three events (D, P, and F) were correlative with S. Were these correlations coincidences or not?

The fact that five other students had the same illness as Ashley allows us to see which, if any, of these correlations were repeated. Let us say that all of the ill students had eaten in the dining hall, but only three of them ate the shellfish and only two had contact with the flu victim. So far, this study shows that the correlations between S and P and between S and F are coincidences, but that the correlation between S and D may not be.

The study, so far, has looked at other events of type S (students getting the stomach illness) to see if they are correlated with other events of type D (students eating in the dining hall). But the correlation can be tested in another way as well. What about beginning with instances in which a type-S event does not occur and seeing if any of them are correlated with instances of type-D events? We could look at a group of students who did not get ill, and see if any of them ate at the dining hall. If not, this strengthens the view that the correlation between S and D is not a coincidence.

Thus, there are two approaches to investigating whether correlative events, x and y, are coincidental. First, look for other instances of type y to see whether they are correlated with instances of type x. Did other students who had the stomach illness also eat in the dining hall? Second, look for instances that are not of type y to see whether any of them are correlated with instances of type x. Did other students who did not get sick eat in the dining hall? These two approaches, along with others, were developed by the nineteenth-century British philosopher John Stuart Mill (1806–1873). He referred to the first as the method of agreement and the second as the method of difference. The **method of agreement** involves studying a number of events of type y to determine whether there is an event of another type (such as x) correlative with each of the type-y events. If so, this supports the claim that x and y are causally connected. The **method of difference** involves studying a number of cases in which there is no event of type y to determine whether any of these cases are correlative with the type of event x that is correlative with y. If not, this further supports the claim that x and y are not coincidental.

Mill's Method of Agreement and Method of Difference

The method of agreement involves studying a number of events of type y to determine whether each of them has an event of another type x correlative with it. If so, this supports the claim that x and y are not coincidental. The method of difference involves studying a number of cases in which there is no event of type y to determine whether any of these cases has correlative with it an event of type x. If not, this further supports the claim that x and y are not coincidental.

If we have determined that events x and y are not coincidental, then we know that they are causally related. The next step is to determine which form their causal relationship takes. To show that x causes y, we need to rule out the alternatives that x and y have a common cause and that y causes x. In contrast, to show that x does not cause y, we need to show either that x and y have a common cause or that y causes x. How do we show that it is true or false that x and y have a common cause or that y causes x?

Consider these examples:

Example 10.25

A. Grandma, I'm as lucky as can be because God made you especially for me![7]

B. "A dog starved at his master's gate predicts the ruin of the state."[8]

The cuteness of sentence A derives from the apparent inconsistency between the causal statement and the implicit temporal relation of the two events. The effect is the creation of the grandmother. The cause is the interests of the grandchild that God creates the grandmother to satisfy. The problem is that the creation occurred many years *before* the child had any interests to satisfy. A basic principle of causation is that a cause never follows its effect in time.[19] A cause always either precedes its effect or occurs simultaneously with it. This provides one way to choose between the two possibilities: that x causes y or that y causes x. If x precedes y, then x must be the cause, and if y precedes x, then y must be the cause. (If they occur simultaneously, we cannot tell.)

Sentence B says that an event, x (a dog's starving at his master's gate), allows us to predict the occurrence of another event, y (the state's ruination). If we can predict one event from another, the two events cannot be coincidental. Thus, if this statement is true, there must be some sort of causal relationship between x and y. But what sort? Does x cause y? This seems highly implausible. Does y cause x? This does not seem to be what the author means, for a prediction usually looks to the future. Because the dog's starving precedes the state's ruination, the latter cannot be the cause of the former. By elimination, then, the relationship between x and y is that they have a common cause.

Indeed, it is quite plausible that events x and y have a common cause in this case. We can find a **plausible causation story** about these events that would make this true, probably something similar to what the author had in mind. We need to consider a possible cause for the one event that could also be a cause of the other. Here is one possibility: The starving of the dog is caused by his master's indifference, an indifference that is part of a general attitude of indifference of the ruling group in society. This indifference would lead to the neglect of small duties, such as feeding dogs, and large duties, such as tending to the welfare of the state. Thus, this indifference could cause both dogs' starvation and the state's ruination. Of course, to say that this is a plausible story is not to say that it is true, and we could criticize it as unlikely or based on a misunderstanding of how a society works. But the key point is that this example shows how plausible stories play an important role in our presentation and evaluation of causal arguments.

This idea about plausible causation stories needs to be generalized. We all have a worldview, largely shared with other members of our culture, that gives us a general understanding of what kinds of events cause what other kinds of events.

That worldview forms a background to the causal statements we make and criticize and to the causal arguments we present and evaluate.

To see how this is the case, consider that when events x and y are correlative our ability to show that x does or does not cause y requires that we argue that the elimination premise is true or false. As we have seen, this requires that we (1) determine whether x and y are coincidental and, if they are not, that we (2) determine whether they are directly causally related (x causes y or y causes x) or have a common cause. But at each of these two steps, our efforts involve an appeal to plausible causation stories based on our general understanding of how the world works.

Our discussion of B in Example 10.25 shows how plausible causation stories apply at the second step. Assuming that these events x and y are not coincidental (in other words, that there is a causal relation between them), we are inclined to agree that their relation is that of having a common cause, because we can find, given our general understanding of how the world works, a cause w that would be common to both. Furthermore, this cause w is such that neither x nor y would be on a causal chain leading from w to the other.

How are plausible causation stories involved in the first step, the one that determines whether events x and y are coincidental? Let us go back to our example of Ashley's illness. Ashley's becoming ill is correlative with a huge number of other events. For example, it might be correlative with a full moon, with the blossoming of Washington's cherry trees, with the birth of a large number of people around the globe, and on and on. We need some way to identify which correlative events to investigate as possible causes. Because we cannot investigate, or even be aware of, most of them, we make this selection based on plausible causation stories. In effect, we ask ourselves which events correlative with the illness are, in our experience with and understanding of the world, potential causes of such illness. It is only those that we choose to investigate.

Most causal arguments do not explicitly have the formal structures, involving the elimination premise, we have discussed in this chapter. Instead, they avoid explicit consideration of the four possibilities mentioned in our earlier discussion and rely directly on plausible causation stories. One example of this is the argument about bicycle helmets presented in Example 10.19. The author presents the causal claim in the second sentence—that bike helmets could be the cause of increasingly fat, immobile children and adults. (Notice that the author presents the claim with modal modification "could be," which may be interpreted as "likely.") The third sentence presents a plausible causation story supporting this claim. That is, having to put on a helmet diminishes the spontaneous pleasure of riding and so causes people to ride less. The strength of this causal argument depends on the plausibility of this story.

Here is the argument structure:

Example 10.26

P1: The declining use of bicycles is correlated with the increasing pressure to wear bicycle helmets.

P2: It is plausible that the increasing pressure to wear helmets takes away the spontaneous pleasure of riding, leading people to ride on fewer occasions.

C: Therefore, likely, the increasing pressure to wear bicycle helmets is causing the decline in bicycle riding.

We may regard P2 as an implicit form of the elimination premise. Clearly, the author would regard this plausible causation story as precluding the other three possibilities: (1) that the events are coincidental, (2) that they have a common cause, or (3) that decline in bike riding is causing the pressure to wear helmets.

Plausible Causation Stories

Plausible causation stories are descriptions of causal relations that seem to us to be plausible given our general understanding of how the world works. When we are presenting a causal argument or subargument, or evaluating one, plausible causation stories play an important role. In particular, defending the truth or falsity of the elimination premise usually involves an appeal at some point in the argument to plausible causation stories, as does an evaluation of that defense.

Of course, a plausible story is not always a true story. Our general understanding of the world may in some respects be mistaken, so that the causation stories we find plausible may be false or the ones we find not to be plausible may be true. This can cause a problem for our causal arguments. Here is one historical example: Hungarian obstetrician Ignaz Semmelweis (1818–1865) was concerned about the high rate of mortality from childbed fever among women in childbirth and devoted himself to finding the cause. There were a number of ideas about the cause, but none of them seemed to be satisfactory.

Noting the death of a fellow physician from the same illness subsequent to his being cut with an autopsy scalpel, Semmelweis thought that the illness might be due to the fact that attending physicians who had been in contact with corpses or other patients with the same illness did not wash their hands prior to delivering the babies. He ordered the physicians to wash their hands first, and the mortality rate plunged. Despite this success, his work was greeted with skepticism. Part of the reason for this skepticism may have been that he advanced his claim that lack of hand washing was the cause of the illness years before the germ theory of disease was developed.

We can imagine that the reason Semmelweis's work met with skepticism is that, prior to the development of germ theory, the claim that a lack of hand washing caused such an illness was not a plausible causation story. The general understanding of the world held by medical personnel in Semmelweis's day was mistaken in a way that only the development of the germ theory would later correct. Until that correction was made, Semmelweis's causal claim simply sounded too implausible for many to accept.[20]

What this discussion of plausible causation stories shows is that in many cases when you are presenting a causal argument, you will find yourself presenting a causation story and proclaiming or defending its plausibility, given the background understanding of how the world works that you share with your audience. Correspondingly, when you are evaluating a causal argument, you will often be called upon to assess the plausibility of the causation story that it contains. In either case, it is important to remember that the plausible causation stories being presented or assessed substitute for a discussion of the factors referred to in the more formal structures presented above (causal argument forms 1 and 2). These factors indicate what a plausible causation story must do, namely, show correlation between the events and eliminate the possibilities of coincidence, common cause, or reversal of direct causal relations. Thus, the plausible causation story is meant implicitly to show correlation of the events and to eliminate the other three possibilities, and the story should be assessed in terms of its success in doing so. Here is the form:

4. Less formal argument to show that x causes y:
   P1: Given the relevant facts (u, v, w), there is a plausible story that x causes y.
   C: Therefore, x causes y.

When causal arguments have this form, there will often be, and usually should be, a subargument supporting the premise. To criticize the argument, through a charge of problematic premise or hasty conclusion on the subargument, you should seek to show that the story is not plausible, or not as plausible as an alternative story, in terms of showing what the elimination premise is designed to show.

EXERCISE SET 10.3

SECTION A: Assume that the events in the following pairs are correlative. For each pair, indicate which of the four alternatives (coincidental, common cause, x causes y, y causes x) is most likely true, and provide a plausible causal story to support the claim. If an alternative other than the one you indicate is also plausible, explain why it is not correct.

EXAMPLE
x: The coming of spring in North America
y: The arrival of migrating birds from South America

ANSWER
Events x and y have a common cause. The same event causes spring to come and causes whatever signals the birds use to know that it is time to migrate north, and this event is the earth's moving into the part of its orbit where the Northern

Hemisphere is tilted toward the sun. Although one might think that x causes y, this is not so because spring is not happening at the place from which the birds begin their migration.

PROBLEMS

1. x: The Summer Olympics occurring in Atlanta in 1996
   y: Bill Clinton being elected president in 1996
2. x: The furnace coming on
   y: The temperature going down
3. x: A person having a morning cup of coffee
   y: That person leaving for work
4. x: A person's hair becoming gray
   y: That person needing bifocals
5. x: A person getting a sore throat
   y: That person getting a cough
6. x: The first snowfall of the year
   y: People buying snow shovels
7. x: An adolescent growing taller
   y: That adolescent acquiring sexual characteristics
8. x: A person quitting her job
   y: That person winning the lottery
9. x: A person being a Taurus
   y: That person having luck when the horoscopes predict he will
10. x: A person dancing
    y: That person enjoying herself
11. x: A person feeling better
    y: That person taking a placebo
12. x: A child committing violent acts
    y: That child watching violence on television
13. x: The large number of gun deaths in the United States
    y: The ready availability of guns in the United States
14. x: Harvard providing a good education
    y: Harvard graduates being intelligent
15. x: The existence of nuclear weapons from 1945 to 1991
    y: The absence of war between the United States and the Soviet Union from 1945 to 1991

SECTION B: The following texts discuss, explicitly or implicitly, the contrast between causes and other conditions. In each case, explain what point the author is making about this contrast. You are invited to comment on the author's claims as well.

EXAMPLE

Background: This letter is in response to a letter about capital punishment. (*New York Times*, 6/97)

The author of a letter contends that the convicted murderer "will go to the electric chair simply because he presents a meritorious legal argument before the courts had agreed on its correctness." Well, no. He will go to the electric chair because he killed somebody.—H.M.A.

ANSWER

There are a number of conditions necessary for a legal execution. The author is responding to someone who singled out one of these conditions, the fact that the merit of the defendant's legal arguments (presumably when the defendant appealed the death sentence to a higher court) was recognized only some time after it had been presented to the court. The author points to another of the conditions, namely, that the defendant was convicted of having killed someone, suggesting that that factor is more important. In effect, the author is claiming that it is more proper to single out as the cause of the execution the condition he cites rather than the other condition.

PROBLEMS

1. Background: This letter is in response to a letter about global warming. (*New York Times*, 8/99)

   The authors miss the key issue about global warming. It is a symptom, not the disease. The disease is overpopulation. If there were many fewer people on Earth, there would be less destruction of the rain forests, which absorb carbon dioxide, and it would matter less how much fossil fuel each person burned. We can treat this problem by demanding that Congress stop obstructing money to assist world population control.—H.T.B.[21]

2. Background: This letter is about computer problems. (*New York Times*, 1/88)

   On behalf of my computer and computers all over the world, I protest your report that "a complex new computer system has continued to delay many payments for Medicaid, food stamps and other public assistance, bringing suffering to thousands of New York's poor." When will people learn that computers do only what people tell them to do? The problem is not the complex new computer system, but the people who installed and programmed it. The problem may have been computer related, but not computer caused.—J.R.V.

3. Background: This letter is in response to a column about gun control. (*New York Times*, 6/98)

   Your columnist is typical of those who would control violence in the world by allowing or banning things. He says that easy access to guns is "one of the biggest factors in violent crime"—apparently, all that is needed to stop crime is to overturn the Second Amendment. Criminals are the source of crime. Proscribing things simply does not work. One of the most illegal things in the world to possess is any illegal drug. One can buy drugs on any street corner in New York City, any time. More crimes are prevented by lawful citizens lawfully protecting themselves with firearms than are prevented by the police. Firearms are not the enemy, criminals are.—W.R.L.

4. Background: This letter is about learning problems of children. (*New York Times*, 4/98)

   One cause of learning problems that is rarely mentioned is the poor diet of countless American children. Diets loaded with sugar and fats are deficient in essential fatty acids, magnesium, vitamins B6 and other important minerals and vitamins. Recent studies show that children who consume such diets are more apt to be troubled by attention deficit disorder and other behavioral and learning problems.—W.G.C.

5. Background: This letter refers to an incident in which a number of young men ran wild, assaulting women. (*New York Times*, 6/00)

Listing "testosterone" as one ingredient fueling the Central Park rampage implies that all men would be capable of engaging in a wolf-pack attack on women. Instead of citing biology as a contributing factor, it would have been more accurate to place the blame on social causes, like the mores that cheapen and dehumanize women while condoning malicious displays of male bravado.—M.S.

6. Background: This letter is in response to a column about a case in which a young mother, D, killed her newborn baby. (*Washington Post*, 6/97)

Take the case of the young girl D who allegedly gave birth in a restroom and then strangled the baby. Your columnist blames the availability of legal abortion for D's act, positing that it led D to see her baby as disposable. But let's take a look at other possible culprits. How about the lessened responsibility fathers are taking for their children? In the past, if a man impregnated his girlfriend, he was expected to marry her. These days, the father usually just walks away. What about the contempt our society has for the children of teenage mothers? Don't conservative columnists constantly say that the babies of teenage girls are mistakes, burdens on society, problems to be prevented? Is it such a surprise that D saw her baby as something to hide, as something worthless? How about the decreased availability of welfare? In the past, abandoned mothers and their children had at least a little help from the government, but even this is taken away. I believe that your columnist has it backward. Making abortion unavailable will just make desperate girls more likely to resort to infanticide. But bear in mind that, throughout the column, abortion is presented as morally equivalent to infanticide.—J.S.

SECTION C: The following texts argue for causal claims or against the causal claims of others. Structure the arguments, using whichever of the four forms of causal argument or some variation of them, is most appropriate. Evaluate the causal arguments, or, if you think that a fallacy charge should not be made, explain how they are strong. Many of the texts involve plausible causation stories.

EXAMPLE

Background: This letter is about suicide by police officers. (*New York Times*, 9/94)

If the rate of suicide among New York police officers is four times that of the general population, isn't it logical to assume that police officers are victims of the ready availability of a gun in a moment of despair? Fortunately, most people do not have access to a gun at such times. This could account for most of the difference in suicide rates.—R.D.

ANSWER

Structure

P1A: There is a correlation between being a police officer and having a higher rate of suicide.

P1B: Police officers have ready access to guns.

P1: There is a correlation between having ready access to guns and having a higher rate of suicide.

P2: It is plausible that a person in despair is more likely to commit suicide if an easy means of suicide is at hand.

C: Therefore, having ready access to guns causes a higher rate of suicide.

EVALUATION

This is a strong argument. The plausible causation story in P2 provides strong support for the causal claim in the conclusion. Moments of despair are often short-lived, and if a person does not have access to an easy means of committing suicide, the moment might pass before suicide could be attempted, so that it is less likely to result.

PROBLEMS

1. Background: This letter is about the effects of immigration. (*New York Times*, 7/00)

   According to your article, immigration is offsetting population lost to death and relocation. Without it, the article says, the city would see "neighborhood abandonment and depopulation." But perhaps it is the other way around: as new population flows into the city, bringing crowded schools, congested streets and housing shortages, long-term residents leave, seeking more habitable space elsewhere. It's hard to know here whether the chicken came first or the egg.—A.K.

2. Background: This letter is about bilingual education. (*New York Times*, 8/00)

   Your article suggests that California's ban on bilingual education has caused test scores to rise. But a chart accompanying the article shows that scores have risen the same or less for non-English-speaking students as for English-speaking students. California has simply improved its education for students.—J.F.

3. Background: This letter is about telephone area codes. (*New York Times*, 11/97)

   The New York State Public Service Commission could have given Manhattan a new area code in a sensible way by splitting the island in half and assigning the new code to everything south of, say, 25th Street. Then area code 646—associated with the coolest and trendiest part of the city—would have quickly developed a cachet equivalent to 212. Devising a system so irrational just to allow people to keep their "glamorous" 212 area codes misunderstands the relationship: it was Manhattan that gave glamour to 212, not 212 that gave glamour to Manhattan.—M.T.

4. Background: This letter is about global warming. (*Washington Post*, 7/97)

Your columnist's discussion of global warming repeats many conventional-wisdom notions that cry out for critical examination. Pretty clearly, eras such as classical antiquity and the high Middle Ages occurred during periods of warmer climates than today. During these times, food-producing areas extended substantially farther north than now, and sea levels were higher—and they were times of great creativity and cultural flowering. In fact, it's possible to argue that eras of cool, drier climates coincide with falling food production, barbarian invasions, wars and plagues—times such as the Homeric period, the fall of Rome and the late Middle Ages. The environment is dynamic, not static, and there is no reason to believe we live in the best of all possible times.—C.M.W.

5. Background: This letter is about the effect of music on behavior. Two students who committed mass murder at Columbine High School in Colorado belonged to a gang called the "trench coat mafia." (*New York Times*, 4/99)

   The deliberate use of loud, disturbing rock music and the abuse it inflicts on our lives in retail settings and schools and on television and radio are certainly in part to blame for the deadly reactions of the adolescents of the "trench coat mafia." Let's bring back classical music education in all schools and in our culture. Many of us studied it in school decades ago, when these kinds of horrible events never occurred. Classical music may not help the bottom line, but it may save lives.—S.S.[22]

6. Background: This letter is about attracting good teachers to the classroom. (*New York Times*, 1/00)

   Raising standards for teacher preparation programs is not a sufficient condition for improving teacher quality, since it does not address the problem of attracting intelligent and talented individuals to the profession. One of the most unattractive features of teaching in public schools is the plethora of moribund bureaucratic regulations imposed routinely by states desperate to appear as if they are doing something to improve public education. As my more talented and dedicated colleagues and I struggle daily with Byzantine state regulations masquerading as "standards," we cannot help but wonder if a dose of academic freedom would not do more to welcome creative and innovative individuals to the profession than would additional state regulations.—N.J.R.

7. Background: This letter is about a proposal to reduce poverty by doing more to encourage marriage in poor communities. (*New York Times*, 7/99)

   The proposal to "revive marriage" to end poverty and protect poor children reverses cause and effect. The "explosion of out-of-wedlock births" among black women closely parallels the decline in job opportunities for the black fathers of these children. In New York, job losses took a high toll among young black men. Their rate of participation in the labor force fell by more than half between 1950 and 1980, and rose only slightly afterwards. The thousands now in prison for drug dealing are exiles from a job market that largely excluded them and a school system that failed them. William Julius

Wilson's research in Chicago showed that black men born in the war years were two and a half times more likely to marry the mothers of their children than were those a generation later. Behavior did not change, but the economy did.—S.M.R.

8. Background: The letter discusses a case in which a mother shot her daughter, who was then put on life support. The daughter's request to be allowed to die was subsequently granted. The question is whether the mother should be charged with murder. (*New York Times*, 5/99)

I was perplexed to find uncertainty over the possibility of bringing murder charges against a mother who allegedly shot her daughter in the neck, leaving her paralyzed. Murder is allowed in many cases in which we would be hard-pressed to say the felon "caused" the victim's death. In many states the death of an innocent bystander occurring during the commission of a felony can result in murder charges brought against the felon. The theory is that the felon set in motion events resulting in the death. The case for murder against the mother is more convincing. Her daughter was kept alive only with the aid of a respirator. Some would argue that such an existence is worse than death and that the daughter had no choice but to plead to be taken off life support. In what sense, then, did the mother not cause the daughter to make this choice?—A.W.R.

❖ 9. Background: This letter is about gun violence. (*New York Times*, 12/93)

Whenever another man decides to go on a rampage and empties his rapid-firing gun into a crowd of uninvolved civilians, his maleness is not considered a motive. It is obvious fact that every single gun-wielding mass murderer in history was a man. Violent rage is an essential feature of the weak male ego. Guns have become a fabulously effective method to combat lingering spinelessness and pathetic lack of conscience. Society and its media do more and more to feed the masculinity myth, which is nothing other than an attenuated version of male homicidal rage. And the solution? Waiting periods, background checks, licenses and testing are only partial answers. They do not challenge the essentially male obsession with guns. It would take a great deal of confidence building and cross-gender communication to mend the millions of thwarted male souls that could inflict mayhem.—P.S.

10. Background: This letter is about the effect of advertising on children. (*Denver Post*, 5/97)

A rumor has it that Budweiser is doing away with its frog and alligator commercials due to pressure from Mothers Against Drunk Driving. Everything geared toward adults suddenly is a no-no because kids might be drawn to the product. What has happened to the days when parents taught their kids right from wrong? In all my years of newspaper reading and TV watching, I have not seen ads condoning cocaine and marijuana use, but their use seems to be on the rise. So it is difficult to believe that a television ad that shows three cool frogs and an alligator will influence and encourage the consumption of beer among children if parents do their job.—J.M.

11. Background: This letter is about the effect of gun control on school violence. (*Boston Globe*, 4/99)

Gun control caused the Colorado massacre by ensuring the murderers that their victims would most likely be unarmed. Guns save lives where the criminals don't know whether their victims are legally armed. This incident could have been stopped almost immediately if a teacher had a concealed handgun. Two of the recent school shootings were stopped by armed citizens. The assistant principal stopped the student gunman in Pearl, Miss., with a handgun retrieved from his car. A bystander held the student gunman at gunpoint until police arrived in Edinboro, Pa. No shots were fired by the armed citizen in either incident. The Colorado Legislature should immediately pass, and the governor should sign into law, the concealed carry bill that is before them. For the children.—P.A.M.

❖ 12. Background: This letter is about magazine covers. (*New York Times*, 5/98)

Although I'm a big admirer of *The New York Times Magazine* and its editor, I found his comment in your article about magazines' catering to celebrities to be smug. It's great that *The Times Magazine* refuses to grant celebrities the kind of quote and photo approval they routinely wrest from other general-interest magazines. In an ideal world all magazines would adhere to that standard. But most magazines are forced to put celebrities on the cover because celebrities drive newsstand sales, a critical source of revenue. By contrast, *The Times Magazine* has no such economic need; since it is bundled inside the rest of the paper, its editors are free to make cover decisions without having to worry about whether that cover will sell on the newsstand.—J.N.

10.4 A Final Word on Implicit Premises

The prior discussion of two main types of nondeductive arguments provides an opportunity for further consideration of distinguishing between deductive and nondeductive arguments. We can do this by saying something more about implicit premises.

We have considered three situations in which an implicit premise should be included in an argument, represented in the rules of addition, numbers 2, 3, and 4.[23] The most important of these for our current purposes is number 3, presented in Chapter 6. When an argument contains a single explicit premise that is a universal statement or a conditional, and there is a statement not included in the text that would link with the premise to show how it supports the conclusion, that statement should be added as an implicit premise. For example, in the case of a single explicit premise that is a conditional, the implicit premise might show how the conditional supports the conclusion by showing the argument to be a case of *modus ponens* or *modus tollens*.

In this kind of case, the implicit premise is a linked premise and reveals the argument to be deductive. As we have seen, all deductive arguments have linked premises (except for immediate inferences). Thus, asking, as we now do, if there are other cases in which implicit premises should be added can be a way of asking if there are other arguments that may not appear to be deductive but are so, because the linked premise is implicit.

Consider these arguments:

Example 10.27

A. All those who are excellent college teachers should be granted tenure. So, Gomez should be granted tenure.

B. Gomez is an excellent college teacher. So, Gomez should be granted tenure.

C. Interest rates have declined. So, the stock market will improve.

D. Lowering the speed limit to 55 MPH would save lives, so we should lower the speed limit to 55 MPH.

E. Buying a new car would impress the neighbors, and it would reduce our frequent trips to the repair shop. So, we should buy a new car.

F. Stalin was only human. So, he had to die someday.

According to the rule of addition, number 3, argument A contains the implicit premise that Gomez is an excellent college teacher. The argument is deductive, as the addition of the implicit premise makes clear. This implicit premise is the same as the explicit premise in argument B. So, the question arises as to whether argument B contains the conditional in argument A as an implicit premise.

If argument B is limited to what the text says explicitly, then it is a nondeductive argument. Including the conditional as an implicit premise would make the argument deductive. This is true for *any* nondeductive argument. If you select one of its premises and add to the argument the appropriate universal statement or conditional that would link with that premise, then the argument becomes deductive.[24] For example, argument C appears to be a nondeductive argument, but it could be turned into a deductive argument by adding the following universal statement: "All situations in which interest rates decline are situations in which the stock market improves." The question of whether argument C has this as an implicit premise is the same as the question of whether it is deductive or nondeductive.

As we have seen, not all arguments with linked premises are deductive. For example, the standard forms of causal arguments and arguments from analogy (discussed in Chapter 11) have linked premises, yet these arguments are nondeductive. But for arguments like B and C, in which the addition of a general statement or a conditional would make the argument deductive, deciding whether the author intends such a statement as an implicit premise involves determining whether the author intends them to be deductive or nondeductive.

A deductive argument is one in which the truth of the premises guarantees the truth of the conclusion. Moreover, when an author presents premises, he or she generally presents them as true. So, when an author intends an argument to be deductive, he or she regards the argument as showing the conclusion to be true without a doubt. There is often a "case closed" character to the way in which an author presents a deductive argument. That is, if there is no doubt about the truth of the conclusion, there is no need to pursue the matter further. In contrast, non-deductive arguments are generally presented in a more open way. An author presenting a nondeductive argument recognizes that the truth of the premises is consistent with the falsity of the conclusion, and this recognition is often revealed in contextual clues.

Two contextual clues are the most important. First, when an author intends an argument to be nondeductive, there are often two or more convergent premises, as in argument E. The presence of these convergent premises shows that the author believes that one premise is not enough. But if the argument were deductive, with a universal statement or conditional as an implicit premise, one premise would be enough. That is, one premise, along with the implicit universal statement or conditional with which it is linked, would, given the truth of the premises, establish the conclusion with certainty. There would be no need for other convergent premises. So, the presence of two or more convergent premises usually indicates that the argument does not have an implicit premise and that the author does not intend the argument to be deductive.[25] In the case of E, if the author meant the argument to be deductive with an implicit premise, there would have been no need to include the second convergent premise.

The second clue concerns the acceptability of the universal statement or conditional that would link with the explicit premise to make the argument deductive. If that statement is a claim that people would readily believe, it is more likely that the argument has that statement as an implicit premise and is meant to be deductive. However, if that statement is not acceptable, it is less likely that the argument has an implicit premise and is meant to be deductive.

Consider arguments C and D. The statement that would, if included as an implicit premise, make C deductive is as follows: "All situations in which interest rates decline are situations in which the stock market improves." This is not an acceptable statement. Most people recognize that interest rates are only one factor that influences the stock market, but according to this statement interest rates are the only factor. The statement that would make argument D deductive is as follows: "All actions we can take that would save lives are actions we should take." While this initially might seem to be an acceptable value claim, on reflection it is not. For example, if we lowered all speed limits to 25 MPH, we would save even more lives, but the inconveniences of this policy would be so great that few would regard it as acceptable. So, the second kind of clue suggests that arguments C and D do not have an implicit premise and are not meant to be deductive.

Contrast these cases with argument F. Here, there is a single premise, and the universal statement that would make the argument deductive ("all humans are mortal") is certainly an acceptable one. As a result, the available contextual clues suggest that argument F has that statement as an implicit premise and is meant to be deductive.

When a universal statement or conditional is explicitly included as a premise, this usually indicates that the argument is meant to be deductive, and if the argument needs the inclusion of an implicit premise to make it clearly so, then one should be added. This is the rule of addition, number 3, from Chapter 6. But if the text does not contain a universal statement or conditional (and does not fall under one of the other two rules of addition pertaining to premises), this usually means that it is not intended as a deductive argument and so contains no implicit premise, unless the contextual clues indicate otherwise. The two main contextual clues indicating that an argument is meant to be deductive are that (1) there is only one premise, as in arguments C, D, and F, and (2) the universal statement or conditional that would make the argument deductive is acceptable, as in argument F. In most cases, unless both of these conditions are satisfied, the argument should be regarded as nondeductive. This is the rule of addition, number 5. Accordingly, arguments C and D are probably not deductive, and argument F probably is.

> ### Rule of Addition, Number 5
>
> An implicit premise is a linked premise and often reveals an argument to be deductive. Some arguments other than those to which the rule of addition, number 3, applies—that is, some arguments without an explicit universal statement or conditional as a premise—may contain such an implicit premise. In the case of such arguments, contextual clues may indicate that the argument contains such a statement as an implicit premise and is meant by the author to be deductive. The two main contextual clues indicating that such an implicit premise exists are (1) that there is only one premise and (2) the universal statement or conditional that would make the argument deductive is an acceptable claim. In most cases in which both of these clues are present, the implicit premise should be included and the argument treated as deductive. Otherwise, the argument is likely nondeductive.

Based on this rule, what should we say about argument B? Given the absence of one of the contextual clues, no implicit premise should be added. It is true that there is only one premise, but the statement that would make the argument deductive is not acceptable. The statement is that " all excellent teachers should be granted tenure" would not be regarded as true by most people because there is a recognition that other factors besides teaching should be considered in the granting of tenure. For example, college teachers are expected to be scholars as well as teachers.

While it is not always easy to tell whether an argument of the sort we are discussing has an implicit premise, this is not, in one respect, a serious problem. The evaluation of an argument is not in general seriously impaired by our decision whether to regard it as having an implicit premise. The reason for this has to do with the **transformation of fallacy charge.** That is, a fallacy charge that would be made against an argument under one of the interpretations (no implicit premise) is transformed into a different fallacy charge under the other interpretation (an implicit premise). For instance, what is a hasty conclusion charge under one interpretation becomes a problematic premise charge under the other. More importantly, the same critical point can be used in the justification for either fallacy charge.

Consider how argument B would be evaluated under both interpretations:

Example 10.28

A. Evaluation of argument B interpreted as having no implicit premise:

> I charge this argument with the fallacy of hasty conclusion. The premise is not sufficient to show that the conclusion is true. More evidence is needed to show that Gomez should get tenure. Tenure at a college or university is granted based on several factors. Although teaching is one, and perhaps the most important, other factors are the person's activities as a scholar and commitment to the life of the college community. These factors would have to be considered in additional premises before a judgment about tenure for Gomez could be made.

B. Evaluation of argument B interpreted as having an implicit premise:

> I charge this argument with the fallacy of problematic premise. The implicit premise, that all those who are excellent college teachers should be granted tenure, is not acceptable. Support for it is needed. Tenure at a college or university is granted based on several factors. Although teaching is one, and perhaps the most important, other factors are the person's activities as a scholar and commitment to the life of the college community. The author needs to address these points in a subargument to show that the premise is acceptable.

Identical language is used in these two evaluations to show that the same critical point can be made against the argument, whichever fallacy is charged. Thus, this problem with the argument will be revealed, whichever of the two interpretations is adopted.

The Transformation of Fallacy Charges

There is sometimes doubt about whether an argument should be interpreted as having an implicit premise. But in such cases, weaknesses in the argument will reveal themselves under either interpretation, due to the transformation of fallacy charges. If the argument is interpreted as not having an implicit premise, the charge of hasty conclusion may be appropriate. But if it is given the other interpretation, a charge of problematic premise against the implicit premise will be appropriate, and the same critical point will be part of the justification for either charge. The same weakness in the argument is revealed because the hasty conclusion charge is transformed into a problematic premise charge, or vice versa.

Summary

Nondeductive arguments are of several kinds, two of which are inductive and causal. In an inductive argument, we reason from singular claims based on observation to an empirical generalization, from what we know to what we do not know. We reason from a sample, the cases referred to in the singular statements of the premises, to a population, the cases referred to in the general statement of the conclusion. In a statistical inductive argument, the premises indicate that a portion, rather than all, of the sample has some characteristic, and the conclusion indicates that the same portion of the population has that characteristic.

The evaluation of an inductive argument usually focuses on how the sample is selected. When the sample has not been adequately selected, a hasty conclusion charge is appropriate. Two features are especially important in sample selection, size and representativeness. Representativeness is assured when the sample is selected randomly, but a truly random selection is seldom possible. When a sample is not random, there is bias in the selection that may seriously compromise representativeness. When considering a charge of problematic premise against an inductive argument, we must pay special attention to the reliability of human observation and to the differences in the way people can categorize their experience in their description of it.

Causal arguments have conclusions that are causal statements. A causal statement indicates that two events or states of affairs, the cause and effect, stand in a causal relation. A cause may be proximate (close) to its effect or remote from it. A remote cause is normally connected to its effect by a series of intervening causes and effects, known as a causal chain. Causal statements may be singular, indicating a causal relation between two particular events, or general, indicating a causal relation between events of one kind and events of another kind.

A cause is often understood to be a necessary condition for its effect, in which case the cause is normally chosen from among other conditions necessary for that effect. Sometimes, however, a cause is understood to be a sufficient condition for its effect, in which case the cause is normally considered to be the entire set of conditions of the effect.

When one event (or state) causes another, they are correlated, meaning that they occur together. But events may be correlated without being causally related. To argue from mere correlation to causation is to commit the fallacy of *post hoc ergo propter hoc*. When two events x and y are correlated, there are four possibilities: x causes y, y causes x, x and y have a common cause, or x and y are coincidental, in which case there is no causal relation between them.

Assuming that two events x and y are correlated, the causal argument that x causes y must rule out the other three possibilities, based on the elimination premise. There are two basic forms of causal argument for singular causal statements, one concluding that x causes y and the other that x does not cause y.

Given the assumption that there is regularity to nature, causation operates according to rules (called causal laws) guaranteeing that if two events are causally related their causal relationship in the one case will be matched by events of that kind being causally related, and hence correlated, in other cases as well. We can look for other such correlations either by passively observing the world or by actively intervening through experiments, deliberately setting up opportunities for other such correlations, if they exist, to reveal themselves. These efforts can be aided by applying Mill's method of agreement and method of difference.

If we find no correlations between other events of kind x and kind y, then we may conclude that x does not cause y. If we do find them, then we must investigate whether they have a common cause or whether y causes x. We can often rule out the possibility that y causes x based on temporal considerations. In investigating whether the events have a common cause, we need to consider events or states that might be a common cause of x and y, while ensuring that neither is on a causal chain with the other. This requires that we apply our general understanding of how the world works. In attempting to show that the elimination premise is true or false, we rule in or out causal scenarios based largely on their plausibility in the light of this general understanding, even though that understanding may in some respects be mistaken.

Because implicit premises are linked premises, the inclusion of an implicit premise often indicates that the argument is deductive, whereas without that premise it would be nondeductive. An implicit premise should also be included when an argument contains no explicit premise that is a universal statement or a conditional but it is clear nonetheless that the author intends the argument to be deductive. Most such arguments are not intended to be deductive, but some are.

When we judge that such an argument is intended to be deductive, the universal statement or conditional that would reveal it to be deductive should be included as an implicit premise. There are two contextual clues that together strongly suggest that an author intends such an argument to be deductive: (1) The argument contains a single explicit premise, and (2) the universal statement or conditional that would make the argument deductive is an acceptable claim.

Whether we correctly interpret such an argument as deductive or nondeductive does not interfere with our ability to evaluate it, due to the transformation of fallacy charges. The same critical points that would be included in the justification of a hasty conclusion charge, if the argument is interpreted as nondeductive, can be included in the justification of a problematic premise charge against the implicit premise, if the argument is interpreted as deductive.

Key Terms

inductive argument

empirical
  generalization

population

sample

induction by
  enumeration

condensed premise

regularity of nature

statistical inductive
  argument

collective property

sample size

sample
  representativeness

sample selection

random sample

bias

stratified sample

causal statement

causal argument

proximate cause

remote cause

causal chain

singular causal
    statement

general causal
    statement

causal verb

conditions

correlation

*post hoc ergo propter
    hoc*

elimination premise

causal explanation

method of
    agreement

method of difference

plausible causation
    story

transformation of
    fallacy charge

Notes

1. George Santayana, *Life of Reason, Reason in Common Sense* (New York: Scribner, 1905), p. 284.
2. In addition to the case of Kosovo, some people argue that the atomic bombing of Hiroshima also was effective at forcing the Japanese to surrender in World War II.
3. Moreover, who knows what genetics has in store for our children and grandchildren?
4. Unless we travel to one of the polar regions, where we would find 24 hours of darkness.
5. Sometimes, this point is made by saying that the argument has an implicit premise with which the three explicit premises are linked, namely, that Joe, Bill, and John are the only men in my family.
6. The exceptional cases are mainly those in which all the members of the sample have the characteristic, but the author then cautiously draws the conclusion only that most of the members of the population do.
7. It would be a mistake to think that Einstein derived his theory of motion from an inductive argument. It used to be thought that induction was the principal method of science. Instead, the view now is that science operates principally through deduction. A scientist will come up with a hypothesis—a possible natural law—and test the hypothesis by deriving conclusions deductively from it and testing those conclusions. If a conclusion proves to be false, then the hypothesis from which it is derived is shown to be false by *modus tollens.*
8. On certain metaphysical views, objects are simply events of a certain kind. For example, some claim that persons are events when viewed from the perspective of four-dimensional space-time.
9. General causal statements that include the phrase "tends to cause," or some equivalent, are nonuniversal generalizations. Those without such a phrase, explicit or implicit, are universal generalizations.
10. There is a third way of understanding a cause. Sometimes, what is labeled a cause is not a necessary or a sufficient condition, but instead a nonnecessary contributing factor in bringing about the effect. This applies frequently in the case of general causal statements. For example, smoking is a nonnecessary condition (often called a contributing condition) for lung cancer, in the sense that smoking is a condition for some cases of lung cancer but not for others. This might be due to our not distinguishing more pre-

cisely among different kinds of effects. In other words, it may be that smoking is a necessary condition for some kinds of lung cancer and not a condition at all for others. If we are speaking of causation between particular events, the following kind of situation can arise: A and B simultaneously shoot C, who dies, each shot having been sufficient, in conjunction with the other existing conditions, to kill C. Then neither shooting is a necessary condition for the death. This is referred to as overdetermination. But, unfortunately, given space limitations, we must ignore such complexities.

11. For the discussion of conditionals, see Chapter 5, section 5.2. The conditional in A, by the way, makes clear that the conditional relationship is not necessarily "directional" in the sense that the direction of the horseshoe might lead you to suspect. Events move from cause to effect, but the "movement" in the conditional representing this is the other way, from effect to cause.

12. See note 9 for another aspect of the explanation.

13. The last part of this sentence is necessary because, for us, events having a common cause is meant to be an alternative to either of them causing the other. Any event in a causal chain is the cause of all the events later in the chain, but this kind of "common cause" is not what we mean to include. When we speak of events having a common cause, we mean that they are not directly causally related. This is true of the coming up of the snowdrops and the crocuses.

14. When the conclusion is itself a general causal statement, the premise would include a *more general* general causal statement.

15. See note 14.

16. Partly for this reason, those who study causal laws often treat causes as sufficient conditions rather than as necessary conditions.

17. Adapted from a plaque given to a grandmother by her grandchild.

18. William Blake.

19. God, of course, may have the ability to violate this principle.

20. For a colorful account of Semmelweis, see Victor Robinson, *Pathfinders in Medicine* (New York: Medical Life Press, 1929).

21. The author of this letter is Howard T. Bellin, M.D.

22. The author of this letter is Stephen Starkman.

23. The rule of addition, number 1, is about implicit conclusions.

24. Recall that when we discussed the strength of nondeductive arguments in Chapter 6 we said that adding relevant premises could make the argument formally stronger, but never strong enough to be valid. But we included the qualification that the added premises had to be of the same kind as the premises already in the argument. This qualification was meant to exclude the addition of premises of the kind that would make the argument deductive and valid—that is, a universal statement or conditional that would link with one of the premises already part of the argument.

25. It does not prove that this is the author's intention, however, for otherwise there would be no such thing as mixed arguments, which, as discussed earlier, are arguments with both linked and convergent premises.

CHAPTER 11

All-Things-Considered Arguments and Analogies

He who knows only his own side of the case, knows little of that. His reasons may be good, and no one may have been able to refute them. But if he is equally unable to refute the reasons on the opposite side; if he does not so much as know what they are, he has no ground for preferring either opinion.

—JOHN STUART MILL[1]

In this chapter, we consider two other forms of nondeductive argument: all-things-considered arguments and arguments from analogy.

11.1 All-Things-Considered Arguments

The quotation from Mill reminds us that we need to examine and understand all sides of an issue, both the side we agree with and the side or sides we disagree with. We use an **all-things-considered (ATC) argument** to examine issues that have different sides.

11.1.1 Considering All Things

An ATC argument is useful in considering issues that have different sides. But an ATC argument is not appropriate for all issues because not all issues have different sides. In general, an issue has different sides when it is plausible to hold different views on the issue. For example, the issue of affirmative action has different sides because it is plausible to hold a position favoring or opposing this social policy. To understand the difference between issues that have different sides and those that do not, recall our discussion of the hasty conclusion fallacy in Chapter 6. To charge an argument with a hasty conclusion is to say that it does not consider factors (or evidence) that it should have, and those factors may be of the same type as or a different type from the ones considered in the premises. When an argument should consider factors of different types, the related issue generally has more than one side. The reason is that the different types of factors tend to support different positions on the issue, thereby making it plausible to hold different positions on that issue, depending on which of the factors are emphasized.

Because an ATC argument is used for issues that have different sides, the premises of that argument should refer to the different types of factors involved. The "all" in "all-things-considered" refers to the fact that ATC arguments present different types of factors. (It would be more accurate, though more awkward, to call these "all-types-of-things-considered arguments.") Issues that have different sides and that are best treated by an ATC argument are known as **ATC issues.**

Consider these two arguments on the topic of euthanasia:

Example 11.1

A. P1: Euthanasia is the killing of a human being.
    C: Therefore, euthanasia is wrong.

B. P1: Euthanasia is the killing of a human being.
    P2: Euthanasia requires doctors to become killers.
    P3: Euthanasia may lead to the ill being killed against their wishes.
    P4: Euthanasia is getting rid of the bothersome and the burdensome.
    P5: Euthanasia may be abused by those wishing to be rid of the ill.
    P6: A cure or recovery is always possible for any illness.
    P7: Those drugged and fearful cannot give full consent.
    P8: The pain of the terminally ill can be controlled with painkillers.
    C: Therefore, euthanasia is wrong.

Argument B does a better job of treating the issue of euthanasia, not only because it considers more factors than argument A but also because it considers factors of different types. For instance, whereas P1 frames the issue of euthanasia in terms of killing, P2 considers a factor of a different type, namely, the standing of euthanasia in relation to the role and responsibilities of physicians. The other premises raise other types of factors, including the possibility of people being killed against their will, the problematic nature of a patient's consent to euthanasia, the possibility of a cure should the patient remain alive, and the intense pain that may afflict the terminally ill. In contrast, argument A considers only one type of factor.

Argument B is a better way of addressing the issue of euthanasia than argument A because euthanasia is an issue that requires us to consider factors of many different types. Euthanasia is an issue about which it is plausible to hold different positions, and the different types of factors tend to support different positions. For example, the factor of killing tends to oppose the practice of euthanasia, whereas the factor of patient's choice tends to favor the practice.

As the euthanasia example suggests, ATC issues are often social, political, and moral in nature. In these cases, many types of factors or kinds of evidence are relevant to the conclusion, which is often an action recommendation. But ATC issues may be personal as well. That is, many of the issues we face as individuals in our day-to-day lives involve a variety of types of factors that need to be considered through an ATC argument.

Not all ATC arguments are value arguments; rather, many factual issues are also ATC issues. For example, arguments about whether birds descended from dinosaurs might appeal to different types of factors such as the fossil record, the physiology of the bird wing, and DNA studies. Or, arguments about long-range weather forecasts might involve different types of factors such as the historical record, current meteorological data, and the behavior of the wooly caterpillar. In fact, ATC arguments are probably the most common kind of argument you will encounter. Many of the arguments given earlier in this book are ATC arguments.

ATC arguments may be contrasted with inductive arguments, which we discussed in Chapter 10. In general, inductive arguments consider only one type of factor or kind of evidence, whereas ATC arguments consider several types. But there is no sharp line separating ATC arguments from inductive arguments. This is because it is not always clear whether different factors are of the same type. This means that there is not a clear distinction between ATC issues and other issues, nor between issues that have different sides and those that do not. Nonetheless, many issues are obviously ATC issues, and this makes it important to understand ATC arguments.

In an ATC issue, the different types of factors support different positions on the issue. There can be good reasons supporting opposing conclusions—this is why issues have different sides. What characterizes ATC issues is not simply that different kinds of factors are relevant to their consideration, but that the different types of factors tend to support opposing positions. Thus, in reaching a conclusion on these issues, you have to consider *all* the relevant factors, favorable and unfavorable.

All-Things-Considered Arguments and ATC Issues

An all-things-considered (ATC) argument is a nondeductive argument with premises that consider or should consider factors of different types or evidence of different kinds. An ATC argument is appropriate for ATC issues—that is, issues that have different sides. It is plausible to take different sides on ATC issues because the different types of factors involved tend to support different positions.

In an ATC argument, you need to compare the factors on all sides of the issue to avoid a hasty conclusion charge. For controversial issues that have good reasons on different sides, arriving at a conclusion requires balancing the various relevant factors. In this sense, constructing a strong argument on an ATC issue requires weighing the factors on all sides and then showing that the factors favoring your conclusion outweigh the factors on the other side. If you fail to address some of the different types of factors, you might reach a hasty conclusion.

Consider this letter:

Example 11.2

Background: This letter is in response to an editorial on federal policy regarding air quality and the advisability of adopting a set of clean-air standards proposed by the Environmental Protection Agency (EPA). (*Atlanta Constitution*, 3/97)

> Your recent editorial implied that the industries and organizations that were against more stringent air-quality standards were "against better air." I seriously doubt that anyone is truly against clean air and the attendant health benefits. However, many sensible and responsible people are concerned about striking a reasonable balance between the need to protect public health and avoiding the burdens of unbridled government regulation. The proposed air-quality standards would gain only marginal health benefits in return for enormous economic and social costs.—J.C.

The author does two things. First, he criticizes the editorial for implying that anyone opposed to the EPA standards is also opposed to clean air. In other words, he argues, it is inappropriate to address this issue in terms of a single type of factor—in this case, the cleanness of the air. The social and economic cost of the government regulations should be considered as well. Thus, the factor of clean air counts in favor of the EPA regulations, and the factor of the cost of regulation counts against it. Second, the author argues that, when the proper balance is struck between these factors, the costs of the regulations outweigh the cleanness of the air, so the EPA standards should not be adopted.

The primary way in which ATC arguments compare opposing factors is through the inclusion of counterpremises.

11.1.2 Counterpremises

In the case of an ATC issue, those factors that tend to support a particular conclusion are known as **considerations.** Those factors that tend to oppose the conclusion are known as counterconsiderations, as discussed in Chapter 6. Reasons count as considerations or counterconsiderations depending on the conclusion of the argument. Thus, what would be considerations with regard to one conclusion might be counterconsiderations with regard to another, and vice versa. Here is an example:

Example 11.3

ATC issue: whether to place further restrictions on the sale of cigarettes
One conclusion: Further restrictions should be placed on cigarette sales.
    Consideration: the need to reduce teen smoking
    Counterconsideration: the right of adults to freely buy cigarettes

Another conclusion: No further restrictions should be placed on cigarette sales.
Consideration: the right of adults to freely buy cigarettes
Counterconsideration: the need to reduce teen smoking

Notice how a consideration becomes a counterconsideration when an opposing conclusion is adopted, and vice versa.

Arguing for a particular conclusion involves presenting the considerations and showing that the counterconsiderations are not sufficient to show that the conclusion is false. But how can counterconsiderations be included in the argument, given that they support a different conclusion? How can the considerations and counterconsiderations be compared? The answer to both of these questions lies in the use of counterpremises, also discussed in Chapter 6. Recall that a counterpremise is a premise claiming that a particular counterconsideration should not lead to the abandonment of the conclusion. An ATC argument includes counterpremises corresponding to the counterconsiderations. Through the use of counterpremises, an author seeks to show that the conclusion is true despite the counterconsiderations.

Considerations and Counterconsiderations

In ATC arguments, considerations are reasons that tend to support a particular conclusion, in contrast to counterconsiderations, which are reasons that tend to oppose that conclusion. If an opposing conclusion is adopted, considerations often become counterconsiderations, and vice versa. ATC arguments incorporate counterpremises, which are premises showing how the counterconsiderations are not sufficient to show the conclusion to be false.

The euthanasia argument B in Example 11.1 is an ATC argument with counterpremises. The conclusion is that euthanasia should not be allowed. Two counterconsiderations to this conclusion are that patients' choices should be respected and that terminally ill patients are often in great pain. These are counterconsiderations because they are factors that tend to support the opposing conclusion, that euthanasia should be allowed. The author seeks to show that the conclusion is true despite the counterconsiderations by including a counterpremise corresponding to each one. For instance, P7 is a counterpremise corresponding to the counterconsideration that a patient's choice should be respected. In P7, the author claims that this factor does not show the conclusion to be false because terminally ill patients are often not in a position to make fully voluntary choices. P8 is the counterpremise corresponding to the counterconsideration that a terminally ill patient is often in great pain. In P8, the author claims that such pain can be controlled through medication.

In the next example, the list of factors relevant to the issue of whether we should send astronauts to Mars is broken down into considerations and counter-considerations, based on the conclusion that we should send astronauts to Mars.

Example 11.4

Conclusion: Astronauts should be sent to Mars.

Considerations:

1. Mars may hold the secret to life on Earth.
2. If the human race does not keep pushing the frontiers of space, it will stagnate.
3. A Mars expedition could unite the nations of the Earth.
4. The human race may need a place to go should Earth become uninhabitable.

Counterconsiderations:

5. A Mars expedition would be very expensive.
6. Machines can discover as much as humans on Mars.
7. Humans could contaminate the pristine Martian environment.
8. A Mars expedition would be a distraction from problems on Earth.

It is easy to see how an argument for sending astronauts to Mars would include these four considerations, or premises. The argument takes the counterconsiderations into account by including premises claiming that the counterconsiderations do not, for one reason or another, show that the conclusion is false. These are the counterpremises. Through the inclusion of counterpremises, an author seeks to defeat the counterconsiderations or to take from them the threat they pose to the conclusion. Counterpremises represent the author's response to the factors or reasons that favor an opposing conclusion.

11.1.3 Formulating Counterpremises

How are counterpremises formulated? There are different ways to do this, depending on the nature of the counterconsideration in question. I refer to these different ways as **defusing strategies.** The job of a counterpremise is to "defuse" a counterconsideration, because a counterconsideration is like a bomb that could explode and destroy your argument. Thus, in presenting a strong argument, your job is to defuse the bomb.

There are four basic ways to defuse a counterconsideration, and so four defusing strategies. Each strategy indicates how the counterpremise corresponding to a counterconsideration should be formulated. One strategy, called the falseness defusing strategy, is based on the claim that the counterconsideration in question is false or very likely false. Another strategy, the irrelevance defusing strategy, is based on the claim that the counterconsideration is not relevant to the conclusion, that it does not count either for or against it. A third strategy, the positive-relevance defusing strategy, is based on the claim that the counterconsideration not only does not count against the conclusion but actually supports it. Finally, there is the insufficiency defusing strategy, based on the claim that the counterconsideration, while counting against the conclusion, does not count against it sufficiently to show that the conclusion should not be accepted. Each defusing strategy involves a claim about the counterconsideration, and the counterpremise is formulated to make this claim. Here is how counterpremises might be formulated according to each of the strategies (labeling the counterconsideration "x" and the conclusion "c"):

1. Falseness defusing strategy: "x is false (or very likely false)."
2. Irrelevance defusing strategy: "x does not count against c."
3. Positive-relevance defusing strategy: "x actually supports c."
4. Insufficiency defusing strategy: "Although X counts against c, it is not sufficient to show that c should not be accepted."

Defusing Strategies

In an ATC argument, counterconsiderations are addressed by the inclusion of counterpremises. A counterpremise claims that a counterconsideration does not show that the conclusion should not be accepted. The four ways that such a claim can be made are the defusing strategies: (1) the falseness defusing strategy, (2) the irrelevance defusing strategy, (3) the positive-relevance defusing strategy, and (4) the insufficiency defusing strategy.

An author of an ATC argument has to choose which of the strategies to adopt with regard to each of the counterconsiderations she or he faces in constructing an argument for a particular conclusion. The question is, which strategy is the most effective at defusing the counterconsideration in question? Which strategy is most defensible? Most counterpremises will be supported by a subargument that makes a case for the claim made in the counterpremise, that the counterconsideration is false, irrelevant, positively relevant, or insufficient. The actual wording of counterpremises can vary greatly, and the wordings given previously are only rough models. Although there may be considerable variation in the phrasing of actual counterpremises, each of them will be an example of one of the four defusing strategies. Thus, these models can be helpful when you are structuring an argument with counterpremises and reformulating those premises.

Let us see the strategies in action from the point of view of an author, using as our examples the counterconsiderations to the proposal to send astronauts to Mars in Example 11.4. How might an author use counterpremises and subarguments to support the conclusion that astronauts should be sent to Mars?

The first counterconsideration is that a Mars expedition would be very expensive. The first three strategies do not seem to work here because it clearly would be very expensive to send an expedition to Mars, and the cost is clearly a reason for not doing it. So, the strategy of choice is the insufficiency defusing strategy. One response is to claim that the benefits will outweigh the costs. How can this be supported in a subargument? One way is to call attention to how the technology developed in mounting the expedition will have great value in other areas of human endeavor.

The second counterconsideration is that machines could discover as much about Mars as humans could. Here, the best strategy seems to be the falseness defusing strategy. How might this counterpremise be supported in a subargument? One way is to point out that humans are more adaptable than machines.

The third counterconsideration is that humans could contaminate the environment of Mars. Again, the first three strategies do not seem to work here, because the risk is real, and it is a reason for not going to Mars. But the insufficiency defusing strategy works well here because the risk is low due to the availability of procedures for sterilizing the spacecraft.

The fourth counterconsideration is that a Mars expedition would be a distraction from problems on Earth. Certainly, a Mars expedition might be a distraction. Many people would likely become interested in the space program, just as they did with the lunar landing of 1969, and this might take their minds off of other things. But the question is whether such a distraction would be good or bad. Viewing this as a counterconsideration assumes that such a distraction would be bad, but it can plausibly be argued that it would be good. Thus, the strategy to adopt here is the positive-relevance defusing strategy, with the counterpremise that the point does not count against the conclusion but actually supports it. How could a subargument for such a premise be constructed? One way is to claim that humans need distractions that unite them and show them how humanity can overcome great problems, such as getting humans to Mars.

So, here is the argument for sending astronauts to Mars, including the considerations from the original list and the counterpremises and their subarguments:

Example 11.5

P1: Mars may hold the secret to life on Earth.

P2: If the human race does not keep pushing the frontiers of space, it will stagnate.

P3: A Mars expedition could unite the nations of the Earth.

P4: The human race may need a place to go should the Earth become uninhabitable.

    P5A: The technology developed in the efforts to send humans to Mars would be of great value in other human activities.

P5: The claim that a Mars expedition would be very expensive is not sufficient to show that the conclusion is false.

    P6A: Machines cannot deal with the unexpected, nor can they discover what they were not programmed to discover.

P6: It is false that machines can discover as much on Mars as humans.

    P7A: The reliable and well-tested procedures for sterilizing spacecraft would make the risk of contamination slight.

P7: The claim that humans might contaminate Mars is not sufficient to show that the conclusion is false.

    P8A: Humans need a distraction from their problems that will lift their spirits and show them what great feats humans can achieve.

P8: The claim that a Mars expedition would be a distraction from problems on Earth is a reason to go to Mars.

C: Therefore, astronauts should be sent to Mars.

11.1.4 Identifying and Reformulating Counterpremises

Counterpremises occur in many forms in argumentative texts. You need to be able to identify them when they occur and to reformulate them in your argument structures. Consider this letter:

Example 11.6

Background: The following letter, written by an older couple, is on the issue of whether older drivers should be periodically tested. (*Boston Globe,* 4/98)

> ① Drivers over a certain age should be required to undergo stringent testing. ② It is true that many seniors, including us, are capable and safe drivers—for now. ③ Can anyone predict, however, when some disability may develop that will change that situation? ④ Who is going to be the one to tell us to give up our licenses? ⑤ We hope we will be wise enough ourselves to do so. ⑥ But giving up a driver's license, and the independence that goes with it, is a difficult decision to make. ⑦ Official agencies such as the Registry of Motor Vehicles must take the initiative and make it mandatory for seniors to be tested yearly in order to see to it that they do not become a danger to themselves and to others.—I.H. & G.H.

The conclusion of this argument, represented in sentences 1 and 7a, is that the government motor vehicle agency should test senior drivers yearly. But the authors refer to two counterconsiderations in the text. In sentence 2, the authors point out that many senior drivers are capable, and in sentence 5, they point out that seniors themselves could choose to stop driving when they are no longer capable. Both of these are counterconsiderations because they count against the conclusion that senior drivers need to be tested. But the authors mention these counterconsiderations in order to defuse them. It is the resulting counterpremises that should be included in the argument structure.

What are the corresponding counterpremises? Consider the first counterconsideration, that many seniors are capable drivers. The authors respond to this in sentence 3, claiming that disabilities might arise for seniors at any time, hindering their ability to drive. The authors are adopting the insufficiency defusing strategy. Because disability can strike seniors at any time, the fact that many seniors are capable drivers is not sufficient to show that they should not be regularly tested. How, then, should the counterpremise be formulated? Here are two possibilities:

Example 11.7

A. P1A: Seniors are prone to acquiring disabilities that can turn them from competent into incompetent drivers.

   P1: The fact that many seniors are competent drivers is not sufficient to show that they should not be tested yearly.

B. P1: While many seniors are competent drivers, the disabilities to which they are prone can cause them to become incompetent at any time.

Example A makes it clear, by the wording of the main premise, that the author is following the insufficiency strategy. The claim offered in sentence 3 in support of this is then included as a subargument. Example B is a looser formulation of the counterpremise in which the reason offered in the subargument in A is incorporated into the main premise itself. Although a reformulation like that in A makes it clearer what defusing strategy the author is employing, the looser reformulation represented by B is entirely appropriate for the argument structure.

What about the second counterconsideration, that seniors themselves will choose to stop driving when they are no longer capable? The authors address this in sentence 6. In stating here that it is difficult for people to give up the independence of driving, the authors are adopting the falseness strategy toward this counterconsideration. The difficulty that people have in giving up the independence of driving shows that it is likely false that seniors would choose to stop driving when they are no longer capable. As before, this counterpremise can be reformulated in a stricter or a looser manner, as shown here:

Example 11.8

A. P2A: It is difficult for people to give up the independence of driving.

   P2: The claim that seniors would themselves choose to stop driving when they are incapable is likely false.

B. P2: Given the difficulty people have in giving up the independence of driving, it is unlikely that seniors would themselves choose to stop driving when they are incapable.

An ATC argument can be charged with hasty conclusion if there are considerations or counterconsiderations that the author does not discuss. If an ATC argument has counterpremises, the author has presented some counterconsiderations. But there may be other counterconsiderations that should have been included but were not. For example, in the argument in Example 11.6, one counterconsideration is the cost of administering yearly tests to all senior drivers. The authors should have included a counterpremise addressing this concern, and their failure to do so can be used to help justify a hasty conclusion charge.

The presence of a counterpremise is often indicated by certain phrases, which we can refer to as **counterpremise indicators.** In Example 11.6, sentence 2 begins with the phrase "it is true that." Such a phrase usually introduces a counterconsideration and signals that the author is going to present a counterpremise. (In this case, the nature of the defusing strategy for the counterpremise is indicated in sentence 3.) Seldom does an author introduce a consideration with the phrase "it is true that," even though the author presents considerations as true. The phrase "it is true that" represents a concession to the opposition, a recognition that what follows counts in favor of the opposition, even as it signals that the author intends to show in the counterpremise how the point does not show the conclusion to be false.

Counterpremise Indicators

Certain phrases are used in an argumentative text to indicate a counterpremise. Some of these phrases precede a reference to a counterconsideration, to which the author then goes on to respond. Examples of such phrases include "it is true that," "granted that," "although," "while," and "admittedly." Other of these phrases follow a sentence or clause referring to a counterconsideration and precede the author's response. Examples of such phrases include "but," "however," and "nevertheless." The author's response indicates the content of the counterpremise.

The second counterconsideration in this argument is mentioned in sentence 5. Sentence 6, which indicates the defusing strategy for the counterpremise, begins with "but." This is another counterpremise indicator. In grammatical terms, the term "but" introduces a response to what comes just before it in a text. Thus, when this term appears in a text, the sentence or clause that precedes it often indicates a counterconsideration, and the sentence or clause that follows it indicates how the author chooses to defuse the counterconsideration. There are other counterpremise indicators that, like "it is true that," precede a reference to a counterconsideration; examples include "granted that," "although," "while," and "admittedly." There are also other counterpremise indicators that, like "but," follow a reference to a counterconsideration and precede the author's response; examples include "however" and "nevertheless."

But not all counterpremises are signaled by such phrases. Here is an example:

Example 11.9

Background: This letter is about voting on the Internet. (*New York Times,* 11/98)

① Voting on the Internet should be considered as a tool to help get out the vote.
② The Internet allows us to file taxes with the Internal Revenue Service, view Congress on C-Span, read newspaper reports, trade stocks, shop and read election

results. ③ The same kind of technology used to insure the confidentiality of money transactions could guarantee the sanctity of the ballot. ④ And the frequent problems associated with absentee ballots could be ameliorated by allowing people to vote on the Net.—F.W.R.

In this case, there are no counterpremise indicators because the counterconsideration is referred to implicitly rather than explicitly. The conclusion, represented in sentence 1, is that we should adopt a policy of Internet voting. The counterconsideration, implicit in sentence 3, is that voting must be confidential. This factor counts against the conclusion because of the confidentiality problems associated with the Internet. Sentence 3 also provides the response to this concern, pointing out that there are ways of ensuring confidentiality on the Internet. This suggests that the author is adopting the irrelevance defusing strategy. The demonstrated possibility of confidential transactions on the Internet makes the claim that voting must be confidential irrelevant to the conclusion. The counterpremise and subargument are as follows:

Example 11.10

P3A: The technology used to guarantee the confidentiality of Internet financial transactions could also be used to guarantee the confidentiality of voting.

P3: The claim that voting must be confidential does not count against the claim that Internet voting should be allowed.

A basic feature of ATC arguments is that, whenever an author introduces a counterconsideration, he should be understood as intending to provide a counterpremise, even though the nature of the counterpremise and the defusing strategy involved may not always be clear. Suppose it is not clear to you what the counterpremise is and what defusing strategy is involved. Try placing "while" or "although" in front of a formulation of the counterconsideration, creating a subordinate clause in a longer sentence, and ask yourself, based on your understanding of the text, how the author might complete the sentence. This should indicate the nature of the counterpremise and the defusing strategy.

The most common of the four defusing strategies is the insufficiency strategy. When an author adopts an insufficiency defusing strategy, she is saying that the factor referred to in the counterconsideration is less weighty than factors that favor the conclusion. This means that factors cited in other main premises often will be included in the subargument for the counterpremise as well.

It is not always clear which of the four strategies an author is using for a counterpremise. Often, for example, when an author mentions a counterconsideration, he could be understood as responding with a counterpremise that uses either an insufficiency strategy or an irrelevance strategy. In structuring ATC arguments, you simply need to do the best you can in the formulation of the counterpremises and their subarguments, recognizing that the formulations will not always be clear from the text.

11.1.5 Qualified Conclusions

Statements in arguments are often qualified in one way or another, and it is important, as we have discussed, to represent accurately in reformulation such qualifications. Some qualifications, as discussed in Chapter 5, are in the scope of a statement ("all," "some," "few") or in the modality of its assertion ("possibly," "certainly," "likely").[2] Other qualifications involve the inclusion of a limiting phrase. Examples of this include: "*Hawaiian* mornings are delightful," "students *who want to excel* need to study hard," and "*first- and second-trimester* abortions should be allowed." The italicized phrases qualify the statements these sentences are expressing. In ATC arguments, the qualification of the conclusion, if any, is especially important.

In ATC arguments, authors can choose to qualify their conclusions as a way of helping them deal with counterconsiderations. In response to counterconsiderations, authors can qualify their conclusions in order to help them formulate defensible counterpremises. For example, if you were presenting an argument in favor of the pro-choice position on the issue of abortion, you might face the following counterconsideration: There is little difference between a third-trimester fetus and a newborn baby. If you adopted the qualified conclusion—that "first- and second-trimester abortions should be allowed"—this would make it possible for you to formulate a counterconsideration using the irrelevance defusing strategy.

Here is an example of how a qualified conclusion can help to handle counterconsiderations:

Example 11.11

Background: This is a portion of a letter written in response to criticisms of rap music. (*Atlanta Constitution,* 3/97)

> Violence is prevalent in most inner-city neighborhoods, but to blame this rash of violence solely on rap music is unjust. Admittedly, rap lyrics and videos do send out violent images to youths, but so do many action-adventure movies. Long before I heard rap, I saw guns in movies. Why place the blame on rap artists when there are so many other ills that contribute to this senseless society?—R.B.

The conclusion, represented in the first sentence, is that rap music is not solely to blame for the violence in inner-city neighborhoods. The term "solely" is a qualification of the conclusion. The unqualified conclusion is that rap music plays no role in causing youth violence. But the author does not assert this; rather, he claims only that rap music is not the sole factor causing such violence.

Consider how the difference between the unqualified and the qualified forms of the conclusion makes a difference in the counterpremises the author would offer:

Example 11.12

A. Unqualified conclusion: Rap music plays no role in causing youth violence.

    P1: The fact that rap music presents violent images to youths is not sufficient to show that rap plays a role in causing youth violence.

B. Qualified conclusion: Rap music is not the sole factor in youth violence.
      PIA: Action-adventure movies present violent images to youths.
    PI: The fact that rap music presents violent images to youths does not count against the claim that it is not the sole factor in youth violence.

With the unqualified form of the conclusion (in A), the author would have had to adopt the insufficiency defusing strategy for the counterpremise. But P1 in A is a very difficult claim to defend. It is hard to see how the author could have provided a plausible subargument for it. In contrast, with the qualified conclusion in B, the author is able to use the irrelevance defusing strategy. The first part of the second sentence introduces the counterconsideration, that rap music presents violent images to youths. (Note the counterpremise indicator "admittedly.") The second part of the sentence indicates the subargument for the counterpremise, that movies do this as well. The defusing strategy the author adopts is irrelevance. The counterpremise in B is much more defensible than that in A.

    The general point is that authors of ATC arguments deal with counterconsiderations in two ways: (1) They formulate counterpremises to defuse the counterconsiderations, and (2) they add qualifications to their conclusions in order to make defensible counterpremises easier to formulate. Authors often craft their conclusions in the light of the counterconsiderations. Instead of defending a preordained conclusion on some ATC issue, they use the process of creating the ATC argument to fashion the precise conclusions they choose to defend. They are open to qualifying their conclusions based on their assessment of the counterconsiderations.

EXERCISE SET 11.1

SECTION A: For each of the following arguments, first formulate the conclusion and then list the counterconsideration(s) referred to in the argument. Some of the arguments may refer to more than one counterconsideration, and some may have a qualified conclusion. (You may want to do these exercises in conjunction with those in Section B, in which you formulate counterpremises for the same arguments.)

EXAMPLE
Background: This letter is on the issue of nuclear power. (*New York Times*, 12/97)

① In discussions about global warming and measures to mitigate its consequences, nuclear power is often overlooked. ② Nuclear power does not produce carbon emissions, the major contributor to global warming. ③ France is a dramatic example of what can be done. ④ Its use of nuclear power to generate nearly 80 percent of its electricity allows it to maintain the lowest per-capita carbon dioxide emissions level among members of the Organization for Economic Cooperation and Development. ⑤ True, nuclear power produces radioactive waste, which must be isolated for hundreds of years. ⑥ But the amounts are relatively small and can be safely and economically managed, as shown in Europe. ⑦ The impediments to the resolution of nuclear waste management in the United States are largely political, not technical or economic.—S.G.

ANSWER

Conclusion: The conclusion, indicated in sentence 1, is that nuclear power should be used to lessen the problem of global warming.

Counterconsideration: A counterconsideration, indicated in sentence 5, is that nuclear power produces dangerous radioactive waste.

PROBLEMS

1. Background: This letter is about the practice of selling the organs of executed prisoners for transplantation. (*New York Times,* 2/98)

   Why should the sale of kidneys and other organs from executed Chinese prisoners be deemed immoral and criminalized? While China's criminal justice system and overzealous use of capital punishment stand out as immoral and severe human rights abuses, does the cremation or interring of life-sustaining organs ameliorate those violations? The thousands whose lives are sustained by dialysis simply because there are too few donated kidneys may see the moral arguments differently.—T.M.

2. Background: This letter is about the plan of Harvard to create a professorship in Holocaust studies. (*New York Times,* 7/97)

   The Holocaust needs to be remembered, but the proposed Harvard chair in Holocaust studies and other such efforts that cast the Holocaust as the defining Jewish experience assign all Jews to victim status. Along with all groups with a history of political or religious persecution, Jews have always regarded and conducted themselves as survivors, contributing enormously to every society they dwelt in and asking for nothing except the basic human right to live.—R.P.

3. Background: This letter is about whether a testing company should be allowed to indicate on the test scores it sends to colleges and universities whether the test taker had special accommodation status in taking the test (such as being allowed more time due to a diagnosed learning disability). The Americans with Disabilities Act is a set of federal regulations designed to protect the rights of the disabled. (*New York Times,* 2/01)

   I was sorry to read that the Educational Testing Service has been pressured to stop reporting the special accommodation status of certain test-takers. That information might help universities make better decisions on behalf of their students. I agree that the Americans with Disabilities Act may limit the use of this information, but surely the restrictions should apply to the educational institutions' actions, not to the testing company's words. Preventing the Educational Testing Service from saying what it wants is a blatant violation of its freedom of speech.—D.S.

4. Background: This letter is on the issue of whether African Americans should be given reparations for the injustices of slavery. (*New York Times,* 8/00)

   It is counter-productive for African Americans to insist upon reparations. Of the several arguments made against reparations, one that is often overlooked is the fact that Americans, North and South, have already paid a debt for slavery in blood. Hundred of thousands of soldiers lost their lives in the Civil War, and a greater number were wounded and maimed. While the chief motive of Northern soldiers may have been preservation of the Union and most Northerners regarded blacks as inferior, soldiers were aware of slavery as a moral issue and as a root cause of the war. A significant percentage of the Northern volunteers were committed abolitionists. Among those who helped pay the debt in blood was the commander in chief, Abraham Lincoln.—J.N.R.

5. Background: This letter is about political campaign advertising. (*New York Times*, 12/99)

However misleading, campaign advertising offers one of the few unmediated outlets for political candidates. Without advertising, voters in large states would rely almost exclusively on media-filtered glimpses of the candidates. If commercials necessarily rely on sound bites, at least they are of the candidates' own choosing.—R.B.

6. Background: This letter is in response to articles on the role of the Scholastic Aptitude Tests (SATs) in college admissions. (*San Francisco Chronicle*, 11/97)

Your recent series on the SAT left me puzzled. Most of the people interviewed criticized college admissions officers for relying on the SAT, which is alleged to be "culturally biased." I grant that the SAT drafters have not perfected a means of writing questions which clearly distinguish raw intelligence from culture, but they have done a pretty good job of it. And what is the alternative? The "GPA"—the student's high school teachers! And who reviews these tests to see if they are culturally biased? No one. Indeed, it is much more likely that biases will infect the GPA than the SAT, for one simple reason: high school teachers know who submits each answer, while the SAT graders do not.—M.M.

7. Background: This letter is in response to a column on the New Orleans School Board's decision to change the names of schools that had been named for slave owners, including George Washington. (*New York Times*, 12/97)

The columnist faults the New Orleans School Board for deciding to rename schools named for slave owners. She questions the appropriateness of changing George Washington Elementary to Dr. Charles Drew Elementary. Perhaps the simple answer is that yes, there is reason to be ashamed of Washington's ownership of fellow humans. This deed will not eclipse his greatness, nor will his greatness eclipse the deed. It is, however, reasonable to suppose his value as role model for black children is somewhat tarnished.—N.S.

8. Background: This is in response to a letter on gun control. (*San Francisco Chronicle*, 4/98)

The letter writer supports the curious notion that the Second Amendment to the Constitution guarantees citizens the right to bear arms for private purposes. That is simply not the law and never has been, the federal courts having consistently interpreted the Second Amendment according to what it actually says: "A well-regulated Militia, being necessary to the security of a free State, the right of the people to keep and bear Arms, shall not be infringed." It is a legitimate issue for public debate whether people should have the legal right to bear arms for personal protection, sport, hunting, collecting or other personal reasons. But it has never been a constitutional right.—S.H.B.

9. Background: This letter is about vegetarianism. (*Boston Globe*, 6/98)

I disagree with the position that man was meant to and should be vegetarian. Certainly our dental anatomy would indicate otherwise. Unlike the horses and elephants, we have multipurpose machinery in our mouths; cuspids, incisors, and canines for ripping and tearing and molars for grinding. Further, our anthropological record indicates that as nomadic hunter-gatherers we are omnivorous by design; staying in one place eating vegetation while it was plentiful and opting for higher-protein meat while on the move. While I decry wanton cruelty, that shouldn't be used as an argument for the vegetarian position. There is a natural designation called the carnivore. Without being overly flippant, I'll stop eating meat when I can enter the lion's den without fear of becoming his primary source of protein.—C.L.T.

10. Background: This letter is in response to the proposal that the automobiles of individuals convicted of drunk driving should be confiscated. (*Washington Post*, 5/97)

I'm for it, but there is a problem: In many areas of our car-addicted country, losing one's car can make it impossible to get to work. The possibility of swelling the unemployment rolls makes legislators nervous. A few years ago a friend made an inspired suggestion: Impound the car or not, but do not take away the driver's license. Instead, restrict it to motorcycles of 10 or fewer horsepower. The offenders still can get to work, but they are unlikely to hurt anyone else even when drunk. Considering Washington weather, the "cruel and unusual" clause may be invoked, but it's not as cruel as forbidding one to drive. But by having a legal way to get around, the offender will not be so tempted to get into the driver's seat without a license.—S.P.

11. Background: This is in response to a letter commenting on the public's reaction to a murder. (*New York Times*, 2/01)

The letter writer said it is cold to dismiss the tragedies that strike those we don't know, and she suggested that we would be a better society if we cared more about our fellow citizens even when we don't know them. While it is hard to quarrel with such sentiments, it is also true that we'd be in tears and deep depression at all times if we actually took to heart the tragedies that afflict those we don't know. We are steeped in news of murder, genocide and earthquakes. We watch these stories unfolding on the TV news as we eat popcorn and enjoy soft drinks. It's callous and macabre, but psychic numbing seems necessary if we are to go to work in the morning and function.—C.J.P.

12. Background: This is in response to a letter pointing out the value of street fire-alarm boxes, given the important role they had played in the quick reporting of a recent fire. (*New York Times*, 9/95)

    The letter writer makes a valid point about the use of a street alarm box to report a recent fire in a New York City office building. Yet viewed against the 250,000 or more false alarms from alarm boxes, which translate into a million or more unit responses—two engines and two ladder companies and a battalion chief generally respond to street alarms—the situation demands redress. Eliminating most street alarms, save for isolated areas or ones of public concern, makes sense. False alarms delay responses to real fires and emergencies. They have caused accidents, injuries and even death to fire-fighters and civilians. They also create unnecessary hardship on firefighters and accelerate wear on the apparatus. Phone alarms, from the myriad phones in the city, allow the fire dispatcher to ascertain the response needed, in many cases less than what is standard for a street alarm box.—J.K.

13. Background: This letter is about the value of methadone treatment for heroin addiction. (*New York Times*, 8/98)

    There is certainly merit to the characterization of methadone treatment as a substitution of one addiction for another. However, when it is legally available, methadone reduces crime and permits an addict to live a relatively productive life. The alternative, in the case of heroin, is a totally wasted life of crime and imprisonment. While I strongly believe in the restoration of personal responsibility in American life, available alternative therapies have a poor record of ending heroin addiction. Methadone at least protects the rest of us and helps an addict become self-supporting.—R.W.

14. Background: This letter addresses the issue of gun control. (*New York Times*, 3/00)

    The latest gun violence has once again brought out the apologists who assure us that gun control is not the answer. How would they know? It's not as if the idea has been tried and found wanting. One writer says he grew up with guns and such violence was unthinkable. Yet, society has changed since then—so aren't new restrictions a logical response? Another writer invokes "constitutional" gun rights. The licensing and registration of automobiles hasn't led us down any "slippery slope" of tyranny. A third writer says gun control absolves us of responsibility, suggesting instead that we reach out "to our neighbors with acceptance and support." This isn't likely to be achieved any time soon. While we wait, I'll settle for licensing and registration of every handgun.—A.M.

15. Background: This letter is part of the debate over the exploration of space. (*Boston Globe*, 7/97)

    Scientists are probing Mars to discover new clues about our solar system. Discovering more about our solar system is a grandiose achievement for all mankind, which gives us reasons to celebrate. However, when I look at the condition of the earth, I wonder if it is getting any better? We have famine in some parts of the world, teenage violence and pregnancies are high, and single-parent families raising children are on the rise. Since Galileo, we have come a long way in understanding our solar system, and maybe it is time that we look at the earth as the center of the universe— the place where human beings live. I really think that our obsession with outer space is a psychological scapegoat for running away from our own earthly problems.—C.D.

16. Background: The following letter is in response to a statement by former Democratic presidential candidate George McGovern. (*Los Angeles Times*, 7/97)

McGovern quotes George Washington as saying, "I had rather be in my grave than endure another four years in the White House." Never happened. Washington never lived in the White House. He did not want another term, true. He probably said so many times. But he never said what was attributed to him in that quote.—G.R.

17. Background: This letter, written in response to another letter, is about the acceptability of evolutionary theory. (*Houston Chronicle*, 8/97)

The statement that "evolution is one of the most thoroughly researched and documented scientific facts" is just not correct. It is true that evolution within a species has been demonstrated to occur via Darwin's mechanism of natural selection, both in the field and in the laboratory. But evolution of one species into another has never been tested or demonstrated, but only speculated. In fact, within the last several years, mathematical analyses of biological processes have shown conclusively that evolution between species is physically impossible if natural selection is the mechanism. If evolution between species is occurring, the mechanism is unknown and therefore, as yet, scientifically untestable.—J.S.S.

❖ 18. Background: This letter is about the opposition of the U.S. government to the International Criminal Court, based on the fear that other nations would bring politically motivated charges against U.S. citizens. (*New York Times*, 7/98)

It is hard to understand why Washington failed to support the creation of a permanent International Criminal Court. The concern that American citizens, and particularly service members stationed abroad, would be subject to politically motivated prosecution before an alien tribunal overlooks the realities of the modern world. American service members have already been subject to the jurisdiction of foreign tribunals, although without the protection fundamental to the proposed court. Businesses incorporated and headquartered in the United States are subjected to litigation before foreign courts if they export goods or services. The United States is bound by extradition treaties to turn over Americans for prosecution in appropriate cases. The issue is not whether Americans can be insulated from foreign courts; they cannot be. Rather, it is whether the United States can exercise its influence to help institutionalize the rule of law in which we believe and for which we have in the past had to fight. An effective International Criminal Court, holding out the prospect of punishment for those inclined toward ethnic cleansing, genocide and other crimes against humanity, would make this a safer world for Americans and, not the least, American servicemen. Trial by law, with all its defects, is vastly preferable to trial by combat.—R.S.R.

19. Background: This letter is in response to an article on motorcycle helmet laws. (*San Francisco Chronicle*, 3/98)

   I have several problems with the article in support of the current helmet law. (1) It treats the issue of personal freedom as unimportant, an annoyance, an afterthought. This is disrespectful to the memories of the many who died fighting for freedom. Were they irrelevant? (2) The report that motorcycle deaths had decreased by half since the helmet took effect is true. What the article doesn't say is that the number of accidents also decreased by half. The number of deaths per 100 accidents is 2.8. That's the same as it was before the law took effect. (3) The article says the helmet law saves money, but it has been six years now since the law went into effect, and my taxes haven't gone down.—I.M.

20. Background: This letter is about a congressional committee's consideration of impeachment charges against former President Clinton for his actions in the Monica Lewinsky scandal. The author suggests that a censure of the president would be a viable alternative to impeachment. (*New York Times*, 11/98)

   Although it may be true that a censure by itself has no constitutional basis, the scholars who testified before the House Judiciary Committee missed the point. An impeachment is nothing other than a two-part legal process with the House acting as a grand jury and the Senate acting as a jury hearing the trial. This process is thus akin to ordinary criminal trials, many of which result in a plea bargain. The President's counsel could negotiate a plea bargain with Congressional leaders on the determination of the President's guilt and the terms of his punishment. If a majority of both the House and the Senate agree, then the Chief Justice of the Supreme Court could order that the agreement be put into effect, provided that he deems it consistent with the requirements of the Constitution.—H.R.B.

❖ 21. Background: This is in response to a letter about eating disorders of women. (*Boston Globe*, 7/97)

   I was angered by the letter, which suggested that women simply need to take control of their own bodies to avoid eating disorders. The writer's oversimplification of this problem demonstrates how little understood is the power of the media and society to influence women's self-images. I would like to suggest that the writer pay careful attention the next time he is in the company of his wife, sister, mother, daughter, or female co-worker. Listen for the self-deprecating comments that many women make about their own bodies. Poor body image, which for a small percentage will lead to an eating disorder, is unfortunately the norm for most women in our society. I agree that women would do well to think independently about their bodies and not hate themselves for not meeting society's too-slender norm. It is neither realistic nor fair to expect women to bear the full burden of making society's standards for women's bodies more real.—A.S.

22. Background: This letter concerns the proper punishment for Timothy McVeigh, the man found guilty in the 1995 bombing of the Federal Building in Oklahoma City. (*San Francisco Chronicle*, 6/97)

Timothy McVeigh is a monster. This is incontrovertible. Therefore, a monster such as he should receive the harshest possible sentence. So why then am I against him receiving the death penalty? Because to do so makes us no better than he. The initial reaction I hear when I state such an opinion is "Well, what if your wife/mother/etc., died in the building? How then would you feel?" To be sure, I'd want McVeigh dead. And not just dead, but I'd want him to die slowly and painfully. I'd hardly be human if I felt any differently. But that's not justice, it's vengeance! And that is not and cannot be the point where the state is involved in punishing its citizens. I return to Timothy McVeigh. As much as his execution may somehow satisfy those victims who lost loved ones, we need to remember that justice isn't about revenge. It's about doing what is right. To execute Timothy McVeigh makes the state —and by association, all of us—as guilty as he.—T.E.

SECTION B: Go back to the exercises in Section A. For each of the counterconsiderations you have identified, state which defusing strategy the author has adopted, and construct the counterpremise that the author intends, including a subargument, if any.

EXAMPLE
See the example in Section A.

ANSWER
Counterconsideration: See the answer in Section A.
Counterpremise: Sentences 6 and 7 indicate that the author adopts the insufficiency defusing strategy:

P2A: The amounts of waste are relatively small and can be safely and economically managed, as in Europe.

P2B: The impediments to proper nuclear waste management in the United States are largely political, not technical or economic.

P2: Although nuclear power produces radioactive waste, this is not sufficient to show that nuclear power should not play a greater role in power generation.

SECTION C: Again, go back to the exercises in Section A. Structure the arguments (a tree diagram is optional), including the conclusions and the counterpremises from your work in Sections A and B, and evaluate the main arguments for hasty conclusion. Include in the justifications for any hasty conclusion charges you make the counterconsiderations that the author should have considered but did not.

EXAMPLE
See the example in Section A.

ANSWER

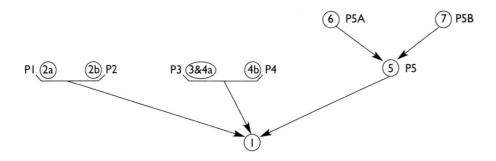

P1: Nuclear power does not produce carbon emissions.
P2: Carbon emissions are the major contributor to global warming.
P3: France generates nearly 80 percent of its electricity with nuclear power.
P4: This allows France to have the lowest per-capita carbon dioxide emissions level among members of the OECD.

  P5A: The amounts of waste are relatively small and can be safely and economically managed, as in Europe.

  P5B: The impediments to proper nuclear waste management in the United States are largely political, not technical or economic.

P5: Although nuclear power produces radioactive waste, this is not sufficient to show that nuclear power should not play a greater role in power generation.

C: Therefore, nuclear power should be used to lessen the problem of global warming.

Evaluation

I charge the main argument with hasty conclusion. The premises are not sufficient to prove the conclusion because important relevant issues are not considered. Nothing is said about renewable energy resources, like wind power and solar power, that would also not emit greenhouse gases but would not have the nuclear waste problem. In addition, nothing is said about conservation, which would also address the energy problem without increasing the production of greenhouse gases or creating dangerous waste products. Moreover, nothing is said about the cost of nuclear power, which is quite high. These are all counter-considerations that the argument should have addressed.

SECTION D: Pick a controversial social or political issue that you have a strong and clear position on (for example, you may favor or oppose the death penalty). Take your position as your initial conclusion, and come up with three or four considerations and three or four counterconsiderations. (You may want to generate the counterconsiderations by working with a classmate who has an opposing position on the issue.) Second, decide whether the counterconsiderations would lead you to qualify your position, and, if so, how you would formulate your qualified conclusion. Third, create a PC structure for your argument, including premises corresponding to your considerations and counterpremises formulated in response to your counterconsiderations. In formulating your counterpremises, include any subargument you think appropriate, and be sure to take account of any qualifications you made in your conclusion.

11.2 Arguments from Analogy

As a thinking being, you have the ability to compare one thing with another and to draw conclusions about the one based on your understanding of the other. This ability is one of the principal ways in which you increase your understanding of the world. The comparison you make is an **analogy.** When you use an analogy to increase your understanding of the world, you are using an **argument from analogy.** In an argument from analogy, the claims that the two things are alike and that one of them has some characteristic supports the conclusion that the other thing has that characteristic as well.

Consider these examples:

Example 11.13

A. Background: This letter concerns the policy of investments in support of China's economical modernization. (*San Francisco Chronicle*, 6/97)

> Doesn't anyone read history? Both the Soviet Union and Nazi Germany feigned moderation and liberalization to successfully entice foreign capital. Once factories were built, the Russians and Nazis dropped the facade and resumed their true identity as bellicose military dictatorships. They nationalized all the foreign facilities and, in some recorded cases, kidnapped key personnel. What evidence exists to prove that the Red Chinese will act any differently?—J.A.W.

B. Background: This letter is about the use of the Internet in education. (*Los Angeles Times*, 5/97)

> Employing the Internet to educate secondary school students is much like sending them on a field trip to the mall, assuming they will head to the bookstore.—J.G.

Each of these texts makes a comparison between two (or among three) things. In text A, communist China is compared with the Soviet Union and Nazi Germany. In text B, turning secondary school students loose on the Internet to further their education is compared with turning them loose to find the bookstore in a mall. These are the analogies.

In text A, the argument from analogy proceeds in this way: The author claims that the Soviet Union and Nazi Germany are like communist China and that the former two shared the characteristic of feigning moderation to entice foreign investment, and then reverting to hostile militarism. The conclusion, represented in the rhetorical question in the final sentence, is that communist China will show this characteristic as well. In text B, the analogy is between kids using the Internet at school and kids being turned loose at a shopping center. The implicit conclusion is that secondary school students turned loose on the Internet to further their education will not spend their time at educational sites. An implicit premise is that a characteristic of the situation in which students are released in a mall to shop at the bookstore is that they would spend their time elsewhere in the mall instead. So, secondary students turned loose on the Internet to further their education, has a similar characteristic, namely, that the students will not spend their time at educational sites.[3]

> ### Argument from Analogy
>
> An analogy is a comparison between two things, a claim that two things are alike. An argument from analogy begins with an analogy and draws a conclusion about one of the things based on a claim about a characteristic of the other. The reasoning is that x has (or should have) some characteristic because y, which is like x, has that characteristic.

An argument from analogy compares two things and concludes that one of them has a certain characteristic because the other does. The two "things" that are compared in an analogy can be objects, events, people, actions, policies, situations, states of affairs, institutions, and so forth. They can also be groups of any of these, as when, for example, dolphins are compared with people. The characteristic (or property, feature, or attribute) is any description that could be given of the things being compared, anything that could be said about them. In addition, as the example about China shows, in an analogy, one thing can be compared with two or more other things.

Often, an argument from analogy includes a separate argument, or subargument, to support the claim that the two things are alike. Consider how this works in the case of one of the best-known arguments from analogy, the **design argument,** which is meant to prove the existence of God. The analogy is between the universe and a machine, such as a watch. Because they are alike and because one of them, the machine, has the characteristic of having an intelligent designer, the conclusion is that the other has that characteristic as well, the intelligent designer being God. But the design argument also includes a subargument providing support for the analogy. It argues that the universe is like a machine because each exhibits a complicated regularity in its operation. In each case, the parts fit together into a functioning whole.

> ### The Design Argument
>
> The design argument is based on an analogy between the universe and a human machine. The two are alike because each is a whole composed of parts that work together in a regular, recurring process. The claim is that a characteristic of the machine is that it has an intelligent designer. The conclusion is that the universe has an intelligent designer as well, namely, God.

Arguments from analogy concern not only what characteristics things *do* have but also what characteristics they *should* have. Figure 11.1 shows an example of such an argument from analogy from a public service advertisement. In this case, the two things being compared involve baseball and politics: (1) a batter giving money to an umpire in the expectation of favorable calls and (2) people or corporations giving money to political parties or candidates in the expectation of favorable rulings or legislation. A characteristic of the baseball situation is that it is against the rules. The conclusion is that this kind of behavior should be illegal in politics as well.

The conclusion of this argument is not that political contributions are illegal, but rather that they should be. As this example shows, arguments from analogy can be value arguments. The argument is for the action recommendation that we should make political contributions illegal. We often use analogies to argue about how the world should be, and therefore, how we should act to change it. The conclusions of arguments from analogy are often action recommendations.

For example, people often decide how to act based on an argument from analogy. Think about it: As you make your way through the world, you frequently face new situations to which you are unsure how to respond. You seek to understand new situations by comparing them with situations from your past. In other words, you figure out how to act based on analogies between new situations and old ones. Such analogies help you decide how to respond to new situations by suggesting that you respond in a way that worked in old situations that are like the new ones.

We now consider further the role of analogies in value arguments.

11.2.1 Consistency, Justice, and the Law

Analogies and analogical reasoning figure prominently not only in our efforts to understand the world but also in our efforts to change it. How should we seek to change the world? We often find the answer in arguments from analogy. When we talk about what changes we should make in our social world, in the relations among human beings, we are in the realm of ethics and the law, and analogical reasoning plays an important role in this realm.

Money to the Umpire?

In Politics, It's Legal

You can't give money to the umpire. Can't give money to a judge.

Yet it's perfectly legal for special interests to give money to members of Congress. In fact, it happens all the time.

Of course, some members of Congress say that collecting big bucks from people trying to influence their legislative decisions is just "the American Way."

But that's not the way we play America's favorite pastime, or run our system of justice. It *is* the way Congress gives out special favors, costing *us* a bundle.

Clean Money. We can change all that with Clean Money Campaign Reform.

Candidates who agree to strict spending limits, and refuse private contributions, would receive full and equal funding of their campaigns from a publicly financed election fund.

That would free the candidates from having to depend on special interest money. And also level the playing field, so more good candidates will have a real chance to win.

Last fall, voters in Maine made Clean Money the law in their state. It's long overdue at the federal level too.

It's time to make members of Congress play by the rules that apply to the rest of us.

PUBLIC CAMPAIGN

**It's Time for
Clean Money Campaign Reform**

A message from Public Campaign • To find out more, call toll-free 1-888-293-5755 • Or visit our web site: www.publicampaign.org

FIGURE 11.1   Real-Life Example of an Argument from Analogy

A key value of our actions in the social world is **consistency** in our treatment of others. That is, if x has been properly treated one way, and y is like x, then y should be treated in the same way. Not to do so is to show favoritism or to discriminate; it is to adopt a double standard or be hypocritical. In other words, we should treat like cases alike. This idea of maintaining consistency and treating like cases alike, which means treating people fairly, is at the foundation of our idea of justice and fairness, in both ethics and the law.[4]

Claims about consistency are, in effect, arguments from analogy. Consider the phrase "treat like cases alike." To claim that two cases are alike is to find an analogy between them. To claim that such cases should be treated alike is to claim that a characteristic that one has—namely, that we treat it in a certain way—is a characteristic the other should have. For each case to have this characteristic, we must treat them in the same way.

Consider these cases:

Example 11.14

A. Background: This letter concerns a death reported in the press. (*New York Times*, 7/97)

> An unmuzzled pit bull left alone in a backyard is able to escape and attack a passing 70-year-old neighbor, who dies of a heart attack. The pit bull's owner receives only summonses for having an unlicensed dog and for not keeping it on a leash. In contrast, anyone else causing the death of another by negligent action (for example, driving a vehicle while intoxicated) is charged with negligent homicide. The negligence of the pit bull's owner directly led to a death. A jury of the owner's peers should be allowed to decide the extent of his negligence.—E.J.K.

B. Background: This letter is in response to an editorial about cigarette advertising. (*San Francisco Chronicle*, 6/97)

> Your editorial supports the right of R.J. Reynolds to air Joe Camel advertisements on the basis of First Amendment right of free speech. I disagree. When executives of a tobacco company, using Joe Camel advertisements, induce children into nicotine addiction, it causes them injury and premature death and is fully as damaging as falsely crying "Fire" in a crowded hall. Your editorial admits such a cry is not speech covered by the First Amendment.—H.J.

Text A is a call for the law to be applied consistently. The analogy is between a person who caused a death by failing to keep his pit bull leashed and other people who cause deaths through their negligent actions, such as drunk drivers. The two cases are alike because both involve a negligently caused death, and like cases should be treated alike. In other words, the law should be consistently applied. This argument from analogy is an appeal to consistency, justice, and fairness.

Text B is also from the legal realm—in this case, constitutional law. The Supreme Court in an opinion has suggested that, if someone falsely shouts "fire" in a crowded theater, the free-speech guarantee of the Constitution does not protect that person from prosecution for any harm that results.[5] The argument in B is that falsely shouting fire in a crowded theater is akin to aiming cigarette advertising at children. And because the one is not constitutionally protected, the other should not be, either. That is, the cigarette companies should not be able to use the claim of free-speech protection to avoid legal regulation of their advertising.

As these examples suggest, many legal arguments consist in the presentation and criticism of arguments from analogy. The law puts analogies front and center through the doctrine of precedent, the idea that cases should be decided consistent with previous decisions. Of course, arguments from analogy, like all arguments, may be strong or weak. A good part of ethical and legal debate involves both presenting arguments from analogy and criticizing arguments from analogy put forth by others. The key issue here is whether the analogies are good ones or are faulty. For example, the pit bull owner and the tobacco companies would probably dispute the arguments in Example 11.14, claiming that the analogies are faulty. For an analogy to work, not only must the two things be alike, but they must be alike in a relevant way. We will address the evaluation of arguments from analogy later in the chapter.

Consistency

The role of arguments from analogy in value arguments centers on the idea of consistency. Consistency, which involves treating like cases alike, is the basis of justice and fairness. If we treat one case in a certain way, and a second case is like the first, then we should treat the second case in the same way. Not to do so would be inconsistent, unjust, and unfair.

Another area in which consistency plays a role in our actions concerns how we label things. This often involves value arguments in that we make action recommendations about how one kind of thing should be labeled consistent with how other kinds of things are labeled. These are arguments from analogy. Because two kinds of things are alike, how one is labeled should determine how the other is labeled. Consider this case:

Example 11.15

Background: This letter is about what to call the units of time added to keep our timekeeping in line with the Earth's motions. (*New York Times*, 1/96)

In your Dec. 31 issue, two references are made to the "leap second" that was to be added to the last hour of 1995. Both draw an analogy between the periodic addition of a second at the end of a year to the insertion of any extra day in leap years. There appears to be a logical disconnect in the use of the term "leap second" and linking it to the term "leap year." The addition of an extra day to the calendar once in four years defines a leap year, not a leap day, week or month. Linguistic consistency

demands, therefore, that the additional second added at the end of the year not be referred to as a leap second nor should we lend the "leap" designation to the last minute or hour but rather to the last day. Dec. 31, 1995, should be called a leap day.
—J.E.G.

Because the addition of a day to the calendar is like the addition of a second, the basis of our labeling of one of these situations (yielding the phrase "leap year") should also govern the labeling of the other, which should therefore be designated a "leap day."[6] This is required for the sake of consistency.

Arguments from analogy about how something should be labeled play a role in the law as well. Here is a recent important example: In the disputed 2000 presidential election, the race between George Bush and Al Gore came down to who won Florida. In certain contested Florida counties, where the punch card votes were counted by machine, the Gore forces requested a hand count. The Bush forces argued against this, claiming that the votes had already been counted. The Gore forces used an analogy to argue that it was false that the votes had already been counted. In the machine count, the machine rejected some votes that it could not decipher. Had these votes been counted? If you go to a supermarket with checkout scanner technology, and some of your items do not register on the scanner, these items clearly have not been "counted" on the grocery bill. But this is like the vote-counting situation in the contested counties. Thus, the machine rejects should not be labeled as counted, either.

11.2.2 Analogues—Real and Hypothetical

It is helpful in discussing an argument from analogy to label its different parts. As you know, an analogy is a comparison between two things. In an argument from analogy, one of the things is the **primary subject,** and the other is the **analogue.** The primary subject is the one the conclusion is about, and the analogue is the other. For instance, in Example 11.14A, the primary subject is the owner of the pit bull, and the analogue is the people who kill others while driving intoxicated. The dog owner is the primary subject because the conclusion is about him. The primary subject is compared with the analogue so that a conclusion can be drawn about the primary subject.

> ### Primary Subjects, Analogues, and Selected Characteristics
>
> In an argument from analogy, the two things being compared are referred to as the primary subject and the analogue. The primary subject is the one that the conclusion is about, and the analogue is the other. The selected characteristic is what the conclusion claims is true of the primary subject. The argument is that a characteristic of the analogue (the selected characteristic) is also a characteristic of the primary subject.

Another part of an argument from analogy is the **selected characteristic,** what the conclusion claims is (or should be) true of the primary subject. It is (or should be) true of the primary subject because it is true of the analogue. In other words, the conclusion is that a particular characteristic of the analogue is also present (or should be present, in the case of a value argument) in the primary subject. Thus, the pit bull owner should be charged with negligent homicide because others who negligently cause a person's death are so charged. Here is a schematic structure of an argument from analogy:

Example 11.16

P1: The primary subject is like the analogue.
P2: The analogue has the selected characteristic.
C: Therefore, the primary subject has the selected characteristic.

In arguments from analogy, there are two types of analogues: real analogues and hypothetical analogues.[7] **Real analogues** are things that actually exist or have existed in the past; **hypothetical analogues** are fictional, things made up or invented by the author. Consider these examples:[8]

Example 11.17

A. Background: This letter is about the war on drugs. (*USA Today,* 2/99)

> The casualties and costs of our war on drugs continue to mount, and one of its major leaders now is saying we are both unwilling and unable to fight. We have been here before. Thirty years ago, the Vietnam conflict was sucking us dry. There seemed to be no end to the human suffering, and we apparently were addicted to that horrible war. How did it end? Eventually, when the leaders of the war and media realized that our country was unwilling and unable to win the battle, we just said "no" to the war. Couldn't we apply the lessons so painfully learned in the Vietnam conflict to our present situation in the drug war? How long must we suffer before we say enough? End the drug war now.—G.T.

B. Background: This letter is part of the debate over school vouchers, a proposed policy to provide state funds for parents to send their children to private schools. (*New York Times,* 6/98)

> It is disingenuous for advocates of school vouchers to argue that public schools would be forced to improve if they had to compete with private and religious schools. Imagine a floundering corporation from which the most competent managers are removed. Now imagine a public school from which the students from the most positive home environments are removed. Public schools, which serve the whole community, need taxpayer support, as opposed to schools that enjoy the advantage of a self-selecting population.—S.L.

Text A refers to a real analogue, to a situation that actually occurred, namely, the war in Vietnam. The primary subject is the war on drugs, and the analogy is between the two struggles. The selected characteristic, which the analogue possesses and the primary subject does as well, is that the struggle is unwinnable and should be ended. As the United States came to realize that the war in Vietnam was unwinnable and withdrew from it, so we should do with the war on drugs.

Text B refers not to a real analogue, but to a fictional one made up by the author for the sake of the argument. The primary subject is a school system that has lost its best-prepared students, and the analogue is a foundering corporation that has lost all of its competent managers. The author introduces the analogue with the term "imagine." There is no indication that he is referring to any actual corporation. Rather, he invented the example in order to create an analogy for the argument. The argument is that, since this fictional corporation would have the characteristic of being unable to improve, so would a school system from which the best-prepared students had been removed. The larger conclusion of text B is that we should not adopt a policy of vouchers.[9]

At first, it may seem puzzling that there can be arguments from analogy in which the analogue is fictional. After all, the point of an argument from analogy is that a characteristic of the analogue is also possessed by the primary subject, and if the analogue is invented, of what argumentative force is the fact that it has a certain characteristic (the selected characteristic)? In other words, if the analogue is hypothetical, how can the argument work? The argument can work because the claim that the analogue has the selected characteristic is not itself part of the invention. The author makes up the analogue and them claims both that it is like the primary subject and that it has the selected characteristic. The author does not stipulate in the hypothetical analogue that the analogue has the selected characteristic. Rather, he invites the audience to recognize that, if it had the characteristics that are part of the invention, then it would also have the selected characteristic. For instance, if someone says, "If Michael Jordan still played for the Chicago Bulls, the Bulls would still be a championship team," the analogue is fictional (a Bulls team with Jordan still playing for it), but the claim is that if this fiction existed then it would have the characteristic of still being a championship team.

In text B, the fictional analogue is a floundering corporation from which the most competent managers are removed. This is the part that the author makes up. But he then makes the claim that if this example existed then it would have the selected characteristic. This claim is not itself part of the invention. The author does not stipulate that the analogue has the selected characteristic, as he stipulates its other characteristics. Rather, he claims that if something had those other characteristics then it would also have the selected characteristic. Thus, if there were a floundering corporation from which the most competent managers were removed, then such a corporation would also have the characteristic of being unable to improve. The last two sentences demonstrate why the fictional analogue is referred to as hypothetical.

Here is a well-known example of an argument from analogy with a hypothetical analogue:

Real and Hypothetical Analogues

In an argument from analogy, the analogue may be real or hypothetical. A real analogue is something that actually exists or has existed. A hypothetical analogue is something that the author makes up for the sake of the argument. A hypothetical analogue is designed to have characteristics that ensure that it would also have the selected characteristic.

Example 11.18

Background: This excerpt is from a famous essay by Judith Jarvis Thompson on the issue of abortion. The primary subject is women who wish to have abortions.[10]

> But now let me ask you to imagine this. You wake up in the morning and find yourself back to back in bed with an unconscious violinist. A famous unconscious violinist. He has been found to have a fatal kidney ailment, and the Society of Music Lovers has canvassed all the available medical records and found that you alone have the right blood type to help. They have therefore kidnapped you, and last night the violinist's circulatory system was plugged into yours, so that your kidneys can be used to extract poisons from his blood as well as your own. The director of the hospital now tells you, "Look, we're sorry the Society of Music Lovers did this to you—we would never have permitted it if we had known. But still, they did it, and the violinist now is plugged into you. To unplug you would be to kill him. But never mind, it's only for nine months. By then he will have recovered from his ailment, and can safely be unplugged from you." Is it morally incumbent on you to accede to this situation? [The director continues:] "All persons have a right to life, and violinists are persons. Granted you have a right to decide what happens in and to your body, but a person's right to life outweighs your right to decide what happens in and to your body. So you cannot be unplugged from him." I imagine that you would regard this as outrageous.

The hypothetical analogue is a situation in which a person who is kidnapped and hooked up to a famous violinist in order to keep the violinist alive wishes to disconnect herself. Clearly, there is an analogy between this and a situation in which a woman is seeking an abortion, and the analogue is, of course, designed for this purpose. The selected characteristic is the claim, contained in the final sentence, that the kidnapped person would have no moral obligation to remain hooked up to the violinist, even if the unhooking would kill the violinist. Thompson does not invent the hypothetical analogue with that characteristic, but rather claims that if it had the other characteristics she attributes to it then it would also have this characteristic. The conclusion, of course, is that the primary subject also has this characteristic. That is, a woman who wishes to have an abortion has no obligation not to have one.

Thompson's imaginative analogue is carefully constructed to resemble the primary subject and to make her point about abortion. She might have found a real analogue to make her point, but if a real one cannot be found, a hypothetical one can do as well. An argument from analogy is often used to make a complex point, and finding a real analogue that is sufficiently like the primary subject to make the argument can be difficult. The creativity involved in producing arguments is most clearly revealed in the case of arguments from analogy with hypothetical analogues. Coming up with hypothetical analogues requires a great deal of imagination, because the analogue must make precisely the point that the arguer is trying to make.

Hypothetical analogues often consist of little episodes of science fiction involving strange beings and fantastic technological apparatus. Hypothetical analogues, especially the more complicated and imaginative ones, are often referred to as **thought experiments.** These can play a major role in the creative process in all areas of human endeavor. Consider this example:

Example 11.19

Background: Albert Einstein used the following thought experiment in an explication of his theories. This passage is from a popular exposition by Einstein of his general theory of relativity. The situation is that a large chest is suspended in a region of space far removed from any bodies, so that there is little or no gravitational forces on the chest and its contents.[11]

> Let us imagine a spacious chest resembling a room with an observer inside who is equipped with apparatus. Gravitation naturally does not exist for this observer. . . . To the middle of the lid of the chest is fixed externally a hook with rope attached, and now a "being" (what kind of being is immaterial to us) begins pulling at this with a constant force. The chest together with the observer then begin to move "upwards" with a uniformly accelerated motion. . . . How does the man in the chest regard the process? The acceleration of the chest will be transmitted to him by the reaction of the floor of the chest. He must therefore take up this pressure by means of his legs if he does not wish to be laid out full length on the floor. He is then standing in the chest in exactly the same way as anyone stands in a room of a house on our earth. . . . The man in the chest will thus come to the conclusion that he and the chest are in a gravitational field. . . . Ought we to smile at the man and say that he errs in his conclusion? I do not believe we ought to if we wish to remain consistent; we must rather admit that his mode of grasping the situation violates neither reason nor known mechanical laws.

Here is one way to interpret this complicated argument: The primary subject is a proper understanding of gravitation. The analogue is the understanding of gravitation held by the person in the chest. The selected characteristic is that the force of gravitation cannot be distinguished from the force of acceleration. The conclusion is that the forces of gravitation and acceleration are indistinguishable for us as well. Einstein claimed that analogies like this played a role not only in his explication of his theories for others but also in the thought processes by which he came up with his theories. Great human discoveries are often the result of a creative mind hitting upon an analogy that shows the way.

11.2.3 Structuring an Argument from Analogy

An analogy is a claim that two things are alike, and an argument from analogy draws a conclusion from this claim. However, to provide a strong argument from analogy, it is not enough merely to claim that two things are alike. After all, everything is like everything else in at least some respect. In a strong argument from analogy, an author will claim not simply that the two things are alike, but that they are alike in respects relevant to the conclusion of the argument. The strength of an analogy in an argument from analogy is always dependent on what conclusion the author seeks to draw.

For example, is the statement "a bicycle is like an automobile" a good analogy? It depends on what the conclusion is of the argument of which it is a part. If the conclusion is that bicycles need regular maintenance, the analogy is a good one. Bicycles are like automobiles in ways that indicate the need for regular maintenance. But if the conclusion is that bicycles contribute to global warming, it is a bad one. Bicycles are not like automobiles in ways that indicate a contribution to global warming. In fact, the two things are unalike in the relevant respect, namely, that automobiles have a gas-burning motor. Thus, the way in which a bicycle is like an automobile is relevant to the maintenance issue but not to the global warming issue.

This important point about arguments from analogy needs to be represented in the structuring of them. Here is the earlier schematic form (from Example 11.16) modified to incorporate this point. In this version, x is the primary subject, y the analogue, and z the selected characteristic.

Example 11.20

>   P1A, etc. [subargument for P1]
> ⎡ P1: x is *relevantly* like y.
> ⎣ P2: y has characteristic z.
>   C: Therefore, x has characteristic z.

The need to assess the strength of the analogy relative to the conclusion is indicated by the term "relevantly" in P1, which presents the analogy. When you make an argument from analogy, you claim that the primary subject and the analogue are similar in a way that supports the claim that they both possess the selected characteristic. This aspect of the claim is represented by the term "relevantly." P2 indicates that the analogue has the selected characteristic, so P1 and P2 are linked premises.

As mentioned previously, a subargument for P1 may or may not be present. Whereas the main argument is an argument *from* analogy, the subargument for P1 is an **argument to analogy,** in that it seeks to show that there is an analogy relevant to the conclusion. This argument usually consists of claims that the primary subject and the analogue share additional common characteristics (other than the selected characteristic). And these claims support the claim in P1 that the analogue and the primary subject are relevantly similar.

This is the case with the design argument. Recall that the design argument includes a subargument supporting the analogy between the universe and a machine. The subargument claims that both the universe and a machine are composed of parts that function together in a regular and harmonious way. The presence of this common characteristic supports the claim that the two things are relevantly alike because this is the sort of characteristic that, were it associated with the selected characteristic (having an intelligent designer) in one case (the machine) would be associated with that characteristic in the other case (the universe).

Arguments to Analogy

Often, an argument from analogy will include a subargument that supports the premise indicating the analogy. This subargument is an argument *to* analogy because its conclusion is a claim that there is an analogy. This argument usually consists of claims that the primary subject and the analogue have common characteristics (other than the selected characteristic) that are associated with the selected characteristic, thereby showing that the way in which the two things in the analogy are alike is relevant to the main conclusion.

Here is an example of an argument from analogy that contains a subargument to the analogy:

Example 11.21

Background: This letter is about drug policy. (*Miami Herald*, 4/97)

> We are losing the battle against drugs. Drug abuse is a lethal weapon that is surreptitiously destroying our progeny—sons and daughters. This infusion of drugs into our nation's mainstream is as effective as bombs, machine guns, or chemicals in destroying our beloved homeland. We are at war for our national survival. Our armed forces are supposed to defend, protect, and secure our nation. They should be deployed immediately. If authorized to use force, they can stop illegal immigration, restore our borders, abolish the traffic of illegal drugs, and safeguard the greatest country on Earth.—G.C.D.

The conclusion of this argument is that the military should be used to handle the drug problem. The primary subject is drug abuse, the analogue is war, and the selected characteristic is that the military is used to deal with it. Because drug abuse is like war, and the military is used to deal with war, the military should be used to deal with drug abuse. In addition to presenting this main argument from analogy, however, the author provides support for the claim that war and drug abuse are alike in relevant ways. Here is a structure indicating the subargument:

Example 11.22

> P1A: Both drug abuse and war destroy our progeny and homeland.
> P1B: In both drug abuse and war, national survival is at stake.
> P1: Drug abuse is relevantly like war.
> P2: War is a problem that the military deals with.
> C: Therefore, drug abuse is a problem the military should deal with.

Two other features are sometimes present in arguments from analogy: (1) Sometimes there will be a subargument for P2, and (2) sometimes there will be additional premises supporting the main conclusion that are not part of the argument from analogy itself. For example, if the drug abuse argument had included the claim that the military is the only government agency with adequate funding to tackle the drug problem, this would have been an additional main premise not connected with the argument from analogy.

11.2.4 Even-More-So Arguments and Counteranalogies

There are two special versions of argument from analogy that deserve our attention. Consider these examples:

Example 11.23

A. Background: This letter is in response to a newspaper column about treason and American history. (*New York Times,* 1/00)

> Your columnist asserts that those who fought under the Confederate flag were guilty of treason. If so, then Thomas Jefferson and George Washington and his army were traitors. Southerners had the logical argument that as previously independent states they voluntarily entered into union with other states and thus had the right to withdraw from that union. The colonists rebelled against duly constituted British authority with their only justification their desire to be independent.—H.M.G.

B. Background: This letter is in response to a newspaper column arguing that television is not a danger to society. (*New York Times,* 9/93)

> Your columnist argues that past societies survived the effects of new technologies, and that we will also survive television. He brings in Socrates, movies and comic books to defend his point. A more fitting analogy for television might be the Roman waterworks. The aqueducts were a great accomplishment. The pipes were made of

> lead. Slowly, imperceptibly the population was poisoned. Some historians consider lead poisoning a major cause of the fall of the Roman Empire. I hope future historians will not look back on television in the 20th century as the pollutant that caused the failure of American democracy.—A.P.

The author of text A rejects the claim of the columnist that those who fought in the Confederacy were traitors. In this argument from analogy, the primary subject is those who fought in the Confederacy. The selected characteristic is not being traitors. The analogue is those who fought for American independence. Because those who fought for American independence were not traitors, neither were those who fought in the Confederacy. But this argument has a special feature. In the third and fourth sentences, the author claims that the Confederacy more clearly had right on its side than did the thirteen colonies. Specifically, the Confederate states had the legal right to leave the union, but the colonies did not have the legal right to separate from Britain. This means that the selected characteristic (not being traitors) would apply even more to the members of the Confederacy than to the American revolutionaries. This strengthens the argument's support for the conclusion.

Arguments from analogy that include this extra element are known as **even-more-so arguments.** The primary subject would have the selected characteristic even more so than does the analogue. In the PC structure, this can be represented by including the idea in the structured argument by inserting the phrase "even more so" at an appropriate place in the premise stating the analogy (P1) and in the conclusion.

Text B is another kind of argument from analogy, an **argument from counteranalogy,** in which an author critically responds to an argument from analogy by proposing a different argument from analogy. This second argument has the same primary subject but (usually) a different analogue, whose conclusion is inconsistent with the conclusion of the original argument. The issue in this case is the effect of television on society. We can gather from this text that in the original argument the conclusion was that society would survive television because analogues like comic books, movies, and Socrates all had the characteristic that society had survived their presence.[12] The author calls this conclusion into question by presenting a different argument from analogy. The analogue in this case is the ancient Roman waterworks, which used lead-lined pipes, and the selected characteristic is being a likely cause of the destruction of society. Because the Roman waterworks had this characteristic, television has it, too.

Argument from counteranalogy can be a rhetorically effective way to respond when someone uses an argument from analogy to support a conclusion with which you disagree. But note that this is not an evaluation of the original argument. The nature of the response offered by an argument from counteranalogy is a criticism of a conclusion itself, and not of the argument offered for that conclusion, an important distinction we discussed in Chapter 6. An argument from counteranalogy does not attempt to show that the original argument is weak or that the analogy of that argument is defective. It ignores the argument and attacks the con-

> **Even-More-So Arguments**
> **and Arguments from Counteranalogy**
>
> Two kinds of argument are variants on argument from analogy. In an
> even-more-so argument, an author claims that the selected characteristic
> would apply more so to the primary subject than to the analogue, which
> strengthens the conclusion that the primary subject has the selected
> characteristic. In an argument from counteranalogy, an author responds
> to another's argument from analogy by presenting a different analogy with
> the same primary subject, thereby drawing a conclusion at odds with that
> of the other's argument.

clusion. An evaluation of an argument from analogy involves showing that the
analogy is weak or questionable in some way. This is the topic of the next section.

EXERCISE SET 11.2

SECTION A: For each of the following arguments from analogy, list the primary subject, the analogue, and the selected characteristic. Then structure the argument,
including a subargument to analogy if there is one. Some of the arguments may have
implicit conclusions and/or implicit premises, and the wording of the text may need to
be reformulated.

EXAMPLE
Having to suffer the poverty of a low-wage job is a violation of human rights.
After all, it is like slavery.

ANSWER
Primary subject: having to suffer the poverty of a low-wage job
Analogue: slavery
Selected characteristic: a violation of human rights
P1: Suffering the poverty of having a low-wage job is relevantly like slavery.
IP2: Slavery is a violation of human rights.
C: Having to suffer the poverty of a low-wage job is a violation of human rights.

PROBLEMS
1. In the current crisis, we cannot afford not to reelect Jones as president. You
   should not change horses in the middle of a stream.
2. Children require benevolent authority from their parents. So, we should not
   worry about a benevolent authoritarian ruler.
3. I know that my friend has a conscious mind that directs her behavior
   because she behaves like I do and I know that I have a conscious mind
   directing my behavior.

4. I would advise against marriage. Being married to someone is like wearing a ball and chain.

5. Thinking creatively is like prospecting for gold. You come up with nothing much more often than you come up with something.

❖ 6. When a nation makes military threats against other nations, it is like when the law makes threats of punishment against citizens of a nation. And we know that legal threats work.

7. Civil disobedience is never justified. Living in a country is like signing a contract promising always to obey its laws.

8. If a nation is invaded, it is entitled to defend itself, just as an individual is allowed to use force in self-defense.

❖ 9. If you have too much information in your head, you need to forget something before you can learn something new, because the brain is like a computer. After all, the nerve cells of the brain are like the circuits on a computer chip.

10. The Internet is like a vast library. Soon we will be able to get any information we desire from the comfort of our own home.

11. Our nation with so many people seeking to immigrate to it is like a lifeboat with many people in the water trying to get in it. Our resources are limited, as are the provisions in a lifeboat. The conclusion is clear. We should not let immigrants in.

SECTION B: For the following arguments from analogy, list the primary subject, the analogue, and the selected characteristic. Then structure the argument (tree diagram optional), including subarguments and additional premises, if any. Some may be subarguments and some arguments from counteranalogy or even-more-so arguments.

EXAMPLE
Background: This letter is critical of the 1997 budget agreement between Congress and the president. (*Los Angeles Times*, 8/97)

> The new budget agreement is like a family paying off the mortgage (the deficit), while taking an expensive vacation (tax cuts for the wealthy), with little regard for the education of their elementary-school kids.—S.S.L.

ANSWER
Primary subject: the new budget agreement
Analogue: a family paying off the mortgage while taking an expensive vacation and giving little regard to the education of their elementary school kids
Selected characteristic (implicit): is not acceptable

P1A: The new budget agreement pays off the deficit, gives tax cuts to the wealthy, and does not include enough money for education.

P1: The new budget agreement is relevantly like a family paying off the mortgage while taking an expensive vacation and giving little regard to the education of their elementary school kids.

IP2: A family paying off the mortgage while taking an expensive vacation and giving little regard to the education of their elementary school kids is not acceptable.

IC: Therefore, the new budget agreement is not acceptable.

PROBLEMS

1. Background: This letter comments on the response to live TV news coverage of a suicide. (*Los Angeles Times*, 5/98)

   Why do so many who are bent out of shape over live TV coverage of the tragic freeway suicide April 30 passively accept far more graphic portrayals of violence on so-called entertainment programs? And why do spokesmen for TV stations "deeply regret" that their viewers saw this tragedy as it happened but feel no remorse for subjecting viewers to far more gruesome portrayals of murder and mayhem on a daily basis in the name of entertainment?—R.D.N.

2. Background: This letter is about the efforts by the United States to build a "Star Wars" defense system to defend against missile attack. (*New York Times*, 4/00)

   Even if the United States built a defense system that could identify and shoot down missiles, our adversaries could work around it by delivering bombs by plane, boat or truck. Our borders are porous. Putting bars on our windows won't reduce the probability of intruders if our doors are wide open. Surely we can think of better ways to spend $60 billion.—H.T.[13]

❖ 3. Background: This letter is about capital punishment. (*Los Angeles Times*, 6/97)

   We don't rape women to prevent rape; we don't steal to prevent theft. Why is it OK to murder people to prevent murder? And don't kid yourself, the death penalty is murder.—R.S.C.

4. Background: This letter is about South Carolina flying the Confederate flag over its capitol. (*New York Times*, 3/00)

   The South Carolina Legislature should stop hiding behind the notion that the Confederate flag flying atop the state capitol is a symbol of heritage. The only heritage that the flag represents is that of white South Carolinians whose ancestors fought in the Civil War. Flying a flag that celebrates only one portion of its citizens is as exclusionary as placing an Irish or a Jamaican flag atop the dome. South Carolina is a multiracial, multiethnic state, and it's time that its legislators realize this fact.—R.E.

5. Background: This letter is about the problems of alcohol. (*New York Times*, 6/00)

   As much as smoking or even secondhand smoking is bad for your health, it does not compare with the terrible health and social consequences that alcohol creates in our society. Where is the social outrage, and when is Congress going to do something about the problem?—G.S.

❖ 6. Background: This letter comments on one of the lawsuits brought against tobacco companies. (*Miami Herald*, 6/97)

   Now that the flight attendants are also suing the tobacco companies because they were allegedly damaged from passengers' cigarette smoke, which airlines permitted, I have a suggestion: Why don't we have a class-action lawsuit against automobile manufacturers because some automobiles were driven too fast or the driver was drunk and people were killed?—R.B.W.

7. Background: This letter is in response to a column about smoking in public places. (*Boston Globe*, 6/97)

   Your columnist states: "Restaurant diners are not a captive audience. Those unwilling to share a room with smokers can complain to the owners or switch to another restaurant. Enough complaints or switches, and restaurateurs will get the message." I wonder if he would suggest that if car manufacturers sold cars with defective brakes, we should wait for complaints from drivers to persuade the manufacturers to follow responsible practices?—W.B.

8. Background: This is another letter about tobacco. (*New York Times*, 3/00)

   The Supreme Court, in this unfortunate 5-to-4 decision finding that the Food and Drug Administration, part of the executive branch, does not have the authority to regulate tobacco as a drug, said that "owing to its unique place in American history and society, tobacco has its own unique political history," and that Congress must speak on the matter. Slavery, too, held a "unique place in American history and society," and the executive branch, through President Lincoln's Emancipation Proclamation, resolved to free the slaves when Congress would not act. The executive branch's decision to exercise jurisdiction to limit tobacco sales to minors should have been applauded by the Court, not undermined.—T.K.

❖ 9. Background: This passage is from Charles Darwin's *On the Origin of Species*.[14]

   I cannot doubt that the theory of descent with modification embraces all the members of the same class. . . . Analogy would lead me one step further, namely, to the belief that all animals and plants have descended from some one prototype. . . . All living things have much in common, in their chemical composition, their germinal vesicles, their cellular structure, and their laws of growth and reproduction. . . . Therefore, I would infer from analogy that probably all organic beings which have ever lived on this earth have descended from some one primordial form, into which life was first breathed.

10. Background: This letter is in response to a newspaper column discussing whether the news photographers (the paparazzi) were responsible for the death of Princess Diana of England when they gave chase to her car before it crashed. (*Boston Globe*, 9/97)

   Your columnist finds no fault with the paparazzi in Princess Diana's death when he writes, "It is not up to the celebrity to draw the line after he or she has opened the door." This has the curious ring of a date rapist's plea that his victim didn't have the right to say no once she agreed to have a kiss.—J.H.

11. Background: This letter is about the news reporting policies of the *Boston Globe*. (*Boston Globe*, 7/97)

   When reporting boating accident fatalities, the *Globe* usually states whether the victim was wearing a life jacket. When reporting traffic accident fatalities, the *Globe* usually reports whether the victims were wearing seat belts.

When reporting pedestrian fatalities, the *Globe* would do a great public service if you mentioned whether the pedestrian was walking (or jogging) with his or her back to the oncoming traffic. This would certainly raise public awareness of the dangers.—P.H.T.

❖ 12. Background: This letter, part of the debate on gun control, is about a bill introduced in Congress, the child safety lock bill. (*New York Times*, 5/97)

Countless deaths and injuries of children occur every year because of accidental shooting. Something must be done to prevent such senseless accidents. The child safety lock bill would require that every new handgun be sold with a child safety lock and a warning detailing the dangers of improperly storing a firearm. The idea of a locking device on a gun is really no different from providing a child safety cap on a bottle of aspirin or a seat belt in a car. It would seem unthinkable for such basic safety measures as those not to exist. Our children's lives are worth the $10 cost.—H.K.

13. Background: This letter is about the controversial sentence given to Jonathan Pollard, convicted of spying for Israel. (*New York Times*, 12/00)

A letter urging clemency for the convicted spy Jonathan J. Pollard repeats the overused and underexamined argument that Mr. Pollard was spying for an ally and that his life sentence is "almost unheard of." Julius and Ethel Rosenberg were executed after being convicted of spying for the Soviet Union during World War II, when Moscow was our ally. Thus, the Pollard lobby does not seem to realize the comparative leniency of his sentence, as well as another salient difference: Mr. Pollard spied more for money than for principle.—M.D.

14. Background: This letter is about computer viruses. (*New York Times*, 5/00)

The latest virus invasion, particularly through the Microsoft Outlook program, illustrates yet another aspect of the problems of monopoly. In effect, the Windows monopoly is a computer monoculture with all the same problems of other monocultures. In agriculture, one of the worries of the widespread planting of monoculture crops is higher susceptibility to insects and disease, since specialized bugs can rapidly increase their numbers. We might well want to encourage diversity in our computer software not just for economic reasons but to avoid future outbreaks of disease and bug infestation. —R.C.L.

❖ 15. Background: This letter is in response to an article about people protesting gun violence by placing the shoes of a victim of the steps of the headquarters of a gun manufacturer. (*Los Angeles Times*, 5/98)

While the grief of the families who have lost loved ones to gun violence is understandable, their logic is not. Taking the shoes of a victim to the headquarters of a gun manufacturer is like taking the shoes of a drunk driver's victim to the steps of General Motors or Ford: The car's not to blame, it's just an apparatus, a mechanism; the culprit is the driver, the operator of the apparatus. Likewise, the relationship between guns and their operators. If your paper ran a story about families of drunk-driving victims putting shoes in front of a car company's headquarters almost all your readers would say, "Gee, that's goofy. Why blame the car?"—J.R.

16. Background: This letter is critical of the legal action taken against Microsoft on the grounds of its alleged monopolistic practices in the software market. (*New York Times*, 5/98)

There is a simpler alternative: a change in copyright law. Microsoft's domination exists because the law allows it. If Windows 98 could be copied and sold freely and legally, Microsoft's monopoly would evaporate overnight. Computer operation systems are inherently different from other intellectual property, like song lyrics. They are more like languages. If the law allowed a copyright on English, we would have to pay royalties whenever we opened our mouths.—M.B.B.

17. Background: This is another letter about the legal action taken by the government against Microsoft for monopolistic practices. It responds to a column suggesting that no action be taken because technological advances will soon undo Microsoft's monopoly. (*New York Times*, 4/00)

Your columnist implies that technological progress in a free market somehow heals all wounds. This notion is flawed, in my view. By that reasoning, a guy who stole a horse in the early part of the 20th century was blameless, since horses were soon to be replaced by cars. Has technology created a virtual statute of limitations for what's right and what's wrong? I always thought that a guy who steals a horse on Monday remains a thief, come Tuesday.—C.S.

❖ 18. Background: This letter is in response to a columnist who criticized a proposal to use statistical sampling to achieve a more accurate census count. (*New York Times*, 12/97)

Your columnist's attempt to discredit census sampling by comparing it to pre-election polling is based on an inaccurate comparison. A more reasonable association would be with exit polling, where information is collected about actual behavior, not predictions about actions (which those polled may not wish to disclose). Sampling, in both exit polling and census taking, derives from large quantities of substantiated data, from which projections are then made about the much smaller unrecorded portion.—J.R.

19. Background: This letter is about campaign finance reform and free-speech guarantees. (*New York Times*, 2/00)

In the context of campaign finance reform legislation, the regulation of the expenditure of money has a direct impact on the exercise of speech. To argue by analogy: few would contend that a local ordinance limiting the amount of land one may own to one-quarter acre is an infringement on free speech; but a local ordinance limiting the amount of land one may use to place placards supporting political candidates to one-quarter acre would come under some constitutional scrutiny. It is not the limitation on the ownership or use of property generally that raises concerns, but the limitation on the use of property to exercise constitutional rights.—M.J.M.

20. Background: This letter about the North Atlantic Treaty Organization (NATO), an alliance of mostly western European nations founded in 1949 to counteract the military power of the former Soviet Union. The letter addresses the issue of whether to expand NATO to include some of the nations in eastern Europe that during the Cold War were allies of the Soviet Union. (*Boston Globe*, 6/97)

We would all do well to remember that it was the humiliation of Germany by the Western allies after World War I that allowed Adolf Hitler to rise to power and plunge the world into a war that cost tens of millions of lives. The humiliation of Russia by the same Western powers could ultimately cost billions of lives. Russia, after all, still has thousands of nuclear weapons. Our insistence on expanding the alliance eastward is likely to strengthen nationalist elements in Russia. What possible benefit can be achieved from adding a few weak nations to NATO that would justify incurring risks this great?—W.B.

❖ 21. Background: This letter is about the activities of the tobacco companies. It also refers to Ted Kaczynski, who was convicted of the "unabomber" crimes of sending bombs through the mail in the 1980s and 1990s. (*Chicago Tribune*, 5/97)

Federal prosecutors will seek the death penalty for Ted Kaczynski, suspected "Unabomber," since he "intentionally killed the victims, lacks remorse and has a low potential for rehabilitation." This for a series of offenses that spanned 20 years and resulted in three deaths and 21 injuries. During the same 20 years, cigarette smoking has killed roughly 6 million people and injured millions more. Tobacco executives have shown no remorse and a low potential for rehabilitation. They have lied to the American public and targeted our children for their poison. Although Kaczynski's actions may have been the product of a mentally ill individual, the tobacco companies have been motivated strictly by greed and have continued to market illness and death. If Ted Kaczynski deserves the death penalty for his actions, which killed three people, why should cigarette company executives, who are responsible for more deaths than occurred in the Nazi Holocaust, be rewarded with respectability and financial success? These men and women are guilty of a much worse crime. They kill without remorse strictly for money.—D.W.

22. Background: This is part of a letter about U.S. policy in the late 1990s toward Iraq. This passage follows a portion of the letter that described the deaths of three Iraqi children caused by U.S. policy. (*Boston Globe*, 12/98)

It seems to me this conveys with terrible clarity that Saddam Hussein and the leaders of our government have much in common: They are both visiting death and suffering on the people of Iraq. In response to the possibility that Saddam Hussein may have "weapons of mass destruction" and the additional possibility that he may use them in the future, the United States, in the present, is using weapons of mass destruction: cruise missiles, B-52 bombers, and, most of all, economic sanctions that have resulted in the deaths of hundreds of thousands of Iraqi children. We have taken the lives, among others, of three Iraqi children in order to "send a message" (as our leaders have said) to Saddam Hussein. Would we be willing to take the lives of three American children to "send a message"? Are Iraqi children less worthy of living than our own?—H.Z.

23. Background: This 1980 letter is in response to claims by then President Ronald Reagan that the U.S. participation in the war in Vietnam was "a noble cause." The author refers to the attempt by the former Soviet Union to defeat an anti-Soviet uprising in the neighboring nation of Afghanistan, an effort that Reagan opposed. (*New York Times*, 8/80)

If Ronald Reagan believes our Vietnam intervention was "a noble cause," he can have no logical objection to the Soviet invasion of Afghanistan. In both cases, a puppet dictator, placed in office by the superpower, officially requested military help from the superpower to subdue subversive elements. Like Mr. Reagan, the average Russian superpatriot must regard his country's intervention as "a noble cause," and since Afghanistan, unlike Vietnam, borders the interventionist power, the Russian may have a shade more logic on his side.—I.N.W.

11.3 The Fallacy of Faulty Analogy

When the analogy in an argument from analogy is weak, the argument commits the **fallacy of faulty analogy.** As mentioned previously, an analogy in an argument from analogy is strong or weak only relative to the conclusion of the argument. This is the reason for including the term "relevantly" in P1 of the schematic structure for this kind of argument. The fallacy of faulty analogy, in its stronger form, is a specific version of the basic fallacy of false premise.[15] To claim that the analogy is faulty is to claim that P1 is false, that the primary subject is not relevantly like the analogue. In its weaker form, the fallacy is a version of problematic premise; the claim that the two things are relevantly alike is doubtful and needs support.

Just as you make an analogy by citing how two things are alike, you generally criticize an analogy by pointing out how the two things are, in fact, unlike. Consider how this works in this evaluation of an argument from analogy:

Example 11.24

Background: This letter comments on Microsoft's response to the claim that it should not be allowed to include its Internet browser as part of its Windows operating system. (*New York Times*, 10/97)

In its defense, Microsoft said, "Ford would not allow one of its dealers to pull the factory installed engine out of a Mustang and substitute a Chevy engine." The analogy is flawed. First, the Internet browser does not "drive" the computer. Second, auto retailers will allow the customer to pull the factory installed stereo system from a

> delivered car and will give the customer a credit. If anything, Microsoft's argument works against it.—R.A.L.

First, what is the argument from analogy to which the author is responding? Because Microsoft's removing its Internet browser from its operating system is like the dealer's taking the factory-installed engine out of a new Ford car and replacing it with a Chevy engine, Microsoft may prohibit dealers from removing its browser. The author criticizes this argument on the grounds that the analogy is weak. The author points out that the browser does not drive the operating system as the engine drives the car and that the dealer often replaces the radios in new cars with different radios.

In effect, the author is making a charge of faulty analogy. To justify such a charge, he must show that it is false that taking the browser out of the operating system is *relevantly* like putting a Chevy engine in a new Ford. He seeks to do this by showing that the two things are unalike in a way that is relevant to the conclusion. That is, the two are unalike in that one (the car engine) drives the machine it is in and the other (the Internet browser) does not—a difference that is clearly relevant to the conclusion. Whether it is appropriate to replace a part of something depends to some extent on how important that part is to the functioning of the whole. That which drives something is generally its most important part. This argument is bolstered by the author's point about the radio. When parts are less important (like a radio in a car), replacing them is more acceptable.

This is the most common way in which a fallacy charge of faulty analogy is justified. To show how an analogy is weak involves pointing out how the two things are unalike, not simply in any old way, but in ways that are relevant to the conclusion. To counter the claim in P1 that the primary subject and analogue are alike in ways relevant to the conclusion, the person charging faulty analogy argues that the two things are unalike in ways relevant to the conclusion. The strategy is to imply that for the analogy to work the two things have to be alike in certain ways, and they are not alike in those ways.

Recall the design argument: A machine and the universe are alike, and because the machine has an intelligent designer, so does the universe. The claim that the two are relevantly alike is supported by a subargument that both have the characteristic of being composed of parts that function together in a consistent and regular way. How might we make a faulty analogy charge against this argument? First, think about some ways in which a machine and the universe are *unalike:* (1) The universe is much larger than any machine, (2) the universe is much longer lasting than any machine, and (3) a machine always has a discernible purpose, whereas the universe has no discernible purpose. The first and second ways are not relevant to the conclusion; that is, the size and age of something is not relevant to its having or not having an intelligent designer. In contrast, the third way is relevant to the claim that something has an intelligent designer. Something's having a purpose is closely associated with its having an intelligent designer, so much so that the lack of purpose shows the lack of intelligent design. Thus, the third way could be cited in the justification of a faulty analogy charge against the design argument.[16]

> ### The Fallacy of Faulty Analogy
>
> The fallacy of faulty analogy is charged against an argument from analogy
> when the analogy is weak relative to the conclusion of the argument, that
> is, when the primary subject and the analogue are not alike in ways rele-
> vant to the selected characteristic. The fallacy is a specific version of
> either false premise or problematic premise.

Let us try an evaluation of our own:

Example 11.25

Background: This letter refers to then President Clinton's claim that, until the campaign finance laws were changed, the Democrats had to continue to seek large
donations to keep up with the Republicans. (*Boston Globe*, 2/97)

> Clinton on campaign finance offers the response of a child who has done something
> wrong, as in: "Daddy, I did it because the other kids were doing it." Most of us wouldn't
> accept this excuse from a child. Why should we accept it from the president?—P.B.

To structure and evaluate an argument from analogy, it is helpful to first list the
primary subject, the analogue, and the selected characteristic.

Example 11.26

Primary subject: President Clinton's justification when he is criticized for his ques-
tionable political fund-raising
Analogue: a child who justifies questionable behavior by saying that other kids do it
Selected characteristic: being unacceptable
Argument

> P1: President Clinton's justification when he is criticized for his questionable
>   political fund-raising is relevantly like a child justifying questionable behav-
>   ior by saying that other kids do it.
> P2: A child justifying questionable behavior by saying that other kids do it is
>   not acceptable.
> C: Therefore, Clinton's justification when he is criticized for his questionable
>   political fund-raising is unacceptable.

Evaluation

> I charge this argument from analogy with faulty analogy. The argument com-
> mits this fallacy because P1 is false. There is a crucial relevant respect in
> which the primary subject and analogue are unalike. In politics, in a two-party
> situation in which one party gives up questionable fund-raising tactics that the
> other party continues to practice, it would become difficult or impossible for
> the first party to win elections. It would not be fair to a party's supporters
> for that party to commit political suicide in this way. One party should aban-
> don questionable fund-raising tactics only when the other party agrees to as

> well. There would seldom be anything like this characteristic in the case of a child's questionable behavior.

This justification asserts that the claim of relevant similarity is false, making the charge in this case a version of false premise. But you can also make the charge as a version of problematic premise by arguing that the author needs to provide support for the claim that the two things are relevantly alike.

When arguments from analogy are criticized, their authors often come back with a revised argument designed to overcome the criticism. For example, recall Judith Thompson's argument from analogy about abortion in Example 11.18. Her analogy involves a hypothetical situation in which a person is kidnapped and hooked up to a famous violinist to keep him alive. Her conclusion is that a woman getting an abortion, like the kidnap victim unhooking herself from the violinist, is morally acceptable.

However, many have argued that the analogy is weak because the pregnant woman (unless a victim of rape or incest) has voluntarily behaved in a way that resulted in the pregnancy, whereas the woman hooked up to the violinist is the victim of a kidnapping. This is a strong response because whether the woman was in the situation voluntarily is relevant to whether she has an obligation not to unhook herself from the violinist. But, because the analogue is hypothetical, Thompson is free to change the details in order to overcome this criticism, and, in fact, she does so.[17] In the revised version of the analogue, the public knows that the kidnappers are in a certain part of town looking for a victim to hook up to the violinist, and the woman who is kidnapped is grabbed while wandering in that part of town. This revision brings the analogue into line with the situation in which a woman wanting an abortion had sexual intercourse knowing that she might become pregnant. Because, Thomson argues, the woman in the revised analogue will still be morally permitted to unhook herself from the violinist, the conclusion of the argument from analogy remains that a woman is not morally required to continue the pregnancy. The point is that the woman who wanders in that part of town is still kidnapped against her will, just as the woman who becomes pregnant after voluntary intercourse may still be pregnant against her will.

≡ EXERCISE SET 11.3

SECTION A: Each of the following texts criticizes an argument from analogy. Based on the information given, indicate the analogy being criticized and the conclusion it is being used to argue for. Then express in your own words the justification for the charge of faulty analogy offered by the author.

EXAMPLE

Background: This letter is in response to an argument for the feasibility of building an effective limited defense shield against missiles. (*New York Times*, 4/00)

> Your columnist cites our technological success in landing a man on the moon to answer the doubters of our ability to achieve an effective limited

missile defense. His analogy is flawed. The moon is a passive target; it does not try to dodge from the oncoming manned rocket ship. But once our missile defense system is in place, the reputed enemy can "fake out" our defense system.—B.S.

ANSWER

The analogy is that the technological task of landing men on the moon is relevantly like the technological challenge of building an effective limited defense against missile attack, leading to the conclusion that the missile defense, like the moon landing, can be achieved. The author criticizes this analogy on the grounds that the two are unlike in that what the moon rocket was aimed at is not evasive, whereas what the defensive rocket is aimed at would be designed to be evasive. This unlikeness is relevant to the conclusion because evasiveness would make the technological challenge of the missile defense much more difficult.

PROBLEMS

1. Background: This is a response to a letter that criticized the United States for being much more vigorous in its response to a humanitarian crisis in Europe than to one in Africa. (*New York Times*, 3/00)

   A letter writer suggests that we "contrast our government's tepid response to the humanitarian disaster in Mozambique with last year's onslaught in Kosovo." But a distinction should be made between situations like Kosovo and the floods in Mozambique: it was important for the United States to intervene in Kosovo not only to avert a humanitarian disaster but also to send a clear message that aggression would not be tolerated. This second factor is not applicable to the natural disaster in Mozambique.—J.S.W.

2. Background: This letter is about a court decision that allowed the Boy Scouts to continue their refusal to admit homosexuals. (*San Francisco Chronicle*, 3/98)

   In the decision upholding the right of the Boy Scouts to discriminate against gays, lesbians and bisexuals, the Justice wrote the following: "Could the NAACP be compelled to accept as a member a Ku Klux Klansman? Could B'nai B'rith be required to admit an anti-Semite?" I find such an attitude by the Justice to be reprehensible and disgraceful. She owes a public apology to the people of California for her intemperate and hateful remarks in comparing gays, lesbians and bisexual people to these hateful groups.—M.S.

3. Background: This letter is in response to a column arguing that stay-at-home mothers should get preferential treatment in rehiring, just as veterans do. (*Chicago Tribune*, 12/97)

   Your columnist uses faculty logic when comparing rehiring preferences given to veterans to her proposed three-year rehiring preference for women who choose to stay home with children. The fault is that while having children is entirely voluntary, service to our country is often not. Just ask a Vietnam vet. Comparing women who choose to have children and then wish to return to the work force to those men and women who served our country and lost arms, legs and lives is a huge insult.—J.B.

4. Background: This is on the issue of alcohol advertising. (*New York Times*, 7/97)

   One government official, explaining why she voted to block a proposal to investigate the effects of hard liquor television advertising on children, said that she saw no distinction between alcoholic beverages and products such as "air bags" and "sugared cereals" where safety concerns have been raised. Do air bags contribute to violent crime? How many people are arrested for driving under the influence of sugared cereals?—N.A.P.

5. Background: This letter is about a comparison between students who sought out the reclusive author J.D. Salinger and news photographers (paparazzis) who constantly stalked the late Princess Diana of Great Britain. (*Boston Globe*, 9/97)

   Students who made the pilgrimage to see J.D. Salinger cannot be compared to the paparazzis stalking Princess Diana. It was not the same because the motivation was different. The students' was based on admiration for Salinger, while the photographers had only dollar signs in their eyes. Carried to an extreme, you would not have children worship a hero, fall in love with an icon, or seek an autograph from a role model. The difference is between adoration and greed.—D.R.L.

6. Background: This letter is about the 1997 chess match between the world chess champion, Garry Kasparov, and a computer programmed to play chess. (*New York Times*, 5/97)

   Your columnist described the chess match as "man versus computer." In fact, the contest was between men with computers and men without them. We discovered that a man with a computer can beat a man without one. This is like discovering that a man with a pole can jump higher than a man without one. Give Mr. Kasparov a cram course in computer programming and a computer of his own. Then we will have Deep Blue vs. Deep Garry. I know on whom to lay my money.—D.P.L.

7. Background: This letter is a response to a proposal by football great Joe Montana that professional football players be eligible for workers' compensation, which is financial support workers receive when injured on the job. (*San Francisco Chronicle*, 5/97)

   Joe Montana maintains that police officers and firefighters are aware of the risks inherent in their jobs and still receive workers' compensation. He asks for the same benefits for professional football players, who know the risks associated with the sport. Joe misses a critical point in making the comparison: police officers, firefighters, soldiers and the like are providing safety and security essential to every member of society, while professional athletes are basically offering a form of entertainment.—R.L.

8. Background: This letter is about the mind. It is critical of a hypothesis about how human consciousness works. (*New York Times*, 3/95)

   The hypothesis sounds reasonable but is not. There is a glaring flaw in its idea that proximity in time binds perceptions and events in the brain. To me, the time-binding theory is based on an analogy between brains and computers. Ordinary computers do indeed operate by way of "instruction" and "execution" cycles over time, and more advanced parallel computing systems can generate time-dependent carrier waves. However, a computer is not a brain; it is only, as it were, a brain-child. The human mind invented both computers and the concept of time. If these products of human thought also constitute thought's origin, then a vicious cycle of cause and effect results. There has to be a more reasonable way of linking the mind and brain.—D.M.

❖   9. Background: This letter is about the value of Microsoft. (*New York Times*, 7/99)

An article on Microsoft's $500 billion market value says that if Microsoft were a country, its gross national product would rank right behind Spain's, the ninth-largest economy in the world. This is misleading and only feeds the hype surrounding Microsoft and Internet stocks. Gross national product measures a country's annual output of goods and services, a number more akin to a company's revenue than to its market value. With Microsoft revenue at about $20 billion a year, a better comparison would be to the economies of Uruguay and the Slovak Republic, the 61st and 62nd largest economies in the world.—R.W.M.

10. Background: This letter is in response to a column arguing in favor of workfare, which seeks to get welfare recipients off welfare. The WPA was a Depression-era federal program to give the unemployed work. (*New York Times*, 5/98)

Your columnist's analogy between New York City's workfare and the Works Progress Administration is an ingenious maneuver, but it won't stand much scrutiny. The W.P.A. was premised on providing jobs and dignity. New York City insists that workfare recipients are not employees, lest they imagine they have any job-related rights. The W.P.A. grew out of a vision of social solidarity and compassion; workfare is motivated primarily by a desire to trim the welfare rolls. The W.P.A. assumed that people wanted to work, while workfare assumes that welfare recipients don't want to work.—P.L.

11. Background: This letter is about a legal case involving Autumn Jackson, who claimed to be the illegitimate daughter of the actor Bill Cosby and who tried to get money from Cosby by threatening to reveal his alleged paternity. (*New York Times*, 7/97)

Your columnist sees nothing wrong with Autumn Jackson's demanding money from Bill Cosby under threat of telling the tabloids he might be her father. He says that if she had hired a lawyer to ask for her, and the lawyer threatened to sue for child support while only hinting he might tell the tabloids, that would have been all right. Right analogy, wrong conclusion. A lawyer who helps a client commit a wrong is as much to blame as the client. The columnist is right that a clever lawyer will disguise the threat so that prosecution is impossible. But morally, blackmail is blackmail is blackmail, whether the threat is obvious or only implied.—R.W.G.

❖   12. Background: This letter is in response to the argument that, because the male-impotence drug Viagra is covered by health insurance, birth control pills should be as well. (*New York Times*, 8/98)

Impotence is defined in medical dictionaries as the inability of the male to achieve or maintain an erection. Usually, this is caused by a defect that can be remedied and thus should be considered a treatable condition. Pregnancy, on the other hand, is a normal outcome of sexual intercourse that is open to the possibility of new life. It is never an abnormality. Why should health insurance companies that cover Viagra, which can improve a treatable condition, be asked to cover contraceptives, which are man-made chemicals ingested by women who fear the possibility of a child? Equity is one thing, but this is ridiculous. Women who are not prepared to bear a child can practice abstinence, which costs nothing.—J.B.

13. Background: This letter is about sport utility vehicles. (*New York Times*, 11/97)

Your columnist seems to believe that the ballooning sales of sport utility vehicles are a throwback to the "fat and sassy 50's" when big cars were the norm. Our parents can be forgiven for their passion for big cars—smaller cars weren't then available, and people knew little about air pollution, crash tests and our dependence on foreign oil. People who purchase these vehicles now do it in the face of such consequences. This speaks of a selfish generation, not one tugged by longings for yesteryear.—M.E.T.

14. Background: This letter is about the policy of affirmative action. (*New York Times*, 11/97)

The letter writer asks, "How can we condemn the use of race, religion and gender criteria for denying students admission while at the same time using these criteria to artificially enhance diversity?" The answer is not far to seek. When people are excluded on the basis of race or ethnicity, it usually means that they are being treated as inherently unworthy or unqualified. We say the discrimination is invidious. Although some people are excluded who might have been admitted under a different policy, many laws affect people unequally and provide benefits only to some. Such "discrimination" may restrict opportunities, but we live with it if it is justified by legitimate public purpose and if it does not exclude us on grounds that are arbitrary and irrelevant. Affirmative action may be opposed as divisive or costly, but not because we cannot see the difference between benign and evil ways of taking race or ethnicity into account.—P.S.

❖   15. Background: This letter concerns Israeli policy in the Palestinian areas of East Jerusalem which, at the time, were controlled by Israel politically and militarily though the area was populated primarily by Palestinians. (*New York Times*, 10/97)

The writer, who justifies the purchase of property in Arab East Jerusalem to house Israeli Jews on the grounds that Arabs buy housing in West Jerusalem, makes an insufficient case. The major fault is that when an Arab owns a home in Israel, he is subject to Israeli law and lives in his home as a foreign guest, just the way Americans do who own vacation homes in Canada or France. But when an Israeli occupies a home in East Jerusalem, he is not acting like a foreigner subject to local law, because there is no Palestinian government; he is simply trying to enhance his own country's presence in an occupied country. As long as Palestinians are not allowed to form a nation with its own boundaries, laws and sovereignty, they have every right to complain about incursions by Israelis.—R.S.

SECTION B: Return to the problems in Section A and discuss in each case how the author being criticized might respond.

SECTION C: Structure and evaluate the following arguments from analogy. Include a list of the primary subject, the analogue, and the selected characteristic. Remember that you can criticize an argument even when you agree with its conclusion.

EXAMPLE
Background: This letter is about a schoolteacher who requested special precautions on the part of others in the school due to her high degree of chemical intolerance. (*Los Angeles Times*, 1/98)

It is not as though schools don't have enough to deal with, without the Culver City teacher with chemical intolerance. If you can't lift 20 pounds, you can't be a delivery person; if you can't be around people without breaking into flu-like symptoms, you can't be a teacher.—C.H.

ANSWER
Primary subject: a schoolteacher with chemical intolerance
Analogue: a delivery person who cannot lift 20 pounds
Selected characteristic: cannot perform the work

P1: A schoolteacher with a high degree of chemical intolerance is relevantly like a delivery person who cannot lift 20 pounds.
P2: A delivery person who cannot lift 20 pounds cannot perform the work.
C: Therefore, a schoolteacher with a high degree of chemical intolerance cannot perform the work.

I charge this argument with faulty analogy. The argument commits this fallacy because the primary subject and analogue are unlike in a way relevant to the selected characteristic. A delivery person who cannot lift 20 pounds lacks the skills necessary to perform the work of that job, but this is not the case with the teacher with chemical intolerance. Chemical intolerance is a condition unrelated to the skills of teaching. A person with chemical intolerance could still be a good teacher, but a person unable to lift 20 pounds could not be a good delivery person. The selected characteristic, not being able to perform the work, depends on whether a person has the skills necessary for the job.[18]

PROBLEMS
1. Background: This letter is about gun control. (*Miami Herald*, 6/97)

   When a group of people contract a contagious disease, we mobilize (sometimes slowly) people and resources to eliminate it. We don't just blame some of those infected. Gun ownership is a contagious disease.—M.M.

2. Background: This letter was written when the United States and its allies were fighting Yugoslavia over its conduct in Kosovo while at the same time sending a baseball team to Cuba, ruled by Fidel Castro. (*USA Today*, 5/99)

It is unbelievable that we are fighting one dictator in Kosovo while pampering another in Cuba. How would the world and the American people have reacted if in 1940 we would have taken a baseball team to Germany to play a game in front of Adolf Hitler?—C.F.

❖ 3. Background: This letter is about smokers filing lawsuits against tobacco companies for illnesses caused by smoking. (*Miami Herald*, 5/97)

I have recently read that people who look directly at the sun without wearing sunglasses tend to develop early cataracts. I presume that all cataract sufferers soon will file a class-action suit against the sun. Of course, no one forced them to look directly at the sun, any more than anyone forced people to smoke.—J.F.

4. Background: This is a portion of a letter criticizing the idea that the government should provide universal health insurance. (*USA Today*, 11/98)

Universal Health Care isn't civilized, because it takes away the rights and choices of both providers and patients. Imagine Universal Food Care, where diners can eat all they want after waiting a week for a table, but choose from only one menu, and the chefs are told by a bureaucrat what to serve. Oh, and by the way, cooking for yourself is illegal.—J.S.

5. Background: This letter is about whether protesters who burn the American flag should be protected under free-speech guarantees.[19] (*New York Times*, 7/98)

Physically desecrating the American flag is not speech but physical action, and should not be protected under the First Amendment. Burning the flag is no more speech than vandalizing our national monuments, which is punishable by law. Why is this action worse than desecrating our flag? Where is the logic in the Supreme Court's decision that protects flag desecration as freedom of speech? Our national symbol deserves better!—A.L.

❖ 6. Background: This is a portion of a letter about capital punishment. The letter's final conclusion is different from the one in this portion of the text. (*New York Times*, 6/98)

Society often permits action be taken that creates the statistical probability —even the statistical certainty—of death for what is perceived to be a greater good. We build bridges, knowing that fatal accidents are inevitable. We raise automobile speed limits, although we know that thousands more drivers and passengers will be killed as a result. And we send soldiers into combat with the awful knowledge that many of them will not survive. If all these are ethical decisions, then why is it not also ethical to execute convicted killers to deter other potential murderers from taking the lives of others? If the loss of human life can ever be justified by a greater good, then mob hit men and other violent criminals must surely be more suitable subjects of sacrifice than construction workers, automobile passengers and marines.—R.G.

7. Background: This letter is about zoning. (*Los Angeles Times*, 5/98)

If the government passed a law that said no person could change their profession, that whatever they are doing now is the use to which they must put the rest of their life, such a law would not be tolerated for long. However, with zoning the government tells us we cannot change the profession of our property, the use to which we put our land, and intolerance in this case is negligible. Why?—J.R.

8. Background: This is a letter about atheism. (no publication data)

In the age-old allegory about the emperor who had no clothes, it is necessary that the townsfolk wanted to be seen as virtuous and "saw" the emperor's invisible "new suit." This represents most people who want to prove how virtuous they are by acknowledging an invisible God. The tailors who conned the emperor into buying that invisible suit represent all the priests, ministers, rabbis and imams. The little boy, like all atheists, did not have to prove his virtue. The little boy, who perceived reality, said the emperor was naked. He represents the atheist, who by the same process of observing reality, can say there is no God.—N.J.

❖   9. Background: This letter is in response to a column suggesting that the person who turned in the ball hit by Mark McGwire to break Roger Maris's record for the most home runs in a year was foolish not to sell it instead. (*New York Times*, 9/98)

How sad that your columnist can only judge the value of an act by how much money it will bring on the open market rather than appreciate a simple, selfless gesture. Tim Forneris, the St. Louis Cardinals' groundskeeper who sent Mark McGwire's 62d home run ball to the Baseball Hall of Fame, recognizes values other than greed. This hardly makes him a "pigeon." Some people feel better knowing that they did what they believe to be right rather than what would make them wealthy. I wonder if the columnist would similarly disparage someone who returned a lost wallet without stealing the money inside.—L.K.

10. Background: This letter is an argument in favor of allowing euthanasia. (*Los Angeles Times*, 6/97)

Is there indeed a "duty to die"? We don't hesitate to enact laws that force our healthiest young men and women to sacrifice their lives "for the greater good." Our best and brightest young people are conscripted, often unwillingly, to fight our wars and die so that we may protect our way of life. Why can we not allow our older citizens to personally and voluntarily decide to ease their suffering and relieve their families of the financial and emotional burden of such suffering? Just as we recognize the sacrifice of our war heroes, we should also honor those who willingly and voluntarily make such a sacrifice for the benefit of their families.—A.W.S.

11. Background: This letter is in response to a column critical of the complexity of computer commands. (*New York Times*, 8/98)

If computer users have indeed been frustrated by symbols and commands like "COPY B: SUBDIR**C:JEEPERSIMLOST," how come millions of ordinary business people have been able to master this arcana? If your columnist wishes to decry something that's opaque, frustrating, and difficult to use, he might start with the English language. All those different parts and terms: verbs, cases, subjects, objects, clauses, prepositions, punctuation! And why have tens of thousands of words when a core of around 5,000 words meets the needs of most people? There are difficulties in mastering English, but the effort is regarded as one that's both necessary and rewarding; so it is with powerful computers.—H.A.K.

12. Background: This letter is about local taxation. (*Miami Herald*, 5/97)

Why does your paper consistently endorse higher taxes to solve municipal problems? If, years ago, the auto industry had not been forced to make more efficient engines, cars would now get seven miles to a gallon to handle the increase in electrical devices and greater horsepower. Instead, we have engines that do more, use less gas, and last longer. County government is an engine—a gas guzzler. Make it more efficient.—P.E.

13. Background: This letter discusses the way smokers are treated by others. (*Atlanta Constitution*, 3/97)

As I peruse the classified ads, searching for that "just right" job, I keep facing a new form of discrimination: numerous ads for jobs that are open only to nonsmokers. When did we stop accessing an individual on his or her skills and qualifications? What's next? Should we not hire a person because he chews his nails, coughs without covering his mouth or owns a white poodle? How can a company advertise as an "equal opportunity employer" and not give equal opportunity?—D.D.D.

14. Background: This letter is in response to an article reporting that a group of prominent African American scholars were supporting the idea of a lawsuit to seek reparations for injuries incurred during slavery. (*Boston Globe*, 3/00)

Have they thought through the mind-boggling implications of this proposed class-action lawsuit on behalf of the descendants of those injured by slavery? To test the legal and moral viability (as one of them puts it) of such a lawsuit, I invite these prominent black academics to consider another infamous historical wrong, albeit one on a much smaller scale. In 1692, 20 men and women of Salem were tried, convicted and executed—or judicially murdered, as some would say today—on charges of witchcraft. I am distantly related to two of these pitiable victims, Alice Parker and Mary Parker. So, who could sue whom for these cruel murders, on what grounds, and for what damages? If we Parkers won, how would we distribute any proceeds from this action? Who would decide who gets what? And so on, endlessly. It would be another lawyers' Klondike.—H.P.

❖   15. Background: This letter is in response to a discussion of the war against Yugoslavia, which was suppressing and engaging in ethnic cleansing against the ethnic Albanians in its own province of Kosovo. (*USA Today*, 3/99)

Your writer pointed out that the United States and NATO are setting a precedent by siding with the rebels who operate inside a sovereign nation. I wonder what our history would have been like if, during our Civil War, a group of nations decided to bomb the North unless it stopped its war against the South and accepted an autonomous Confederacy? Of course, the group of nations could have justified its actions with some high-flung "moral" phrase. Would the North have accepted the conditions? I think not. The USA has no business taking military action against a sovereign nation involved in a civil war. Such action has always been viewed as an act of war, and rightly so.—S.H.

Summary

Two kinds of nondeductive arguments are all-things-considered (ATC) arguments and arguments from analogy. ATC arguments consider all sides of an issue to address issues that have more than one side, or ATC issues. For ATC issues, different types of factors, and not simply factors of the same type, are relevant to the conclusion. ATC issues include matters of social, moral, and political controversy, such as euthanasia and human cloning, but not all ATC issues are value issues. ATC issues have different sides because the different types of factors relevant to the conclusion tend to support opposing conclusions.

Because the different types of factors in an ATC argument support conflicting conclusions, a particular conclusion has both considerations—factors that tend to support it—and counterconsiderations—factors that tend to oppose it. Arguing for a particular conclusion is often a matter of "balancing" the considerations and counterconsiderations. This balancing is represented in the structure of the argument by counterpremises. Each counterconsideration has associated with it a counterpremise, in which an arguer claims in one way or another that that counterconsideration does not show that the conclusion should be rejected. In the counterpremises, the arguer seek to "defuse" the counterconsiderations, to render them incapable of showing the conclusion to be false. Anytime an argumentative text mentions a counterconsideration, a counterpremise should be included in the structure.

There are four defusing strategies, or ways that counterpremises can be used to defuse counterconsiderations. An author can claim in a counterpremise that a counterconsideration is (1) false, (2) irrelevant to the conclusion, (3) positively relevant to the conclusion, or (4) insufficient to overcome the reasons in favor of the conclusion. The fourth, the insufficiency defusing strategy, is the most common. In addition to using counterpremises, an author will often qualify a conclusion in response to a counterconsideration.

An analogy is a comparison of two things, a claim that they are alike. An argument from analogy infers from an analogy and a claim that one of the things has a certain characteristic that the other has (or should have) that characteristic as well. One of the main venues for arguments from analogy is ethics and the law, where these arguments are involved in demands for consistency or fairness. The first premise of an argument from analogy states the analogy, which holds between what are called the primary subject and the analogue. The second premise is that the analogue has a certain characteristic, referred to as the selected characteristic. The conclusion is that the primary subject has that characteristic as well. Analogues can be real or hypothetical. Hypothetical analogues are fictional examples, sometimes bizarre, designed to be an analogue to the primary subject and to have characteristics showing that it would also have the selected characteristic. Arguments from analogy often include a subargument supporting the first premise; these are referred to as arguments to analogy.

But the first premise must state not simply that the primary subject and the analogue are alike in some respects but that they are alike in respects relevant to the conclusion of the argument. The two things must be *relevantly* alike, that is, alike in a way that supports the inference from the claim that the analogue has the selected characteristic to the conclusion that the primary subject has that characteristic. In evaluation, the main way to criticize an argument from analogy is to claim that the primary subject and analogue are not relevantly alike, in which case the argument may be charged with the fallacy of faulty analogy. The justification for this charge will usually point to ways in which the primary subject and the analogue are unalike. But not just any unlikenesses will do. The two must be unalike in ways relevant to the selected characteristic.

Key Terms

all-things-considered (ATC) argument

ATC issue

considerations

defusing strategy

counterpremise indicator

analogy

argument from analogy

design argument

consistency

primary subject

analogue

selected characteristic

real analogue

hypothetical analogue

thought experiment

argument to analogy

even-more-so argument

argument from counteranalogy

fallacy of faulty analogy

Notes

1. John Stuart Mill, *On Liberty* (New York: Norton, 1975), p. 36.

2. As discussed in Chapter 5, these two forms of qualification can be represented in strength space.

3. In both A and B, the arguments from analogy can be interpreted as subarguments. In A, the conclusion of the argument from analogy can be understood as a premise supporting the (implicit) main conclusion that we should withhold capital investment from China. In B, the conclusion of the argument from analogy can be understood as a premise supporting the (also implicit) main conclusion that we should doubt the educational value of the Internet.

4. The idea of fairness or treating like cases alike is especially important in American law, given the constitutional foundation of the principle of equality.

5. The 1919 Supreme Court case is *Schenck v. U.S.* (249 U.S. 47). The decision was written by Justice Oliver Wendell Holmes.

6. Such questions about how things should be labeled are closely connected with our discussion of conceptual issues in Chapter 9.

7. What I call real analogues are also referred to as inductive analogues, and what I call hypothetical analogues are also referred to as *a priori* analogues.

8. Another pair of examples like this can be found in Example 11.13, where A has a real analogue and B has a hypothetical analogue.

9. The whole argument from analogy is, then, a subargument of the main argument with this conclusion.

10. Judith Jarvis Thompson, "A Defense of Abortion," *Philosophy and Public Affairs* 1, 1 (1973): 48–49.

11. Albert Einstein, *Relativity: The Special and General Theories* (New York: Crown, 1961), pp. 66–67.

12. The way in which movies and comic books were meant to be analogues in this argument is reasonably clear, but we can only surmise how Socrates, the famous philosopher of ancient Athens, was meant to be one. Perhaps it was that Athenian society survived his constant public questioning of it, though it was fear of the effect of this questioning that led that society to try and execute him.

13. The author of this letter is Howard Tomb.

14. Charles Darwin, *On the Origin of Species* (Cambridge, MA: Harvard University Press, 1964), pp. 483–484.

15. This can serve as another illustration of the transformation of fallacy charges discussed in the previous chapter. Arguments from analogy may be structured without the term "relevantly" in P1. This would save P1 from a false premise or problematic premise charge, but at the cost of creating the possibility of a charge of irrelevant reason regarding P1. The same points used to support one charge would also support the other. An alternative structuring transforms the fallacy charge.

16. One reaction to this argument might be that the universe has a purpose because God has given it one. But to assume that the universe has a God-given purpose in arguing for God's existence is to commit the fallacy of begging the question.

17. Thomson, "A Defense of Abortion." In her fascinating article, Thomson considers as well further revisions in the hypothetical analogue to deal with other objections to her argument.

18. As is often the case, this discussion only initiates what could be a longer debate on this issue. How might the letter writer respond to this justification?

19. After completing your answer to this exercise, you might want to compare it with a response to this letter. The letter addresses the question A.L. asks: why vandalizing a national monument is worse than desecrating a flag. (*New York Times*, 7/98)

> The question deserves an answer, since it reflects a confusion that seems to be widespread. If I burn a flag flown at one of our national monuments, I have indeed committed an act of vandalism punishable by law. Others—taxpayers in this instance—paid for the flag and must pay again to replace it. If I buy a flag with my own money, the situation is entirely different. If I burn it, it is my own money I have squandered. Few object to burning an old and tattered flag in an act of reverence to save it from disposal in a landfill. Objections to burning the flag come from those who dislike the message of the flag burner. While freedom of speech does not include the freedom to destroy the property of others, it emphatically includes the freedom to deliver a hateful message in a hateful way.—D.S.D.

Argument Structuring:
Steps, Rules, and a Principle

Structuring Steps

An argument structure consists of a tree diagram and a PC structure. To structure an argument, do the following:

1. Number the sentences of the text.
2. Pick out the sentence that expresses the main conclusion, putting its number in a circle at the base of a tree diagram. The conclusion may be expressed in part of a sentence or in more than one sentence, and it may be implicit.
3. Pick out the sentences that express the main premises, putting their numbers in circles above that of the conclusion and drawing arrows from those circles to the conclusion circle. Connect the circles of convergent premises individually, and the circles of linked premises in bracketed groups, to the conclusion circle. If the argument is complex, continue the process by including in the tree diagram the subarguments supporting the premises. A premise may also be expressed in part of a sentence or in more than one sentence, and it may be implicit.
4. Create the PC structure by writing down sentences expressing the main premises above a sentence expressing the conclusion, labeling the premise sentences as P1, P2, and so forth, and the conclusion sentence as C. The sentences should be reformulated versions of the text sentences, when reformulation is necessary to express the statements clearly. Groups of linked premises should be bracketed. If the argument is complex, add the subarguments in the same way.

Special Rules for Structuring

Rule of Addition, Number 1

If an argumentative text contains no sentence expressing the point the author is making, the conclusion is implicit. You must then figure out the author's point and formulate it as a sentence in the PC structure. In the tree diagram, label the implicit conclusion as IC in the conclusion circle.

Rule of Omission

Often, there are sentences or parts of sentences in an argumentative text that do not express any part of the argument and are not included in the argument structure. When identifying premises, you should not assume that all of the text sentences other than the one expressing the conclusion express premises.

Rule of Fairness

In structuring an argument, you should give a fair interpretation of the argument. To achieve this, after structuring the argument, you should return to the text to compare it again with the tree diagram and the PC structure, including the reformulations you have given, to ensure that they are faithful to the argument the author intended.

Rule of Addition, Number 2

An intermediate implicit premise, which occurs in some complex arguments, is an implicit premise that is both supported by a subargument and linked with an explicit premise. When one or more premises (often themselves linked) support a statement that can be linked with an explicit premise, you should add that statement as an implicit premise, with the premises supporting it constituting a subargument.

Rule of Addition, Number 3

A second kind of implicit premise occurs when an argument contains a conditional statement or a universal statement as an explicit premise and an additional statement, not expressed in the text, could be linked with the explicit premise showing how it supports the conclusion and making the argument deductive. In that case, you may include the statement as an implicit premise.

Rule of Addition, Number 4

When an argument includes a vague term that needs to be clarified by a conceptual premise, but none is explicitly included, you can include the appropriate conceptual statement as an implicit premise. The content of the implicit premise is usually evident from the text's internal and external context.

Rule of Addition, Number 5

Sometimes, when an argumentative text contains no explicit conditional statement or universal statement, you can include such a statement as an implicit premise to make the argument deductive. This is the case when contextual clues indicate that the author intended the argument to be deductive. Two contextual clues are that there is only one explicit premise and that the conditional statement or universal statement that would make the argument deductive is an acceptable claim.

The Principle of Reasonable Alternative Interpretations

An argument often may be interpreted in different ways; it can be given alternative reasonable interpretations. This means that in many cases different interpretations or structurings of an argument may be reasonably viewed as correct. When you give an interpretation of an argument, you should be prepared to argue in favor of that interpretation. A reasonable interpretation is one that has a strong argument in its favor. The reasonable interpretation with the strongest argument in its favor is the best interpretation. An interpretation without a strong argument in its favor is an unreasonable, or incorrect, interpretation.

APPENDIX B

Fallacies

Four Basic Fallacies

Formal Fallacies (concerning the relationship between premises and conclusion)

1. Irrelevant reason: A premise by itself has no support relationship with the conclusion or it supports the claim that the conclusion is false. In other words, the premise is not relevant to the conclusion or is relevant to the claim that the conclusion is false.
2. Hasty conclusion: All of the premises taken together, assuming they are true, do not provide sufficient support for the conclusion. The premises do not show that the conclusion is true or likely true.

Content Fallacies (concerning the truth or falsity of premises by themselves)

1. False premise: A premise is false.
2. Problematic premise: A premise is not supported by a subargument, and there are doubts about the truth of that premise, either in the view of the audience or in its own terms.

Some Specific Fallacies

Versions of Hasty Conclusion

1. Fallacy of argument by anecdote: This fallacy is committed when the conclusion of an argument is a general statement and the only premise offered is an anecdote, that is, a report of one instance, or a very small number of instances, to which the generalization applies.
2. Fallacy of affirming the consequent: This is a formal fallacy, an invalid argument form in which one premise is a conditional statement, another premise is the consequent of that conditional, and the conclusion is the antecedent.

3. Fallacy of denying the antecedent: This is a formal fallacy, an invalid argument form in which one premise is a conditional statement, another premise asserts the falsity of the antecedent, and the conclusion asserts the falsity of the consequent.

4. Fallacy of *post hoc ergo propter hoc:* This fallacy occurs in a causal argument when the only support given for the conclusion that A causes B is that B follows A.

A Version of Irrelevant Reason

1. *Ad hominem* fallacy: This fallacy occurs when the support for a conclusion that some claim is false includes a premise that "attacks the person," that is, that makes claims of a negative kind about a person or group that believes or advocates that claim.

Versions of Problematic Premise and False Premise

1. Fallacy of faulty appeal to authority: This fallacy occurs when a claim is supported by an appeal to authority that fails to satisfy all of the conditions for an acceptable appeal to authority. These are, briefly, that the claim is from an area in which there are authorities and the person cited is such an authority, that there is not significant disagreement among the authorities about that claim, and that the authority does not have a substantial personal stake in getting others to believe the claim.

2. Fallacy of false dilemma: A dilemma is a statement of alternatives claimed to be exhaustive, and an argument by dilemma contains a dilemma as a premise. The fallacy of false dilemma occurs when a premise stating the dilemma can be shown to be either false or not acceptable.

3. Slippery slope fallacy: In a slippery slope argument, an author opposes an action by claiming in a premise that the action would either lead through a series of events to a bad outcome or serve as a precedent that could justify a series of bad actions. The fallacy occurs when that premise is unacceptable or false.

4. Fallacy of ambiguity: This fallacy occurs when a term or a sentence that expresses part of an argument in an argumentative text can have different meanings, and the context does not resolve the ambiguity.

5. Fallacy of equivocation: This fallacy occurs when an ambiguous term is used in two different ways (that is, according to two of its meanings) in the same argumentative text, and the force of the reasoning in the argument depends on the term's being understood in the two different ways.

6. Fallacy of tendentiousness: This fallacy occurs when the premises of an argument are tendentious, that is, expressed with language that has strong expressive meaning, and this meaning would lead the audience to accept the conclusion by appealing to their feelings or emotions. Such

use of tendentious language masks the fact that reasons need to be offered in support of the claim that is implied by the language.

7. Fallacy of faulty analogy: This fallacy occurs when an argument is based on an analogy in which the two things being compared are not relevantly alike, in relation to the conclusion of the argument.

Some Special Cases

1. Straw man fallacy: A straw man is a misinterpretation of an argument, a major misunderstanding of what the author intended an argument to be, and the straw man fallacy occurs when someone misinterprets an argument. The straw man fallacy is sometimes deliberate, as when an argument is misinterpreted on purpose to provide an easier critical target.

2. Fallacy of begging the question: This fallacy occurs when an author assumes, in an effort to argue for something, the truth of the conclusion. The fallacy is committed when an argument has a premise that either is identical with or assumes the truth of the conclusion.

3. Fallacy of appeal to force: This fallacy occurs when the premise of an argument is a threat made by the author against the audience.

Note: Every fallacy charge should be supported by an argument to justify the charge.

Answers to Selected Exercises

Note: In most cases, your answers will not be exactly like the ones given here. This does not necessarily mean that your answers are incorrect. Due to the nature of interpreting a text, different correct answers may be possible. This is the idea of alternative reasonable interpretations, discussed in Chapter 5. Most of the exercises in this book (with some exceptions, as in some of the formal exercises in Chapter 7) have alternative reasonable interpretations. When there are alternative reasonable interpretations, the purpose of doing an exercise is not to arrive at one single interpretation, but to develop skill in understanding and evaluating argumentative texts. To do this, you need to be able to argue that the interpretation you have given is correct. What is most important is the quality of that argument, not the specific answer. It would be of no use to you, for example, to get a correct answer by accident.

When you find, as you will, that your answers differ from the ones given here, first try to determine whether the difference is trivial (for example, an insignificant variation in the wording of the sentence expressing a statement) or important (for example, your giving as a premise what is presented as a conclusion). If the difference is trivial, it is probably of no matter. If the difference is important, seek to understand why I have interpreted the text as I have. If you have a stronger argument for your interpretation than I do for mine, yours is the better interpretation.

EXERCISE SET 1.1A

3. Expressive use. The sentence is used to express resignation in the face of the rain. (Although the sentence may seem directive, it is better to view it as expressive because there is no agent that the speaker is directing—the rain is not a being with the ability to understand direction.)

6. Descriptive use. The sentence describes a person as male, young, charming, and capable of being intimidating. (The sentence does not have an argumentative use because none of the different claims made about the person support any of the others.)

9. Descriptive use. The sentence describes the person being addressed as someone who is irritating to the speaker. (The sentence may also have an expressive use, expressing the speaker's irritation at the person addressed.)

12. Descriptive use or expressive use. In this sentence, the speaker describes the predicted future event of the deaths of a group of people and also expresses despair at his upcoming death.

15. Directive use. The sentence directs some people to think about a particular subject, namely, a psychological fact about barricades.

EXERCISE SET 2.1A

3. (1) A support relationship exists between a and b.
   (2) The relationship is negative, since, if a is true, then b must be false.

6. (1) A support relationship exists between a and b.
   (2) The relationship is positive.
   (3) The relationship is implication, since one cannot excel on a soccer team without knowing how to kick a ball.

9. (1) A support relationship exists between a and b.
   (2) The relationship is positive.
   (3) The relationship is weaker than implication, since a person does not have to be poor to dress in second-hand clothes.

12. (1) There is no support relationship between a and b, since the odds of heads or tails for any toss is independent of the results of other tosses. (The

belief that things are otherwise is known as the "gambler's fallacy.")

15. (1) A support relationship exists between a and b.
    (2) The relationship is positive.
    (3) The relationship is weaker than implication, since the killing of another human being is sometimes justified.

18. (1) A support relationship exists between a and b.
    (2) The relationship is positive.
    (3) The relationship is weaker than implication, since there may be other reasons sufficient to justify the patenting of genes.

EXERCISE SET 2.1B

3. (1) The premises are linked. Because muggles are nonwizards, each premise shows how the other supports the conclusion.

6. (1) The premises are linked, since the fact that Socrates is a man shows how the fact that all men are mortal applies to him.

EXERCISE SET 2.2A

3. (1) There is no greatness without the capacity to suffer. [*Therefore,*] an easy life breeds complacency.
    An easy life breeds complacency. [*Therefore,*] there is no greatness without the capacity to suffer.
    (2) The second revision makes sense, so the text is argumentative, with the first sentence expressing the conclusion. (Both revisions make some sense, but the second makes more sense than the first.)

6. (1) Some are morning people and some are night people. [*Therefore,*] morning people do their best work when the sun rises, just as the night people are finished theirs.
    Morning people do their best work when the sun rises, just as the night people are finished theirs. [*Therefore,*] some are morning people and some are night people.
    (2) Neither revision makes sense, so the text is not argumentative.

9. (1) TV today is filled with sex, violence, and trivial pandering. [*Therefore,*] it is a vast wasteland.
    TV today is a vast wasteland. [*Therefore,*] it is filled with sex, violence, and trivial pandering.
    (2) The first revision makes sense, so the text is argumentative, with the second sentence expressing the conclusion.

12. (1) Microsoft should be condemned for putting solitaire into Windows. [*Therefore,*] millions of hours have been wasted playing that stupid game.
    Millions of hours have been wasted playing that stupid solitaire game on Windows. [*Therefore,*] Microsoft should be condemned for putting it into Windows.
    (2) The second revision makes sense, so the text is argumentative, with the first sentence expressing the conclusion.

15. (1) Fairy tales always begin with the same phrase, "once upon a time." [*Therefore,*] children can always tell at the beginning that a story is a fairy tale.
    Children can always tell at the beginning that a story is a fairy tale. [*Therefore,*] fairy tales always begin with the same phrase, "once upon a time."
    (2) The first revision makes sense, so the text is argumentative, with the second sentence expressing the conclusion.

EXERCISE SET 2.2B

3. (1) The text has the reasoning indicator "thus" between the two parts of the sentence, indicating that the conclusion is expressed by sentence 1b and the premise by sentence 1a.
    (2) The conclusion is: The body part that is most constant is used to classify varieties of animals.

6. (1) The text seems to express an argument, but it has no reasoning indicators. Sentence 2 is a likely candidate for the conclusion, and sentence 3 a likely candidate for a premise. Applying the test: ③ TF ②. This makes sense, so the text is argumentative.
    (2) The conclusion is: Often, when parents forbid their children to watch action-adventure films, it only spurs kids to see them on the sly.

9. (1) The text seems to express an argument, but it has no reasoning indicators. Sentence 1 is a likely candidate for the conclusion, and sentence 2 is a likely candidate for a premise. Applying the test: ② TF ①. This makes sense, so the text is argumentative.
    (2) The conclusion is: The transfer of Hong Kong to Chinese rule, and with it, the effective end of the greatest empire in human history, leaves several ironies in its wake.

12. (1) This text is not an argument. None of the sentences has a support relationship with any of the others. Applying the reasoning indicator test does not yield a text that makes sense.

15. (1) The text has the reasoning indicator "because" between the two parts of sentence 3, indicating that the conclusion is expressed by sentence 3a and the premise by sentence 3b.
    (2) The conclusion is: The NEA should be abolished.

18. (1) The text has the reasoning indicator "since," indicating that what follows is a premise, but it is not a premise that directly supports the conclusion. Rather, the first part of sentence 2 supports the second part of the sentence, which is a premise supporting the conclusion, expressed in sentence 1. This is confirmed by applying the reasoning indicator test: ②b TF ①. This makes sense.
    (2) The conclusion is: Failure to reach 67 votes to convict President Clinton on the impeachment charge is not tantamount to acquittal.

21. (1) This text is not an argument. None of the sentences has a support relationship with any of the others. Applying the reasoning indicator test does not yield a text that makes sense.

24. (1) The text seems to express an argument, but it has no reasoning indicators. Sentence 1 is a likely candidate for the conclusion, and sentence 2 is a likely candidate for a premise. But before applying the reasoning indicator test, we need to reword sentence 2 to change it from the interrogative to the indicative ("An artist must show a particular expression in painting and sculpture so that it will be successfully understood by the viewer.") Applying the test, using the reworded sentence: ② TF ①. This makes sense, so the text is argumentative.
    (2) The conclusion is: The study of facial expressions is vital to the artist.

EXERCISE SET 3.1A

3. (1) The conclusion is expressed in second sentence, as indicated by the reasoning indicator. The text is argumentative, because many in the audience would probably not believe this.
   (2) P1: The legal costs of death penalty appeals are tremendous.
       C: Therefore, executing a person costs more than keeping him in jail for life.

6. (1) The conclusion is expressed in the first sentence, and the text is argumentative because most of the audience would not believe this.
   (2) P1: An ice pick can kill as many people as an atomic bomb, though it takes longer.
       C: Therefore, an atomic bomb is no more deadly than an ice pick.

9. (1) The explanandum is expressed in the first sentence, as suggested by the reasoning indicator at the start of the next sentence. The text is explanatory because the conclusion is something most of the audience would attest to. "It is no wonder that . . ." would make sense in front of the first sentence.
   (2) Explanans: When you are having a good time, you are less likely to think about what time it is.
       Explanandum: Time seems to go faster when you are having a good time.

EXERCISE SET 3.1B

3. (1) Explanans: Weather reporters have little sense of the needs of farmers for rain and snow.
       Partly explains.
       Explanandum: Television weather reporters describe cloudy days and precipitation in negative terms.
   (2) In addition to this explanation, there is an argument offered for the explanans. The claim that weather reporters have little sense of the needs of farmers for rain and snow is supported by the claim that they are usually young and city-bred.

6. Explanans:
   1. Countries with less income disparity have longer life expectancies and lower rates of mortality from specific diseases.
   2. The United States has greater income disparity.
   Partly explains.
   Explanandum: People in countries less well off than the United States are in better health and live longer.

9. Explanans: Plumage has evolved to aid sexual selection.
   Likely explains.
   Explanandum: The plumage of breeding-age birds differs from the plumage of young birds.

12. Explanans:
    1. Liberal ideology has guided our educational system, judicial system, and cultural compass for more than 30 years.
    2. This ideology has produced failing schools, a failing judicial system, and an unrelenting assault on our religious foundations and values.
    Explanandum: Our culture can produce young people capable of evil that we could previously only imagine.

15. Explanans:
    1. There is no substantive political debate.
    2. A more informed and engaged electorate would be more difficult to sway with negative campaigning.

Partly explains.
Explanandum: Negative campaigning is effective.

18. Explanans:
    1. Fourteen black students were admitted to the law school this year but subsequently declined.
    2. Now that the university has adopted race-neutral policies, well-qualified black law school applicants are at a premium and can command preferential treatment for scholarships and other benefits outside of California.
    Explanandum: The decline in black enrollments at the law school is not due to discrimination.

21. (1) Explanans:
    1. With the demise of the Soviet Union, Eurasia's natural resources are being rediscovered by the rest of the industrialized world.
    2. There is a need for monitoring, containing, and countering threats to foster businesses in these mineral-, oil-, and natural gas-rich regions.
    3. The United Nations is turning out to be unwieldy with its global scope and focus.
    4. A regional NATO is a viable substitute for the United Nations.
    Explanandum: NATO survives and expands.
    (2) In addition to the explanation, the second premise is supported by a subargument, the premises of which are that the Middle East is potentially uncertain and unstable in the years to come and that the fragmentation of Russia is probable.

24. (1) Explanans: There has been an increase in the availability of guns.
    Explanandum: There has been an increase in deadly school violence.
    (2) In addition to the explanation, there is an argument. The argument is that the explanation offered is better than an alternative explanation, namely, that the school violence is due to violent TV shows and the lack of police in schools. The premises are that angry people will always seek to harm others and that they will use a gun if one is available.

EXERCISE SET 3.2A

3. This is a factual statement because it describes Max's prices in comparison with other muffler shops.

6. This is a value statement because it is a comparative evaluation of two kinds of computer.

9. This is a factual statement because it describes what may happen to those who live fast.

12. This is a factual statement because it describes how the world is as a result of the advent of the Internet.

15. This is a value statement because it involves a comparative evaluation of Wright's buildings versus those of others.

18. This is a factual statement because it describes how the world is, namely, a place where daily exercise promotes health.

EXERCISE SET 3.2B

3. (1) The conclusion is expressed in sentences 4 and 5: If the adverse reactions from medical treatment bring children close to death or cause them to be severely diminished, parents should be respected in their decision to withhold treatment.
   (2) A value premise is expressed in sentence 6: Allowing terminally ill children to live full lives unencumbered by debilitating treatment may be the most humane thing we can do for them.
   (3) A value statement on the other side of the issue is that any treatment that might save a child's life should be required.

6. (1) The conclusion is expressed in the last part of sentence 3: President Clinton should strike an agreement with Russia to remove all nuclear weapons from high-alert status.
   (2) There is no explicit value premise. An implicit value premise is that we should do what we can to avoid an accidental nuclear attack.
   (3) A value statement on the other side is that we should not lessen the deterrent value of our nuclear weapons.

9. (1) The conclusion is expressed in sentence 4: We should reduce, not expand, the copyright period.
   (2) There is no explicit value premise. An implicit value premise, parallel to the statement in sentence 1, is that we should have copyrights only to the extent that they encourage invention and innovation.
   (3) A value statement on the other side is that a person should be allowed to profit from all the wealth created by her inventions whether or not this encourages more invention.

EXERCISE SET 4.1A

Note: Each of the sayings in this exercise could be expressed in different ways, so answers other than the ones given may be acceptable.

3. Those who are foolish engage in activities that those who are wise avoid.

6. A small mistake may cause the failure of a large project.

9. Those who are more powerful cause more damage when they fall from power.

12. Once something is broken, it may be impossible to make it whole again.

15. As time passes, the future is a constant source of new opportunity.

18. You should think in unconventional ways.

EXERCISE SET 4.2A

3. <u>Buying a baseball team is a good investment.</u> After all, baseball is America's national pastime.

6. <u>There is no joy in Mudville.</u> Mighty Casey has struck out.

9. <u>I had better take voice lessons.</u> I would like to teach the world to sing in perfect harmony.

12. Time seems to pass quickly when you're having fun. <u>If you want to feel like you're having a long life, don't have any fun.</u>

15. What doth it profit a man to win the world but lose his soul? <u>Everyone needs to attend to matters spiritual.</u>

EXERCISE SET 4.2B

3. George is a liar.

6. Good things may now happen.

9. The animal in my backyard is a possum.

12. There is no feasible solution to global warming.

15. Elizabeth is prejudiced against Mr. Darcy.

18. The first atomic bombs were 1000 times more powerful than the Blockbuster.

21. Jane is in Cuba.

EXERCISE SET 4.2C

3. (1) With an energy shortage in New York, <u>why is there no law prohibiting retail establishments from running air conditioners full blast, with their doors wide open?</u>
   (2) There should be a law prohibiting retail establishments in New York from running air conditioners full blast with their doors wide open.

6. (1) Implicit conclusion.
   (2) Gov. Ryan should not have imposed a moratorium on executions.

9. (1) The former director of central intelligence, John M. Deutch, is called "sloppy" by security officials and his security clearance is suspended. Wen Ho Lee, a Los Alamos weapons scientist, was indicted and is now held without bail. <u>Has</u>

<u>the concept of equal treatment before the law been discarded?</u>
   (2) The differences in treatment for John Deutch and Wen Ho Lee show a disregard for the concept of equal treatment before the law.

12. (1) <u>Your reference to "the Old Testament credo of an eye for an eye and a tooth for a tooth" is out of place.</u> The commandment originally was intended as a response to "might makes right," as expressed in Lamech's song of Genesis. Long before Jesus proposed nonretaliation, the Jewish people had substituted fines for such acts of retaliation.
   (2) Your suggestion that the Old Testament credo of an eye for an eye and a tooth for a tooth refers to retaliation is incorrect.

15. (1) <u>The letter regarding the "unfairness" in granting higher salaries to sanitation workers than to teachers exposed the "degree syndrome" all too prevalent today.</u> Participation in numerous pedagogical sessions does not entitle a person to a higher pay scale than others. Societal forces alone determine this.
   (2) Teachers should not get higher salaries than sanitation workers simply because teachers have more education.

18. (1) The octopus is a living, feeling animal of fairly advanced intelligence. Tossing dead octopuses on the ice demonstrates a fundamental disregard for the sanctity of life and teaches children that life, especially animal life, is a disposable commodity. Is this the lesson we want our children to take with them to school? Furthermore, whether one eats them or not, octopuses are a source of food. Hockey fans who toss them away like garbage would do well to remember that there are hungry and starving people in the world, including here in the United States, and that food should not be wasted in such a nonchalant manner. <u>This senseless, destructive ritual ought to end.</u>
   (2) The practice of throwing octopuses onto the ice at hockey games should end.

EXERCISE SET 4.3A

3.

6.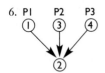

9.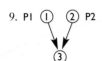

12.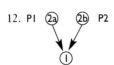

15.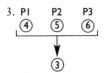

EXERCISE SET 4.3B

3.

6.

9.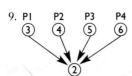

12.

EXERCISE SET 4.3C

3.

6.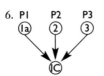

9.

12.

15.

18.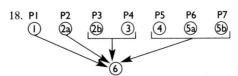

EXERCISE SET 4.3D

3.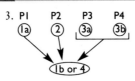

6.

9.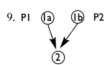

12.

15.
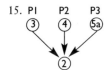

18.
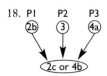

21.
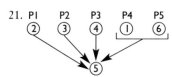

24.
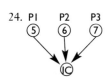

EXERCISE SET 5.1B

3. Many European colonial officials at the height of imperialism were cruel toward the native populations of their colonies. ("Many" because the policy of colonialism as a whole exploited and abused native populations.)

6. Many human actions are selfish. ("Many" because, while humans often act selfishly, they also often act directly out of concern for others; this is, however, a controversial issue.)

9. Some genetic engineering experiments are harmful. ("Some" because, of the experiments that have been done to date, most have not had any obvious harmful effects.)

12. All houses of brick are stronger than houses of straw. ("All" because of the nature of the two materials, brick and straw.)

EXERCISE SET 5.1C

3. Position H: *Likely, few* labor-saving devices have failed to save us time.

6. Position E: *Likely, many* places on Earth will be warmer 50 years from now.

9. Position D: *Possibly, many* of Mozart's early works were written with his sister.

12. Position I: *Certainly,* few presidential elections have been as close as the 2000 election.

EXERCISE SET 5.2A

3. Not a conditional.

6. If a dog is a pit bull, then it cannot be trusted around children.

9. Not a conditional.

EXERCISE SET 5.2B

3. Sentence 4: If we meant to do justice, then we should have forced Timothy McVeigh to live.

6. Sentence part 3b: If the baseball teams want to be more considerate of the fans, then they should speed up the game.

9. Sentence part 1c: If America is not connected at all, or is connected only by the feeble tie of a simple league offensive and defensive, then it would by the operation of such opposite and jarring alliances be gradually entangled in all the pernicious labyrinths of European politics and wars.

12. Sentence 1: If the expansion of NATO does not undermine the transformation of Europe, then the expansion will complicate that transformation.
    Sentence 2: If the expansion of NATO will undermine or complicate the transformation of Europe, then there would be significant opposition to the expansion from the European members of NATO.

15. Sentence 2: If the Park Service started charging foreigners a couple of dollars more than it charges American taxpayers, then it could easily solve a lot of its problems.
    Sentence 3: If the parks are really the property of the American people, then charging foreigners a couple of dollars more than American taxpayers is only fair.

EXERCISE SET 5.3A

3. P1: The first nation to do something that leads inexorably to war is to blame for the war.
   P2: Germany was the first nation to mobilize its forces.
   P3: The mobilization of forces leads inexorably to war.
   C: Therefore, Germany was to blame for World War I.

6. P1: Acrobats must work long, hard hours to develop the strength, stamina, and flexibility their work requires.
   P2: If a person must work long, hard hours to develop the physical skills needed for her or his vocation or avocation, then she or he is an athlete.
   C: Therefore, circus acrobats are athletes.

9. P1: Canada's cities are cleaner.
   P2: Canada has a lower crime rate than the United States.
   P3: It is more generous with its foreign aid.
   P4: It has a government-run universal health insurance system.
   C: Therefore, Canada is more civilized than the United States.

12. P1: Sun exposure can cause premature aging of the skin.
   P2: Severe sunburns can increase the risk of skin cancer.
   C: Therefore, sun exposure is not healthy.

≡ EXERCISE SET 5.3B

3. P1: There is an energy shortage in New York.
   C: Therefore, there should be a law prohibiting retail establishments in New York from running air conditioners full blast with their doors wide open.

6. P1: Governor Ryan's moratorium on executions thwarts the will of the people.
   P2: Since the beginning of the republic we have accepted the possibility that innocent people will be convicted of capital crimes and executed.
   P3: We also accept that parole and bail will result in additional crimes, even the murder of innocent people.
   C: Therefore, Governor Ryan should not have imposed a moratorium on executions.

9. P1: When the former director of central intelligence, John M. Deutch, abused classified data, he was called "sloppy" by security officials and his security clearance was suspended.
   P2: When Wen Ho Lee, a Los Alamos weapons scientist, abused classified data, he was indicted and held without bail.
   C: Therefore, the differences in treatment between John Deutch and Wen Ho Lee show a disregard for the concept of equal treatment before the law.

12. P1: The commandment "an eye for an eye and a tooth for a tooth" originally was intended as a response to "might makes right," as expressed in Lamech's song of Genesis.
   P2: Long before Jesus proposed nonretaliation, the Jewish people had substituted fines for such acts of retaliation.
   C: Therefore, your suggestion that the Old Testament credo of an eye for an eye and a tooth for a tooth refers to retaliation is incorrect.

15. P1: Participation in numerous pedagogical sessions does not entitle a person to a higher pay scale than others.
   P2: Societal forces alone determine this.
   C: Therefore, teachers should not get higher salaries than sanitation workers simply because teachers have more education.

18. P1: The octopus is a living, feeling animal of fairly advanced intelligence.
   P2: Tossing dead octopuses on the ice demonstrates a fundamental disregard for the sanctity of life.
   P3: It teaches children that life, especially animal life, is a disposable commodity.
   P4: This is not the lesson we want our children to take with them to school.
   P5: Octopuses are a source of food.
   P6: Hockey fans toss them away like garbage.
   P7: They should remember that there are hungry and starving people in the world, including here in the United States.
   C: Therefore, the practice of throwing octopuses onto the ice at hockey games should end.

≡ EXERCISE SET 5.3C

3. P1: The *Seinfeld* actors labored for years before hitting it big.
   P2: Their salaries are not at the expense of the poor.
   P3: *Seinfeld* generates tremendous wealth.
   P4: That wealth is in part based on the talents of these actors.
   C: Therefore, the actors should not voluntarily work for less than they can get in negotiations.

6. P1: History is not encouraging to those who would predict the future of innovation.
   P2: Future breakthroughs in information technology may well come from research in optics, polymer chemistry, or biology.
   C: Therefore, the best we can do is support the research and training of talented people in a wide range of fields, not just computers and telecommunications.

9. P1: The best colleges have always practiced social engineering in addition to considering merit in the admissions process.
   P2: Merit is a far from simple concept.
   C: Therefore, it is inconsistent of those now complaining about affirmative action not to have complained when the social engineering was done to further the advantages of the already privileged.

12. P1: The space that the *Tribune* has devoted to the death and funeral of Princess Diana seems to rival the space it devoted to the death and funeral of John F. Kennedy.

IC: Therefore, the *Tribune* has given too much attention to the death and funeral of Princess Diana.

15. P1: In its golden age (mid-1950s to mid-60s), at least, "Peanuts" was a brilliant, quasi-surrealistic explosion of language and imagination.

P2: Many of its situations bore no resemblance at all to our lives.

P3: The cartoonist, Charles Schulz, made ingenious use of sophisticated language.

C: Therefore, in its golden age, it is not true that "Peanuts" was a sweet, simple comic strip that reflected its readers' lives.

18. P1: Electrocution is a repulsive way of putting anyone to death.

P2 Lethal injection is procedurally not different from other injections.

P3: Lethal injection is a painless and nonrepulsive way of doing justice.

C: Therefore, executions should be carried out by injection rather than electrocution.

21. P1: Knowing the material, not speed-reading, should be what the grade is based on for the SAT, Graduate Record Exam, and the Medical College Admissions Test.

P2: Many students are simply slow readers, but are tops academically.

P3: Slow reading results not only from attention deficit disorders, dyslexia, etc. but also from English as a second language and simply from being a normal kid who is not a speed reader.

P4: These examinations discriminate against slower readers.

P5: Doubling the time for these exams would result in a fair evaluation of knowledge and ability, not one based on discriminatory speed-reading.

C: Therefore, all students should be given double time on all these exams.

24. P1: If women are not doing what is best for their family, they should change it.

P2: If women are doing what is best for their family, they should not complain about it.

P3: No self-respecting woman should care what some stranger thinks about the way she has chosen to care for her family.

IC: Therefore, women should focus on doing what is best for their families and not worry about what other people think.

EXERCISE SET 5.3D

3. P1: The recently published reports concerning the worst rioting in the history of England do not include mention of a single death.
   P2: England is gun-free.
   C: Therefore, reducing the availability of guns can reduce deaths.

6. P1: Women have far less upper-body strength than men.
   P2: Women are less inclined to engage in physically risky activities than men.
   P3: Assuming fair selection, a city with more female firefighters is no better than one with fewer.
   C: Therefore, the fire department should not seek to increase the number of women firefighters by providing physical training for female applicants to improve their test performance.

9. P1: Oxford Health Plan pays for six Viagra tablets a month for its patients.
   P2: The plan often refuses to cover oral contraceptives for female patients, even when prescribed for the treatment of other medical problems like premature menopause and polycystic ovary disease or as a prophylaxis for women with a family history of ovarian cancer.
   P3: While impotence is not a life-threatening condition, unwanted pregnancies, certain uterine cancers, and ovarian cancer certainly are.
   C: Therefore, this policy of Oxford Health Plan cannot be justified.

12. P1: Based on the headline that moderate drinking can lower the risk of heart disease, people are likely to infer that habitual drinking is not only benign but good for you.
    P2: If people took this inference, it would encourage incipient alcoholism.

P3: According to your article, virtually the only people who benefit from regular drinking are people at special risk of heart disease (like sedentary, stressed-out, obese smokers).

P4: There are infinitely healthier and even more pleasurable ways than drinking to relax and reduce every known risk factor for cardiovascular disease.

C: Therefore, the headline has horrible implications for public health.

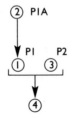

15. P1: If we tolerate the educational advantage of wealthy school districts, then this creates a mass of second-class citizens mired in poverty and despair.

P2: Americans believe in fair play and a level playing field.

P3: The belief that only the rich deserve to get richer is a violation of equal opportunity.

C: Therefore, we should not tolerate the educational advantage of wealthy school districts.

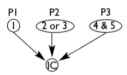

18. P1: Newspapers, magazines, and corrugated cardboard are recycled, but gray cardboard, brown paper bags, and general paper scrap are not.

P2: Plastics labeled 1 and 2 are recycled, but other plastics, including those clearly labeled with higher numbers, are not.

P3: Recycling cannot gain intelligent or enthusiastic support from the citizen who is required to recycle certain materials and yet forbidden to recycle others of a seemingly identical nature.

C: Therefore, we need an explanation for the apparent inconsistency in what New York City allows to be recycled.

21. P1: The World Trade Organization seeks to increase protection for intellectual property claims like copyrights and patents, helping big corporations like Microsoft.

P2: These forms of protectionism are enormously costly to developing nations.

P3: When patent protection involves vital drugs, it could cost lives.

P4: The WTO also seeks to make Internet commerce tax-free.

P5: This idea has no economic or ethical justification.

C: Therefore, the WTO agenda is clearly designed to help big corporations like Microsoft, to the detriment of much of the world's population.

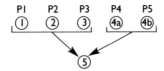

EXERCISE SET 5.4A

3. Sentence 3 expresses the conclusion.

A. ① TF ② TF ③

B. ② TF ① TF ③

Neither makes sense, so the argument is simple.

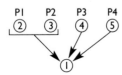

6. Sentence 4 expresses the conclusion.

A. ② TF ③ TF ④

B. ③ TF ② TF ④

C. ② TF ① TF ④

D. ① TF ② TF ④

E. ③ TF ① TF ④

F. ① TF ③ TF ④

Application C makes sense, so the argument is complex.

9. Sentence 1 expresses the conclusion, and sentence 2 expresses two premises.

    A. ② TF ② TF ①

    B. ② TF ② TF ①

Neither makes sense, so the argument is simple.

12. The implicit conclusion is that you are a fool.

    A. ② TF ③ TF ©

    B. ③ TF ② TF ©

    C. ① TF ② TF ©

    D. ② TF ① TF ©

    E. ③ TF ① TF ©

    F. ① TF ③ TF ©

Application D makes sense, so the argument is complex.

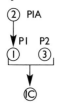

EXERCISE SET 5.4C

3. IIP: Any problem created by humans is not something to worry too much about.

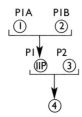

EXERCISE SET 5.4D

3.   P1A: If cigarette taxes were imposed at the time of manufacture and before shipment to distributors, then the distribution system would pass the tax on through the retailing network.

P1: If the distribution system passes the tax on through the retailing network, then smugglers would be forced to pay the tax.

C: Therefore, if cigarette taxes were imposed at the time of manufacture and before shipment to distributors, then concerns about contraband cigarettes and smuggling cigarettes as a result of proposed tax increases to help discourage teenage smoking could be alleviated.

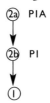

6.   P1A: A stamp that was 3 cents in 1945 is now 32 cents.

    P1B: Milk that was 16 cents is now $1.20.

    P1C: Bread that was 9 cents is now $1.

    P1D: The minimum wage that was 40 cents is now $5.15.

    P1E: A house that was $10,131 is now $180,000.

IIP1: Since 1945, common consumer items have risen in price from 7 to 17 times.

P2: Gasoline has risen in price since 1945 less than 7 times.

C: Therefore, gasoline is a bargain today compared with other items.

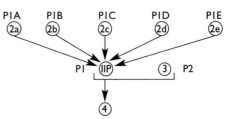

9.   P1A: The Confederate flag was placed atop the South Carolina statehouse only in 1962, as a rebuke to the civil rights movement.

P1: The flag's flying in that location is not a holdover from the Civil War.

C: Therefore, there is hardly an argument for preserving "heritage" in continuing to fly the flag there.

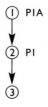

12. P1A: His efforts led eventually to a Nuclear Test Ban Treaty between Russia and the United States.
P1: Due to his efforts, the air that we breathe today is less contaminated.
P2: By lending his presence to peace demonstrations, he made protests respectable and civil disobedience acceptable.
P3: He had a gifted mind and an intrepid heart.
C: Therefore, Dr. Benjamin Spock should be awarded a posthumous Nobel Peace Prize.

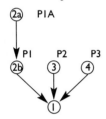

15. P1A: For the foreseeable future, the threats to European stability from ethnic discord and Islamic fundamentalism exceed any risk of Russian expansionism.
P1Bi: The Holy Roman Empire was a multinational entity that combated Muslim autocracies.
P1B: The Holy Roman Empire would be better suited to manage these threats than an alliance whose purpose is to contain Russia.
P1: The Holy Roman Empire is more relevant to current European security problems than is NATO.
C: Therefore, rather than entering NATO, Poland and Hungary should be admitted to the Holy Roman Empire.

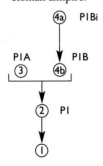

18. P1A: The Vatican suppresses opinions that contradict its doctrine on subjects like birth control and gay rights.
P1: The Vatican displays authoritarian tendencies.
P2Ai: The Pope has had his views on the ordination of women declared infallible.

P2A: The Pope has ruled out discussion of the ordination of women.
P2: The Pope has been an enthusiastic censor.
P3A: Honest and unfettered intellectual activity cannot be bound by doctrinal barriers, even when its results cause discomfort.
P3: The key ingredient in rational inquiry is skepticism, not faith.
C: Therefore, the Vatican is a source whose credentials on the subject of free inquiry are certainly suspect.

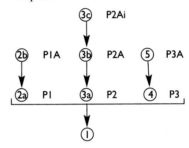

21. P1A: In the 1960s the birth control pill caused an increase in sexual activity despite its role in decreasing female fertility.
P1: It is not the biological feature of fertility that makes women sexually attractive.
P2A: The popularity of the impotence drug Viagra casts doubt not only on the fertility of older men but also on their ability to perform sexually.
P2: Likely, biology is not the basis for older men seeming more sexually attractive than older women.
C: Therefore, the film roles coupling older men with younger women are a reflection of stereotypes, not biology.

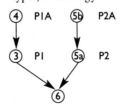

24. P1A: Historically, legislation regarding health insurance intends to cover more people.
P1B: Under the federal bipartisan commission's proposal to delay Americans receiving Medicare to age 67, fewer people would be covered.
P1C: Under the proposal, the number of uninsured (already more than 40 million) would go up.
P1: The federal bipartisan commission's proposal is a regressive idea.

P2: Social legislation should help more, not fewer, people.
IC: Therefore, the commission's proposal should be rejected.

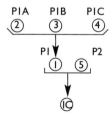

EXERCISE SET 6.1

3. Both a formal and a content criticism can be made of this argument. The content criticism is that the premise is false. Jimmy Carter, a Democrat, won in 1976. The formal criticism is that, even if it were true that the Republicans had won six presidential elections in a row, this is not sufficient evidence to predict that they will win the next election. In U.S. history, the party controlling the presidency has changed many times, even when one party has controlled it for a number of elections.

6. A content criticism cannot be made of this argument, since the two premises are clearly true, but a formal criticism can. While the conclusion is in fact true, the truth of these premises does not guarantee it. What if the first premise were "all Parisians are Europeans"? In that case, the argument would have the same form and both premises would still be true, but the conclusion, that all Parisians are Germans, would be false.

EXERCISE SET 6.2A

3. Valid; pattern 5.
 P1: All those who participate in class discussion get good grades.
 P2: Cain participates in class discussion.
 C: Therefore, Cain gets good grades.

6. Valid; pattern 6.
 P1: All who surf the Internet are socially isolated.
 P2: Diane is not socially isolated.
 C: Therefore, Diane does not surf the Internet.

9. Valid; pattern 3.
 P1: Either those who are now young will be denied Social Security when they retire or the government will go bankrupt.
 P2: The government cannot go bankrupt.
 IC: Therefore, those who are now young will be denied Social Security when they retire.

12. Valid; pattern 5.
 P1: All those who put others' lives in danger should be sent to prison.
 P2: Drunk drivers put others' lives in danger.
 C: Therefore, drunk drivers should be sent to prison.

15. Valid; pattern 4.
 P1: If a person is dead, then that person has no experience.
 P2: If a person has no experience, then that person cannot be harmed.
 C: Therefore, if a person is dead, then that person cannot be harmed.

EXERCISE SET 6.2B

3. P1: If x, then y.
 P2: If y, then z.
 P3: z.
 C: Therefore, x.
This argument is invalid, as this counterexample shows.
 P1: If a city has the world's tallest building, then it gets much publicity.
 P2: If a city gets much publicity, then it attracts many tourists.
 P3: Philadelphia attracts many tourists.
 C: Therefore, Philadelphia has the world's tallest building.
The premises of this argument are true, but the conclusion is false. Philadelphia attracts many tourists for other reasons, for example, the presence of Independence Hall.

EXERCISE SET 6.2C

3. This has the form of the double conditional argument. It is valid.
 P1: If our municipal government made a real commitment to reducing the amount of garbage we create, then New York City's plan to dump its garbage in other states' landfills would engender less ill will.
 P2: If the legislation pending in the City Council is passed, then our municipal government would make a real commitment to reducing the amount of garbage we create.
 C: Therefore, if the legislation is passed, then New York City's plan to dump its garbage in other states' landfills would engender less ill will.

6. This has the form of the double conditional argument. It is valid.
 P1: If soft money restrictions were applicable only to political parties, then wealthy individuals and organizations would merely channel their donations to private groups.

P2: If wealthy individuals and organizations chan-
neled their donations to private groups, then
the already weakened political parties would
grow weaker while shadowy issue groups and
their financial supporters would increase their
political influence over candidates.

IC: Therefore, if soft money restrictions were
applicable only to political parties, then the
already weakened political parties would grow
weaker while shadowy issue groups and their
financial supporters would increase their political influence over candidates.

9. This has the form of the double conditional argument. It is valid.

P1: If young people feel worthless, then everything
around them seems worthless.

P2: If everything around young people seems
worthless, then the consequences will often be
disastrous.

C: Therefore, if young adults are victimized, marginalized, and made to feel worthless by their
peers, then the rage that we have seen will continue.

EXERCISE SET 6.3A

3. P1: If an animal is the king of the jungle, then it is
the largest animal.
IP2: The lion is not the largest animal.
C: Therefore, the lion is not the king of the jungle.
Valid; *modus tollens.*

6. P1: All intellectuals are absent-minded.
IP2: Henry is absent-minded.
C: Therefore, Henry is an intellectual.
Invalid; pattern 3.

9. P1: If an actor comes from Indiana University, then
he is a great actor.
IP2: Kevin comes from Indiana University.
C: Therefore, Kevin is a great actor.
Valid; *modus ponens.*

12. P1: The only way to get someone to do something
he initially does not want to do is to persuade
him or coerce him.
P2: Ed did something he initially did not want to
do, and he was not coerced into it.
C: Therefore, Ed was persuaded into doing what he
initially did not want to do.
Valid; disjunctive argument.

EXERCISE SET 6.3B

3. The pattern is *modus tollens.*

P1: If we the people accept the settlement with the
tobacco companies, then future elected officials
will not be so willing to control the marketing
of this murderous drug.

IP2: Future officials should control the marketing
of this drug.

IC: We should not accept the settlement with the
tobacco companies.

6. The pattern is *modus tollens.*

P1: If the United States keeps on using intemperate
language in dealing with countries, then it will
find itself, sooner or later, the victim of a self-
inflicted credibility loss when the bluff is called.

IP2: The United States should not suffer credibility
loss.

C: Therefore, the United States should not conduct
policy by the use of threats.

9. The pattern is *modus ponens.*

P1: If joblessness is necessary for maintaining economic stability, then the unemployed should be
suitably rewarded for doing the job that is
assigned them.

P2: Joblessness is necessary for maintaining economic stability.

IC: Therefore, the unemployed should be suitably
rewarded for doing the job that is assigned
them.

EXERCISE SET 6.4A

3. P1: Lincoln's speech-making abilities were
unparalleled.
C: Therefore, Abraham Lincoln is the greatest
president.
Premises to add to strengthen the argument:
P2: Lincoln issued the Emancipation Proclamation.
P3: Lincoln preserved the Union by winning the
Civil War.

6. P1: When ships sailing away reach the horizon,
their masts are the last part to disappear.
C: Therefore, certainly, the world is round.
Premises to add to strengthen the argument:
P2: From outer space, the world appears round.
P3: If a person travels straight in any direction, he
will eventually return to the point from which
he started.

9. P1: Driving drunk can lead to expensive body work
on your automobile.
C: Therefore, you should not drive drunk.
Premises to add to strengthen the argument:
P2: Driving drunk greatly increases the likelihood
of fatal accidents.

≡ EXERCISE SET 6.6A

3. P1: If the Earth warmed up, growing seasons would be longer.
   C: Therefore, we should encourage global warming.

I charge this argument with hasty conclusion. The premise provides some support for the conclusion, but not enough. Much more needs to be said about this important topic. Other factors need to be considered. Some are factors of the same kind. Would global warming damage agriculture in some areas by making them too hot for the crops currently grown there, or damage agriculture generally by leading to more violent weather? Some are factors of a different kind. Would global warming lead to the extinction of many species? Would it inundate low-lying cities by causing the melting of the polar ice? Would it lead to massive famines?

6. P1: Insects are a nuisance.
   P2: Insects spread disease.
   P3: Insects damage crops.
   C: Therefore, we should try to destroy all insects.

I charge this argument with hasty conclusion. Even assuming that all of the premises are true, many other factors must be considered before such a conclusion can be drawn. For example, while some insects damage crops, other insects, such as bees, are necessary for the success of many crops. In addition, some insects play a crucial role in keeping the populations of harmful insects in check. More generally, insects may be vital for many of the services provided by the environment that are important for human well-being.

9. P1: Everybody deserves a day of rest.
   C: Therefore, all businesses should by law be closed on Sundays.

I charge this argument with irrelevant reason. The premise does not support the conclusion. The need to give everyone a day of rest can be satisfied without closing businesses on Sundays, or on any other particular day. Businesses can, and do, stay open every day by rotating their employees in such a way that their days off are not on the same day.

≡ EXERCISE SET 6.6B

3. P1: According to Blaise Pascal, the inability of people to sit still in a room is the source of all human evil.
   C: Therefore, one should not object to a culture in which people sit alone at home using a computer to conduct their banking transactions rather than wait in line to complete a transaction with a real person.

I charge this argument with irrelevant reason. Pascal was not speaking about any activity done alone. Rather, he was likely speaking about the value of people being able to appreciate solitude and engage in private meditation. So, his comments have no bearing on whether it is valuable for a person to use a computer while alone. In fact, he probably would have thought that the use of a computer interferes with the kind of solitude he thought valuable. Thus, his thoughts are irrelevant to the conclusion of this argument.

6. P1: If we avoided everything that interrupts a natural process, then we would abandon our efforts to combat disease with medicine.
   C: Therefore, the claim that abortion is wrong because it interrupts a natural process is false.

I charge this argument with hasty conclusion. The premise does not offer sufficient support for the conclusion because there is an aspect of the "natural process" referred to in the conclusion that is not considered in the premise. Pregnancy, like disease, is a part of nature, but pregnancy is also natural in the sense that it is part of the normal functioning of the human species and necessary for its survival, which is not the case with illness. Without addressing this aspect of natural process, the premises do not sufficiently support the conclusion.

   (As we discuss in Chapter 9, this argument could instead be charged with the fallacy of equivocation, which is a specific version of the content fallacy of false premise, because the argument equivocates on the term "natural process," that is, uses it in two different ways in the argument.)

9. P1: That Bill Clinton became governor of Arkansas and president of the United States shows that he is not an idiot.
   P2A: He has a reputation as a womanizer.
   P2B: He is being sued for sexual harassment.
   P2: If the allegations that Clinton had an affair with a 21-year-old intern at the White House are true, he would have to be the dumbest man the world has ever seen.
   C: Therefore, the allegations must be false.

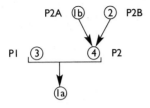

I charge this argument with hasty conclusion against the subargument at P2. These claims alone (P2A and P2B) are not sufficient to show that Clinton would have to be lacking in political intelligence to carry on the alleged relationship with the intern. The fact that many very successful politicians have had private lives that are scandalous and would be highly damaging to them if revealed to the public shows that political intelligence is not incompatible with such activities. This is a consideration that the author would need to address to sufficiently support P2.

(An interesting feature of this argument is that it was written before it became public knowledge that the allegations about Clinton's relationship with the intern were true. But the fact that the conclusion is now known to be false is not in itself, in the case of a nondeductive argument at least, a criticism of the argument. We still need to look to see where the fallacies lie.)

12. P1: A high school sophomore chooses to sit out reciting the pledge because she "thinks the U.S. government is corrupt and that American society is too violent, so she shouldn't have to show respect for a country that has so many problems."

P2: In doing so, she is invoking her First Amendment free speech rights guaranteed her by the government and society she believes to be violent and corrupt.

C: Therefore, this student is inconsistent in refusing to recite the pledge.

I charge this argument with hasty conclusion. The premises are not sufficient to support the conclusion that her actions are inconsistent. Most people approve of some things about their government and society and disapprove of others. It is not inconsistent to approve of some things and disapprove of others. If this student were refusing to pledge allegiance to protest those things about her government and society of which she strongly disapproved, she could do this consistent with her approving the free speech guarantees of the government. In fact, the free speech guarantees are endorsed when they are exercised in protest of what we disagree with, as in the actions of this student. To avoid a hasty conclusion charge, the author would need to take account of such considerations.

15. P1: Polls show that most U.S. adults would prefer to leave the smoking/nonsmoking issue to the marketplace rather than government regulation.

P2: The air quality problem in this country lies in its addiction to fossil fuels.

P3: The health problem in this country lies in the way we eat and exercise (or, rather, don't exercise).

IC: The government should not regulate smoking in restaurants.

I charge this argument with hasty conclusion. The premises are not sufficient to support the conclusion because there is an important factor that the author does not address, namely, the harmful effects of secondhand smoke in restaurants. This issue must be considered in judging whether government regulation should be avoided. In addition, while it may be true, as P2 and P3 suggest, that fossil fuel pollution and our poor eating and exercise habits are the major factors affecting our health, this does not imply that second-hand smoke is not an important health consideration as well.

18. P1: Eliminating concerns about race would be more enlightened.

P2: Nearly all of us have mixed ancestry.

P3: Existing laws—and new ones—could protect us against crimes committed because of prejudice based on skin color, ethnicity, sex, or sexual preference, without relying on "race" as a basis for anything.

C: Therefore, the Census Bureau should eliminate the question about race.

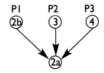

I charge this argument with hasty conclusion. Even if all of the premises are true, they do not provide sufficient support for the conclusion. An important factor that the author does not consider is the value of our having information about the racial composition of society in order to help to ensure that the forms of racial discrimination of our past are being successfully overcome. In our past, such discrimination has been so pervasive and subtle that simply having laws to deal with the individual identifiable cases of discrimination that P3 mentions may not be enough to fight the vestiges of that past. This is a factor that should have been addressed before this conclusion was drawn.

21. P1: If the government were smaller, then there would be less money and power in the public domain
P2: If there were less money and power in the public domain, then there would be less influence money trying to control that power.
C: Therefore, a better way to fix the corrupt campaign finance system is to create smaller government.

I charge this argument with hasty conclusion. The premises are not sufficient to support the conclusion because an important consequence of smaller government is not addressed. Small government means more decentralized government. But corruption can happen at the local level as well as at the national level, and one of the roles of a national government is to fight abuses of power at the local level. This suggests that it is not automatic that smaller government leads to less governmental corruption. This issue needs to be considered before this conclusion can be drawn.

≡ EXERCISE SET 6.7

3. P1: The opposition of the fundamentalists to the movie *The Last Temptation of Christ*, given their claim to an unshakable, rocklike faith, seems to be psychological abnormal behavior.
C: Therefore, the fundamentalists' opposition to the film and their demand that it should be censored should be rejected.

I charge this argument with the fallacy of argument *ad hominem*. The conclusion of the argument is that

the view of a group of people (that a movie should be censored) should be rejected, and the support for this is an attack on that group, a claim that the basis of the group's view is a psychological abnormality. But, even if true, that claim is irrelevant to the conclusion.

6. P1: In America, road rage is part of a larger phenomenon, winning at all costs.
   P2A: The centrality of winning is seen on the football field, on the basketball court, in politics, and in business.
P2: Winning at all costs is becoming the highest value in our society.
P3: This value is to the detriment of a sense of justice, decency, and what some call "family values."
P4: As Paul Joseph Goebbels proclaimed, "Important is not what is right but what wins."
IC: We should seek to deemphasize the value of winning at all costs.

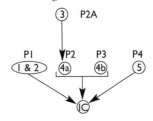

I charge this argument with the fallacy of argument *ad hominem* regarding P4. Goebbels was the propaganda minister of the Nazi regime in Germany. As such, he is an appropriate symbol of evil. The author seeks to get the audience to reject the idea of winning at all costs by associating it with this evil person. But P4 is irrelevant. The evilness of a person does not support the claim that what he believes is false.

9. P1: The Court might try to arraign Yasir Arafat, the Palestinian leader, for complicity in undoubted Palestinian atrocities or Ariel Sharon, the Israeli cabinet minister, for complicity in what many believe to be atrocities against the Palestinian people.
P2: If the Court did this, then it would not help the search for peace on terms acceptable to the constituents of both.
C: Therefore, if the world community takes responsibility for dealing with atrocities through the International Criminal Court, then the peace process will suffer.

This argument cites two anecdotes—specifically, the possibility that Arafat or Sharon might be indicted by the International Criminal Court—and uses these to support the conclusion that the Court would hinder the search for peace. But it is not appropriate to charge this argument with the fallacy of argument by anecdote because it is plausible to understand the author as using the anecdotes as a stand-in for a general claim, namely, that the indictment of leaders by the Court would often interfere with achieving peace by interfering with achieving the compromises necessary for peace.

12. P1: Both of my children, one with Down's syndrome, bring our family equal happiness.
   P2: Our disabled child has challenged us to think about what it means to be human, regardless of achievement.
   C: Therefore, Singer's claim is wrong that a disabled infant has lesser prospects for a happy life.

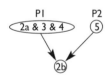

I charge this argument with the fallacy of argument by anecdote. In the author's criticism of Singer's views, she cites her own experience with a disabled child, but the conclusion is that her experience is generally the case, and we cannot infer this from the one instance alone.

(In addition, the argument could be charged with irrelevant reason, on the grounds that Singer, as the quotation makes clear, is speaking about the prospects of happiness for the child. But the author counters this by speaking about the prospects for happiness of the child's family.)

15. P1: In the emergency room where I work, they recently brought in a man who had been beaten silly by his wife while he was sleeping.
   P2: They also brought in a man with a bullet lodged in his head from being shot by his wife while he was asleep.
   P3: They also brought in a young baby boy with bruises all over his body from a beating by his mother.

C: Therefore, likely, women are at least as brutal and aggressive as men are.

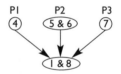

I charge this argument with the fallacy of argument by anecdote. The author cites three anecdotes of brutality by women and concludes that women are likely at least as brutal and aggressive as men are. But these three instances do not establish the generalization of the conclusion. A much more careful survey of violence by both sexes would need to be done to draw this conclusion. There is a related weakness in the argument. The author does not consider the possibility that the women in the first two anecdotes did not initiate the violence they perpetrated, but were retaliating for violence earlier perpetrated on them by the men. The fact the violence was done while the men were asleep supports the plausibility of this possibility.

EXERCISE SET 7.2A

3. Some family gatherings are activities that tend to go on and on.
   Type I: Some S are P.

6. All generalizations are claims that are false.
   Type A: All S are P.

9. All categorical statements are statements that have one of four forms.
   Type A: All S are P.

12. All critical thinking textbooks are textbooks that have exercise sets.
    Type A: All S are P.

15. No playwrights are writers who can surpass Shakespeare.
    Type E: No S are P.

18. Some dogs are not pets who obey their masters.
    Type O: Some S are not P.

EXERCISE SET 7.2B

3. Some family gatherings are activities that tend to go on and on.
   S = family gatherings; P = activities that tend to go on and on.

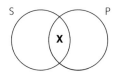

6. All generalizations are claims that are false.
   S = generalizations; P = claims that are false.

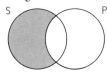

9. All categorical statements are statements that have one of four forms.
   S = categorical statements; P = statements that have one of four forms.

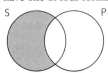

12. All critical thinking textbooks are textbooks that have exercise sets.
   S = critical thinking textbooks; P = textbooks that have exercise sets.

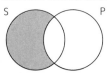

15. No playwrights are writers who can surpass Shakespeare.
   S = playwrights; P = writers who can surpass Shakespeare.

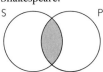

18. Some dogs are not pets who obey their masters.
   S = dogs; P = pets who obey their masters.

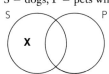

EXERCISE SET 7.2C

3. Some stories are things that are boring.
   Some stories are boring.
6. All buses are vehicles with more than one wheel.
   All buses have more than one wheel.

EXERCISE SET 7.2D

3. All parents are people older than their children.
6. Some fathers are people who know best.
9. All jobs are tasks worth doing well.
12. All chains are objects only as strong as their weakest link.
15. All homes are places where the heart is.
18. All military drafts are institutions preferable to an all-volunteer fighting force.
21. Some prizes are not benefits worth having.
24. All sewage is a substance to be avoided.
27. All years are times when prices go up.

EXERCISE SET 7.2E

3. No society that began its history by defining a black person as less than a full person is a society that can expect the damage from this to be eliminated in one generation.
6. Some of our military heroes are people who were involved in long-term amorous relationships while in combat.
9. Some people on the jury were people who knew firsthand the fears of Mr. Goetz.
12. Some bureaucrats are people who think that any writing style other than one that's turgid, impersonal, and convoluted will undermine their authority.
15. Some religions are organizations that do a great service to women by encouraging men to behave.
18. All fractions on our rulers and ounces and pounds on our scales are measurement units that are silly, unwieldy, and should be gotten rid of.
21. All events in life are compromises.
24. Some religions are organizations that do not concern themselves with the worship of God.

EXERCISE SET 7.3A

3. O: Some intelligent actions are not things a computer can do better. True (as stipulated)

A: All intelligent actions are things a computer can do better. False

E: No intelligent actions are things that a computer can do better. Undetermined

I: Some intelligent actions are things a computer can do better. Undetermined

6. E: No octogenarians are mountain climbers. True (as stipulated)

A: All octogenarians are mountain climbers. False

I: Some octogenarians are mountain climbers. False

O: Some octogenarians are not mountain climbers. True

9. E: No breakfast foods are tasty meals. True (as stipulated)

A: All breakfast foods are tasty meals. False

I: Some breakfast foods are tasty meals. False

O: Some breakfast foods are not tasty meals. True

12. O: Some oysters are not creatures bearing pearls. True (as stipulated)

A: All oysters are creatures bearing pearls. False

E: No oysters are creatures bearing pearls. Undetermined

I: Some oysters are creatures bearing pearls. Undetermined

EXERCISE SET 7.3B

3. Given sentence: No appliances are heirlooms.
Converse: No heirlooms are appliances. Valid inference.
Obverse: All appliances are nonheirlooms. Valid inference.
Contrapositive: No nonheirlooms are non-appliances. Invalid inference.

6. Given sentence: Some immigrants are Democrats.
Converse: Some Democrats are immigrants. Valid inference.
Obverse: Some immigrants are not non-Democrats. Valid inference.
Contrapositive: Some non-Democrats are non-immigrants. Invalid inference.

9. Given sentence: Some wrestlers are women.
Converse: Some women are wrestlers. Valid inference.
Obverse: Some wrestlers are not nonwomen. Valid inference.
Contrapositive: Some nonwomen are nonwrestlers. Invalid inference.

12. Given sentence: Some gamblers are not winners.
Converse: Some winners are not gamblers. Invalid inference.
Obverse: Some gamblers are nonwinners. Valid inference.

Contrapositive: Some nonwinners are not non-gamblers. Valid inference.

EXERCISE SET 7.3C

Given claim: All lizards are reptiles.

3. Some lizards are not reptiles. False (square of opposition)

6. All nonreptiles are nonlizards. True (contrapositive)

9. No nonreptiles are nonlizards. False (contrapositive, square of opposition)

EXERCISE SET 7.4A

3. Table of symbols:
   P = people with power
   C = people who are corrupted
   O = politicians
   P1: All P are C.
   P2: All O are P.
   C: Therefore, all O are C.

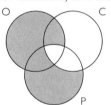

The argument is valid.

6. Table of symbols:
   S = software
   U = product that is user-friendly
   M = product that should be on the market
   P1: Some S is not U.
   P2: All M are U.
   C: Therefore, some S are not M.

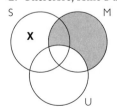

The argument is valid.

9. Table of symbols:
   M = male legislators
   P = people who know what it is like to be pregnant
   J = people who should pass judgment on abortion

P1: No M are P.
P2: All J are P.
C: Therefore, no M are J.

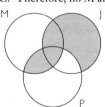

The argument is valid.

12. Table of symbols:
S = students
W = people who do not take their work seriously
E = people who should do something else instead
P1: Some S are W.
P2: Some W are E.
C: Therefore, some S are E.

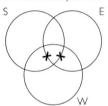

The argument is invalid.

15. Table of symbols:
G = greens
E = people concerned about the environment
D = people who drive fuel-efficient cars
R = people subject to road rage
P1A: All G are E.
P1B: All E are D.
P1: All G are D.
P2: No D are R.
C: Therefore, no G are R.

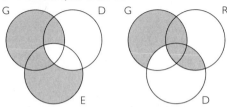

Both the subargument and the main argument of this sorites are valid.

EXERCISE SET 7.4B

3. Implicit premise: All problems that cannot be solved at the national level require a limited global authority.
Table of symbols:
G = global problems
S = problems that cannot be solved at the national level
L = problems whose solution requires a limited global authority
P1: Some G are S.
P2: All S are L.
C: Therefore, some G are L

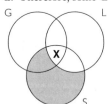

The argument is valid.

6. Implicit premise: Hero worship of Elvis Presley is hero worship of a confirmed drug addict.
Table of symbols:
H = hero worship of a confirmed drug addict
N = something we need
P = hero worship of Elvis Presley
P1: No H are N.
P2: All P are H.
C: Therefore, no P are N.

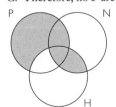

The argument is valid.

EXERCISE SET 7.5A

3. Table of symbols:
P = The shooters' parents did not notice warning signs in their behavior.
T = The shooters' teachers did not notice warning signs in their behavior.
P · T

6. Table of symbols:
H = I am having a heart attack.
S = Send a volunteer—or a slew of former presidents—with a box of Band-Aids.
H ⊃ ~S

9. Table of symbols:
   A = This is appropriate for off-road vehicles.
   D = This is what the sport utilities were designed for.
   A · D

12. Table of symbols:
    C = Congress appropriates money explicitly for such grants.
    S = The grants are subject to closer scrutiny than the tax breaks.
    B = There is better government.
    (C ⊃ S) ⊃ B

15. Table of symbols:
    C = Children pay for their own college education.
    R = Children become much more responsible.
    P = Children take pride in their achievements.
    C ⊃ (R · P)

18. Table of symbols:
    P = Proof of the efficiency of rail service is needed.
    L = One should look at two of our greatest economic competitors, Germany and Japan.
    T = One should notice that in Germany and Japan fast, dependable trains are an integral part of the economy and are taken for granted.
    P ⊃ (L · T)

21. Table of symbols:
    G = The problem with the militia "movement" is that it is antigovernment.
    D = The problem with the militia "movement" is that it is antidemocratic government.
    ~ G · D

24. Table of symbols:
    D = You are not certain about your definition of a human being.
    Q = You are not certain what constitutes quality living and what does not.
    S = It is better to err on the side of saving a life, rather than destroying it.
    (D · Q) ⊃ S

EXERCISE SET 7.5B

3. Table of symbols:
   A = You have the ability.
   D = You have the drive.
   S = You succeed in our firm.
   P1: (A · D) ⊃ S
   P2: D
   P3: ~A
   IC: Therefore, ~S

A	D	S	~A	~S	A · D	(A · D)⊃S
T	T	T	F	F	T	T
T	T	F	F	T	T	F
T	F	T	F	F	F	T
T	F	F	F	T	F	T
F	T	T	T	Ⓕ	F	T
F	T	F	T	Ⓣ	F	T
F	F	T	T	F	F	T
F	F	F	T	T	F	T
P			P		C	P

This argument is invalid.

6. Table of symbols:
   I = In this business, you sink.
   W = In this business, you swim.
   P1: I ∨ W
   P2: ~W
   C: Therefore, I

I	W	~W	I ∨ W
T	T	F	T
Ⓣ	F	T	T
F	T	F	T
F	F	T	F
C		P	P

This argument is valid.

9. Table of symbols:
   P = We permit human cloning.
   D = The human race is doomed.
   P1: P ⊃ D
   P2: ~P
   C: Therefore, ~D

P	D	~P	~D	P ⊃ D
T	T	F	F	T
T	F	F	T	F
F	T	T	Ⓕ	T
F	F	T	Ⓣ	T
		P	C	P

This argument is invalid (denying the antecedent).

EXERCISE SET 7.5C

3. Table of symbols:
   R = Leni Riefenstahl is honored for her propaganda films.
   O = Lee Harvey Oswald should be honored for sharpshooting.
   P1: R ⊃ O
   IP2: ~O
   C: Therefore, ~R

R	O	~R	~O	R ⊃ O
T	T	F	F	T
T	F	F	T	F
F	T	T	F	T
F	F	Ⓣ	T	T
		C	P	P

The argument is valid (*modus tollens*).

6. Table of symbols:

V = It is morally right to give preference to veterans.

D = It is morally right to give preference to groups that have been denied full opportunity.

P1: V ⊃ D
P2: V
IC: Therefore, D

V	D	V⊃D
T	(T)	T
T	F	F
F	T	T
F	F	T
P	C	P

This argument is valid (*modus ponens*).

9. Table of symbols:

A = The lifestyle aspirations of the majority of the participants in antipoverty programs like Project New Hope can be satisfied with an annual package of earnings, wage subsidies, and welfare amounting to less that $12,000.

D = These programs that rely on personal drive and ambition are indeed doomed.

P1: A ⊃ D
P2: A
C: Therefore, D

A	D	A⊃D
T	(T)	T
T	F	F
F	T	T
F	F	T
P	C	P

This argument is valid (*modus ponens*)

12. This text criticizes the columnist's argument by charging false premise (against P2), but no justification is offered for the charge. Here is the columnist's argument:

Table of symbols:

S = There is no sane or sensible way of using nuclear weapons.

N = Nuclear weapons cannot be used.

P = Nuclear weapons cannot have prevented war.

P1: S
P2: S ⊃ N
P3: N ⊃ P
C: Therefore, P

S	N	P	S⊃N	N⊃P
T	T	(P)	T	T
T	T	F	T	F
T	F	T	F	T
T	F	F	F	T
F	T	T	T	T
F	T	F	T	F
F	F	T	T	T
F	F	F	T	T
P		C	P	P

The argument is valid.

15. Table of symbols:

P = Federal, state, and private health plans are willing to pay for many of these scientifically unproven techniques.

D = Research and proof of efficacy is discouraged.

P1: P ⊃ D
P2: ~D
C: Therefore, ~P

P	D	~P	~D	P⊃D
T	T	F	F	T
T	F	F	T	F
F	T	T	F	T
F	F	(T)	T	T
		C	P	P

This is a valid argument (*modus tollens*).

EXERCISE SET 8.1A

3. I have seen many different maps that locate Nigeria in Africa. I have read news accounts of happenings in Africa. I regard all of these sources as reliable. In addition, I have known a person from Nigeria who has referred to himself as being African.

6. I have been treated since infancy as male. I have observed many times that I have typical male sexual characteristics. People beyond my family have also treated me as male. This is certainly one of my beliefs that I regard as extremely reliable.

9. I have observed repeatedly in recent years how the private lives of politicians have often been extensively discussed in the press. A significant recent example of this is the discussion of the private relationships of former president Bill Clinton. At the same time, it has been made clear to me by the comments of many informed people that the press refused to report what they knew about the extramarital relationships of former president John Kennedy.

EXERCISE SET 8.1B

3. Value claim: This is a claim about how the world should be.

6. *A posteriori* truth: This is a truth that has been discovered recently by medical researchers.

9. *A posteriori* truth: A statement known to be true through our understanding of history.

12. *A posteriori* truth or *a posteriori* falsehood: This statement is an *a posteriori* claim, in that it is something we have learned from experience, with its truth or falsehood depending on whether it is understood to have the implicit quantifier "all." With that quantifier, it is probably false.

15. *A posteriori* falsehood: If this is understood as having an implicit quantifier "all," as seems a reasonable interpretation, then experience would almost certainly reveal it to be false. Likely most of those with pierced noses listen to rock, but very likely not all.

18. Analytic falsehood: This is *a priori* false by the definition of "sanctimonious."

EXERCISE SET 8.2A

3. P1: The automobile is the most expensive thing that most of us will ever buy.
   C: Therefore, people should think carefully about their automobile purchase.

I charge this argument with false premise at P1. This is a universal generalization about the things people buy (though not about the people who buy them). The claim is that all things most people will buy will be less expensive than an automobile. This can be shown to be false by a counterexample. More than 50 percent of people in our society buy their own home, which is more expensive than a car. (Remember, the fact that the conclusion is true has no bearing on the strength of the argument.)

6. P1: The higher a college in the *U.S. News & World Report* ranking of colleges, the better the educational experience it provides.
   C: Therefore, of all the colleges a student is admitted to, she should attend the one highest on that list.

I charge this argument with false premise at P1. While it may generally be true that the higher a college is in that ranking, the better the education experience, this is certainly not always the case. Different students have different educational needs, and often the educational needs of a particular student will not match the factors that are used by the magazine to rank colleges. (There is also a hasty conclusion charge that could be made against this argument, because there are other factors, such as cost, that often need to be considered as well.)

9. P1: The Sears Tower in Chicago is the tallest building in the world.
   C: Therefore, the tallest building in the world is in the United States.

I charge this argument with false premise at P1. While the tallest building in the world used to be the Sears Tower, the tallest building is now the Petronas Towers in Kuala Lumpur, Malaysia, at 1483 feet (the Sears Tower is 1450 feet).

EXERCISE SET 8.2B

3. P1: If the philosophy that whites cannot write about blacks is pushed to its fullest conclusion, then only autobiographies will become acceptable representations of a life.
   P2: It is false that autobiographies should be the only acceptable representations of life.
   C: Therefore, it is false that whites should not write about blacks.

This is a case of *reductio ad absurdum* because the consequence of the conditional in P1 is not simply false, but an absurdity. (In addition, the argument could also be charged with the specific content fallacy of slippery slope, discussed later in the chapter.)

6. P1: If, as the columnist claims, "government intervention in the labor market to mandate wage rates and other employer practices does not work even at a national level," then minimum wage laws, laws mandating the 8-hour day, laws restricting child labor, laws regulating health and safety, and laws regulating pension management have not been successful government interventions in the labor market to mandate wage rates and other employer practices at the national level.
   P2: These laws have been so successful.
   C: Therefore, the columnist's claim is false.

This is a case of refutation by counterexample. The columnist makes a universal statement, and the author cites several examples in which the generalization does not apply.

9. P1: If no citizen ought to be compelled to support expression to which he or she objects, then no citizen should be compelled to have the government support with his or her taxes anything with which he or she disagrees.
   P2: It is false that no citizens should be compelled to have the government support with their taxes anything with which they disagree.

C: Therefore, it is false that no citizen ought to be compelled to support expression to which he or she objects.

This is a case of *reductio ad absurdum* because the consequent of P1, that no one should be compelled to support through taxes any government spending with which they disagree, is an absurd result. Taxpaying would become purely voluntary, and government would cease to function.

12. P1: If manufacturers should not be required to install certain safety features in automobiles because of the expense involved, as the Reagan administration claims, then manufacturers should not be required to install brakes on automobiles either.
P2: The government should require auto manufacturers to install brakes.
C: Therefore, the Reagan administration claim is false.

This is a case of refutation by false implication. While the consequent of P1 is false, it is not an absurdity. The claim that cars should not have brakes is an absurdity, but the claim that the government should not require cars to have brakes is not, because it is likely that cars would have brakes even if the government did not require this.

EXERCISE SET 8.2C

3. P1: Almost all social science textbooks are characterized by shallowness and simplicity.
P2: They make no attempt to intellectually engage students.
P3: They have no "life" beyond the classroom.
C: Therefore, almost all social science textbooks numb students' minds and turn them off to education.

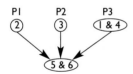

I charge this argument with problematic premise on all three premises. The justification is the same for all three charges. None of the premises is supported, and none of them are acceptable to the audience without support. Most members of the audience have little contact with a range of social science textbooks and thus are not in a position to affirm the truth of these claims. They may be true, but we need to be shown that they are true by a subargument.

6. P1: The war on drugs is insane.
P2: It has accomplished nothing by way of solving the drug problem.
P3: It has severely eroded the constitutional rights on which this country was founded.
C: Therefore, if we stopped the war on drugs and instead devoted all those billions to drug and alcohol rehabilitation, then we would all be better off.

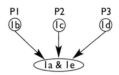

I charge this argument with problematic premise on all three premises:

(1) P1 is problematic because its truth is not evident and it needs support. To label a policy "insane" is a strong charge. It may be accurate in this case, but we need a subargument to show exactly what the author means by the term "insane" and how the resulting claim would be supported.

(2) P2 is problematic in terms of a conventional assessment, as P1 is, because the audience would not regard this statement as likely true. But it is also so chargeable on a critical assessment. Many defenders of the war on drugs argue that the rate of drug consumption would be much greater were drugs decriminalized, so that the war on drugs is having at least the negative effect of keeping the rate of consumption much lower than it would otherwise be.

(3) P3 is chargeable with problematic premise on a conventional assessment. Most members of the audience would probably not regard this statement as likely true, so the author needs to provide support for it.

9. P1: The Congressional Budget Office found years ago that reducing the number of insurance payers to 1 (the government) from 1500 would save more than $100 billion a year in administrative costs.
P2: Only 70 percent to 75 percent of health maintenance organizations' premium dollars go to benefits, with the rest going to administration, advertising, huge executive salaries, and profit.
P3: Both Medicare and the Canadian single-payer system spend 97 percent of their income on benefits.
C: Therefore, for-profit health insurance is inherently costly.

Answers-26

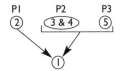

I charge this argument with problematic premise at P2 and P3. These claims are not common knowledge and need support. They are a matter of detailed statistics that the audience would not know, and so each requires a subargument. (Note the contrast with these premises and P1. P1 also contains a detailed statistical claim that the audience would not know, but in P1 an authority is cited in support of the claim, namely, the Congressional Budget Office. As we discuss in the next section, citing an authority like this can take the place of a subargument, thereby avoiding a problematic premise charge. One issue of interpretation of this argument is whether the author is claiming that P2 and P3 are also derived from the same Congressional Budget Office study. If so, they would avoid a problematic premise charge as well. But the charge is appropriate because the text does not make clear that P2 and P3 are claims from that study.)

12. P1: This redrawing of the male-female design involved in the effort to grant rights to gays and lesbians does not make life more fruitful, only more barren.
    P2: The effort to grant such rights is a mind game, cloaked in the false raiment of the discrimination issue.
    P3: The effort dares to exempt humankind from the sexual bipolarity that runs up the evolutionary ladder of earthy beings.
    IC: Therefore, we should oppose efforts to grant rights to gays and lesbians.

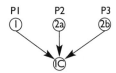

I charge this argument with problematic premise at P1 and P2.

(1) There is reason to doubt the truth of P1, so a critical assessment is in order. First, granting gays and lesbians rights shows respect for their autonomy and for their choices, and this seems to make life more fruitful and less barren. Also, granting such rights adds to the diversity of society, which too seems to make life more fruitful and less barren. Second, if the author, in using these phrases, is referring to the issue of sexual reproduction, it is clear that, given population problems, lack of additional procreation may be

a positive rather than a negative. Given these points, the author needs to include a subargument in support of this premise.

(2) P2 claims that the issue of rights for gays and lesbians is not a true discrimination issue. This is doubtful as well. It certainly seems to be an issue of discrimination, similar to other legal discrimination issues. Given this appearance, the author's claim that it is not requires support, support which should also explain what he means by "mind game" in this context. (Should P3 be charged with problematic premise as well? The audience would likely believe this claim, but should it be subject to a critical assessment? If there is widespread evidence of homosexual behavior among nonhuman animals, then it should.)

15. P1: Being tried for a serious crime knowing that those charged with determining your guilt have all expressed a willingness to kill you if you are guilty is a violation of the Sixth Amendment guarantee of an impartial jury.
    IC: Therefore, opponents of capital punishment should not be excluded from juries in capital cases.

I charge this argument with problematic premise at P1. There is reason to doubt that this claim is true, so the author should have supported it. The impartiality of juries the Sixth Amendment refers to concerns a lack of prejudgment of the guilt of the defendant, a willingness to base the verdict only on the evidence presented at trial. It is not clear that the impartiality extends to beliefs about what punishments are appropriate. The author needs to argue that this is the case.

EXERCISE SET 8.3A

3. The authority (x) is Mr. Simon, who (y) is a celebrated lawyer and legal expert. The claim (z) is that the death penalty is not an effective punishment.

I charge this argument with faulty appeal to authority. It violates two of the three conditions for an acceptable appeal to authority. While the first condition is satisfied, because Mr. Simon is a genuine authority in the appropriate area, the second is not, because the authorities are in disagreement on this question. Some argue that the death penalty is an effective deterrent, and others argue that it is not. The third condition is violated because the authority has a substantial personal interest in getting others to believe the truth of z.

6. The authority (x) is Dr. Spaulding, who (y) is a professor of chemistry. The claim (z) is that Argon is a noble gas.

   This is an acceptable appeal to authority. Spaulding is a genuine authority in the relevant area, chemistry, and the matter is one that the authorities agree upon. There is no personal interest at stake.

9. The personal authority (x) is Gilbert, who (y) was an eyewitness to the bank robbery. The claim (z) is that the robber had blonde hair.

   I charge this argument with faulty appeal to authority. Although Gilbert is a genuine personal authority on the matter in question, and one who seems to have no personal interest at stake, the fact that other eyewitnesses disagreed with her indicates that the second condition is violated.

EXERCISE SET 8.3B

3. The authority is Supreme Court Justice Robert Jackson, and the claim is that the purpose of the Bill of Rights is to guarantee that certain subjects will not be decided by majority rule but by an independent judiciary.

   This is an acceptable appeal to authority. Justice Jackson, as a member of the Supreme Court, is clearly an authority in this area, and he has no personal interest at stake. It seems as well that the authorities are in substantial agreement on this question. While the authorities may disagree on whether it is acceptable to have judicial elections, which is what the conclusion of the argument is about, Jackson is not being cited in support of this claim, but rather of a premise supporting that claim.

6. The authority cited is an unnamed study, and the claim is that weak students often use evaluations to get back at "difficult" professors.

   I charge this argument with faulty appeal to authority. Because the study is unnamed, we cannot tell whether it is an authority that satisfies the first and third conditions. In addition, it seems likely that the second condition would not be satisfied in any case, since this is a matter about which the experts are not likely to agree.

9. The authority cited is the president of the world's largest educational testing organization, and the claim is that college admission test scores should not be used as the sole yardstick of individual merit.

   This is an acceptable appeal to authority. The person cited is presumably an authority on the use of test scores, and this is probably an area in which the experts would agree. The third condition, the authority's having no personal interest in getting the audience to believe the claim, is satisfied as well. (In fact, this text applies the frequently used tactic of playing on the third condition to make the argument more forceful. Because this authority would likely have a personal interest in the audience's *not* believing the claim, since this would seem to be to the benefit of the testing industry, this appeal to authority has added strength.)

EXERCISE SET 8.4A

3. P1: The final examination is a course requirement.
   C: Therefore, you must take the final examination.

   This is an acceptable argument, not chargeable with the fallacy of appeal to force. The premise should not be understood as a threat, but simply the statement of existing policy, and, in any case, there is no indication that the instructor of the course is the author of the argument.

6. P1: Your boss Jones said that if you do not sleep with him, you will be fired.
   C: Therefore, you had better sleep with him.

   This is not chargeable with the fallacy of appeal to force because, though P1 is a threat, the author of the argument is not Jones, the person issuing the threat.

9. P1: Either there will be 6 feet or more of snow this winter or there will not be.
   P2: If there is, the skiers will be happy.
   P3: If there is not, snow shovelers will be happy.
   C: Therefore, either skiers or snow shovelers will be happy

   This argument is not chargeable with the fallacy of false dilemma because the dilemma in P1 is genuine. It is a tautology.

12. P1: Either aliens frequently visit Earth or the many who claim to have been abducted by aliens are all lying.
    P2: But so many people could not all be lying.
    C: Therefore, aliens must frequently visit Earth.

    I charge this argument with the fallacy of false dilemma. The two alternatives presented in P1 are not exhaustive. There are other possible explanations. For example, consider that to lie is to say what you believe to be false. It could be that many of those who claim to have been abducted believe what they are saying, even though what they are saying is false, because the experience was a hallucination or some other kind of illusion.

15. P1: You should love America or you should leave it.
    P2: You protesters do not love America.
    C: Therefore, you protesters should leave America.

I charge this argument with the fallacy of false dilemma. The two alternatives presented in P1 are not exhaustive. A person is under no obligation to love the nation of which she is a citizen. She should fulfill her obligations as a citizen, but loving the nation is not an obligation of citizenship. Thus, it is not the case that a person who does not love her country should leave it. (There is also a fallacy charge of problematic premise or false premise against P2. One can argue that to protest the shortcomings of one's country is to show a genuine love for the country, a desire to see it improve.)

EXERCISE SET 8.4B

3. This is a complicated argument to interpret. Perhaps the best interpretation is to regard the text as containing two arguments by dilemma, one in each sentence and both subarguments, and an implicit conclusion. Each of the dilemmas is expressed in an implicit premise.

> IP1A: Either moral disapproval of an act or lifestyle is bigotry, or it is freedom of conscience.
> P1B: Moral disapproval of an act or lifestyle is freedom of conscience.

P1: Moral disapproval of an act is not bigotry.

> IP2A: Either publishing one's views on such matters is inciting others to violence, or it is free speech.
> P2B: Publishing one's views on such matters is free speech.

P2: Publishing one's views on such matters is not inciting others to violence.

IC: Therefore, publishing one's moral disapproval of an act or lifestyle should not be restricted.

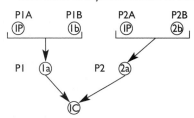

The fallacy charge will require that we explore more deeply the nature of arguments by dilemma.

I charge this argument with the fallacy of false dilemma at P1A and P2A. In both cases, the error is the same. The standard form of an argument by dilemma is that the linked premise claims that one of the alternatives presented in the dilemma is not the case, and the conclusion is that the other one is the case. These two arguments by dilemma do not follow that pattern. Instead, the linked premise in each case claims that one of the alternatives is the case, and the conclusion (P1 and P2) is that the other is not the case. For this form of the argument to be valid, the alternatives must be not *exhaustive* (as they must be for the standard form), but *exclusive*, meaning that both alternatives cannot be true. The fallacy in these cases is that there is reason in the case of both dilemmas to doubt that the two alternatives are exclusive. Perhaps bigotry is sometimes also freedom of conscience, and incitement to violence is sometimes also free speech. It is not implausible that this may be the case. As a result, the author should have provided further argumentation to show that these alternatives are exclusive.

6. P1: If New York City sues tobacco companies to recover money spent caring for cancer patients, then there is no reason they should not also sue General Motors and the Ford Motor Company to recover all the money spent on fuel for gas-guzzling city vehicles or Anheuser-Busch for money spent caring for liver patients in city hospitals.

  IP2: It would be absurd to sue these other companies for these reasons.

  C: Therefore, New York City should not sue tobacco companies to recover money spent caring for cancer patients.

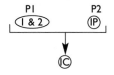

I charge this argument with the slippery slope fallacy. P1 claims that the city's suing tobacco companies would be a precedent to justify suing auto manufacturers for producing gas-guzzlers used by the city or beer companies for health expenses due to alcoholism that the city must cover. There is good reason to doubt the truth of this claim. The cases are different in relevant ways. The tobacco companies sold a product that they knew would often lead to serious illness when used as expected, and such illness caused expenses for the city. This is not the case for the auto manufacturers or the beer companies. In the case of the auto manufacturers, the city chose to purchase the autos it purchased, while it did not choose for the smokers to smoke. In the case of the beer companies, the beer did not cause serious health problems when used as expected, only when it was abused.

9.   P1A: History indicates that the name was intended as an honor and not as a slur.

P1: The crusade to force the Washington Redskins National Football League franchise to change its name describes a perfect example of political correctness run amok.

P2: Regardless of past usage of the word, to most Americans today, the word "redskin" connotes a member of the Washington football team.

P3: The radical agenda behind this crusade is to change all team names that refer to Native Americans.

P4: If the names of teams referring to Native Americans were changed, then this would serve as a precedent to change other team names as well, such as Notre Dame's "Fighting Irish" and basketball's Boston "Celtics" (referring to the Irish), hockey's Vancouver "Canucks" and Montreal "Canadiens" (referring to French Canadians and Canadians generally), baseball's San Diego "Padres" and Anaheim "Angels" and football's New Orleans "Saints" (referring to Catholics), and football's New York "Giants" and baseball's San Francisco "Giants" (referring to very large people).

C: Therefore, the Washington Redskins should not be forced to change their name.

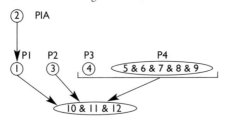

I charge this argument with the fallacy of slippery slope at P4. P4 claims that if team names referring to Native Americans were changed then this would serve as a precedent justifying demands for changes in many other team names where the names refer to other groups of individuals. There is good reason to doubt the truth of this claim. The cases are different in relevant ways. There is a history of extreme discrimination and, some would argue, attempted extermination of Native Americans that has caused nicknames given to them by the dominant culture (such as "Redskins") to be traditionally used in a very derogatory way. This is not the case for the other groups. While there has been discrimination against and mistreatment of these other groups, it in no way compares with what has been done to the Native Americans. Thus, P4 is false.

EXERCISE SET 9.1B

3. Conceptual statement: If a child is assaulted so as to cause physical injury or deprived of some basic necessities of life, then that child has been a victim of child abuse.

Resolution: Because the children were not fed for long periods, they were deprived of some basic necessities of life, were the victims of child abuse, and should be removed from the home.

EXERCISE SET 9.1C

3. Conceptual statement: If a child is assaulted so as to cause physical injury or deprived of some basic necessities of life, then that child has been a victim of child abuse.

Conceptual argument: The principal obligation of a child's caregiver is to help the child develop into a normal adult. So, child abuse is the failure on the part of a caregiver to live up to this obligation. If a child is assaulted so as to cause physical injury or deprived of some basic necessities of life, then the child has been treated in a way that will substantially interfere with that child's developing into a normal adult. The injury or deprivation is likely to cause physical or psychological trauma that will make it more difficult for the child to develop into a normal adult. Thus, if a child is assaulted so as to cause physical injury or deprived of some basic necessities of life, then the child has been subjected to child abuse.

EXERCISE SET 9.1D

3. Conclusion: In the last half of 1999, workers were exploited.

Conceptual premise: If workers become more productive and their pay is not increased, then they are exploited.

There is no conceptual argument offered for this premise. I charge this argument with problematic premise at the conceptual premise. Like all conceptual statements, this one is controversial, and so the author should have offered a conceptual argument in support of it. This premise goes to the root of the debate over capitalism versus socialism. From a capitalist perspective, if the means of increased productivity is new machinery (like computers) introduced by management, then workers do not necessarily have a right to share in the results of increased productivity and, as a result, are not necessarily being exploited. The author should have addressed this objection in a conceptual subargument.

6. Conclusion: Corporate tax reductions are not welfare.

Conceptual premise: A government subsidy is welfare if and only if the recipient of the subsidy is not a net contributor of money to the government.

The author offers a conceptual argument for this premise. Three premises are offered for the conclusion that corporate tax reductions are not welfare. First, someone receiving welfare lives off the fruit of others' labor. Second, if an entity (person or corporation) is a net contributor of money to the government, the recipient is not living off the fruit of others' labor. Third, corporations that receive tax reductions remain net contributors of money to the government. I charge this argument with false premise at the second premise. Corporations, like people, receive services from the government. If a corporation is not paying enough to support those services, not paying its fair share, then it is living off the fruit of others' labor, even if it is paying some taxes. Thus, when a corporate tax reduction means that the corporation is paying less than its fair share, then that tax reduction can be regarded as welfare.

9. Conclusion: Bicycles are a part of traffic and should be given greater consideration.
   Conceptual premise: If a vehicle can move people from place to place, then it is a part of traffic.

   No conceptual argument is offered. The argument offered is in support of the conclusion rather than the conceptual premise. Problematic premise can be charged against the premise. There is reason to doubt the premise. Lots of vehicles, such as baby buggies and tricycles, can move people but would not be considered part of traffic, mainly because they are too cumbersome or slow to fit in with the flow of traffic. This is an issue that the author should have addressed in a subargument.

12. This letter is an ironic criticism of the idea that population increases are always improvements. The concept to be clarified is, therefore, that of the improvement of a society, but the conceptual premise is implicit. The author may be appealing to some idea such as the density of the population in determining what is an improvement.

   Conclusion: An increase in population growth is not necessarily an improvement in the society.
   Conceptual premise: If an event is an improvement in a society, then it does not increase the density of the population.

   There is no argument for the conceptual premise. I charge false premise against this premise. While an increase in the density of a population would sometimes not be an improvement, other times it would be. If a society has a small population and the addition of more people would lead to a more vital economy and a more thriving cultural life, then an increase in the density of the population would be an improvement. This is an issue the author should have addressed in a subargument. To defend this conclu-

sion, the author will need to come up with a better conceptual premise.

15. The author is questioning the acceptability of hormone replacement therapy as a medical treatment. So, the concept at issue is that of an acceptable medical treatment.

   Conclusion: Hormone replacement therapy is not an acceptable medical treatment.
   Conceptual premise: If a drug increases the risk of harm from any source, then it is not an acceptable medical treatment.

   No argument is offered for the conceptual premise. I charge false premise against this premise. The appropriate measure of acceptability is not whether a treatment causes or risks harm from any source, but whether it causes or risks harm overall. All medical treatments (even aspirin, for example) carry some risk of harm, yet if the risk is substantially less than the benefit, the treatment is acceptable. So, if a treatment were acceptable only if it carried no risk of harm from any source, no medical treatment would be acceptable. To defend this conclusion, the author will need to come up with a better conceptual premise.

18. Conclusion: We should place in the Tomb of the Vietnam Unknown Soldier a scroll or book inscribed with all 58,000 names of those who did not return from Vietnam.
   Conceptual premise: If someone or something is unknown, then it is not known and cannot be known.

   There is no argument for this conceptual premise. I charge false premise against the premise. Many things are currently unknown, but may become known. For example, the perpetrators of many crimes are referred to as unknown, even though we expect that in many or most cases they will become known after police investigation. To defend this conclusion, the author will need to come up with a better conceptual premise.

21. Conclusion: A more accurate way to describe crime in winter is to say, "Usually the type of crime changes in this kind of weather."
   Conceptual premise: If an action causes harm or risk of harm to someone, then it should be regarded as a crime.

   There is no argument for the conceptual premise. I charge false premise against this premise. Many actions we do that should not be considered crimes harm or risk harm to other persons. For example, when we drive a car, we put our passengers and pedestrians along our route at risk, but driving a car should not be considered a crime. To defend this conclusion, the author will need to come up with a better conceptual premise.

EXERCISE SET 9.2A

Note: There are different answers possible for each of these exercises.

3. Overcoat
    Genus: an outer garment
    Species: for cold weather
6. Computer
    Genus: machine
    Species: that calculates
9. Hearing aid
    Genus: device
    Species: that helps a person hear better

EXERCISE SET 9.2B

Note: There are different answers possible for each of these exercises.

3. Counterexample: a class held outdoors or on the Internet. These show the definition to be too narrow.
    Revision: A class is an educational activity that is part of a structured set of activities designed to teach.
6. Counterexample: An action that causes a person to be called for jury duty or to appear as a trial witness. These show the definition to be too broad.
    Revision: A crime is any action that can cause a person to be required to appear in court as a defendant.

EXERCISE SET 9.3A

3. The double meaning in this headline results from ambiguity in the verb "try." One meaning, the intended one, is to determine legal guilt in court, in which case the headline means that the shooting defendant will have his legal guilt determined in juvenile court. Another meaning is to attempt, in which case the term "shooting" is not an adjective but a verb, and the headline means that the court will attempt to shoot the defendant.

6. The double meaning in this headline results from ambiguity in the verb "run down." One meaning, the intended one, is to discover and give a citation or ticket to. The other meaning is to strike with an automobile. What brings this second meaning to mind is that jaywalkers are at risk of being run down by automobiles.

9. The double meaning in this headline results from ambiguity in the term "Farmer Bill." On one meaning of the term, the intended one, the term refers to

a piece of legislation before Congress, and "House" refers to the House of Representatives. On the other meaning, the term is a combination of a person's name (Bill) and an indication of his occupation (farmer), in which case the meaning is that Bill died in his house rather than out in his fields.

12. The double meaning in this headline results from ambiguity in the phrase "left waffles." On one meaning, the intended one, "left" labels a part of the political spectrum in Britain and "waffles" is a verb meaning to avoid taking a clear position on an issue. (The issue in this case is the war that Britain fought with Argentina in 1982 over the Falkland Islands.) On the other meaning, "left" means not to take with one and "waffles" refers to the breakfast item usually eaten with syrup.

EXERCISE SET 9.3B

3. P1: The end of things is their perfection.
    P2: The end of human beings is their death.
    C: Therefore, the perfection of human beings is their death.

    I charge this argument with the fallacy of equivocation. The term "end" has a different meaning in each of the premises in which it occurs, and the reasoning depends on this shift in meaning. In P1, the term means goal, and in P2, it means conclusion.

6. P1: Everyone's birth is an accident.
    C: Therefore, you should not be concerned that your birth was an accident.

    I charge this argument with the fallacy of equivocation. The term "accident" has a different meaning in the premise and in the conclusion, and the reasoning depends on this shift in meaning. In the premise, the term means that the original meeting of the two people who conceive a child, however much the conception is intended and the child wanted, might not have happened, in which case the child would never have existed. In the conclusion, the term means that the two people who conceive a child do not intend their sexual intercourse to result in a conception, implying that the resulting child is in some sense unwanted.

EXERCISE SET 9.3C

3. The author criticizes the newspaper for referring to the medical treatment President Clinton received after a knee injury as a "grueling rehab." The author argues that the term "rehabilitation" applies only when an injury is serious and long-term. The author regards the use of the term as tendentious because it is, in his view, sensationalistic.

6. The author suggests that it would be more appropriate to refer to what President Clinton was alleged in the Starr report to have done not as "having and concealing an affair in the White House," but as "repeated lying, and encouraging other witnesses to lie, in grand jury and discovery proceedings." The author argues that the latter phrase makes clearer than the former the impact of the alleged activities on the judicial process. The author implies that the phrase used by the columnists is euphemistic because it conceals the real impact of the alleged activities.

9. The author criticizes a scientist for using certain terms to discuss the relationship between a pregnant woman and her fetus, terms such as "conflict," "tug-of-war," "move," and "countermove," arguing that there is no justification for using such terms to refer to chemical reactions in the body. The author clearly regards the use of such terms as tendentious and as warlike metaphors, and suggests that their use reflects the status of women in patriarchal societies.

EXERCISE SET 9.3D

3. P1A: The decision of Dartmouth's Board of Trustees to require its fraternities and sororities to go co-ed was profound and rash.

   P1B: The decision was made without input from alumni or the student body.

   P1C: The decision was a case of pandering to a small, vocal minority while sacrificing the needs and wishes of the majority.

   P1: The decision was irresponsible.

   C: Therefore, the members of the Board should be removed from office.

I charge this argument with the fallacy of tendentiousness at P1A and P1C. At P1A, the author refers to the decision as rash. This tendentious term has a negative expressive meaning that bolsters the claim that the decision was irresponsible. It may be true that the decision was rash, but this needs to be defended in a subargument. At P1C, the author refers to the decision as a case of pandering. This also is a tendentious term with a negative expressing meaning that bolsters the claim that the decision was irresponsible. Its accuracy needs to be defended in a subargument.

6. P1: Execution deters convicted murderers from killing again.

   C: Therefore, the district attorney's claim that there is no credible evidence that execution deters crime is false.

I charge this argument with the fallacy of equivocation. There is an equivocation on a key term in the argument, "deters." It is used in one way in the premise, where it refers to the effect of punishment in ensuring that the person punished does not commit the crime again. It is used another way in the conclusion. The district attorney, as the author suggests, clearly meant the term to refer to the effect of punishment in ensuring that *other* people do not commit the crime. The force of the argument depends on this shift in meaning. If the term had the same meaning in the premise that it does in the conclusion, the premise would not make sense.

9. P1: The essence of any art form is freedom of expression.

   P2: Government funding would allow artists the freedom of expression to make art without the constraints of the commercial marketplace.

   C: Therefore, the government should fund artists.

I charge this argument with the fallacy of equivocation. The argument equivocates on the key term "freedom of expression." In P1, the term refers to the right guaranteed in the Bill of Rights to express oneself free of government constraint. In P2, the term refers to the ability to express oneself through art free of the need to make a living with one's art by producing art that is commercially viable. The force of the argument depends on this shift in meaning.

EXERCISE SET 10.1A

3. This is an empirical generalization, best interpreted as nonuniversal. The implicit quantifier is "many" or "most." Reformulation: Many new medical technologies present us with difficult moral choices.

6. This is a nonuniversal empirical generalization. No reformulation needed.

9. There are two ways to interpret this sentence:

   (1) The first way ignores the opening phrase, which would probably not be part of the statement if the statement were part of an argument. The remainder of the sentence is best interpreted as being about the configuration of continents, not about the continents themselves. So understood, this is a singular empirical statement. Reformulation: The configuration of the continents used to be different.

   (2) The second way includes the opening phrase. So understood, the sentence expresses an empirical generalization about geologists. Since the claim about the continents seems to be non-controversial within geology, the sentence is best interpreted as expressing a universal generalization, with an implicit quantifier "all." Reformulation: All geologists believe that the

configuration of the continents used to be different.

12. This is a universal empirical generalization and needs no reformulation.

EXERCISE SET 10.1B

Note: Many different answers are possible for these exercises.

3. P1: The technology for cloning humans presents us with difficult moral choices.
   P2: The technology for organ transplants presents us with difficult moral choices.
   P3: The technology for determining the presence of genetic defects prior to birth presents us with difficult moral choices.
   P4: The technology for keeping brain-dead individuals alive indefinitely presents us with difficult moral choices.
   C: Therefore, many new medical technologies present us with difficult moral choices.

6. P1: Fifty-six people who attend our college have the name "Jennifer."
   P2: A number of well-known celebrities have the name "Jennifer."
   P3: The number of people named "Jennifer" listed in the New York City phone book is very large.
   C: Therefore, many people have the name "Jennifer."

9. P1: All the major geology texts claim that the configuration of the continents used to be different.
   P2: There has been no article in a major geology journal in recent years questioning the claim that the configuration of the continents used to be different.
   C: Therefore, all geologists believe that the configuration of the continents used to be different.

12. P1: Her IQ is at the very high tail end of the bell curve of IQs.
    P2: No member of Mensa has a higher IQ than she does.
    P3: Her IQ is higher than the estimated IQs of Einstein, Mozart, and Newton.
    C: Therefore, no one comes close to her in IQ.

EXERCISE SET 10.1C

3. Features: condensed premise
   P1: All societies throughout history that I can think of have fought wars.
   C: Therefore, at all times in the future, societies will have wars.

6. Features: no special features
   P1: I saw *Cosi Fan Tutti* and I did not like it.
   P2: I saw *Aida* and I did not like it.
   P3: I saw *La Boheme* and I did not like it.
   C: Therefore, all times will be times when I do not like opera.

9. Features: induction to a collective property; possibility a complete enumeration
   P1: Carl is a member of our shop and does engine work.
   P2: Betty is a member of our shop and works on transmissions.
   P3: Grady is a member of our shop and handles suspensions and electrical systems.
   P4: Lewis is a member of our shop and his specialty is cooling systems.
   C: Therefore, our shop has your whole car covered.

EXERCISE SET 10.2A

3. Two methods of selection would lead to harmful bias:
   (1) If your method of selection favors males over females, the bias would probably be harmful. Being male is probably relevant to the characteristic of watching wrestling because it is likely that a higher proportion of males watch wrestling than females.
   (2) If your method of selection favors young people over older people, the bias would probably be harmful. Being young is probably relevant to the characteristic of watching wrestling because it is likely that a higher proportion of young people watch wrestling than older people.

Two methods of selection would not lead to harmful bias:
   (3) If your method of selection favors those whose last names begin with letters in the first half of the alphabet, the bias would probably not be harmful. There is no reason to think that having a last name in the first half of the alphabet is relevant to the characteristic of watching wrestling.
   (4) If your method of selection favors tall people over short people, the bias would probably not be harmful. There is no reason to think that being tall is relevant to the characteristic of watching wrestling.

EXERCISE SET 10.2B

3. P1: All societies throughout history that I can think of have fought wars.
   C: Therefore, at all times in the future, societies will have wars.

I charge this inductive argument with the fallacy of hasty conclusion. First, it is not clear that the sample size is sufficiently large because it is not clear how many societies the author knows about. Second, there is a harmful bias in the method of sample selection, making the sample not sufficiently representative. The sample includes only societies that have existed in the past, whereas the population includes only societies of the future. This is a harmful (though inescapable) bias because social organization may change in the future (for example, in economic terms or in terms of global organization) in ways that eliminate the possibility of war.

6. P1: I saw *Cosi Fan Tutti* and I did not like it.
   P2: I saw *Aida* and I did not like it.
   P3: I saw *La Boheme* and I did not like it.
   C: Therefore, all times will be times when I do not like opera.

I charge this inductive argument with hasty conclusion. The sample size is probably large enough, but the sample is not sufficiently representative. The bias in the sample selection is that all the members of the sample occur when the author is young, whereas the population includes times from all the stages of the author's life. We know a person's cultural tastes tend to change and mature with age, so that what a person does or does not like as a youth is not necessarily a reliable indicator of what she will like or not like as an adult.

9. P1: Carl is a member of our shop and does engine work.
   P2: Betty is a member of our shop and works on transmissions.
   P3: Grady is a member of our shop and handles suspensions and electrical systems.
   P4: Lewis is a member of our shop and his specialty is cooling systems.
   C: Therefore, our shop has your whole car covered.

I charge this inductive argument with hasty conclusion. This is a special case of inductive argument. It is induction to a collective property, and it may be a complete enumeration. Whether or not this is a complete enumeration, the premises do not provide sufficient support to show that the shop has the collective property. The braking system is an important part of a car, and the premises give no indication that this area is covered among the members of the shop. If the premises represent a complete enumeration of the shop employees, then brakes are not covered. If the premises, like those of most inductive arguments, represent only a partial enumeration, they give us no reason to think that anyone else at the shop covers brakes.

EXERCISE 10.2C

3. P1: In my garden, the deer did not eat American holly, which is prickly.
   P2: In my garden, the deer did not eat Chinese juniper, which is scratchy.
   P3: In my garden, the deer did not eat Japanese andromeda, which is distasteful and possibly poisonous.
   C: Therefore, short of starvation, deer will avoid many thorny, fuzzy, aromatic, and toxic plants.

I charge this inductive argument with hasty conclusion. The sample size is small. But, more importantly, there are questions about its representativeness. The number of deer that visit this author's garden may be quite small, and their tastes may not represent the tastes of deer in general. In addition, it is not clear that the author has categorized the plants correctly. It may be that the feature of the plants that kept the deer from eating them were not the obvious ones that the author has picked out.

6. P1A: The once efficient handgun-licensing process in New York City has developed over the years into a 9-month ordeal costing prospective gun owners hundreds of dollars.
    P1: The creation of a new government bureaucracy could turn the right to keep and bear arms into an overly arduous undertaking for honest citizens.
    P2: The handgun control measure would be intrusive.
    P3: The measure would not prevent criminals from obtaining guns.
    P4: It would not serve the interests of a free society.
    C: Therefore, the handgun control measure should not be adopted.

I charge inductive subargument at P1 with the fallacy of hasty conclusion. The sample, a single instance, is too small and not representative. It is not representative because the jurisdiction of New York City may not be typical of the places that the measure would be applied. The fact that the jurisdiction is New York City may be relevant to the characteristic because the size of the government may make it more prone to developing oversized bureaucracies.

9. P1: Salmon that were genetically engineered with growth hormones developed deformities and bone overgrowth, and, though they were designed to be sterile, the injected sterility gene did not take effect.
   P2: A genetically engineered bacterium, created to produce ethanol from agricultural waste as a way of generating fuel, when added to soil caused a significant decrease in the growth of

both roots and shoots of wheat and a decease in beneficial soil fungi, which are necessary for fertile soil and healthy plants.

C: Therefore, sometimes when a new gene is introduced into an organism through genetic engineering, unpredicted effects can occur.

The conclusion of this argument is a nonuniversal generalization. Moreover, it uses the quantifier "some." So, it is not really an inductive argument at all. It is deductive rather than nondeductive. (It is valid.)

EXERCISE SET 10.3A

3. These two events have a common cause. They are causally related, but neither causes the other. Instead, they are both caused by the person's getting up on a workday. This is the only one of the four alternatives that is plausible.

6. For most purchases of snow shovels coincident with the first snowfall, the most plausible of the four alternatives in this case is that x causes y. The snowfall reminds people that they need a snow shovel (if they do not already have one), thus causing them to buy one. But for some such purchases, the two events would have a common cause, namely the onset of winter. In such cases, the purchasers realize that winter is beginning and so buy a snow shovel, and the beginning of winter also then causes the first snowfall.

9. There is, of course, disagreement about the presence or absence of causal relations in such cases. Those who believe in astrology believe that x causes y. Those who dismiss astrology believe that the two events are coincidental. This kind of case represents a real divide in the basic worldviews of members of our society. Which causal story is plausible depends on which side of the divide a person is on. In my view, only the claim that x and y are coincidental is plausible. Given what science tells us about how the world works, it is not plausible that the positions of the stars can have a significant impact on people's everyday lives.

12. This is another case in which the causal relationship varies from case to case. When children who have watched violence on TV commit violent acts, some will be cases in which y causes x and some will be cases in which x and y are coincidental. Perhaps the most plausible causal story is that y causes x. Because we know that children are imitative, we can readily imagine how y would cause x. But this may be one of those cases in which what is most plausible is not true. Certainly many children who watch violence on television do not commit violent acts.

Given that there are many cases in which events of kind x and y are correlative, the important question, much debated by social scientists, is whether a high proportion of such cases of correlation are cases of y causing x, as opposed to x and y being coincidental. Another possibility, by the way, is that, in some of the cases at least, x and y have a common cause. Whatever psychological constitution leads children to violence also leads them to seek out violence in their television viewing.

15. There is much debate about the causal relationship between these two events. The question is whether nuclear weapons were successful as a deterrent. Did nuclear deterrence really work? Perhaps the most plausible causal story for most people is that it did work, that x caused y. But, while many people argue that x caused y, others argue that x and y were coincidental. One way to describe this debate is this: Was there a sufficient level of antagonism between the U.S. and the USSR that they likely would have gone to war if there had been no nuclear weapons? Those who claim that there was not argue that this necessary condition for war was lacking, so that x could not be the cause of y, even though, under different circumstances (that is, if there were a sufficient level of antagonism), x might have been the cause of y. This is a good example of the complexity of many causal questions.

EXERCISE SET 10.3B

3. Violent crime exists in society, and the causes of this crime are complicated and difficult to determine. If someone perpetrates violence using a gun, both the person's action and his access to a gun are necessary conditions for the particular violent result. Either of them could be labeled as the cause, depending on our purposes. If the question is who do we blame, certainly the criminal's act should be singled out as the cause. This seems to be the view of the author. But if our purpose is to reduce the number of such acts of violence, the easiest way to do this may be to seek to limit access to guns. In that case, the availability of the gun would be labeled as the cause. In the author's view, this would not be an effective way to reduce such crime, and it has serious drawbacks as well.

6. The author discusses various factors that may be conditions for the action of D's killing her newborn infant. She criticizes a columnist who singled out as the cause the legal availability of abortions. In response, the author makes two points. First, she lists other alternatives (such as the lessened responsibility of fathers) that might more appropriately be regarded as the cause. Second, she suggests that the factor

cited by the columnist might not be a condition of D's action at all. On the contrary, the unavailability of abortions may tend to cause such actions. The argument that the author seems to have in mind is that if abortions are available, young women are less likely to find themselves in the kind of situation that D did.

▤ EXERCISE SET 10.3C

3. P1A: There is a correlation between the glamour of area code 212 and the glamour of Manhattan.

P1B: It is plausible that what gives area code 212 its glamour is that it is the area code of Manhattan, not the other way around.

P1: The glamour of a location causes the glamour of its area code, rather than the glamour of an area code causing the glamour of its location.

C: Therefore, the New York State Public Service Commission should have given the new, as yet unglamorous area code to the trendiest part of Manhattan.

The causal argument is the subargument at P1. It is a strong argument. In particular, P1B, the premise indicating the plausible causal story, is acceptable without subargument support. I would make no fallacy charges against the subargument at P1.

6. P1A: It is plausible that academic freedom would draw creative and innovative individuals to the teaching profession.

P1: A dose of academic freedom would cause more creative and innovative individuals to enter the teaching profession.

P2: Raising standards for teacher preparation programs is an example of the moribund bureaucratic regulations that drive good people away from a teaching career.

C: Therefore, to improve teacher quality, governments should allow more academic freedom rather than imposing more bureaucratic regulations.

The causal argument is the subargument at P1. It is a strong argument (as opposed to the main argument, against which some fallacies could be charged). Given what we know of creative and innovative people, namely, that they like freedom in their work, allowing academic freedom would cause such people to be drawn to the teaching profession.

9. P1Ai: Obviously, every single gun-wielding mass murderer in history has been a man.

P1A: There is a correlation between being male and committing mass violence.

P1Bi: Violent rage is an essential feature of the weak male ego.

P1Bii: Guns are a fabulously effective method to combat male spinelessness and lack of conscience.

P1Biii: Society and its media feed the masculinity myth.

P1Biv: This myth is nothing other than an attenuated version of male homicidal rage.

P1B: It is plausible that being male is the reason perpetrators of acts of mass violence commit those acts.

P1: The maleness of perpetrators of acts of mass violence causes those acts.

P2: Waiting periods, background checks, licenses, and testing do not challenge the essentially male obsession with guns.

P3: Only a great deal of confidence building and cross-gender communication could mend the millions of thwarted male souls that could inflict mayhem.

C: Therefore, beyond waiting periods, background checks, licenses, and testing, we should seek to bring about for men a great deal of confidence building and cross-gender communication.

The causal argument is the subargument at P1. Although the causal statement at P1 is a controversial claim, the argument for it seems quite strong. The premises of the subargument are themselves both supported. One problem, which could be the basis of a hasty conclusion charge against the subargument, is that the author does not distinguish clearly between maleness as an innate biological category and maleness as a socially conditioned gender role. Much of the language suggests that the author has the biological category in mind, but the conclusion of the main argument suggests that the author understands maleness as a socially acquired characteristic, for otherwise, it would not make sense to talk of its being healed.

12. P1A: There is a correlation between general-interest magazines' depending on newsstand sales and their putting celebrities on the cover.

P1Bi: For such magazines, newsstand sales are a critical source of revenue.

P1Bii: Celebrities on the cover of such magazines drive their newsstand sales.

P1B: It is plausible that the dependence of such magazines on newsstand sales is the cause of their putting celebrities on their covers.

P1: The cause of such magazines' putting celebrities on their covers is that celebrities drive newsstand sales.

P2: Celebrities demand some control over the content of a magazine in exchange for their allowing their photographs to appear on the cover.

P3A: The *New York Times Magazine* is bundled inside the rest of the paper.

P3: The *Times Magazine* does not depend on newsstand sales.

C: Therefore, the editor of the *Times Magazine* should not be smug about the fact that it does not allow celebrities control over content the way that other magazines do.

The causal argument is the subargument at P1. It is a strong argument. The causation story at P1B is plausible, especially given the subargument for it. We all understand how people want to read about celebrities, how celebrities on the cover attract the eye of newsstand customers, and how general-interest magazines want to sell as many newsstand copies as possible.

EXERCISE SET 11.1A

3. Conclusion: The Educational Testing Service should not be pressured to stop reporting the special accommodation status of certain test-takers.
Counterconsideration (sentence 3): The Americans with Disabilities Act may limit the use of this information.

6. Conclusion: The SAT examinations should not be rejected on the grounds that they are culturally biased.
Counterconsideration (sentence 3): The SAT drafters have not perfected a means of writing questions that clearly distinguish raw intelligence from culture

9. Conclusion: Humans were not meant to be and should not be vegetarian.
Counterconsideration (sentence 5): We should avoid wanton cruelty.

12. Conclusion: Most street fire alarm boxes in New York City, except those in isolated areas and those of public concern, should be eliminated.
Counterconsideration (sentence 1): A street fire alarm box was used recently to report a fire in a New York City office building.

15. Conclusion: We should focus all of our energies on Earth, not giving any to space.
Counterconsideration (sentence 2): Discovering more about our solar system is a grandiose achievement for all mankind.

18. Conclusion: The United States should support the creation of a permanent international criminal court.
Counterconsideration (sentences 2 and 6): It would be good if American citizens, and particularly service members stationed abroad, were not subject to politically motivated prosecution before an alien tribunal.

21. Conclusion: It is an oversimplification that women simply need to take control of their own bodies to avoid eating disorders.
Counterconsideration (sentence 6): Women would do well to think independently about their bodies and not hate themselves for not meeting society's too-slender norm.

EXERCISE SET 11.1B

Note: "Px" is used to label the counterpremises, since we do not yet know what number x would be.

3. Counterconsideration: The Americans with Disabilities Act may limit the use of this information.
Counterpremise and subargument (sentence 3, irrelevance strategy):
PxA: Surely the Americans with Disabilities Act restrictions should apply to the educational institutions' actions, not to the testing company's words.
Px: The claim that the Americans with Disabilities Act may limit the use of this information does not count against the conclusion.

6. Counterconsideration: The SAT drafters have not perfected a means of writing questions that clearly distinguish raw intelligence from culture.
Counterpremise and subargument (sentence 3, insufficiency strategy):
PxA: The SAT drafters have done a pretty good job of writing questions that distinguish raw intelligence from culture.
Px: The claim the SAT drafters have not perfected a means of writing questions that clearly distinguish raw intelligence from culture is not sufficient to show that the conclusion should not be accepted.

9. Counterconsideration: We should avoid wanton cruelty.
Counterpremise and subargument (sentences 5 and 6, irrelevance strategy):
PxAi: Humans are natural carnivores.
PxA: Human cruelty to the animals they eat is not wanton.
Px: The claim that we should avoid wanton cruelty does not count against the conclusion.

12. Counterconsideration: A street fire alarm box was used recently to report a fire in a New York City office building.
Counterpremise and subargument (sentences 2 through 6, insufficiency strategy):

> PxA: There are 250,000 or more false alarms from street fire alarm boxes in New York City each year.
> PxB: False alarms delay responses to real fires and emergencies.
> PxC: They cause accidents, injuries, and even death to firefighters and civilians.
> PxD: They create unnecessary hardship on firefighters.
> PxE: They accelerate wear on the apparatus.

Px: The fact that some street fire alarm boxes are used to report fires is not sufficient to show that the conclusion should not be accepted.

15. Counterconsideration: Discovering more about our solar system is a grandiose achievement for all mankind.
Counterpremise and subargument (sentences 2, 3, and 4, insufficiency strategy):

> PxAi: We have famine in some parts of the world, teenage violence and pregnancies are high, and single-parent families raising children are on the rise.
> PxA: Problems on Earth are getting worse.

Px: The fact that discovering more about our solar system is a grandiose achievement for all mankind is not sufficient to show that the conclusion should not be accepted.

18. Counterconsideration: It would be good if American citizens, and particularly service members stationed abroad, were not subject to politically motivated prosecution before an alien tribunal.
Counterpremise and subargument (sentences 2 through 6, irrelevance strategy):

> PxAi: American service members have already been subject to the jurisdiction of foreign tribunals.
> PxAii: Business incorporated and headquartered in the United States are subject to litigation before foreign courts if they export goods or services.
> PxAiii: The United States is bound by extradition treaties to turn over Americans for prosecution in appropriate cases.
> PxA: American citizens cannot be protected from prosecution before alien tribunals.

Px: The claim that American citizens, especially servicemen, should not be subject to prosecu-

tion before alien tribunals does not count against the conclusion.

21. Counterconsideration: Women would do well to think independently about their bodies and not hate themselves for not meeting society's too-slender norm.
Counterpremise and subargument (sentences 2, 6, and 7, insufficiency strategy):

> PxAi: The media and society have great power to influence women's self-images.
> PxA: It is neither realistic nor fair to expect women to bear the full burden of making society's standards for women's bodies more real.

Px: The claim that women would do well to think independently about their bodies and not hate themselves for not meeting society's too-slender norm is insufficient to show that the conclusion should not be accepted.

EXERCISE SET 11.1C

3. P1: Information from the Educational Testing Service on the special accommodation status of certain test-takers might help universities make better decisions on behalf of their students.
P2A: Surely the Americans with Disabilities Act restrictions should apply to the educational institution's actions, not to the testing company's words.
P2: The claim that the Americans with Disabilities Act may limit the use of this information does not count against the conclusion.
P3: Preventing the Educational Testing Service from saying what it wants is a blatant violation of its freedom of speech.
C: Therefore, the Educational Testing Service should not be pressured to stop reporting the special accommodation status of certain test-takers.

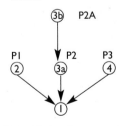

I charge the main argument with hasty conclusion. The main premises are not sufficient to support the conclusion. An important counterconsideration is not addressed. The argument does not address the concern that many students with special accommodation needs have that letting educational institutions know that they had this status while taking the test would lead the institutions to discount their test scores. If the special accommodation status put them on an equal footing with other students in taking the test, as the ETS claims, then their scores should not be discounted. The author needs to address this concern.

6. P1A: The SAT drafters have done a pretty good job of writing questions that distinguish raw intelligence from culture.

 P1: The claim that the SAT drafters have not perfected a means of writing questions that clearly distinguish raw intelligence from culture is not sufficient to show that the conclusion should not be accepted.

 P2A: There is no one to review the students' grades for cultural bias.

 P2Bi: High school teachers know who submits each answer, whereas the SAT graders do not.

 P2B: Bias is much more likely to affect the student's grades than their SAT scores.

 P2: There is no good alternative to relying on SAT scores for admission decisions.

 C: Therefore, the SAT examinations should not be rejected on the grounds that they are culturally biased.

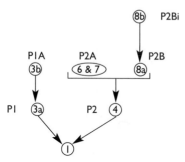

I charge the main argument with hasty conclusion. The main premises are not sufficient to support the conclusion because an important relevant issue is not addressed, namely, the counterconsideration that there is great cultural diversity in our immigrant society. It seems that, the more culturally diverse a society is, the more difficult it is to avoid cultural bias in a test that is given to young people from across the cultural spectrum. Even if, as P1 claims, the drafters of the SAT tests try their best to avoid cultural bias, the great diversity of our society may mean that their best efforts are not good enough. This is something the author needs to consider.

9. P1A: Unlike horses and elephants, humans have multipurpose machinery in our mouths; cuspids, incisors, and canines for ripping and tearing and molars for grinding.

 P1: Certainly our dental anatomy indicates that humans are not meant to be vegetarian.

 P2A: The anthropological record indicates that as nomadic hunter-gathers, humans stayed in one place eating vegetation while it was plentiful and opting for higher-protein meat while on the move.

 P2: Humans are omnivorous by design.

 P3Ai: Humans are natural carnivores.

 P3A: Human cruelty to the animals they eat is not wanton.

 P3: The claim that we should avoid wanton cruelty does not count against the conclusion.

 C: Therefore, humans were not meant to be and should not be vegetarian.

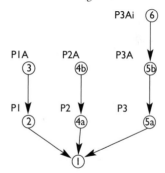

I charge the main argument with hasty conclusion. The main premises do not provide sufficient support for the conclusion. The conclusion claims both that humans are not meant to be vegetarians and that they should not be vegetarians. But the main premises do not provide sufficient support for either of these aspects of the conclusion. Regarding the claim that humans are not meant to be vegetarians, something cannot be meant to be some way unless there is some intelligence that designed the thing with that purpose in mind. The author says nothing to show that this is the case. Regarding the claim that humans should not be vegetarians, the author does not address all of the value statements that would be counterconsiderations to this. For example, many people argue that we should be vegetarian because this would eliminate hunger and starvation in the world (because the grains not fed to animals would be available for human consumption).

12. P1A: There are 250,000 or more false alarms from street fire alarm boxes in New York City each year.

P1B: False alarms delay responses to real fires and emergencies.

P1C: They cause accidents, injuries, and even death to firefighters and civilians.

P1D: They create unnecessary hardship on firefighters.

P1E: They accelerate wear on the apparatus.

P1: The fact that some street fire alarm boxes are used to report fires is not sufficient to show that the conclusion should not be accepted.

P2: Phone alarms from the myriad phones in the city allow the fire dispatcher to ascertain the response needed.

P3: Street fire alarm boxes often lead the fire dispatcher to send a greater response than is needed.

C: Therefore, most street fire alarm boxes in New York City, except those in isolated areas and those of public concern, should be eliminated.

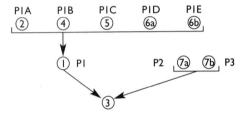

I charge the main argument with hasty conclusion. The main premises do not provide sufficient support for the conclusion because some important counter-considerations are not raised. The author does address the claim that in poor neighborhoods, where the danger of fire is greatest, many people may not have access to a telephone. Also, the author does not consider ways to reduce the number of false alarms from street boxes, such as installing cameras that would photograph anyone who pulled an alarm.

15.   P1Ai: We have famine in some parts of the world, teenage violence and pregnancies are high, and single-parent families raising children are on the rise.

P1A: Problems on Earth are getting worse.

P1: The fact that discovering more about our solar system is a grandiose achievement for all mankind is not sufficient to show that the conclusion should not be accepted.

P2: Since Galileo, we have come a long way in understanding our solar system.

P3: Our obsession with outer space is a psychological scapegoat for running away from our own earthly problems.

C: Therefore, we should focus all of our energies on Earth and not devote our energies to space.

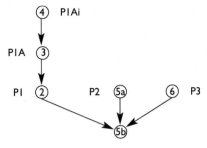

I charge the main argument with hasty conclusion. The main premises do not provide sufficient support for the conclusion because several counterconsiderations are not addressed. The author does not consider that only a very small part of our national wealth goes into space exploration. Nor does the author consider that the knowledge achieved in space exploration is both valuable for its own sake, because people enjoy learning more about our universe, and valuable for the potential benefits that can come from it, such as the greater knowledge of our own planet (for example, knowledge of its weather and geology) that may follow from our knowledge of other planets. These points would have to be addressed before the conclusion could be acceptable.

18.   P1Ai: American service members have already been subject to the jurisdiction of foreign tribunals.

P1Aii: Business incorporated and headquartered in the United States are subject to litigation before foreign courts if they export goods or services.

P1Aiii: The United States is bound by extradition treaties to turn over Americans for prosecution in appropriate cases.

P1A: American citizens cannot be protected from prosecution before alien tribunals.

P1: The claim that American citizens, especially servicemen, should not be subject to prosecution before alien tribunals does not count against the conclusion.

P2: The United States should exercise its influence to help institutionalize the rule of law in which we believe and for which we have in the past had to fight.

P3A: An effective international criminal court would hold out the prospect of punishment for those inclined toward ethnic cleansing, genocide, and other crimes against humanity.

P3: An effective international criminal court would make this a safer world for Americans and, not the least, American servicemen.

P4: Trial by law, with all its defects, is vastly preferable to trial by combat.

C: Therefore, the United States should support the creation of a permanent international criminal court.

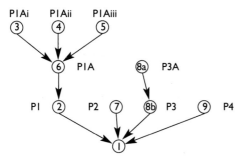

I charge the main argument with hasty conclusion. The premises do not provide sufficient support for the conclusion because an important counterconsideration is not adequately addressed. This is the issue of loss of national sovereignty. This issue is partially addressed by the counterpremise, but there is more to it than that. In formally supporting the international criminal court, the United States would not only be acknowledging the existing international realities, as the author claims, but also inviting expansion of international governing structures and further restrictions on its sovereignty down the road. This is a concern that the author should address.

21. P1Ai: If you listen to women you know, you will find them making self-deprecating remarks about their bodies.

 P1A: Many women make self-deprecating comments about their bodies.

P1: Poor body image, which for a small percentage will lead to an eating disorder, is the norm for most women in our society.

  P2Ai: The media and society have great power to influence women's self-images.

 P2A: It is neither realistic nor fair to expect women to bear the full burden of making society's standards for women's bodies more realistic.

P2: The claim that women would do well to think independently about their bodies and not to hate themselves for failing to meet society's too-slender norm is insufficient to show that the conclusion should not be accepted.

C: Therefore, it is an oversimplification that women simply need to take control of their own bodies to avoid eating disorders.

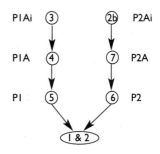

I charge the main argument with the fallacy of hasty conclusion. The premises do not provide sufficient support for the conclusion. In this case, what the author has not taken into account is not a counterconsideration but an important consideration, namely, the idea characteristic of our society that women must always be pleasing in appearance to men. It is another factor, in addition to the power of the media, that shows why it is not the case that women can simply take control of their own bodies without some social changes to make this possible. Including discussion of this point in the premises would provide a stronger case for the conclusion.

EXERCISE SET 11.2A

3. Primary subject: my friend
Analogue: me
Selected characteristic: having a conscious mind that directs one's behavior
 P1A: My friend behaves like I do.
 [P1: My friend is relevantly like me.
 P2: I have a conscious mind that directs my behavior.
 C: Therefore, my friend has a conscious mind that directs her behavior.

6. Primary subject: military threats by one nation against others
Analogue: legal threats of punishment by a nation against its citizens
Selected characteristic: the threats' working
 [P1: Military threats by one nation against others are relevantly like legal threats of punishment by a nation against its citizens.
 P2: Legal threats work.
 IC: Therefore, military threats work.

9. Primary subject: the human brain
Analogue: a computer
Selected characteristic: having to delete something from memory when the memory is full to remember something new
 P1A: The nerve cells of the brain are like the circuits on a computer chip.
 [P1: The human brain is relevantly like a computer.

IP2: In a computer, if the memory is full, something must be deleted from it before new
information can be added.

C: Therefore, if you have too much information in
your head, you need to forget something before
you can learn something new.

EXERCISE SET 11.2B

3. Primary subject: murdering people to prevent
murder
Analogue: raping to prevent rape; stealing to prevent theft
Selected characteristic: not effective or acceptable

P1: Murdering people to prevent murder is relevantly like raping to prevent rape or stealing to
prevent theft.

P2: It is ineffective and/or unacceptable to rape to
prevent rape or to steal to prevent theft.

P3: The death penalty is murdering people to prevent murder.

IC: Therefore, it is ineffective and/or unacceptable
to impose the death penalty.

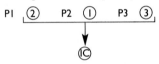

6. Primary subject: flight attendants suing tobacco
companies to recover for harm caused by smoking
passengers
Analogue: us suing automobile manufacturers to
recover for harm caused by dangerous drivers
Selected characteristic (implicit): a silly thing to do

P1: Flight attendants suing the tobacco companies
to recover for harm caused by smoking passengers is relevantly like our suing automobile
manufacturers to recover for harm caused by
dangerous drivers

IP2: It would be silly for us to sue automobile manufacturers for this reason.

IC: Therefore, it is silly for flight attendants to sue
tobacco companies for this reason.

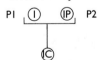

9. Primary subject: all animals and plants
Analogue: all members of the same class of animal
or plant
Selected characteristic: having descended from a
single prototype

P1Ai: All living things are similar in their
chemical composition, their germinal vesicles, their cellular structure, and their laws of growth and
reproduction

P1A: All living things, like all members of a
class of living things, have much in
common.

IP1: All members of the group of all animals and
plants are relevantly like all members of the
same class of animal or plant.

P2: All members of the same class of animal or
plant descended from a single prototype.

C: Therefore, probably all animals and plants have
descended from some one prototype.

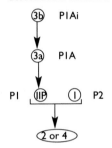

12. Primary subject: putting child safety locks on guns
Analogue: putting a child safety cap on a bottle of
aspirin or a seat belt in a car
Selected characteristic: being unthinkable not to do
so

P1A: Putting child safety locks on guns is relevantly like putting child safety caps on
bottles of aspirin or seat belts in cars.

P1B: It is unthinkable not to put child safety
caps on bottles of aspirin or seat belts in
cars.

IP1: It is unthinkable not to put child safety locks
on guns.

P2A: Countless deaths and injuries of children
occur every year because of accidental
shootings.

P2: Something must be done to prevent such
accidents.

P3A: The child safety lock bill would require
that every new handgun be sold with a
child safety lock and a warning detailing
the dangers of improperly storing a
firearm.

IP3: The child safety lock bill would help prevent
such accidents.

P4: Our children's lives are worth the $10 cost.

IC: Therefore, the child safety lock bill should be
approved.

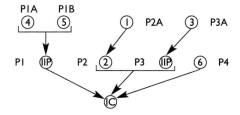

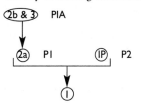

15. Primary subject: taking the shoes of a victim of gun violence to the headquarters of a gun manufacturer
Analogue: taking the shoes of a drunk driver's victim to the steps of General Motors or Ford
Selected characteristic: being inappropriate (a goofy idea)

> P1A: In both cases, the apparatus is not to blame.
> P1B: In both cases, the culprit is the operator of the apparatus.

P1: Taking the shoes of a victim of gun violence to the headquarters of a gun manufacturer is relevantly like taking the shoes of a drunk driver's victim to the steps of General Motors or Ford.
P2: It would be inappropriate to take the shoes of a drunk driver's victim to the steps of General Motors or Ford.
IC: Therefore, it is inappropriate to take the shoes of a victim of gun violence to the headquarters of a gun manufacturer.

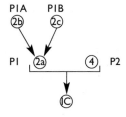

18. This is an argument from counteranalogy.
Primary subject: census sampling
Analogue: exit polling (not pre-election polling)
Selected characteristic: a reliable way to arrive at a count statistically

> P1A: With both census sampling and exit polling, information is collected about actual behavior, and is not, as with pre-election polling, based on predictions about actions that those polled may not wish to disclose.

P1: Census sampling is relevantly like exit polling, not like pre-election polling.
P2: Exit polling, unlike pre-election polling, is a reliable statistical way of arriving at an accurate count.

C: Therefore, census sampling is a reliable statistical way of arriving at an accurate count.

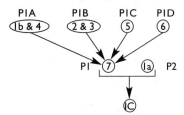

21. This is an even-more-so argument.
Primary subject: tobacco company executives
Analogue: the unibomber Ted Kaczynski
Selected characteristic: someone for whom the death penalty was sought

> P1A: Both unabomber Ted Kaczynski and tobacco executives killed people intentionally, lack remorse, and are poor candidates for rehabilitation.
> P1B: Kaczynski caused 3 deaths, and the tobacco executives have caused over 5 million deaths and continue to cause more.
> P1C: Unlike Kaczynski, the tobacco executives lied and targeted children.
> P1D: Unlike Kaczynski, who was probably mentally ill, the tobacco executives have acted out of greed.

P1: The tobacco executives are relevantly like Kaczynski, but the executives are that way even more so.
P2: The death penalty was sought against Kaczynski.
IC: Therefore, even more so, the death penalty should be sought against tobacco executives.

EXERCISE SET 11.3A

3. The analogy being criticized is between rehiring preferences given to veterans and rehiring preferences for women who choose to stay home with their young children, and the conclusion of the argument from analogy is that women, like veterans, should have such preferences. The author argues that the analogy is faulty because the

women's staying at home is voluntary, whereas the veterans' serving often was not, and because the veterans were injured and put at great risk, whereas the women were not.

6. The analogy being criticized is between a human chess player and a chess-playing computer, and the conclusion of the argument from analogy is that the computer won the chess match. The author argues that the analogy is faulty because the opponent is not simply a computer, but rather a group of people (the programmers) using a computer to play. The author poses a counteranalogy, between a person playing chess using a computer and a person jumping using a pole, and concludes that it is not surprising that a person playing chess with a computer can beat a person playing chess without one.

9. The analogy being criticized is between the market value of a company and the size of a national economy, and the conclusion of the argument from analogy is that Microsoft would rank behind Spain as the ninth-largest economy in the world. The author argues that the analogy is faulty because market value of a company is more like the total wealth of a country. The author poses a counteranalogy, between the size of a national economy and the revenue of a company, and concludes from this that Microsoft would rank with Uruguay and the Slovak Republic, the sixty-first- and sixty-second-largest economies.

12. The analogy being criticized is between drugs to treat male impotence and drugs to prevent pregnancy, and the conclusion of the argument from analogy is that drugs to prevent pregnancy should be covered by health insurance. The author argues that the analogy is faulty because male impotence is an abnormal and treatable condition, whereas pregnancy is not an abnormality and is not treated by contraceptives.

15. The analogy being criticized is between Jews purchasing property from Arabs in East Jerusalem and Arabs purchasing property from Jews in West Jerusalem, and the conclusion of that argument from analogy is that Jews should be allowed to purchase property from Arabs in East Jerusalem. The author argues that the analogy is faulty because the Arab purchaser would come under Israeli sovereignty, whereas the Jewish purchaser would not come under Palestinian sovereignty but would be enhancing Israeli presence in an occupied country.

EXERCISE SET 11.3B

3. The original presenter of the argument from analogy might respond to the letter in the following way.

Contrary to the conclusion of the letter writer, there are several ways in which being a woman who has stayed home with her young children is like being a veteran in ways relevant to the claim that the woman, like the veteran, should receive a rehiring preference. First, both are doing something that is for the benefit of society. Second, both are doing something that society wants to encourage people to do: to protect the country, on the one hand, and to strengthen families and raise better children, on the other.

6. The original presenter of the argument from analogy might respond to the letter in the following way. The letter writer argues that the computer is not the winner of the match; rather, the winner is the programmers using the computer. On the contrary, being a human chess player and being a very sophisticated chess-playing computer are alike in an important way relevant to the claim that either can be said to have won a chess match. The computer chooses how to move on its own. It has been given programming that makes it capable of independent thought, at least so far as chess moves go. This is no different from the way that a human can go beyond the lessons given by her chess teacher and become capable of playing independently. Student can surpass teacher in chess ability, as the computer can surpass the chess ability of its programmers.

9. This is a very strong argument, and I do not think that the letter writer could have anything forceful to say in response.

12. The original presenter of the argument from analogy might respond to the letter in the following way. Drugs to prevent impotence and drugs to prevent pregnancy are alike in a crucial way relevant to the claim that both should be covered by health insurance or that if one is the other should be as well. Both drugs allow humans to have and enjoy sexual relations. Both drugs overcome a problem that interferes with the ability to have and enjoy sex. This is obvious in the case of drugs to prevent impotence, but it is also true for drugs to prevent pregnancy. A woman who does not want to become pregnant cannot have sex, or cannot fully enjoy having sex, unless she can be assured that pregnancy will not result.

15. The original presenter of the argument from analogy might respond to the letter in the following way. The basis of the criticism in the letter is that, because there is an Israeli state but currently no Palestinian state, the Israeli seeking property in East Jerusalem (in Israeli-occupied territory) is in a different legal situation than the Palestinian seeking property in West Jerusalem (in Israel proper). While this is true, it does not undermine the analogy between them that, if one has the right to make such

a purchase, so does the other. If the two are acting as individuals and not as representatives of political entities, then the difference in the legal situations should not undermine their equal right to purchase property.

≣ EXERCISE SET 11.3C

3. Primary subject: smokers filing lawsuits against tobacco companies because of illnesses caused by smoking

Analogue: people filing lawsuits against the sun because of cataracts caused by looking at the sun

Selected characteristic (implicit): an absurd thing to do

P1A: No one forces people to smoke or to look at the sun.

P1: Smokers filing lawsuits against tobacco companies because of illnesses caused by smoking is relevantly like people filing lawsuits against the sun because of cataracts caused by looking at the sun.

IP2: People filing lawsuits against the sun because of cataracts caused by looking at the sun is absurd.

IC: Therefore, smokers filing lawsuits against tobacco companies because of illnesses caused by smoking is absurd.

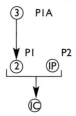

I charge this argument with the fallacy of faulty analogy. The argument commits this fallacy because the primary subject and the analogue are unlike in ways relevant to the selected characteristic. The author's point is that looking at the sun and smoking are both voluntary actions, so that the person acting should bear full responsibility for any negative consequences, like cataracts or lung cancer. But this ignores important differences between the two cases. First, the tobacco companies enticed people to smoke through advertising and creating an addiction, and for many years they did not inform consumers of the fact, known to them, that smoking is harmful to health. In contrast, the sun does nothing to entice. Second, and a related point, the sun is not a moral agent, whereas the tobacco companies are composed of moral agents, and only a moral agent can be blamed for something it caused to happen.

6. This is an even-more-so argument.

Primary subject: executing convicted murderers to deter others

Analogue: adopting various beneficial social policies

Selected characteristic: is morally acceptable

P1A: We build bridges, knowing that fatal accidents are inevitable.

P1B: We raise automobile speed limits, although we know that thousands more drivers and passengers will be killed as a result.

P1C: We send soldiers into combat with the awful knowledge that many of them will not survive.

P1D: Certainly, mob hitmen and other violent criminals are more suitable subjects of sacrifice than construction workers, automobile passengers, and marines.

P1: Executing convicted murderers to deter others is relevantly like adopting various beneficial social policies, and even more so.

P2: Adopting these social policies is morally acceptable.

C: Therefore, executing convicted murderers to deter others is even more acceptable morally.

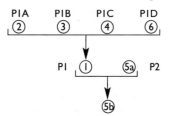

I charge this argument with the fallacy of faulty analogy. The argument commits this fallacy because the primary subject and the analogue are unlike in a way relevant to the selected characteristic. It is indeed true that we adopt beneficial social policies knowing that some deaths will result, but the "social policy" of the death penalty is fundamentally different from the other cases. It is the difference between a person's intentionally killing a particular person and creating a dangerous situation that causes someone's death. Think of the contrast between murder and manslaughter. The former is morally worse than the latter, and this same moral difference applies in the case of the death penalty and beneficial social policies that put some people at risk of death. The even-more-so aspect of the argument does not work because the issue is not how much the people who die deserve to die, but whether the state kills a particular person or simply creates a condition in which some might die.

9. Primary subject: Tim Forneris returning Mark McGwire's sixty-second home run ball to the baseball Hall of Fame
   Analogue: someone who returns a lost wallet without stealing the money inside
   Selected characteristic: has done the right thing
   P1: Tim Forneris returning Mark McGwire's sixty-second home run ball to the baseball Hall of Fame is relevantly like someone who returned a lost wallet without stealing the money inside.
   P2: Someone who returns a lost wallet without stealing the money inside has done the right thing.
   P3: In returning the ball to the baseball Hall of Fame, Forneris recognized a value other than greed.
   C: Therefore, when Forneris returned the home run ball to the baseball Hall of Fame, he did the right thing.

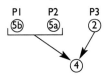

I charge this argument with the fallacy of faulty analogy. The argument commits this fallacy because the primary subject and the analogue are unalike in a way relevant to the selected characteristic. When you return a lost wallet, you are returning something to its rightful owner, but it is not clear that the baseball Hall of Fame is the rightful owner of the baseball in question. It is a tradition in baseball that fans are allowed to keep any balls hit into the stands. This suggests that Mr. Forneris may have been the rightful owner of the ball, so that he was under no obligation to turn it in instead of keeping it or selling it.

12. Primary subject: county government
    Analogue: gas-guzzling automobiles
    Selected characteristic: becoming more efficient by being forced to become more efficient
    P1A: County government is relevantly like gas-guzzling automobiles.
    P1B: Gas-guzzling automobiles became more efficient by being forced to become more efficient.
    IIP1: County government would become more efficient by being forced to become more efficient.
    P2: County government should be made more efficient.
    C: Therefore, the newspaper should not endorse higher taxes to solve municipal problems.

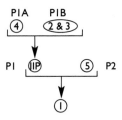

I charge this argument with the fallacy of faulty analogy at P1. The argument commits this fallacy because the primary subject and the analogue are unalike in ways relevant to the selected characteristic. Governments deliver services, whereas automobiles deliver mechanical power, so improving the efficiency of each is quite a different matter. The efficiency of auto engines can be improved by technological innovation, but such innovation plays a much more limited role in improving the efficiency of organizations that deliver services. There is another respect in which the analogy is weak. What forced the automakers to make more efficient autos was government regulation and/or foreign and domestic competition. The increase in efficiency required great capital investment. In contrast, the author wants to reduce the amount of money available to government, a very different way of attempting to improve efficiency.

15. Primary subject: NATO's attacking Yugoslavia to protect Kosovo
    Analogue: a nation's attacking the Union to protect the Confederacy during the U.S. Civil War
    Selected characteristic: is unacceptable
    P1A: Yugoslavia and the United States are sovereign nations.
    P1B: The conflict in Yugoslavia and the struggle between the North and the South are both civil wars.
    P1C: Attack on a sovereign nation has always been seen as an act of war.
    P1: NATO's attacking Yugoslavia to protect Kosovo is relevantly like a nation's attacking the Union to protect the Confederacy during the U.S. Civil War.
    P2: A nation's attacking the Union to protect the Confederacy during the U.S. Civil War would have been unacceptable.
    C: Therefore, NATO's attacking Yugoslavia to protect Kosovo is unacceptable.

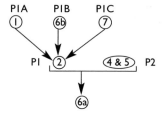

I charge this argument with the fallacy of faulty analogy. The argument commits this fallacy because the primary subject and the analogue are unlike in ways relevant to the selected characteristic. First, it is misleading to call the conflict in Kosovo a civil war. While some Kosovars were fighting for independence from the rest of Yugoslavia, the main military activity was the Yugoslav central government seeking to ethnically cleanse Kosovo of its Albanian population. This was what NATO was trying to stop. Nothing like this was happening in the case of the American Civil War. Second, the violation of human rights that was at stake in the American Civil War was southern slavery, so the Union had a moral justification to suppress the Confederacy in the same way that NATO had a moral justification for interfering in the Yugoslav conflict. In fact, this contrast between the two cases is the basis of a counteranalogy. In this case, the two things compared in the counteranalogy are the military struggle of the Union and NATO's interference in Kosovo. The selected characteristic is that the Union struggle was morally justified, and the conclusion is that the NATO interference is morally justified as well.

Index